On Stage, America!

Blanche Bates as The Girl
in David Belasco's *The Girl of the Golden West*, 1905

On Stage, America!

A Selection of
Distinctly American Plays

edited and introduced

by

Walter J. Meserve

Feedback Theatrebooks & Prospero Press

For my friend, Richard Moody (1911-1996)

Library of Congress Catalog Card Number: 96-85294

Copyright © 1996 by Feedback Theatrebooks

Manufactured in the United States of America.

Feedback Theatrebooks & Prospero Press
305 Madison Avenue, Suite 1146
New York, NY 10165

ISBN   0-937657-20-4

96-2403
PB
812.008
m ES

CONTENTS

LIST OF ILLUSTRATIONS

An Introduction

America, the beautiful, the boastful, the brave;
Adventurer, socialite, idealist, knave --
"Of thee I sing!"

And nowhere is this *song* sung more poignantly than in the theatre. A ready mirror for a country's faults and foibles, a constant source of opinion on the topics of any day, the theatre of a free society provides one of the most reliable reflections of that society.

On the stages of America the playwrights of America have unfurled a panorama of American life: its cultural yearnings and insufficiencies (*The Contrast, Fashion*), its singular people and their distinctive voices (*The Stage-Struck Yankee, Glance at New York, The Old Homestead*), its concern for history and fantasy (*Metamora, Rip Van Winkle*), its social problems (*Young Mrs. Winthrop, Margaret Fleming*), its fascination with the spectacular (*Under the Gaslight, The Girl of the Golden West*), and its frivolous nature (*A Trip to Chinatown*). In a more complex manner than this listing suggests, however, and far more intricately woven into the character, action, and thought of these plays, a broad view of American life appears. Chosen to exhibit the best efforts of pre-World War I American dramatists reflecting the American scene in its cultural, economic, and political diversity, as well as to illustrate the major movements in American theatre history and the development of American dramatic literature, the twelve plays in this anthology form a basic core for an understanding of America through its theatre.

Heroes and hero-worship absorbed the interests of several 19th century writers, English and American. Thomas Carlyle wrote a book on the subject in 1841; Ralph Waldo Emerson selected his "Representative Men" in 1850. For Royall Tyler in *The Contrast* the American hero is a soldier--well-spoken, polite, self-assured, and a gentleman, proud to love and serve his country. Although young Walter in John Augustus Stone's

Metamora lacks Col. Manly's sophistication, he has a gentleman's courage, appropriate manners, and a respect for others. Col. Howard in *Fashion* gains stature through his military bearing and moral character. Interestingly enough, the roughneck Mose in *Glance at New York* was widely admired and imitated by the younger male denizens of that city, although the playwright almost certainly did not conceive of him as a "role model." Ray Trafford, Augustin Daly's hero in *Under the Gaslight*, appears at first to be an effete if well-mannered young man, but he is soon recognized as capable of substantive feelings and both physical and moral action. By the time David Belasco needed a worthy companion for his Girl of the Golden West, he could create an anti-hero, a contemptible villain in the minds of the men in Cloudy Mountain--a road-agent named Dick Johnson.

In many great plays throughout history, heroines dominate the action and speak the dramatists' thoughts. This is true on the American stage. From the very proper and respectful Maria in *The Contrast* to Belasco's straightforward, idealistic Girl, women are guardians of the heavenly virtues and promoters of goodness in men and society. In *Fashion*, for example, Gertrude's social and moral superiority to every other character in the play underscores Anna Cora Mowatt's message. Perhaps both Laura Courtland in *Under the Gaslight* and Margaret Fleming in Herne's play deserve stronger men, but in securing their positions in life they exhibit the moral courage that identified the 19th century heroine as the lodestar of family love and understanding. Combining dignity with native guile and a resolute fortitude, Nahmeokee fulfills her role as the appropriate mate for the heroic Metamora. Constance Winthrop (*Young Mrs. Winthrop*) lacks that necessary self-possession and would flounder without the wit and wisdom of an old friend, but she has the good sense to take his advice. Margaret Fleming possesses a mysterious inner power which allows her to transcend the problems of a real world quite beyond the purview of her own morality.

The ethnic minorities among America's struggling masses were a distinctive part of the theatre from its own struggling beginnings. During the 19th century the portrayal of Indians underwent the greatest change. As Edwin Forrest, the actor, proved repeatedly, it was difficult to enact a greater dignity or strength of purpose on stage than through Metamora. The opposite end of the spectrum appears with Billy Jackrabbit and Wowkle in *The Girl of the Golden West*, but not without some tenderness. The Negro, a servant and an object of humor (*The Contrast, Fashion, The Stage-Struck Yankee, Under the Gaslight*) until the liberal implications of Mrs. Stowe's *Uncle Tom's Cabin* became acceptable in the theatre, reached heroic proportions in Edward Sheldon's *The Nigger*, 1909. The stage Yankee, often placed alongside the stage Irishman and the stage German, is more regional--like the Backwoodsman or the Westerner--than ethnic. Throughout the 19th century, however, the Yankee's progress was phenomenal--from Jonathan to Zachariah to Uncle Josh.

As might be expected in a nation as geographically expansive as the United States, the potential for hostile comparison between city and country life was blatant in the 19th century. Royall Tyler set the stage admirably with *The Contrast,* and others eagerly followed his example. The Doubles play upon country simplicity in *The Stage-Struck Yankee*; Mrs. Mowatt constantly reminds her audiences of the differences between Catteraugus County and New York City; Ben Baker gives his audiences a "glance at New York" to show how George, the upstate greenhorn, contends with various opportunities for fun and corruption. Even in the social problem play *Young Mrs. Winthrop*, a sharp distinction is drawn between the pressures of the city and life in a rural town. Joshua Whitcomb in *The Old Homestead* becomes another greenhorn in New York. On the West Coast, the sophistication of Monterey, as revealed in Dick Johnson's language and manners, overwhelms the citizens of Cloudy Mountain where The Girl can only say, "'Tain't no use. I lay down my hand to you," and run into his arms. This is one of the few plays in which "the city" apparently prevails.

It is not always "America, the beautiful!" on stage. The piteous cry of Metamora--"I am weary of the world for ye are dwellers in it."--brings no credit to his conquerors. The crusade for temperance that began in the 1820s and flourished throughout the century claimed a painful reason for its existence. Such plays as *The Drunkard*, 1844, by William H. Smith, were deadly serious. *The Old Homestead* takes a similar view. In *Fashion* drunkenness is associated with corruption and criminal behavior. Rip Van Winkle's mellow "good humor" may ease the conscience of the audience, but Gretchen appropriately describes the terrible effects of alcohol on family life. Only in *A Trip to Chinatown* does intemperance become part of the frivolity of successful farce. Although divorce, another social problem appearing on the 19th century stage, is averted as a personal disaster for the Winthrops, it is clearly shown as a potential menace for the business world. Contemporary audiences, appalled by the ugliness of the situation presented in *Margaret Fleming*, rejected the play.

America, "land that I love"--in spite of inadequacies, attracted the attention of most pre-World War I playwrights. Being serious mainly in their obligation "to entertain" and, therefore, to make money, they were concerned with America's bigness, its energy, its opportunities--America, the spectacular! There was the spectacle of Edwin Forrest as Metamora, the spectacle of the various Yankee performers, the costume spectacle in *Rip Van Winkle*, the revue spectacle of *Glance at New York*, the vaudeville acts in *Under the Gaslight*, and the "hilarious confusion" that always brought cheers at productions of *A Trip to Chinatown*. Theatregoers demanded to be both amused and amazed, and 19th century American playwrights tried their best to satisfy them. For sensational melodrama--sweet and sentimental, vivid and violent--from the railroad scene in *Under the Gaslight* to the drifting snow and howling wind in *The Girl of the Golden West*, American playwrights had no peers.

These plays *are* America--On Stage!

WJM

Royall Tyler (1757-1826) and *The Contrast*

With a self-confessed reputation for "dissipation" as a young man, Royall Tyler quite naturally prepared himself for dual careers in theatre and in law. If the frivolous endeavors that his youthful nature dictated did not advance his romantic pursuit of John Adams' daughter, they did enhance his status at Harvard College as an amusing, quick-witted conversationalist. A thoughtful man, interested in society and politics, he possessed a natural flair for literature and enjoyed writing light verse, a novel, and sprightly satiric essays, some of which he collected in *The Yankey in London*, 1809. As a lawyer, he ended his career on Vermont's Supreme Court.

Tyler experienced amateur theatre in the Boston of his youth, but it is reasonably certain that he did not see a professional production until March of 1787, when, finding himself in New York, he undoubtedly witnessed *The School for Scandal* and met the actor Thomas Wignell. In *The Contrast*, his first play, he created for Wignell the part of Jonathan, whose tale in Act III clearly mirrors Tyler's own initiation into the professional theatre.

There is evidence of thirty-eight performances of *The Contrast* by the Old American Company in New York, Baltimore, and Philadelphia from 1787 through 1804. Other companies occasionally produced *The Contrast*, and songs were introduced, changes made, and a subtitle--"The American Son of Liberty"--added. But time passed and tastes changed. Few later productions were documented until World War II, when university theatres began to stage the play to support an academic interest in the history of the American theatre.

The success of *The Contrast* can be measured only by the standards of its day. A talky play with little action and slight plot, *The Contrast*, nevertheless, satisfied the demands of theatregoers in 1787: exultant nationalism, a Yankee character, a strong moral, and the broad satire that American audiences had enjoyed for more than a century. Tyler wrote nine other plays but none with the skill or appeal of *The Contrast*, and it is this play which earns him a place in the history of American dramatic literature.

Royall Tyler

Scene from *The Contrast*, Act V, Scene 2

THE CONTRAST

(1787)

by Royall Tyler

CHARACTERS

Col. Manly	Charlotte
Dimple	Maria
Van Rough	Letitia
Jessamy	Jenny
Jonathan	Servants

The scene is New-York.

PROLOGUE.
Written by a young gentleman of New-York; spoken by Mr. Wignell.

EXHULT each patriot heart!--this night is shewn
A piece, which we may fairly call our own;
Where the proud titles of "My Lord! Your Grace!"
To humble Mr. and plain Sir give place.
Our Author pictures not from foreign climes
The fashions or the follies of the times;
But has confin'd the subject of his work
To the gay scenes--the circles of New-York.
On native themes his Muse displays her pow'rs;
If ours the faults, the virtues too are ours.
Why should our thoughts to distant countries roam,
When each refinement may be found at home?
Who travels now to ape the rich or great,
To deck an equipage and roll in state;
To court the graces, or to dance with ease,
Or by hypocrisy to strive to please?
Our free-born ancestors such arts despis'd;
Genuine sincerity alone they priz'd;
Their minds, with honest emulation fir'd,
To solid good--not ornament--aspir'd;

Or, if ambition rous'd a bolder flame,
Stern virture throve, where indolence was shame.

But modern youths, with imitative sense,
Deem taste in dress the proof of excellence;
And spurn the meanness of your homespun arts,
Since homespun habits would obscure their parts;
Whilst all, which aims at splendour and parade,
Must come from Europe, and be ready made.
Strange! we should thus our native worth disclaim,
And check the progress of our rising fame.
Yet one, whilst imitation bears the sway,
Aspires to nobler heights and points the way,
Be rous'd, my friends! his bold example view;
Let your own Bards be proud to copy you!
Should rigid critics reprobate our play,
At least the patriotic heart will say,
"Glorious our fall, since in a noble cause.
The bold attempt alone demands applause."
Still may the wisdom of the Comic Muse
Exhult your merits, or your faults accuse.
But think not, 'tis her aim to be severe;--
We all are mortals and as mortals err.

If candour pleases, we are truly blest;
Vice trembles, when compell'd to stand confess'd.
Let not light Censure on your faults, offend,
Which aims not to expose them, but amend.
Thus does our Author to your candour trust;
Conscious, the free are generous, as just.

ACT I.

Scene 1. An Apartment at Charlotte's. (*Charlotte and Letitia discovered.*)

LETITIA.   And so, Charlotte, you really think the pocket-hoop unbecoming.

CHARLOTTE. No, I don't say so: It may be very becoming to saunter round the house of a rainy day; to visit my grand-mamma, or to go to Quakers' meeting: but to swim in a minuet, with the eyes of fifty well-dressed beaux upon me, to trip it in the Mall, or walk on the battery, give me the luxurious, jaunty, flowing, bell-hoop. It would have delighted you to have seen me the last evening, my charming girl! I was dangling o'er the battery with Billy Dimple; a knot of young fellows were upon the platform; as I passed them I faultered with one of the most bewitching false steps you ever saw, and then recovered myself with such a pretty confusion, flirting my hoop to discover a jet black shoe and brilliant buckle. Gad! how my little heart thrilled to hear the confused raptures of--"*Demme, Jack, what a delicate foot!*" "*Ha! General, what a well-turn'd--*"

LETITIA. Fie! fie! (*Stopping her mouth.*) Charlotte, I protest you are quite a libertine.

CHARLOTTE. Why, my little prude, are we not all such libertines? Do you think, when I sat tortured two hours under the hands of my friseur, and an hour more at my toilet, that I had any thoughts of my aunt Susan, or my cousin Betsey? though they are both allowed to be critical judges of dress.

LETITIA. Why, who should we dress to please, but those who are judges of its merit?

CHARLOTTE. Why a creature who does not know *Buffon* from *Souflee*--Man!--my Letitia--Man! for whom we dress, walk, dance, talk, lisp, languish, and smile. Does not the grave Spectator assure us, that even our much bepraised diffidence, modesty, and blushes, are all directed to make ourselves good wives and mothers as fast as we can. Why, I'll undertake with one flirt of this hoop to bring more beaux to my feet in one week, than the grave Maria, and her sentimental circle, can do, by sighing sentiment till their hairs are grey.

LETITIA. Well, I won't argue with you; you always out talk me; let us change the subject. I hear that Mr. Dimple and Maria are soon to be married.

CHARLOTTE. You hear true. I was consulted in the choice of the wedding clothes. She is to be married in a delicate white sattin, and has a monstrous pretty brocaded lutestring for the second day. It would have done you good to have seen with what an affected indifference the dear sentimentalist arranged her dress with such apathy, as if she did not know that plain white sattin, and a simple blond lace, would shew her clear skin, and dark hair, to the greatest advantage.

LETITIA. But they say her indifference to dress, and even to the gentleman himself, is not entirely affected.

CHARLOTTE. How?

LETITIA. It is whispered, that if Maria gives her hand to Mr. Dimple, it will be without her heart.

CHARLOTTE. Though the giving of the heart is one of the last of all laughable considerations in the marriage of a girl of spirit, yet I should like to hear what antiquated notions the dear little piece of old fashioned prudery has got in her head.

LETITIA. Why, you know that old Mr. John-Richard-Robert-Jacob-Issaac-Abraham-Cornelius Van Dumpling, Billy Dimple's father (for he has thought fit to soften his name, as well as manners, during his English tour), was the most intimate friend of Maria's father. The old folks, about a year before Mr. Van Dumpling's death, proposed this match: the young folks were accordingly introduced, and told they must love one another. Billy was then a good natured, decent, dressing young fellow, with a little dash of the coxcomb, such as our young fellows of fortune usually have. At this time, I really believed she thought she loved him; and had they then been married, I doubt not, they might have jogged on to the end of the chapter, a good kind of a sing-song lack-a-daisical life, as other honest married folks do.

CHARLOTTE. Why did they not then marry?

LETITIA. Upon the death of his father, Billy went to England to see the world, and rub off a little of the patroon rust. During his absence, Maria like a good girl, to keep herself constant to her *own true-love*, avoided company, and betook herself, for her amusement, to her books, and her dear Billy's letters. But, alas! how many ways has the mischievous demon of inconstancy of stealing into a woman's heart! Her love was destroyed by the very means she took to support it.

CHARLOTTE. How? Oh! I have it--some likely young beau found the way to her study.

LETITIA. Be patient, Charlotte--your head so runs upon beaux. Why, she read Sir Charles Grandison, Clarissa Harlow, Shenstone, and the Sentimental Journey; and between whiles, as I said, Billy's letters. But as her taste improved, her love declined. The contrast was so striking betwixt the good sense of her books, and the flimsiness of her love-letters, that she discovered she had unthinkingly engaged her hand without her heart; and then the whole transaction managed by the old folks, now appeared so unsentimental, and looked so like bargaining for a bale of goods, that she found she ought to have rejected, according to every rule of romance, even the man of her choice, if imposed upon her in that manner--Clary Harlow would have scorned such a match.

CHARLOTTE. Well, how was it on Mr. Dimple's return? Did he meet a more favourable reception than his letters?

LETITIA. Much the same. She spoke of him with respect abroad, and with contempt in her closet. She watched his conduct and conversation, and found that he had by travelling acquired the wickedness of Lovelace without his wit, and the politeness of Sir Charles Grandison without his generosity. The ruddy youth who washed his face at the cistern every morning, and swore and looked eternal love and constancy, was now metamorphosed into a flippant, palid, polite beau, who devotes the morning to his toilet, reads a few pages of Chesterfield's letters, and then minces out to put the infamous principles in practice upon every woman he meets.

CHARLOTTE. But, if she is so apt at conjuring up these sentimental bugbears, why does she not discard him at once?

LETITIA. Why, she thinks her word too sacred to be trifled with. Besides, her father, who has a great respect for the memory of his deceased friend, is ever telling her how he shall renew his years in their union, and repeating the dying injunctions of old Van Dumpling.

CHARLOTTE. A mighty pretty story! And so you would make me believe, that the sensible Maria would give up Dumpling manor, and the all-accomplished Dimple as a husband, for the absurd, ridiculous reason, forsooth, because she despises and abhors him. Just as if a lady could not be privileged to spend a man's fortune, ride in his carriage, be called after his name, and call him her *own dear lovee* when she wants money, without loving and respecting the great he-creature. Oh! my dear girl, you are a monstrous prude.

LETITIA. I don't say what I would do; I only intimate how I suppose she wishes to act.

CHARLOTTE. No, no, no! A fig for sentiment. If she breaks, or wishes to break, with Mr. Dimple, depend upon it, she has some other man in her eye. A woman rarely discards one lover, until she is sure of another. (*Aside.*) Letitia little thinks what a clue I have to Dimple's conduct. The generous man submits to render himself disgusting to Maria, in order that she may leave him at liberty to address me. I must change the subject. (*Rings a bell. Enter Servant.*) Frank, order the horses to-- Talking of marriage--did you hear that Sally Bloomsbury is going to be married next week to Mr. Indigo, the rich Carolinian?

LETITIA. Sally Bloomsbury married! Why, she is not yet in her teens.

CHARLOTTE. I do not know how that is, but, you may depend upon it, 't is a done affair. I have it from the best authority. There is my aunt Wyerley's Hannah (you know Hannah--though a black, she is a wench that was never caught in a lie in her life); now Hannah has a brother who courts Sarah, Mrs. Catgut the milliner's girl, and she told Hannah's brother and Hannah, who, as I said before, is a girl of undoubted veracity, told it directly to me, that Mrs. Catgut was making a new cap for Miss Bloomsbury, which, as it was very dressy, it is very probable is designed for a wedding cap: now, as she is to be married, who can it be to, but to Mr. Indigo? Why, there is no other gentleman that visits her at papa's.

LETITIA. Say not a word more, Charlotte. Your intelligence is so direct and well grounded, it is almost a pity that it is not a piece of scandal.

CHARLOTTE. Oh! I am the pink of prudence. Though I cannot charge myself with ever having discredited a tea-party by my silence, yet I take care never to report any thing of my acquaintance, especially if it is to their credit--*discredit*, I mean--until I have searched to the bottom of it. It is true, there is infinite pleasure in this charitable pursuit. Oh! how delicious to go and condole with the friends of some backsliding sister, or to retire with some old dowager or maiden aunt of the family, who loves scandal so well, that they cannot forbear gratifying their appetite at the expense of the reputation of their nearest relations! And then to return full fraught with a rich collection of circumstances, to retail to the next circle of our acquaintance under the strongest injunctions of secrecy--ha, ha, ha!--interlarding the melancholy tale with so many doleful shakes of the head, and more doleful, "Ah! who would have thought it! so amiable, so prudent a young lady, as we all thought her, what a monstrous pity! well, I have nothing to charge myself with; I acted the part of a friend, I warned her of the principles of that rake, I told her what would be the consequence; I told her so, I told her so." Ha, ha, ha!

LETITIA. Ha, ha, ha! Well, but Charlotte, you don't tell me what you thing of Miss Bloomsbury's match.

CHARLOTTE. Think! why I think it is probable she cried for a plaything, and they have given her a husband. Well, well, well, the puling chit shall not be deprived of her plaything: 'tis only exchanging London dolls for American babies-- Appropos, of babies, have you heard what Mrs. Affable's high-flying notions of delicacy have come to?

LETITIA. Who, she that was Miss Lovely?

CHARLOTTE. The same; she married Bob Affable of Schenectady. Don't you remember? (*Enter Servant.*)

SERVANT. Madam, the carriage is ready.

LETITIA. Shall we go to the stores first, or visiting?

CHARLOTTE. I should think it rather too early to visit; especially Mrs. Prim: you know she is so particular.

LETITIA. Well, but what of Mrs. Affable?

CHARLOTTE. Oh, I'll tell you as we go; come, come, let us hasten. I hear Mrs. Catgut has some of the prettiest caps arrived you every saw. I shall die if I have not the first sight of them. (*Exeunt.*)

Scene 2. A Room in Van Rough's House.

MARIA. (*sitting disconsolate at a table, with books, etc., sings*)
> The sun sets in night and the stars shun the day;
> But glory remains when their lights fade away!
> Begin, ye tormentors! your threats are in vain,
> For the son of Alknomook shall never complain.
>
> Remember the arrows he shot from his bow;
> Remember your chiefs by his hatchet laid low:
> Why so slow?--do you wait till I shrink from the pain?
> No--the son of Alknomook will never complain.
>
> Remember the wood where in ambush we lay;
> And the scalps which we bore from your nation away:
> Now the flame rises fast, you exult in my pain;
> But the son of Alknomook can never complain.
>
> I go to the land where my father is gone;
> His ghost shall rejoice in the fame of his son:
> Death comes like a friend, he relieves me from pain;
> And thy son, Oh Alknomook! has scorn'd to complain. (*Song ends.*)

There is something in this song which ever calls forth my affections. The manly virtue of courage, that fortitude which steels the heart against the keenest misfortunes, which interweaves the laurel of glory amidst the instruments of torture and death, displays something so noble, so exalted, that in despite of the prejudices of education, I cannot but admire it, even in a savage. The prepossession which our sex is supposed to entertain for the character of a soldier, is, I know, a standing piece of raillery among the wits. A cockade, a lapell'd coat, and a feather, they will tell you, are irresistible by a female heart. Let it be so. Who is it that considers the helpless situation of our sex, that does not see we each moment stand in need of a protector, and that a brave one, too. How inconsistent! that man should be leagued to destroy that honour, upon which, solely rests his respect and esteem.

Ten thousand temptations allure us, ten thousand passions betray us; yet the smallest deviation from the path of rectitude is followed by the contempt and insult of man, and the more remorseless pity of woman; years of penitence and tears cannot wash away the stain, nor a life of virtue obliterate its remembrance. Heaven grant that the man with whom I may be connected--may be connected! Whither has my imagination transported me--whither does it now lead me? Am I not indissolubly engaged to a man who can never share my affections, and whom a few days hence, it will be criminal for me to disapprove--to disapprove! would to heaven that were all--to despise. For, can the most frivolous manners, actuated by the most depraved heart, meet, or merit, anything but contempt from every woman of delicacy and sentiment?

VAN ROUGH. (*without*) Mary.

MARIA. Ha, my father's voice-- Sir! (*Enter Van Rough.*)

VAN ROUGH. What, Mary, always singing doleful ditties, and moping over these plaguy books.

MARIA. I hope, Sir, that it is not criminal to improve my mind with books; or to divert my melancholy with singing at my leisure hours.

VAN ROUGH. Why, I don't know that, child; I don't know that. They us'd to say when I was a young man, that if a woman knew how to make a pudding, and to keep herself out of fire and water, she knew enough for a wife. Now, what good have these books done you? Have they not made you melancholy, as you call it? Pray, what right has a girl of your age to be in the dumps? Hav'n't you every thing your heart can wish; an't you going to be married to a young man of great fortune; an't you going to have the whit-rent of twenty miles square?

MARIA. One hundredth part of the land, and a lease for life of the heart of a man I could love, would satisfy me.

VAN ROUGH. Pho, pho, pho! child; nonsense, downright nonsense, child. This comes of your reading your story-books; your Charles Grandisons, your Sentimental Journals, and your Robinson Crusoes, and such other trumpery. No, no, no! child, it is money makes the mare go; keep your eye upon the main chance, Mary.

MARIA. Marriage, Sir, is, indeed, a very serious affair.

VAN ROUGH. You are right, child; you are right. I am sure I found it so to my cost.

MARIA. I mean, Sir, that as marriage is a portion for life, and so intimately involves our happiness, we cannot be too considerate in the choice of our companion.

VAN ROUGH. Right, child; very right. A young woman should be very sober when she is making her choice, but when she has made it, as you have done, I don't see why she should not be as merry as a grig; I am sure she has reason enough to be so-- Solomon says, that "there is a time to laugh, and a time to weep"; now a time for a young woman to laugh is when she has made sure of a good rich husband. Now a time to cry, according to you, Mary, is when she is making choice of him: but, I should think, that a young woman's time to cry was when she despaired of *getting* one. Why, there was your mother now; to be sure when I popp'd the question to her, she did look a little silly; but when she had once looked down on her apron-strings, as all modest young women us'd to do, and drawled out ye-s, she was as brisk and as merry as a bee.

MARIA. My honoured mother, Sir, had no motive to melancholy; she married the man of her choice.

VAN ROUGH. The man of her choice! And pray, Mary, an't you going to marry the man of your choice--what trumpery notion is this? It is these vile books. (*Throws them away.*) I'd have you to know, Mary, if you won't make young Van Dumpling the man of *your* choice, you shall marry him as the man of *my* choice.

MARIA. You terrify me, Sir. Indeed, Sir, I am all submission. My will is yours.

VAN ROUGH. Why, that is the way your mother us'd to talk. "My will is yours, my dear Mr. Van Rough, my will is yours": but she took special care to have her own way though for all that.

MARIA. Do not reflect upon my mother's memory, Sir--

VAN ROUGH. Why not, Mary, why not? She kept me from speaking my mind all her *life*, and do you think she shall henpeck me now she is dead, too? Come, come; don't go to sniveling: be a good girl, and mind the main chance. I'll see you well settled in the world.

MARIA. I do not doubt your love, Sir; and it is my duty to obey you. I will endeavor to make my duty and inclination go hand in hand.

VAN ROUGH. Well, well, Mary; do you be a good girl, mind the main chance, and never mind inclination. Why, do you know that I have been down in the cellar this very morning to examine a pipe of Madeira which I purchased the week you were born, and mean to tap on your wedding day. That pipe cost me fifty pounds sterling. It was well worth sixty pounds; but I over-reached Ben Bulkhead, the supercargo: I'll tell you the whole story. You must know that-- (*Enter Servant.*)

SERVANT. Sir, Mr. Transfer, the broker, is below. (*Exit.*)

VAN ROUGH. Well, Mary, I must go. Remember, and be a good girl, and mind the main chance. (*Exit.*)

MARIA. (*alone*) How deplorable is my situation! How distressing for a daughter to find her heart militating with her filial duty! I know my father loves me tenderly, why then do I reluctantly obey him? At a parent's command I could wed awkwardness and deformity. At a father's command I could embrace poverty. Were the poor man my husband, I would learn resignation to my lot; I would enliven our frugal meal with good humour, and chase away misfortune from our cottage with a smile. At a father's command, I could almost submit, to what every female heart knows to be the most mortifying, to marry a weak man, and blush at my husband's folly in every company I visited. But to marry a depraved wretch, whose only virtue is a polished exterior; whose laurels are the sighs and tears of the miserable victims of his specious behavior. Can he, who has no regard for the peace and happiness of other families, ever have a due regard for the peace and happiness of his own? Would to heaven that my father were not so hasty in his temper! Surely, if I were to state my reasons for declining this match, he would not compel me to marry a man--whom, though my lips may solemnly promise to honour, I find my heart must ever despise.

   (*Exit Maria.*)

ACT II.

Scene 1. (*Enter Charlotte and Letitia.*)

CHARLOTTE. (*at entering*) Betty, take those things out of the carriage and carry them to my chamber; see that you don't tumble them. My dear, I protest, I think it was the homeliest of the whole. I declare I was almost tempted to return and change it.

LETITIA. Why would you take it?

CHARLOTTE. My dear, what could I do? Did not Mrs. Catgut say it was the most fashionable; and if I had not taken it, was not that awkward gawky, Sally Slender ready to purchase it immediately?

LETITIA. Then did you take notice, with what an affected warmth of friendship she and Miss Wasp met? when all their acquaintances know how much pleasure they take in abusing each other in every company?

CHARLOTTE. Lud! Letitia, is that so extraordinary? Why, my dear, I hope you are not going to turn sentimenatlist. Scandal, you know, is but amusing ourselves with the faults, foiblies, follies and reputations of our friends. Indeed, I don't know why we should have friends, if we are not at liberty to make use of them. But no person is so ignorant of the world as to suppose, because I amuse myself with a lady's faults, that I am obliged to quarrel with her person every time we meet; believe me, my dear, we should have very few acquaintances at that rate.

(*Enter Servant, delivers a letter to Charlotte, and exit.*)

You'll excuse me, my dear.

(*Charlotte opens the letter and reads to herself.*)

LETITIA. Oh, quite excusable.

CHARLOTTE. As I hope to be married, my brother Henry is in the city.

LETITIA. What, your brother, Colonel Manly?

CHARLOTTE. Yes, my dear; the only brother I have in the world.

LETITIA. Was he never in this city?

CHARLOTTE. Never nearer than Harlem Heights, where he lay with his regiment.

LETITIA. What sort of a being is this brother of yours? If he is as chatty, as pretty, as sprightly as you, half the belles in the city will be pulling caps for him.

CHARLOTTE. My brother is the very counterpart and reverse of me: I am gay, he is grave; I am airy, he is solid; I am ever selecting the most pleasing objects for my laughter, he has a tear for every pitiful one. And thus, whilst he is plucking the briars and thorns from the path of the unfortunate, I am strewing my own path with roses.

LETITIA. My sweet friend, not quite so poetical, and a little more particular.

CHARLOTTE. Hands off, Letitia. I feel the rage of simile upon you; I can't talk to you in any other way. My brother has a heart replete with the noblest sentiments, but then, it is like--it is like-- Oh! you provoking girl, you have deranged all my ideas--it is like-- Oh! I have it--his heart is like an old maiden lady's band-box; it contains many costly things, arranged with the most scrupulous nicety, yet the misfortune is, that they are too delicate, costly, and antiquated, for common use.

LETITIA. By what I can pick out of your flowery description, your brother is no beau.

CHARLOTTE. No, indeed; he makes no pretention to the character. He'd ride, or rather fly, an hundred miles to relieve a distressed object, or to do a gallant act in the service of his country: but, should you drop your fan or bouquet in his presence, it is ten to one that some beau at the farther end of the room would have the honour of presenting it to you, before he had observed that it fell. I'll tell you one of his antiquated, anti-gallant notions. He said once in my presence, in a room full of company--would you believe it--in a large circle of ladies, that the best evidence a gentleman could give a young lady of his respect and affection, was, to endeavour in a friendly manner to rectify her foibles. I protest I was crimson to the eyes, upon reflecting that I was known as his sister.

LETITIA. Insupportable creature! tell a lady of her faults! If he is so grave, I fear I have no chance of captivating him.

CHARLOTTE. You captivate him! Why, my dear, he would as soon fall in love with a box of Italian flowers. There is Maria now, if she were not engaged, she might do something. Oh! how I should like to see that pair of pensorosos together, looking as grave as two sailors' wives on a stormy night, with a flow of sentiment meandering through their conversation like purling streams in modern poetry.

LETITIA. Oh! my dear fanciful--

CHARLOTTE. Hush! I hear some person coming through the entry.

(*Enter Servant.*)

SERVANT. Madam, there's a gentleman below who calls himself Colonel Manly; do you chuse to be at home?

CHARLOTTE. Shew him in. (*Exit Servant.*) Now for a sober face.

(*Enter Colonel Manly.*)

MANLY. My dear Charlotte, I am happy that I once more enfold you within the arms of fraternal affection. I know you are going to ask (amiable impatience!) how our parents do--the venerable pair transmit you their blessing by me--they totter on the verge of a well-spent life, and wish only to see their children settled in the world, to depart in peace.

CHARLOTTE. I am very happy to hear that they are well. (*Coolly.*) Brother, will you give me leave to introduce you to our uncle's ward, one of my most intimate friends.

MANLY. (*saluting Letitia*) I ought to regard your friends as my own.

CHARLOTTE. Come, Letitia, do give us a little dash of your vivacity; my brother is so sentimental, and so grave, that I protest he'll give us the vapours.

MANLY. Though sentiment and gravity, I know, are banished in the polite world, yet, I hoped, they might find some countenance in the meeting of such near connections as brother and sister.

CHARLOTTE. Positively, brother, if you go one step further in the strain, you will set me crying, and that, you know, would spoil my eyes; and then I should never get the husband which our good papa and mama have so kindly wished me--never be established in the world.

MANLY. Forgive me, my sister--I am no enemy to mirth; I love your sprightliness; and I hope it will one day enliven the hours of some worthy man; but when I mention the respectable authors of my existence--the cherishers and protectors of my helpless infancy, whose hearts glow with such fondness and attachment, that they would willingly lay down their lives for my welfare, you will excuse me, if I am so unfashionable as to speak of them with some degree of respect and reverence.

CHARLOTTE. Well, well, brother; if you won't be gay, we'll not differ; I will be as grave as you wish. (*Affects gravity.*) And so, brother, you have come to the city to exchange some of your commutation notes for a little pleasure.

MANLY. Indeed, you are mistaken; my errand is not of amusement, but business; and as I neither drink nor game, my expenses will be so trivial, I shall have no occasion to sell my notes.

CHARLOTTE. Then you won't have occasion to do a very good thing. Why, there was the Vermont General--he came down some time since, sold all his musty notes at one stroke, and then laid the cash out in trinkets for his dear Fanny. I want a dozen pretty things myself; have you got the notes with you?

MANLY. I shall be ever willing to contribute as far as it is in my power, to adorn, or in any way to please my sister; yet, I hope, I shall never be obliged for this, to sell my notes. I may be romantic, but I preserve them as a sacred deposit. Their full amount is justly due to me, but as embarrassments, the natural consequences of a long war, disable my country from supporting its credit, I shall wait with patience until it is rich enough to discharge them. If that is not in my day, they shall be transmitted as an honourable certificate to posterity, that I have humbly imitated our illustrious WASHINGTON, in having exposed my health and life in the service of my country, without reaping any other reward than the glory of conquering in so arduous a contest.

CHARLOTTE. Well said heroics. Why, my dear Henry, you have such a lofty way of saying things, that I protest I almost tremble at the thought of introducing you to the polite circles in the city. The belles would think you were a player run mad, with your head filled with old scraps of tragedy: and, as to the beaux, they might admire, because they would not understand you. But, however, I must, I believe, venture to introduce you to two or three ladies of my acquaintance.

LETITIA. And that will make him acquainted with thirty or forty beaux.

CHARLOTTE. Oh! brother, you don't know what a fund of happiness you have in store.

MANLY. I fear, sister, I have not refinement sufficient to enjoy it.

CHARLOTTE. Oh! you cannot fail being pleased.

LETITIA. Our ladies are so delicate and dressy.

CHARLOTTE. And our beaux so dressy and delicate.

LETITIA. Our ladies chat and flirt so agreeably.

CHARLOTTE. And our beaux simper and bow so gracefully.

LETITIA. With their hair so trim and neat.

CHARLOTTE. And their faces so soft and sleek.

LETITIA. Their buckles so tonish and bright.

CHARLOTTE. And their hands so slender and white.

LETITIA. I vow, Charlotte, we are quite poetical.

CHARLOTTE. And then, brother, the faces of the beaux are of such a lily white hue! None of that horrid robustness of constitution, that vulgar corn-fed glow of health, which can only serve to alarm an unmarried lady with apprehensions, and prove a melancholy memento to a married one, that she can never hope for the happiness of being a widow. I will say this to the credit of our city beaux, that such is the delicacy of their complexion, dress, and address, that, even had I no reliance upon the honour of the dear Adonises, I would trust myself in any possible situation with them, without the least apprehensions of rudeness.

MANLY. Sister Charlotte!

CHARLOTTE. (*interrupting him*) Now, now, now, brother, now don't go to spoil my mirth with a dash of your gravity; I am so glad to see you, I am in tip-top spirits. Oh! that you could be with us at a little snug party. There is Billy Simper, Jack Chassé, and Colonel Van Titter, Miss Promonade, and the two Miss Tambours, sometimes make a party with some other ladies, in a side-box at the play. Everything is conducted with such decorum. First, we bow round to the company in general, then to each one in particular; then we have so many inquiries after each other's health, and we are so happy to meet each other, and it is so many ages since we last had that pleasure. Then the curtain rises, then our sensibility is all awake, and then by the mere force of apprehension, we torture some harmless expression into a double meaning, which the poor author never dreamt of, and then we have recourse to our fans, and then we blush, and then the gentlemen jog one another, peep under the fan, and make the prettiest remarks; and then we giggle and they simper, and they giggle and we simper, and then the curtain drops, and then for nuts and oranges, and then we bow, and it's pray Ma'am take it, and pray Sir keep it, and oh! not for the world, Sir: and then the curtain rises again, and then we blush and giggle, and simper, and bow, all over again. Oh! the sentimental charms of a side-box conversation! (*All laugh.*)

MANLY. Well, sister, I join heartily with you in the laugh; for, in my opinion, it is as justifiable to laugh at folly, as it is reprehensible to ridicule misfortune.

CHARLOTTE. Well, but brother, positively, I can't introduce you in these clothes: why, your coat looks as if it were calculated for the vulgar purpose of keeping yourself comfortable.

MANLY. This coat was my regimental coat in the late war. The public tumults of our state have induced me to buckle on the sword in support of that government which I once fought to establish. I can only say, sister, that there was a time when this coat was respectable, and some people even thought that those men who had endured so many winter campaigns in the service of their country, without bread, clothing, or pay, at least deserved that the poverty of their appearance should not be ridiculed.

CHARLOTTE. We agree in opinion entirely, brother, though it would not have done for me to have said it: it is the coat makes the man respectable. In the time of war, when we were almost frightened to death, why, your coat was respectable, that is, fashionable; now another kind of coat is fashionable, that is, respectable. And pray direct the tailor to make yours the height of fashion.

MANLY. Though it is of little consequence to me of what shape my coat is, yet, as to the height of the fashion, there you will please to excuse me, sister. You know my sentiments on that subject. I have often lamented the advantage which the French have over us in that particular. In Paris, the fashions have their dawnings, their routine and declensions, and depend as much upon the caprice of the day as in other countries; but there every lady assumes a right to deviate from the general *ton*, as far as will be of advantage to her own appearance. In America, the cry is, what is the fashion? and we follow it, indiscriminately, because it is so.

CHARLOTTE. Therefore it is, that when large hoops are in fashion, we often see many a plump girl lost in the immensity of a hoop petticoat, whose want of height and *em-bon-point* would never have been remarked in any other dress. When the high head-dress is the mode, how then do we see a lofty cushion with a profusion of gauze, feathers, and ribband, supported by a face no bigger than an apple; whilst a broad full-faced lady, who really would have appeared tolerably handsome in a large head-dress, looks with her smart chapeau as masculine as a soldier.

MANLY. But remember, my dear sister, and I wish all my fair country-women would recollect, that the only excuse a young lady can have for going extravagantly into a fashion, is, because it makes her look extravagantly handsome. Ladies, I must wish you a good morning.

CHARLOTTE. But, brother, you are going to make home with us.

MANLY. Indeed, I cannot. I have seen my uncle, and explained that matter.

CHARLOTTE. Come and dine with us, then. We have a family dinner about half past four o'clock.

MANLY. I am engaged to dine with the Spanish ambassador. I was introduced to him by an old brother officer; and instead of freezing me with a cold card of compliment to dine with him ten days hence, he, with the true old Castilian frankness, in a friendly manner, asked me to dine with him to-day--an honour I could not refuse. Sister, adieu-- Madam, your most obedient. (*Exit.*)

CHARLOTTE. I will wait upon you to the door, brother; I have something particular to say to you. (*Exit.*)

LETITIA. (*alone*) What a pair! She the pink of flirtation, he the essence of everything that is *outré* and gloomy. I think I have completely deceived Charlotte by my manner of speaking of Mr. Dimple; she's too much the friend of Maria to be confided in. He is certainly rendering himself disagreeable to Maria in order to break with her and proffer his hand to me. This is what the delicate fellow hinted in our last conversation. (*Exit.*)

Scene 2. The Mall.

JESSAMY. (*at entering*) Positively this Mall is a very pretty place. I hope the city won't ruin it by repairs. To be sure, it won't do to speak of in the same day with Ranelagh or Vauxhall; however, it's a fine place for a young fellow to display his person to advantage. Indeed, nothing is lost here; the girls have taste, and I am very happy to find they have adopted the elegant London fashion of looking back, after a genteel fellow like me has passed them. Ah! who comes here? This, by his awkwardness, must be the Yankee colonel's servant. I'll accost him. (*Enter Jonathan.*) Votre très--humble serviteur, Monsieur. I understand Colonel Manly, the Yankee officer, has the honour of your services.

JONATHAN. Sir!

JESSAMY. I say, Sir, I understand that Colonel Manly has the honour of having you for a servant.

JONATHAN. Servant! Sir, do you take me for a neger? I am Colonel Manly's waiter.

JESSAMY. A true Yankee distinction, egad, without a difference. Why, Sir, do you not perform all the offices of a servant? Do you not even blacken his boots?

JONATHAN. Yes; I do grease them a bit sometimes; but I am a true blue son of liberty, for all that. Father said I should come as Colonel Manly's waiter to see the world, and all that; but no man shall master me: my father has as good a farm as the Colonel.

JESSAMY. Well, Sir, we will not quarrel about terms upon the eve of an acquaintance, from which I promise myself so much satisfaction-- therefore sans ceremonie--

JONATHAN. What?

JESSAMY. I say, I am extremely happy to see Colonel Manly's waiter.

JONATHAN. Well, and I vow, too, I am pretty considerably glad to see you--but what the dogs need of all this outlandish lingo? Who may you be, Sir, if I may be so bold?

JESSAMY. I have the honour to be Mr. Dimple's servant, or, if you please, waiter. We lodge under the same roof, and should be glad of the honour of your acquaintance.

JONATHAN. You a waiter! By the living jingo, you look so topping, I took you for one of the agents to Congress.

JESSAMY. The brute has discernment notwithstanding his appearance. Give me leave to say I wonder then at your familiarity.

JONATHAN. Why, as to the matter of that, Mr.-- Pray, what's your name?

JESSAMY. Jessamy, at your service.

JONATHAN. Why, I swear we don't make any great matter of distinction in our state between quality and other folks.

JESSAMY. This is, indeed, a levelling principle. I hope, Mr. Jonathan, you have not taken part with the insurgents.

JONATHAN. Why, since General Shays has sneaked off, and given us the bag to hold, I don't care to give my opinion; but you'll promise not to tell--put your ear this way--you won't tell? I vow, I did think the sturgeons were right.

JESSAMY. I thought, Mr. Jonathan, you Massachusetts men always argued with a gun in your hand. Why did n't you join them?

JONATHAN. Why, the Colonel is one of those folks called the Shin-- shin--dang it all, I can't speak them lignum vitae words--you know who I mean--there is a company of them--they wear a China goose at their button-hole--a kind of gilt thing. Now the Colonel told father and brother--you must know there are, let me see--there is Elnathan, Silas, and Barnabas, Tabitha--no, no, she's a she--tarnation, now I have it--there's Elnathan, Silas, Barnabas, Jonathan, that's I--seven of us, six went into the wars, and I staid at home to take care of mother. Colonel said that it was a burning shame for the true blue Bunker-hill sons of liberty, who had fought Governor Hutchinson, Lord North, and the Devil, to have any hand in kicking up a cursed dust against a government, which we had every mother's son of us a hand in making.

JESSAMY. Bravo! Well, have you been abroad in the city since your arrival? What have you seen that is curious and entertaining?

JONATHAN. Oh! I have seen a power of fine sights. I went to see two marbled-stone men and a leaden horse, that stands out of doors in all weathers; and when I came where they was, one had got no head, and t'other wer'n't there. They said as how the leaden man was a damn'd tory, and that he took wit in his anger and rode off in the time of the troubles.

JESSAMY. But this was not the end of your excursion.

JONATHAN. Oh, no; I went to a place they call Holy Ground. Now I counted this was a place where folks go to meeting; so I put my hymn-book in my pocket, and walked softly and grave as a minister; and when I came there, the dogs a bit of a meeting-house could I see. At last I spied a young gentlewoman standing by one of the seats, which they have here at the doors--I took her to be the deacon's daughter and she looked so kind, and so obliging, that I thought I would go and ask her the way to lecture, and would you think it--she called me dear, and sweeting, and honey, just as if we were married; by the living jingo, I had a month's mind to buss her.

JESSAMY. Well, but how did it end?

JONATHAN. Why, as I was standing talking with her, a parcel of sailor men and boys got round me, the snarl headed curs fell a-kicking and cursing of me at such a tarnal rate, that, I vow, I was glad to take to my heels and split home, right off, tail on end like a stream of chalk.

JESSAMY. Why, my dear friend, you are not acquainted with the city; that girl you saw was a-- (*Whispers.*)

JONATHAN. Mercy on my soul! was that young woman a harlot! Well, if this is New York Holy Ground, what must the Holy-day Ground be!

JESSAMY. Well, you should not judge of the city too rashly. We have a number of elegant fine girls here, that make a man's leisure hours pass very agreeably. I would esteem it an honour to announce you to some of them. Gad! that announce is a select word; I wonder where I picked it up.

JONATHAN. I don't want to know them.

JESSAMY. Come, come, my dear friend, I see that I must assume the honour of being the director of your amusements. Nature has give us passions, and youth and opportunity stimulate to gratify them. It is no shame, my dear Blueskin, for a man to amuse himself with a little gallantry.

JONATHAN. Girl huntry! I don't altogether understand. I never played at that game. I know how to play hunt the squirrel, but I can't play anything with the girls; I am as good as married.

JESSAMY. Vulgar, horrid brute! Married, and above a hundred miles from his wife, and think that an objection to his making love to every woman he meets! He never can have read, no, he never can have been in a room with a volume of the divine Chesterfield. So you are married?

JONATHAN. No, I don't say so; I said I was as good as married, a kind of promise.

JESSAMY. As good as married!

JONATHAN. Why, yes; there's Tabitha Wymen, the deacon's daughter, at home, she and I have been courting a great while, and folks say as how we are to be married; and so I broke a piece of money with her when we parted, and she promised not to spark it with Solomon Dyer while I am gone. You would n't have me false to my true love, would you?

JESSAMY. May be you have another reason for constancy; possibly the young lady has a fortune? Ha! Mr. Jonathan, the solid charms; the chains of love are never so binding as when the links are made of gold.

JONATHAN. Why, as to fortune, I must needs say her father is pretty dumb rich; he went representative for our town last year. He will give her--let me see--four times seven is--seven times four--nought and carry one; he will give her twenty acres of land--somewhat rocky though--a bible and a cow.

JESSAMY. Twenty acres of rock, a bible, and a cow! Why, my dear Mr. Jonathan, we have servant maids, or, as you would more elegantly express it, wait'resses, in this city, who collect more in one year from their mistresses' cast clothes.

JONATHAN. You don't say so!

JESSAMY. Yes, and I'll introduce you to one of them. There is a little lump of flesh and delicacy that lives at next door, wait'ress to Miss Maria; we often see her on the street.

JONATHAN. But are you sure she would be courted by me?

JESSAMY. Never doubt it; remember a faint heart never--blisters on my tongue--I was going to be guilty of a vile proverb; flat against the authority of Chesterfield. I say there can be no doubt, that the brilliancy of your merit will secure you a favourable reception.

JONATHAN. Well, but what must I say to her?

JESSAMY. Say to her! why, my dear friend, though I admire your profound knowledge on every other subject, yet, you will pardon my saying, that your want of opportunity has made the female heart escape the poignancy of your penetration. Say to her! Why, when a man goes a-courting, and hopes for success, he must begin with doing, and not saying.

JONATHAN. Well, what must I do?

JESSAMY. Why, when you are introduced, you must make five or six elegant bows.

JONATHAN. Six elegant bows! I understand that; six, you say? Well--

JESSAMY. Then you must press and kiss her hand; then press and kiss, and so on to her lips and cheeks; then talk as much as you can about hearts, darts, flames, nectar and ambrosia--the more incoherent the better.

JONATHAN. Well, but suppose she should be angry with I?

JESSAMY. Why, if she should pretend--please to observe, Mr. Jonathan--if she should pretend to be offended, you must-- But I'll tell you how my master acted in such a case: He was seated by a young lady of eighteen upon a sopha, plucking with a wanton hand the blooming sweets of youth and beauty. When the lady thought it necessary to check his ardour, she called up a frown upon her lovely face, so irresistibly alluring, that it would have warmed the frozen bosom of age: remember, said she, putting her delicate arm upon his, remember your character and my honour. My master instantly dropped upon his knees, with eyes swimming with love, cheeks glowing with desire, and in the gentlest modulation of voice, he said-- My dear Caroline, in a few months our hands will be indissolubly united at the altar; our hearts I feel are already so--the favours you now grant as evidence of your affection, are favours indeed; yet when the ceremony is once past, what will now be received with rapture, will then be attrubuted to duty.

JONATHAN. Well, and what was the consequence?

JESSAMY. The consequence! Ah! forgive me, my dear friend, but you New England gentlemen have such a laudable curiosity of seeing the bottom of every thing--why, to be honest, I confess I saw the blooming cherub of a consequence smiling in its angelic mother's arms, about ten months afterwards.

JONATHAN. Well, if I follow all your plans, make them six bows, and all that; shall I have such little cherubim consequences?

JESSAMY. Undoubtedly. What are you musing upon?

JONATHAN. You say you'll certainly make me acquainted? Why, I was thinking then how I should contrive to pass this broken piece of silver--won't it buy a sugar-dram?

JESSAMY. What is that, the love-token from the deacon's daughter? You come on bravely. But I must hasten to my master. Adieu, my dear friend.

JONATHAN. Stay, Mr. Jessamy--must I buss her when I'm introduced to her?

JESSAMY. I told you, you must kiss her.

JONATHAN. Well, but must I buss her?

JESSAMY. Why, kiss and buss, and buss and kiss, is all one.

JONATHAN. Oh! my dear friend, though you have a profound knowledge of all, a pugnancy of tribulation, you don't know everything.

(*Exit Jonathan.*)

JESSAMY. (*alone*) Well, certainly I improve; my master could not have insinuated himself with more address into the heart of a man he despised. Now will this blundering dog sicken Jenny with his nauseous pawings, until she flies into my arms for very ease. How sweet will the contrast be, between the blundering Jonathan, and the courtly and accomplished Jessamy!

ACT III.

Scene 1. Dimple's room.

DIMPLE. (*at a toilet, reading*) "Women have in general but one object, which is their beauty." Very true, my lord; positively very true. "Nature has hardly formed a woman ugly enough to be insensible to flattery upon her person." Extremely just, my lord; every day's delightful experience confirms this. "If her face is so shocking that she must, in some degree, be conscious of it, her figure and air, she thinks, make ample amends for it." The sallow Miss Wan is a proof of this. Upon my telling the distasteful wretch the other day, that her countenance spoke the pensive language of sentiment, and that Lady Wortley Montague declared, that if the ladies were arrayed in the garb of innocence, the face would be the last part which would be admired as Monsieur

Milton expresses it, she grin'd horribly a ghastly smile. "If her figure is deformed, she thinks her face counterbalances it." (*Enter Jessamy with letters.*) Where got you these, Jessamy?

JESSAMY. Sir, the English packet is arrived.

DIMPLE. (*opens and reads a letter enclosing notes*)

"Sir,

I have drawn bills on you in favour of Messrs. Van Cash and Co. as per margin. I have taken up your note to Col. Piquet, and discharged your debts to my Lord Lurcher and Sir Harry Rook. I herewith enclose you copies of the bills, which I have no doubt will be immediately honoured. On failure, I shall empower some lawyer in your country to recover the amounts.

I am, Sir, Your most humble servant,

John Hazard."

Now, did not my lord expressly say, that it was unbecoming a well-bred man to be in a passion, I confess I should be ruffled. (*Reads.*) "There is no accident so unfortunate, which a wise man may not turn to his advantage; nor any accident so fortunate, which a fool will not turn to his disadvantage." True, my lord: but how advantage can be derived from this, I can't see. Chesterfield himself, who made, however, the worst practice of the most excellent precepts, was never in so embarrassing a situation. I love the person of Charlotte, and it is necessary I should command the fortune of Letitia. As to Maria!--I doubt not by my *sang-froid* behaviour I shall compel her to decline the match; but the blame must not fall upon me. A prudent man, as my lord says, should take all the credit of a good action to himself, and throw the discredit of a bad one upon others. I must break with Maria, marry Letitia, and as for Charlotte--why, Charlotte must be a companion to my wife. Here, Jessamy!

(*Enter Jessamy. Dimple folds and seals two letters.*)

Here, Jessamy, take this letter to my love.

JESSAMY. (*taking the letter*) To which of your honour's loves? Oh! (*Reading.*) To Miss Letitia, you honour's rich love.

DIMPLE. (*delivers another*) And this to Miss Charlotte Manly. See that you deliver them privately.

JESSAMY. Yes, you honour. (*Going.*)

DIMPLE. Jessamy, who are these strange lodgers that came to the house last night?

JESSAMY. Why, the master is a Yankee colonel; I have not seen much of him; but the man is the most unpolished animal your honour ever disgraced your eyes by looking upon. I have had one of the most *outré* conversations with him! He really has a most prodigious effect upon my risibility.

DIMPLE. I ought, according to every rule of Chesterfield, to wait upon him and insinuate myself into his good graces. Jessamy, wait upon the colonel with my compliments, and if he is disengaged, I will do myself the honour of paying him my respects. Some ignorant unpolished boor--

(*Jessamy goes off and returns.*)

JESSAMY. Sir, the colonel is gone out, and Jonathan, his servant, says that he is gone to stretch his legs upon the Mall--stretch his legs! what an indelicacy of diction!

DIMPLE. Very well. Reach me my hat and sword. I'll accost him there on my way to Letitia's, as by accident, pretend to be struck with his person and address, and endeavor to steal into his confidence. Jessamy, I have no business for you at present. (*Exit.*)

JESSAMY. (*taking up the book*) My master and I obtain our knowledge from the same source, though--gad!--I think myself much the prettier fellow of the two. (*Surveying himself in the glass.*) That was a brilliant thought, to insinuate that I folded my master's letters for him; the folding is so neat, that it does honour to the operator. I once intended to have insinuated that I wrote his letters too; but that was before I saw them; it won't do now; no honour there, positively. (*Reading affectedly.*) "Nothing looks more vulgar, ordinary, and illiberal, than ugly, uneven, and ragged nails; the ends of which should be kept even and clean, not tipped with black, and cut in small segments of circles." Segments of circles! Surely my lord did not consider that he wrote for the beaux. Segments of circles! What a crabbed term! Now I dare answer, that my master, with all his learning, does not know that this means, according to the present mode, to let the nails grow long, and then cut them off even at top. (*Laughter without.*) Ha! that's Jenny's titter. I protest I despair of ever teaching that girl to laugh; she has something so execrably natural in her laugh, that I declare it absolutely discomposes my nerves. How came she into our house! (*Calls.*) Jenny! (*Enter Jenny.*) Prythee, Jenny, don't spoil your fine face with laughing.

JENNY. Why, must n't I laugh, Mr. Jessamy?

JESSAMY. You may smile; but, as my lord says, nothing can authorise a laugh.

JENNY. Well, I can't help laughing-- Have you seen him, Mr. Jessamy? Ha, ha, ha!

JESSAMY. Seen whom?

JENNY. Why, Jonathan, the New England colonel's servant. Do you know he was at the play last night, and the stupid creature don't know where he has been. He would not go to a play for the world; he thinks it was a show, as he calls it.

JESSAMY. As ignorant and unpolished as he is, do you know, Miss Jenny, that I propose to introduce him to the honour of your acquaintance.

JENNY. Introduce him to me! for what?

JESSAMY. Why, my lovely girl, that you may take him under your protection, as Madam Rambaoulliet did young Stanhope; that you may, by your plastic hand, mold this uncouth cub into a gentleman. He is to make love to you.

JENNY. Make love to me!

JESSAMY. Yes, Mistress Jenny, make love to you; and, I doubt now, when he shall become domesticated in your kitchen, that this boor, under your auspices, will soon become *un aimable petit Jonathan.*

JENNY. I must say, Mr. Jessamy, if he copies after me, he will be vastly monstrously polite.

JESSAMY. Stay here one moment, and I will call him. (*Calls.*) Jonathan!--Mr. Jonathan!

JONATHAN. (*within*) Holla! there. (*Enters.*) You promise to stand by me--six bows you say. (*Bows.*)

JESSAMY. Mrs. Jenny, I have the honour of presenting Mr. Jonathan, Colonel Manly's waiter, to you. I am extremely happy that I have it in my power to make two worthy people acquainted with each other's merit.

JENNY. So, Mr. Jonathan, I hear you were at the play last night.

JONATHAN. At the play! why, did you think I went to the devil's drawing-room!

JENNY. The devil's drawing-room!

JONATHAN. Yes; why an't cards and dice the devil's device; and the play-house the shop where the devil hangs out the vanities of the world, upon the tenterhooks of temptation. I believe you have not heard how they were acting the old boy one night, and the wicked one came among them sure enough; and went right off in a storm, and carried one quarter of the play-house with him. Oh! no, no, no! You won't catch me at a play-house, I warrant you.

JENNY. Well, Mr. Jonathan, though I don't scruple your veracity, I have some reasons for believing you were there; pray, where were you about six o'clock?

JONATHAN. Why, I went to see one Mr. Morrison, the *hocus pocus* man; they said as how he could eat a case knife.

JENNY. Well, and how did you find the place?

JONATHAN. As I was going about here and there, to and again, to find it, I saw a great crowd of folks going into a long entry that had lantherns over the door; so I asked a man, whether that was not the place where they played *hocus pocus*. He was a very kind civil man, though he did speak like the Hessians; he lifted up his eyes and said-- "they play *hocus pocus* tricks enough there, Got knows, mine friend."

JENNY. Well--

JONATHAN. So I went right in, and they shewed me away clean up to the garret, just like a meeting-house gallery. And so I saw a power of topping folks, all sitting round in little cabbins--and then there was such a squeaking with the fiddles, and such a tarnal blaze with the lights, my head was near turned. At last the people that sat near me set up such a hissing--hiss--like so many mad cats; and then they went thump, thump, thump, just like our Peleg threshing wheat, and stampt away, just like the nation; and called out for one Mr. Langolee--I suppose he helps act the tricks.

JENNY. Well, and what did you do all this time?

JONATHAN. Gor, I--I liked the fun, and so I thumpt away, and hiss'd as lustily as the best of 'em. One sailor-looking man that sat by me, seeing me stamp, and knowing I was a cute fellow, because I could make a roaring noise, clapt me on the shoulder and said, you are a d-----d hearty cock, smite my timbers! I told him so I was, but I thought he need not swear so, and make use of such naughty words.

JESSAMY. The savage! Well, and did you see the man with his tricks?

JONATHAN. Why, I vow, as I was looking out for him, they lifted up a great green cloth, and let us look right into the next neighbour's house. Have you a good many houses in New York made so in that 'ere way?

JENNY. Not many: but did you see the family?

JONATHAN. Yes, swamp it; I see'd the family.

JENNY. Well, and how did you like them?

JONATHAN. Why, I vow they were pretty much like other families: there was a poor, good natured, curse of a husband, and a sad rantipole of a wife.

JENNY. But did you see no other folks?

JONATHAN. Yes. There was one youngster, they called him Mr. Joseph; he talked as sober and as pious as a minister; but like some ministers that I know, he was a sly tike in his heart for all that: He was going to ask a young woman to spark it with him, and--the Lord have mercy on my soul!--she was another man's wife.

JESSAMY. The Wasbash!

JENNY. And did you see any more folks?

JONATHAN. Why, they came on as thick as mustard. For my part, I thought the house was haunted. There was a soldier fellow, who talked about his row de dow dow, and courted a young woman: but of all the cute folk I saw, I liked one little fellow--

JENNY. Aye! who was he?

JONATHAN. Why, he had red hair, and a little round plump face like mine, only not altogether so handsome. His name was Darby--that was his baptizing name, his other name I forgot. Oh! it was, Wig--Wag--Wag-all, Darby Wag-all--pray, do you know him? I should like to take a sling with him, or a drap of cyder with a pepper-pod in it, to make it warm and comfortable.

JENNY. I can't say I have that pleasure.

JONATHAN. I wish you did, he is a cute fellow. But there was one thing I did n't like in that Mr. Darby; and that was, he was afraid of some of them 'ere shooting irons, such as your troopers wear on training days. Now, I'm a true born Yankee American son of liberty, and I never was afraid of a gun yet in all my life.

JENNY. Well, Mr. Jonathan, you were certainly at a play-house.

JONATHAN. I at the play-house! Why did n't I see the play then?

JENNY. Why, the people you saw were players.

JONATHAN. Mercy on my soul! did I see the wicked players? Mayhap that 'ere Darby that I liked so, was the old serpent himself, and had his cloven foot in his pocket. Why, I vow, now I come to think on 't, the candles seemed to burn blue, and I am sure where I sat it smelt tarnally of brimstone.

JESSAMY. Well, Mr. Jonathan, from your account, which I confess is very accurate, you must have been at the play-house.

JONATHAN. Why, I vow I began to smell a rat. When I came away, I went to the man for my money again: you want your money, says he; yes, says I; for what, says he; why, says I, no man shall jocky me out of my money; I paid my money to see sights, and the dogs a bit of a sight have I seen, unless you call listening to people's private business a sight. Why, says he, it is the School for Scandalization. The School for Scandalization! Oh! ho! no wonder you New York folks are so cute at it, when you go to school to learn it: and so I jogged off.

JESSAMY. My dear Jenny, my master's business drags me from you;

would to heaven I knew no other servitude than to your charms.

JONATHAN. Well, but don't go; you won't leave me so.

JESSAMY. Excuse me. (*Aside to him.*) Remember the cash. (*Exit.*)

JENNY. Mr. Jonathan, won't you please to sit down. Mr. Jessamy tells me you wanted to have some conversation with me.

(*Having brought forward two chairs, they sit.*)

JONATHAN. Ma'am!

JENNY. Sir!

JONATHAN. Ma'am!

JENNY. Pray, how do you like the city, Sir?

JONATHAN. Ma'am!

JENNY. I say, Sir, how do you like New York?

JONATHAN. Ma'am!

JENNY. (*aside*) The stupid creature! but I must pass some little time with him, if it is only to endeavour to learn, whether it was his master that made such an abrupt entrance into our house, and my young mistress's heart this morning. (*Aloud.*) As you don't seem to like to talk, Mr. Jonathan--do you sing?

JONATHAN. (*aside*) Gor, I--I am glad she asked that, for I forgot what Mr. Jessamy bid me say, and I dare as well be hanged as act what he bid me do, I'm so ashamed. (*Aloud.*) Yes, ma'am, I can sing--I can sing Mear, Old Hundred, and Bangor.

JENNY. Oh! I don't mean psalm tunes. Have you no little song to please the ladies; such as Roslin Castle or the Maid of the Mill?

JONATHAN. Why, all my tunes go to meeting tunes, save one, and I count you won't altogether like that 'ere.

JENNY. What is it called?

JONATHAN. I am sure you have heard folks talk about it, it is called Yankee Doodle.

JENNY. Oh! it is the tune I am fond of; and, if I know anything of my mistress, she would be glad to dance to it. Pray, sing?

JONATHAN. (*sings*)

> Father and I went up to camp,
> Along with Captain Goodwin;
> And there we saw the men and boys,
> As thick as hasty pudding.
>   Yankee Doodle do, etc.
> And there we saw a swamping gun,
> Big as log of maple,
> On a little deuced cart,

A load for father's cattle.
>Yankee Doodle do, etc.

And every time they fired it off,
It took a horn of powder,
It made a noise like father's gun,
Only a nation louder.
>Yankee Doodle do, etc.

There was man in our town,
His name was-- (*Stops singing.*)

No, no, that won't do. Now, if I was with Tabitha Wymen and Jemima Cawley, down at father Chase's, I should n't mind singing this all out before them--you would be affronted if I was to sing that, though that's a lucky thought; if you should be affronted, I have something dang'd cute, which Jessamy told me to say to you.

JENNY. Is that all! I assure you I like it of all things.

JONATHAN. No, no; I can sing more, some other time, when you and I are better acquainted, I'll sing the whole of it--no, no--that's a fib--I can't sing but a hundred and ninety verses: our Tabitha at home can sing it all. (*Sings.*)

Marblehead's a rocky place,
And Cape-Cod is sandy;
Charleston is burnt down,
Boston is the dandy.
>Yankee Doodle do, etc. (*Song ends.*)

I vow, my own town song has put me into such topping spirits, that I believe I'll begin to do a little, as Jessamy says we must when we go a courting-- (*Runs and kisses her.*) Burning rivers! cooling flames! red hot roses! pig-nuts! hasty-pudding and ambrosia!

JENNY. What means this freedom! you insulting wretch. (*Strikes him.*)

JONATHAN. Are you affronted?

JENNY. Affronted! with what looks shall I express my anger?

JONATHAN. Looks! why, as to the matter of looks, you look as cross as a witch.

JENNY. Have you no feeling for the delicacy of my sex?

JONATHAN. Feeling! (*Rubbing his cheek.*) Gor, I--I feel the delicacy of your sex pretty smartly, though, I vow, I thought when you city ladies courted and married, and all that, you put feeling out of the question. But I want to know whether you are really affronted, or only pretend to be so? 'Cause, if you are certainly right down affronted, I am at the end of my tether; Jessamy did n't tell me what to say to you.

JENNY. Pretend to be affronted!

JONATHAN. Aye, aye, if you only pretend you shall hear how I'll go to work to make cherubim consequences. (*Runs up to her.*)

JENNY. Begone, you brute!

JONATHAN. That looks like mad; but I won't lose my speech. My dearest Jenny--your name is Jenny, I think? My dearest Jenny, though I have the highest esteem for the sweet favours you have just now granted me-- (*Aside.*) Gor, that's a fib though, but Jessamy says it is not wicked to tell lies to the women. (*Aloud.*) I say, though I have the highest esteem for the favours you have just now granted me, yet, you will consider, that as soon as the dissolvable knot is tied, they will no longer be favours, but only matters of duty, and matters of course.

JENNY. Marry you! you audacious monster! get out of my sight, or rather let me fly from you. (*Exit hastily.*)

JONATHAN. Gor! she's gone off in a swinging passion, before I had time to think of consequences. If this is the way with your city ladies, give me the twenty acres of rock, the bible, the cow, and Tabitha, and a little peaceable bundling.

Scene 2. The Mall.

MANLY. (*at entering*) It must be so, Montague! and it is not all the tribe of Mandevilles shall convince me, that a nation, to become great, must first become dissipated. Luxury is surely the bane of a nation: Luxury! which enervates both soul and body, by opening a thousand new sources of enjoyment, opens, also, a thousand new sources of contention and want: Luxury! which renders a people weak at home, and accessible to bribery, corruption, and force from abroad. When the Grecian states knew no other tools than the axe and saw, the Grecians were a great, a free, and a happy people. The kings of Greece devoted their lives to the service of their country, and her senators knew no other superiority over their fellow-citizens than a glorious pre-eminence in danger and virtue. They exhibited to the world a noble spectacle: a number of independent states united by a similarity of language, sentiment, manners, common interest, and common consent, in one grand mutual league of protection. And, thus united, long might they have continued the cherishers of arts and sciences, the protectors of the oppressed, the scourge of tyrants, and the safe asylum of liberty: But when foreign gold, and still more pernicious, foreign luxury, had crept among them, they sapped the vitals of their virtue. The virtues of their ancestors were only found in their writings. Envy and suspicion, the vices of little minds, possessed them. The various states engendered jealousies of each other; and, more unfortunately, growing jealous of their great federal council, the Amphictyons, they forgot that their common safety had existed, and would exist, in giving them an honourable extensive prerogative. The common good was lost in the pursuit of private interest; and that people, who, by uniting, might have stood against the world in arms, by dividing, crumbled into ruin; their name is now only known in the page of the historian, and what they once were, is all we have left to admire. Oh! that America! Oh! that my country, would in this her day, learn the things which belong to her peace! (*Enter Dimple.*)

DIMPLE. You are Colonel Manly, I presume?

MANLY. At your service, Sir.

DIMPLE. My name is Dimple, Sir. I have the honour to be a lodger in the same house with you, and hearing you were in the Mall, came hither to take the liberty of joining you.

MANLY. You are very obliging, Sir.

DIMPLE. As I understand you are a stranger here, Sir, I have taken the liberty to introduce myself to your acquaintance, as possibly I may have it in my power to point out some things in this city worthy your notice.

MANLY. An attention to strangers is worthy a liberal mind, and must ever be gratefully received. But to a soldier, who has no fixed abode, such attentions are particularly pleasing.

DIMPLE. Sir, there is no character so respectable as that of a soldier. And, indeed, when we reflect how much we owe to those brave men who have suffered so much in the service of their country, and secured to us those inestimable blessings that we now enjoy, our liberty and independence, they demand every attention which gratitude can pay. For my own part, I never meet an officer, but I embrace him as my friend, nor a private in distress, but I insensibly extend my charity to him. (*Aside.*) I have hit the Bumkin off very tolerably.

MANLY. Give me your hand, Sir! I do not proffer this hand to everybody; but you steal into my heart. I hope I am as insensible to flattery as most men; but I declare (it may be my weak side), that I never hear the name of soldier mentioned with respect, but I experience a thrill of pleasure, which I never feel on any other occasion.

DIMPLE. Will you give me leave, my dear colonel, to confer an obligation on myself, by shewing you some civilities during your stay here, and giving a similar opportunity to some of my friends?

MANLY. Sir, I thank you; but I believe my stay in this city will be very short.

DIMPLE. I can introduce you to some men of excellent sense, in whose company you will esteem yourself happy; and, by way of amusement, to some fine girls, who will listen to your soft things with pleasure.

MANLY. Sir, I should be proud of the honour of being acquainted with those gentlemen;--but as for the ladies, I don't understand you.

DIMPLE. Why, Sir, I need not tell you, that when a young gentleman is alone with a young lady, he must say some soft things to her fair cheek--indeed, the lady will expect it. To be sure, there is not much pleasure, when a man of the world and a finished coquet meet, who perfectly know each other; but how delicious is it to excite the emotions of joy, hope, expectation, and delight, in the bosom of a lovely girl, who believes every tittle of what you say to be serious.

MANLY. Serious, Sir! In my opinion, the man, who, under pretensions of marriage, can plant thorns in the bosom of an innocent, unsuspecting girl, is more detestable than a common robber, in the same proportion, as private violence is more despicable than open force, and money of less value than happiness.

DIMPLE. (*aside*) How he awes me by the superiority of his sentiments. (*Aloud.*) As you say, Sir, a gentleman should be cautious how he mentions marriage.

MANLY. Cautious, Sir! How mean, how cruel, is it, by a thousand tender assiduities, to win the affections of an amiable girl, and though you leave her virtue unspotted, to betray her into the appearance of so many tender partialities, that every man of delicacy would suppress his inclination towards her, by supposing her heart engaged! Can any man, for the trivial gratification of his leisure hours, affect the happiness of a whole life! His not having spoken of marriage, may add to his perfidy, but can be no excuse for his conduct.

DIMPLE. Sir, I admire your sentiments; they are mine. The light observations that fell from me, were only a principle of the tongue; they came not from the heart--my practice has ever disapproved these principles.

MANLY. I believe you, Sir. I should with reluctance suppose that those pernicious sentiments could find admittance into the heart of a gentleman.

DIMPLE. I am now, Sir, going to visit a family, where, if you please, I will have the honour of introducing you. Mr. Manly's ward, Miss Letitia, is a young lady of immense fortune; and his niece, Miss

Charlotte Manly, is a young lady of great sprightliness and beauty.

MANLY. That gentleman, Sir, is my uncle, and Miss Manly my sister.

DIMPLE. (*aside*) The devil she is! (*Aloud.*) Miss Manly, your sister, Sir? I rejoice to hear it, and feel a double pleasure in being known to you. (*Aside.*) Plague on him! I wish he was at Boston again, with all my soul.

MANLY. Come, Sir, will you go?

DIMPLE. I will follow you in a moment, Sir. (*Exit Manly.*) Plague on it! this is unlucky. A fighting brother is a cursed appendage to a fine girl. Egad! I just stopped in time; had he not discovered himself, in two minutes more I should have told him how well I was with his sister. Indeed, I cannot see the satisfaction of an intrigue, if one can't have the pleasure of communicating it to our friends.

ACT IV.

Scene 1. Charlotte's apartment.

CHARLOTTE. (*leading in Maria*) This is so kind, my sweet friend, to come to see me at this moment. I declare, if I were going to be married in a few days, as you are, I should scarce have found time to visit my friends.

MARIA. Do you think, then, that there is an impropriety in it? How should you dispose of your time?

CHARLOTTE. Why, I would be shut up in my chamber; and my head would so run upon--upon--upon the solemn ceremony that I was to pass through--I declare it would take me above two hours merely to learn that little monosyllable--*Yes*. Ah! my dear, your sentimental imagination does not conceive what that little tiny word implies.

MARIA. Spare me your raillery, my sweet friend; I should love your agreeable vivacity at any other time.

CHARLOTTE. Why this is the very time to amuse you. You grieve me to see you look so unhappy.

MARIA. Have I not reason to look so?

CHARLOTTE. My dear Maria, you will forgive me; I know your candour and confidence in me; but I have at times, I confess, been led to suppose, that some other gentleman was the cause of your aversion to Mr. Dimple.

MARIA. No, my sweet friend, you may be assured, that though I have seen many gentlemen I could prefer to Mr. Dimple, yet I never saw one that I thought I could give my hand to, until this morning.

CHARLOTTE. This morning!

MARIA. Yes--one of the strangest accidents in the world. The odious Dimple, after disgusting me with his conversation, had just left me, when a gentleman, who, it seems, boards in the same house with him, saw him coming out of our door, and the houses looking very much alike, he came into our house instead of his lodgings; nor did he discover his mistake until he got into the parlour, where I was: he then bowed so gracefully; made such a genteel apology, and looked so manly and noble!

CHARLOTTE. (*aside*) I see some folks, though it is so great an impropriety, can praise a gentleman, when he happens to be the man of their fancy.

MARIA. I don't know how it was--I hope he did not think me indelicate-- but I asked him, I believe, to sit down, or pointed to a chair. He sat down, and instead of having recourse to observations upon the weather, or hackneyed criticisms upon the theatre, he entered readily into a conversation worthy a man of sense to speak, and a lady of delicacy and sentiment to hear. He was not strictly handsome, but he spoke the language of sentiment, and his eyes looked tenderness and honour.

CHARLOTTE. Oh! (*Eagerly.*) You sentimenal grave girls, when your hearts are once touched, beat us rattles a bar's length. And so, you are quite in love with this he-angel?

MARIA. In love with him! How can you rattle so, Charlotte? am I not going to be miserable? (*Sighs.*) In love with a gentleman I never saw but one hour in my life, and don't know his name! No: I only wished that the man I shall marry, may look, and talk, and act, just like him. Besides, my dear, he is a married man.

CHARLOTTE. Why, that was good natured. He told you so, I suppose, in mere charity, to prevent your falling in love with him?

MARIA. He did n't tell me so. (*Peevishly.*) He looked as if he was married.

CHARLOTTE. How, my dear, did he look sheepish?

MARIA. I am sure he has a susceptible heart, and the ladies of his acquaintance must be very stupid not to--

CHARLOTTE. Hush! I hear some person coming.

DIMPLE. (*within*) Upon my honour, Sir!

MARIA. Ha! Dimple's voice! My dear, I must take leave of you. There are some things necessary to be done at our house. Can't I go through the other room? (*Enter Dimple and Manly.*)

DIMPLE. Ladies, your most obedient.

CHARLOTTE. Miss Van Rough, shall I present my brother Henry to you? Colonel Manly, Maria. Miss Van Rough, brother.

MARIA. Her brother! (*Turns and sees Manly.*) Oh! my heart! The very gentleman I have been praising.

MANLY. The same amiable girl I saw this morning!

CHARLOTTE. Why, you look as if you were acquainted.

MANLY. I unintentionally intruded into this lady's presence this morning, for which she was so good as to promise me her forgiveness.

CHARLOTTE. (*aside*) Oh! ho! is that the case! Have these two penserosos been together? Were they Henry's eyes that looked so tenderly? (*Aloud.*) And so you promised to pardon him? and could you be so good natured? Have you really forgiven him? I beg you would do it for my sake. (*Whispering aloud to Maria.*) But, my dear, as you are in such haste, it would be cruel to detain you: I can show you the way through the other room.

MARIA. Spare me, my sprightly friend.

MANLY. The lady does not, I hope, intend to deprive us of the pleasure of her company so soon.

CHARLOTTE. She has only a mantua-maker who waits for her at home. But, as I am to give my opinion of the dress, I think she cannot go yet. We were talking of the fashions when you came in; but I suppose the subject must be changed to something of more importance now. Mr. Dimple, will you favour us with an account of the public entertainments?

DIMPLE. Why, really, Miss Manly, you could not have asked me a question more *mal-apropos*. For my part, I must confess, that to a man who has travelled, there is nothing that is worthy the name of amusement to be found in this city.

CHARLOTTE. Except visiting the ladies.

DIMPLE. Pardon me, Madam; that is the avocation of a man of taste. But, for amusement, I positively know of nothing that can be called so, unless you dignify with that title the hopping once a fortnight to the sound of two or three squeaking fiddles, and the clattering of the old tavern windows, or sitting to see the miserable mummers, whom you call actors, murder comedy, and make a farce of tragedy.

MANLY. Do you never attend the theatre, Sir?

DIMPLE. I was tortured there once.

CHARLOTTE. Pray, Mr. Dimple, was it a tragedy or a comedy?

DIMPLE. Faith, Madam, I cannot tell; for I sat with my back to the stage all the time, admiring a much better actress than any there--a lady who played the fine woman to perfection--though, by the laugh of the horrid creatures around me, I suppose it was a comedy. Yet, on second thoughts, it might be some hero in a tragedy, dying so comically as to set the whole house in an uproar. Colonel, I presume you have been in Europe?

MANLY. Indeed, Sir, I was never ten leagues from the continent.

DIMPLE. Believe me, Colonel, you have an immense pleasure to come; and when you shall have seen the brilliant exhibitions of Europe, you will learn to despise the amusements of this country as much as I do.

MANLY. Therefore I do not wish to see them; for I can never esteem that knowledge valuable, which tends to give me a distaste for my native country.

DIMPLE. Well, Colonel, though you have not traveled, you have read.

MANLY. I have, a little, and by it have discovered that there is a laudable partiality, which ignorant, untravelled men entertain for everything that belongs to their native country. I call it laudable; it injures no one; adds to their own happiness; and, when extended, becomes the noble principle of patriotism. Travelled gentlemen rise superior, in their own opinion, to this: but, if the contempt which they contract for their country is the most valuable acquisition of their travels, I am far from thinking that their time and money are well spent.

MARIA. What noble sentiments!

CHARLOTTE. Let my brother set out from where he will in the fields of conversation, he is sure to end his tour in the temple of gravity.

MANLY. Forgive me, my sister. I love my country; it has its foibles undoutedly--some foreigners will with pleasure remark them, but such remarks fall very ungracefully from the lips of her citizens.

DIMPLE. You are perfectly in the right, Colonel--America has her faults.

MANLY. Yes, Sir; and we, her children, should blush for them in private, and endeavour, as individuals, to reform them. But, if our country has its errors in common with other countries, I am proud to say America, I mean the United States, have displayed virtues and achievements which modern nations may admire, but of which they have seldom set us the example.

CHARLOTTE. But, brother, we must introduce you to some of our gay folks, and let you see the city, such as it is. Mr. Dimple is known to almost every family in town; he will doubtless take a pleasure in introducing you.

DIMPLE. I shall esteem every service I can render your brother as an honour.

MANLY. I fear the business I am upon will take up all my time, and my family will be anxious to hear from me.

MARIA. (*aside*) His family! But what is it to me that he is married! (*Aloud.*) Pray, how did you leave your lady, Sir?

CHARLOTTE. (*observing her anxiety*) My brother is not married; it is only an odd way he has of expressing himself. Pray, brother, is this business, which you make your continual excuse, a secret?

MANLY. No, sister: I came hither to solicit the honourable Congress that a number of my brave old soldiers may be put upon the pension-list, who were, at first, not judged to be so materially wounded as to need the public assistance. (*To Maria.*) My sister says true. I call my late soldiers my family. Those who were not in the field in the late glorious contest, and those who were, have their respective merits; but, I confess, my old brother-soldiers are dearer to me than the former description. Friendships made in adversity are lasting; our countrymen may forget us; but there is no reason why we should forget one another. But I must leave you; my time of engagement approaches.

CHARLOTTE. Well, but brother, if you will go, will you please to conduct my fair friend home? You live in the same street--I was to have gone with her myself. (*Aside.*) A lucky thought.

MARIA. I am obliged to your sister, Sir, and was just intending to go.

MANLY. (*as Maria is going*) I shall attend her with pleasure.

MARIA. (*to Charlotte*) Now, pray don't betray me to your brother.

   (*Exeunt severally.*)

Scene 2. Van Rough's house.

VAN ROUGH. (*alone*) It cannot possibly be true! The son of my old friend can't have acted so unadvisedly. Seventeen thousand pounds! In bills! Mr. Transfer must have been mistaken. He always appeared so prudent, and talked so well upon money matters, and even assured me that he intended to change his dress for a suit of clothes which would not cost so much, and look more substantial, as soon as he married. No, no, no! It can't be; it cannot be. But, however, I must look out sharp. I did not care what his principles or his actions were, so long as he minded the main chance. Seventeen thousand pounds! If he had lost it in trade, why the best men may have ill-luck; but to game it away, as Transfer says--why, at this rate, his whole estate may go in one night, and, what is ten times worse, mine into the bargain. No, no; Mary is right. Leave women to look out in these matters; for all they look as if they did n't know a journal from a ledger, when their interest is concerned, they know what's what; they mind the main chance as well as the best of us. I wonder Mary did not tell me she knew of his spending his money so foolishly. Seventeen thousand pounds! Why, if my daughter was standing up to be married, I would forbid the banns, if I found it was to a man who did not mind the main chance. Hush! I hear somebody coming. 'Tis Mary's voice: a man with her, too! I should n't be surprised if this should be the other string to her bow. Aye, aye, let them alone; women understand the main chance. Though i' faith I'll listen a little. (*Retires into a closet.*)

MANLY. (*leading in Maria*) I hope you will excuse my speaking upon so important a subject, so abruptly; but the moment I entered your room, you struck me as the lady whom I had long loved in imagination, and never hoped to see.

MARIA. Indeed, Sir, I have been led to hear more upon this subject than I ought.

MANLY. Do you then disaprove my suit, Madam, or the abruptness of my introducing it? If the latter, my peculiar situation, being obliged to leave the city in a few days, will, I hope, be my excuse; if the former, I will retire: for I am sure I would not give a moment's inquietude to her, whom I could devote my life to please. I am not so indelicate as to seek your immediate approbation; permit me only to be near you, and by a thousand tender assiduities to endeavour to excite a grateful return.

MARIA. I have a father, whom I would die to make happy--he will disapprove--

MANLY. Do you think me so ungenerous as to seek a place in your esteem without his consent? You must--you ever ought to consider that man as unworthy of you, who seeks an interest in your heart, contrary to a father's approbation. A young lady should reflect, that the loss of a lover may be supplied, but nothing can compensate for the loss of a parent's affection. Yet, why do you suppose your father would disapprove? In our country, the affections are not sacrificed to riches, or family aggrandizement. Should you approve, my family is decent, and my rank honourable.

MARIA. You distress me, Sir.

MANLY. Then I will sincerely beg your excuse for obtruding so disagreeable a subject and retire. (*Going.*)

MARIA. Stay, Sir! your generousity and good opinion of me deserve a return; but why must I declare what, for these few hours, I have scarce suffered myself to think? I am--

MANLY. What?

MARIA. Engaged, Sir. And, in a few days, to be married to the gentleman you saw at your sister's.

MANLY. Engaged to be married! And have I been basely invading the rights of another? Why have you permitted this? Is this the return for the partiality I declared for you?

MARIA. You distress me, Sir. What would you have me say? You are too generous to wish the truth: ought I to say that I dared not suffer myself to think of my engagement, and that I am going to give my hand without my heart? Would you have me confess a partiality for you? If so, your triumph is complete; and can be only more so, when days of misery, with the man I cannot love, will make me think of him whom I could prefer.

MANLY. (*after a pause*) We are both unhappy; but it is your duty to obey your parent, mine to obey my honour. Let us, therefore, both follow the path of rectitude; and of this we may be assured, that if we are not happy, we shall, at least, deserve to be so. Adieu! I dare not trust myself longer with you.

(*Exeunt severally.*)

ACT V.

Scene 1. Dimple's lodgings. (*Enter Jessamy and Jonathan.*)

JESSAMY. Well, Mr. Jonathan, what success with the fair?

JONATHAN. Why, such a tarnal cross tike you never saw! You would have counted she had lived upon crab-apples and vinegar for a fortnight. But what the rattle makes you look so tarnation glum?

JESSAMY. I was thinking, Mr. Jonathan, what could be the reason of her carrying herself so coolly to you.

JONATHAN. Coolly, do you call it? Why, I vow, she was fire-hot angry: may be it was because I buss'd her.

JESSAMY. No, no, Mr. Jonathan; there must be some other cause: I never yet knew a lady angry at being kissed.

JONATHAN. Well, if it is not the young woman's bashfulness, I vow I can't conceive why she shou'd n't like me.

JESSAMY. May be it is because you have not the Graces, Mr. Jonathan.

JONATHAN. Grace! Why, does the young woman expect I must be converted before I court her?

JESSAMY. I mean graces of person; for instance, my lord tells us that we must cut off our nails even at top, in small segments of circles--though you won't understand that-- In the next place, you must regulate your laugh.

JONATHAN. Maple-log seize it! Don't I laugh natural?

JESSAMY. That's the very fault, Mr. Jonathan. Besides, you absolutely misplace it. I was told by a friend of mine that you laughed outright at the play the other night, when you ought only to have tittered.

JONATHAN. Gor! I-- What does one go to see fun for if they can't laugh?

JESSAMY. You may laugh, but you must laugh by rule.

JONATHAN. Swamp it--laugh by rule! Well, I should like that tarnally.

JESSAMY. Why you know, Mr. Jonathan, that to dance, a lady to play with her fan, or a gentleman with his cane, and all other natural motions, are regulated by art. My master has composed an immensely pretty gamut, by which any lady, or gentleman, with a few years' close application, may learn to laugh as gracefully as if they were born and bred to it.

JONATHAN. Mercy on my soul! A gamut for laughing--just like fa, la, sol?

JESSAMY. Yes. It comprises every possible display of jocularity, from an *affettuoso* smile to a *piano* titter, or full chorus *fortissimo* ha, ha, ha! My master employs his leisure-hours in marking out the plays, like a cathedral chanting-book, that the ignorant may know where to laugh, and that pit, box, and gallery may keep time together, and not have a snigger in one part of the house, a broad grin in the other, and a d-----d grum look in the third. How delightful to see the audience all smile together, then look on their books, then twist their mouths into an agreeable simper, then altogether shake the house with a general ha, ha, ha! loud as a full chorus of Handel's, at an Abbey-commemoration.

JONATHAN. Ha, ha, ha! That's dang'd cute, I swear.

JESSAMY. The gentlemen, you see, will laugh the tenor; the ladies will play the counter-tenor; the beaux will squeak the treble; and our jolly friends in the gallery a thorough bass, ho, ho, ho!

JONATHAN. Well, can't you let me see that gamut?

JESSAMY. Oh! yes, Mr. Jonathan; here it is. (*Takes out a book.*) Oh! no, this is only a titter with its variations. Ah! here it is. (*Takes out another.*) Now you must know, Mr. Jonathan, this is a piece written by Ben Jonson, which I have set to my master's gamut. The places where you must smile, look grave, or laugh outright, are marked below the line. Now look over me. "There was a certain man"-- Now you must smile.

JONATHAN. Well, read it again; I warrant I'll mind my eye.

JESSAMY. "There was a certain man, who had a sad scolding wife"-- Now you must laugh.

JONATHAN. Tarnation! That's no laughing matter, though.

JESSAMY. "And she lay sick a-dying"-- Now you must titter.

JONATHAN. What, snigger when the good woman's a-dying! Gor, I--

JESSAMY. Yes; the notes say you must. "And she asked her husband leave to make a will"-- Now you must begin to look grave. "And her husband said"--

JONATHAN. Ay, what did her husband say? Something dang'd cute, I reckon.

JESSAMY. "And her husband said, you have had your will all your life time, and would you have it after you are dead?"

JONATHAN. Ho, ho, ho! There the old man was even with her; he was up to the notch--ha, ha, ha!

JESSAMY. But, Mr. Jonathan, you must not laugh so. Why, you ought to have tittered *piano*, and you have laughed *fortissimo*. Look here; you see these marks, A. B. C. and so on; these are the references to the other part of the book. Let us turn to it, and you will see the directions how to manage the muscles. This--(*turns over*)--was note D you blundered at. "You must purse the mouth into a smile, then titter, discovering the lower part of the three front upper teeth."

JONATHAN. How? Read it again.

JESSAMY. "There was a certain man"-- Very well! "Who had a sad scolding wife"-- Why don't you laugh?

JONATHAN. Now, that scolding wife sticks in my gizzard so pluckily, that I can't laugh for the blood and nowns of me. Let me look grave here, and I'll laugh your belly full where the old creature's a-dying.

JESSAMY. "And she asked her husband"-- (*Bell rings*.) My master's bell! he's returned, I fear-- Here, Mr. Jonathan, take this gamut; and, I make no doubt but with a few years' close application you may be able to smile gracefully.

(*Exeunt severally*.)

Scene 2. Charlotte's apartment.

MANLY. (*at entering*) What, no one at home? How unfortunate to meet the only lady my heart was ever moved by, to find her engaged to another, and confessing her partiality for me! Yet engaged to a man, who, by her intimation, and his libertine conversation with me, I fear, does not merit her. Aye! there's the sting; for, were I assured that Maria was happy, my heart is not so selfish, but that it would dilate in knowing it, even though it were with another. But to know she is unhappy! I must drive these thoughts from me. Charlotte has some books; and this is what I believe she calls her little library.

(Manly enters a closet.   Enter Dimple leading Letitia.)

LETITIA.   And will you pretend to say, now, Mr. Dimple, that you propose to break with Maria? Are not the banns published? Are not the clothes purchased? Are not the friends invited? In short, is it not a done affair?

DIMPLE. Believe me, my dear Letitia, I would not marry her.

LETITIA. Why have you not broke with her before this, as you all along deluded me by saying you would?

DIMPLE. Because I was in hopes she would ere this have broke with me.

LETITIA. You could not expect it.

DIMPLE. Nay, but be calm a moment; 't was from my regard to you that I did not discard her.

LETITIA. Regard to me!

DIMPLE. Yes; I have done everything in my power to break with her, but the foolish girl is so fond of me, that nothing can accomplish it. Besides, how can I offer her my hand, when my heart is indissolubly engaged to you?

LETITIA.   There may be reason in this; but why so attentive to Miss Manly?

DIMPLE. Attentive to Miss Manly! For heavens sake, if you have no better opinion of my constancy, pay not so ill a compliment to my taste. How can you for a moment suppose I should have any serious thoughts of that trifling, gay, flighty coquette, that disagreeable-- *(Enter Charlotte.)* My dear Miss Manly, I rejoice to see you; there is a charm in your conversation that always marks your entrance into company as fortunate.

LETITIA. Where have you been, my dear?

CHARLOTTE. Why, I have been about to twenty shops, turning over pretty things, and so have left twenty visits unpaid. I wish you would step into the carriage and whisk round, make my apology, and leave my cards where our friends are not at home; that you know will serve as a visit. Come, do go.

LETITIA. *(aside)* So anxious to get me out! But I'll watch you. *(Aloud.)* Oh! yes, I'll go; I want a little exercise--positively. *(Dimple offers to accompany her.)* Mr. Dimple, you shall not go--why, half my visits are cake and caudle visits; it won't do, you know, for you to go.

(Exit Letitia, but returns to the door in the back scene and listens.)

DIMPLE. This attachment of your brother to Maria is fortunate.

CHARLOTTE. How did you come to the knowledge of it?

DIMPLE. I read it in their eyes.

CHARLOTTE. And I had it from her mouth. It would have amused you to have seen her! She that thought it so great an impropriety to praise a gentleman, that she could not bring out one word in your favour, found a redundancy to praise him.

DIMPLE. I have done everything in my power to assist his passion there: your delicacy, my dearest girl, would be shocked at half the instances of neglect and misbehaviour.

CHARLOTTE. I don't know how I should bear neglect; but Mr. Dimple must misbehave himself, indeed, to forfeit my good opinion.

DIMPLE. Your good opinion, my angel, is the pride and pleasure of my heart; and if the most respectful tenderness for you and an utter indifference for all your sex besides, can make me worthy of your esteem, I shall richly merit it.

CHARLOTTE. All my sex besides, Mr. Dimple--you forgot your tête-à-tête with Letitia.

DIMPLE. How can you, my lovely angel, cast a thought on that insipid, wry-mouthed, ugly creature!

CHARLOTTE. But her fortune may have charms?

DIMPLE. Not to a heart like mine. The man who has been blessed with the good opinion of my Charlotte must despise the allurements of fortune.

CHARLOTTE. I am satisfied.

DIMPLE. Let us think no more on the odious subject, but devote the present hour to happiness.

CHARLOTTE. Can I be happy, when I see the man I prefer going to be married to another?

DIMPLE. Have I not already satisfied my charming angel that I can never think of marrying the puling Maria. But, even if it were so, could that be any bar to our happiness; for, as the poet sings--

"Love, free as air, at sight of human ties,
    Spreads his light wings, and in a moment flies."

Come then, my charming angel! why delay our bliss! The present moment is ours; the next is in the hand of fate. (*Kissing her.*)

CHARLOTTE. Begone, Sir! By your delusions you had almost lulled my honour asleep.

DIMPLE. Let me lull the demon to sleep again with kisses.

(*Dimple struggles with her; she screams. Enter Manly.*)

MANLY. Turn, villain! and defend yourself--

(*Manly draws. Van Rough enters, beats down their swords, and holds Dimple.*)

VAN ROUGH. Is the devil in you? Are you going to murder one another?

DIMPLE. Hold him, hold him! I can command my passion.

JONATHAN. (*entering*) What the rattle ails you? Is the old one in you? Let the colonel alone, can't you? I feel chock full of fight-- Do you want to kill the colonel?

MANLY. Be still, Jonathan; the gentleman does not want to hurt me.

JONATHAN. Gor! I--I wish he did; I'd shew him Yankee boys play, pretty quick-- Don't you see you have frightened the young woman into the *hystrikes*?

VAN ROUGH. Pray, some of you explain this; what has been the occasion of all this racket?

MANLY. That gentleman can explain it to you; it will be a very diverting story for an intended father-in-law to hear.

VAN ROUGH. How was this matter, Mr. Van Dumpling?

DIMPLE. Sir, upon my honour--all I know is, that I was talking to this young lady, and this gentleman broke in on us, in a very extraordinary manner.

VAN ROUGH. Why, all this is nothing to the purpose. (*To Charlotte.*) Can you explain it, Miss? (*Enter Letitia through the back scene.*)

LETITIA. I can explain it to that gentleman's confusion. (*To Van Rough.*) Though long betrothed to your daughter, yet allured by my fortune, it seems (with shame do I speak it), he has privately paid his addresses to me. I was drawn in to listen to him by his assuring me that the match was made by his father without his consent, and that he proposed to break with Maria, whether he married me or not. But whatever were his intentions respecting your daughter, Sir, even to me he was false; for he has repeated the same story, with some cruel reflections upon my person, to Miss Manly.

JONATHAN. What a tarnal curse!

LETITIA. Nor is this all, Miss Manly. When he was with me this very morning, he made the same ungenerous reflection upon the weakness of your mind as he has so recently done upon the defects of my person.

JONATHAN. What a tarnal curse and damn, too!

DIMPLE. (*aside*) Ha! Since I have lost Letitia, I believe I had as good make it up with Maria-- (*Aloud.*) Mr. Van Rough, at present I cannot enter into particulars; but, I believe I can explain everything to your satisfaction in private.

VAN ROUGH. There is another matter, Mr. Van Dumpling, which I would have your explain: pray, Sir, have Messrs. Van Cash and Co.

presented you those bills for acceptance?

DIMPLE. (*aside*) The deuce! Has he heard of those bills! Nay, then, all's up with Maria, too; but an affair of this sort can never prejudice me among the ladies; they will rather long to know what the dear creature possesses to make him so agreeable. (*To Manly.*) Sir, you will hear from me.

MANLY. And you from me, Sir.

DIMPLE. Sir, you wear a sword.

MANLY. Yes, Sir. This sword was presented to me by that brave Gallic hero, the Marquis De La Fayette. I have drawn it in the service of my country, and in private life, on the only occasion where a man is justified in drawing his sword, in defense of a lady's honour. I have fought too many battles in the service of my country to dread the imputation of cowardice. Death from a man of honour would be a glory you do not merit; you shall live to bear the insult of man, and the contempt of that sex, whose general smiles afforded you all of your happiness.

DIMPLE. You won't meet me, Sir? Then I'll post you for a coward.

MANLY. I'll venture that, Sir. The reputation of my life does not depend upon the breath of a Mr. Dimple. I would have you to know, however, Sir, that I have a cane to chastise the insolence of a scoundrel, and a sword and the good laws of my country, to protect me from the attempts of an assassin.

DIMPLE. Mighty well! Very fine, indeed! Ladies and gentlemen, I take my leave, and you will please to observe, in the case of my deportment, the contrast between a gentleman, who has read Chesterfield and received the polish of Europe, and an unpolished, untravelled American.

(*Exit Dimple. Enter Maria.*)

MARIA. Is he indeed gone?

LETITIA. I hope never to return.

VAN ROUGH. I am glad I heard of those bills; though it's plaguy unlucky: I hoped to see Mary married before I died.

MANLY. Will you permit a gentleman, Sir, to offer himself as a suitor to your daughter? Though a stranger to you, he is not altogether so to her, or unknown in this city. You may find a son-in-law of more fortune, but you can never meet with one who is richer in love for her, or respect for you.

VAN ROUGH. Why, Mary, you have not let this gentleman make love to you without my leave?

MANLY. I did not say, Sir--

MARIA. Say, Sir! I--the gentleman, to be sure, met me accidentally.

VAN ROUGH. Ha, ha, ha! Mark me, Mary; young folks think old folks to be fools; but old folks know young folks to be fools. Why, I knew all about this affair. This was only a cunning way I had to bring it about. Hark ye! I was in the closet when you and he were at our house. (*Turns to the company.*) I heard that little baggage say she loved her old father, and would die to make him happy! Oh! How I love the little baggage! And you talked very prudently, young man. I have inquired into your character, and find you to be a man of punctuality and mind the main chance. And so, as you love Mary, and Mary loves you, you shall have my consent immediately to be married. I'll settle my fortune on you, and go and live with you the remainder of my life.

MANLY. Sir, I hope--

VAN ROUGH. Come, come, no fine speeches; mind the main chance, young man, and you and I shall always agree.

LETITIA. (*advancing to Maria*) I sincerely wish you joy and hope your pardon for my conduct.

MARIA. I thank you for your congratulations, and hope we shall at once forget the wretch who has given us so much disquiet, and the trouble that he has occasioned.

CHARLOTTE. And I--my dear Maria--how shall I look up to you for forgiveness? I, who, in the practice of the meanest arts, have violated the most sacred rights of friendship? I can never forgive myself, or hope charity from the world, but I confess I have much to hope from such a brother; and I am happy that I may soon say, such a sister--

MARIA. My dear, you distress me; you have all my love.

MANLY. And mine.

CHARLOTTE. If repentance can entitle me to forgiveness, I have already much merit; for I despise the littleness of my past conduct. I now find, that the heart of any worthy man cannot be gained by invidious attacks upon the rights and characters of others--by countenancing the addresses of a thousand--or that the finest assemblage of features, the greatest taste in dress, the genteelest address, or the most brilliant wit, cannot eventually secure a coquette from contempt and ridicule.

MANLY. And I have learned that probity, virtue, honour, though they should not have received the polish of Europe, will secure to an honest American the good graces of his fair countrywoman, and, I hope, the applause of the public.

THE END.

John Augustus Stone (1800-1834)
and *Metamora*

Metamora belonged to Edwin Forrest, actor. He initiated the contest with its prize of $500--advertised in *The Critic* on November 22, 1828--for "the best tragedy, in five acts, of which the hero or principal character shall be an aboriginal of this country." He selected the panel of judges, chaired by William Cullen Bryant, who chose *Metamora* as the best of the fourteen entries. For the next forty years, Forrest toured the country with a play skillfully crafted for his robust style of acting and forceful personality. Finally, he confessed that he "utterly despised" the play. It is unlikely, however, that he despised the fortune which *Metamora* brought him.

John Augustus Stone, like other American playwrights of his day, did not fare so well. Beginning his career on the stage in Boston, playing either eccentric comics or old men, he took this line of business to New York and Philadelphia. His first attempt at playwriting, *Restoration; or, The Diamond Cross*, premiered in New York in 1824. In all, he may have written eleven plays: two won Forrest's contests (*Metamora*, premiering December 15, 1829, at the New Park Theater in New York, and *The Ancient Briton*, 1833); two more became popular vehicles for well-known actors. A contemporary actor remembered Stone as a man of "singular temperament" who--despondent, ill, and apparently in debt--leaped from the Spruce Street Wharf in Philadelphia into the Schuylkill River on May 29, 1834.

Stone's source for *Metamora* was historical (King Philip, son of Massasoit), his vision was remarkable, and his research thorough, as evidenced by his reference to the death of John Sassamon (called Sasamond in the play), one of John Eliot's students in the Indian School at Harvard College and recognized by some as the "first Indian Christian martyr." Still, it took a playwright of experience in the theatre and a writer with a wealth of human understanding to create a play of such sublimity and power.

Only incomplete texts of *Metamora* existed until 1960, when Professor Richard Moody discovered the missing fourth act among the Lord Chamberlain's plays in the British Museum.

Edwin Forrest as Metamora

METAMORA
Or, The Last of the Wampanoags

(1829)

by John Augustus Stone

CHARACTERS

Metamora, chief of the Wampanoags
Kaneshine, an Indian prophet
Annawandah, the traitor
Otah, and Indian boy
Indian Boy, child of Metamora
Nahmeokee, wife of Metamora
Indians, warriors, etc.
Lord Fitzarnold
Sir Arthur Vaughan
Errington, chief of the council

Mordaunt
Walter, an orphan
Captain Church
Wolfe
Goodenough
Tramp
Oceana, Mordaunt's
    daughter
Soldiers, Sailors,
    Peasants, etc.

PROLOGUE.

Written by Mr. Prosper M. Wetmore. Spoken by Mrs. Barrett,
New Park Theater, New York, December 15, 1829.

Not from the records of Imperial Rome,
Or classic Greece--the muses' chosen home--
From no rich legends of the olden day
Our bard hath drawn the story of his play;
Led by the guiding hand of genius on,
He here hath painted Nature on her throne;
His eye hath pierced the forest's shadowy gloom,
And read strange lessons from a nation's tomb:
Brief are the annals of that blighted race--
These halls usurp a monarch's resting-place--
Traditions's mist-enshrouded page alone
Tells that an empire was--we know 'tis gone!
From foreign climes full off the muse has brought
Her glorious treasures of gigantic thought;

And here, beneath the witchery of her power,
The eye hath poured its tributary shower:
When modern pens have sought th' historic page,
To picture forth the deeds of former age--
O'er soft Virginia's sorrows ye have sighed,
And dropt a tear when spotless beauty died;
When Brutus "cast his cloud aside"; to stand
The guardian of the tyrant-trampled land--
When patriot Tell his clime from thraldom freed,
And bade th' avenging arrow do its deed,
Your bosoms answered with responsive swell,
For freedom triumph when th' oppressors fell!
These were the melodies of humbler lyres,
The lights of Genius, yet without his fires;
But when the master-spirit struck the chords,
And inspiration breathed her burning words--
When passion's self stalked living o'er the stage,
To plead with love, or rouse the soul to rage--
When Shakespeare led his bright creations forth,
And conjured up the mighty dead from earth--
Breathless--entranced--ye've listened to the line,
And felt the minstrel's power, all but divine!
While thus your plaudits cheer the stranger lay,
Shall native pens in vain the field essay?
To-night we test the strength of native powers,
Subject, and bard, and actor, all are ours--
'Tis yours to judge, if worthy of a name,
And bid them live within the halls of fame!

ACT I.

Scene 1. Sunset. A wild, picturesque scene; high, craggy rocks in distance; dark pine trees, etc. Rocks cross stage, with platform cross behind. Steps, etc., at back. A rude tomb, flowers growing around it. Half dark. (*Mordaunt discovered leaning on tomb. Slow music.*)

MORDAUNT. The sun has sunk beyond yon craggy rocks; and day's last beams are fading from the clouds that fleet in hurrying masses through the sky, like tattered banners of a flying host! England, my home! When will thy parent arms again enfold me? Oh! When for me will dawn a day of hope? Will not sincere repentance from my scathed brow efface the brand of regicide?

TRAMP. (*outside*) What ho! Good Master Mordaunt! (*Cannon.*)

MORDAUNT. Ha! What mean those sounds? (*Enter Tramp.*) Now, your news?

TRAMP. A gallant bark, urged by the favoring breeze, makes for the crowded shore.

MORDAUNT. From England! Ha!

TRAMP. St. George's banner floats from her high mast, and her long signal pennon gleams with green and gold.

MORDAUNT. 'Tis he--he comes and with him hope arrives. Go, hasten, fellow; seek my daughter; say the Lord Fitzarnold comes to greet her. Marshal my followers in their best array--away to the beach and let loud music welcome him ashore. (*Exit Tramp.*) What mingled feelings crowd about my heart, blended so strange and wild? Sunned by her sovereign's smile, Fitzarnold comes to woo and wed my daughter. Born on the heaving deep, the child of storms, and reared in savage wilds, her worth and beauty well may grace the courtly halls of England. And yet, to force her gentle will, whose every thought has been to soothe my sorrows and relieve my cares! Yet must she wed Fitzarnold. His alliance can with oblivion shroud the past, clear from my scutcheon every rebel stain, and give my franchised spirit liberty.

(*Exit Mordaunt. Slow music, four bars. Enter Oceana.*)

OCEANA. (*looking around as if in search*) Sure, 'twas my father's voice, and loud in converse. Father! Dear Father! Not here? And yet I thought-- (*Flute heard, distant.*) Ha! whence that strain? So soft yet strange. Methinks some pious minstrel seeks the moonlight hour to breathe devotion forth in melody. (*Music changes.*) Hark! It changes place and measure, too. Now deeper in the woods it warbles, now it seems aloft floating in plaintive tones through the air. This place--the hour--the day--heavens! 'tis my mother's birthday, and her grave undecked with flowers! Oh my mother, my dear mother! Perhaps her angel spirit hovers here o'er her lone daughter's steps, a guardian still. (*Kneels to tomb.*) Ah, what flower is this? "Forgetmenot!" (*Music ceases.*) My mother, look from thy seraph home upon thy child, and when for those thou lovest on earth thou breathest a prayer, oh, then forget me not. (*Places flower in bosom. Enter Walter.*)

WALTER. Oceana!

OCEANA. Walter, was thine the strain but now I heard?

WALTER. 'Twas but an humble tribute to thy beauty, but could not match the sweetness of thy voice, whose every tone, attuned to dulcet sounds, can melt the soul to nature's harmony.

OCEANA. Walter, this from thee.

WALTER. Nay, blame me not; although dependent on Sir Arthur Vaughan, nameless and poor, yet do I not despair, for in my heart a sacred treasure lies I would not barter for my patron's gold.

OCEANA. What means't thou, Walter?

WALTER. Thine own sweet image, which naught on earth can banish or deface--a whispered hope I dare not speak aloud--a light thine own bright eyes have kindled up.

OCEANA. Nay, Walter, you ask not of the danger I escaped!

WALTER. Danger! What danger? When?

OCEANA. 'Twas yestere'en, when I was lingering on the eastern beach, all heedless of the coming night, a panther growling from the thicket rushed and marked me for his prey. Powerless I stood--my blood stood still--I shrieked as I strove to fly, when at the instant, from a ready hand, swift as the lightning's flash, an arrow came and felled the monster as he crouched to spring.

WALTER. Didst mark who sent it?

OCEANA. Full well I did. High on a craggy rock an Indian stood, with sinewy arm and eye that pierced the glen. His bowstring drawn to wing a second death, a robe of fur was o'er his shoulder thrown, and o'er his long, dark hair an eagle's plume waved in the breeze, a feathery diadem. Firmly he stood upon the jutting height, as if a sculptor's hand had carved him there. With awe, I gazed as on the cliff he turned--the grandest model of a mighty man.

WALTER. 'Twas Haups great chieftain, Metamora called; our people love him not, nor is it strange; he stands between them and extended sway, ready alike with words of power to urge, or gleaming weapon force his princely dues.

METAMORA. (*outside*) Hah! Ha!

OCEANA. (*going up*) Behold his dread encounter with a wolf. His vanquished foe with mighty arm he hurls down the steep height where mortal never trod.

METAMORA. (*entering, on rock*) Hah! Hah! (*Passes across and off.*)

WALTER. (*at Metamora's exit*) 'Tis Metamora, the noble sachem of a valiant race--the white man's dread, the Wampanoag's hope.

(*Enter Metamora, down R.*)

METAMORA. Ha, ha, ha! Turned on me--brave beast; he died like a red man.

OCEANA. Chief, you are hurt; this scarf will staunch the wound.

(*Oceana offers her scarf.*)

METAMORA. No! (*Rejects it.*)

WALTER. 'Tis Oceana--she whose life you saved.

METAMORA. Metamora will take the white maiden's gift.

(*Oceana ties his arm with scarf.*)

OCEANA. But yestere'en thou saved'st my life, great chief; how can I pay thee for the generous deed?

METAMORA. Harken, daughter of the pale face; Metamora forgives not a wrong and forgets not a kindness. In the days of his age, Massasoit, my father, was in the white man's dwelling; while there, the spirit of the grave touched him and he laid down to die. A soft hand was stretched out to save him; it was the hand of thy mother. She that healed him sleeps in yonder tomb; but why should Metamora let his arrows sleep in the quiver when her daughter's life was in danger and her limbs shook with fear? Metamora loves the mild-eyed and the kind, for such is Nahmeokee.

WALTER. Such words, and more than all, such deeds, should win you, chief, the love of all our people. Would you were more among us. Why never seek our homes? Sir Arthur Vaughan's doors will open to the Indian chief.

OCEANA. My sire will thank thee for his daughter's life.

METAMORA. The red man's heart is on the hills where his father's shafts have flown in the chase. Ha! I have been upon the high mountain top where the grey mists were beneath my feet, and the Great Spirit passed by me in his wrath. He spake in anger and the old rocks crumbled beneath the flash of his spear. Then I was proud and smiled, for I had slain the great bird whose wing never tires, and whose eye never shrinks; and his feathers would adorn the long black hair of Nahmeokee, daughter of Miantonemo, the great hunter. The war and the chase are the red man's brother and sister. The storm cloud in its fury frightens him not. Wrapt in the spoils he has won, he lays him down and no one comes near to steal. The Great Spirit hears his evening prayer, and he sleeps admidst the roar of a mighty cataract.

WALTER. Were all thy nation mild and good like thee, how soon the fire of discord might be quenched.

METAMORA. Metamora has been the friend of the white man; yet if the flint be smitten too hard, it will show that in its heart is fire. The Wampanoag will not wrong his white brother who comes from the land that is first touched by the rising sun; but he owns no master, save that

One who holds the sun in his right hand, who rides on a dark storm, and who cannot die. (*Crosses to L.*)

WALTER. That lofty bearing--that majestic mien--the regal impress sits upon his brow, and earth seems conscious of her proudest son.

(*Conch shell heard sounding, R.*)

METAMORA. Ha! My young men return from their evening toil, and their hands are filled with the sweet fish of the lake. Come to my wigwam; ye shall eat of fish that the Great Spirit of the waters sends, and your hearts shall be made glad.

(*Going, R., but returns and takes from his head an eagle plume.*)

Maiden, take this; it means speed and safety; when the startling whoop is heard and the war hatchet gleams in the red blaze, let it be found in thy braided hair. Despise not the red man's gift; it will bring more good to you than the yellow earth the white man worships as his god. Take it--no Wampanoag's hand will e'er be raised against the head or hand that bears the eagle plume. (*Crosses to Walter.*) Young man, be thou like the oak in its spreading power and let thy tough branches shelter the tender flower that springs up under them. Look to the maiden of the eagle plume, and--come to my wigwam. (*Exit.*)

OCEANA. Teach him, Walter; make him like to us.

WALTER. 'Twould cost him half his native virtues. Is justice goodly? Metamora's just. Is bravery virtue? Metamora's brave. If love of country, child and wife and home, be to deserve them all--he merits them.

OCEANA. Yet he is a heathen.

WALTER. True, Oceana, but his worship though untaught and rude flows from his heart, and Heaven alone must judge of it. (*Enter Tramp.*)

TRAMP. Your father, lady, requires your presence.

OCEANA. Say I come. (*A distant drum.*)

WALTER. What is that?

TRAMP. The drum that summons Lord Fitzarnold's escort. He comes a suitor for my lady's hand. (*Exit Tramp.*)

WALTER. Deny it, Oceana--say 'tis false!

OCEANA. It is--

WALTER. Untrue?

OCEANA. Oh, most unwelcome.

WALTER. Heavens! You tremble--and your cheek is pale--my Lord Fitzarnold, that most courtly gentleman, and must my hopes--

OCEANA. Walter, dost thou mean--

WALTER. Obey thy sire. I cannot say farewell. But, oh, when highborn revelers carouse, and proud Fitzarnold lords it at the board, give one

brief thought to me! That blessed thought shall soothe the fond complainings of my heart and hush them to repose.
(*Exit Walter, L. Exit Oceana, R.*)

Scene 2. Lights up. A room in Sir Arthur's house. (*Enter Sir Arthur and Walter.*)

WALTER. Yet hear me, sir.

SIR ARTHUR. Forebear; thou art too hot.

WALTER. 'Tis not the meanness of our state that galls us, but men's opinions. Poverty and toil and consciousness of lowly destiny sit lightly where no scorn is heaped upon them. But yesterday I was indeed content, for none despised, none had learned to scoff the son of charity, the wretched ship boy who could trace existence no further than the wreck from which you plucked him; but now 'tis changed, all suddenly begin to find me base.

SIR ARTHUR. Marry, go to! You wrong yourself and me. Have I not fostered you--like a father tutored you? In early life bereft of wife and child, wearied of discord and fierce civil strife, I left the haunts of wild and factious men, to woo contentment in this wilderness. My heart was vacant and received thee in. Do not by any rash, unworthy act forsake that heart. Who is it finds thee base?

WALTER. All, since Fitzarnold is expected here.

SIR ARTHUR. Fitzarnold! What a plague! There is naught talked of or thought of but Lord Fitzarnold! And yet this noble viscount, but for his coat and title were a man to look with scorn upon--a profligate and spendthrift as fame already has too truly shown him.

WALTER. And 'tis for such a man that Master Mordaunt sets me aside-- for such a man his daughter must cast me off.

SIR ARTHUR. Tut! Master Mordaunt is too wise a man to give his daughter to this Lord Fitzarnold. Patience awhile, and watch the progress of this meteor. Patience, and trust to fortune. (*Exit.*)

WALTER. This lordly suitor comes to wake me from my cherished dreams, and crush the hopes which lately looked so fair. And shall I yield the glorious prize I deemed was wholly mine? Yield, and without a struggle? No, by heaven! Look to thyself, Fitzarnold. Let Oceana be but true, I heed not all thy power, thy wealth, thy titles, backed though they be by Mordaunt's selfish views. (*Exit.*)

Scene 3. The harbor. Ships anchored in the distance. Military music. (*Mordaunt, Errington, Goodenough, Church, Soldiers, Citizens [male and female] discovered. A boat comes on from L., with Fitzarnold, Wolfe, and Sailors, who land. Shout.*)

MORDAUNT. Long live the king! Welcome Fitzarnold! Rest to the sea-worn! Joy to each and all!

FITZARNOLD. I thank thee, Mordaunt! But I did not think to see such faces in the wilderness! Thy woody shores are bright with sparkling eyes, like Argonaut's adverturous sailors. But where's the golden boon we look for, sir? Fair Oceana--Mordaunt, where is she?

(*Enter Walter, L., and stands against wing.*)

MORDAUNT. So please you, my lord, at home, eager to pay your lordship's kindness back, and prove she can discern thy courtesy.

WALTER. (*aside*) Indeed! Dost say so, worldling?

MORDAUNT. Pray thee, regard these gentlemen, my lord--our council's father, Errington--and this our army's leader: elders of the State.

(*Introducing them severally; Fitzarnold salutes them, and at last approaching Walter, extends his hand; Walter bows coldly but not does take it. Music eight bars.*)

FITZARNOLD. How now, young sir? Mordaunt, who is this?

MORDAUNT. My noble lord, I pray thee, heed him not! A wayward youth, somewhat o'er worn with study. (*Crosses to Walter.*) Rash boy! Be wise and tempt me not; I can destroy--

WALTER. Thy daughter's peace and wed her there.

(*Mordaunt gives Walter a look of hate and turns from him.*)

MORDAUNT. Forth to the hall--a strain of music there. (*Crosses to R.*)

FITZARNOLD. Young sir, I shall desire some further converse with you.

WALTER. At injury's prompting, deeds, not words, were best. My lord, you shall find me. (*Touches his sword.*)

FITZARNOLD. Now for thy fair daughter, Mordaunt, come.

(*Music. Exeunt all but Walter and Wolfe. Peasants and Soldiers exeunt, R.*)

WOLFE. Thou goes not with them?

WALTER. No, nor before, nor follow after. But why dost thou ask?

WOLFE. Because I know thee.

WALTER. Then thou knowest one who will not take a lordling by the hand, because his fingers shine with hoops of gold--nor shun the beggar's grasp if it be honest. Thou knowest me?

WOLFE. Yes!

WALTER. To know oneself was thought task enough in olden time. What dost thou know?

WOLFE. That thou wert wrecked and saved.

WALTER. (*aside*) Aye, more's the pity! Had I been drowned I had not lived to love and have no hope.

WOLFE. Thou art a good man's son.

WALTER. A pity, then, again. Were I a rascal's offspring, I might thrive. What more?

WOLFE. Thou shalt possess thy mistress.

WALTER. Didst mark that lord?

WOLFE. He is my master.

WALTER. Then I am dumb. Be faithful to him, and now farewell.

WOLFE. Yet in good time I will say that you will bestow a blessing for.

WALTER. Indeed! What mean you? (*Enter Tramp, L., with packet.*)

TRAMP. News from the Indians. (*Shows packet.*) 'Tis for the council by a horseman left, who bade me see it with all haste delivered. The Indian tribes conspire from east to west and faithful Sasamond has found his grave. This packet must be borne to Mordaunt.

WALTER. Trust it with me.

TRAMP. That I will readily, so thou wilt bear it safely.

WALTER. Aye, and quickly, too. (*Takes packet.*) Let me remember Metamora's words--"Look to the maiden of the eagle plume."

(*Exit hastily, followed by Wolfe and Tramp. Quick curtain.*)

ACT II.

Scene 1. Music. Interior of a wigwam; a skin rolled. Stage covered with skins, etc. (*Child on skin near R. entrance. Nahmeokee near it. Metamora at L. preparing for the chase.*)

NAHMEOKEE. Thou wilt soon be back from the chase.

METAMORA. Yes, before the otter has tasted his midday food on the bank of the stream, his skin shall make a garment for Nahmeokee when the snow whitens the hunting grounds and the cold wind whistles through the trees. Nahmeokee, take our little one from his rest; he sleeps too much.

NAHMEOKEE. Oh, no! But thou, Metamora, sleepst too little. In the still hour of midnight when Wekolis has sung his song, and the great light has gone down behind the hills, when Nahmeokee's arms like the growing vine were round thee--as if some danger lay waiting in the thick wood--thou didst bid me bring thy tomahawk and the spear that Massasoit had borne when the war cry of the Wampanoags was loudest in the place of blood! Why is thy rest like the green lake when the sudden blast passes across its bosom?

METAMORA. Nahmeokee, the power of dreams has been on me, and the shadows of things that are to be have passed before me. My heart is big with a great thought. When I sleep I think the knife is red in my hand, and the scalp of the white man is streaming.

NAHMEOKEE. Metamora, is not the white man our brother? And does not the Great Spirit look on him as he does on us? Do not go towards his home today because thy wrath is kindled and it spreads like the flames which the white man makes in the dark bosom of the forest. Let Nahmeokee clasp her arms around thee; rest thy head upon her bosom, for it is hot and thy eye is red with the thoughts that burn! Our old men counsel peace, and the aim of the white man will spare.

METAMORA. Yes, when our fires are no longer red, on the high places of our fathers; when the bones of our kindred make fruitful the fields of the stranger, which he has planted amidst the ashes of our wigwams; when we are hunted back like the wounded elk far toward the going down of the sun, our hatchets broken, our bows unstrung and war whoop hushed; then will the stranger spare, for we will be too small for his eye to see. (*Trumpet. Enter Otah.*)

OTAH. O son of Massasoit, the power of the white man approaches, and he looks not like one who seeks the Wampanoag's friendship! Look where the bright weapons flash through the clouds of his track.

METAMORA. Ha! Let the paleface come with the calumet or with the knife, Metamora does not fear their power. Where is Annawandah, skilled in talk? Let him approach me. (*Exit Otah.*)

NAHMEOKEE. Our child would not rest in the mid-hour of night for the hidden snake had bitten him as he lay stretched in the rays of the sun. I rose from my seat to get the dried leaves the Good Spirit has filled with power to heal; the moon was bright and a shadow passed me. It was Annawandah passed our wigwam; his step was like the course of the serpent and he paused and listened. My eye followed him to the seaside, and his light canoe shot like an arrow across the slumbering waters.

METAMORA. Humph! Was he alone?

NAHMEOKEE. Alone.

METAMORA. And he went with fear?

NAHMEOKEE. Like one who goes to steal. (*Trumpet. Enter Otah.*)

OTAH. Look! The white warrior comes.

CHURCH. (*entering with Sir Arthur and Goodenough, with Musqueteers*) Although we come unbidden, chieftain, yet is our purpose friendly.

METAMORA. Why do you bring fire weapons if you come to hold a talk of peace?

CHURCH. It is our custom.

METAMORA. Well, speak; my ears are open to hear.

SIR ARTHUR. Philip, our mission is--

METAMORA. Philip! I am the Wampanoag chief, Metamora.

SIR ARTHUR. We are directed by our council's head, for the times are filled with doubt, and to make *sure* our bond of peace and love to urge your presence at the council.

NAHMEOKEE. (*aside*) Do not go.

METAMORA. Daughter of Miantonemo, peace! (*To them.*) I will go.

CHURCH. Our troops shall form thy escort there.

METAMORA. I know the path.

SIR ARTHUR. We must not go without thee, chief.

METAMORA. I have breasted the cold winds of forty winters and to those that spoke kindly to me in words of love I have been pliant--aye, very yielding like the willow that droops over the stream, but till with a single arm you can move the mighty rock that mocks the lightning and the storm seek not to stir Metamora when his heart says no. I will come!

CHURCH. We shall expect thee, chief.

METAMORA. Metamora cannot lie.

CHURCH. Stand to your arms.

(*Trumpet. Exeunt Church, Goodenough, Otah, and Soldiers.*)

SIR ARTHUR. Be thou not rash, but with thy tongue of manly truth dispel all charge that wrongs thy noble nature. Throw not the brand that kindles bloody war lest thou thyself should be the victim. (*Going.*)

METAMORA. My father's deeds shall be my counsellors, and the Great Spirit will hear the words of my mouth. (*Exit Sir Arthur, L.*) Now, Nahmeokee, I will talk to thee. Dost thou not love this little one, Nahmeokee?

NAHMEOKEE. Oh, yes!

METAMORA. When first his little eyes unclosed, thou saidst they were like mine; and my people rejoiced with a mighty joy, that the grandson of Massasoit, the white man's friend, should rule in the high places of his kindred; and hope that his days would be long and full of glory. Nahmeokee, by the blood of his warlike race, he shall not be the white man's slave.

NAHMEOKEE. Thy talk is strange, and fear creeps over me. Thy heart is beating at thy side, as if thy bosom could not hold it.

METAMORA. Because 'tis full of thee--and thee, my little one. Humph! Bring me the knife thy brother wore in battle--my hatchet--the spear that was thy father's when Uncas slew him for the white man's favor. Humph! These things thou gavest me with thyself; thinkest thou this arm can wield them in the fight?

NAHMEOKEE. Ah! Thy bravery will lose thee to me.

METAMORA. Let not thy heart be troubled. If I require assistance from my people, I will lift up a flame on the lofty hill that shall gleam afar through the thick darkness.

NAHMEOKEE. I shall remember thy words.

METAMORA. Take in thy babe; I am going. (*Crosses to L.*)

NAHMEOKEE. Metamora, dost thou go alone?

METAMORA. No; Manito is with me.

(*Exit Metamora. Exit Nahmeokee.*)

Scene 2. A room in the house of Mordaunt. (*Enter Oceana.*)

OCEANA. Free from Fitzarnold's gaze, I feel myself again. Why came he here? His looks appalled [me] yet my father smiled--ah! he comes.

(*Enter Mordaunt.*)

MORDAUNT. How now, my daughter; how is this? Why have you left his lordship thus?

OCEANA. I thought 'twas time.

MORDAUNT. It is not time to play the prude, when noble men confess thy charms and come fair suitors to thee. Fitzarnold loves thee and his alliance is so dear to me, I'll have no scruples of a timid girl to weigh against it. For long years I've nursed this fondness and I now command obedience.

OCEANA. That union must remain unblessed wherein the helpless hand is giving no heart to bear it company. Oh my father, how at the altar can I take that vow my heart now whispers never can be kept.

MORDAUNT. Hear me, rash girl, now that none o'erhear our converse. Learn thy father's destiny--the name I bear is not my own!

OCEANA. My father!

MORDAUNT. Thou didst not know my former life and deeds. Hardy adventure and the shock of arms, civil contention and a monarch's death make up the past, and poison all who come! 'Tis thou alone can clothe my future days with peace and shed one cheering ray o'er a dark scene of terror.

OCEANA. Art thou distraught?

MORDAUNT. Do not deny me, girl, and make me so! I am an outcast and a man forbid. Fitzarnold knows me and he asks my child--has power, and gaining thee preserves thy sire. Speak, Oceana! Thy resolve: what is it?

OCEANA. Thou canst not mean it, father! No, it cannot be!

MORDAUNT. Girl, it is as certain as our earthly doom. Decide, then, now between my honor and my instant death! For by thy mother's memory and by my soul, if my despair do find thee pitiless, my own right hand shall end a wretched life and leave thee nothing for a bridal dower but my curses and a blighted name. (*Crosses to R.*)

OCEANA. My throat is parched! I pray a moment's peace, a moment's pause.

> (*Mordaunt paces the stage in great agitation, at last falls on his knee to Oceana. Enter Walter, starts at seeing them, and remains at back.*)

MORDAUNT. Look at thy father, lowly begging life of thee. I will not swear, I will not rave, my child, but I'll implore thee! If thou hast ever loved me and dost so still, show that affection now! Let not thy father's name forever stand a mark for men to heap their curses on--relent, my child.

OCEANA. I can endure no more--rise, my father.

MORDAUNT. Dost thou promise?

OCEANA. All, all!

MORDAUNT. Swear, by truth! by honor! By the dead--

OCEANA. To wed Fitzarnold--

WALTER. (*comes up*) Hold! Hold, rash girl, forebear! Thou art ensnared and wouldst pronounce thy doom.

MORDAUNT. Lightning consume thee, meddling fool! What bringst thou here?

WALTER. No pleasant duty, sir; a message which the council sends thee here. (*Gives packet to Mordaunt.*) I am no spy, nor do I care to know secrets too dread for thine own heart to hold.

MORDAUNT. Beggar, be gone!

> (*Strikes him with packet. Walter draws sword. Oceana interposes.*)

OCEANA. It is my father, Walter, mine.

WALTER. A blow.

OCEANA. Oh, thou wilt forgive him!

WALTER. Never! I will forth, and ere he shall enforce thee where thou hast no joy, will rend the mask he cheats us with.

OCEANA. And if thou dost, by heaven I'll never be thine.

WALTER. (*sheaths sword*) Old man, an angel's bosom shelters thine. Instruct Fitzarnold in our quarrel's cause. No daughter bars my way to him. (*Exit Walter. Enter Fitzarnold.*)

FITZARNOLD. How now, you tremble; what has chanced?

MORDAUNT. A moody beggar who abused my love and I chastised him for it--that's all.

OCEANA. My father--

MORDAUNT. Go to thy chamber.

OCEANA. Would it were my grave. (*Exit.*)

MORDAUNT. My noble lord, that moody stripling whom you saw last night--whether set on by Vaughan, his patron, or by the vainness of his own conceits, resolves to break my daughter's marriage.

FITZARNOLD. And wilt thou suffer this? What is the villain's state?

MORDAUNT. Dependence on Sir Arthur Vaughan: his wealth, a goodly person, and the love of schools. (*Bell tolls.*) Hark! I am summoned to the council. Wilt thou along?

FITZARNOLD. I trust he finds no favor with your daughter.

MORDAUNT. She shall be thine, my lord; thine with free will and full contentment. Now for the council.

  (*Exeunt.*)

Scene 3. The council chamber. (*Flourish. Errington, Sir Arthur and Church on raised platform. Mordaunt and Fitzarnold seated at table, L. Elders, etc., Goodenough, and Soldiers, R. Villagers, Walter, and Tramp.*)

ERRINGTON. 'Tis news that asks from us most speedy action. Heaven has in sounds most audible and strange, in sights, too, that amaze the lookers-on, forewarned our people of their peril. 'Tis time to lift the arm so long supine, and with one blow cut off this heathen race, who spite of reason and the word revealed, continue hardened in their devious ways, and make the chosen tremble. Colleagues, your voices--speak--are you for peace or war?

SIR ARTHUR. What is your proof your Indian neighbors mean not as fairly towards our settlement as did King Philip's father, Massasoit?

ERRINGTON. Sir, we have full proof that Philip is our foe. Sasamond, the faithful servant of our cause, has been dispatched by Philip's men, set on to murder him. One of his tribe confessed the horrid truth--and will, when time shall call, give horrid proof on't. I say this chieftain is a man of blood, and Heaven will bless the valiant arm that slays him.

  (*Enter Metamora suddenly and remains at C. All start and grasp their* swords. *The Soldiers prepare to fire. All are silent and confused.*)

METAMORA. You sent for me and I am come. Humph! If you have nothing to say, I will go back--if you fear to question, Metamora does not fear to answer.

ERRINGTON. Philip, 'tis thought you love us not, and all unmindful of our league of peace, plot with the Narragansetts, and contrive fatal disorder to our colony.

METAMORA. Do your fears counsel you? What is it makes your old men grave? And your young men grasp their fire weapons as if they awaited the onset of the foe? Brothers, what has Metamora done that doubt is in all your faces and your spirits seem troubled? The good man's heart is a stranger to fear, and his tongue is ready to speak the words of truth.

ERRINGTON. We are informed that thou gavest shelter to a banished man, whose deeds unchristian met our just reproof--one by our holy synod doomed--whom it is said you housed, and thereby hast incurred our church's censure--and given just cause to doubt thy honesty.

METAMORA. Why was that man sent away from the home of his joy? Because the Great Spirit did not speak to him as he had spoken to you? Did you not come across the great waters and leave the smoke of your fathers' hearth because the iron hand was held out against you, and your hearts were sorrowful in the high places of prayer. Why do you that have just plucked the red knife from your own wounded sides, strive to stab your brother?

ERRINGTON. Indian, this is no reply for us. Didst thou not know the sentence of the court on him whom thou didst shelter?

METAMORA. If my rarest enemy had crept unarmed into my wigwam and his heart was sore, I would not have driven him from my fire nor forbidden him to lie down upon my mat. Why then should the Wampanoag shut out the man of peace when he came with tears in his eyes and his limbs torn by the sharp thorns of the thicket? Your great book, you say, tells you to give good gifts to the stranger and deal kindly with him whose heart is sad; the Wampanoag needs no such counselor, for the Great Spirit has with his own fingers written it upon his heart.

MORDAUNT. Why dost thou put arms into thy people's hands, thereby engendering mischief towards us?

METAMORA. If my people do wrong, I am quick to punish. Do you not set a snare for them that they may fall, and make them mad with the fire water the Great Spirit gave you in his wrath? The red man sickens in the house of the palefaces, and the leaping stream of the mountains is made impure by the foul brooks that mingle with it.

SIR ARTHUR. Chieftain, since these things are so, sell us thy lands and seek another biding place.

METAMORA. And if I did, would you not stretch out your hand to seize that also? No! White man, no! Never will Metamora forsake the home of his fathers, and let the plough of the strangers disturb the bones of his kindred.

CHURCH. These are bold words, chief.

METAMORA. They are true ones.

ERRINGTON. They give no token of thy love of peace. We would deal fairly with thee--nay, be generous.

METAMORA. Then would you pay back that which fifty snows ago you received from the hands of my father, Massasoit. Ye had been tossed about like small things upon the face of the great waters, and there was no earth for your feet to rest on; your backs were turned upon the land of your fathers. The red man took you as a little child and opened the door of his wigwam. The keen blast of the north howled in the leafless wood, but the Indian covered you with his broad right hand and put it back. Your little ones smiled when they heard the loud voice of the storm, for your fires were warm and the Indian was the white man's friend.

ERRINGTON. Such words are needless now.

METAMORA. I will speak no more; I am going.

MORDAUNT. Hold! A moment, Philip; we have yet to tell of the death of Sasamond, who fell in secret and by treachery.

METAMORA. So should the treacherous man fall, by the keen knife in the darkness and not ascend from the strife of battle to the bright haven where the dead warrior dwells in glory.

ERRINGTON. Didst thou contrive his murder?

METAMORA. I will not answer.

ERRINGTON. We have those can prove thou didst.

METAMORA. I have spoken.

ERRINGTON. Bring in the witness. (*Exit Goodenough.*) We too long have staid the arm of power from execution. Come, we parley with a serpent and his wiles are deep.

METAMORA. Injurious white man! Do not tread to hard upon the serpent's folds. His fangs are not taken out, nor has its venom lost the power to kill.

ERRINGTON. Approach! (*Goodenough returns with Annawandah.*)

METAMORA. Annawandah!

ERRINGTON. Behold, deceitful man, thy deeds are known.

METAMORA. Let me see his eye. Art thou he whom I snatched from the war club of the Mohegan, when thou hadst sung thy death song, and the lips of the foe were thirsty for thy blood? Has Metamora cherished thee in his wigwam and hast thou put a knife into the white man's hand to slay him! The foul spirit hath entered thee, and the pure blood of the Wampanoag has left thy veins. Thy heart is a lie, and thine eye cannot rest upon the face of truth, when like the great light it shines on thee in unclouded glory. Elders, can he speak to you the words of truth, when he is false to his brother, his country and his god?

ERRINGTON. He was thy trusty agent, Philip, and conscience-smote revealed thy wickedness.

METAMORA. You believe his words?

ERRINGTON. We do, and will reward his honesty.

METAMORA. Wampanoag! No, I will not call thee so. Red man, say unto these people they have bought thy tongue, and thou has uttered a lie!

ERRINGTON. He does not answer.

METAMORA. I am Metamora, thy father and thy king.

ERRINGTON. Philip o'erawes him--send the witness home.

METAMORA. I will do that! Slave of the white man, go follow Sasamond.

> (*Metamora stabs Annawandah, who staggers off, R. All stand up, general movement.*)

ERRINGTON. Seize and bind him.

> (*Soldiers make a forward movement.*)

METAMORA. Come! My knife has drunk the blood of the false one, yet it is not satisfied! White man, beware! The mighty spirits of the Wampanoag race are hovering o'er your heads; they stretch out their shadowy arms to me and ask for vengeance; they shall have it. The wrath of the wronged Indian shall fall upon you like a cataract that dashes the uprooted oak down the mighty chasms. The war whoop shall start you from your dreams at night, and the red hatchet gleam in the blaze of your burning dwellings! From the east to the west, in the north and in the south shall cry of vengeance burst, till the lands you have stolen groan under your feet no more!

ERRINGTON. Secure him!

METAMORA. Thus do I smite your nation and defy your power.

ERRINGTON. Fire on him.

> (*Business. Metamora hurls hatchet into stage and rushes out, C.*

*Soldiers fire after him.   Mordaunt receives a shot and falls in chair.
Tableau.   Drums, trumpets, and general confusion.   Quick curtain.*)

ACT III.

Scene 1. A chamber in Mordaunt's house. (*Enter Fitzarnold.*)

FITZARNOLD. Mordaunt wounded, and perhaps to death, struck by a
shot that was leveled at the chief; and the fierce storm of war at distance
heard, which soon may burst tremendous o'er our heads! This is no
place for me. She must be mine tonight! Aye, this night, for fear his death
may snatch his gold and daughter from me. Within there, Wolfe! (*Enter
Wolfe.*) Go get a surgeon for this Mordaunt's wounds, a scribe and
priest for me--wilt be silent?

WOLFE. I will observe! Does my lord wed tomorrow?

FITZARNOLD. No, this night; and with tomorrow's sun I spread my sail
for England.

WOLFE. Ha!

FITZARNOLD. How now! What meanest thou? Wouldst thou to rival
me?

WOLFE. My lord!

FITZARNOLD. Well, well; go see thy duty done. (*Exit.*)

WOLFE. My lord, be sure on't. Now for young Walter. I will fulfill my
duty but not to thee, my Lord Fitzarnold! Thou wilt not thank me for
the priest I'll bring. (*Exit.*)

Scene 2. An Indian village, deep wood, set wigwam, R. Lights half down.
(*Conch shell heard. Enter Nahmeokee from wigwam.*)

NAHMEOKEE. Sure 'twas the shell of Metamora, and spoke the strain
it was wont when the old men were called to council, or when the scout
returns from his long travel.

METAMORA. (*outside*) Nahmeokee!

NAHMEOKEE. It is--it is Metamora. (*Enter Metamora.*)

METAMORA. Is our little one well, Nahmeokee?

NAHMEOKEE. He is. How didst thou leave the white man with whom
thou hast been to hold a talk?

METAMORA. Like the great stream of the mountain where the spirit of
the storm passes furiously over its bosom. Where are my people?

NAHMEOKEE. Here in the deep woods where Kaneshine, the aged priest, tells them the mighty deeds of their people, and interprets to them the will of the Great Spirit.

METAMORA. Otah! (*Enter Otah.*) Summon my warriors; bid them with speed to council. (*Exit Otah.*) I have escaped the swift flight of the white man's bullets but like the bounding elk when the hunters who follow close upon his heels.

> (*Re-enter Otah with Kaneshine and all the Indians. Indian march, eight bars. Indians form at L.*)

Warriors, I took a prisoner from the uplifted weapon of the Mohegan, when the victor's limbs were bloody and the scalps at his belt had no number. He lived in my wigwam; I made him my brother. When the spirit of sleep was upon me, he crept like a guilty thing away, and put into the white man's hand a brand of fire to consume me, and drive my people far away where there are no hunting grounds and where the Wampanoag has no protecting Spirit.

KANESHINE. Annawandah?

METAMORA. Annawandah!

KANESHINE. Where is he, chief of thy people? And where is the dog whose head the Great Spirit will smite with fire?

METAMORA. Where the ravenous bird of night may eat the flesh of his body. Here is the blood of the traitor's heart! (*Shows knife.*) My people, shall I tell you the thoughts that fill me?

KANESHINE. Speak, Metamora, speak!

METAMORA. When the strangers came from afar off, they were like a little tree; but now they are grown up and their spreading branches threaten to keep the light from you. They ate of your corn and drank of your cup, and now they lift up their arms against you. Oh my people, the race of the red man has fallen away like the trees of the forest before the axes of the palefaces. The fair places of his father's triumphs hear no more the sound of his footsteps. He moves in the region his proud fathers bequeathed him, not like a lord of the soil, but like a wretch who comes for plunder and for prey. (*Distant thunder and lightning.*)

KANESHINE. The chief has spoken truly and the stranger is worthy to die! But the fire of our warriors is burnt out and their hatchets have no edge. Oh son of Massasoit, thy words are to me like the warm blood of the foe, and I will drink till I am full! Speak again!

METAMORA. "Chief of the people," said a voice from the deep as I lay by the seaside in the eyes of the moon--"Chief of the people, wake from thy dream of peace, and make sharp the point of thy spear, for the destroyer's arm is made bare to smite. O son of my old age, arise like the

tiger in great wrath and snatch thy people from the devourer's jaws!"
My father spoke no more; a mist passed before me, and from the mist the
Spirit bent his eyes imploringly on me. I started to my feet and shouted
the shrill battle cry of the Wampanoags. The high hills sent back the
echo, and rock, hill and ocean, earth and air opened their giant throats
and cried with me, "Red man, arouse! Freedom! Revenge or death!"

   (*Thunder and lightning. All quail but Metamora.*)

Hark, warriors! The Great Spirit hears me and pours forth his mighty
voice with mine. Let your voice in battle be like his, and the flash from
your fire weapons as quick to kill. Nahmeokee, take this knife, carry it
to the Narragansett, to thy brother; tell him the hatchet is dug from the
grave where the grass is grown old above it; thy tongue will move him
more than the voice of all our tribe in the loud talk of war.

NAHMEOKEE. Nahmeokee will not fail in her path; and her eyes will
be quick to see where the stranger has set his snare.

METAMORA. Warriors! Your old and infirm must you send into the
country of the Narragansett, that your hearts may not be made soft in
the hour of battle.

NAHMEOKEE. Go you tonight, Metamora?

METAMORA. Tonight! I will not lay down in my wigwam till the foe
has drawn himself together and comes in his height to destroy.
Nahmeokee, I still will be the red man's father and his king, or the sacred
rock whereon my father spoke so long the words of wisdom shall be
made red with the blood of his race.

   (*Hurried music. Metamora and Indians exeunt. Nahmeokee goes in
   wigwam.*)

Scene 3. A chamber in Mordaunt's house. (*Clock strikes twelve as scene
opens. Thunder distant. Enter Oceana in plain attire.*)

OCEANA. I know not how it is but every thunder peal seems to bear
words portentous. The moaning blast has meaning in its sound and tells
of distant horror--it is the hour when I bade Walter come! Can he have
braved the tempest? Hark, I hear a step! (*Knock.*) How my heart beats.
(*Enter Fitzarnold.*) It is--it is Fitzarnold!

FITZARNOLD. Fitzarnold, lady! Why this wonder? Is it fear? Can
she whom thunder frights not shrink from me?

OCEANA. My lord, the hour is late; I feign would know who sent thee
hither.

FITZARNOLD. Thy honored father.

OCEANA. Thy purpose?

FITZARNOLD. Read it there. (*Gives letter.*)

OCEANA. Ha! Tonight! Be thine tonight?

FITZARNOLD. Aye, tonight. I have thy father's secret.

OCEANA. I know thou hast, and in that mean advantage wouldst mar his daughter's happiness forever--away! I blush that thus I parley words with thee--get thee gone. (*Crosses to L.*)

FITZARNOLD. Yes, when thou goest with me; not till then, lady. I will not waste the time that grows more precious every moment to me. (*Thunder.*) What though the lightning flash and thunder roll--what though the tempest pours its fury down, Fitzarnold's soul does swell above the din! Nay more, dares brave the storm within thy breast, and shrinks not from the lightning of thine eye.

OCEANA. Would it could kill thee!

FITZARNOLD. It can do more--can conquer like the fiery serpent. It pierces, and as it pierces charms--Oceana!

OCEANA. Stand back! I will alarm my sire.

FITZARNOLD. And if thou dost, he will not aid thee. My treasures are embarked, aye, all but thee; thy father gives consent, the priest waits and ere morning, father, daughter, son, shall all be riding on the wave for England.

OCEANA. No, never!

FITZARNOLD. Convince thyself-- (*Stamps his foot. Enter Walter, disguised as a priest.*) Now, scornful lady, thy bridal hour has come; thy tauntings do but fan the flame that rages here.

OCEANA. Is there no refuge?

FITZARNOLD. None, but in these arms.

OCEANA. No hope--no rescue!

FITZARNOLD. None! None!

OCEANA. Walter, on thee I call-- Walter, where art thou?

WALTER. (*throws off disguise*) Walter is here.

FITZARNOLD. Villain! Thy life or mine!

  (*Fitzarnold draws, Oceans throws herself between them.*)

OCEANA. Forebear! No blood! (*To Walter.*) Thou must come stainless to these arms.

WALTER. Sayest thou? Wilt thou take me to them?

OCEANA. I will--I do. (*They embrace.*)

FITZARNOLD. Thy father's blood be on thee; he is Fitzarnold's victim.

  (*Exit Fitzarnold, R. Bell rings. Enter Tramp, L.*)

TRAMP. The savages approach! The Wampanoag chieftain and his crew, at distance, peal their startling yell of war! Haste, sir, to meet them.

WALTER. Retire thee for a while, my Oceana--thou, sir, on the instant follow me--your sword! your sword!

(*Exit, R., with Oceana, Tramp follows.*)

Scene 4. A view of Mordaunt's house on the beach, R. Sea in distance, ship on fire. Garden and staircase leading down to the water. Lights down at opening of scene. (*Distant yells heard. Enter Fitzarnold hastily.*)

FITZARNOLD. Almighty powers! Hemmed in on every side! No hope! (*War whoop.*) Hark to their savage yells! No means are left for flight, for on the waves my precious vessel burns--by the fell savage mastered! No retreat!

(*War whoops. Exit Fitzarnold hastily. Metamora and all the Indians enter up staircase entrances. Music hurried, forte till all are on.*)

METAMORA. (*pointing to Fitzarnold*) Follow him! (*To others.*) Go into the white man's dwelling and drag him to me that my eye can look upon his torture and his scalp may tell Metamora's triumph to his tribe--go.

(*Otah and Kaneshine are about to enter the house when Oceana appears.*)

OCEANA. Forebear, ye shall not enter.

METAMORA. Warriors, have I not spoken.

(*Metamora throws Oceana around to L., Indians go in.*)

OCEANA. Great chieftain! Dost thou not know me?

METAMORA. I am a Wampanoag in the home of mine enemy; I ride on my wrongs, and vengeance cries out for blood.

OCEANA. Wilt thou not hear me?

METAMORA. Talk to the rattling storm or melt the high rocks with tears; thou canst not move me. My foe! My foe! My foe!

OCEANA. Have mercy, Heaven! (*Indians return, dragging in Mordaunt.*)

METAMORA. Hah!

MORDAUNT. Mercy! Mercy!

OCEANA. My father! Spare my father! (*Rushes to Mordaunt.*)

METAMORA. He must die! Drag him away to the fire of the sacrifice that my ear may drink the music of his dying groans.

OCEANA. Fiends and murderers!

METAMORA. The white man has made us such. Prepare. (*Business.*)

OCEANA. Then smite his heart through mine; our mangled breasts shall meet in death--one grave shall hold us. Metamora, dost thou remember this? (*Shows eagle plume.*)

METAMORA. Yes.

OCEANA. It was thy father's. Chieftain, thou gavest it to me.

METAMORA. Say on.

OCEANA. Thou saidst it would prove a guardian to me when the conflict raged. Were thy words true when with thy father's tongue thou saidst, whatever being wore the gift, no Indian of thy tribe should do that being harm.

METAMORA. The Wampanoag cannot lie.

OCEANA. Then do I place it here. (*Places it on Mordaunt's bosom.*)

METAMORA. Hah!

OCEANA. The Wampanoag cannot lie, and I can die for him who gave existance to me.

MORDAUNT. My child! My child!

(*Red fire in house.*)

METAMORA. Take them apart!

(*Indians separate them.*)

Old man, I cannot let the tomahawk descent upon thy head, or bear thee to the place of sacrifice; but here is that shall appease the red man's wrath.

(*Metamora seizes Oceana; flames seen in house.*)

The fire is kindled in thy dwelling, and I will plunge her in the hot fury of the flames.

MORDAUNT. No, no, thou wilt not harm her.

OCEANA. Father, farewell! Thy nation, savage, will repent this act of thine.

METAMORA. If thou art just, it will not. Old man, take thy child. (*Throws her to him.*) Metamora cannot forth with the maiden of the eagle plume; and he disdains a victim who has no color in his face nor fire in his eye. (*Bugle sounds.*)

MORDAUNT. Gracious heavens!

METAMORA. Hark! The power of the white man comes! Launch your canoes! We have drunk blood enough. Spirit of my father, be at rest! Thou art obeyed, thy people are avenged.

(*Exit hastily, followed by the Indians. Drums and trumpet till curtain. Enter Walter, Goodenough, Church, Soldiers, Peasants, male and female, all from behind house. Soldiers are about to fire, when Walter throws himself before them and exclaims.*)

WALTER. Forebear! Forebear!

(*Walter and Oceana embrace. Tableau.*)

ACT IV.

Scene 1. A room in Sir Arthur's house. (*Sir Arthur discovered. Enter Errington, Lord Fitzarnold, Walter, and Church, L.*)

SIR ARTHUR. Welcome, my brother.

ERRINGTON. The strife is over: but the wail of those who mourn some captive friend still wounds the ear and fills our hearts with sadness.

FITZARNOLD. The follower of mine, surprised or else too venturous in the fight, was dragged away in bondage.

SIR ARTHUR. Old Wolfe.

FITZARNOLD. The same--a moody but faithful man doomed no doubt to torture or to death.

WALTER. (*aside*) Faithful indeed. But not to him thou thinkst.

ERRINGTON. He will avenge the captives' fall.

WALTER. But must they fall--is there no way to save them?

ERRINGTON. None, young sir, unless thy wisdom find it.

WALTER. They might be ransomed.

SIR ARTHUR. True, they might. And from my wealth I'll pay whatever price the Indians' power will yield them for.

ERRINGTON. But who so rash to bear such offer unto Philip in his present mood?

FITZARNOLD. (*aside*) Could I but tempt this stripling to his death.

ERRINGTON. Say, is there one so reckless and so brave will dare the peril to preserve his fellows?

FITZARNOLD. Grave sirs, I know of none more truly fit than young Walter to achieve the deed. How proud the name required by such an act! How vast the joy his daring heart must feel whose arm against such terror shall prevail and rescue numbers from a lingering death!

WALTER. If my lord so dearly holds the prize, why not himself adventure to attain it? But I will go--for I have reasons, for it would move me, felt I not my lord's great pity for the captives' woe.

SIR ARTHUR. Bravely said; thou deserve'st our thanks, and if thou canst, persuade the hostile chief to draw his arm'd bands away and save the blood that else must flow so terribly.

ERRINGTON. Take swiftest horse, young man, and Heaven protect thee.

WALTER. No tongue so blessed as that which heralds peace-- No heart so mailed as that which beats, warm for his fellow man. Fare you well.

(*Exit Walter.*)

ERRINGTON. Now to our labors--those new levies made-- We may

exterminate, with one full blow, this savage race, hated of man--
unblessed of Heaven-- Surely a land so fair was ne'er designed to feed
the heartless infidel. (*Cry, L.: "Indians! Indians!"*) Hah! More
massacre! Mercy, Heaven! (*Enter Oceana, L.*)

OCEANA. Oh, Sirs, show pity to a captive wretch whom heartless men
abuse with taunts and blows. If ye are men, oh, let the helpless find in
you kind pity--mercy and protection.

ERRINGTON. Maiden, whom dost thou speak of?

OCEANA. An Indian woman and her infant child, by these made
prisoners. Look there, they have ta'en her child from her.

(*Enter Nahmeokee with Officer and two Guards, as prisoner. Enter
Goodenough with the child.*)

ERRINGTON. How now, who hast thou there?

GOODENOUGH. An Indian woman, we captured in the glen. A spy, 'tis
thought sent by the cursed foe.

ERRINGTON. Came she alone?

GOODENOUGH. No, a young and nimble man was with her, but he
'scap'd pursuit. I am sure he is wounded, for I saw him fall.

ERRINGTON. Woman, what art thou?

NAHMEOKEE. Give poor woman her child?

ERRINGTON. Dost thou hear my question?

NAHMEOKEE. Give poor Indian woman her child?

OCEANA. Do so.

GOODENOUGH. Why, 'twas I that caught the creature--and--

OCEANA. Man, didst thou hear me? (*Takes child from him.*)

GOODENOUGH. Hard times indeed to lose so good a prize. The brat is
saleable. 'Tis mine.

OCEANA. Measureless brute!

GOODENOUGH. For what? 'Tis only an Indian boy.

(*Oceana gives the child to Nahmeokee, who, touch'd with her kindness,
takes her scarf to wipe Oceana's eyes. The latter recognizes it to be the
one bound round Metamora's arm in first scene.*)

OCEANA. Nahmeokee!

NAHMEOKEE. Hush!

ERRINGTON. Who art thou, woman?

NAHMEOKEE. I am the servant of the Great Spirit.

ERRINGTON. Who is thy husband?

NAHMEOKEE. One thou dost not love.

ERRINGTON. His name?

NAHMEOKEE. I will not tell thee.

ERRINGTON. We can enforce an answer.

NAHMEOKEE. Poor Indian woman cannot keep her limbs from pain; but she can keep silence.

ERRINGTON. Woman, what is thy nation and thy race?

NAHMEOKEE. White man, the Sun is my father and the Earth my mother-- I will speak no more.

ERRINGTON. Captain, take charge of this same stubborn wretch who neither will her name or purpose tell. If she do prove as alleg'd a spy, nothing shall save her from a public death; we must o'erawe our treacherous foe. And this obdurate and blasphemous witch may in her death, keep death from many more. Summon our Elders--my Lord Fitzarnold--your counsel now may aid us.

FITZARNOLD. 'Tis thine--and my poor service.

ERRINGTON. Take her away. Justice is sometimes slow, yet is she sure.

NAHMEOKEE. Thy nation, white man, yet may find it so.

(*Exeunt Errington, Goodenough, Church, Nahmeokee, and Soldiers.*)

OCEANA. Fitzarnold of the Council--could I move his sympathy? (*Approaching him tremblingly.*) My lord.

FITZARNOLD. Well, lady?

OCEANA. I have offended thee.

FITZARNOLD. I have forgotten it.

OCEANA. I have a boon to ask.

FITZARNOLD. Sayst thou--of me?

OCEANA. It will not cost thee much.

FITZARNOLD. No price too great to purchase thy sweet smiles of thee.

OCEANA. Then be this female's advocate, my lord. Thou canst be eloquent and the heart of good, but much misguided men may by thy speech be moved to pity and to pardon her.

FITZARNOLD. How so--a wandering wretch unknown?

OCEANA. Metamora has helpless prisoners.

FITZARNOLD. 'Tis true--and thou dost deeply feel for them. Young Walter now seeks their enfranchisement.

OCEANA. I know it, sir. (*Aside.*) Be still my throbbing heart. (*To Fitzarnold.*) My lord, what vengeance will her husband take. Think you will aught appease dread Philip's wrath--when he is told-- Chieftain, thy wife's a slave?

FITZARNOLD. His wife--the Queen! Indeed! Dost say so?

OCEANA. Give not the secret unto mortal ear--it might destroy all hopes of unity. Preserve this captive from impending doom, and countless prayers shall pay thee for it.

FITZARNOLD. Thy kind approval is reward enough.

OCEANA. Shall she be saved?

FITZARNOLD. She shall be free--a word of mine can do it.

OCEANA. Thanks! Thanks! My lord, deceive me not.

FITZARNOLD. Fear not, fair lady. I have pledged my word. (*Exit Oceana.*) Thou thinkst me kind--ha! ha! I will be so. Philip has captives--and young Walter's there. The Council dare not take this woman's life, for that would doom their captive countrymen. Imprisoned, she is free from danger, for the law protects her. But turn her loose to the wild fury of the senseless crowd, *she dies* ere justice or the elder's arms can reach her. Ah! This way conducts me straight to the goal I am resolved to reach and seal at once my hated rival's doom. Oh! I will plead as angels do in Heaven for mortals when they err and mourn for it. Her freedom is her death--the zealot crowd will rush upon her like the loosen'd winds and prove as merciless--while the lion husband, madden'd with his loss, sheds blood to surfeiting. Oh yes, dear pleader for the captive one, thy boon is granted. She shall be free!

(*Exit Fitzarnold.*)

Scene 2. An Indian Retreat. (*Lights one-half down. Wolfe bound to a stake, R. Metamora at a distance, leaning on his rifle. Kaneshine and Warriors.*)

KANESHINE. Warriors, our enemies have been met, and the blood of the Stranger has sunk deep into the sand--yet the spirit of those who have fallen by the power of the foe are not yet appeas'd--prepare the captives for their hour of death. Come round the tree of sacrifice and lift up the flame, till it devour in its fiery rage, the abhor'd usurpers (*gun, L.*) of the red man's soil! Come, my lips are dry for the captive's blood.

(*As they are about to fire the pile, a shot is heard. Enter Walter.*)

METAMORA. Hold! Let the young man say why he comes into our country unbidden. Why does he tempt the ire of our warriors, when their weapons are red with the blood of the battle?

WALTER. That I come friendly let this emblem speak: to check the dire advance of bloody war, to urge the Wampanoag to disarm his band and once again renew us with the bond that made the white and red man brothers.

METAMORA. No, young man, the blood my warriors have tasted has made their hearts glad and their hands are thrust out for more. Let the white man fear. The arrow he has shot into the mountain has turned back and pierced his own side. What are the Elders' words?

WALTER. Let Philip take our wampum and our coin, restore his captives and remove his dead, and rest from causeless and destructive war, until such terms of lasting peace are made as shall forever quell our angry feuds and sink the hatchet to be raised no more.

METAMORA. *Humph!* And meanwhile he sharpens his long weapons in secret, and each day grows more numerous. When the great stream of the mountains first springs from the earth, it is very weak, and I can stand up against its waters, but when the great rain descends, it is swift and swollen, death dwells in its white bosom, and it will not spare.

WALTER. By Him who moves the stars and lights the Sun, if thou dost shed the trembling captives' blood, a thousand warlike men will rush to arms and terribly avenge their countrymen.

METAMORA. Well, let them come! Our arms are as strong as the white man's, and the use of the fire-weapon he has taught us. My ears are shut against thee.

WALTER. *(to Wolfe)* Oh, my friend! I will achieve thy rescue if gold or prayers can move them.

WOLFE. I was prepared to die, and only mourned for I am childless and a lonely man. I had not told the secret of thy birth, and shown thy father to thee.

WALTER. My father! Sayst thou?

WOLFE. Walter, listen to me.

OTAH. *(without)* Metamora.

METAMORA. Ha! *(Enter Otah.)*

OTAH. Nahmeokee!

METAMORA. Dead!

OTAH. Our feet grew weary in the path, and we sat down to rest in the dark wood--the fire-weapons blazed in the thicket, and my arm was wounded, with the other I grasped the keen knife you gave Nahmeokee, but I sank down powerless and the white men bore off the queen a captive.

METAMORA. *Humph--* Nahmeokee is the white man's prisoner. Where is thy horse?

WALTER. Beneath yonder tree.

METAMORA. Unbind the captive! Young man! You must abide with the Wampanoag till Nahmeokee returns to her home. Woe unto you if the hard hand has been laid upon her. Take the white man to my wigwam.

WALTER. I thank thee, Chieftain, this is a kindness to me. Come, good Wolfe, tell me my father's name.

METAMORA. If one drop fall from Nahmeokee's eye, one hair from her

head, the axe shall hew your quivering limbs asunder and the ashes of your bones be carried away on the rushing winds. Come, old man.
    (*Exeunt.*)

Scene 3. A room in Sir Arthur's house. (*Enter Fitzarnold.*)

FITZARNOLD. Nahmeokee now is free, and the fanatic herd all cry aloud, "Oh, mad rulers! Mercy to her"--she comes--and "witch," "hag," and "Indian" din her ears. They come this way--I must avoid their clamor. (*Enter Nahmeokee.*)
NAHMEOKEE. Let them not kill the poor Indian woman.
FITZARNOLD. Woman, away.
NAHMEOKEE. They will murder my child.
FITZARNOLD. Hold off--I cannot help thee. (*Exit Fitzarnold.*)
NAHMEOKEE. They come upon me from every side of the path. My limbs can bear me no farther. Mercy! Hah! They have missed my track and seek in the wood, and in the caves for my blood. Who is he that rides a swift horse there, through the narrow pathway of the glen! The shade of the coming night is over him, and he dimly appears a red man riding the swift cloud. (*Shouts heard.*) Ha! they have traced me by the white garment the brambles tore from me in my flight. They come. Cling to me, my child. Cling to thy mother's bosom.
    (*Enter Goodenough and four Peasants.*)
GOODENOUGH. Foul Indian witch, thy race is run. Drag her to the lake. Take her child from her. (*Enter Metamora.*)
METAMORA. Stand back! or the swift death shall take wing. Which of you has lived too long? Let him lift up his arm against her.
GOODENOUGH. How is this? King Philip ventures here? What comest thou for?
METAMORA. Boy! Thou art a child, there is no mark of the war upon thee. Send me thy elder, or thy chief. I'll make my talk to him.
GOODENOUGH. Here comes Master Errington.
ERRINGTON. (*entering with Church and Soldiers*) Philip, a prisoner!
METAMORA. No! He has arms in his hand and courage in his heart; he comes near you of his own will; and when he has done his work, he'll go back to his wigwam.
ERRINGTON. Indian, you answer boldly.
METAMORA. What is there I should fear?
ERRINGTON. Savage! The wrath of him who hates the heathen and the man of blood.

METAMORA. Does he love mercy; and is he the white man's friend?

ERRINGTON. Yes.

METAMORA. How did Nahmeokee and her infant wrong you, that you hunted her through the thorny pathway of the glen, and scented her blood like the fierce red wolf in his hunger?

CHURCH. Why hold parley with him! Call our musqueteers and bear them both to trial and to doom. Heaven smiles on us--Philip in our power. His cursed followers would sue for peace.

METAMORA. Not till the blood of twenty English captives be poured out as a sacrifice. Elders, beware, the knife is sharpened--the stake is fixed--and the captive's limbs tremble under the burning gaze of the prophet of wrath. Woe come to them when my people shall hear their chief has been slain by the palefaces or is bound in the dark place of doom.

NAHMEOKEE. Do not tempt them, Metamora; they are many like the leaves of the forest and we are but as two lone trees standing in their midst.

METAMORA. Which can easier escape the hunter's spear? The tiger that turns on it in his wrath, or the lamb that sinks down and trembles? Thou hast seen me look unmoved at a torturing death--shall mine eye be turned downward when the white man frowns?

ERRINGTON. Philip, the peace our young man offered thee. Didst thou regard his words?

METAMORA. Yes.

ERRINGTON. And wilt thou yield compliance?

METAMORA. I will. Nahmeokee shall bear the tidings to my people that the prisoners may return to their homes, and the war whoop shall not go forth on the evening gale.

ERRINGTON. Let her set forth. Friends, let me advise you. Keep the chieftain prisoner; let's muster men, and in unlook'd for hour with one blow we will overwhelm this accursed race. And furthermore-- (*Apart.*)

NAHMEOKEE. (*to Metamora*) I will remember thy words.

METAMORA. Grieve not that I linger in the dark place of the condemned, for the eye of the Great Spirit will be on me there.

ERRINGTON. We greet thee, Philip, and accept thy love. Nahmeokee may return.

METAMORA. 'Tis very good. The horse stands neath the brow of the hill--speak not--I read thy thought in thy eye. Go--go, Nahmeokee. I am ready to follow you.

ERRINGTON. Conduct him forth to prison.

(*Soldiers attempt to take his gun.*)

METAMORA. No! This shall be to me as my child, and I will talk to it until I go back to my people.

GOODENOUGH. Right well conceived, could it but talk.

METAMORA. It can--when the land of my great fore-fathers is trampled on by the foot of the foe--or when treachery lurks round the Wampanoag, while he bides in the white man's home.

ACT V.

Scene 1. Same as ACT I, Scene 1. Lights down. (*Oceana discovered leaning against tomb. Slow music, four bars.*)

OCEANA. Tomb of the silent dead, thou seemest my only refuge! Oh, Walter, where art thou? Alas! the kindly promptings of thy noble heart have led thee to captivity, perhaps to death! Welcome the hour when these dark portals shall unfold again, and reunite parent and child in the long sleep of death. (*Enter Fitzarnold.*) Ah! Fitzarnold here!

FITZARNOLD. I come with words of comfort to thee and feign would soothe thy sorrow.

OCEANA. I do not ask your sympathy, my lord.

FITZARNOLD. A sea of danger is around thee, lady, and I would be the skillful pilot to guide thy struggling bark to safety.

OCEANA. Nay, but let me rather perish in the waves than reach a haven to be shared with thee.

FITZARNOLD. Thou hast no choice; thy father willed thee mine, and with his latest breath bequeathed thee to me. Walter, my stripling rival in thy love, has left thee here defenseless and alone. I deem as nothing thy unnatural hate, and only see thy fair and lovely form; and though thy flashing eyes were armed with lightning, thus would my arms enfold thee.

OCEANA. (*clings to tomb*) Now, if thou darest, approach me--now whilst with my mother's spirit hovering o'er me--whilst thus with tearful eyes and breaking heart I call on Heaven to blast the bold audacious wretch, who seeks a daughter's ruin o'er her parent's grave.

FITZARNOLD. Aye, despite of all.

METAMORA. (*in tomb*) Hold! Touch her not!

OCEANA. Hark to that voice! Kind Heaven has heard my prayers.

(*The door of the tomb opens, and Metamora appears. Oceana faints.*)

FITZARNOLD. Philip! Here!

METAMORA. He is. The Great Spirit has sent me; the ghosts are waiting for thee in the dark place of doom! Now thou must go. Tremble, for the loud cry is terrible and the blaze of their eyes, like the red fire of war, gleams awfully in the night.

FITZARNOLD. I have not wronged thee.

METAMORA. Not? Didst thou not contrive the death of Nahmeokee, when the treacherous white man thirsted for her blood? Did she not with bended knees, her eyes streaming with woes of the heart, catch hold of thy shining broad garment thinking it covered man? Was not thy hand upraised against her, and thy heart, like thy hand, flint that wounds the weary one who rests upon it?

FITZARNOLD. No! no!

METAMORA. I saw thee when my quick step was on the hills, and the joy of Metamora's eyes felt thy blows. I feel them now! "Revenge!" cried the shadow of my father as he looked on with me. I, too, cried revenge and now I have it! The blood of my heart grows hotter as I look on him who smote the red cheek of Nahmeokee.

FITZARNOLD. As reparation I will give thee gold.

METAMORA. No! Give me back the happy days, the fair hunting ground, and the dominion my great forefathers bequeathed me.

FITZARNOLD. I have not robbed thee of them.

METAMORA. Thou art a white man, and thy veins hold the blood of a robber! Hark! The spirits of the air howl for thee! Prepare--

(*Metamora throws Fitzarnold around to R.*)

FITZARNOLD. Thou shalt not conquer ere thou killest me. This sword a royal hand bestowed! This arm can wield it still.

(*Fitzarnold draws; Metamora disarms and kills him.*)

METAMORA. Metamora's arm has saved thee from a common death. Who dies by me dies nobly! (*Turns to Oceana.*) For thee, Metamora's home shall screen thee from the spreading fury of his nation's wrath.

(*Hurry till change. Exit Metamora, bearing Oceana.*)

Scene 2. A chamber. (*Enter Sir Arthur, meeting Errington and Church.*)

SIR ARTHUR. I have news will startle you.

ERRINGTON. Is't of the chief?

SIR ARTHUR. It is; he has escaped our power!

ERRINGTON. Escaped! Confusion! How?

SIR ARTHUR. But now we sought his prison and found it tenantless.

ERRINGTON. But how escaped he? There was no egress thence, unless some treacherous hand unlocked the door.

SIR ARTHUR. And so we thought, at first; but on minute search we found some stones displaced, which showed a narrow opening into a subterranean passage, dark and deep, through which we crept until, to our surprise, we reached the tomb of Mordaunt.

ERRINGTON. The tomb of Mordaunt?

SIR ARTHUR. The ruined pile which now serves as our prison was, years since, when first he sought these shores, the residence of Mordaunt, and this secret passage, doubtless, was formed by him for concealment or escape in time of danger.

ERRINGTON. Indeed!

SIR ARTHUR. Yes, and he had cause to be so guarded, for once, unseen by him, I heard that wretched man commune with Heaven, and sue for pardon for the heinous sin of Hammond of Harrington!

ERRINGTON. Hammond! The outlawed regicide?

SIR ARTHUR. Even so; it was himself he prayed for, the guilty man who gave to death the king, his lord, the royal martyr Charles. As Mordaunt, he here sought refuge from the wrath of the rightful heir now seated on the throne.

ERRINGTON. Think you the chieftain knew this secret way?

SIR ARTHUR. 'Tis likely that he did, or else by chance discovered it and thus has won his freedom and his life.

CHURCH. We must summon our men. Double the guard and have their range extended. (*Exeunt Church and Errington.*)

WOLFE. (*without*) Where is Sir Arthur Vaughan?

SIR ARTHUR. Who calls? (*Enter Wolfe.*) Now, who art thou?

WOLFE. A suppliant for pardon.

SIR ARTHUR. Pardon--for what?

WOLFE. A grievous sin, I now would feign confess.

SIR ARTHUR. Indeed! Go on! Declare it then; I will forgive thee!

WOLFE. Long years have passed since then, but you must still remember when at Naples with your wife and child.

SIR ARTHUR. Ha! Dost thou mean--

WOLFE. The flames consumed thy dwelling and thou, together with thy wife and boy, escaped almost by miracle.

SIR ARTHUR. Ha!

WOLFE. I there looked on midst the assembled throng, a stranger mariner. Urged by the fiend, and aided by the wild confusion of the scene, I snatched your boy and through the noisy throng I bore him to my anchored bark, thinking his waiting parents soon would claim with gold their darling. Next day came on a tempest and the furious winds far from the city drove us and thy child.

SIR ARTHUR. Heavens! Can this be true?

WOLFE. He grew up the sharer of my sea-born perils. One awful night our vessel stuck upon the rocks near these shores and the greedy ocean swelled over her shattered frame--thy son--

SIR ARTHUR. Go on--go on--

WOLFE. Was by mysterious power preserved and guided to his unconscious father. Walter is thy son.

SIR ARTHUR. Man! Why didst thou not tell me?

WOLFE. I feared thy just anger and the force of law. I became Fitzarnold's follower but to this hour has memory tortured me.

SIR ARTHUR. And Walter is a hostage to the savage foe; perchance they have murdered him!

WOLFE. No! Oceana's kindness to the Indian queen has purchased his freedom and my own.

SIR ARTHUR. Where is he?

WOLFE. Looking for her he loves, fair Oceana! Whom 'tis said, a party of the foe carried off.

SIR ARTHUR. Quick, let us arm and follow him. For thee, this act of justice pardons thee.

    (*Exeunt.*)

Scene 3. Indian village. (*Groups of Indians. Kaneshine and Otah discovered. Kaneshine has been addressing them. His looks are gloomy and bewildered.*)

METAMORA. (*outside, at change of scene*) Where are my people?

KANESHINE. Ha! 'Tis our chief-- I know the sound of his voice, and some quick danger follows him.

    (*Enter Metamora, bearing Oceana. Enter Nahmeokee from wigwam.*)

METAMORA. Nahmeokee, take the white maiden in; I would speak to my people; go in and follow not the track of the warrior's band.

NAHMEOKEE. Come in, my mat is soft, and the juice of the sweet berry shall give joy to thy lips. Come in, thou art pale and yielding, like the lily when it is borne down by the running waters.

    (*Nahmeokee leads Oceana into wigwam.*)

METAMORA. Warriors, I have escaped from the hands of the white man, when the fire was kindled to devour me. Prepare for the approaching hour if ye love the high places your fathers trod in majesty and strength. Snatch your keen weapons and follow me! If ye love the silent spots where the bones of your kindred repose, sing the dread song of war and follow me! If ye love the bright lakes which the Great Spirit gave you when the sun first blazed with the fires of his touch, shout the war song of the Wampanoag race, and on to the battle follow me! Look at the bright glory that is wrapped like a mantle around the slain in battle! Call on the happy spirits of the warriors dead, and cry, "Our lands! Our nation's freedom! Or the grave!"

KANESHINE. O chieftain, take my counsel and hold out to the palefaces the pipe of peace. Ayantic and the great Mohegan join with our foes against us, and the power of our brother, the Narragansett, is no more! List, O Chieftain, to the words that I tell of the time to come.

METAMORA. Ha! Dost thou prophesy?

KANESHINE. In the deep wood, when the moon shone bright, my spirit was sad and I sought the ear of Manito in the sacred places; I heard the sound as of one in pain, and I beheld gasping under a hemlock, the lightning had sometime torn, a panther wounded and dying in his thick red gore. I thought of the tales of our forefathers who told us that such was an omen of coming evil. I spoke loudly the name of Metamora, and the monster's eyes closed instantly and he writhed no more. I turned and mourned, for I said, Manito loves no more the Wampanoag and our foes will prevail.

METAMORA. Didst thou tell my people this?

KANESHINE. Chieftain, yes; my spirit was troubled.

METAMORA. Shame of the tribe, thou art no Wampanoag, thy blood is tainted--thou art half Mohegan, thy breath has sapped the courage of my warriors' hearts. Begone, old man, thy life is in danger.

KANESHINE. I have spoken the words of truth, and the Great Manito has heard them.

METAMORA. Liar and coward! Let him preserve thee now!

(*Metamora is about to stab Kaneshine when Nahmeokee enters from wigwam and interposes.*)

NAHMEOKEE. He is a poor old man--he healed the deep wound of our little one. (*Gets to L. of Metamora.*)

METAMORA. Any breast but Nahmeokee's had felt the keen edge of my knife! Go, corrupted one, thy presence makes the air unwholesome round hope's high places. Begone!

KANESHINE. Metamora drives me from the wigwam before the lightning descends to set it on fire. Chieftain, beware the omen. (*Exit.*)

NAHMEOKEE. (*aside*) Will he not become the white man's friend and

show him the secret path of our warriors?   Manito guard the
Wampanoag!

METAMORA.   Men of Po-hon-e-ket, the palefaces come towards your
dwellings and no warrior's hatchet is raised for vengeance.   The war
whoop is hushed in the camp and we hear no more the triumph of battle.
Manito hates you, for you have fallen from the high path of your
fathers, and Metamora must alone avenge the Wampanoag's wrongs.

OMNES.   Battle!   Battle!

METAMORA.   Ha!   The flame springs up afresh in your bosoms; a
woman's breath has brought back the lost treasure of your souls.

(Distant march, drums and trumpet heard.)

Ha! they come!   Go, warriors, and meet them, and remember the eye of a
thousand ages looks upon you.

(Warriors exeunt silently.)

Nahmeokee, should the palefaces o'ercome our strength, go thou with
our infant to the sacred place of safety.   My followers slain, there with
the last of the Wampanoags pour out his heart's blood on the giant rock,
his father's throne.

NAHMEOKEE.   Oh Metamora!

METAMORA.   Come not near me or thou wilt make my heart soft, when I
would have it hard like the iron and gifted with many lives.   Go in,
Nahmeokee.

(Distant trumpets.   Nahmeokee goes in wigwam.   Metamora kneels.)

The knee that never bent to man I bend to thee, Manito.   As the arm was
broken that was put out against Nahmeokee, so break thou the strength
of the oppressor's nation, and hurl them down from the high hill of their
pride and power, with the loud thunder of thy voice.   Confound them--
smite them with the lightning of thine eye--while thus I bare my red war
arm--while thus I wait the onset of the foe--

(Loud alarm.)

They come!   Death!   Death, or my nation's freedom!

(Metamora rushes off.   Loud shouts.   Drums and trumpets till change.)

Scene 4.   Rocky pass.   *(Trumpet sounds retreat. Enter Errington and
Church.)*

ERRINGTON.   They fly!   They fly--the field is ours!   This blow destroys
them.   Victory cheaply bought at twice our loss; the red man's power is
broken now forever.   *(Enter Walter.)*   Is Oceana slain?

WALTER.   No; the chieftain Metamora rescued her from the base passions of Lord Fitzarnold whom Metamora slew to avenge the wrongs he offered to his wife, and Oceana by the chief was borne in safety to his lodge.

ERRINGTON. In safety?

WALTER. Yes; from the hands of Nahmeokee I received her, just as some Indians maddened by defeat, declared to offer her a sacrifice.

ERRINGTON. Away then, Walter. (*Walter crosses to R.*) Sir Arthur now seeks thee out to claim thee as his own son.

WALTER. My father! I fly to seek him. (*Exit.*)

ERRINGTON. The victory is ours; yet while Philip lives we are in peril! Come, let us find this Indian prophet whom Metamora banished from his tribe. He may be bribed to show us the chieftain's place of safety.

(*Exeunt. Change.*)

Scene 5.   Metamora's stronghold.   Rocks, bridge and waterfall. (*Nahmeokee discovered listening.   The child lies under a tree, R., covered with furs.   Slow music, four bars.*)

NAHMEOKEE. He comes not, yet the sound of the battle has died away like the last breath of a storm! Can he be slain? O cruel white man, this day will stain your name forever.

(*Slow music, sixteen bars.   Enter Metamora on bridge.   Crosses and enter, L.*)

METAMORA. Nahmeokee, I am weary of the strife of blood. Where is our little one? Let me take him to my burning heart, and he may quell its mighty torrent.

NAHMEOKEE. (*with broken utterance*) He is here!

(*Lifts the furs and shows the child dead.*)

METAMORA. Ha! Dead! Dead! Cold!

NAHMEOKEE. Nahmeokee could not cover him with her body, for the white men were around her and over her. I plunged into the stream and the unseen shafts of the fire weapons flew with a great noise over my head. One smote my babe and he sank into the deep water; the foe shouted with a mighty shout, for he thought Nahmeokee and her babe had sunk to rise no more.

METAMORA. His little arms will never clasp thee more; his little lips will never press the pure bosom which nourished him so long! Well, is he not happy? Better to die by the stranger's hand than live his slave.

NAHMEOKEE. Oh Metamora! (*Falls on his neck.*)

METAMORA. Nay, do not bow down thy head; let me kiss off the hot drops that are running down thy red cheeks. Thou wilt see him again in the peaceful land of spirits, and he will look smilingly as--as--as I do now, Nahmeokee.

NAHMEOKEE. Metamora, is our nation dead? Are we alone in the land of our fathers?

METAMORA. The palefaces are all around us, and they tread in blood. The blaze of our burning wigwams flashes awfully in the darkness of their path. We are destroyed--not vanquished; we are no more, yet we are forever--Nahmeokee.

NAHMEOKEE. What wouldst thou?

METAMORA. Dost thou not fear the power of the white man?

NAHMEOKEE. No.

METAMORA. He may come hither in his might and slay thee.

NAHMEOKEE. Thou art with me.

METAMORA. He may seize thee, and bear thee off to the far country, bind these arms that have so often clasped me in the dear embrace of love, scourge thy soft flesh in the hour of his wrath, and force thee to carry burdens like the beasts of the fields.

NAHMEOKEE. Thou wilt not let them.

METAMORA. We cannot fly, for the foe is all about us; we cannot fight, for this is the only weapon I have saved from the strife of blood.

(Metamora draws knife.)

NAHMEOKEE. It was my brother's--Coanchett's.

METAMORA. It has tasted the white man's blood, and reached the cold heart of the traitor; it has been our truest friend; it is our only treasure.

NAHMEOKEE. Thine eye tells me the thought of thy heart, and I rejoice at it. *(Sinks on his bosom.)*

METAMORA. Nahmeokee, I look up through the long path of thin air, and I think I see our infant borne onward to the land of the happy, where the fair hunting grounds know no storms or snows, and where the immortal brave feasts in the eyes of the giver of good. Look upwards, Nahmeokee, the spirit of thy murdered father beckons thee.

NAHMEOKEE. I will go to him.

METAMORA. Embrace me, Nahmeokee--'twas like the first you gave me in the days of our strength and joy--they are gone.

(Places his ear to the ground.)

Hark! In the distant wood I faintly hear the cautious tread of men! They are upon us, Nahmeokee--the home of the happy is made ready for thee.

(Stabs Nahmeokee, she dies.)

She felt no white man's bondage--free as the air she lived--pure as the snow she died! In smiles she died! Let me taste it, ere her lips are cold as the ice.

> (*Loud shouts. Roll of drums. Kaneshine leads Church and Soldiers on bridge, R.*)

CHURCH. He is found! Philip is our prisoner.

METAMORA. No! He lives--last of his race--but still your enemy--lives to defy you still. Though numbers overpower me and treachery surrounds me, though friends desert me, I defy you still! Come to me--come singly to me! And this true knife that has tasted the foul blood of your nation and now is red with the purest of mine, will feel a grasp as strong as when it flashed in the blaze of your burning dwellings, or was lifted terribly over the fallen in battle.

CHURCH. Fire upon him!

METAMORA. Do so, I am weary of the world, for ye are dwellers in it; I would not turn upon my heel to save my life.

CHURCH. Your duty, soldiers.

> (*Soldiers fire. Metamora falls. Enter Walter, Oceana, Wolfe, Sir Arthur, Errington, Goodenough, Tramp, and Peasants. Roll of drums and trumpet till all on.*)

METAMORA. My curses on you, white men! May the Great Spirit curse you when he speaks in his war voice from the clouds! Murderers! The last of the Wampanoag's curse be on you! May your graves and the graves of your children be in the path the red man shall trace! And may the wolf and panther howl o'er your fleshless bones, fit banquet for the destroyers! Spirits of the grave, I come! But the curse of Metamora stays with the white man! I die! My wife! My Queen! My Nahmeokee!

> (*Falls and dies; a tableau is formed. Drums and trumpet sound a retreat till curtain.*)

SLOW CURTAIN.

EPILOGUE.

Written by Mr. James Lawson. Spoken by Mrs. Hilson,
New Park Theater, New York, December 15, 1829.

Before this bar of beauty, taste, and wit,
This host of critics, too, who throng the pit,
A trembling bard has been this night arraigned;
And I am counsel in the cause retained.

Here come I, then, to plead with nature's art,
And speak, less to the law, than to the heart.
   A native bard--a native actor too,
Have drawn a native picture to your view;
In fancy, this bade Indian wrongs arise,
While that embodied all before your eyes;
Inspired by genius, and by judgment led,
Again the Wampanoag fought and bled;
Rich plants are both of our own fruitful land,
Your smiles the sun that made their leaves expand;
Yet, not that they are native do I plead,
'Tis for their worth alone I ask your meed.
How shall I ask ye? Singly? Then I will--
But should I fail? Fail! I must try my skill.
   Sir, I know you--I've often seen your face;
And always seated in that selfsame place;
Now, in my ear--what think you of our play?
That it has merit truly, he did say;
And that the hero, prop'd on genius' wing,
The Indian forest scoured, like Indian king!
   See that fair maid, the tear still in her eye,
And hark! hear not you now that gentle sigh?
Ah! these speak more than language could relate,
The woe-fraught heart o'er Nahmeokee's fate;
She scans us not by rigid rules of art,
Her test is feeling, and her judge the heart.
   What dost thou say, thou bushy-whiskered beau?
He nods approval--whiskers are the go.
   Who is he sits the fourth bench from the stage?
There; in the pit!--why he looks wonderous sage!
He seems displeased, his lip notes a sneer--
O! he's a critic that looks so severe!
Why, in his face I see the attic salt--
A critic's merit is to find a fault.
What fault find you, sir? eh! or you, sir? None!
Then, if the critic's mute, my cause is won.
Yea, by that burst of loud heartfelt applause,
I feel that I have gained my client's cause.
Thanks, that our strong demerits you forgive,
And bid our bard and Metamora live.

Oliver E. Durivage
and *The Stage-Struck Yankee*

Of unclear origin, "Yankee" plays began to appear soon after the turn of the century. In the 1815 preface to his play, *The Yankey in England*, David Humphrey described the "Yankey"; Charles Mathews, the English actor, after his 1822-1823 visit to America, created a popular success with *Jonathan in England*. When Seba Smith and James Russell Lowell began to publish stories about the Yankee, stage actors were quick to exploit the growing popularity of this new American phenomenon.

The fascination with the Yankee began in earnest during the 1820's and continued throughout the 1800's. The character developed and, for a time at mid-century, was accompanied by a Yankee gal. Yankee plays proliferated, and the character went everywhere (*The Yankee in Cuba*) and did everything (*The Yankee Inventor*). Among the popular Yankee actors were James H. Hackett, George Handel "Yankee" Hill, Dan Marble, Joshua Silsbee, and John E. Owens. Their vehicles included *The Forest Rose* (1825, by Samuel Woodworth), *The Yankee Peddler* (1836, by William Bayle Bernard), and *The People's Lawyer* (1839, by Joseph S. Jones).

Oliver Everett Durivage was a Boston-born actor, occasional playwright, journalist, and storyteller, who appeared on New York stages, telling "Original Yankee Stories." During the 1840's he was associated with William Mitchell's Olympic Theatre, as actor and writer of burlesques. His *Richard Number 3*, an obvious burlesque of Shakespeare and clearly reflected in the action of *The Stage-Struck Yankee*, became a stock role for Mitchell.

The Stage-Struck Yankee became a vehicle for Marble, who, according to Joseph Jefferson, dressed "much after the present caricature of Uncle Sam, minus the stars and glorying in stripes." Yankee specialists were gifted storytellers, and stage directions in Scene 2 in this play give the actor his opportunity. Some productions list the hero as Curtis Chunk, but a review in the *Spirit of the Times* of March 22, 1845, reports Marble's role as Zachariah Hotspear, a name which, considering the bawdy nature of much theatre at this time, probably more accurately reflects the interests of contemporary American theatregoers.

No. CCXV.

FRENCH'S MINOR DRAMA.

The Acting Edition.

THE

STAGE-STRUCK YANKEE

A FARCE, IN ONE ACT,

BY O. E. DURIVAGE, ESQ.

TO WHICH ARE ADDED

A description of the Costume—Cast of the Characters—Entrances and Exits—
Relative Positions of the Performers on the Stage, and
the whole of the Stage Business.

AS NOW PERFORMED AT THE PRINCIPAL ENGLISH AND
AMERICAN THEATRES.

PRICE 25 CENTS

New York:
SAMUEL FRENCH
Publisher
25 West 45th Street

London:
SAMUEL FRENCH, Ltd.
26 Southampton Street
Strand

THE STAGE-STRUCK YANKEE

(1840)

by Oliver Everett Durivage

CHARACTERS

Douglas Double	Richard
Captain Hotspear	Fanny Magnet
Zachariah Hotspear	Jedidah

Scene 1. A room; breakfast laid for three; chairs, etc., around. (*Jedidah discovered.*)

JEDIDAH. Oh, dear! Oh, dear! I haven't slept a wink all night, and all for thinking of that good-for-nothing Zachariah Hotspear. What a state he was in when he came home last night, or rather this morning, for it was after twelve when I let him in; and only think that, although I'd saved his supper hot, he wouldn't speak a word to tell me where he had been, but kept talking of murdering, and killing, and such stuff, and then he'd laugh and tell me what a beautiful cretur he'd seen, and how he loved her--the brute! This to me, when to-morrow we are to be married. The more I think of it, the more I am convinced he's been down to that plaguey theatre that's been showing in Squire Josh's barn. What would his father say? He'd be the death of him. But I won't put up with such treatment; I won't have a word to say to him till he makes everything as plain as the nose on his face. But here's his father. Oh, Zachariah Hotspear! Zachariah Hotspear! (*Enter Captain, L.*)
CAPTAIN. Ah, Jedidah, good morning; but how's this? You look as sad as a tombstone. This is no day to be sorrowful; to-day makes my son *my* partner, and to-morrow he's your partner for life. But what is the matter?
JEDIDAH. I--I--didn't sleep well last night.
CAPTAIN. No, I'll be sworn, thinking of the happy day, eh? You sat up late with Zachariah, too--ha, ha! Courting, eh? Ha, ha! Well, Zachariah takes after his father. Just before I was married, the way I courted my gal was ridiculous. But where is Zachariah?
JEDIDAH. I believe he's not up yet.

CAPTAIN. The lazy rascal! But 'tis all your fault. What did you keep him up so late for, last night, eh?

JEDIDAH. Will you have your coffee turned out, sir?

CAPTAIN. Yes, "out with it," as the father said to his boy when he swallowed the nutmeg grater. (*Sits L. of table.*) Ah! Here comes Zachariah; I hear the clatter of his cowhides. But where's the boy's voice? He commonly begins the day with "Yankee Doodle," and ends with "Sally in our Alley," or rather Jedidah in our kitchen. Eh? Ha, ha!

(*Enter Zachariah Hotspear, L.*)

ZACHARIAH. "Who see the sun to-day?"

CAPTAIN. Not you, I'll be bound, until 'twas two hours high.

ZACHARIAH. Ah! I've had such dreams.

CAPTAIN. Dreams! Oh, come, wake up! You are dreaming now--come, rub your eyes and come to your breakfast.

ZACHARIAH. It was only jest a dream--but then such an awful one, such a horrible one. Oh! (*Falls into chair, R.*)

CAPTAIN. I believe you've got the nightmare now. Give him a cup of tea. Come, come, partner of mine, you must wake up. Why, you ought to have been stirring at daybreak, and down at the river to see if the sloop sailed. Do you think she's off, hey?

ZACHARIAH. "I'm busy."

CAPTAIN. Busy! You're crazy. Tell me, will the sloop Polly go this morning?

ZACHARIAH. "Begone, thou troublest me."

CAPTAIN. Troublest! Why, have you turned Quaker or a fool? Zachariah, Zachariah, you've been taking your habituals this morning; your breath smells of wormwood. Now tell me if you are sober, and which way the wind is?

ZACHARIAH. "I'm not in the vein." (*Takes out playbill.*)

CAPTAIN. I'm getting wrathy! But no, it's enough to turn the poor boy's head--partner one day and husband the next. Zachariah, you may talk nonsense till after breakfast, but then we must commence performing our business seriously.

ZACHARIAH. (*reading*) "The performance to commence with the tragedy of----"

JEDIDAH. He's raving, distracted.

CAPTAIN. Yes, and you've helped to make him so. But I must bustle; here, Richard--I suppose, now, that rascal is out of the way. Richard, I say! (*Enter Richard, L., with boots.*) Why, you pimp, I had to call you three times, Richard.

ZACHARIAH. (*reading*) "Richard III."

CAPTAIN. Ah! You've brought my boots, that's all I wanted; now go out, or I'll throw the boot-jack at your head, and will----

ZACHARIAH. (*reading*) "Conclude with the death of Richard."
    (*Exit Richard, L.*)

CAPTAIN. Oh! Go on with your jargon; I'll make you sing another song after breakfast.

ZACHARIAH. (*reading*) "After which a comic song."

CAPTAIN. Jedidah, pass the fool the bread and butter.

ZACHARIAH. (*reading*) "Butter, and cheese, and all."

CAPTAIN. That's right, now you've come to your senses, we'll eat our breakfast; and though you may feel perplexed, I hope, for the rest of the day, you'll conclude to act with a laughing face.

ZACHARIAH. (*reading*) "The whole to conclude with a laughable farce."

CAPTAIN. But come, move your jaws, and leave that account till after breakfast. A memorandum, I suppose, of the auction sales yesterday. By the bye, what did those boxes of sugar fetch?

ZACHARIAH. (*reading*) "Boxes--fifty cents."

CAPTAIN. Don't lie, Zachariah; that's no joke. Think of the punishment of liars--the bottomless pit.

ZACHARIAH. (*reading*) "Pit--twenty-five cents."

CAPTAIN. You are mad or drunk. Never mind, marriage will sober you--it did me, and I was happy--so you will be, when you have been married a year of two.

ZACHARIAH. (*reading*) "Children half price." (*Puts up bill.*) Ha, ha, ha! Oh, dad, you'd ought to have been there. Oh, dad, I see such sights last night.

CAPTAIN. Pshaw!

ZACHARIAH. Yes, you're right there, at the show. Was you ever at a show, dad?

CAPTAIN. Yes, I went out to Brighton Cattle-show.

ZACHARIAH. But did you ever see anything acted right out?

CAPTAIN. If you don't talk common sense, you'll see yourself kicked out.

ZACHARIAH. Oh, you'd ought to seen that show down to Squire Josh's barn. I was there last night. It only cost me twenty-five cents. I sot in the pit.

CAPTAIN. (*starting*) What! You go to see the play-actors? Can I believe my ears? And do you dare to tell your father that you were present at their diabolical abominations?

ZACHARIAH. Oh, dad, you don't know once--I never see such handsome sights. There was a bloody tyrannical sojer, King Richard Three, that made nothing of chopping off heads by the dozens. But then he got rode up Salt Creek at last; for there was another chap, that must have been a *colonel* or a major, tackled him, and fit like murder, and bime-by he run his sword right through his body, so that it stuck out on t'other side, and that 'ere was the death of King Richard Three.

CAPTAIN. Zounds and the devil! I see it all, and this accounts for your conduct. But I'll never forgive you--you shan't sleep another night under this roof! I'm done with you forever, and you shan't have Jedidah!

ZACHARIAH. Look here, dad, you don't know as much as a farrow hen. As for Jedidah, she's been marked at for more than her heft. I used to think that she went ahead of everything on the road, but I see a gal last night that cut Jedidah right out of her swathe.

JEDIDAH. (*rises and comes forward, C.*) Oh, dear, I can hold no longer. You good-for-nothing perjured villain! (*Cries.*)

ZACHARIAH. Well, that's pretty fair; but you don't cry so natural as they did at the show--there they squaked right out.

CAPTAIN. I shall go mad. (*Crosses to C.*) Are you my son? Is your name Zachariah Hotspear?

ZACHARIAH. Yes, Zachariah Hotspear--called for short Zackspear.

CAPTAIN. Out of my way, you rascal! Out of my sight, or I'll be the death of you. I'll strangle you, you dog!

ZACHARIAH. Dad, you'd be a first-rate hand to act out King Richard Three. You're jest about as round-shouldered as him; got jest such bandy legs.

CAPTAIN. Out of my sight, sir!

JEDIDAH. (*crosses to C.*) And out of *my* sight, sir, if you don't want me to drop right down a stiffened corpse, for you'll be the death of me. But if I die, I declare and vow I'll haunt your bedside.

ZACHARIAH. And, Jedidah, you'd do to act one of them women King Richard was so sassy to, for they did nothing but bulloch and beller, and jaw, and blow their noses. But, oh! in the fuss, that 'ere splendiferous angel--oh, Jedidah! wasn't she a buster?

CAPTAIN. Oh, miserable boy!

ZACHARIAH. Dad, I reckon you've got the janders. I ain't miserable; no how you can fix it. I ain't done nothing but laugh all night. You'd ought to have seen the clown there; his name was Gregory. He was a real green one; but he made such sport. He sot out to set the table, and I'll show you how he done it. (*Takes crockery.*)

CAPTAIN. Oh, he's beside himself! Put down the waiter! Where the devil is he carrying it to? (*Follows Zachariah, Jedidah follows Captain.*)

ZACHARIAH. Yes, that's right; now you're acting it right out. Clear the coast!

(*Zachariah turns around, runs against Captain, crockery falls and breaks, Jedidah screams.*)

CAPTAIN. I shall go mad! Oh, you scoundrel!

ZACHARIAH. Yes, that's the idee! Ha, ha! Then all the people laffed, and hurra'd, and clapped, and I couldn't stand it, so I snorted right out, and laffed so much I torn my trousers and my shirt. But why don't you laugh, dad?

CAPTAIN. Laugh! I've made up my mind you shall have a strait-jacket and go to the insane hospital, and as for these play-actors, their license shall be stopped, and bag and baggage they shall leave the town.

ZACHARIAH. Well, I've made up my mind, too: if they leave the town, I go along with them. They are a fine, honorable set of fellows. After the play I took all hands into our store and treated 'em; and they said they'd make a play-actor of me. And as for that 'ere gal I seed, I'm desperate in love with her, and I'll marry her right off. Miss Fanny Magnet is her angelliferous name; I'm going to see her to-day; but first I'm going to write her a love-letter, to let her know how savageously I dote on her. So, Jedidah, you needn't shine up to me any longer.

JEDIDAH. (*crying*) Oh, dear! Oh, dear!

CAPTAIN. I'll go instantly and see this she-devil. (*Puts on his boots.*) Richard! (*Enter Richard, L.*) Saddle my horse directly!

RICHARD. What horse will you have, sir?

CAPTAIN. Saddle the sorrel. (*Exit Richard, L.*)

ZACHARIAH. As Richard Three says, "Saddle the white sorrel for the field to-morrow."

CAPTAIN. Go to the devil, you rascal! (*Throws slipper at him.*) And do you, Jedidah, go to your room; don't remain in the company of this mad man. I'll soon give matters a new turn. Oh, Zachariah, Zachariah Hotspear! (*Exit, L.*)

ZACHARIAH. "Toot away, trumpets, beat the big bass drums,
       And make these women hold their tongues."

JEDIDAH. I'll go and hang myself behind the door in the kitchen. Oh, Zachariah Hotspear! Zachariah Hotspear! (*Cries bitterly, and exit, R.*)

ZACHARIAH. Well, she does take on desperate bad, but I can't help it. What's she, compared to that angelic and splendiferous Fanny? But I mustn't lose no time! I'll write a love-letter and send it right off, and she'll read it while I'm dressing in my Sunday clothes. I'll put on my yaller vest and stiffest shirt collar, and if my rig-out don't take her fancy, then she's fire-proof. (*Sits at table.*) I don't know hardly how to begin. I never wrote a love-letter. I suppose it must be in poetry. Gol darn it, this pen is as blunt as a rolling pin. (*Whittles it with a case knife.*) Now for it. (*Writes.*)

> I write, dear Fanny, for to tell
> How in love with you I fell.
> Except Jedidah, you're the fust
> That ever made my heart to bust.
> Jedidah, I have quit and cussed her
> All for you, you little buster!
> Your eyes like lightning bugs do glitter,
> You most consummate, beautiful critter,
> And I shall be in tarnal torture
> Till you let me come and court you.
> I guess you'll find a lad most dear
> Is Zachariah, called Zackspear.

There's um. "Miss Fanny Magnet, this side up with care." Richard! (*Enter Richard, L.*) Here, Richard, carry this letter down to--to the Columbian Hotel, where the show folks stop. Give it to the barkeeper, and tell him to give it, right straight off, to Miss Fanny Magnet, according to the direction. Now away, away! (*Exit Richard, L.*) I'll walk right through you, if you longer stay. By mighty, I feel kind o' curious; I ain't felt so since last Fourth of July, when I got so swizzled on gin and molasses. I'm afeard to see Miss Fanny. I shan't durst to say half as much as I've written in that letter--though when I get my best clothes on I feel darned fierce. I hate most to see Jedidah take on so. I must be an everlasting loss to her. I hope she ain't got no real notion of committing susanside. If I find her hanging up anywhere round the house, I'll cut her down, by hookey! Then she talks about haunting my bedside--darn it, that would be worse than bedbugs! I've heard of such things! (*Introduces song, and exit, R.*)

Scene 2. Room in a tavern. (*Enter Douglas Double and Fanny Magnet, R.*)

DOUBLE. It's clear that something must be done. We're on the *Road to Ruin*, and there's *The Devil to Pay*. Think but of *Raising the Wind*, and I'm the man *Who wants a Guinea*. The landlord has grown as crusty as his old mouldy bread, and I can't get credit at the bar even for a drink.
FANNY. Well, I've done all I could. You know that I consented to be

called Miss Fanny Magnet, when in fact I'm Mrs. Double, and you've called me a great attraction. Now, I should like to know how much I attracted last night.

DOUBLE. Six dollars, seven shillings and four pence.

FANNY. Well, we've done worse than that--hope for the best.

DOUBLE. Hope! So I do keep hoping. Haven't I been lingering here day after day? Monday was our last night; Tuesday *positively* the last night; Wednesday *definitely* the last night; Thursday the ultimate performance. All depends upon my benefit to-night, when, if you really prove a *great attraction,* we shall quit the town with flying colors.

FANNY. How are you going to play the endless variety of pieces you've advertised? Why, you've put up half a dozen.

DOUBLE. Cut 'em, cut 'em. Cut and come again, my maxim. Ah! To-night I'll astonish them, show them what versatility of talent is! "Richard,"-- "Bombastes,"--"Sylvester Daggerwood,"--"Caleb Quotem,"--hornpipe,-- song,--"Jim Crow,"--I'll do it all.

FANNY. Well, I was so much amused at a country youth who sat in the pit. I think he was smitten with me, or else he had never been to a theatre before; for every word I spoke he cried out, "encore," "encore."

DOUBLE. Damn him!

FANNY. What! "Is he jealous?"

DOUBLE. No! no! no!

FANNY. Well, I think you may count upon his patronage to-night for fifty cents.

DOUBLE. No, twenty-five; he sits in the pit.

CAPTAIN. (*without, L.*) I tell you I will come up; offer to stop me and I'll knock you down.

DOUBLE. Eh! What's the meaning of this noise upon the stairs?

FANNY. I say, Double, if it's anyone to see me, I'm not at home, you know.

DOUBLE. It may be somebody for tickets--business is business. (*Exit, R.*)

FANNY. Well, well, I cannot easily forget the comical actions of that Yankee. Ah! Who comes here? (*Enter Captain, L.*)

CAPTAIN. (*aside*) Ah! There she stands, the sarpent. I can't bear to look upon the critter, for I never was in such company before. I dare say she's some old harridan, all paint and wrinkles. (*Fanny turns to him.*) Why, she's as likely a looking girl as Jedidah. I thought I'd blaze away the moment I saw her, but somehow my spirit is leaking away as fast as it can. Oh! I'm so tender-hearted.

FANNY. To what am I endebted for the honor of this visit?

CAPTAIN. (*aside*) I'll put myself into a bit of a passion.

FANNY. Pray be seated. (*They sit.*)

CAPTAIN. (*aside*) Dear me, how very polite! However, she can't fool me. (*Aloud.*) Pray, madam, is your name Fanny Magnet?

FANNY. Yes, sir, that's my name--at your service.

CAPTAIN. (*aside*) Yes, and anybody else's, I suppose. (*Aloud.*) Pray, ma'am, do you know my son?

FANNY. Why, what a strange question! I don't even know you.

CAPTAIN. My name is Hotspear, old Captain Hotspear. I'm selectman and captain of militia. My son, a good-for-nothing fellow, came to see you act out last night.

FANNY. Well, sir, I trust he was pleased with the performance?

CAPTAIN. Pleased, ma'am! Why, the boy's as crazy as a coot. He has done nothing but holler and scream all the forenoon, and call for his horse, and talk about Richard, and Catesby, and the devil knows who.

FANNY. Ha, ha! This must be the youth of last night. Well, sir, is this all?

CAPTAIN. No, ma'am--it isn't all, ma'am--he has engaged to marry Jedidah Pratt, his cousin, ma'am, and till last night he liked her very well; but since he's seen you, he's treated poor Jedidah shamefully, and talks of nothing but Miss Fanny Magnet.

FANNY. La, sir, what could he see in my face to admire?

CAPTAIN. Well, I don't know what--ha, ha, ha! You're not so bad-looking, after all. Now I look at you again, you're a smart, nice gal. But don't try to get Zachariah away from Jedidah--it would break her heart.

FANNY. My dear sir, I could not do it. (*Smiles.*)

CAPTAIN. I don't know that; egad, if you smiled on him as you did on me just now, it would be all over with him. You pretty little--I mean, Miss Fanny Magnet.

FANNY. Well, now, I declare, you're a nice old gentleman!

CAPTAIN. Am I, though? Well, perhaps I am, though I never found it out.

FANNY. Yes, you are; and if your son is only half as well bred, and as good–

CAPTAIN. Come, now, none of that, Miss Fanny Magnet, or you'll make me wrathy again. But between you and I, I should very much like to know what you did to tickle Zachariah so, last night? What did you act out?

FANNY. Why, first I spouted, for instance, and then I danced, and then I sang a little.

CAPTAIN. Sang! What, can you sing? I dare say you can, you little rogue. I beg your pardon, ma'am. I love singing, and as far as Old

Hundred goes, I'm something of a fist at it myself. Pray, let's hear you.

FANNY. (*singing*) "An old man will never do for me,

For May and December can never agree."

CAPTAIN. Why, will nothing but a young man serve your turn? Egad! You sing like a bobolink. You've made me feel so merry, I verily believe I could dance.

FANNY. So could I, you dear old man.

(*Sings "Buy a Broom" and waltzes him round the stage.*)

CAPTAIN. Dear me, young woman, how improper. I declare, you've set my head whirling, and my brain keeps whizzing like the in'ards of a clock in a quinsy. You've absolutely turned my head. If you acted out so with my son, no wonder he came home last night as crazy as a coot.

DOUBLE. (*without, R.*) "Limbs, do your office, and support me well;

Bear me but to her, then fail me, if you can."

FANNY. There's my manager! For Heaven's sake go, old man--if he sees you here, he'll be in a dreadful passion.

CAPTAIN. Well, well, I'll be gone. I can't find it in my heart to scold you--but just try and don't love Zachariah Hotspear. I know it's hard to resist him, for he takes after me--but now don't spile him. I'm off. Think about Jedidah--I'm going; it will be the death of her--I'm gone. (*Exit, L.*)

FANNY. Well, this is truly whimsical. (*Enter Double, R.*)

DOUBLE. "The sun of heaven methought was lothe to set." Pray, Fanny, who was that tiresome old man, and what were you talking about? Your conversation was full five lengths.

FANNY. He's the father of the youth I captivated last night, so now you know the secret.

DOUBLE. The deuce he was! Here, there came a letter to you, which I assumed a husband's privilege of reading. It contains a request to see you, enclosing the following verses. (*Reads and laughs.*)

FANNY. Oh! Do let me see them.

DOUBLE. When he comes, I'll kick him out.

FANNY. No, Double, don't play the farce of *Turn Out*; leave him to me, and I'll show him how to play the *Double Dealer*.

DOUBLE. What! Trust you with a fascinating young man?

FANNY. Yes, you must, Double. "Believe me for mine honor, and have respect for mine honor, that you may believe so." (*Exit, R.*)

DOUBLE. Devilish fine woman, though I say it that shouldn't. In the metropolis she'd draw--she'd be a great attraction. So should I, I'm sure. We'd have a smashing benefit, and when we were called out before the curtain, I should take her by the hand, and, advancing to the footlights,

say: Ladies and gentlemen, we return you our most sincere thanks for
your patronage this evening, and believe us when we say-- (*Enter
Zachariah Hotspear.*) Who the devil are you?

ZACHARIAH. By Jehoshaphat! It's Richard Three!

DOUBLE. Douglas Double, at your service--Manager of the Eagle
Circuit Company.

ZACHARIAH. And I'm Zachariah Hotspear. By beeswax, I'm glad to see
you! You acted out that 'ere tyrant first-rate; but you got an almighty
thrashing at the last. If that 'ere fellow with the tin coffee-pot on his
head, and the pot-kiver on his arm, didn't walk into you with that 'ere
ironspit, then it ain't no matter.

DOUBLE. "A sweeter and a lovelier gentleman,
        Framed in the prodigality of Nature,
        Young, valiant, wise, and no doubt quite royal,
        The spacious world cannot again afford."

ZACHARIAH. Bravo! Bravo! Hurrah for Richard Three!

DOUBLE. You seem to be a lover of dramas?

ZACHARIAH. No, I'm a lover of Jedidah's; and as for drams, I don't make
it a practice to, though I do get swizzled Fourth of July, and muster,
regular as a tea-pot.

DOUBLE. I mean, you're fond of shows?

ZACHARIAH. I want to know if I ain't? Though father keeps one up so
darned tight, I can't get a lick at 'em once in a hundred years. Last night
was the first time I ever seen a play acted right out. At first I thought
you were all swizzled, and you might have heard me sing out,
"Tomatoes! Do they act so day-times, or are they all tight?" But bimeby
I began to see through it. Come to think, it wasn't the first big show I
ever see, 'cause I carried Jedidah to see the Mammoth Caravan, and
wasn't that a snorter! (*Tells a story.*)

DOUBLE. Ha, ha, ha! You are no greenhorn.

ZACHARIAH. I want to know if I am not? No, no, not I? Don't I know
a thing or two? I rather guess I do. I can manufacture cat-skin into
outer kids, and turn half a dozen wooden bacon hams in an hour, and,
twixt you and I, if I could act out as you do, I shouldn't wonder.

DOUBLE. Nor I, upon my soul! You have a noble figure for the stage.

ZACHARIAH. I've a darned good mind to go along with you. What
wages do you give a green hand?

DOUBLE. Well, that depends upon circumstances.

ZACHARIAH. Try before you buy, that's father's maxim. Well, I don't
think I could act without a little practice. Guess I could go Richard

Three, arter I'd learned the lesson. (*Strikes an attitude.*) A hoss! A hoss!

DOUBLE. Bravo! Bravo! You could do it very well.

ZACHARIAH. And then when it came to the fightin' part--by mighty!-- wouldn't I jump around and lick everybody I come across? I wouldn't let that tarnal Richmond lick me like he did you. I'd have that old skewer out of his hand and kick him out darn quick.

DOUBLE. But, as you say, you couldn't have done it without practice or study. Now, I'll be your instructor. Come, let's rehearse a speech or two. I'll spout a line and you repeat it. Are you ready? Now, you must take the stage.

ZACHARIAH. Where to--tarnation?

DOUBLE. Pshaw! Observe me.

ZACHARIAH. Go ahead, I'll follow you. Give us something solid, now.

(*Double speaks and Zachariah repeats every line.*)

DOUBLE. "A thousand hearts are great within my bosom.
            Advance your standards! Set upon our foes!
            Our ancient word of courage, Good St. George!
            Inspire us with the spleen of fiery dragons!
            Upon them! Charge!"

ZACHARIAH. By gosh! This is as hard work as hoeing corn! I'm all out of breath. But I tell you what, I want you to introduce me to that splendiferous critter, Miss Fanny Magnet. I'll shin up to her like a hero, court her like I did Jedidah, and if she don't surrender, then it ain't no matter. Go ahead!

DOUBLE. "Was ever woman in this humor wooed?" (*Exeunt, L.*)

Scene 3. A room meanly furnished; chairs, table, tumbler of water, band- box with bonnet, shoe brushes, men's shoes, theatrical dresses scattered about in disorder. (*Fanny discovered. Dress similar to "Nelly's," in "No Song, No Supper"; pipe in mouth brushing a man's shoe.*)

FANNY. Well, I think this disguise will somewhat disgust my ardent lover. At any rate, he'll not think me so beautiful as when he saw me on the stage last night. I shouldn't wonder if the scene between us would be worth dramatizing; but, eh! He is here!

(*Fanny puts pipe in her mouth and brushes shoe. Enter Zachariah, L.*)

ZACHARIAH. How d'ye do?

FANNY. Who are you?

ZACHARIAH. My name is Zachariah Hotspear; called for short Zackspear.

FANNY. Well, you can squat down, I s'pose?

ZACHARIAH. Well, I can't stop, not now; I come to see Miss Fanny Magnet.

FANNY. Say, you're her sweetheart, ain't you?

ZACHARIAH. I love her most extemporaneously. You're her servant gal, ain't you?

FANNY. Say, you bean't afraid of me, be you? (*She smuts her face.*)

ZACHARIAH. I ain't afeared of no white gal, or nigger either, and your face is six of one and about half a dozen of t'other.

FANNY. Say, don't give me no sass.

ZACHARIAH. I thought you might like to know you've got a gob of blacking on it.

FANNY. Say, did you come to see Miss Fanny Magnet?

ZACHARIAH. Yes, that lovely, all-thunderin' fine gal.

FANNY. Take hold and brush that shoe, then.

ZACHARIAH. Darn it, I just washed my hands, and I shall spatter my trousers all over.

FANNY. Them's Miss Fanny's shoes.

ZACHARIAH. These 'ere? Go along.

FANNY. Yes, they are--why not?

ZACHARIAH. Why, darn it, they'd fit me, and my foot's a foot and a half.

FANNY. Don't you know who I am?

ZACHARIAH. Yes--you're the ugliest white gal I ever see.

FANNY. Well, I'm Miss Fanny Magnet.

ZACHARIAH. You git out!

FANNY. Is this your love for me?

ZACHARIAH. Love for you? Why, you're no more like Miss Fanny Magnet than a sowbug's like a woodchuck.

FANNY. Will you just examine my face?

ZACHARIAH. I can hardly see through that coat of Day & Martin. Why, no!--yes!--it is, by golly!--I'm blamed if it ain't!

FANNY. Are you satisfied?

ZACHARIAH. Yes, ma'am; I hope I see you fine.

FANNY. If you are my sweetheart, just take my hand and kiss it.

ZACHARIAH. Oh, Miss Fanny, that would be taking too extravagant a liberty. (*Aside.*) I don't fancy the taste of Day & Martin.

FANNY. Why don't you take hold?

ZACHARIAH. Well, here goes. (*Kisses her hand. Aside.*) It's Japan blacking, and I've got a mouthful.

FANNY. Ha, ha, ha! You are a proper nice man. (*Falls on his neck.*)

ZACHARIAH. No, I ain't, by a jugful.

FANNY. Yes! You are a dear man.

ZACHARIAH. Hollo! This is more than I bargained for. Damn it! You'll smother me!

FANNY. What! Do you disdain me?

ZACHARIAH. No, I don't want nothing to do with you.

FANNY. Didn't you write me a letter telling me how much you loved me?

ZACHARIAH. Yes! But I've rather concluded pretty much to change my mind.

FANNY. Oh! I shall faint right off.

ZACHARIAH. Now, don't you; it will make such a muss.

FANNY. I will! Oh, you deceiver! oh! oh!

ZACHARIAH. Here's a flare-up. What on earth shall I do? Here's some water. I reckon that will fetch her to.

(Brings down tumbler of water; Fanny takes it, chases him round the stage, and finally throws it in his face.)

Darn your picter! What are you about? You've taken all the stiffening out of my dickey, and now I shall tumble right though my shirt.

FANNY. You traitor, won't you marry me?

ZACHARIAH. I'll see you darned first.

(Fanny takes broom and chases him round stage, Zachariah crying.)

Help! Help! Murder! Take her off!

DOUBLE. *(entering with sword)* Ha! What do I see? *(Strikes attitude.)*

FANNY. Douglas! Save me, save me!

DOUBLE. Villain, let go thy hold. *(Rushes forward, throws Fanny round to L., strikes another attitude.)* Base ravisher, draw and defend thyself!

ZACHARIAH. Draw! Why, I ain't got nothing to draw.

DOUBLE. Ha! Coward! Then die the death of a dog! *(Drives Zachariah round the stage, thrusting at him; he defends himself with band-box.)*

FANNY. Oh! I'm ruined! Undone!

DOUBLE. And you shall be avenged! I demand satisfaction!

ZACHARIAH. Why, look here, King Richard, I never tackle no woman, nor wild cats neither, but I ain't a might afeared of you; but put down that spit, and I'll plough and harrow you in less than no time.

JEDIDAH. *(without, L.)* I tell you I'll see her face to face, and I'll tear her all to pieces!

DOUBLE. The plot thickens; here is one of the legitimate wild cats.

JEDIDAH. *(rushing in)* Where is the minx? Where is this Fanny Magnet?

ZACHARIAH. I tell you what, Jedidah, you'd better keep clear of her. She'll walk right through you like soap-suds down a sink.

JEDIDAH. Stand out of the way, you perjured wretch! Where is Fanny Magnet, I say?

FANNY. Here she is. What have you got to say?

JEDIDAH. Be you she? And did you forsake your true love for this wretch, Zachariah Hotspear?

FANNY. Yes, he has, and what have you got to say to that?

JEDIDAH. I came here to give you a piece of my mind.

FANNY. He promised to marry me, and marry me he shall, and if you ain't careful what you say, I'll slap your face.

JEDIDAH. If you do, I'll scratch your eyes out.

FANNY. Take that, then! (*Slaps her face.*)

JEDIDAH. And you take that, and that. (*They fight.*)

DOUBLE. Ladies! Pray don't expose yourselves.

JEDIDAH. I'll be the death of her.

ZACHARIAH. I say, King Richard Three, we must choke them off.
  (*Jedidah and Fanny try to fight each other. Double holds Fanny, Zachariah holds Jedidah, who turns and beats him.*)
  Hollo! Thunder and lightning!

FANNY. Oh! If I could but get at her!

JEDIDAH. Let me go, you vile deceiver!

ZACHARIAH. No, you don't, by thunder!

DOUBLE. Fanny, my dear, retire and compose yourself.

FANNY. I will, dear Double, but if there's law in the land, I'll have it. I'll sue for breach of promise. (*Exit, R.*)

ZACHARIAH. Good riddance, too! Now look here, King Richard Three, these women have raised my dander, I've been so jofiredly--

DOUBLE. Beaten, bobbed and thumped.

ZACHARIAH. Exactly so. Come on, King Richard Three, and I'll lick you pretty darn supple.

DOUBLE. No, it must not be. The lady has shown you the preference, and I'll resign all claims. You'll marry her, of course?

ZACHARIAH. If I do, may I be drained through a sawmill and converted into slabs. She talks of damages, though, and I s'pose she can recover, though I didn't make her any decided offer of marriage. But then a chap in York State had to pay three hundred dollars just for dreaming he promised to marry a gal; but I wouldn't marry her, not if she was a conglomeration of specie.

JEDIDAH. You wouldn't?--sartin true? And do you love me?

ZACHARIAH. Tremendously!

JEDIDAH. And will you marry me?

ZACHARIAH. Sartin, you little domesticated wild cat. Kiss me and make up.

JEDIDAH. Ain't you ashamed?

ZACHARIAH. Not a mite. Now don't be squeamish. (*Kisses her.*) There wasn't no Day & Martin about that. That was the raw material. Darn it, let's have another squeeze. (*Kisses her again. Enter Captain, L.*)

CAPTAIN. That's right! Keep at it! Keep at it! Tol lol! (*Dances.*)

ZACHARIAH. Hello, dad! Have you got the spring-halt?

CAPTAIN. No; but I'm the happiest old fellow alive--that is, if my eyes don't deceive me. You've come to your senses. You'll have Jedidah, won't you?

ZACHARIAH. Yes, dad, I reckon I've come to my oats. But I ain't got off so easily. This 'ere Fanny swears she'll marry me whether I will or no, or else she'll sue me for a breach of promise. Now, I don't like the idea of going to law. Damages would make considerable of a hole in our specie, partner.

CAPTAIN. Never mind; what can't be cured must be endured! But perhaps we can compromise. Can't you give us a word of advice in the matter, Mr. Manager?

DOUBLE. I think I can. I have a little interest in the lady in question. The fact is, since we opened our establishment for the gratification of your enlightened community, we have met with considerable opposition from many who asserted that our performances were of an immoral tendency.

CAPTAIN. A parcel of bigoted boobies. I was one, but my eyes are open.

DOUBLE. Well, sir, our receipts have been so uncomfortably small, that we are in considerable arrears. Now, one crowded house would set us afloat, and if, through your influence--

CAPTAIN. I understand, and I'll patronize you. I'll take every ticket, and pay you cash, and Jedidah shall come and see the beautiful rival.

JEDIDAH. Beautiful! She's as homely as sin.

DOUBLE. Jealousy! Nothing but jealousy! But don't be alarmed; Miss Fanny Magnet will give you no further cause for uneasiness.

CAPTAIN. That's right. But, Zachariah, you had a narrow escape. It's lucky you didn't see Miss Fanny; it would have been all over with you.

ZACHARIAH. Well, I have seen her, and she was pretty nigh the death of me.

CAPTAIN. She's most angelical.

ZACHARIAH. She's most diabolical.

CAPTAIN. Come, come, Zachariah, you shan't slander her. She's an angel, I say! Such languishing eyes, such ruby lips, such polished skin--

ZACHARIAH. Yes, polished with Knapp's Japan blacking.

DOUBLE. Heyday! Here's playing at cross-purposes with a vengeance. But here comes the lady to decide the dispute.

(*Enter Fanny, in her first dress, R.*)

ZACHARIAH. I hope she's cooled off a bit.

FANNY. Am I a welcome visitor here, or shall I make my courtesy and retire?

ZACHARIAH. This is her in right down earnest, I swow!

CAPTAIN. Well, is she diabolical?

ZACHARIAH. No; she's as angelical as when I first see her. Then that *was* your servant gal I see?

FANNY. (*imitating*) Here, take hold of that shoe and brush it, can't you? And as for you, minx, I'll slap your face, I will.

ZACHARIAH. By mighty, how cute!

JEDIDAH. And then it *was* you, and in fun all along?

ZACHARIAH. Yes, Jedidah, she was acting out.

FANNY. Yes; and now, dear girl, let us embrace in token of friendship.

(*Fanny and Jedidah embrace.*)

ZACHARIAH. I rather guess that was a little tenderer than you embraced jest now. Now, what do you think, Jedidah? Ain't she a buster? By mighty! I love her just as bad as ever!

FANNY. My friend, were I ever so much inclined to favor your suit, it is not in my power. My hand is not at my disposal. I am not single.

DOUBLE. No, you are *Double*. Ladies and gentlemen--(*taking her hand*)-- Mrs. Fanny Double, wife of Douglas Double, Esquire.

ZACHARIAH. What! Married? Dad, I guess we are walked into rather scrumptiously.

DOUBLE. Not so; as some deception has been practiced, you are at liberty to withdraw your liberal offer.

CAPTAIN. No, I shan't; I won't grudge a cent of it. Gad! I'd be willing to double it, to have the pleasure of hearing that charming creature sing, with fal-lal-lal. (*Dances.*)

ZACHARIAH. And I'd give twenty-five cents extra to rip out once more, A hoss! A hoss!

DOUBLE. Thanks, generous friends! And now may fortune favor us, and grant that our unceasing efforts to please may indeed prove a great attraction.

THE END.

Anna Cora Mowatt (1819-1870)
and *Fashion*

Closing a letter from London to her old friend Henry W. Longfellow a few months before her death, the author of *Fashion* signed herself "Anna Cora Mowatt Ritchie," and so she was--a respected member of New York and American high society. When her background and her chosen profession clashed in the minds of some mid-19th century sophisticates, breeding prevailed, encouraging a spirit of cooperation between theatre professionals and the literati. For all of her active years in the theatre, she was Anna Cora Mowatt. Retiring from the stage in 1854--three years after the death of James Mowatt, whom she had married when she was fifteen years old--she married William Ritchie, whom she left in 1860 to spend her remaining years in Europe.

In her *Autobiography of an Actress* (1854), Mrs. Mowatt explained how her early prejudices against the theatre "melted" away as she grew older and circumstances required that she have an income. Few writers were in a better position to know New York society, and none had the wit and skill to satirize it more effectively on stage. *Fashion*, which Mrs. Mowatt herself called "a good-natured satire upon some of the follies incident to a new country," held something for every mid-19th century theatregoer: moral commentary and patriotic sentiments, romantic episodes, the pervasive city versus country conflict, a temperance issue, social caricatures, a melodramatic villain, a country Yankee, a stalwart American hero, a negro servant--even a phony count and a French maid.

Edgar Allan Poe twice reviewed *Fashion* in *The Broadway Journal*, finding it "theatrical but not dramatic" and "in many respects . . . superior to any American play." Encouraged by her success, Mrs. Mowatt ventured into an acting career--to considerable acclaim. Poe, enchanted by her "profusion of rich auburn hair," found "no actress in America her equal." She also wrote other plays, but only *Fashion*, catching the attention of a generation and reflecting the charm of its author, has lasted.

A number of critics hoped that *Fashion* would stimulate a more meaningful American theatre. Perhaps it did, as it became a landmark of American social comedy.

Anna Cora Mowatt, c. 1845

E. L. Davenport as Adam Trueman

FASHION
Or, Life in New York

(1845)

by Anna Cora Mowatt

CHARACTERS

Adam Trueman
Count Jolimaitre, a fashionable European importation
Colonel Howard, an officer in the United States Army
Mr. Tiffany, a New York merchant
T. Tennyson Twinkle, a modern poet
Augustus Fogg, a drawing-room appendage
Snobson, a rare species of confidential clerk
Zeke, a colored servant
Mrs. Tiffany, a lady who imagines herself fashionable
Prudence, a maiden lady of a certain age
Millinette, a French lady's maid
Gertrude, a governess
Seraphina Tiffany, a belle

PROLOGUE.
Written by Epes Sargent.

(*Enter a gentleman, reading a newspaper.*)
"*Fashion, A Comedy.*"
I'll go; but stay--
Now I read farther, 'tis a Native play!
"Bah! home-made calicoes are well enough,
But home-made dramas must be stupid stuff.
Had it the London stamp, 'twould do--but then,
For plays, we lack the manners and the men!"
Thus speaks *one* critic. Here *another's* creed:--
"*Fashion!*--what's here? (*Reads.*) It never can succeed!
What! from a *woman's* pen? It takes a *man*
To write a comedy--no woman can."
Well, sir, and what say *you*? And why that frown?

His eyes uprolled, he lays the paper down:--
"Here! take," he says, "the unclean thing away!
'Tis tainted with a notice of a *play!*"
But, sir!--but, gentlemen!--you, sir, who think
No comedy can flow from *native* ink--
Are we such *perfect* monsters, or such *dull,*
That wit no traits for ridicule can cull?
Have we no follies here to be redressed?
No vices jibetted? no crimes confessed?
"But then, a female hand can't lay the lash on!"
"How know you *that,* sir, when the theme is Fashion?"
And now, come forth, thou man of sanctity!
How shall I venture a reply to thee?
The *Stage*--what is it, though beneath thy ban,
But a *Daguerreotype* of life and man?
Arraign poor human nature, if you will,
But let the *Drama* have her mission still!
Let her, with honest purpose, still reflect
The faults which keen-eyed Satire may detect.
For there *be* man, who fear not an hereafter,
Yet tremble at the Hell of public laughter!
Friends, from these scoffers we appeal to you!
Condemn the *false*, but O! applaud the *true.*
Grant that *some* wit may grow on native soil,
And Art's fair fabric rise from woman's toil--
While we exhibit but to reprehend
The social vices, 'tis for *you* to mend!

ACT I.

A splendid drawing room in the house of Mrs. Tiffany. Open folding doors, discovering a conservatory. On either side glass windows down to the ground. Doors on right and left. Mirror, couches, ottomans, a table with albums, etc., beside it an armchair. (*Millinette dusting furniture, etc. Zeke in a dashing livery, scarlet coat, etc.*)

ZEKE. Dere's a coat to take de eyes ob all Broadway! Ah! Missy, it am de fixin's dat make de natural *born* gemman. A libery for ever! Dere's a pair ob insuppressibles to 'stonish de colored population.

MILLINETTE. (*very politely*) Oh, *oui,* Monsieur Zeke. (*Aside.*) I not *comprend* one word he say!

ZEKE. I tell 'ee what, Missy, I'm 'stordinary glad to find dis a bery 'spectabul like situation! Now as you've made de acquaintance ob dis here family and dere you've had a supernumerary advantage ob me-- seeing dat I only receibed my appointment dis morning. What I wants to know is your publicated opinion, privately expressed ob de domestic circle.

MILLINETTE. You mean vat *espèce*, vat kind of *personnes* are Monsieur and Madame Tiffany? Ah! Monsieur is not de same ting as Madame-- not at all.

ZEKE. Well, I 'spose he ain't altogether.

MILLINETTE. Monsieur is man of business--Madame is lady of fashion. Monsieur make de money--Madame spend it. Monsieur nobody at all--Madame everybody altogether. Ah! Monsieur Zeke, de money is all dat is *necessaire* in dis country to make one lady of fashion. Oh! it is quite anoder ting in *la belle France!*

ZEKE. A bery lucifer explanation! Well, now we've disposed ob de heads of de family, who comes next?

MILLINETTE. First, dere is Mademoiselle Seraphine Tiffany. Mademoiselle is not at all one proper *personne*. Mademoiselle Seraphina is one coquette. Dat is not de mode in *la belle France;* de ladies dere never learn *la coquetrie* until dey do get one husband.

ZEKE. I tell 'ee what, Missy, I disreprobate dat proceeding altogeder!

MILLINETTE. Vait! I have not tell you all *la famille* yet. Dere is Ma'mselle Prudence--Madame's sister, one very *bizarre* personne. Den dere is Ma'mselle Gertrude, but she not anybody at all; she only teach Mademoiselle Seraphina *la musique.*

ZEKE. Well now, Missy, what's your own special defunctions?

MILLINETTE. I not understand, Monsieur Zeke.

ZEKE. Den I'll amplify. What's de nature ob your exclusive services?

MILLINETTE. *Ah, oui! Je comprend.* I am Madame's *femme de chambre*-- her lady's maid, Monsieur Zeke. I teach Madame *les modes de Paris,* and Madame set de fashion for all New York. You see, Monsieur Zeke, dat it is me, *moi-même,* dat do lead de fashion for all de American *beau monde!*

ZEKE. Yah! yah! yah! I hab de idea by de heel. Well now, p'raps you can 'lustrify my officials?

MILLINETTE. Vat you will have to do? Oh! much tings, much tings. You vait on de table--you tend de door--you clean de boots--you run de errands--you drive de carriage--you rub de horses--you take care of de flowers--you carry de water--you help cook de dinner--you wash de dishes--and den you always remember to do everyting I tell you to!

ZEKE. Wheugh, am dat *all*?

MILLINETTE. All I can tink of now. To-day is Madame's day of reception, and all her grand friends do make her one *petite* visit. You mind run fast ven de bell do ring.

ZEKE. Run? If it wasn't for dese superfluminous trimmings, I tell 'ee what, Missy, I'd run--

MRS. TIFFANY. (*outside*) Millinette!

MILLINETTE. Here comes Madame! You better go, Monsieur Zeke.

ZEKE. (*aside*) Look ahea, Massa Zeke, doesn't dis open rich!

(*Exit Zeke. Enter Mrs. Tiffany, dressed in the most extravagant height of fashion.*)

MRS. TIFFANY. Is everything in order, Millinette? Ah! very elegant, very elegant, indeed! There is a *jenny-says-quoi* look about this furniture--an air of fashion and gentility perfectly bewitching. Is there not, Millinette?

MILLINETTE. Oh, *oui*, Madame!

MRS. TIFFANY. But where is Miss Seraphina? It is twelve o'clock; our visitors will be pouring in, and she has not made her appearance. But I hear that nothing is more fashionable than to keep people waiting. None but vulgar persons pay any attention to punctuality. Is it not so, Millinette?

MILLINETTE. Quite *comme il faut*. Great persons always do make little *personnes* wait, Madame.

MRS. TIFFANY. This mode of receiving visitors only upon one specified day of the week is a most convenient custom! It saves the trouble of keeping the house continually in order and of being always dressed. I flatter myself that *I* was the first to introduce it amongst the New York *ee-light*. You are quite sure that it is strictly a Parisian mode, Millinette?

MILLINETTE. Oh, *oui*, Madame; entirely *mode de Paris*.

MRS. TIFFANY. (*aside*) This girl is worth her weight in gold. (*Aloud.*) Millinette, how do you say *arm-chair* in French?

MILLINETTE. *Fauteuil*, Madame.

MRS. TIFFANY. *Fowtool*! That has a foreign--an out-of-the-wayish sound that is perfectly charming--and so genteel! There is something about our American words decidedly vulgar. *Fowtool*! how refined. *Fowtool*! *Arm-chair*! What a difference!

MILLINETTE. Madame have one charmante pronunciation. (*Aside, mimicking.*) *Fowtool!* (*Aloud.*) Charmante, Madame!

MRS. TIFFANY. Do you think so, Millinette? Well, I believe I have. But a woman of refinement and of fashion can always accommodate herself to everything foreign! And a week's study of that invaluable work-- "*French without a Master,*" has made me quite at home in the court language of Europe! But where is the new valet? I'm rather sorry that he is black, but to obtain a white American for a domestic is almost impossible; and they call this a free country! What did you say was the name of this new servant, Millinette?

MILLINETTE. He do say his name is Monsieur Zeke.

MRS. TIFFANY. Ezekiel, I suppose. Zeke! Dear me, such a vulgar name will compromise the dignity of the whole family. Can you not suggest something more aristocratic, Millinette? Something *French!*

MILLINETTE. Oh, *oui,* Madame; *Adolph* is one very fine name.

MRS. TIFFANY. A-dolph! Charming! Ring the bell, Millinette. (*Millinette rings the bell.*) I will change his name immediately, besides giving him a few directions.

(*Enter Zeke. Mrs. Tiffany addresses him with great dignity.*)

Your name, I hear, is *Ezekiel.* I consider it too plebeian an appellation to be uttered in my presence. In future you are called A-dolph. Don't reply-- never interrupt me when I am speaking. A-dolph, as my guests arrive, I desire that you inquire the name of every person, and then announce it in a loud, clear tone. *That* is the fashion in Paris.

(*Millinette retires up the stage.*)

ZEKE. (*speaking very loudly*) Consider de office discharged, Missus.

MRS. TIFFANY. Silence! Your business is to obey and not to talk.

ZEKE. I'm dumb, Missus!

MRS. TIFFANY. (*pointing*) A-dolph, place that *fowtool* behind me.

ZEKE. (*looking about him*) I habn't got dat far in de dictionary yet. No matter, a genus gets his learning by nature.

(*Takes up the table and places it behind Mrs. Tiffany, then expresses in dumb show great satisfaction. Mrs. Tiffany discovers the mistake.*)

MRS. TIFFANY. You dolt! Where have you lived not to know that *fowtool* is the French for *arm-chair*? What ignorance! Leave the room this instant.

(*Mrs. Tiffany draws forward an arm-chair and sits. Millinette comes forward suppressing her merriment at Zeke's mistake and removes the table.*)

ZEKE. Dem's de defects ob not having a libery education.

(*Exit Zeke. Prudence peeps in.*)

PRUDENCE. I wonder if any of the fine folks have come yet. Not a soul--
I knew they hadn't. There's Betsy all alone. (*Walks in.*) Sister Betsy!

MRS. TIFFANY. Prudence! How many times have I desired you to call
me *Elizabeth*? *Betsy* is the height of vulgarity.

PRUDENCE. Oh! I forgot. Dear me, how spruce we do look here, to be
sure--everything in first-rate style now, Betsy. (*Mrs. T. looks at her
angrily.*) *Elizabeth*, I mean. Who would have thought, when you and I
were sitting behind that little mahogany-colored counter, in Canal
Street, making up flashy hats and caps--

MRS. TIFFANY. Prudence, what do you mean? Millinette, leave the
room.

MILLINETTE. *Oui*, Madame.

   (*Millinette pretends to arrange the books upon a side table, but lingers
   to listen.*)

PRUDENCE. But I always predicted it--I always told you so, Betsy--I
always said you were destined to rise above your station!

MRS. TIFFANY. Prudence! Prudence! Have I not told you that--

PRUDENCE. No, Betsy, it was *I* that told you, when we used to buy our
silks and ribbons of Mr. Antony Tiffany--"*talking Tony*," you know we
used to call him. And when you always put on the finest bonnet in our
shop to go to his--and when you staid so long smiling and chattering
with him, I always told you that *something* would grow out of it--and
didn't it?

MRS. TIFFANY. Millinette, send Serafina here instantly. Leave the room.

MILLINETTE. *Oui*, Madame. (*Aside.*) So dis Americaine ladi of fashion
vas one *milliner*? Oh, vat a fine country for *les marchandes des modes*!
I shall send for all my relations by de next packet! (*Exit Millinette.*)

MRS. TIFFANY. Prudence! Never let me hear you mention this subject
again. Forget what we *have* been, it is enough to remember that we *are* of
the *upper ten thousand*!

   (*Prudence goes up and sits down. Enter Seraphina, very extravagantly
   dressed.*)

MRS. TIFFANY. How bewitchingly you look, my dear! Does Millinette
say that that head dress is strictly Parisian?

SERAPHINA. Oh yes, Mamma, all the rage! They call it a *lady's
tarpaulin*, and it is the exact pattern of one worn by the Princess
Clementina at the last court ball.

MRS. TIFFANY. Now, Seraphina my dear, don't be too particular in
your attentions to gentlemen not eligible. There is Count Jolimaitre,
decidedly the most fashionable foreigner in town--and so refined--so

much accustomed to associate with the first nobility in his own country that he can hardly tolerate the vulgarity of Americans in general. You may devote yourself to him. Mrs. Proudacre is dying to become acquainted with him. By the by, if she or her daughters should happen to drop in, be sure you don't introduce them to the Count. It is not the fashion in Paris to introduce. Millinette told me so. (*Enter Zeke.*)

ZEKE. (*in a very loud voice*) Mr. T. Tennyson Twinkle.

MRS. TIFFANY. Show him up. (*Exit Zeke.*)

PRUDENCE. I must be running away! (*Going.*)

MRS. TIFFANY. Mr. T. Tennyson Twinkle--a very literary young man and a sweet poet! It is all the rage to patronize poets! Quick, Seraphina, hand me that magazine. Mr. Twinkle writes for it.

(*Seraphina hands the magazine; Mrs. Tiffany seats herself in an armchair and opens the book.*)

PRUDENCE. (*returning*) There's Betsy trying to make out that reading without her spectacles.

(*Takes a pair of spectacles out of her pocket and hands them to Mrs. Tiffany.*)

There, Betsy, I knew you were going to ask for them. Ah! They're a blessing when one is growing old!

MRS. TIFFANY. What do you mean, Prudence? A woman of *fashion* never grows old! Age is always out of fashion.

PRUDENCE. Oh, dear! What a delightful thing it is to be fashionable.

(*Exit Prudence. Mrs. Tiffany resumes her seat. Enter Twinkle. He salutes Seraphina.*)

TWINKLE. Fair Seraphina! the sun itself grows dim,
　　　　Unless you aid his light and shine on him!

SERAPHINA. Ah! Mr. Twinkle, there is no such thing as answering you.

TWINKLE. (*looks around and perceives Mrs. Tiffany, aside*) The "New Monthly Vernal Galaxy." Reading my verses by all that's charming! Sensible woman! I won't interrupt her.

MRS. TIFFANY. (*rising and coming forward*) Ah! Mr. Twinkle, is that you? I was perfectly *abimé* at the perusal of your very *distingué* verses.

TWINKLE. I am overwhelmed, Madame. Permit me. (*Taking the magazine.*) Yes, they do read tolerably. And you must take into consideration, ladies, the rapidity with which they were written. Four minutes and a half by the stop watch! The true test of a poet is the *velocity* with which he composes. Really they do look very prettily and they read tolerably-- *quite* tolerably--*very* tolerably--especially the first verse. (*Reads.*) "To Seraphina T----."

SERAPHINA. Oh! Mr. Twinkle!

TWINKLE. (*reads*) "Around my heart"--

MRS. TIFFANY. How touching! Really, Mr. Twinkle, quite tender!

TWINKLE. (*recommencing*) "Around my heart"--

MRS. TIFFANY. Oh! I must tell you, Mr. Twinkle! I heard the other day that poets were the aristocrats of literature. That's one reason I like them, for I do dote on all aristocracy!

TWINKLE. Oh, Madame, how flattering! Now pray lend me your ears! (*Reads.*) "Around my heart thou weavest"--

SERAPHINA. That is such a *sweet* commencement, Mr. Twinkle!

TWINKLE. (*aside*) I wish she wouldn't interrupt me! (*Reads aloud.*) "Around my heart thou weavest a spell"--

MRS. TIFFANY. Beautiful! But excuse me one moment, while I say a word to Seraphina! (*Aside to Seraphina.*) Don't be too affable, my dear! Poets are very ornamental appendages to the drawing room, but they are always as poor as their own verses. They don't make eligible husbands!

TWINKLE. (*aside*) Confound their interruptions. (*Aloud.*) My dear Madame, unless you pay the utmost attention, you cannot catch the ideas. Are you ready? Now you shall hear it to the end! (*Reads.*) "Around my heart thou weavest a spell/Whose"-- (*Enter Zeke.*)

ZEKE. Mister Augustus Fogg! (*Aside.*) A bery misty lookin' young gemman?

MRS. TIFFANY. Show him up, A-dolph! (*Exit Zeke.*)

TWINKLE. This is too much!

SERAPHINA. Exquisite verses, Mr. Twinkle--exquisite!

TWINKLE. Ah, lovely Seraphina! Your smile of approval transports me to the summit of Olympus.

SERAPHINA. Then I must frown, for I would not send you so far away.

TWINKLE. Enchantress! (*Aside.*) It's all over with her.

(*Twinkle and Seraphina retire up and converse.*)

MRS. TIFFANY. Mr. Fogg belongs to one of our oldest families--to be sure he is the most difficult person in the world to entertain, for he never takes the trouble to talk, and never notices anything or anybody--but then I hear that nothing is considered so vulgar as to betray any emotion, or to attempt to render oneself agreeable!

(*Enter Mr. Fogg, fashionably attired but in very dark clothes.*)

FOGG. (*bowing stiffly*) Mrs. Tiffany, your most obedient. Miss Seraphina, yours. How d'ye do, Twinkle?

MRS. TIFFANY. Mr. Fogg, how do you do? Fine weather--delightful, isn't it?

FOGG. I am indifferent to weather, Madame.

MRS. TIFFANY. Been to the opera, Mr. Fogg? I hear that the *bow monde* make their *debutt* there every evening.

FOGG. I consider operas a bore, Madame.

SERAPHINA. (*advances*) You must hear Mr. Twinkle's verses, Mr. Fogg!

FOGG. I am indifferent to verses, Miss Seraphina.

SERAPHINA. But Mr. Twinkle's verses are addressed to me!

TWINKLE. Now pay attention, Fogg. (*Reads.*) "Around my heart thou weavest a spell/Whose magic I"-- (*Enter Zeke.*)

ZEKE. Mister-- No, he say he ain't no Mister--

TWINKLE. "Around my heart thou weavest a spell/Whose magic I can never tell!"

MRS. TIFFANY. Speak in a loud, clear tone, A-dolph!

TWINKLE. This is terrible!

ZEKE. Mister Count Jolly-made-her!

MRS. TIFFANY. Count Jolimaitre! Good gracious! Zeke, Zeke-- A-dolph, I mean. (*Aside.*) Dear me, what a mistake! (*Aloud.*) Set that chair out of the way--put that table back. Seraphina, my dear, are you all in order? Dear me! dear me! Your dress is so tumbled! (*Arranges her dress. To Zeke.*) What are you grinning at? Beg the Count to honor us by walking up! (*Exit Zeke. Aside to Seraphina.*) Seraphina, my dear, remember now what I told you about the Count. He is a man of the highest--good gracious! I am so flurried; and nothing is so ungenteel as agitation! What will the Count think! (*Aloud.*) Mr. Twinkle, pray stand out of the way! Seraphina, my dear, place yourself on my right! Mr. Fogg, the con-servatory--beautiful flowers--pray amuse yourself in the conservatory.

FOGG. I am indifferent to flowers, Madame.

MRS. TIFFANY. (*aside*) Dear me! The man stands right in the way--just where the Count must make his *entray*! (*Aloud.*) Mr. Fogg--pray--

(*Enter Count Jolimaitre, very dashingly dressed, wears a moustache.*)

MRS. TIFFANY. Oh, Count, this unexpected honor--

SERAPHINA. Count, this inexpressible pleasure--

COUNT. Beg you won't mention it, Madame! Miss Seraphina, your most devoted! (*Crosses.*)

MRS. TIFFANY. (*aside*) What condescension! (*Aloud.*) Count, may I take the liberty to introduce-- (*Aside.*) Good gracious! I forgot. (*Aloud.*) Count, I was about to remark that we never introduce in America. All our fashions are foreign, Count.

(*Twinkle, who has stepped forward, shows great indignation.*)

COUNT. Excuse me, Madame, our fashions have grown antediluvian before you Americans discover your existence. You are lamentably behind the age--lamentably! 'Pon my honor, a foreigner of refinement finds great difficulty in existing in this provincial atmosphere.

MRS. TIFFANY. How dreadful, Count! I am very much concerned. If there is anything which I can do, Count--

SERAPHINA. Or I, Count, to render your situation less deplorable--

COUNT. Ah! I find but one redeeming charm in America--the superlative loveliness of the feminine portion of creation-- (*Aside.*) And the wealth of their obliging papas.

MRS. TIFFANY. How flattering! Ah! Count, I am afraid you will turn the head of my simple child here. She is a perfect child of nature, Count.

COUNT. Very possibly, for though you American women are quite charming, yet, demme, there's a deal of native rust to rub off!

MRS. TIFFANY. *Rust*? Good gracious, Count! Where do you find any rust? (*Looking about the room.*)

COUNT. How very unsophisticated!

MRS. TIFFANY. Count, I am so much ashamed--pray excuse me! Although a lady of large fortune, and one, Count, who can boast of the highest connections, I blush to confess that I have never travelled--while you, Count, I presume are at home in all the courts of Europe.

COUNT. *Courts*? Eh? Oh, yes, Madame, very true. I believe I am pretty well known in some of the courts of Europe. (*Aside, crossing.*) Police courts. (*Aloud.*) In a word, Madame, I had seen enough of civilized life-- wanted to refresh myself by a sight of barbarous countries and customs--had my choice between the Sandwich Islands and New York-- chose New York!

MRS. TIFFANY. How complimentary to our country! And, Count, I have no doubt you speak every conceivable language? You talk English like a native.

COUNT. Eh, what? Like a native? Oh, ah, demme, yes, I am something of an Englishman. Passed one year and eight months with the Duke of Wellington, six months with Lord Brougham, two and half with Count d'Orsay--knew them all more intimately than their best friends--no heroes to me--hadn't a secret from me, I assure you. (*Aside.*) *Especially of the toilet.*

MRS. TIFFANY. (*aside to Seraphina*) Think of that, my dear! Lord Wellington and Duke Broom!

SERAPHINA. (*aside to Mrs. Tiffany*) And only think of Count d'Orsay, Mamma! (*Aloud.*) I am so wild to see Count d'Orsay!

COUNT. Oh! A mere man milliner. Very little refinement out of Paris!

Why, at the very last dinner given at Lord--Lord Knowswho, would you believe it, Madame, there was an individual present who wore a *black* cravat and took *soup twice!*

MRS. TIFFANY. How shocking! The sight of him would have spoilt my appetite! (*Aside to Seraphina.*) Think what a great man he must be, my dear, to despise lords and counts in that way. (*Aside.*) I must leave them together. (*Aloud.*) Mr. Twinkle, your arm. I have some really very *foreign exotics* to show you.

TWINKLE. I fly at your command. (*Aside, and glancing at the Count.*) I wish all her exotics were blooming in their native soil!

MRS. TIFFANY. Mr. Fogg, will you accompany us? My conservatory is well worthy a visit. It cost an immense sum of money.

FOGG. I am indifferent to conservatories, Madame; flowers are such a bore!

MRS. TIFFANY. I shall take no refusal. Conservatories are all the rage--I could not exist without mine! Let me show you--let me show you.
(*Places her arm through Mr. Fogg's, without his consent. Exeunt Mrs. Tiffany, Fogg, and Twinkle into the conservatory, where they are seen walking about.*)

SERAPHINA. America, then, has no charms for you, Count?

COUNT. Excuse me--some exceptions. I find you, for instance, particularly charming! Can't say I admire your country. Ah! if you had ever breathed the exhilarating air of Paris, ate creams at Tortoni's, dined at the Café Royale, or if you had lived in London--felt at home at St. James's, and every afternoon driven a couple of lords and a duchess through Hyde Park, you would find America--where you have no kings, queens, lords nor ladies--insupportable!

SERAPHINA. Not while there was a Count in it?
(*Enter Zeke, very indignant.*)

ZEKE. Where's de missus?
(*Enter Mrs. Tiffany, Fogg, and Twinkle from the conservatory.*)

MRS. TIFFANY. Whom, do you come to announce, A-dolph?

ZEKE. He said he wouldn't trust me--no, not even wid so much as his name; so I wouldn't trust him up stairs, den he ups wid *his stick* and I *cuts mine.*

MRS. TIFFANY. (*aside*) Some of Mr. Tiffany's vulgar acquaintances. I shall die with shame. (*Aloud.*) A-dolph, inform him that I am *not at home.* (*Exit Zeke.*) My nerves are so shattered, I am ready to sink. Mr. Twinkle, that *fowtool*, if you please!

TWINKLE. What? What do you wish, Madame?

MRS. TIFFANY. (*aside*) The ignorance of these Americans! (*Aloud.*)
Count, may I trouble you? That *fowtool*, if you please!

COUNT. (*aside*) She's not talking English, nor French, but I suppose it's
American.

TRUEMAN. (*outside*) Not at home!

ZEKE. No, Sar--Missus say she's not at home.

TRUEMAN. Out of the way, you grinning nigger!

> (*Enter Trueman, dressed as a farmer, a stout cane in his hand, his boots
> covered with dust. Zeke jumps out of his way as he enters. Exit Zeke.*)

Where's this woman that's not *at home* in her own house? May I be
shot! if I wonder at it! I shouldn't think she'd ever feel *at home* in such a
show-box as this! (*Looking around.*)

MRS. TIFFANY. (*aside*) What a plebeian looking old farmer! I wonder
who he is? (*Aloud.*) Sir-- (*Advancing very agitatedly.*) What do you
mean, Sir, by this owdacious conduct? How dare you intrude into my
parlor? Do you know who I am, Sir? (*With great dignity.*) You are in
the presence of Mrs. Tiffany, Sir!

TRUEMAN. Antony's wife, eh? Well now, I might have guessed that--
ha! ha! ha!--for I see you make it a point to carry half your husband's
shop upon your back! No matter; that's being a good helpmate--for he
carried the whole of it once in a pack on his own shoulders--now you
bear a share!

MRS. TIFFANY. How dare you, you impertinent, owdacious, ignorant
old man! It's all an invention. You're talking of somebody else. (*Aside.*)
What will the Count think!

TRUEMAN. Why, I thought folks had better manners in the city! This is
a civil welcome for your husband's old friend, and after my coming all
the way from Catteraugus to see you and yours! First, a grinning nigger
tricked out in scarlet regimentals--

MRS. TIFFANY. Let me tell you, Sir, that liveries are all the fashion!

TRUEMAN. The fashion, are they? To make men wear the *badge of
servitude* in a free land--that's the fashion, is it? Hurrah for republican
simplicity! I will venture to say now, that you have your coat of arms,
too!

MRS. TIFFANY. Certainly, Sir; you can see it on the panels of my
voyture.

TRUEMAN. Oh! no need of that. I know what your escutcheon must be!
A band-box *rampant* with a bonnet *couchant*, and a peddlar's pack
passant! Ha, ha, ha! That shows both houses united!

MRS. TIFFANY. Sir! You are most profoundly ignorant--what do you mean by this insolence, Sir? (*Aside.*) How shall I get rid of him?

TRUEMAN. (*looking at Seraphina, aside*) I hope that is not Gertrude!

MRS. TIFFANY. Sir, I'd have you know that--Seraphina, my child, walk with the gentlemen into the conservatory.

(*Exeunt Seraphina, Twinkle, and Fogg into conservatory.*)

Count Jolimaitre, pray make the due allowances for the errors of this rustic! (*Whispers to him.*) I do assure you, Count--

TRUEMAN. (*aside*) Count! She calls that critter with a shoe brush over his mouth "Count"! To look at him, I should have thought he was a tailor's walking advertisement!

COUNT. (*addressing Trueman, whom he has been inspecting through his eye glass*) Where did you say you belonged, my friend? Dug out of the ruins of Pompeii, eh!

TRUEMAN. I belong to a land in which I rejoice to find that you are a foreigner.

COUNT. What a barbarian! He doesn't see the honor I'm doing his country! Pray, Madame, is it one of the aboriginal inhabitants of the soil? To what tribe of Indians does he belong--the Pawnee or Choctaw? Does he carry a tomahawk?

TRUEMAN. Something quite as useful--do you see that?

(*Shaking his stick. Count runs behind Mrs. Tiffany.*)

MRS. TIFFANY. Oh, dear! I shall faint! Millinette! (*Approaching.*) Millinette! (*Enter Millinette, without advancing into room.*)

MILLINETTE. *Oui*, Madame.

MRS. TIFFANY. A glass of water! (*Exit Millinette. Mrs. Tiffany crosses to Trueman.*) Sir, I am shocked at your plebeian conduct! This is a gentleman of the highest standing, Sir! He is a *Count*, Sir!

(*Enter Millinette, bearing a salver with a glass of water. In advancing towards Mrs. Tiffany, she passes in front of the Count, starts and screams. The Count, after a start of surprise, regains his composure, plays with his eye glass, and looks perfectly unconcerned.*)

MRS. TIFFANY. What is the matter? What is the matter?

MILLINETTE. Noting, noting--only-- (*Looks at Count and turns away her eyes again.*) Only--noting at all!

TRUEMAN. Don't be afraid, girl! Why, did you never see a live Count before? He's tame--I dare say your mistress there leads him about by the ears.

MRS. TIFFANY. This is too much! Millinette, send for Mr. Tiffany instantly! (*Crosses to Millinette, who is going.*)

MILLINETTE. He just come in, Madame!

TRUEMAN. My old friend! Where is he? Take me to him--I long to have one more hearty shake of the hand!

MRS. TIFFANY. (*crosses to Count*) Count, honor me by joining my daughter in the conservatory. I will return immediately.

(*Count bows and walks towards conservatory, Mrs. Tiffany following part of the way and then returning to Trueman.*)

TRUEMAN. What a Jezebel! These women always play the very devil with a man, and yet I don't believe such a damaged bale of goods as *that*--(*looking at Mrs. Tiffany*)--has smothered the heart of little Antony!

MRS. TIFFANY. This way, Sir, *sal vous plait.* (*Exit with great dignity.*)

TRUEMAN. *Sal vous plait.* Ha, ha, ha! We'll see what Fashion has done for him.

ACT II.

Scene 1. Inner apartment of Mr. Tiffany's counting house. (*Mr. Tiffany, seated at a desk looking over papers. Mr. Snobson, on a high stool at another desk, with a pen behind his ear.*)

SNOBSON. (*rising, advances to the front of the stage, regards Tiffany and shrugs his shoulders*) How the old boy frets and fumes over those papers, to be sure! He's working himself into a perfect fever--ex-actly--therefore *bleeding's* the prescription! So here goes! (*Aloud.*) Mr. Tiffany, a word with you, if you please, Sir?

TIFFANY. (*sitting still*) Speak on, Mr. Snobson, I attend.

SNOBSON. What I have to say, Sir, is a matter of the first importance to the credit of the concern--the *credit* of the concern, Mr. Tiffany!

TIFFANY. Proceed, Mr. Snobson.

SNOBSON. Sir, you've a handsome house--fine carriage--nigger in livery--feed on the fat of the land--everything first rate--

TIFFANY. Well, Sir?

SNOBSON. My salary, Mr. Tiffany!

TIFFANY. It has been raised three times within the last year.

SNOBSON. Still it is insufficient for the necessities of an honest man--mark me, an *honest* man, Mr. Tiffany.

TIFFANY. (*aside*) What a weapon he has made of that word! (*Aloud.*) Enough--another hundred shall be added. Does that content you?

SNOBSON. There is one other subject, which I have before mentioned, Mr. Tiffany--your daughter--what's the reason you can't let the folks at home know at once that I'm to be *the man*?

TIFFANY. (*aside*) Villain! And must the only seal upon this scoundrel's lips be placed there by the hand of my daughter? (*Aloud.*) Well, Sir, it shall be as you desire.

SNOBSON. And Mrs. Tiffany shall be informed of your resolution?

TIFFANY. Yes.

SNOBSON. Enough said! That's the ticket! The CREDIT *of the concern's safe*, Sir! (*Returns to his seat.*)

TIFFANY. (*aside*) How low have I bowed to this insolent rascal! To rise himself he mounts upon my shoulders, and unless I can shake him off, he must crush me! (*Enter Trueman.*)

TRUEMAN. Here I am, Antony, man! I told you I'd pay you a visit in your money-making quarters. (*Looks around.*) But it looks as dismal here as a cell in the State's Prison!

TIFFANY. (*forcing a laugh*) Ha, ha, ha! State's Prison! You are so facetious! Ha, ha, ha!

TRUEMAN. Well, for the life of me I can't see anything so amusing in that! I should think the State's Prison plaguy uncomfortable lodgings. And you laugh, man, as though you fancied yourself there already.

TIFFANY. Ha, ha, ha!

TRUEMAN. (*imitating him*) Ha, ha, ha! What on earth do you mean by that ill-sounding laugh, that has nothing of a laugh about it! This *fashion*-worship has made heathens and hypocrites of you all! *Deception* is your household god! A man laughs as if he were crying and cries as if he were laughing in his sleeve. Everything is something else from what it seems to be. I have lived in your house only three days, and I've heard more lies than were ever invented during a Presidential election! First, your fine lady of a wife sends me word that she's not at home--I walk up the stairs, and she takes good care that *I* shall not be *at home*--wants to turn me out of doors. Then *you* come in--take your old friend by the hand--whisper, the deuce knows what in your wife's ear, and the tables are turned in a tangent! Madame curtsies--says she's enchanted to see me—and orders her grinning nigger to show me a room.

TIFFANY. We were exceedingly happy to welcome you as our guest!

TRUEMAN. Happy? *You* happy? Ah, Antony! Antony! that hatchet face of yours, and those criss-cross furrows tell quite another story! It's many a long day since you were *happy* at anything! You look as if you'd melted down your flesh into dollars, and mortgaged your soul in the bargain! Your warm heart has grown cold over your ledger--your light spirits heavy with calculation! You have traded away your youth --your hopes--your tastes, for wealth! And now you *have* the wealth you coveted, what does it profit you? Pleasure it cannot buy; for you have lost your *capacity* for enjoyment-- Ease it will not bring; for the love of gain is never satisfied! It has made your counting house a penitentiary, and your home a fashionable *museum* where there is no niche for you! You have spent so much time *ciphering* in the one that you find yourself at last a very *cipher* in the other! See me, man! Seventy-two last August! Strong as a hickory and every whit as sound!

TIFFANY. I take the greatest pleasure in remarking your superiority, Sir.

TRUEMAN. Bah! no man takes pleasure in remarking the superiority of another! Why the deuce can't you speak the truth, man? But it's not the *fashion* I suppose! I have not seen one frank, open face since--no, no, I can't say that either, though lying *is* catching! There's that girl, Gertrude, who is trying to teach your daughter music--but Gertrude was bred in the country!

TIFFANY. A good girl; my wife and daughter find her very useful.

TRUEMAN. Useful? Well, I must say you have queer notions of *use*! But come, cheer up, man! I'd rather see one of your old smiles, than know you'd realized another thousand! I hear you are making money on the true, American, high pressure system--better go slow and sure-- the more steam, the greater danger of the boiler's bursting! All sound, I hope? Nothing rotten at the core?

TIFFANY. Oh, sound--quite sound!

TRUEMAN. Well, that's pleasant, though I must say you don't look very pleasant about it!

TIFFANY. My good friend, although I am solvent, I may say, perfectly solvent--yet you--the fact is, can be of some assistance to me!

TRUEMAN. That's the *fact*, is it? I'm glad we've hit upon one *fact* at last! Well--

(Snobson, who during this conversation has been employed in writing, but stops occasionally to listen, now gives vent to a dry chuckling laugh.)

Hey? What's that? Another of those deuced ill-sounding, city laughs!
(Sees Snobson.)

Who's that perched up on the stool of repentance--eh, Antony?

SNOBSON. *(aside and looking at Tiffany's seat)* The old boy has missed his text there--*that's* the stool of repentance!

TIFFANY. One of my clerks--my confidential clerk!

TRUEMAN. Confidential? Why, he looks for all the world like a spy-- the most inquisitorial, hang-dog face--ugh! The sight of it makes my blood run cold! *(Crosses.)* Come, let us talk over matters where this critter can't give us the benefit of his opinion! Antony, the next time you choose a confidential clerk, take one that carries his credentials in his face--those in his pocket are not worth much without!

(*Exeunt Trueman and Tiffany.*)

SNOBSON. (*jumping from his stool and advancing*) The old prig has got the tin, or Tiff would never be so civil! All right--Tiff will work every shiner into the concern--all the better for me! Now I'll go and make love to Seraphina. The old woman needn't try to knock me down with any of her French lingo! Six months from to-day if I ain't driving my two footmen tandem, down Broadway--and as fashionable as Mrs. Tiffany herself, then I ain't the trump I thought I was! That's all. (*Looks at his watch.*) Bless me! Eleven o'clock and I haven't had my julep yet! Snobson, I'm ashamed of you! (*Exit.*)

Scene 2. The interior of a beautiful conservatory; walk through the center; stands of flower pots in bloom; a couple of rustic seats. (*Gertrude, attired in white, with a white rose in her hair, watering the flowers. Colonel Howard regarding her.*)

HOWARD. I am afraid you lead a sad life here, Miss Gertrude?

GERTRUDE. (*turning round gaily*) What! Amongst the flowers?

(*She continues her occupation.*)

HOWARD. No, amongst the thistles with which Mrs. Tiffany surrounds you; the tempests, which her temper raises!

GERTRUDE. They never harm me. Flowers and herbs are excellent tutors. I learn prudence from the reed, and bend until the storm has swept over me!

HOWARD. Admirable philosophy! But still this frigid atmosphere of fashion must be uncongenial to you? Accustomed to the pleasant companionship of your kind friends in Geneva, surely you must regret this cold exchange?

GERTRUDE. Do you think so? Can you suppose that I could possibly prefer a ramble in the woods to a promenade in Broadway? A wreath of scented flowers to a bouquet of these sickly exotics? The odour of new-mown hay to the heated air of this crowded conservatory? Or can you imagine that I could enjoy the quiet conversation of my Geneva friends, more than the edifying chit-chat of a fashionable drawing room? But I see you think me totally destitute of taste?

HOWARD. You have a merry spirit to jest thus at your grievances!

GERTRUDE. I have my *mania*--as some wise person declares that all mankind have--and mine is a love of independence! In Geneva, my wants were supplied by two kind old maiden ladies, upon whom I know not that I have any claim. I had abilities, and desired to use them. I came here at my own request; for here I am no longer *dependent*! *Voila tout*, as Mrs. Tiffany would say.

HOWARD. Believe me, I appreciate the confidence you repose in me!

GERTRUDE. Confidence! Truly, Colonel Howard, the *confidence* is entirely on your part, in supposing that I confide that which I have no reason to conceal! I think I informed you that Mrs. Tiffany only received visitors on her reception day--she is, therefore, not prepared to see you. Zeke--Oh! I beg his pardon--Adolph made some mistake in admitting you.

HOWARD. Nay, Gertrude, it was not Mrs. Tiffany, nor Miss Tiffany, whom I came to see; it--it was--

GERTRUDE. The conservatory perhaps? I will leave you to examine the flowers at leisure. (*Crosses.*)

HOWARD. Gertrude--listen to me. (*Aside.*) If I only dared to give utterance to what is hovering upon my lips! (*Aloud.*) Gertrude!

GERTRUDE. Colonel Howard!

HOWARD. Gertrude, I must--must--

GERTRUDE. Yes, indeed you *must* leave me! I think I hear somebody coming--Mrs. Tiffany would not be well pleased to find you here--pray, pray leave me--that door will lead you into the street.

> (*She hurries him out through door; takes up her watering pot, and commences watering flowers, tying up branches, etc.*)

What a strange being is man! Why should he hesitate to say--nay, why should I prevent his saying, what I would most delight to hear? Truly, man *is* strange--but woman is quite as incomprehensible!

> (*Walks about gathering flowers. Enter Count Jolimaitre.*)

COUNT. There she is--the bewitching little creature! Mrs. Tiffany and her daughter are out of ear-shot. I caught a glimpse of their feathers floating down Broadway not ten minutes ago. Just the opportunity I have been looking for! Now for an engagement with this captivating little piece of prudery! 'Pon honor, I am almost afraid she will not resist a Count long enough to give value to the conquest. (*Approaching her.*) *Ma belle petite*, were you gathering roses for me?

GERTRUDE. (*starts on first perceiving him, but instantly regains her self-possession*) The roses here, Sir, are carefully guarded with thorns-- If you have the right to gather, pluck for yourself!

COUNT. Sharp as ever, little Gertrude! But now 'that we are alone, throw off the frigidity, and be at your ease.

GERTRUDE. Permit me to *be alone*, Sir, that I *may* be at my ease.

COUNT. Very good, *ma belle*, well said. (*Applauding her.*) Never yield too soon, even to a title! But as the old girl may find her way back before long, we may as well come to particulars at once. I love you; but that you know already. (*Rubbing his eye glass unconcernedly with his handkerchief.*) Before long I shall make Mademoiselle Seraphina my wife, and, of course, you shall remain in the family!

GERTRUDE. (*indignantly*) Sir--

COUNT. 'Pon my honor you shall! In France we arrange these little matters without difficulty!

GERTRUDE. But I am an American! Your conduct proves that you are not one! (*Going, crosses.*)

COUNT. (*preventing her*) Don't run away, my immaculate *petite Americaine!* Demme, you've quite overlooked my condescension--the difference of our stations--you a species of upper servant--an orphan-- no friends. (*Enter Trueman unperceived.*)

GERTRUDE. And therefore more entitled to the respect and protection of every *true gentleman!* Had you been one, you would not have insulted me!

COUNT. My charming little orator, patriotism and declamation become you particularly! (*Approaches her.*) I feel quite tempted to taste--

TRUEMAN. (*thrusting him aside*) An American hickory switch! (*Strikes him.*) Well, how do you like it?

COUNT. (*aside*) Old matter-of-fact! (*Aloud.*) Sir, how dare you?

TRUEMAN. My stick has answered that question!

GERTRUDE. Oh! Now I am quite safe!

TRUEMAN. Safe! not a bit safer than before! All women would be safe, if they knew how virtue became them! As for you, Mr. Count, what have you to say for yourself? Come, speak out!

COUNT. Sir--aw--aw--you don't understand these matters!

TRUEMAN. That's a fact! Not having had *your* experience, I don't believe I *do* understand them!

COUNT. A piece of pleasantry--a mere joke--

TRUEMAN. A joke was it? I'll show you a joke worth two of that! I'll teach you the way we natives joke with a puppy who don't respect an honest woman! (*Seizing him.*)

COUNT. Oh! oh! demme--you old ruffian! Let me go! What do you mean?

TRUEMAN. Oh! a piece of pleasantry--a mere joke-- Very pleasant isn't it?

(*Attempts to strike him again; Count struggles with him. Enter Mrs. Tiffany hastily, in her bonnet and shawl.*)

MRS. TIFFANY. What is the matter? I am perfectly *abimé* with terror. Mr. Trueman, what has happened?

TRUEMAN. Oh! we have been joking!

MRS. TIFFANY. (*to Count, who is re-arranging his dress*) My dear Count, I did not expect to find you here--how kind of you!

TRUEMAN. Your *dear* Count has been showing his kindness in a very *foreign* manner. Too *foreign*, I think he found it, to be relished by an *unfashionable native*! What do you think of a puppy, who insults an innocent girl all in the way of *kindness*? This Count of yours--this importation of--

COUNT. My dear Madame, demme, permit me to explain. It would be un-becoming--demme--particular unbecoming of you--aw--aw--to pay any attention to this ignorant person. (*Crosses to Trueman.*) Anything that he says concerning a man of my standing--aw--the truth is, Madame--

TRUEMAN. Let us have the truth by all means--if it is only for the novelty's sake!

COUNT. (*turning his back to Trueman*) You see, Madame, hoping to obtain a few moments' private conversation with Miss Seraphina--with *Miss Seraphina* I say and--aw--and knowing her passion for flowers, I found my way to your very tasteful and *recherché* conservatory. (*Looks about him approvingly.*) *Very* beautifully arranged--does you great credit, Madame! Here I encountered this young person. She was inclined to be talkative; and I indulged her with--with a--aw--demme--a few *common places*! What passed between us was mere *harmless badinage*--on *my* part. You, Madame, you--so conversant with our European manners--you are aware that where a man of fashion--that is, when a woman--a man is bound--amongst noblemen, you know--

MRS. TIFFANY. I comprehend you perfectly--*parfittement*, my dear Count.

COUNT. (*aside*) 'Pon my honor, that's very obliging of her.

MRS. TIFFANY. I am shocked at the plebeian forwardness of this conceited girl!

TRUEMAN. (*walking up to Count*) Did you ever keep a reckoning of the lies you tell in an hour?

MRS. TIFFANY. Mr. Trueman, I blush for you! (*Crosses to Trueman.*)

TRUEMAN. Don't do that--you have no blushes to spare.

MRS. TIFFANY. It is a man of rank whom you are addressing, Sir!

TRUEMAN. A rank villain, Mrs. Antony Tiffany! *A rich one* he would be, had he as much *gold* as *brass*!

MRS. TIFFANY. Pray pardon him, Count; he knows nothing of *how ton*!

COUNT. Demme, he's beneath my notice. I tell you what, old fellow--

(*Trueman raises his stick as Count approaches, the latter starts back.*)
The sight of him discomposes me--aw--I feel quite uncomfortable--aw--
let us join your charming daughter? (*To Trueman.*) I can't do you the
honor to shoot you, Sir--you are beneath me--a nobleman can't fight a
commoner! Good bye, old Truepenny! I--aw--I'm insensible to your
insolence! (*Exeunt Count and Mrs. Tiffany.*)

TRUEMAN. You won't be insensible to a cow hide in spite of your
nobility! The next time he practises any of his foreign fashions on you,
Gertrude, you'll see how I'll wake up his sensibilities!

GERTRUDE. I do not know what I should have done without you, Sir.

TRUEMAN. Yes, you do--you know that you would have done well
enough! Never tell a lie, girl! Not even for the sake of pleasing an old
man! When you open your lips, let your heart speak. Never tell a lie!
Let your face be the looking-glass of your soul--your heart its clock--
while your tongue rings the hours! But the glass must be clear, the clock
true, and then there's no fear but the tongue will do its duty in a
woman's head!

GERTRUDE. You are very good, Sir!

TRUEMAN. That's as it may be! (*Aside.*) How my heart warms
towards her! (*Aloud.*) Gertrude, I hear that you have no mother?

GERTRUDE. Ah! no, Sir; I wish I had.

TRUEMAN. (*aside and with emotion*) So do I! Heaven knows, so do I!
(*Aloud.*) And you have no father, Gertrude?

GERTRUDE. No, Sir--I often wish I had!

TRUEMAN. (*hurriedly*) Don't do that, girl! Don't do that! Wish you
had a mother--but never wish that you had a father again! Perhaps the
one you had did not deserve such a child! (*Enter Prudence.*)

PRUDENCE. Seraphina is looking for you, Gertrude.

GERTRUDE. I will go to her. (*Crosses.*) Mr. Trueman, you will not
permit me to thank you, but you cannot prevent my gratitude! (*Exit.*)

TRUEMAN. (*looking after her*) If falsehood harbours there, I'll give up
searching after truth!

(*Trueman retires up the stage musingly, and commences examining the
flowers.*)

PRUDENCE. (*aside*) What a nice old man he is to be sure! I wish he
would say something!

(*She walks after him, turning when he turns--after a pause, aloud.*)

Don't mind *me*, Mr. Trueman!

TRUEMAN. Mind you? Oh! no, don't be afraid. (*Crosses.*) I wasn't minding you. Nobody seems to mind you much!

(*Continues walking and examining the flowers, Prudence follows.*)

PRUDENCE. Very pretty flowers, ain't they? Gertrude takes care of them.

TRUEMAN. Gertrude? So I hear-- (*Advancing.*) I suppose you can tell me now who this Gertrude--

PRUDENCE. Who she's in love with? I *knew* you were going to say that! I'll tell you all about it! Gertrude, she's in love with--Mr. Twinkle! and he's in love with her. And Seraphina, she's in love with Count Jolly-what-d'ye-call-it: but Count Jolly don't take to her at all-- but Colonel Howard--he's the man--he's desperate about her!

TRUEMAN. Why, you feminine newspaper! Howard in love with that quintessence of affectation! Howard--the only frank, straightforward fellow that I've met since-- I'll tell him my mind on the subject! And Gertrude hunting for happiness in a rhyming dictionary! The girl's a greater fool than I took her for! (*Crosses.*)

PRUDENCE. So she is--you see I know all about them!

TRUEMAN. I see you do! You've a wonderful knowledge--wonderful-- of *other people's concerns*! It may do here, but take my word for it, in the county of Catteraugus you'd get the name of a great *busy-body*. But perhaps you know that too?

PRUDENCE. Oh! I always know what's coming. I feel it beforehand all over me. I knew something was going to happen the day you came here-- and what's more, I can always tell a married man from a single--I felt right off that you were a bachelor!

TRUEMAN. Felt right off I was a bachelor, did you? You were sure of it--sure? Quite sure? (*Prudence assents delightedly.*) Then you felt wrong! A bachelor and a widower are not the same thing!

PRUDENCE. Oh! but it all comes to the same thing--a widower's as good as a bachelor any day! And besides, I knew that you were a farmer *right off*.

TRUEMAN. On the spot, eh? I suppose you saw cabbages and green peas growing out of my hat?

PRUDENCE. No, I didn't--but I knew all about you. And I knew-- (*Looking down and fidgeting with her apron.*) I knew you were for getting married soon! For last night I dream't I saw your funeral going along the streets, and the mourners all dressed in white. And a funeral is a sure sign of a wedding, you know! (*Nudging him with her elbow.*)

TRUEMAN. (*imitating her voice*) Well, I can't say that I *know* any such thing, you know! (*Nudging her back.*)

PRUDENCE. Oh! it does, and there's no getting over it! For my part, I like farmers--and I know all about setting hens and turkeys, and feeding chickens, and laying eggs, and all that sort of thing!

TRUEMAN. (*aside*) May I be shot! if mistress newspaper is not putting in an advertisement for herself! (*Aloud.*) This is your city mode of courting I suppose, ha, ha, ha!

PRUDENCE. I've been west, a little; but I never was in the county of Catteraugus, myself.

TRUEMAN. Oh! you were not? And you have taken a particular fancy to go there, eh?

PRUDENCE. Perhaps, I shouldn't object--

TRUEMAN. Oh! Ah! So I suppose. Now pay attention to what I'm going to say, for it is a matter of great importance to yourself.

PRUDENCE. (*aside*) Now it's coming--I know what he's going to say!

TRUEMAN. The next time you want to tie a man for life to your apron-strings, pick out one that don't come from the country of Catteraugus--for greenhorns are scarce in those parts, and modest women plenty!
  (*Exit Trueman.*)

PRUDENCE. Now who'd have thought he was going to say that! But I won't give him up yet--I won't give him up. (*Exit.*)

ACT III.

Scene 1. Mrs. Tiffany's parlour. (*Enter Mrs. Tiffany, followed by Mr. Tiffany.*)

TIFFANY. Your extravagance will ruin me, Mrs. Tiffany!

MRS. TIFFANY. And your stinginess will ruin me, Mr. Tiffany! It is totally and *toot a fate* impossible to convince you of the necessity of *keeping up appearances*. There is a certain display which every woman of fashion is forced to make!

TIFFANY. And pray who made *you* a woman of fashion?

MRS. TIFFANY. What a vulgar question! All women of fashion, Mr. Tiffany--

TIFFANY. In this land are *self-constituted*, like you, Madame--and *fashion* is the cloak for more sins than charity ever covered! It was for *fashion's* sake that you insisted upon my purchasing this expensive house--it was for *fashion's* sake that you ran me in debt at every exorbitant upholsterer's and extravagant furniture warehouse in the city--it was for *fashion's* sake that you built that ruinous conservatory--hired more servants than they have persons to wait upon--and dressed your footman like a harlequin!

MRS. TIFFANY. Mr. Tiffany, you are thoroughly plebeian, and insufferably *American*, in your grovelling ideas! And, pray, what was the occasion of these very *mal-ap-pro-pos* remarks? Merely because I requested a paltry fifty dollars to purchase a new style of head-dress--a *bijou* of an article just introduced in France.

TIFFANY. Time was, Mrs. Tiffany, when you manufactured your own French head-dresses--took off their first gloss at the public balls, and then sold them to your short-sighted customers. And all you knew about France, or French either, was what you spelt out at the bottom of your fashion plates--but now you have grown so fashionable, forsooth, that you have forgotten how to speak your mother tongue!

MRS. TIFFANY. Mr. Tiffany, Mr. Tiffany! Nothing is more positively vulgarian--more *unaristocratic* than any allusion to the past!

TIFFANY. Why I thought, my dear, that *aristocrats* lived principally upon the past--and traded in the market of fashion with the bones of their ancestors for capital?

MRS. TIFFANY. Mr. Tiffany, such vulgar remarks are only suitable to the counting house; in my drawing room you should--

TIFFANY. Vary my sentiments with my locality, as you change your *manners* with your *dress*!

MRS. TIFFANY. Mr. Tiffany, I desire that you will purchase Count d'Orsay's "Science of Etiquette," and learn how to conduct yourself--especially before you appear at the grand ball, which I shall give on Friday!

TIFFANY. Confound your balls, Madame; they make *footballs* of my money, while you dance away all that I am worth! A pretty time to give a ball when you know that I am on the very brink of bankruptcy!

MRS. TIFFANY. So much the greater reason that nobody should suspect your circumstances, or you would lose your credit at once. Just at this crisis a ball is absolutely *necessary* to save your reputation! There is Mrs. Adolphus Dashaway--she gave the most splendid fête of the season --and I hear on very good authority that her husband has not paid his baker's bill in three months. Then there was Mrs. Honeywood--

TIFFANY. Gave a ball the night before her husband shot himself-- perhaps you wish to drive me to follow his example? (*Crosses.*)

MRS. TIFFANY. Good gracious, Mr. Tiffany! How you talk! I beg you

won't mention anything of the kind. I consider black the most
unbecoming color. I'm sure I've done all that I could to gratify you.
There is that vulgar old torment, Trueman, who gives one the lie fifty
times a day--haven't I been very civil to him?

TIFFANY. Civil to his *wealth*, Mrs. Tiffany! I told you that he was a
rich old farmer--the early friend of my father--my own benefactor--and
that I had reason to think he might assist me in my present
embarrassments. Your civility was *bought*--and like most of your *own*
purchases has yet to be *paid* for. (*Crosses.*)

MRS. TIFFANY. And will be, no doubt! The condescension of a woman
of fashion should command any price. Mr. Trueman is insupportably
indecorous--he has insulted Count Jolimaitre in the most outrageous
manner. If the Count was not so deeply interested--so *abimé* with
Seraphina, I am sure he would never honor us by his visits again!

TIFFANY. So much the better--he shall never marry my daughter! I am
resolved on that. Why, Madame, I am told there is in Paris a regular
matrimonial stock company, who fit out indigent dandies for this
market. How do I know but this fellow is one of its creatures, and that
he has come here to increase its dividends by marrying a fortune?

MRS. TIFFANY. Nonsense, Mr. Tiffany. The Count, the most fashionable young man in all New York--the intimate friend of all the dukes and
lords in Europe--not marry my daughter? Not permit Seraphina to
become a Countess? Mr. Tiffany, you are out of your senses!

TIFFANY. That would not be very wonderful, considering how many
years I have been united to you, my dear. Modern physicians pronounce
lunacy infectious!

MRS. TIFFANY. Mr. Tiffany, he is a man of fashion--

TIFFANY. Fashion makes fools, but cannot *feed* them. By the bye, I have
a request--since you are bent upon ruining me by this ball, and there is
no help for it--I desire that you will send an invitation to my
confidential clerk, Mr. Snobson.

MRS. TIFFANY. Mr. Snobson! Was there ever such an *you-nick* demand!
Mr. Snobson would cut a pretty figure amongst my fashionable friends!
I shall do no such thing, Mr. Tiffany.

TIFFANY. Then, Madame, the ball shall not take place. Have I not told
you that I am in the power of this man? That there are circumstances
which it is happy for you that you do not know--which you cannot
comprehend--but which render it essential that you should be civil to
Mr. Snobson? Not you merely, but Seraphina also? He is a more
appropriate match for her than your foreign favorite.

MRS. TIFFANY. A match for Seraphina, indeed! (*Crosses.*) Mr. Tiffany, you are determined to make a *fow pas.*

TIFFANY. Mr. Snobson intends calling this morning. (*Crosses.*)

MRS. TIFFANY. But, Mr. Tiffany, this is not reception day--my drawing rooms are in the most terrible disorder--

TIFFANY. Mr. Snobson is not particular--he must be admitted.
     (*Enter Zeke.*)

ZEKE. Mr. Snobson. (*Enter Snobson, exit Zeke.*)

SNOBSON. How dye do, Marm? (*Crosses.*) How are you?   Mr. Tiffany, your most--

MRS. TIFFANY. (*formally*) *Bung jure. Comment vow portè vow, Monsur Snobson?*

SNOBSON. Oh, to be sure--very good of you--fine day.

MRS. TIFFANY. (*pointing with great dignity to a chair*) *Sassoyez vow, Monsur Snobson.*

SNOBSON. (*aside*) I wonder what she's driving at? I ain't up to the fashionable lingo yet! (*Aloud.*) Eh? what? Speak a little louder, Marm?

MRS. TIFFANY. (*aside*) What ignorance!

TIFFANY. I presume Mrs. Tiffany means that you are to take a seat.

SNOBSON. Ex-actly--very obliging of her--so I will. (*Sits.*) No ceremony amongst friends, you know--and likely to be nearer--you understand? O.K., all correct. How *is* Seraphina?

MRS. TIFFANY. Miss Tiffany is not visible this morning. (*Retires up.*)

SNOBSON. (*jumping up*) Not visible? I suppose that's the English for can't see her? Mr. Tiffany, Sir-- (*Walking up to him.*) What am I to understand by this *de-fal-ca-tion,* Sir? I expected your word to be as good as your bond--beg pardon, Sir--I mean *better*--considerably better-- ·no humbug about it, Sir.

TIFFANY. Have patience, Mr. Snobson. (*Rings bell. Enter Zeke.*) Zeke, desire my daughter to come here.

MRS. TIFFANY. (*coming down*) A-dolph--I say, A-dolph--
     (*Zeke straightens himself and assumes foppish airs as he turns to Mrs. Tiffany.*)

TIFFANY. Zeke.

ZEKE. Don't know any such nigga, Boss.

TIFFANY. Do as I bid you instantly, or off with your livery and quit the house!

ZEKE. Wheugh! I'se all dismission! (*Exit.*)

MRS. TIFFANY. (*calling after him*) A-dolph, A-dolph!

SNOBSON. (*aside*) I brought the old boy to his bearings, didn't I though! Pull that string, and he is sure to work right. (*Aloud.*) Don't make any stranger of me, Marm--I'm quite at home. If you've got any odd jobs about the house to do up, I sha'n't miss you. I'll amuse myself with Seraphina when she comes--we'll get along very cosily by ourselves.

MRS. TIFFANY. Permit me to inform you, Mr. Snobson, that a French mother never leaves her daughter alone with a young man--she knows your sex too well for that!

SNOBSON. Very *dis*-obliging of her--but as we're none French--

MRS. TIFFANY. You have to learn, Mr. Snobson, that the American *ee-light*--the aristocracy--the *how-ton*--as a matter of conscience, scrupulously follow the foreign fashions.

SNOBSON. Not when they are foreign to their interest, Marm--for instance-- (*Enter Seraphina.*) There you are at last, eh, Miss? How dye do? Ma said you weren't visible. Managed to get a peep at her, eh, Mr. Tiffany?

SERAPHINA. I heard you were here, Mr. Snobson, and came without even arranging my toilette; you will excuse my negligence?

SNOBSON. Of everything but *me*, Miss.

SERAPHINA. I shall never have to ask your pardon for *that*, Mr. Snobson.

MRS. TIFFANY. (*approaching Seraphina*) Seraphina--child--really--
    (*Mr. Tiffany plants himself in front of his wife.*)

TIFFANY. Walk this way, Madame, if you please. (*Aside.*) To see that she fancies the surly fellow takes a weight from my heart.

MRS. TIFFANY. Mr. Tiffany, it is highly improper and not at all *distingué* to leave a young girl-- (*Enter Zeke.*)

ZEKE. Mr. Count Jolly-made-her!

MRS. TIFFANY. Good gracious! The Count-- Oh, dear! Seraphina, run and change your dress--no there's not time! A-dolph, admit him. (*Exit Zeke.*) Mr. Snobson, get out of the way, will you? Mr. Tiffany, what are you doing at home at this hour?
    (*Enter Count Jolimaitre, ushered by Zeke.*)

ZEKE. (*aside*) Dat's de genuine article ob a gemman. (*Exit.*)

MRS. TIFFANY. My dear Count, I am overjoyed at the very sight of you.

COUNT. Flattered myself you'd be glad to see me, Madame--knew it was not your *jour de reception*.

MRS. TIFFANY. But for you, Count, all days--

COUNT. I thought so. Ah, Miss Tiffany, on my honor, you're looking beautiful. (*Crosses.*)

SERAPHINA. Count, flattery from you--

SNOBSON. What? Eh? What's that you say?

SERAPHINA. (*aside to him*) Nothing but what etiquette requires.

COUNT. (*regarding Mr. Tiffany through his eye glass*) Your worthy papa, I believe. Sir, your most obedient.

> (*Mr. Tiffany bows coldly; Count regards Snobson through his glass, shrugs his shoulders and turns away.*)

SNOBSON. (*to Mrs. Tiffany*) Introduce me, will you? I never knew a Count in all my life--what a strange-looking animal!

MRS. TIFFANY. Mr. Snobson, it is not the fashion to introduce in France!

SNOBSON. But, Marm, we're in America. (*Mrs. T. crosses to Count. Aside.*) The woman thinks she's somewhere else than where she is. She wants to make an *alibi*?

MRS. TIFFANY. I hope that we shall have the pleasure of seeing you on Friday evening, Count?

COUNT. Really, Madame, my invitations--my engagements--so numerous--I can hardly answer for myself: and you Americans take offense so easily--

MRS. TIFFANY. But, Count, everybody expects you at our ball--you are the principal attraction--

SERAPHINA. Count, you *must* come!

COUNT. Since you insist--aw--there's no resisting you, Miss Tiffany.

MRS. TIFFANY. I am so thankful. How can I repay your condescension? (*Count and Seraphina converse.*) Mr. Snobson, will you walk this way? I have *such* a cactus in full bloom--remarkable flower! Mr. Tiffany, pray come here--I have something particular to say.

TIFFANY. Then speak out, my dear-- (*Aside to her.*) I thought it was highly improper just now to leave a girl with a young man?

MRS. TIFFANY. Oh, but the Count--that is different!

MR. TIFFANY. I suppose you mean to say there's nothing of *the man* about him? (*Enter Millinette with a scarf in her hand.*)

MILLINETTE. (*aside*) Adolph tell me he vas here. (*Aloud.*) Pardon, Madame, I bring dis scarf for Mademoiselle.

MRS. TIFFANY. Very well, Millinette; you know best what is proper for her to wear.

> (*Mr. and Mrs. Tiffany and Snobson retire up; she engages the attention of both gentlemen. Millinette crosses toward Seraphina, gives the Count a threatening look, and commences arranging the scarf over Seraphina's shoulders.*)

MILLINETTE.   Mademoiselle, *permettez-moi*. (*Aside to Count*.) *Perfide!*
(*Aloud*.) If Mademoiselle vil stand *tranquille* one *petit moment*. (*Turns
Seraphina's back to the Count, and pretends to arrange the scarf. Aside to
Count*.) I must speak vid you to-day, or I tell all--you find me at de foot
of de stair ven you go. *Prends garde!*

SERAPHINA. What is that you say, Millinette?

MILLINETTE. Dis scarf make you so very beautiful, Mademoiselle-- *Je
vous salue, Mesdames*. (*Curtsies. Exit*.)

COUNT. (*aside*) Not a moment to lose! (*Aloud*.) Miss Tiffany, I have an
unpleasant--a particularly unpleasant piece of intelligence--you see, I
have just received a letter from my friend--the--aw--the Earl of Airshire;
the truth is, the Earl's daughter--beg you won't mention it--has
distinguished me by a tender *penchant*.

SERAPHINA. I understand--and they wish you to return and marry the
young lady; but surely you will not leave us, Count?

COUNT. If *you* bid me stay--I shouldn't have the conscience-- (*Aside*.) I
couldn't *afford* to tear myself away. I'm sure that's honest.

SERAPHINA. Oh, Count!

COUNT. Say but one word--say that you shouldn't mind being made a
Countess--and I'll break with the Earl tomorrow.

SERAPHINA. Count, this surprise--but don't think of leaving the
country, Count--we could not pass the time without you! I--yes--yes,
Count--I do consent!

COUNT. (*aside, while he embraces her*) I thought she would! (*Aloud*.)
Enchanted, rapture, bliss, ecstacy, and all that sort of thing--words
can't express it, but you understand. But it must be kept a secret--
positively it *must!* If the rumour of our engagement were whispered
abroad--the Earl's daughter--the delicacy of my situation, aw--aw--you
comprehend? It is even possible that our nuptials, my charming Miss
Tiffany, *our nuptials* must take place in private!

SERAPHINA. Oh, that is quite impossible!

COUNT. It's the latest fashion abroad--the very latest. Ah, I knew that
would determine you. Can I depend on your secrecy?

SERAPHINA. Oh, yes! Believe me.

SNOBSON. (*coming forwards in spite of Mrs. Tiffany's efforts to detain
him*) Why, Seraphina, haven't you a word to throw to a dog?

TIFFANY. (*aside*) I shouldn't think she had after wasting so many upon a
puppy. (*Enter Zeke, wearing a three-cornered hat*.)

ZEKE. Missus, de bran new carriage am below.

MRS. TIFFANY. Show it up--I mean, very well, A-dolph. (*Exit Zeke*.)

Count, my daughter and I are about to take an airing in our new
voyture-- Will you honor us with your company?

COUNT. Madame, I--I have a most *pressing* engagement. A letter to
write to the *Earl of Airshire*--who is at present residing in the *Isle of
Skye*. I must bid you good morning.

MRS. TIFFANY. Good morning, Count. (*Exit Count.*)

SNOBSON. (*crosses to Mrs. T.*) *I'm* quite at leisure, Marm. Books
balanced--ledger closed--nothing to do all the afternoon--I'm for you.

MRS. TIFFANY. (*without noticing him*) Come, Seraphina, come!

  (*As they are going, Snobson follows them.*)

SNOBSON. But, Marm--I was saying, Marm, I am quite at leisure--not a
thing to do; have I, Mr. Tiffany?

MRS. TIFFANY. Seraphina, child--your red shawl--remember--Mr.
Snobson, *bon swear*! (*Exit, leading Seraphina.*)

SNOBSON. Swear! Mr. Tiffany, Sir, am I to be fobbed off with a *bon
swear*? D--n it, I will swear!

TIFFANY. Have patience, Mr. Snobson, if you will accompany me to the
counting house--

SNOBSON. Don't count too much on me, Sir. I'll make up no more
accounts until these are settled! I'll run down and jump into the carriage
in spite of her *bon swear*. (*Exit.*)

TIFFANY. You'll jump into a hornet's nest, if you do! Mr. Snobson, Mr.
Snobson! (*Exit after him.*)

Scene 2. Housekeeper's room. (*Enter Millinette.*)

MILLINETTE. I have set dat bête, Adolph, to vatch for him. He said he
would come back as soon as Madame's *voiture* drive from de door. If he
not come--but he vill--he vill--he *bien etourdi*, but he have *bon coeur*.

  (*Enter Count.*)

COUNT. Ah! Millinette, my dear, you see what a good-natured dog I am
to fly at your bidding--

MILLINETTE. Fly? Ah! *trompeur*! Vat for you fly from Paris? Vat for
you leave me--and I love you so much? Ven you sick--you almost die--
did I not stay by you--take care of you--and you have no else friend?
Vat for you leave Paris?

COUNT. Never allude to disagreeable subjects, *mon enfant*! I was forced
by uncontrollable circumstances to fly to the land of liberty--

MILLINETTE. Vat you do vid all de money I give you? The last sou I
had--did I not give you?

COUNT. I dare say you did, *ma petite*-- (*Aside.*) Wish you'd been better supplied! (*Aloud.*) Don't ask any questions here--can't explain now--the next time we meet--

MILLINETTE. But, ah! ven shall ve meet--ven? You not deceive me, not any more.

COUNT. Deceive you! I rather deceive myself-- (*Aside.*) I wish I could! I'd persuade myself you were once more washing linen in the Seine!

MILLINETTE. I vil tell you ven ve shall meet-- On Friday night Madame give one grand ball--you come *sans doute*--den ven de supper is served--de Americans tink of noting else ven de supper come--den you steal out of de room, and you find me here--and you give me one grand *explanation*! (*Enter Gertrude, unperceived.*)

COUNT. Friday night--while supper is serving--*parole d'honneur* I will be here--I will explain every thing--my sudden departure from Paris--my--my--demme, my countship--every thing! Now let me go--if any of the family should discover us--

GERTRUDE. (*who during the last speech has gradually advanced*) They might discover more than you think it advisable for them to know!

COUNT. The devil!

MILLINETTE. *Mon Dieu*! Mademoiselle Gertrude!

COUNT. (*recovering himself*) My dear Miss Gertrude, let me explain--aw--nothing is more natural than the situation in which you find me--

GERTRUDE. I am inclined to believe that, Sir.

COUNT. Now--'pon my honor, that's not fair. Here is Millinette will bear witness to what I am about to say--

GERTRUDE. Oh, I have not the slightest doubt of that, Sir.

COUNT. You see, Millinette happened to be lady's-maid in the family of--of--the Duchess Chateau d'Espagne--and I chanced to be a particular friend of the Duchess--*very particular* I assure you! Of course I saw Millinette, and she, demme, she saw me! Didn't you, Millinette?

MILLINETTE. Oh, *oui*-- Mademoiselle, I knew him ver vell.

COUNT. Well, it is a remarkable fact that--being in correspondence with this very Duchess--at this very time--

GERTRUDE. That is sufficient, Sir--I am already so well acquainted with your extraordinary talents for improvisation, that I will not further tax your invention--

MILLINETTE. Ah! Mademoiselle Gertrude, do not betray us--have pity!

COUNT. (*assuming an air of dignity*) Silence, Millinette! My word has been doubted--the word of a nobleman! I will inform my friend, Mrs. Tiffany, of this young person's audacity. (*Going.*)

GERTRUDE. (*aside*) His own weapons alone can foil this villain! (*Aloud.*) Sir--Sir--Count! (*At the last word, the Count turns.*) Perhaps, Sir, the least said about this matter the better!

COUNT. (*delightedly*) The least said? We won't say anything at all. (*Aside.*) She's coming round--couldn't resist me. (*Aloud.*) Charming Gertrude--

MILLINETTE. *Quoi?* Vat that you say?

COUNT. (*aside to her*) My sweet, adorable Millinette, hold your tongue, will you?

MILLINETTE. (*aloud*) No, I vill not! If you do look so from out your eyes at her again, I vill tell all!

COUNT. (*aside*) Oh, I never could manage two women at once--jealousy makes the dear creatures so spiteful. The only valor is in flight! (*Aloud.*) Miss Gertrude, I wish you good morning. Millinette, *mon enfant, adieu.* (*Exit.*)

MILLINETTE. But I have one word more to say. Stop, stop! (*Exit.*)

GERTRUDE. (*musingly*) Friday night, while supper is serving, he is to meet Millinette here and explain--what? This man is an imposter! His insulting me--his familiarity with Millinette--his whole conduct--prove it. If I tell Mrs. Tiffany this, she will disbelieve me, and one word may place this so-called Count on his guard. To convince Seraphina would be equally difficult, and her rashness and infatuation may render her miserable for life. No--she shall be saved! I must devise some plan for opening their eyes. Truly, if I *cannot* invent one, I shall be the first woman who was ever at a loss for a stratagem--especially to punish a villain or to shield a friend. (*Exit.*)

ACT IV.

Scene 1. Ballroom splendidly illuminated. A curtain hung at the further end. (*Mr. and Mrs. Tiffany, Seraphina, Gertrude, Fogg, Twinkle, Count, Snobson, Colonel Howard, a number of guests--some seated, some standing. As the curtain rises, a cotillion is danced; Gertrude dancing with Howard, Seraphina with Count.*)

COUNT. (*advancing with Seraphina to the front of the stage*) To-morrow then--to-morrow--I may salute you as my bride--demme, my Countess!

(*Enter Zeke, with refreshments.*)

SERAPHINA. Yes, to-morrow.

(*The Count is about to reply.*)

SNOBSON. (*thrusting himself in front of Seraphina*) You said you'd dance with me, Miss--now take my fin, and we'll walk about and see what's going on.

(*Count raises his eye glass, regards Snobson, and leads Seraphina away; Snobson follows, endeavoring to attract her attention, but encountering Zeke, bearing a waiter of refreshments; stops him, helps himself, and puts some in his pockets.*)

Here's the treat! Get my to-morrow's luncheon out of Tiff.

(*Enter Trueman, yawning and rubbing his eyes.*)

TRUEMAN. What a nap I've had, to be sure! (*Looks at his watch. To Tiffany, who approaches.*) Eleven o'clock, as I'm alive! Just the time when country folks are comfortably *turned in*, and here your grand *turn-out* has hardly begun yet.

GERTRUDE. (*advancing*) I was just coming to look for you, Mr. Trueman. I began to fancy that you were paying a visit to dream-land.

TRUEMAN. So I was, child--so I was--and I saw a face--like yours--but brighter--even brighter! (*To Tiffany.*) There's a smile for you, man! It makes one feel that the world has something worth living for in it yet! Do you remember a smile like that, Antony? Ah! I see you don't--but I do-- (*Much moved.*) I do!

HOWARD. (*advancing*) Good evening, Mr. Trueman. (*Offers his hand.*)

TRUEMAN. That's right, man; give me your whole hand! When a man offers me the tips of his fingers, I know at once there's nothing in him worth seeking beyond his fingers ends.

(*Trueman and Howard, Gertrude and Tiffany converse.*)

MRS. TIFFANY. (*advancing*) I'm in such a fidget lest that vulgar old fellow should disgrace us by some of his plebeian remarks! What it is to give a ball, when one is forced to invite vulgar people!

(*Mrs. Tiffany advances towards Trueman; Seraphina stands conversing flippantly with the gentlemen who surround her; amongst them is Twinkle who, having taken a magazine from his pocket, is reading to her, much to the undisguised annoyance of Snobson.*)

Dear me, Mr. Trueman, you are very late--quite in the fashion, I declare!

TRUEMAN. Fashion! And pray what is *fashion*, Madame? An agreement between certain persons to live without using their souls! to substitute etiquette for virtue--decorum for purity--manners for morals! to affect a shame for the works of their Creator! and expend all their rapture upon the works of their tailors and dressmakers!

MRS. TIFFANY. You have the most *ou-tray* ideas, Mr. Trueman--quite rustic, and deplorably *American*! But pray walk this way.

(*Mrs. Tiffany and Trueman go up.*)

COUNT. (*advancing to Gertrude, Howard a short distance behind her*) Miss Gertrude--no opportunity of speaking to you before--in demand, you know!

GERTRUDE. (*aside*) I have no choice, I must be civil to him. (*Aloud.*) What were you remarking, Sir?

COUNT. Miss Gertrude--charming Ger--aw--aw-- (*Aside.*) I never found it so difficult to speak to a woman before.

GERTRUDE. Yes, a very charming ball--many beautiful faces here.

COUNT. Only one! Aw--aw--one--the fact is-- (*Talks in dumb show.*)

HOWARD. What could old Trueman have meant by saying she fancied that puppy of a Count--that paste jewel thrust upon the little finger of society.

COUNT. Miss Gertrude--aw--'pon my honor--you don't understand-- really--aw--aw--will you dance the polka with me?

(*Gertrude bows and gives him her hand; he leads her to the set forming; Howard remains looking after them.*)

HOWARD. Going to dance with him, too? A few days ago she would hardly bow to him civilly--(*retiring up*)--could old Trueman have had reasons for what he said?

(*Dance, the polka; Seraphina, after having distributed her bouquet, vinaigrette, and fan amongst the gentlemen, dances with Snobson.*)

PRUDENCE. (*peeping in as dance concludes*) I don't like dancing on Friday; something strange is always sure to happen! I'll be on the look out.

(*Peeping and concealing herself when any of the company approach.*)

GERTRUDE. (*advancing hastily*) They are preparing the supper--now if I can only dispose of Millinette while I unmask this insolent pretender!

(*Exit Gertrude.*)

PRUDENCE. (*peeping*) What's that she said? It's coming!

(*Re-enter Gertrude, bearing a small basket filled with bouquets; approaches Mrs. Tiffany; they walk to the front of the stage.*)

GERTRUDE. Excuse me, Madame--I believe this is just the hour at which you ordered supper?

MRS. TIFFANY. Well, what's that to you! So you've been dancing with the Count--how dare you dance with a nobleman--*you*?

GERTRUDE. I will answer that question half an hour hence. At present I have something to propose, which I think will gratify you and please your guests. I have heard that at the most elegant balls in Paris, it is customary--

MRS. TIFFANY. What? What?

GERTRUDE. To station a servant at the door with a basket of flowers. A bouquet is then presented to every lady as she passes in--I prepared this basket a short time ago. As the company walk in to supper, might not the flowers by distributed to advantage?

MRS. TIFFANY. How *distingué*! You are a good creature, Gertrude-- there, run and hand the *bokettes* to them yourself! You shall have the whole credit of the thing.

GERTRUDE. (*aside*) Caught in my own net! (*Aloud.*) But, Madame, I know so little of fashions--Millinette, being French herself, will do it with so much more grace. I am sure Millinette--

MRS. TIFFANY. So am I. She will do it a thousand times better than you--there, go call her.

GERTRUDE. (*giving basket*) But, Madame, pray order Millinette not to leave her station till supper is ended--as the company pass out of the supper room she may find that some of the ladies have been overlooked.

MRS. TIFFANY. That is true--very thoughtful of you, Gertrude. (*Exit Gertrude.*) What a *recherché* idea! (*Enter Millinette.*) Here, Millinette, take this basket. Place yourself there, and distribute these *bokettes* as the company pass in to supper; but remember not to stir from the spot until supper is over. It is a French custom, you know, Millinette. I am so delighted to be the first to introduce it. It will be all the rage in the *bow-mande*!

MILLINETTE. (*aside*) *Mon Dieu*! Dis vill ruin all! (*Aloud.*) Madame, let me tell you, Madame, dat in France, in Paris, it is de custom to present *les bouquets* ven every body first come--long before de supper. Dis vould be *outré*! *Barbare*! Not at all *la mode*! Ven dey do come in--dat is de fashion in Paris!

MRS. TIFFANY. Dear me! Millinette, what is the difference? Besides, I'd have you to know that Americans always improve upon French fashions! Here, take the basket, and let me see that you do it in the most *you-nick* and genteel manner.

(*Millinette poutingly takes the basket and retires upstage. A march. Curtain hung at the further end of the room is drawn back, and discloses a room, in the center of which stands a supper table, beautifully decorated and illuminated; the company promenade two by two into the supper room; Millinette presents bouquets; Count leads Mrs. Tiffany.*)

TRUEMAN. (*encountering Fogg, who is hurrying alone to the supper room*) Mr. Fogg, never mind the supper, man! Ha, ha, ha! Of course, you are indifferent to suppers!

FOGG. Indifferent! Suppers--oh, ah--no, Sir--suppers? No--no--I'm not indifferent to suppers! (*Hurries away towards table.*)

TRUEMAN. Ha, ha, ha! Here's a new discovery I've made in the fashionable world! Fashion don't permit the critters to have *heads* or *hearts*, but it allows them to have stomachs! (*To Tiffany, who advances.*) So it's not fashionable to *feel*, but it's fashionable to *feed*, eh, Antony? ha, ha, ha!

(*Trueman and Tiffany retire towards supper room. Enter Gertrude, followed by Zeke.*)

GERTRUDE. Zeke, go to the supper room instantly--whisper to Count Jolimaitre that all is ready, and that he must keep his appointment without delay--then watch him, and as he passes out of the room, place yourself in front of Millinette in such a manner that the Count cannot see her nor she him. Be sure that they do not see each other--every thing depends upon that. (*Crosses.*)

ZEKE. Missey, consider dat business brought to a scientific conclusion.

(*Exit into supper room. Exit Gertrude.*)

PRUDENCE. (*who has been listening*) What can she want of the Count? I always suspected that Gertrude, because she is so merry and busy! Mr. Trueman thinks so much of her, too--I'll tell him this! There's something wrong--but it all comes of giving a ball on a Friday! How astonished the dear old man will be when he finds out how much I know! (*Advances timidly towards the supper room.*)

Scene 2. Housekeeper's room; dark stage; table, two chairs. (*Enter Gertrude, with a lighted candle in her hand.*)

GERTRUDE. So far the scheme prospers! And yet this imprudence--if I fail? Fail! To lack courage in a difficulty, or ingenuity in a dilemma are not woman's failings!

(*Enter Zeke, with a napkin over his arm, and a bottle of champagne in his hand.*)

Well, Zeke--Adolph!

ZEKE. Dat's right, Missey; I feels just now as if dat was my legitimate title; dis here's de stuff to make a nigger feel like a gemman!

GERTRUDE. But he is coming?

ZEKE. He's coming! (*Sound of a champagne cork.*) Do you hear dat, Missey? Don't it put you all in a froth, and make you feel as light as a cork? Dere's nothing like the *union brand* to wake up de harmonies ob de heart. (*Drinks from bottle.*)

GERTRUDE. Remember to keep watch upon the outside--do not stir from the spot; when I call you, come in quickly with a light--now, will you be gone!

ZEKE. I'm off, Missey, like a champagne cork wid de strings cut. (*Exit.*)

GERTRUDE. I think I hear the Count's step. (*Crosses, dark stage; she blows out candle.*) Now if I can but disguise my voice, and make the best of my French. (*Enter Count.*)

COUNT. Millinette, where are you? How am I to see you in the dark?

GERTRUDE. (*imitating Millinette's voice in a whisper*) Hush! *Parle bas.*

COUNT. Come here and give me a kiss.

GERTRUDE. *Non--non--* (*Retreating alarmed, Count follows.*) Make haste, I must know all.

COUNT. You did not use to be so deuced particular.

ZEKE. (*without*) No admission, gemman! Box office closed, tickets stopped!

TRUEMAN. (*without*) Out of my way; do you want me to try if your head is as hard as my stick?

GERTRUDE. What shall I do? Ruined, ruined!

(*She stands with her hands clasped in speechless despair.*)

COUNT. Halloa! they are coming here, Millinette! Millinette, why don't you speak? Where can I hide myself? (*Running about stage, feeling for a door.*) Where are all your closets? If I could only get out--or get in somewhere; may I be smothered in a clothes' basket, if you ever catch me in such a scrape again!

(*His hand accidentally touches the knob of a door opening into a closet.*)

Fortune's favorite yet! I'm safe!

(*Count gets into closet and closes door. Enter Prudence, Trueman, Mrs. Tiffany, and Howard, followed by Zeke, bearing a light; lights up.*)

PRUDENCE. Here they are, the Count and Gertrude! I told you so!

(*Prudence stops in surprise on seeing only Gertrude.*)

TRUEMAN. And you see what a lie you told!

MRS. TIFFANY. Prudence, how dare you create this disturbance in my house? To suspect the Count, too--a nobleman!

HOWARD. My sweet Gertrude, this foolish old woman would--

PRUDENCE. Oh! you needn't talk--I heard her make the appointment--I know he's here--or he's been away. I wonder if she hasn't hid him away! (*Runs peeping about the room.*)

TRUEMAN. (*following her angrily*) You're what I call a confounded--troublesome--meddling--old--prying--

(*As he says the last word, Prudence opens the closet.*)

Thunder and lightning!

PRUDENCE. I told you so!

(*They all stand aghast; Mrs. Tiffany, with her hands lifted in surprise and anger; Trueman, clutching his stick; Howard, looking with an expression of bewildered horror from the Count to Gertrude.*)

MRS. TIFFANY. (*shaking her fist at Gertrude*) You depraved little minx! This is the meaning of your dancing with the Count!

COUNT. (*stepping from the closet and advancing, aside*) I don't know what to make of it! Millinette not here! Miss Gertrude--oh! I see--a disguise--the girl's desperate about me--the way with them all.

TRUEMAN. (*partly aside*) I'm choking--I can't speak--Gertrude--no--no-- it is some horrid mistake! (*Changes his tone suddenly.*) The villain! I'll hunt the truth out of him, if there's any in-- (*Approaches Count threateningly.*) Do you see this stick? You made its first acquaintance a few days ago; it is time you were better known to each other.

(*As Trueman attempts to seize him, Count escapes, and shields himself behind Mrs. Tiffany, Trueman following.*)

COUNT. You ruffian! Would you strike a woman? Madame--my dear Madame--keep off that barbarous old man, and I will explain! Madame, with--aw--your natural *bon gout*--aw--your fashionable refinement-- aw--your--aw--your knowledge of *foreign customs*--

MRS. TIFFANY. Oh! Count, I hope it ain't a *foreign custom* for the nobility to shut themselves up in the dark with young women? We think such things *dreadful* in America.

COUNT Demme--aw--hear what I have to say, Madame--I'll satisfy all sides--I am perfectly innocent in this affair--'pon my honor I am! That young lady shall inform you that I am so herself--can't help it, sorry for her. (*Aside.*) Old matter-of-fact won't be convinced any other way-- that club of his is so particularly unpleasant! (*Aloud.*) Madame, I was summoned here *malgré moi*, and not knowing whom I was to meet-- Miss Gertrude, favor the company by saying whether or not you directed-- that--aw--aw--that colored individual to conduct me here?

GERTRUDE. Sir, you well know--

COUNT. A simple yes or no will suffice.

MRS. TIFFANY. Answer the Count's question instantly, Miss.

GERTRUDE. I did--but--

COUNT. You hear, Madame--

TRUEMAN. I won't believe it--I can't! Here, you nigger, stop rolling up your eyes, and let us know whether she told you to bring that critter here?

ZEKE. I'se refuse to gib evidence; dat's de device ob de skilfullest counsels ob de day! Can't answer, Boss--neber git a word out ob dis child-- Yah! yah! (*Exit.*)

GERTRUDE. Mrs. Tiffany--Mr. Trueman, if you will but have patience--

TRUEMAN. Patience! Oh, Gertrude, you've taken from an old man something better and dearer than his patience--the one bright hope of nineteen years of self-denial--of nineteen years of--

(*He throws himself upon a chair, his head leaning on table.*)

MRS. TIFFANY. Get out of my house, you owdacious--you ruined--you *abimé* young woman! You will corrupt all my family. Good gracious! Don't touch me--don't come near me. Never let me see your face after to-morrow. Pack. (*Goes up.*)

HOWARD. Gertrude, I have striven to find some excuse for you--to doubt--to disbelieve--but this is beyond all endurance!

(*Exit Howard. Enter Millinette in haste.*)

MILLINETTE. I could not come before-- (*Stops in surprise at seeing the persons assembled.*) Mon Dieu! Vat does dis mean?

COUNT. (*aside to her*) Hold your tongue, fool! You will ruin everything, I will explain to-morrow. (*Aloud.*) Mrs. Tiffany--Madame--my dear Madame, let me conduct you back to the ball-room. (*She takes his arm.*) You see I am quite innocent in this matter; a man of my standing, you know, aw--aw--you comprehend the whole affair.

(*Exit Count leading Mrs. Tiffany.*)

MILLINETTE. I vill say to him von vord, I vill! (*Exit.*)

GERTRUDE. Mr. Trueman, I beseech you--I insist upon being heard--I claim it as a right!

TRUEMAN. Right? How dare you have the face, girl, to talk of rights? (*Comes down.*) You had more rights than you thought, but you have forfeited them all! All right to love, respect, protection, and to not a little else that you don't dream of. Go, go! I'll start for Catteraugus to-morrow--I've seen enough of what fashion can do! (*Exit.*)

PRUDENCE. (*wiping her eyes*) Dear old man, how he takes on! I'll go and console him! (*Exit.*)

GERTRUDE. This is too much! How heavy a penalty has my imprudence cost me! His esteem, and that of one dearer--my home--my-- (*Burst of lively music from ball-room.*) They are dancing, and I--I should be weeping, if pride had not sealed up my tears.

(*She sinks into a chair. Band plays the polka behind till curtain falls.*)

ACT V.

Scene 1. Mrs. Tiffany's drawing room--same scene as Act I. (*Gertrude seated at a table, with her head leaning on her hand; in the other hand she holds a pen. A sheet of paper and an inkstand before her.*)

GERTRUDE. How shall I write to them? What shall I say? Prevaricate I cannot. (*Rises and comes forward.*) And yet if I write the truth--simple souls! how can they comprehend the motives for my conduct? Nay--the truly pure see no imaginary evil in others! It is only vice that, reflecting its own image, suspects even the innocent. I have no time to lose--I must prepare them for my return. (*Resumes her seat and writes.*) What a true pleasure there is in daring to be frank! (*After writing a few lines, more pauses.*) Not so frank either--there is one name that I cannot mention. Ah! that he should suspect--should despise me. (*Enter Trueman.*)
TRUEMAN. (*aside*) There she is! If this girl's soul had only been as fair as her face--yet she dared to speak the truth--I'll not forget that! A woman who refuses to tell a lie has one spark of heaven in her still. (*Approaches and speaks to her.*) Gertrude. (*Gertrude starts and looks up.*) What are you writing there? Plotting more mischief, eh, girl?
GERTRUDE. I was writing a few lines to some friends in Geneva.
TRUEMAN. The Wilsons, eh?
GERTRUDE. (*surprised, rising*) Are you acquainted with them, Sir?
TRUEMAN. I shouldn't wonder if I was. I suppose you have taken good care not to mention the dark room--that foreign puppy in the closet--the pleasant surprise--and all that sort of thing, eh?
GERTRUDE. I have no reason for concealment, Sir! for I have done nothing of which I am ashamed!
TRUEMAN. Then I can't say much for your modesty.
GERTRUDE. I should not wish you to say more than I deserve.
TRUEMAN. (*aside*) There's a bold minx!
GERTRUDE. Since my affairs seem to have excited your interest--I will not say *curiosity*, perhaps you even feel a desire to inspect my correspondence? There. (*Handing the letter.*) I pride myself upon my good nature--you may like to take advantage of it?
TRUEMAN. (*aside*) With what an air she carries if off! (*Aloud.*) Take advantage of it? So I will. (*Reads.*) What's this? "French chamber-maid-- Count-- Imposter-- Infatuation-- Seraphina-- Millinette-- Disguised myself-- Expose him." Thunder and lightning! I see it all! Come and kiss me, girl! (*Gertrude evinces surprise. Aside.*) No, no--I

forgot--it won't do to come to that yet! She's a rare girl! I'm out of my senses with joy! I don't know what to do with myself! (*Capers and sings.*) Tol, de rol, de rol, de ra!

GERTRUDE. (*aside*) What a remarkable old man! (*Aloud.*) Then you do me justice, Mr. Trueman?

TRUEMAN. I say I don't! Justice? You're above all dependence upon justice! Hurrah! I've found one true woman at last? *True?* (*Pauses.*) Humph! I didn't think of that flaw! Plotting and manoeuvering--not much truth in that? An honest girl should be above stratagems!

GERTRUDE. But my *motive*, Sir, was good.

TRUEMAN. That's not enough--your *actions* must be *good* as well as your *motives*! Why could you not tell the silly girl that man was an imposter?

GERTRUDE. I did inform her of my suspicions--she ridiculed them; the plan I chose was an imprudent one, but I could not devise--

TRUEMAN. I hate devising! Give me a woman with the *firmness* to be *frank*! But no matter--I had no right to look for an angel out of Paradise; and I am as happy--as happy as a Lord! that is, ten times happier than any Lord ever was! Tol, de rol, de rol! Oh! you--you--I'll thrash every fellow that says a word against you!

GERTRUDE. You will have plenty of employment then, Sir, for I do not know of one just now who would speak in my favor!

TRUEMAN. Not *one*, eh? Why, where's your dear Mr. Twinkle? I know all about it--can't say that I admire your choice of a husband! but there's no accounting for a girl's taste.

GERTRUDE. Mr. Twinkle! Indeed, you are quite mistaken!

TRUEMAN. No--really? Then you're not taken with him, eh?

GERTRUDE. Not even with his rhymes.

TRUEMAN. Hang that old mother meddle-much! What a fool she has made of me. And so you're quite free, and I may choose a husband for you myself? Heart-whole, eh?

GERTRUDE. I--I--I trust there is nothing *unsound* about my heart.

TRUEMAN. There it is again. Don't prevaricate, girl! I tell you an *evasion* is a *lie in contemplation*, and I hate lying! Out with the truth! Is your heart *free* or not?

GERTRUDE. Nay, Sir, since you *demand* an answer, permit *me* to demand by what right you ask the question? (*Enter Howard.*) Colonel Howard here!

TRUEMAN. (*aside*) I'm out again! What's the Colonel to her?
(*He retires up.*)

HOWARD. (*crosses to her*) I have come, Gertrude, to bid you farewell. To-morrow I resign my commission and leave this city, perhaps for ever. You, Gertrude, it is you who have exiled me! After last evening--

TRUEMAN. (*coming forward to Howard*) What the plague have you to say about last evening?

HOWARD. Mr. Trueman!

TRUEMAN. What have you got to say about last evening? And what have you to say to that little girl at all? It's Tiffany's precious daughter you're in love with.

HOWARD. Miss Tiffany? Never! I never had the slightest pretention--

TRUEMAN. That lying old woman! But I'm glad of it! Oh! Ah! Um! (*Looking significantly at Gertrude and then at Howard.*) I see how it is. So you don't choose to marry Seraphina, eh? Well now, whom do you choose to marry? (*Glancing at Gertrude.*)

HOWARD. I shall not marry at all!

TRUEMAN. You won't? (*Looking at them both again.*) Why, you don't mean to say that you don't like-- (*Points with his thumb to Gertrude.*)

GERTRUDE. Mr. Trueman, I may have been wrong to boast of my good nature, but do not presume too far upon it.

HOWARD. You like frankness, Mr. Trueman, therefore I will speak plainly. I have long cherished a dream from which I was last night rudely awakened.

TRUEMAN. And that's what you call speaking plainly? Well, I differ with you! But I can guess what you mean. Last night you suspected Gertrude there of--(*angrily*)--of what no man shall ever suspect her again while I'm above ground! You did her injustice--it was a mistake! There, now that matter's settled. Go, and ask her to forgive you--she's woman enough to do it! Go, go!

HOWARD. Mr. Trueman, you have forgotten to whom you dictate.

TRUEMAN. Then you won't do it? You won't ask her pardon?

HOWARD. Most undoubtedly, I will not--not at any man's bidding. I must first know--

TRUEMAN. You won't do it? Then if I don't give you a lesson in politeness--

HOWARD. It will be because you find me your *tutor* in the same science. I am not a man to brook an insult, Mr. Trueman! but we'll not quarrel in presence of the lady.

TRUEMAN. Won't we? I don't know that-- (*Crosses.*)

GERTRUDE. Pray, Mr. Trueman--Colonel Howard-- (*Crosses.*) Pray desist, Mr. Trueman, for my sake! (*Taking hold of his arm to hold him back.*) Colonel Howard, if you will read this letter, it will explain everything. (*Hands letter to Howard, who reads.*)

TRUEMAN. He don't deserve an explanation! Didn't I tell him that it was a mistake? Refuse to beg your pardon! I'll teach him, I'll teach him!

HOWARD. (*after reading*) Gertrude, how have I wronged you!

TRUEMAN. (*between them*) Oh, you'll beg her pardon now?

HOWARD. Hers, Sir, and yours! Gertrude, I fear--

TRUEMAN. You needn't--she'll forgive you. You don't know these women as well as I do--they're always ready to pardon; it's their nature, and they can't help it. Come along, I left Antony and his wife in the dining room; we'll go and find them. I've a story of my own to tell! As for you, Colonel, you may follow. Come along. Come along!

(*Trueman leads out Gertrude, followed by Howard. Enter Mr. and Mrs. Tiffany, Mr. Tiffany with a bundle of bills in his hand.*)

MRS. TIFFANY. I beg you won't mention the subject again, Mr. Tiffany. Nothing is more plebeian than a discussion upon economy—nothing more *ungenteel* than looking over and fretting over one's bills!

TIFFANY. Then I suppose, my dear, it is quite as ungenteel to *pay* one's bills?

MRS. TIFFANY. Certainly! I hear the *ee-light* never consescend to do anything of the kind. The honor of their invaluable patronage is sufficient for the persons they employ!

TIFFANY. *Patronage* then is a newly invented food upon which the working classes fatten? What convenient appetites poor people must have! Now listen to what I am going to say. As soon as my daughter marries Mr. Snobson--

(*Enter Prudence, a three-cornered note in her hand.*)

PRUDENCE. Oh, dear! oh, dear! what shall we do! Such a misfortune! Such a disaster! Oh, dear! oh, dear!

MRS. TIFFANY. Prudence, you are the most tiresome creature! What *is* the matter?

PRUDENCE. (*pacing up and down the stage*) Such a disgrace to the whole family! But I always expected it. Oh, dear! oh, dear!

MRS. TIFFANY. (*following her up and down the stage*) What are you talking about, Prudence? Will you tell me what has happened?

PRUDENCE. (*still pacing, Mrs. Tiffany following*) Oh! I can't, I can't! You'll feel so dreadfully! How could she do such a thing! But I expected nothing else! I never did, I never did!

MRS. TIFFANY. (*still following*) Good gracious! what do you mean, Prudence? Tell me, will you tell me? I shall get into such a passion!

What *is* the matter?

PRUDENCE. (*still pacing*) Oh, Betsy, Betsy! That your daughter should have come to that! Dear me, dear me!

TIFFANY. Seraphina? Did you say Seraphina?
   (*Following Prudence up and down the stage on the opposite side from Mrs. Tiffany.*)
What has happened to her? What has she done?

MRS. TIFFANY. (*still following*) What *has* she done?

PRUDENCE. Oh! something dreadful--something--shocking!

TIFFANY. (*still following*) Speak quickly and plainly--you torture me by this delay--Prudence, be calm, and speak! What is it?

PRUDENCE. (*stopping*) Zeke just told me--he carried her travelling trunk himself--she gave him a whole dollar! Oh, my!

TIFFANY. Her trunk? where? where?

PRUDENCE. Round the corner!

MRS. TIFFANY. What did she want with her trunk? You are the most vexatious creature, Prudence! There is no bearing your ridiculous conduct!

PRUDENCE. Oh, you will have worse to bear--worse! Seraphina's gone!

TIFFANY. Gone! Where?

PRUDENCE. Off! Eloped--eloped with the Count! Dear me, dear me! I always told you she would!

TIFFANY. Then I am ruined! (*Stands with his face buried in his hands.*)

MRS. TIFFANY. Oh, what a ridiculous girl! And she might have had such a splendid wedding! What could have possessed her?

TIFFANY. The devil himself possessed her, for she has ruined me past all redemption! Gone, Prudence, did you say gone? Are you *sure* they are gone?

PRUDENCE. Didn't I tell you so! Just look at this note--one might know by the very fold of it--

TIFFANY. (*snatching the note*) Let me see it! (*Opens the note and reads.*)
   "My dear Ma--
      When you receive this, I shall be a *countess*! Isn't it a sweet title? The Count and I were forced to be married privately, for reasons which I will explain in my next. You must pacify Pa, and put him in a good humour before I come back, though now I'm to be a countess I suppose I shouldn't care!"
Undutiful huzzy! (*Reads.*)
   "We are going to make a little excursion and will be back in a week. Your dutiful daughter--Seraphina."

A man's curse is sure to spring up at his own hearth--here is mine! The sole curb upon that villain gone, I am wholly in his power! Oh! the first downward step from honor--he who takes it cannot pause in his mad descent and is sure to be hurried on to ruin!

MRS. TIFFANY. Why, Mr. Tiffany, how you do take on! And I dare say to elope was the most fashionable way after all!

(*Enter Trueman, leading Gertrude, and followed by Howard.*)

TRUEMAN. Where are all the folks? Here, Antony, you are the man I want. We've been hunting for you all over the house. Why--what's the matter? There's a face for a thriving city merchant! Ah! Antony, you never wore such a hang-dog look as that when you trotted about the country with your pack upon your back! Your shoulders are no broader now, but they've a heavier load to carry--that's plain!

MRS. TIFFANY. Mr. Trueman, such allusions are highly improper! What would my daughter, *the Countess*, say!

GERTRUDE. The Countess? Oh! Madame!

MRS. TIFFANY. Yes, the Countess! My daughter Seraphina, the Countess *dee* Jolimaitre! What have you to say to that? No wonder you are surprised after your *recherché, abimé* conduct! I have told you already, Miss Gertrude, that you were not a proper person to enjoy the inestimable advantages of my patronage. You are dismissed--do you understand? Discharched!

TRUEMAN. Have you done? Very well, it's my turn now. Antony, perhaps what I have to say don't concern you as much as some others-- but I want you to listen to me. You remember, Antony--(*his tone becomes serious*)--a blue-eyed, smiling girl--

TIFFANY. Your daughter, Sir? I remember her well.

TRUEMAN. None ever saw her to forget her! Give me your hand, man. There--that will do! Now let me go on. I never coveted wealth--yet twenty years ago I found myself the richest farmer in Catteraugus. This cursed money made my girl an object of speculation. Every idle fellow that wanted to feather his nest was sure to come courting Ruth. There was one--my heart misgave me the instant I laid eyes upon him--for he was a city chap, and not over fond of the truth. But Ruth--ah! she was too pure herself to look for guile! His fine words and his fair looks--the old story--she was taken with him--I said, "no"--but the girl liked her own way better than her old father's--girls always do! and one morning--the rascal robbed me--not of my money, he would have been welcome to that--but of the only treasure I cherished--my daughter!

TIFFANY. But you forgave her!

TRUEMAN. I did! I knew she would never forgive herself--that was punishment enough! The scoundrel thought he was marrying my gold with my daughter--he was mistaken! I took care that they should never want; but that was all. She loved him--what will not woman love? The villain broke her heart--mine was tougher, or it wouldn't have stood what it did. A year after they were married, he forsook her! She came back to her old home--her old father! It couldn't last long--she pined-- and pined--and--then--she died! Don't think me an old fool--though I am one--for grieving won't bring her back. (*Bursts into tears.*)

TIFFANY. It was a heavy loss!

TRUEMAN. So heavy, that I should not have cared how soon I followed her, but for the child she left! As I pressed that child in my arms, I swore that my unlucky wealth should never curse it, as it had cursed its mother! It was all I had to love--but I sent it away--and the neighbors thought it was dead. The girl was brought up tenderly but humbly by my wife's relatives in Geneva. I had her taught true independence--she had hands--capacities--and should use them! Money should never buy her a husband! for I resolved not to claim her until she had made her choice, and found the man who was willing to take her for herself alone. She turned out a rare girl! And it's time her old grandfather claimed her. Here he is to do it! There stands Ruth's child! Old Adam's heiress! Gertrude, Gertrude! My child! (*Gertrude rushes into his arms.*)

PRUDENCE. (*after a pause*) Do tell; I want to know! But I knew it! I always said Gertrude would turn out somebody, after all!

MRS. TIFFANY. Dear me! Gertrude an heiress! My dear Gertrude, I always thought you a very charming girl--quite *you-nick*--an heiress! (*Aside.*) I must give her a ball! I'll introduce her into society myself--of course, an heiress must make a sensation!

HOWARD. (*aside*) I am too bewildered even to wish her joy. Ah! there will be plenty to do that now--but the gulf between us is wider than ever.

TRUEMAN. Step forward, young man, and let us know what you are muttering about. I said I would never claim her until she had found the man who loved her for herself. I *have* claimed her--yet I never break my word--I think I *have* found that man! and here he is. (*Strikes Howard on the shoulder.*) Gertrude's yours! There--never say a word, man--don't bore me with your thanks--you can cancel all obligations by making that child happy! There--take her! Well, girl, and what do you say?

GERTRUDE. That I rejoice too much at having found a parent for my first act to be one of disobedience! (*Gives her hand to Howard.*)

TRUEMAN. How very dutiful! and how disinterested!

(*Tiffany retires up--and paces the stage, exhibiting great agitation.*)

PRUDENCE. (*to Trueman*) All the *single* folks are getting married!

TRUEMAN. No they are not. You and I are single folks, and we're not likely to get married.

MRS. TIFFANY. My dear Mr. Trueman--my sweet Gertrude, when my daughter, the Countess, returns, she will be delighted to hear of this *deenooment*! I assure you that the Countess will be quite charmed!

GERTRUDE. The Countess? Pray, Madame, where *is* Seraphina?

MRS. TIFFANY. The Countess *dee* Jolimaitre, my dear, is at this moment on her way to--to Washington! Where after visiting all the fashionable curiosities of the day--including the President--she will return to grace her native city!

GERTRUDE. I hope you are only jesting, Madame? Seraphina is not married?

MRS. TIFFANY. Excuse me, my dear, my daughter had this morning the honor of being united to the Count *dee* Jolimaitre!

GERTRUDE. Madame! He is an imposter!

MRS. TIFFANY. Good gracious! Gertrude, how can you talk in that disrespectful way of a man of rank? An heiress, my dear, should have better manners! The Count-- (*Enter Millinette, crying.*)

MILLINETTE. Oh! Madame! I vill tell you everyting--oh! dat monstre! He break my heart!

MRS. TIFFANY. Millinette, what is the matter?

MILLINETTE. Oh! he promise to marry me--I love him much--and now Zeke say he run away vid Mademoiselle Seraphina!

MRS. TIFFANY. What insolence! The girl is mad! Count Jolimaitre marry my *femmy de chamber*!

MILLINETTE. Oh! Madame! He is not one Count, not at all! Dat is only de title he go by in dis country. De foreigners always take de large title ven dey do come here. His name *à Paris* vas Gustave Treadmill. But he not one Frenchman at all, but he do live one long time *à Paris*. First he live vid Monsieur Vermicelle--dere he vas de head cook! Den he live vid Monsieur Tire-nez, de barber! After dat he live vid Monsieur Le Comte Frippon-fin--and dere he vas le Comte's valet! Dere, now I tell everyting I feel one great deal better!

MRS. TIFFANY. Oh! good gracious! I shall faint! Not a Count! What will everybody say? It's no such thing! I say he *is* a Count! One can see the foreign *jenny says quoi* in his face! Don't you think I can tell a Count when I see one? I say he *is* a Count!

(*Enter Snobson, his hat on--his hands thrust into his pockets--evidently a little intoxicated.*))

SNOBSON. I won't stand it! I say I won't!

TIFFANY. (*rushing up to Snobson, aside to him*) Mr. Snobson, for heaven's sake--

SNOBSON. Keep off! I'm a hard customer to get the better of! You'll see if I don't come out strong!

TRUEMAN. (*quietly knocking off Snobson's hat with his stick*) Where are your manners, man?

SNOBSON. My business ain't with you, Catteraugus; you've waked up the wrong passenger! (*Aside.*) Now the way I'll put it into Tiff will be a caution. I'll make him wince! That extra mint julep has put the true pluck in me. Now for it! (*Aloud.*) Mr. Tiffany, Sir--you needn't think to come over me, Sir--you'll have to get up a little earlier in the morning before you do *that*, Sir! I'd like to know, Sir, how you came to assist your daughter in running away with that foreign loafer? It was a downright swindle, Sir. After the conversation I and you had on that subject, she wasn't your property, Sir.

TRUEMAN. What, Antony, is that the way your city clerk bullies his boss?

SNOBSON. You're drunk, Catteraugus--don't expose yourself--you're drunk! Taken a little too much toddy, my old boy! Be quiet! I'll look after you, and they won't find it out. If you want to be busy, you may take care of my *hat*--I feel so deuced weak in the chest, I don't think I *could* pick it up myself. (*Aside.*) Now to put the screws to Tiff. (*Aloud.*) Mr. Tiffany, Sir--you have broken your word, as no virtuous individual--no honorable member--of--the--com--mu--ni--ty--

TIFFANY. (*aside to him*) Have some pity, Mr. Snobson, I beseech you! I had nothing to do with my daughter's elopement! I will agree to anything you desire--your salary shall be doubled--tripled--

SNOBSON. (*aloud*) No you don't. No bribery and corruption.

TIFFANY. (*aside to him*) I implore you to be silent. You shall become partner of the concern--if you please--only do not speak. You are not yourself at this moment.

SNOBSON. Ain't I, though? I feel *twice* myself. I feel like two Snobsons rolled into one, and I'm chock full of the spunk of a dozen! Now Mr. Tiffany, Sir--

TIFFANY. (*aside to him*) I shall go distracted! Mr. Snobson, if you have one spark of manly feeling--

TRUEMAN. Antony, why do you stand disputing with that drunken

jackass? Where's your nigger? Let him kick the critter out, and be of
use for once in his life.

SNOBSON. Better be quiet, Catteraugus. This ain't your hash, so keep
your spoon out of the dish. Don't expose yourself, old boy.

TRUEMAN. Turn him out, Antony!

SNOBSON. He daren't do it! Ain't I up to him? Ain't he in my power?
Can't I knock him into a cocked hat with a word? And now he's got my
steam up--I *will* do it!

TIFFANY. (*beseechingly*) Mr. Snobson--my friend--

SNOBSON. It's no go--steam's up--and I don't stand at anything!

TRUEMAN. You won't *stand* here long unless you mend your manners--
you're not the first man I've *upset* because he didn't know his place.

SNOBSON. I know where Tiff's place is, and that's in the *State's Prison*!
It's bespoke already. He would have it! He wouldn't take pattern of me,
and behave like a gentleman! He's a *forger*, Sir!
    (*Tiffany throws himself into a chair in an attitude of despair; the others
    stand transfixed with astonishment.*)
He's been forging Dick Anderson's endorsements of his notes these ten
months. He's got a couple in the bank that will send him to the wall
anyhow--if he can't make a raise. I took them there myself! Now you
know what he's worth. I said I'd expose him, and I have done it!

MRS. TIFFANY. Get of the house! You ugly, little, drunken brute, get out!
It's not true. Mr. Trueman, put him out; you have got a stick--put him out!
    (*Enter Seraphina, in her bonnet and shawl--a parasol in her hand.*)

SERAPHINA. I hope Zeke hasn't delivered my note.
    (*She stops in surprise at seeing the persons assembled.*)

MRS. TIFFANY. Oh, here is the Countess! (*Advances to embrace her.*)

TIFFANY. (*starting from his seat, and seizing Seraphina violently by the
arm*) Are--you--married?

SERAPHINA. Goodness, Pa, how you frighten me! No, I'm not married,
quite.

TIFFANY. Thank heaven.

MRS. TIFFANY. (*drawing Seraphina aside*) What's the matter? Why did
you come back?

SERAPHINA. The clergyman wasn't at home--I came back for my jewels--
the Count said nobility couldn't get on without them.

TIFFANY. I may be saved yet! Seraphina, my child, you will not see me
disgraced--ruined! I have been a kind father to you--at least I have tried
to be one--although your mother's extravagance made a *madman* of me!
The Count is an imposter--you seemed to like him--(*pointing to Snobson,*

aside)--Heaven forgive me! (*Aloud.*) Marry *him* and save *me*. You, Mr. Trueman, you will be my friend in this hour of extreme need--you will advance the sum which I require--I pledge myself to return it. My wife-- my child--who will support them were I--the thought makes me frantic! You will aid me? You had a child yourself.

TRUEMAN. But I did not *sell* her--it was her own doings. Shame on you, Antony! Put a price on your own flesh and blood! Shame on such foul traffic!

TIFFANY. Save me--I conjure you--for my father's sake.

TRUEMAN. For your *father's* SON'S sake I will *not* aid you in becoming a greater villain than you are!

GERTRUDE. Mr. Trueman--Father, I should say-save him--do not embitter our happiness by permitting this calamity to fall upon another--

TRUEMAN. Enough--I did not need your voice, child. I am going to settle this matter my own way.

(*Goes up to Snobson--who has seated himself and fallen asleep--tilts him out of the chair.*)

SNOBSON. (*waking up*) Eh? Where's the fire? Oh! it's you, Catteraugus.

TRUEMAN. If I comprehend aright, you have been for some time aware of your principal's forgeries?

(*As he says this he beckons to Howard, who advances as witness.*)

SNOBSON. You've hit the nail, Catteraugus! Old chap saw that I was up to him six months ago; left off throwing dust into my eyes--

TRUEMAN. Oh, he did!

SNOBSON. Made no bones of forging Anderson's name at my elbow.

TRUEMAN. Forged at your elbow? You saw him do it?

SNOBSON. I did.

TRUEMAN. Repeatedly.

SNOBSON. Re--pea--ted--ly.

TRUEMAN. Then you, Rattlesnake, if he goes to the State's Prison, you'll take up your quarters there, too. You are an accomplice, an *accessory*!

(*Trueman walks away and seats himself, Howard joins Gertrude. Snobson stands for some time bewildered.*)

SNOBSON. The deuce, so I am! I never thought of that! I must make my- self scarce. I'll be off! Tiff, I say, Tiff! (*Confidentially.*) That drunken old rip has got us in his power. Let's give him the slip and be off. They want men of genius at the West--we're sure to get on! You--you can set up for a writing master, and teach copying *signatures*; and I--I'll give lectures on *temperance*! You won't come, eh? Then I'm off without you. Good bye, Catteraugus! Which is the way to California? (*Steals off.*)

TRUEMAN. There's one debt your city owes me. And now let us see what other nuisances we can abate. Antony, I'm not given to preaching, therefore I shall not say much about what you have done. Your face speaks for itself--the crime has brought its punishment along with it.

TIFFANY. Indeed, it has, Sir! In *one year* I have lived a *century* of misery.

TRUEMAN. I believe you, and upon one condition I will assist you--

TIFFANY. My friend--my first, ever kind friend--only name it!

TRUEMAN. You must sell your house and all these gew gawes, and bundle your wife and daughter off to the country. There let them learn economy, true independence, and home virtues, instead of foreign follies. As for yourself, continue your business--but let moderation, in future, be your counsellor, and let *honesty* be your confidential clerk.

TIFFANY. Mr. Trueman, you have made existence once more precious to me! My wife and daughter shall quit the city to-morrow, and--

PRUDENCE. It's all coming right! It's all coming right! (*Walking up to Trueman.*) We'll go to the county of Catteraugus.

TRUEMAN. No, you won't--I make that a stipulation, Antony; keep clear of Catteraugus. None of your fashionable examples there!

(*Count appears in Conservatory and peeps into the room unperceived.*)

COUNT. (*aside*) What can detain Seraphina? We ought to be off!

MILLINETTE. (*turns round, perceives him, runs and forces him into the room*) Here he is! Ah, Gustave, *mon cher* Gustave! I have you now and we never part no more. Don't frown, Gustave, don't frown--

TRUEMAN. Come forward, Mr. Count! and for the edification of fashionable society confess that you're an imposter.

COUNT. An imposter? Why, you abominable old--

TRUEMAN. Oh, your feminine friend has told us all about it, the cook-- the valet--barber and all that sort of thing. Come, confess, and something may be done for you.

COUNT. Well, then, I do confess I am no count; but really, ladies and gentlemen, I may recommend myself as the most capital cook.

MRS. TIFFANY. Oh, Seraphina!

SERAPHINA. Oh, Ma! (*They embrace and retire up.*)

TRUEMAN. Promise me to call upon the whole circle of your fashionable acquaintances with your own advertisements and in your cook's attire, and I will set you up in business to-morrow. Better turn stomachs than turn heads!

MILLINETTE. But you vill marry me?

COUNT. Give us your hand, Millinette! Sir, command me for the most delicate *paté*--the dantiest *croquette à la royale*--the most transcendent

omelette souflée that ever issued from a French pastry-cook's oven. I
hope you will pardon my conduct, but I heard that in America, where
you pay homage to titles while you profess to scorn them--where
Fashion makes the basest coin current--where you have no kings, no
princes, no *nobility*--

TRUEMAN. Stop there! I object to your use of that word. When justice
is found only among lawyers--health among physicians--and patriotism
among politicians, *then* may you say that there is no *nobility* where there
are no titles! But we *have* kings, princes, and nobles in abundance--of
Nature's stamp, if not of *Fashion's*--we have honest men, warm hearted
and brave, and we have women, gentle, fair, and true, to whom no *title*
would add *nobility*.

EPILOGUE.

PRUDENCE. I told you so! And now you hear and see.
  I told you *Fashion* would the fashion be!
TRUEMAN. Then both its point and moral I distrust.
COUNT. Sir, is that liberal?
HOWARD.   Or is it just?
TRUEMAN. The guilty have escaped!
TIFFANY.   Is, therefore, sin
  Made charming? Ah! there's punishment within!
  Guilt ever carries its own scourge along.
GERTRUDE. Virtue her own reward!
TRUEMAN.   You're right, I'm wrong.
MRS. TIFFANY. How we have been deceived!
PRUDENCE.   I told you so.
SERAPHINA. To lose at once a title and a beau!
COUNT. A count no more. I'm no more of *account*.
TRUEMAN. But to a nobler title you may mount,
  And be in time--who knows?--an honest man!
COUNT. Eh, Millinette?
MILLINETTE.   Oh, *oui*--I know you can!
GERTRUDE. (*to audience*) But ere we close the scene, a word with you--
  We charge you answer-- Is this picture true?
  Some little mercy to our efforts show,
  Then let the world your honest verdict know.
  Here let it see portrayed its ruling passion,
  And learn to prize at its just value--

FASHION!

Benjamin A. Baker (1818-1896)
and *Glance at New York*

In his *Annals of the New York Stage*, George C. D. Odell called it "one of the greatest successes ever known in the history of the New York stage"; a contemporary described it as an "unmitigated conglomeration of vulgarity and illiteracy." The play was *Glance at New York*, which opened at William Mitchell's Olympic Theatre in that city on February 2, 1848, as *New York in 1848*. Immediately undergoing a change of title, it brought pandemonium to the pit and gallery for four months.

Mitchell opened his Olympic Theatre on December 9, 1839, advertising "the production of Vaudevilles, Burlesques, Extravaganzas, Farces, Etc.," and closed it on March 9, 1850, having been extremely successful in achieving his goal. He did this in two ways. He surrounded himself with a stable of exemplary actors and writers (William K. Northall, Alexander Allan, Charles Walcot, Henry Horncastle, and Ben Baker), and he shrewdly targeted the sensational topics of the day. Charles Dickens came to town--Mitchell created *Boz*; William Macready brought *MacBeth* to America--Mitchell burlesqued his acting style; Dion Boucicault's *London Assurance* played at the Park Theater--Mitchell responded with *Olympic Insurance*. His fare changed rapidly: Odell lists 107 pieces performed during the 1845-1846 season alone.

Baker joined Mitchell in 1839 as actor and prompter, a street-wise New Yorker, whose first job in the theatre was as a lamplighter in Natchez. Writing only slight farces on "the follies of the day," he created *Glance at New York* hastily for his own benefit, featuring Frank S. Chanfrau, whom he had promised the role of a fire boy. It was such a success that Baker wrote a second play for Chanfrau--*New York As It Is*, which spawned imitations: *Glance at Philadelphia, Philadelphia As It Is, Mose in China, Mose in California, Mose in a Muss*.

The man who gained most from Baker's creations was Frank Chanfrau, another New York native, who became the darling of the town. Chanfrau claimed that his fame as Mose lasted for more than three and a half years. "His likeness pervaded every window, and his sayings were uttered by every urchin of the city."

Lize and Mose, the Bowery B'hoy

GLANCE AT NEW YORK

(1848)

by Benjamin A. Baker

CHARACTERS

Mose	Eliza Stebbins
Harry Gordon	Mrs. Morton
Jake	Mary
George Parsells	Jane
Major Gates	Jenny Bogert
Mike	Men and Women
Bill Sykes	Boys and Girls

ACT I.

Scene 1. View of Steamboat Pier, foot of Barclay Street. (*A number of newsboys, porters, apple-women, etc., discovered. During the chorus, a profile steamboat crosses upstage from U.E.L. to R.*)

Opening Chorus.
"Jolly Young Waterman."
The folks are all waiting to see the fast steamer
    That's coming from Albany down to this pier;
Ah! here she is! now, you, sir, ain't she a screamer?
    In New York, the fastest boats always land here.

CABMAN. Hire a cab to ride through the city, sir?
MAN. No, sir, I thank you; no, sir, I thank you!
WOMAN. Try some cakes. (*Man shakes head.*) Sure 'tis a pity!
CABMAN. No, he's too cranky; no, he's too cranky!

Chorus.
Ah! here comes the boat! Get out of the way!
We've been waiting to see her best part of the day!
    (*At end of chorus, steamboat bell rings.*)

OMNES. There's the Albany boat!

(*Omnes rush off, U.E.R. Passengers cross from U.E.R. to L. Boys following, crying: "Take your baggage, sir?" Cabmen offer cards. Enter Harry and George, U.E.R. George has a valise. Boys follow them on.*)

BOY. Shall I carry your valise, sir?

GEORGE. No, I'll take care of it myself.

(*Exeunt Boys, quarreling, U.E.R.*)

HARRY. Ha! ha! ha! Bravo! George. I see you have not forgotten my advice. No tricks upon travelers, eh? Well, here we are, in the great metropolis of the Western World, where you can realize all I have told you of it; here you can purchase amusements of all kinds, from the Astor Place Opera, to the far famed "Hall of Novelty"; five minutes' walk will take you from the extreme of wealth to the extreme of poverty. Here you can see all sorts of life. How much better it is to live here, than in your stupid village in the back woods, with no society but that of Bumpkins and old women; to be sure, you have some pretty girls there--your cousin Jane, for instance; but what are your country girls, compared to our dashing New York belles? I declare, during the two months I have passed with you there, I have grown almost as verdant as yourself.

GEORGE. Well, Harry, you must admit that your visit to our village has somewhat improved your health. Poor father! It was a long time before he'd give his consent for me to visit New York. The old gentleman has a great regard for my morals, and I believe nothing but your promise to look after me would have induced him to let me come.

HARRY. Never mind, George, you have not only got his consent, but his dollars into the bargain. We must now look about us for a conveyance to the Astor House. To be sure, it is only at the head of the street, but fashion, my boy, won't allow us to walk there; we must ride. Egad! while we've been talking, the cabs and carriages have all deserted us. Remain you here till I find one. I'll not be long.

(*Exit Harry, L.1E. Enter Jake and Mike, U.E.R.H.*)

MIKE. I say, Jake, there's a greenhorn. I knew it the minute he stepped ashore. I've been watching every moment since. Try it on.

JAKE. All right.

GEORGE. How delighted my poor old dad will be, when I return and tell him of my adventures, and the New York sights.

JAKE. (*advancing and touching George on the shoulder*) I beg your pardon, sir: if I mistake not, you're from the country?

GEORGE. Yes, sir, I am.

JAKE. So am I. I belong up the river. I came here about two months ago, in hopes of getting a situation in a store, but can't make it out. I've spent all the money my father gave me, and have nothing left but this gold watch. (*Shows watch.*) I wouldn't part with it if I could help it, but I've been turned out of my boarding-house, and had nothing to eat these two days. Wouldn't you like to buy it?

GEORGE. I don't know as I can afford it; besides, I have a very good silver one, that answers my purpsose. (*Shows it.*)

JAKE. I will sell it to you cheap, sir. As I am in want of money to take me home, I wouldn't mind trading with you for a little to boot. It almost breaks my heart to part with it, as my father gave it to me. I'll tell you what I'll do--I'll swop with you, if you give me ten dollars to boot!

GEORGE. (*aside*) Egad, I'll do it. (*Aloud.*) As you say you're very much in want of money, I'll trade with you. But is it good gold?

JAKE. If you have any doubts, you can go with me to the jeweler's and ask him.

GEORGE. No, my friend, I will take your word. There!
(*Gives him silver watch and money, and receives gilt watch from Jake.*)

JAKE. Thank 'ye, sir. You've got a great bargain!
(*Goes up and joins Mike.*)

GEORGE. (*puts watch in pocket*) What a swell I will cut when I get home! Father and mother will open their eyes wider than ever, and all the neighbors will be anxious to see my gold watch! (*Struts about.*)

JAKE. I've done it, Mike. Here's your five. (*They divide money.*) I think you can come the drop game there, while I go and sell the silver one.
(*Exeunt Jake and Mike, U.E.L.H. Re-enter Harry, L.1E.*)

HARRY. I hope you are not tired of waiting for me, George. I had to go two blocks before I could find a coach; now I'll go and get my valise out of the Captain's office, and be with you in a minute. (*Going, U.E.R.*)

GEORGE. Stop one minute, Harry! I want to show you what a glorious bargain I've made! (*Shows watch.*) What do you think of that?

HARRY. You don't mean to say you've been buying that?

GEORGE. Yes, my boy! I got it dirt cheap. I gave my silver lever and ten dollars to boot!

HARRY. George, you've been sadly victimized! This watch is not worth ten cents!

GEORGE. Nonsense! Don't you see it's gold?

HARRY. All is not gold that glitters. You've been the dupe of a scoundrel!

GEORGE. Do you really mean to say I have been deceived in this watch?

HARRY. I do! Why, my dear George, I thought you too cunning for the watch-stuffers.

GEORGE. I tell you, Harry, the poor fellow who sold it to me was from the country and almost starving.

HARRY. Nonsense! this is the old stereotyped tale! But console yourself--you are not the first greenhorn that has been taken in by that manoeuvre. There's about as much gold in that watch as you can put in your eye!

GEORGE. Let's after the rascal, and have him arrested!

HARRY. Pooh! pooh! you may as well look for a needle in a haystack! Besides, you have no proof. Your watch he has sold ere this. You must be content with your bargain. Stop here till I return from the boat.

   (*Exit Harry, U.E.R.*)

GEORGE. Deuce take the fellow! A pretty laughing-stock he's made of me. The old adage--"Experience requires to be bought"--is beginning to be verified in my case. I have made a good beginning, at any rate. Egad! I'd like to see 'em try it again--that's all!

   (*Re-enter Jake and Mike, U.E.L., dressed as cartmen. Mike drops pocket-book between George's legs, then stoops and picks it up.*)

JAKE. Let me look at that.

MIKE. No you don't! No doubt it belongs to some gentleman who arrived by the Albany boat.

JAKE. Maybe it belongs to some of the cartmen about here?

MIKE. I tell you it ain't possible! It's full of papers, etc.

   (*Jake goes up. Mike offers it to George.*)

Here's your pocket-book, sir: I've just picked it up, and that man wanted to claim it.

GEORGE. (*feeling pockets*) You are mistaken, friend; it does not belong to me.

MIKE. Indeed, sir! Well, I could have sworn it did. (*Opens pocket-book and shows George.*) You see, it's full of papers, besides a number of bank-bills. You see, as I can't read, you'd better take it, and keep it till a reward is offered, which, I dare say, will be something handsome--fifty dollars at the least! Then we'll go halves. You can always find me at 300 Robinson Street.

GEORGE. (*aside*) Egad! Here's a speculation. (*Aloud.*) Very well, my friend, I will take it. (*Offers to take it.*)

MIKE. Stop a minute! You see, I'm going to trust you with almost a fortune--as I don't know you, suppose you let me have ten dollars now, and when you get the remainder, you can call at my boarding house and let me have the balance of my share.

GEORGE. Well, that's fair enough.

(*Takes out pocket-book and gives him a ten dollar bill.*)
There.

MIKE. And there's the pocket-book. Good day.

GEORGE. Good day, friend. (*Exeunt Jake and Mike, U.E.L.*) Well, here's a good speculation! This will make up for the money I lost with my watch. (*Looks at book.*) What's this? Invoice of boots and shoes, hardware, etc., and here's a quantity of bills--Globe Bank--Globe Bank--Atlas Bank--egad! I'm in luck.

(*Re-enter Harry, with valise, U.E.R.*)

HARRY. Come, George, let's be off.

GEORGE. Now, Harry, laugh if you dare. I think I have fully redeemed myself.

HARRY. In what way?

GEORGE. See! (*Shows book.*) This will make up for my loss.

HARRY. Where did you get that?

GEORGE. A man found it, and placed it in my hands until a reward is offered for it.

HARRY. Well?

GEORGE. I advanced him ten dollars.

HARRY. Ha! ha! ha! duped again! They have initiated you into the drop business! Ha! ha! ha!

GEORGE. Don't laugh, Harry. See, here are a number of bank bills--Globe Bank, and Hoboken Banking & Grazing Company.

HARRY. Globe Bank bills are as worthless as chaff! Ha! ha! ha! you have been done capitally! Come--if you stay here much longer, you'll not have a cent left.

(*Enter a number of Boys. They crowd round George.*)

BOY. Pocket-combs--cent a pair!

NEWSBOY. Extra Sun, sir--with a full account of the great meeting in the Park to regulate the price of putty.

(*They crowd round him so fast that he runs off. They follow, U.E.L.H. Scene closes.*)

Scene 2. Front Street, Broadway. (*Enter Mrs. Morton, Mary, and Jane, L.H.1E.*)

MRS. MORTON. My dear girls, 'tis time we were at home; it's past five o'clock, and dinner will be waiting for us.

JANE. Dear me, aunt, how the time passes! I declare, I was never so delighted in my life! Such a never-ending display of silks, jewelry, and shawls as this Broadway boasts of! 'Tis enough to turn my brain!

MARY. If the windows of the stores put you in such ecstacies, what will a visit to the interior accomplish?

JANE. Oh, dear! don't mention it! I should go wild! I know I should!

MRS. MORTON. (*reprovingly*) Jane!

JANE. Excuse me, aunt; but everything I see is so much superior to our village, that I don't know whether New York belongs to this world of not.

MRS. MORTON. Talking of your village, how nicely you contrived to give your cousin George the slip, and arrive here a day before him.

JANE. Yes, George, poor fellow, was so delighted with the prospect of his visit to New York--which induced me to write word I would visit you; how surprised he will be to find me here before him!

MRS. MORTON. No doubt he will meet you at our house, where, of course, he'll call, together with his friend, Harry Gordon.

JANE. (*confused*) Harry Gordon?

MARY. Why, Jane, what ails you? Is there anything so terrible in the name of Harry Gordon?

JANE. No; why do you ask?

MARY. No matter. By the way you mentioned his name I suspect there is some truth in the little bit of scandal afloat.

JANE. Scandal!

MARY. Harmless, I assure you. 'Tis said a certain gentleman paid marked attention to a pretty village lass, on the occasion of his visit, for the double purpose of seeing his relations and recruiting his health.

MRS. MORTON. And you think he lost no time in recruiting his heart?

(*Jane runs off, R.H.*)

Come, girls.

MARY. Ma! I hope you intend to take Jane with us to our bowling saloon?

MRS. MORTON. Of course, I do; while she is in the city I intend to show her every place of amusement. Bless the girl! There she is, staring into that shop window, as usual.

(*Exeunt Mrs. Morton, Mary, and Jane, R.H. Enter Newsboy, L.H., and crosses R.H.*)

BOY. Here's the Extra Herald--arrival of the ferry boat Jamaica--four days late from Brooklyn!

(*Re-enter George and Jake, L.H.*)

GEORGE. (aside) Our apartments are secured, and everything seen to; Harry has left me until he arranges a little business of his own; meantime, my new-found friend will show me the Elephant-- He looks like an honest fellow.

JAKE. If you want me, sir, I have an hour to spare, and will be happy to serve you.

GEORGE. Your calling, my friend, is rather a new one. Pray, do you find many customers?

JAKE. Oh, yes; I sometimes have a job that lasts three or four days. I'm a city pilot; my line of business hasn't been long established, and, I'm sorry to say, it's been sadly cut into by outsiders.

GEORGE. By what?

JAKE. By outsiders--fellows who live upon other people's ideas. You see, I and two or three others struck upon this idea, to offer our services to gentlemen unacquainted with the city to show them the Elephant, and have so far been well patronized. We have earned a good name for honesty, and I hope you will recommend me to your friends.

GEORGE. What are your terms?

JAKE. One dollar an hour, payable in advance.

GEORGE. I suppose that means you want me to pay before we say any more?

JAKE. One dollar an hour for services, and you are to pay the entrance fees for any place we may visit.

GEORGE. Very good. (Gives a bill.) Now, what open space is that with the large building in the center?

JAKE. That's the Park. The admission is fifty cents apiece.

GEORGE. Indeed! Do all these people pay that! They seem to walk in and out free.

JAKE. That's because they're regular subscribers.

GEORGE. Oh! (Gives money.) There's a dollar; that will pay for us two; take it; you know more about it than I do.

JAKE. I'll give it to the gate-keeper myself, and as you'll want to visit the Battery soon after we get through the Park, suppose you give me another dollar? Then you won't be troubled when we get there.

GEORGE. I've nothing less than a ten dollar bill--suppose you give me the change? (Gives bill.)

JAKE. I'll run to the corner and get it changed, if you'll stop here a minute.

GEORGE. Certainly. (Exit Jake, laughing aside, R.1E.) That seems an honest fellow enough; he will be of great service to me while Harry is absent. (*Looks off.*) Egad! Here comes Harry; he has returned sooner than I expected.

(*Re-enter Harry, L.1E.*)

HARRY. Well, here I am, George; I've finished my business for the day; now, suppose we take a turn through the city. But how came you to leave the sitting-room at the Astor before my return?

GEORGE. I met a gentleman who informed me that his business was to show up the Elephant to country people, or, in other words, take them about town to see the sights.

HARRY. Well?

GEORGE. I engaged him, paid him one dollar an hour for his services, paid for two tickets for the Park; and he has just gone to get a ten dollar bill changed to take out for two Battery tickets.

HARRY. Ha! ha! ha! you innocent lamb! I shall certainly have to put you under lock and key while I am absent. You'll never see him or your money again; and as for the Park and Battery, they are public grounds and open to all!

GEORGE. Do you mean to say these people now walking in and out are not subscribers?

HARRY. Subscribers! Pooh! They pay enough taxes, if that's what you mean. Ha! ha! ha!

GEORGE. Don't laugh, Harry. It seems to me there hasn't been a countryman in New York in ten years, by the way the sharpers set upon me.

HARRY. They do seem to have a design upon your pockets; but I will look after you in the future.

GEORGE. Thank you--but who is this coming?

HARRY. Why, as I live, it's one of the b'hoys--an old schoolfellow of mine! He seems to be talking confidentially to himself. Step aside for a minute.

(*Retires up. Enter Mose, smoking, R.1E.*)

MOSE. (*spits*) I've made up my mind not to run wid der machine any more. There's that Corneel Anderson don't give de boys a chance. Jest 'cause he's Chief Ingineer he thinks he ken do as he likes. Now, last night when de fire was down in Front Street, we was a-takin' 40's water; I had hold ov de butt, and seed she was gittin' too much fur us; and I said to Bill Sykes: "Skyesy, take de butt." Seys he, "What fur?" Seys I, "Never you mind, but take de butt." And he took de butt; so I goes down de street a little, and stood on 40's hose. Corneel Anderson cum along and seed me. Seys he, "Get off de hose!" Seys I, "I won't get off de hose!" Seys he, "If you don't get off de hose, I'll hit you over de gourd wid my trumpet!" Seys I, "What! I won't get off de hose!" And he did hit me over de gourd!

(*Harry advances and taps him on the shoulder.*)

I say, lookye here! What yer mean by that?

HARRY. Why, Mose, don't you remember me?

MOSE. No sir-ree, I don't.

HARRY. What! Don't remember Harry Gordon that used to go to Evans' school with you, in Bayard Street?

MOSE. (*taking his hand*) Well, I don't know anybody else! How are you? How have you been for the last ten years?

HARRY. Oh! hearty. But how comes it I find you in this part of the town? I heard that you held Broadway in such contempt that you could'n be persuaded even to cross it.

MOSE. I've got over dat now. The fact is, I'm agoin' to give up runnin' to fires. I arn't been used well, so I'm goin' to locate somewhere in this quarter, if I can find a good boardin'-house.

HARRY. I'm glad of that, for we can then renew an old acquaintance. You used to fight all my battles for me at school, and we were firm friends! But allow me to introduce you to my friend, George Parsells, from the country.

MOSE. (*shakes hands*) How are you, old hoss?

GEORGE. Proud of your acquaintance.

HARRY. Mose, we want to take a little spree to-night--have you any objection to accompany us?

MOSE. No sir-ree! I'm open fur a spree! Where'll you go fust?

HARRY. I have a capital idea. Let's carry it through, just for the fun of the thing.

GEORGE and MOSE. What is it?

HARRY. Sometime since I visited some lady friends of mine, and by hook or crook I obtained tickets of admission to a ladies' bowling saloon. Now, if we can go there and disquise ourselves in the uniform they wear, while playing, I think I can warrant some fun. What say you?

MOSE. I say I'm there, hoss. I can play pretty if I'm a mind to!

GEORGE. But where to find these dresses?

HARRY. A five dollar bill to the wardrobe-keeper will procure them, I think.

OMNES. Ha! ha! ha! That's capital! Let's be off at once.

MOSE. Let's do it up pretty.

(*Exeunt, R.H.1E.*)

Scene 3. Ladies' Bowling Saloon. Bar at Back. (*A number of ladies playing at ten-pins, dressed in plain white pants and blue blouses, and little black caps. Mrs. Morton, Jane, and Mary are discovered, all smoking cigars.*)

Chorus.
"*Fra Diavalo*," Second Act.
For pleasure there's no denying;
Who can boast such a city as this?
We've no cause at our lot to be sighing--
So come, take a game with me, Miss:
I am sure, I am sure, you cannot resist!
(*All laugh at end of chorus.*)

JANE. (*comes forward with Mrs. Morton*) Really, aunt, you New York ladies are not at a loss for amusements.

MRS. MORTON. And exercise. What do you think of our saloon? All to ourselves—no men admitted, my dear.

JANE. Indeed?

MRS. MORTON. Yes; I have found that card-playing, dancing, theaters, etc., were a bore; and the continual cry of the doctor was, "You should take exercise!" So I determined on a bowling alley, and with the assistance of a few lady friends carried it into effect. Our club now numbers fifty ladies, of the first families in New York.

JANE. 'Tis indeed capital fun.

MARY. (*who has been playing, comes forward*) Come, mamma, play a game with me. I have beat Miss Wilson one string.

GIRL. (*playing*) A ten-strike!

SECOND GIRL. Good!
   (*Mrs. Morton and Jane go up to play. Enter Harry, George, and Mose, dressed in uniform, L.*)

HARRY. Here we are! Mind, Mose, no ecstacies, or you'll betray us.

MOSE. Don't be alarmed about me. I can shuffle through.

HARRY. (*to George, who is gaping about*) What do you think of this, George? Don't the New York ladies deserve great credit for their exertions to promote health?

GEORGE. And is this place exclusively reserved for ladies? I say, we better go back again.

HARRY. You're a pretty fellow, to talk in that way! No, we'll have it out, come what come may. There are some friends of mine--I must not acknowledge them, or they'll betray us.

(*Mose spits, Harry pulls his dress.*)

Mose, dispense with your tobacco for the present, or you'll betray us.

MOSE. Them is hard lines, but I suppose I must. I say, arn't dere goin' to be any fitein'?

HARRY. Nonsense, Mose! Go pick out a partner, and take a game of ten-pins.

(*They go up to alleys. Mose rolls extravagantly twice, and marks a spare. Mrs. Morton, Jane, and Mary come forward.*)

MRS. MORTON. Girls, you saw the last three persons who entered?

GIRLS. Yes.

MRS. MORTON. I've a secret to tell you. But promise not to scream, or give the alarm in any way.

GIRLS. We promise.

MRS. MORTON. Well, you must know that these people I suspect to be men.

GIRLS. Men!

MRS. MORTON. And one of them no other than Harry Gordon!

MARY. Indeed! How did they get in?

MRS. MORTON. I can't tell for the life of me.

JANE. I declare, if the stout one isn't cousin George! Let's bother them; they dare not avow their sex.

MRS. MORTON and MARY. Agreed!

(*Mary goes to George, Jane to Harry, and Mrs. Morton to Mose.*)

JANE. (*comes forward with Harry*) Excuse me, Miss, I've had no introduction, but I imagine it's all the same. I challenge you to play a game with me.

HARRY. (*aside*) How very like the little girl I used to make love to in the country! (*Aloud.*) As you seem disposed to play, I don't care if I do. You will pardon me, I hope, if I ask one question. Have you any relations living in the country?

JANE. Oh, yes! my sister Jane lives in a small village, just out of Newburgh.

HARRY. Jane? Do you know, Madam, I love--

JANE. (*quickly*) A game of ten-pins--so do I. Come, the players have ceased--now's our time. (*They go up.*)

MARY. (*comes forward with George*) You seem a stranger in this saloon. May I ask if you've long been a member of this club?

GEORGE. (*aside*) Hang me if I know what to say! (*Aloud.*) No, Miss, I have just joined it; indeed, this is my first visit here.

MARY. Oh! we'll soon make you acquainted. When once within these walls, we are secure from the intrusion of horrid men.

GEORGE. (*aside*) There's a dig for me. She's devilish pretty.

MARY. Come, let me beat you.

GEORGE. With all my heart!

MARY. Eh?

GEORGE. If you can. (*They go up to play.*)

MRS. MORTON. (*comes forward with Mose*) Have you ever played bowls before?

MOSE. You can bet your life I have!

MRS. MORTON. You appear to be a stranger in our saloon. And I had no idea there were others.

MOSE. There's a lots ov 'em in de Bowery, beside a whole load ov 'em in Broadway.

MRS. MORTON. I thought they were for gentlemen?

MOSE. Ov course dey are. (*Aside.*) I almost let de cat out ov de bag. (*Aloud.*) As I wus a sayin', I've seen de signs a-hangin' out: dat's de way I cum to know 'em.

MRS. MORTON. (*aside*) What an odd creature Harry has chosen for a companion. (*Aloud.*) What sort of a game do you play?

MOSE. Why, a fair game ov course. Jest look a-here!
(*Takes her around the waist and kisses her. Mrs. Morton screams and shouts, "A man!" Women all scream. Harry and George come forward.*)
Yes sir-ree, I am a man, and no mistake--and one ov de b'hoys at dat!
(*Squares off.*)

HARRY and GEORGE. Come, Mose, you've betrayed us--let's be off!
(*Women scream and run upstage. Men run off, L.H.1E. Music hurried. Scene closes.*)

Scene 4. Front Street. (*Enter Jake and Mike, L.1E.*)

MIKE. Well, Jake, how about the greenhorn? Have you bled him since we joined in the spec with the pocket-book and watch?

JAKE. Oh! haven't I? Let me alone for that! He's too good game to let slip so easy. I saw how willing he was to fork out the mopusses, so I came the Elephant dodge on him.

MIKE. Well, how did you make out?

JAKE. Glorious! I bled him to the tune of twelve dollars' worth.

MIKE. Why, you don't say so!

JAKE. Yes, I got one dollar for my services, and one dollar for two Park tickets. Then what do you think he was green enough to do?

MIKE. I can't imagine.

JAKE. Why, he sent me to get a ten dollar bill changed.

MIKE. You brought the change back, of course?

JAKE. Oh, yes, I did, over the left.

MIKE. Ha! ha! ha! I say, Jake, I have been doing a little myself in the dog line.

JAKE. The dog line! What do you mean?

MIKE. I'll explain. I was walking on the Battery, and I saw a fine large dog. There was a gentleman just a-head--of course, it didn't belong to him. Well, I was walking along, whistling, and the dog came up along side. I walked off the Battery, and the dog followed. I turned round and looked for the owner, but he wasn't there. I've taken him up to my cellar, and am going to keep him there till a reward is offered.

JAKE. Why, Mike, I'm ashamed of you! How can you condescend to the dog line, when the legitimate business pays so well?

MIKE. There was a chance to make a few shiners. Why shouldn't I do it?

JAKE. You'd better starve than make money in that low way. Stuff watches, drop pocket-books, or do anything in a genteel way, but never condescend to smug dogs. But be off to Loafer's Paradise, and I'll follow you. (*Mike crosses, R.*) And Mike, keep up your respectability as long as possible. Get the reward for the dog, and, seeing its you, why, I'll take half.

MIKE. (*aside*) No, you don't. (*Exit, R.1E.*)

Song. JAKE.
"Bow-wow-wow."

I'm sure the world can't blame a man
        For getting an honest living, sirs;
The game of life is catch who can--
        Each for himself is striving, sirs.
There's many a one who walks about
        With airs like a grand Turk, sirs,
So neatly dressed, his form so stout--
        And yet, he'll never work, sirs!
                Bow-wow-wow, etc.

He speculates in pocket-books,
        And other curious wears, sirs,

And with an honest man's shrewd looks,
    Ne'er taken unawares, sirs.
The simple he imposes on,
    With quite an easy grace, sirs,
And picks their pockets just for fun,
    While looking in their face, sirs!
          Bow-wow-wow, etc.

Sometimes he's caught, and brought before
    The Justice of the Peace, sirs;
The charge is made--when that is o'er,
    They give him a release, sirs.
The reason is, there's some mistake,
    And settled in a crack, sirs--
How can a man be proved a rogue,
    With a fine coat on his back, sirs?
          Bow-wow-wow, etc.
    (*Exit Jake, R.H. Enter Harry, George, and Mose, laughing, L.H.*)

HARRY. Ha! ha! ha! We escaped just in time to save our bacon! I wouldn't have liked Mrs. Morton to discover us.

MOSE. Well, I confess I stuck my foot in it; but I couldn't help tryin' to give dat old woman a smack.

GEORGE. (*annoyed*) I should think you might have refrained from such rudeness.

MOSE. Now, look a-here--I don't know what you mean by rudeness--but if you want satisfaction, I s'pose you can take it! (*Stands menacingly.*)

HARRY. Mose, you misunderstand him. He don't want satisfaction, as you call it.

MOSE. Oh! I thought he did: as if he wants to make a muss, I'm on hand.

HARRY. I'll have no quarreling, boys; we are out on a little spree, and all must bear good feelings.

GEORGE. I'm sure, Harry, I did not mean to hurt the feelings of our friend in any way.

HARRY. I knew it, George. So, shake hands with him, Mose, and let's be jolly.

MOSE. You didn't mean to make a muss?

GEORGE. No.

MOSE. Put it there. (*Offers his hand.*)

HARRY. Where shall we go next?

MOSE. Why don't you go to de theater?

HARRY. Which theater?

MOSE. Why, de Bowery Theater. Look a-here--did you ever see old Jack Jack Scott take Don Keyser de Bassoon? When he takes out dat sword, and comes down to de front and says something--ain't dat high?

HARRY. It's too late for the theater. Where else can we go?

MOSE. I'm bilein' over for a rousin' good fight with some one somewhere. What do you say for Loafer's Paradise?

GEORGE. Loafer's Paradise?

HARRY. Where's that, Mose?

MOSE. That's tellins. But if you say so, I'll take you there. It's a smash-in' place for a fight, anyway, and if I don't have a muss soon, I'll spile.

HARRY. What say you, George?

GEORGE. I'll go.

MOSE. That's right; you're a perfect brick! Come along, for I'm itchin' for a regular knock-down and drag-out!

(*Exit Harry, R.1E. George stands a moment.*)

Why don't yer come along?

(*Exeunt, R.H.*)

Scene 5. Loafer's Paradise. A dirty bar-room. Large Stove in the Center, with Pipe off Wing, R.H. (*A number of Loafers about. One sitting on a long bench by stove. Major Gates, a literary loafer, standing by stove. Bar U.E.L.H.*)

Chorus.
"Irish Air."

Here we are, a precious crew, that's always on hand
For a theft or a frolic, at any man's command;
And a poor deserted lot, too, of late we have been,
'Cos we cannot get a visitor that is at all green.

For the green 'uns pay the score
That's kept behind the door--
When once rubbed off, we can get trust for
Just as much more!

JAKE. (*entering, U.E.R.H., looking around to Loafers*) Come, you Johnny Stokes and Billy Waters, time's up--move yourselves--come!

VOICE. (*without*) Three insiders!

(*Enter Mose, followed by George and Harry, C.D.*)

HARRY. Mose, is this Loafer's Paradise?

MOSE. 'Tain't nuthin' else. Now, if you want ter fight, say the word.

HARRY. Not yet, Mose. Let's take a drink.

MOSE. I'm a'goin' to have a fight in this crib--I am! (*They all go up to bar.*)

JAKE. (*beckons Mike forward*) I say, Mike, do you know his knibbs?

MIKE. No; who is he?

JAKE. Don't you remember the chap we did at the foot of Barclay Street?

MIKE. My eye, so it is. Do you think he knows us?

JAKE. No matter if he does: we're at home here.

MIKE. I don't mind them much, but there's fightin' Mose along with 'em; I'm rather afraid of him.

JAKE. Pshaw! You fool. We must make something more out of that greenhorn before he leaves here. His watch ain't worth lifting; if you can't do anything better, you must prig his wipe.

MIKE. I'm down. Are you going to speechify to-night?

JAKE. I am that; it pays well when we have genteel visitors: for while I speechifys, you picks their pockets. Ha! ha!

MIKE. Ha! ha! ha!

(*They retire up. Harry, Mose, and George come forward. Mose goes to bench at stove, tilts it up, and spills Loafers off it, and sits with cigar.*)

HARRY. This, George, is the renowned Loafer's Paradise, the abode of many worthies, who would not be at home in any other place, who never think of the past or care for the future, never miss an opportunity of committing a small theft, nor keep the proceeds thereof till to-morrow. So long as they can raise a few pennies for a warm by the stove and a glass of that poisonous liquor, they are happy.

GEORGE. And is it possible that such dens as this exist in the very heart of New York?

HARRY. Not only possible, but, alas! too true. But where's Mose all this time? (*Turns and sees him.*) Mose!

MOSE. (*advances slowly*) Well, what yer want?

HARRY. Why did you throw that man off the bench?

MOSE. 'Cos I want to pick up er muss!

HARRY. Nonsense, Mose! They all seem peaceably disposed: don't bother 'em.

MOSE. (*contemptiously*) What? (*Turns a little up.*)

JAKE. (*to Loafers*) Come, Bill Waters and Johnny Stokes, I told you once before, time's up. Now toddle. (*Two Loafers exeunt slowly.*)

MOSE. (*to Harry, pointing after Loafers*) Them's foo-foos!

GEORGE. What's foo-foos?

MOSE. Why, foo-foos is outsiders, and outsiders is foo-foos.

GEORGE. I'm as wise now as ever.

MOSE. Well, as you're a greenhorn, I'll enlighten you. A foo-foo, or outsider, is a chap wot can't come de big figure.

GEORGE. What's the big figure?

MOSE. The big figure here, is three cents for a glass of grog and a night's lodging.

HARRY. Do you mean on those benches?

MOSE. Yes.

GEORGE. A queer bed they must make.

MOSE. I don't know; I never tried it.

JAKE. (*to Major Gates, who is advancing*) Come, Major, time's up--toddle!

MAJOR. (*indignant*) Permit me to observe, Mr. Jake, that if the wings of time have already swept over the course of two hours since I became one of us, he travels much faster now-a-days than formerly.

JAKE. Remember the rules, Major. If you don't slope when the word is given, a dozen on the ventilator.

MAJOR. (*to George and Harry*) Allow me to remark that I believe you to be strangers here, and, consequently, not *au fait* in the rules and regulations. Hence I must evacuate these premises unless I can lay myself under a deep and lasting obligation to someone.

GEORGE. For what, Major?

MAJOR. Alexander sighed for a second world to conquer, Solomon for the wings of a dove, but Major Gates would be as happy as either of them, if he could only mortgage his boots, or otherwise, to quote the profane, "raise the wind for a snifter."

MOSE. (*knocking Major's hat over his eyes*) Come out--you don't come over this crowd, though we are a little raw.

HARRY. Hold on, Mose; the poor fellow seems hard up; here's a sixpence for you.

(*He gives it to Major, who walks up to bar, looking scornfully at Mose.*)

MOSE. Well, if de greenhorn had done dat, I could have looked over it, but you!

HARRY. Have you no pity for the unfortunate?

MOSE. Yes, sir; I feel as much for a poor fellow as any body livin', but not for a lazy one. There's plenty of work in this village for everybody, if they're only a mind to look for it; and helpin' such fellows as him is only encouraging 'em.

HARRY. What you say is true, Mose.

MOSE. True! I believe you--you can bet high on it.

HARRY. Come, Mose, let's be off--

MOSE. (*astonished*) What! Widout a fight? No sir-ree--I'm goin' to have a speech from the landlord--den for a knock-down and a drag-out--den I retires like a gentleman.

HARRY. Well, I suppose we must oblige you this time.

MAJOR. Gentlemen, allow me to propose a speech from our worthy landlord.

OMNES. Aye, aye! a speech! a speech!

(Jake mounts bench. Mose sits beside him.)

MOSE. Now, landlord, if you're game, let's hear you cackle.

JAKE. Fellow citizens, of everywhere in particular, and nowhere in general--I appear before you to say what I shall say; and I say, to begin, that I am opposed to all governments: I am opposed to all laws!

(Applause.)

MOSE. Louder, old puddin'-head! louder!

JAKE. I goes in for the first-come-first-served principle! I goes for human natur', fellow citizens! (*Applause.*) Up with no work, up with no watch-house! (*Applause.*) Up with lashing of grog and insiders! (*Hurrah!*) Foo-foos be blowed! Any man be blowed who can't raise three cents for an insider! Them as will snooze in the market, when such an establishment as this is open, is no gentleman!

MOSE. Oh, gas!

JAKE. Who said gas?

MOSE. I did--d'ye want tu take it up?

JAKE. No, sir; I don't want to take any such liberties.

MOSE. Go in, lemons!

(Mose upsets bench, and pitches into Jake. General row, stove upset, etc. Scene closes.)

Scene 6. Front Street. Music Hurried. Dark Stage. (*George runs across from L. to R., followed by a Loafer, beating him. Harry crosses, fighting Loafer. Enter Mose, L.1E.*)

MOSE. Them fellers have been followin' me long enough. Now I'm goin' in!

(Enter two Fellows, who attack Mose. He knocks them down, and after one or two rounds, they fight each other. Mose runs off, laughing, R.1E. Two men roll about stage, fighting, till they discover their mistake. Then they run off, L.1E.)

ACT II.

Scene 1. Front Street. (*Enter George and Harry, R.1E. George has his hat smashed in and a black eye.*)

HARRY. Ha! ha! ha! There he goes. I hope he's got enough of a row to last him some time.

GEORGE. I hope so, too; for my part, I'm beginning to get sick of this fun. I'm satisfied with New York.

HARRY. Pooh! pooh! You haven't seen half yet.

GEORGE. No--nor do I intend to see it. I'm off by the first boat to-morrow. My visit to New York has cost me over fifty dollars, and a black eye into the bargain--I'm hanged if my watch ain't gone!

HARRY. A black eye? (*Looks at it.*) So it is! Your eye has gone into mourning, sure enough! Never mind--we'll go over to the druggist's--he'll soon take that away.

GEORGE. What! My eye?

HARRY. No, no! the black off it. (*Enter Mose, L.*)

MOSE. Any of 'em round? When them fellers come mussin' round me, I'll lam 'em.

HARRY. No--come in, Mose--the coast is clear.

MOSE. I tell you what it is, I escaped by the skin of my teeth this time! I wouldn't liked to have slept in de station-house; I've always managed to escape that business, and I ain't goin' to begin to be tuck up now. (*To George.*) Well, what do yer think of that fur a muss?

GEORGE. I don't know what to think of it. All I know is, I have something to make me remember it.

MOSE. What's that, Rip?

GEORGE. (*shows eye*) Look here.

MOSE. That's a blinker--you wasn't quick enough--you ought to hit out strong--so! (*Boxes.*)

GEORGE. I say--stop that fun!

HARRY. Easy, Mose--you'll hurt him.

MOSE. I wouldn't hurt him for the world.

(*Enter woman with a covered basket, L.1E.*)

WOMAN. (*to George*) I beg your pardon, sir--can you tell me where-abouts Henry Street is?

GEORGE. I cannot, my good woman; maybe this gentleman can.

(*He points to Mose.*)

MOSE. You're a long way off Henry Street, ma'am.

WOMAN. Oh, dear! I've carried this basket a long way, and am so tired! Will you hold it for me till I fix my shawl a bit?

MOSE. Yes, ma'am.

(Woman gives Mose basket, and runs off quick, R.1E.)

HARRY. What the deuce ails the woman?

MOSE. I don't know. She can't mean to leave the basket with me!

HARRY. It seems she has left it. *(Child cries in basket.)*

OMNES. What's that?

MOSE. It sounds like a baby crying. Maybe it's in the basket.

(Uncovers basket and discovers baby. Baby cries. To Harry.)

Here, you hold this for me, will yer?

HARRY. *(puts finger to nose)* No you don't--ha! ha! ha!

MOSE. What yer afeard of? I only want to roll down my trousers. *(To George.)* Here, you take hold.

GEORGE. D'ye see anything green? Ha! ha! ha!

MOSE. *(gets angry and shakes basket, baby cries louder)* Shut up, ye little varment! Order!

HARRY and GEORGE. *(going)* Good-bye, old fellow.

MOSE. Sa-a-y--look a'here--you ain't a-goin' to leave me with this young one--are you?

HARRY. Why not? You've got another friend now--you don't want us anymore. Good night--ha! ha! ha!

(Exeunt Harry and George, R.1E.)

MOSE. *(looking after them)* I'd like to give you one!

(Shaking his fist, sets basket down.)

I got nothing to do wid de baby.

(Walks away and returns.)

It ain't de little baby's fault.

(Takes up basket.)

Dis baby puts me in mind when de fire was down in Spruce Street; dere was a lot of shanties burning; I had de pipe, 'cos I rolled de ingine dat night--and I saw a woman cryin' and a hollerin'. Seys I, "What's de matter, good woman?" Seys she, "My baby's in de house, and it's burnin'!" Seys I, "What!" I turned my cap hindside afore, and buttoned my old fire-coat, and I went in and fetched out dat baby. I never forgot dat woman's countenance wen I handed de baby to her. She fell down on her knees and blessed me.

(Wipes his eye with sleeve.)

Ever since dat time I've had a great partiality for little babies. The fire-b'hoys may be a little rough outside, but they're all right here.

(*Touches breast.*)

It never shall be said dat one of de New York b'hoys deserted a baby in distress.

(*Exit Mose, R.H.1E. Enter Jake and Mike, L.H.1E.*)

MIKE. Well, Jake, was there much broke?

JAKE. Nothing to hurt; the stove was upset, and the lodgers scattered a few: but I put all to rights again before I left; Sam got the greenhorn's ticker--to be sure, it wasn't worth much, but it's better than nothing, you know--he made a dive for his pocket-book, but couldn't make it out.

MIKE. So much the better; we might have got the one I dropped on him this morning; then what would we have done?

JAKE. Why, in a case like that, turn virtuous, and return the gentleman his property. (*Enter Major Gates and Joe, R.1E.*) Ha! ha! ha! Here's a couple of the scape goats. Well, Major, how have you fared?

MAJOR. Oh! sadly, Mr. Jake; I've been badly used.

JAKE. Serves you right, Major; if you had conformed with the rules of the cellar, and walked your trotters when the word was given, you would have escaped a good drubbing. But I can't stand here talking-- I've some work to do.

MAJOR. Stay, most potent sir: have you the price of a glass of refreshment to loan me, till some remittances arrive from my uncle?

JAKE. (*puts finger to nose*) No, you don't! Go to your old bunk, and maybe the clerk of the market will stand treat to you for patronizing his shop. (*Exit Jake, R.1E.*)

Trio. MIKE, MAJOR and JOE.
"*Canadian Boat Song.*"

MIKE.   Go, Major, go, for half the night's past;
           Seek your stall in the market, or you'll sure be the last!

MAJOR.   No, no, Mr. Mike--I'll find plenty of room,
           For that is the common loafer's home!

TRIO.   Home, home, home, the loafer's home--
           For that is the common loafer's home!

MIKE.   There's dark, and there's light, there's brown and there's fair:
           All sleep in the market to enjoy the fresh air!

MAJOR.   When the clerk comes round, you'll cut out like fun,
           To avoid a good shower-bath, how quick you run!

TRIO.   Home, home, home, the loafer's home--
           How large is the common loafer's home!

(*Exit Mike, R.1E. Exeunt Major and Joe, L.1E. Scene closes.*)

Scene 2. New Street. Lights up house, U.E.R.H. (*Several Street Sweepers discovered. Enter Mose, dressed as a butcher, with check sleeves, carrying a basket, with meat, on his shoulders. Men sweep.*)

MOSE. (*to Sweepers*) Say, look a-here, you--if you kick up such a dust as that when I'm passin', to spile my beef, I'll lam you!

1ST MAN. We ain't kickin' up as much dust as you are.

MOSE. None of your lip, old fellow; I can't give my customers gritty beef all along o' you.

    (*Knocks at door, and gives beef to servant girl. Enter Newsboy, R.1E.*)

NEWSBOY. Here's the Sun, Herald and Tribune--got the last telegraph news from Williamsburgh! (*To Mose.*) Have a paper, sir?

MOSE. Go long wid yer.

NEWSBOY. I say, butcher, who do yer kill for?

MOSE. What d'ye say?

    (*Newsboy runs off, L.1E. Mose picks up a stone and throws after him. Enter Lize, R.2E., with an open book and a reticule.*)

LIZE. Hello, Mose! What's the matter?

MOSE. Is dat you, Lize? I was a-tryin' to plump one of dem saucy newsboys. What brings you out so early in de mornin'?

LIZE. You see, Mose, we're a little hurried down to the shop, so I turned out sooner than usual.

MOSE. What book have you got there?

LIZE. *Matilda, the Disconsolate.*

MOSE. How do you like it as far as you've got?

LIZE. Oh, it's prime.

MOSE. Have you come to where Lucinda stabs de Count yet? Ain't dat high?

LIZE. No, Mose, I ain't; and I just wish you wouldn't spile the story by tellin' me.

MOSE. Say, Lize, you're a gallus gal, anyhow.

LIZE. I ain't nothin' else.

MOSE. What do yer say for Waxhall to-night?

LIZE. What's a-goin' on? Is de wawdeville plays there?

MOSE. No--there's going to be a first-rate shin-dig; some of our b'hoys'll be there.

LIZE. Will Sykesy be on hand?

MOSE. S'posen he is--what den?

LIZE. Nothin'.

MOSE. Now, look a-here, Lize, I go in fur Bill Sykesy 'cos he runs wid our merchaine--but he mustn't come foolin' round my gal, or I'll give him fits!

LIZE. La! Mose, don't get huffy 'cause I mentioned him; but I'd rather go to Christy's. Did you ever see George Christy play de bones? Ain't he one of 'em?

MOSE. Well, he ain't nothin' else.

LIZE. And that feller with the tambourine musn't be sneezed at neither.

MOSE. Yes, he's some.

LIZE. Do you know I've been learnin' one of their songs--and if it wasn't for bein' in the street, I'd sing it for you.

MOSE. It's too early in de mornin' for many folks to be out--so you're safe. Blow your horn.

   (*Song.* LIZE. *"Lovely Mae," published.*)

MOSE. (*affected*) Well, I'm blowd if that ain't slap up. Lize, you can sing a few.

LIZE. You ought to hear Jenny Bogert and I sing at the shop. We can come it a few, I tell you. But I can't stand talking here--I must go to the shop. Drive on with your meat, Mose.

MOSE. What time will I come up to your shanty?

LIZE. Any time after tea. (*Going.*)

MOSE. Nuff ced--I'm there. (*Exit Lize, L.H.*) She's a gallus gal--she is; I've strong suspicions I'll have to get slung to her one of these days. But I musn't forget my butcher-cart. (*Goes up.*) I say, boy, yer better drive the cart right up to de slaughter-house. The customers are all sarved. What! Yer don't know where de slaughter-house is yet? Well, drive up Chrystie Street till you smell blood, and dere stop.

   (*Exit Mose, U.E.L. Enter Mike, L.1E., meeting Major, R.H.*)

MIKE. Hallo! Major; where have you been?

MAJOR. Been, Mike? Where should I go to lay my laureled head but in the market? Ever since I evacuated the premises, I have had a most ardent desire to imbibe some of the elixir of life; but somehow, my finances will not allow of such extravagance. (*Enter Jake L.H.*) Good morning, Mr. Jake. The eastern sun has scarce lighted the hemisphere, but I find you on the go, like the far-famed Achilles.

JAKE. Oh! stow your gab, Major. Mike, I've a plan to bleed the greenhorn a little more. I watched him to his lodgings last night, and from sundry little circumstances, found out that his bank is not broke yet. I shall enlist the Major in our cause. I'm afraid he'll smoke if I go it on him too strong. I wonder if he's seen the shark in the Park fountain yet? Ha! ha! ha!

MIKE. Ha! ha! ha! Suppose I go to the auction-room and drum up the Peters?

JAKE. Do! I'll be along presently--going--going--gone! We know. (*Exit Mike, laughing, L.H.*) Come, Major, I will want your services for the day--let's take a drink; there's a crib open.

MAJOR. Ah! that word has given me new spirits. Figuratively speaking, I am your slave for life.

JAKE. Oh, none of your nonsense! Come along--cut your poetry and play-acting stuff for a little while, or I'll change my mind.

MAJOR. Change your money as much as you like, but still adhere to your mind.

(*Exeunt Jake and Major, R.1E. Enter George, U.E.R., looking about.*)

GEORGE. Well, the New Yorkers are the laziest mortals I ever met with.

(*A cry of "Fire" heard.*)

What's that? Fire?

(*The bell rings. "Fire" is cried. Boys and men cross the stage from one side to the other. George is looking off U.E.R.H. Mose, L.U.E., pulling on hose. He runs against George, who falls. Scene closes.*)

Scene 3. Front Street. St. Paul's Church. (*Enter Jake and Major, L.1E.*)

JAKE. Now, Major, mind my instructions; pitch it strong; come the dodge well and I'll give you a share.

MAJOR. But do you think he'll recognize me?

JAKE. Pooh! pooh! stuff! It was too dark in the cellar last night, and he has had too much since to think about, so I think you are pretty safe; he's sure to pass this way, so look out.

(*Exit Jake, R.1E. Major takes out a roll of bills and throws them down; then pretends to be looking for them. Enter George, L.H.1E.*)

GEORGE. I'd give anything to find Harry. I've been knocked down in the dirt, had a fire-engine to run along within an inch of my nose; then they told me to get up, as I was in the way. Where shall I go, to get out of the way, I wonder? (*Sees roll of bills.*) What's this? (*Picks them up.*) What a lot of money! (*Sees Major.*) What's the matter, my good man? What are you looking for?

MAJOR. Oh, sir, I am a ruined man! I have just lost all the money I possessed in the world. I have been saving it up for the last twelve years, depriving myself of almost all the necessities of life for the sake of having a little for my family to live on. Oh, dear! oh, dear! what shall I do!

GEORGE. Don't take on, my good man. Here is your money. I've just picked it up--here, take it.

MAJOR. Oh, bless you, sir! (*Takes it.*) Allow me to reward you for your kindness.

GEORGE. It's of no consequence.

MAJOR. But I insist upon it. You have saved me from the poor house in my old age; I can in justice do no more than present you with five dollars for your honesty.

GEORGE. Oh, well, if you like, I'll take it.

MAJOR. (*opening roll*) Here, sir--no, that is a ten! I'm sorry I've not a five dollar bill here.

GEORGE. Oh! never mind.

MAJOR. Yes, sir, I insist upon doing you justice. If you have a five in your possession, give it to me, and take my ten.

GEORGE. Well, if you insist, there.

(*Gives five dollar bill, and takes Major's ten.*)

MAJOR. I wish you a very good morning.

GEORGE. Good morning, sir. (*Exit Major, R.1.E.*) City Trust Bank--that's all right. (*Puts bill into his pocket.*) What a lucky thing it was for him that I happened to find his money; many a one would have kept it all without saying a word. (*Enter Newsboy, L.1E.*)

NEWSBOY. Here's the Sun, Herald, and Tribune--got another battle in Mexico. (*Crosses to R.*)

GEORGE. (*calls him*) Here, boy, let me have a newspaper.

NEWSBOY. Yes, sir!

(*Helps him. George pays him. Newsboy is going. George opens paper and looks at it. Calls Newsboy.*)

GEORGE. I say--this paper is dated August 3d, 1847. How's this?

NEWSBOY. Is it, sir? (*Looks at it.*) So it is; it must be a mistake of the printer; you'll find it all right, sir. (*Exit Newsboy, R.1.E., laughing.*)

GEORGE. It would take me some time to get the hang of this city, if I once set about it. Well, I'll put the paper in my pocket and look it over bye and bye. Now, I'll go and see if I can find Harry.

(*Exit George, R.1E. Enter Mose, L.1E.*)

MOSE. It was a loafer fire, after all; we give 28's fellers fits, though I guess dey won't undertake to race wid our machine any more. We had de rope manned good and strong, and de way de b'hoys laid out of de old bunk-room was sinful. I did think yesterday I'd leave de machine, but I can't do it; I love that ingine better than my dinner; last time she was at de corporation-yard, we plated de brakes and put in new condensil pipes; and de way she works is about right, I tell you. She throws a three-inch stream de prettiest in town. I'd like to see any machine wash us now: I only wish dere'd come a good fire onst just to try; I must be off to de market, or boss'll get cross-grained. (*Going, R.H.*)

HARRY. (*entering, L.H.*) Hello, Mose! Where are you going?

MOSE. Back to de market.

HARRY. Where was the fire?

MOSE. Dere was none; it was only a false alarm.

HARRY. What became of the basket you had last night?

MOSE. Go 'long--I left de little baby in the Park Alms-house.

HARRY. Have you seen anything of George this morning?

MOSE. What George? (*Recollecting.*) Oh! de greenhorn?

HARRY. Yes; have you seen him?

MOSE. Well, I have; I tumbled over him wid de butt. I haven't seen him since.

HARRY. Mose, if you have no objection, I'll walk down Chatham Street with you.

MOSE. Come along! But I say--I seed Lizey when she was goin' to work dis mornin', and I'm bound to take her to Waxhall to-night; we're goin' up to have a sore eye there; will yer come up?

HARRY. Well, Mose, I see nothing at present to prevent me. I presume that Lize, as you call her, is your Dulcinea?

MOSE. I don't know what yer mean by that; but she's one of de gals.

HARRY. She is, eh?

MOSE. Well, she ain't nothin' else. But I say, if you want my company, you'll have to hurry up your cakes.

HARRY. Ha! ha! ha! (*Exeunt.*)

Scene 4. A Mock Auction Store. Counter and Rostrum, L.H. Placards about store. (*Several Peter Funks discovered. Jake, as auctioneer, behind counter. Mike, as a Peter, outside, at end of counter. At end of counter, next the audience, a man is keeping books. George is standing with his hands in his pockets, looking on.*)

JAKE. (*holding a card of knives*) And an aff--and an aff--shall I say five-eighths? (*Bid.*) Five-eighths--five-eighths--going--going. (*Bid.*) Thank 'ye, sir--six--six--six--only six cents for that beautiful card of knives-- it's really too great a sacrifice--going--going--gone! (*Knocks them down.*) Mr. Jacques! Mr. Jacques, one card of knives.

GEORGE. (*aside*) I wish I had bid on 'em.

JACK. (*producing a box of jewelry, pair of pistols, and a piece of cloth*) Gentlemen, allow me to call your attention to this valuable lot; that box of jewelry belongs to the widow of an American officer who was killed in Mexico. What shall I say, gentlemen? Give me a bid.

(*All look at box; George among the rest.*)

GEORGE. Are these real diamonds?

JAKE. Really, sir, I can't say; the lady appeared to be so overcome by her sufferings, that she hadn't time to tell me; but such as they are, gentlemen, give me a bid. If they are real diamonds, think what a bargain you have made; and if they are not, you have surely got the worth of your money. Come, bid, gentlemen--examine for yourselves, gentlemen; here's a splendid pair of pistols--real London make--what do you say a piece for the lot--together with this remnant of superb broadcloth? Give me a bid.

MIKE. Twenty cents a piece.

JAKE. Twenty cents! Really, gentlemen, this is too bad. Here's as valuable a lot of jewelry as there is in New York, and I am only offered twenty cents a piece! Going--going!

GEORGE. Twenty-five!

(*George keeps bidding against himself until the lot is knocked down at fifty cents a piece.*)

JAKE. What name shall I say, sir?

GEORGE. Mr. Parsells.

JAKE. Mr. Parsells, fifty cents a piece. Gentlemen, the next thing I have to offer you is a splendid gold watch, makers, Tobias & Co., London--there's the name; warranted eighty-three holes jeweled--how much will I have?

MIKE. (*takes watch and examines it, says, loud enough for George to hear*) That's a splendid watch, and I shall go in for it!

(*George takes it and examines it.*)

JAKE. (*to Mike*) Well, Mr. Wilson, what is your opinion of that watch?

MIKE. Good!

JAKE. Gentlemen, here's Mr. Wilson, who keeps a large jewelry store in Novagambia, who has come down to purchase stock, pronounces it good. I'll tell you the history of it; that watch was smuggled into this country by a mate of one of our packet ships, and was left here to be sold, on account of his mother dying in Boston, and wants to raise money enough to pay her funeral expenses. How much shall I say for the watch? Remember, gentlemen, I have already advanced him forty dollars on it; so make your bids; don't be afraid; if you should purchase it, and change your mind after, only bring it to me on Monday next, and we will enter it again on our catalogue; so you are safe; come, make a bid; don't waste time.

MIKE. Well, I will say thirty dollars.

JAKE. Thirty dollars, gentlemen--here is a jeweler who bids thirty dollars--thirty--thirty--do I hear any advance on thirty?

GEORGE. Thirty-five.

JAKE. Thank 'ye, sir--thirty five. The sacrifice is too great--literally throwing goods into the street.

(*George continues bidding till runs up to fifty dollars, when Jake knocks it down.*)

Mr. Parsells, fifty dollars. Really, sir, you have a bargain. I'm sorry to inform you, gentlemen, that the sales are closed for the day--trade is so dull. There will be a book auction here this evening, to commence at seven o'clock--the regular sales to-morrow at ten, as usual. Mr. Parsells, if you will step to the book-keeper, he will hand you your bill. (*To boy.*) William, sweep out the store.

(*George goes to Clerk at end of counter.*)

CLERK. Your bill, Mr. Parsells, is four hundred dollars! One lot of jewelry, etc., three hundred and fifty dollars! One gold watch, fifty dollars! Total, four hundred dollars!

GEORGE. There must be some mistake.

JAKE. No, sir, there is no mistake here, sir.

GEORGE. Why, there was not over a dozen pieces of jewelry at fifty cents a piece.

JAKE. Oh, you're in error, sir--there were seven hundred pieces, at fifty cents a piece.

GEORGE. What will I do? I haven't as much money about me as that.

JAKE. Why, sir, in these cases, a deposit is always left.

GEORGE. (*giving bill*) Here's a ten dollar bill.

JAKE. (*takes it*) This bill is bad, sir.

GEORGE. Bad, sir! What do you mean?

JAKE. I mean what I say, sir.

GEORGE. That bill was given me in change, a few minutes before I came in here.

JAKE. Have you no other money by you?

GEORGE. I have--but I must first go and see if you tell the truth about this bill.

JAKE. No--you don't leave here without making a deposit--we ain't going to be swindled, no how.

GEORGE. Do you mean to insult me, sir?

JAKE. I want my dues.

(*They prevent George from going. Enter Harry, C.D.*)

GEORGE. Oh, Harry, I'm glad you're come!

HARRY. What's the matter?

GEORGE. They say that bill is bad.

HARRY. (*looks at it*) So it is--stop a minute.

(*Goes to C.D., and calls "Mose!" Enter Mose, C.D.*)

MOSE. What's up? Say, Bubby, what's de matter?

GEORGE. Why, I bought about a dozen pieces of jewelry and a gold watch, and they make my bill out four hundred dollars!

MOSE. *What!* Say--which is the chap that wanted to charge you four hundred dollars?

GEORGE. That man behind the counter.

MOSE. I'll give him four hundred dollars! (*Goes up to Jake.*) You want four hundred dollars, do you?

(*Peter Funks seize Mose. He throws them off, and knocks Jake down. Tears up counter. General confusion. Scene closes.*)

Scene 5. Front Street. (*Enter Mose and George, L.H.1E.*)

MOSE. Now, look a-here, greenhorn, if you keep running your head in the noose so often, you've got to strangle--dere ain't no fun in fightin' dem auction chaps.

GEORGE. I am really obliged to you, and am sorry if I have caused you any trouble. You didn't get hurt?

MOSE. What! There ain't one in dat crowd can floor me-- I like a good fight, but not one with a parcel of foo-foos like them-- But I must go home-- I've got to get ready for de ball to-night. Ye comin' up?

GEORGE. Yes, if Harry will go, too. I wonder where he is? I lost sight of him in the fight.

MOSE. Oh! he's safe enough. There's no real pluck in dem auction chaps. Only come up to-night, and I'll show you as gallus a piece of calico as any on de floor.

GEORGE. Show me what?

MOSE. I'll show you my prize lamb--she's one of 'em.

(*Exit Mose, 1E.R. It begins to grow gradually dark.*)

GEORGE. I think I'll go up to this place, for I am a connoiseur in cattle-- they may trick me in almost anything in New York, but they can't beat me in judging of cattle.

(*A bright blue light appears, as if from the top of the Museum.*)

What's that? What a singular light! (*It dies away.*) I wonder what it is! (*Flashes up again.*) There it is again! (*Mike saunters on from L.H.1E.*) I beg your pardon, sir, but can you tell me what that is?

MIKE. Oh! That is the comet.

GEORGE. The comet!

MIKE. Yes, sir--it's a great curiosity--only seen once in a lifetime.

(*Light dies away, and them brightens.*)

You see, sir, how regular it keeps time. The first time that comet was seen was on the night Christopher Columbus discovered America.

GEORGE. Indeed!

MIKE. Fact, sir. Do you know how to see it to advantage?

GEORGE. How?

MIKE. Why, you must put your hands up so.

(*Puts up his hands to show him.*)

Then you must take out your watch and count every five minutes.

GEORGE. (*puts up his hands*) There now--how can I look at my watch with both hands up to my eyes?

MIKE. The best way for you, would be to let me hold it, while you look.

GEORGE. No, you don't! (*Puts his finger to his nose.*)

MIKE. Oh! very well. (*Calling.*) Here, Broadway and Bleecker Street!

(*Exit Mike, R.1E.*)

GEORGE. Ha! ha! ha! I was too much for him that time--I'm beginning to get up to their tricks. I shall certainly go home to-morrow, and be satisfied that, however sharp a stranger to New York may be, he'll find plenty of folks ready and willing to teach him. (*Enter Harry, L.H.1E.*) Why, Harry, what has kept you so long?

HARRY. To tell you the truth, George, I saw your cousin Jane, along with Mary and Mrs. Morton, and have prevailed on them to come up to Vauxhall to-night.

GEORGE. Well, I'd like to go--Mose promised to show me some fat cattle there.

HARRY. Cattle? Why, it's a ball in the gardens.

GEORGE. Ball or not, Mose said he had a prize lamb to show me, and then he said something about a piece of gallus calico.

HARRY. Ha! ha! ha! You unsophisticated mortal; he means his sweetheart!

GEORGE. What a guess name for a sweetheart.

HARRY. What's in a name? The rose, by any other name, would smell as sweet. Those honest fellows have a peculiar way of their own.

GEORGE. I should think they had--calling a sweetheart a calico lamb!

HARRY. Let's be off. (*Light flashes up.*)

GEORGE. Stay, Harry! look--at the comet!

HARRY. Ha! ha! ha! Be off with you.

 (*Drags him off, laughing, R.H.1E.   Enter Lize and Jenny, L.1E.*)

LIZE. Come, Jenny, hurry up--I promised Mose to be ready for Waxhall soon after tea!

JENNY. Say, Lizey, can't you wring me in?

LIZE. I s'pose I can, with hard squeezin'--but that Mose of mine is such a dear fellow--he don't care for expense--not he--he thinks there's no gal like me in this village. You ought see him in de market once, I tell you--how killin' he looks! De way he takes hold of de cleaver and fetches it down is sinful! Dere's no mistake but he's one of de b'hoys!

JENNY. He is that! Some one told me that Bill Sykes was cuttin' round you.

LIZE. Sykesy tried, but I bluffed him off. He's got to look a little more gallus, like my Mose, afore he can commence to shine. Do you know, ever since I've been to Christy's that duett has been haunting me.

JENNY. What--the one your learnt me?

LIZE. Yes--let's run over it--no one's about.

Duet. LIZE and JENNY.

"*Oh Lud, Gals.*"

LIZE. Here we are, as you diskiver,
     All the way from roaring river--
     My wife dies--I'll get another
     Pretty yaller gal--just like t'other;
     Oh Lud, Gals, give me chaw tobacco!

JENNY. Oh, dear--fotch along de whisky,
     My head swims when I get tipsy!

 (*Exeunt, R.1E.*)

Scene 6. Vauxhall Garden. Arches of variegated lamps. Refreshment tables, R. and L. (*Company discovered dancing a gallopade. Harry and Jane, George and Mary, Mr. and Mrs. Morton, and another couple form the first set. All go up at end of dance. Enter Mose and Lize, U.E.L.*)

MOSE. Say, Lizey, ain't this high?

LIZE. Well, it ain't nothin' else.

HARRY. (*advances to Mose*) Good evening, Mose--how are you enjoying yourself?

MOSE. Oh, great! How are you gettin' on?

HARRY. Capital. (*To Mose, aside.*) Can't you introduce me?

MOSE. Oh, I forgot--Lize, this is Mr. Gordon. (*She curtsies.*) Don't you feel like eatin' something?

LIZE. I do that.

(*They go to table, R.H., and sit. Harry turns upstage.*)

MOSE. (*knocking on the table*) Say, ain't somebody comin' soon? (*Enter Waiter, U.E.L.*) Oh! Look a-here--take de lady's order. Lize, what'll you have?

LIZE. A cup of coffee, and nine doughnuts!

MOSE. Look a-here--you got any pork and beans?

WAITER. Yes, sir.

MOSE. Bring me a plate of pork and beans. (*Waiter is going.*) Say, a large piece of pork, and don't stop to count de beans.

WAITER. Anything else, sir?

MOSE. Yes--a brandy skin!

(*Enter Sykesy and Jenny, U.E.L., and take seats at table, L.H. Re-enter Waiter with refreshments for Mose and Lize, and is going, when Sykesy calls him.*)

SYKESY. Here, Napoleon--take a slight order from that lady.

JENNY. I'll take a veal cutlet--round bone.

SYKESY. Give me a corner roll and some fried liver.

HARRY. (*advancing with Jane*) Really, your condescension in honoring this place with your presence makes me indeed happy, for I feel assured that it was partly to please me that you came here.

JANE. Indeed! You flatter yourself.

HARRY. I do flatter myself that the vows I have already made to you have not been unheeded.

JANE. Well, I accept you on condition that you give up roaming.

HARRY. I swear it! (*They retire a little.*)

MARY. (*advancing with George, L.H.*) Do you still hold your determination to sail from New York in the first boat?

GEORGE. I must say--since becoming acquainted with you, I am sadly tempted to remain.

MARY. Indeed, sir!

MR. MORTON. (*advancing with Mrs. Morton*) Well, young folks, you seem to be quite at home in each other's company--but for all that, let's have no billing or cooing in corners. Come--out with it at once! Mary, you seem fond of my friend, Mr. Parsells. His father is an old friend of mine, and a substantial one--so, take him! Jane, you have Mr. Gordon's arm--keep it! We'll have your weddings both on the same day!

MRS. MORTON. But, Mr. Morton, maybe you'll ask if the young folks are agreeable?

MR. MORTON. There's no occasion to ask that--I see they are satisfied--so let's be jolly!

HARRY. Stay, Mr. Morton--I have a friend here I would like you to know, for, in spite of his *outré* manners, he has a noble heart. (*Calls.*) Mose!

MOSE. What yer want?

HARRY. Come here a minute.

MOSE. (*comes forward, sucking his fingers*) Well, here I am.

HARRY. Mr. Morton, Mose--Mose, Mr. and Mrs. Morton.

MOSE. (*turns and sees Mrs. Morton, takes Harry aside*) Say, ain't that the old woman I tried to kiss in the ten-pin alley? (*To her.*) I would apologize, ma'am, but I'm afraid of making a muss of it.

MRS. MORTON. I forgive you, sir.

MOSE. Thank 'ye, ma'am! I want to show you something--Lize! (*Calls her.*) Lize! Why don't you come along? Don't be eatin' up all de man has in de house!

LIZE. (*comes down*) Here I am, Mose.

MOSE. (*introducing her*) Ain't she gallus?

(*A great row is heard outside, U.E.L. Waiter rushes on.*)

WAITER. I beg your pardon, sir, but is your name Mose?

MOSE. It ain't nothin' else.

WAITER. There's a gentleman outside who has got into a little trouble, and has been calling for you--I think he calls himself Mr. Sykes.

MOSE. What! Sykesy in a muss? (*To Harry.*) Look here! You just take care of my gal! I'll lam some of 'em, I know!

LIZE. Bravo! Mose, go to it! I'll hold your coat!

(*Mose is going up. Harry stops him.*)

HARRY. Mose, don't go in that manner. (*Points to audience.*) Remember them!

MOSE. Oh, yes--I forgot. (*To audience.*) Look a-here, ladies and gentlemen--don't be down on me 'cos I'm goin' to leave you--but Sykesy's got in a muss, and I'm bound to see him righted, 'cos he runs wid our machine, you know--and if you don't say no, why, I'll scare up this crowd again to-morrow night, and then you can take another . . .

GLANCE AT NEW YORK!

Rip Van Winkle
as acted by Joseph Jefferson III (1829-1905)

For many late 19th century Americans with a Rogers statue of Washington Irving's character on Victorian tables in their front parlors, Joseph Jefferson *was* Rip Van Winkle. And with good reason. In 1881 Jefferson confessed that he had played "Rip" about 2,500 times, and he continued to perform that role almost exclusively until he retired from the stage in 1904.

It all started with Irving's story in *The Sketchbook* in 1819. Over the next forty years, at least four dramatizations appeared: an anonymous version in Albany, New York, in 1828; an adaptation in 1829 by John Kerr; a version in 1850 by Charles Burke, Jefferson's half-brother; and an English version by Thomas H. Lacy. Jefferson--the last of three actors of this name--became interested in Rip during the summer of 1858, fully aware of the story's theatrical history. Drawing from past versions, Jefferson created a play which he performed in Washington, D.C., in 1859 and occasionally on a later tour to Australia. But he was disappointed with his work.

Still dissatisfied after some periodic tinkering with his play, Jefferson met Dion Boucicault in London and commissioned him to rework the script. An accomplished actor, manager, and playwright, Boucicault was also a skillful "play doctor," but it is impossible to determine his exact contributions. This new version opened at the Adelphi Theatre in London on September 5, 1865, and was an instant success with an initial run of 170 nights. From that time on, Jefferson, a pleasantly intelligent human being, sensitive to the idiosyncrasies of his public, dominated the American stage in a starring vehicle *par excellence*. The play was first published in 1895.

Joseph Jefferson thrived as Rip Van Winkle, but in a little poem to a friend, he revealed a wry attitude toward his success, as he commented on his "future."

> For myself when I knock at the gate with some fear,
> I know that St. Peter will say
> Walk in, young comedian, and act with us here,
> But for Heaven's sake get a new play.

Joseph Jefferson

Joseph Jefferson as Rip Van Winkle in Act IV

RIP VAN WINKLE

(1865)

as acted by Joseph Jefferson

CHARACTERS

Rip Van Winkle	Jacob Stein
Derrick Von Beekman	Gretchen
Nicholas Vedder	Meenie
Hendrick	Kätchen
Cockles	Villagers
Seth Slough	Demons

ACT 1.

Scene. The village of Falling Waters, set amid familiar and unmistakable Hudson River scenery, with the shining river itself and the noble heights of the Kaatskills visible in the distance. In the foreground, to the left of the stage, is a country inn bearing the sign of George III. In the wall of the inn, a window closed by a solid wooden shutter. To the right of the stage, an old cottage with a door opening into the interior; before the cottage stands a bench holding a wash-tub, with a washboard, soap and clothes in the tub. In the center of the stage, a table and chairs, and on the table a stone pitcher and two tin cups. (*As the curtain rises, Gretchen is discovered washing, and little Meenie sitting nearby on a low stool. The sound of a chorus and laughter comes from the inn.*)

GRETCHEN. Shouting and drinking day and night. (*Laughter is heard from the inn.*) Hark how they crow over their cups while their wives are working at home, and their children are starving.
 (*Enter Derrick from the inn with a green bag, followed by Nick Vedder. Derrick places his green bag on the table.*)
DERRICK. Not a day, not an hour. If the last two quarters' rent be not paid by this time tomorrow, out you go!
NICK. Oh, come, Derrick, you won't do it. Let us have a glass, and talk the matter over; good liquor opens the heart. Here, Hendrick! Hendrick!
 (*Enter Hendrick.*)

HENDRICK. Yes, father.

DERRICK. So that is your brat?

NICK. Yes, that is my boy.

DERRICK. Then the best I can wish him is that he won't take after his father, and become a vagabond and a penniless outcast.

NICK. Those are hard words to hear in the presence of my child.

HENDRICK. Then why don't you knock him down, father?

GRETCHEN. I'll tell you why--

DERRICK. Gretchen!

GRETCHEN. (*wiping her arms and coming to front of tub*) It is because your father is in that man's power. And what's the use of getting a man down, if you don't trample on him?

NICK. Oh, that is the way of the world.

GRETCHEN. (*to Hendrick*) Go in, boy. I want to speak to your father, and my words may not be fit for you to hear. Yonder is my little girl; go and play with her. (*Hendrick and Meenie exeunt into the cottage.*) Now, Derrick, Vedder is right; you won't turn him out of his house yonder.

DERRICK. And why not? Don't he owe me a year's rent?

GRETCHEN. And what do you owe him? Shall I sum up your accounts for you? Ten years ago, this was a quiet village, and belonged mostly to my husband, Rip Van Winkle, a foolish, idle fellow. That house yonder has since been his ruin. Yes; bit by bit, he has parted with all he had, to fill the mouths of sots and boon companions, gathered around him in yonder house. And you, Derrick--you supplied him with the money to waste in riot and drink. Acre by acre, you've sucked in his land to swell your store. Yonder miserable cabin is the only shelter we have left; but that is mine. Had it been his, he would have sold it you, Derrick, long ago, and wasted its price in riot.

   (*Vedder, who has been enjoying Derrick's discomfiture during this speech, is unable to control himself, and at the end of the speech, bursts into a loud laugh.*)

Aye, and you too, Nick Vedder; you have ruined my husband between you.

NICK. Oh, come, Mrs. Van Winkle, you're too hard. I couldn't refuse Rip's money in the way of business; I had my rent to pay.

GRETCHEN. And shall I tell you why you can't pay it? It is because you have given Rip credit, and he has ended by drinking you out of house and home. Your window-shutter is not wide enough to hold the score against him; it is full of chalk. Deny it if you can.

NICK. I do deny it. There now!

GRETCHEN. Then why do you keep that shutter closed? I'll show you why. (*Goes to inn, opens shutter, holds it open, pointing at Rip's score.*) That's why, Nick Vedder, you're a good man in the main, if there is such a thing. (*Derrick laughs.*) Aye, and I doubt it. (*Turning on him.*) But you are the pest of this village, and the hand of every woman in it ought to help pull down that drunkard's nest of yours, stone by stone.

NICK. Come, Dame Van Winkle, you're too hard entire; now a man must have his odd time, and he's none the worse for being a jolly dog.

GRETCHEN. No, none the worse. He sings a good song; he tells a good story--oh, he's a glorious fellow! Did you ever see the wife of a jolly dog? Well, she lives in a kennel. Did you ever see the children of a jolly dog? They are the street curs, and their home is the gutter.

(*Goes up to the wash-tub, and takes revenge on the clothing she scrubs.*)

NICK. (*getting up and approaching Gretchen timidly*) I tell you what it is, Dame Van Winkle, I don't know what your home may be, but judging from the rows I hear over there, and the damaged appearance of Rip's face after having escaped your clutches-- (*Gretchen looks up angrily; Nick retreats a few paces hastily.*) I should say that a gutter was a luxurious abode compared with it, and a kennel a peaceful retreat.

(*Exit Nick hurriedly, laughing, to the inn. Gretchen looks up angrily, throws the cloth she has been wringing after him, and resumes washing. Derrick laughs, walks up, and puts one foot on the bench.*)

DERRICK. Is it true, Gretchen? Are you truly miserable with Rip?

GRETCHEN. Ain't you pleased to hear it? Come, then and warm your heart at my sorrow. Ten years ago I might have had you, Derrick. But I despised you for your miserly ways, and threw myself away on a vagabond.

DERRICK. You and I shared him between us. I took his estate, and you took his person. Now, I've improved my half. What have you done with yours?

GRETCHEN. I can't say that I have prospered with it. I've tried every means to reclaim him, but he is as obstinant and perverse as a Dutch pig. But the worst in him--and what I can't stand--is his good-humour. It drives me frantic when, night after night, he comes home drunk and helplessly good-humoured! Oh, I can't stand that!

DERRICK. Where is he now?

GRETCHEN. We had a tiff yesterday, and he started. He has been out all night. Only wait until he comes back! The longer he stops out, the worse it will be for him.

DERRICK. Gretchen, you've made a great mistake, but there is time enough to repair it. You are comely still, thrifty, and that hard sort of grain that I most admire in woman. (*Looks cautiously around. Leans on tub.*) Why not part with Rip for ever, and share my fortune?

GRETCHEN. Oh, no, Derrick; you've got my husband in your clutches, but you can't get them around me. If Rip would only mend his ways, he would see how much I love him; but no woman could love you, Derrick; for woman is not a domestic animal, glad to serve and fawn upon a man for the food and shelter she can get; and that is all she would ever get from you, Derrick.

(*Piling the clothes on the washboard and shouldering it.*)

DERRICK. The time may come when you'll change your tune.

GRETCHEN. Not while Rip lives, bad as he is. (*Exit into cottage.*)

DERRICK. Then I'll wait until you've killed him. Her spirit is not broken yet. But patience, Derrick, patience; in another month I'll have my claws on all that remains of Rip's property--yonder cottage and grounds; then I'll try you again, my lady.

(*Enter Cockles, with papers in his hand, running towards the inn.*)

How now, you imp? What brings you here so full of a hurry? Some mischief's in your head, or your heels would not be so busy.

COCKLES. I've brought a letter for you from my employer. There it is.

DERRICK. (*examining letter*) Why, the seal is broken!

COCKLES. Yes, I read it as I came along.

DERRICK. Now I apprenticed this vagabond to my lawyer, and this is his gratitude.

COCKLES. Don't waste your breath, nunky, for you'll want it; for when you read that, if it don't take you short in the wind, I'll admire you.

DERRICK. (*reads*) "You must obtain from Rip Van Winkle a proper conveyance of the lands he has sold to you. The papers he has signed are in fact nothing but mortgages on his estate. If you foreclose, you must sell the property, which has lately much advanced in value; and it would sell for enough to pay off your loan, and all your improvements would enure to the benefit of Rip Van Winkle."

COCKLES. There, now, see what you've been doing of--wasting your money and my expectations on another chap's property. Do you want to leave me a beggar?

DERRICK. (*reads*) "I enclose a deed for him to sign that will make him safe."

COCKLES. Of course he'll sign it; he won't wait to be asked--he'll be in such a hurry.

DERRICK. All my savings--all my money--sunk in improving this village!

COCKLES. Yes, instead of physicking Rip, as you thought, you've been coddling him all the while.

DERRICK. All these houses I've built are on another man's land. What shall I do?

COCKLES. Pull them down again; pull them down.

DERRICK. Ass--dolt that I have been!

COCKLES. Calling yourself names won't mend it, nunky.

DERRICK. The imp is right. Rip must be made to sign this paper. But how--how?

COCKLES. How? How? How's a big word sometimes, ain't it, nunky?

DERRICK. Rip would not do it if he knew what he was about. But he can't read--nor write, for the matter of that. But he can make his cross, and I can cajole him.

COCKLES. Look sharp, nunky. The man that's looking round for a fool and picks up Rip Van Winkle, will let him drop again very quick.

DERRICK. He is poor; I'll show him a handful of money. He's a drunkard; I'll give him a stomachful of liquor. Go in, boy, and leave me to work this; and let this be a lesson to you hereafter; beware the fatal effects of poverty and drink.

COCKLES. Yes--and parting with my money on bad security.

(*Exit Cockles. Laughter outside.*)

DERRICK. Here he comes now, surrounded by all the dogs and children in the district. They cling around him like flies around a lump of sugar.

(*Enter Rip, running and skipping, carrying one small child pickaback, and surrounded by a swarm of others hanging on the skirts of his coat. He is laughing like a child himself. His merry blue eyes twinkle with delight. He is dressed in an old deerskin coat, a pair of breeches which had once been red, now tattered, patched, and frayed, leather gaiters and shoes equally dilapidated, a shapeless felt hat with a bit of the brim hanging loose--the whole stained and weather-worn to an almost uniform clay-colour, except for the bright blue of his jean shirt and the scarlet of his long whisp of a necktie. One of the boys carries his gun.*)

RIP. (*taking his gun from the boy*) There, run along mit you; run along.

(*The children scamper off. Rip stands laughing and watching them.*)

DERRICK. The vagabond looks like the father of the village.

RIP. (*calls after children*) Hey! you let my dog Schneider alone there; you hear that. Sock de Jacob de bist eine for donner spits poo--yah--

DERRICK. Why, what's the matter, Rip?

RIP. (*coming down and shaking hands with Derrick*) Oh, how you was, Derrick? How you was?

DERRICK. You seem in trouble.

RIP. Oh, yah; you know them fellers. Vell, I tole you such a funny thing. (*Laughing.*) Just now, as me and Schneider was comin' along through the willage--Schneider's my dawg; I don't know whether you know him?

> (*Rip always speaks of Schneider as if he were a person, and one in whom his hearer took as profound an interest as himself.*)

Well, them fellers went and tied a tin kettle mit Schneider's tail, and how he did run then, mit the kettle banging about. Well, I didn't hi him comin'. He run betwixt me and my legs, an' spilt me an' all them children in the mud--yah, that's a fact. (*Rip leans his gun against the cottage.*)

DERRICK. (*aside*) Now's my time. (*Aloud.*) Vedder! Vedder!

> (*Vedder appears at the door of the inn.*)

Bring us a bottle of liquor. Bring us your best, and be quick.

NICK. What's in the wind now? The devil's to pay when Derrick stands treat!

> (*Exit Nick, then re-enter with bottle and cups in left hand. Hands bottle to Derrick. Rip lounges forward, and perches on the corner of the table.*)

DERRICK. (*rising and approaching Rip*) Come, Rip, what do you say to a glass?

RIP. (*takes a cup and holds it to be filled*) Oh, yah; now what do I generally say to a glass? I say it's a fine thing--when there's plenty in it. Ve gates! Ve gates! (*Shakes hands with Nick.*) And then I says more to what's in it than I do to the glass. Now you wouldn't believe it--that's the first one I've had today.

DERRICK. How so?

RIP. (*dryly*) Because I couldn't get it before, I suppose.

DERRICK. Then let me fill him up for you.

RIP. No, that is enough for the first one.

NICK. Come, Rip, a bumper for the first one.

RIP. That is enough for the first one.

DERRICK. Come, Rip, let me fill him up for you.

RIP. (*with ludicrous decision and dignity*) I believe I know how much to drink. When I says a thing, I mean it.

DERRICK. Oh, well-- (*Turns aside, and starts to fill his own cup.*)

RIP. All right; come along.

> (*Holding out his glass, and laughing at his own inconsistency.*)

Here's your good health, and your families', and may they live long and prosper!

> (*They all drink. At the end, Nick smacks his lips and exclaims "Ah!" Derrick repeats the same and Rip repeats after Derrick. To Nick, sadly.*)

Ah, you may well go "Ah!" and smack your chops over that. You don't give me such schnapps when I come. Derrick, my score is too big now.

(*Jerking his head towards the shutter, he notices that it is open.*)

What you go and open that window for? That's fine schnapps, Nick. Where you got that?

NICK. That's high Dutch, Rip--high Dutch, and ten years in bottle. Why, I had that in the very day of your wedding. We broached the keg under yonder shed. Don't you recollect?

RIP. Is that the same?

NICK. Yes.

RIP. I thought I knowed that licker. You had it ten years ago? (*Laughing suddenly.*) I would not have kept it so long. But stop, mein freund; that's more than ten years ago.

NICK. No, it ain't.

RIP. It's the same day I got married?

NICK. Yes.

RIP. Well, I know by that. You think I forgot the day I got married? Oh, no, my friend; I remember that day long as I live.

(*Serious for a moment, takes off his hat, and puts it on the table.*)

DERRICK. Ah! Rip, I remember Gretchen then, ten years ago. Zounds, how I envied you!

RIP. (*looking up, surprised*) Did you? (*Winks at Nick. Then, suddenly remembering.*) So did I. You didn't know what was comin', Derrick.

DERRICK. She was a beauty.

RIP. What? Gretchen? Yes, she was. She was a pretty girl. My! my! Yah! we was a fine couple altogether. (*Holding out his cup to Derrick, who fills it from the bottle.*) Well, come along.

NICK. Yes, come along.

(*Nick takes water pitcher from the table and starts to fill up Rip's cup. Rip stops him.*)

RIP. (*who has been lounging against the table, sits on it, and puts his feet on the chair*) Stop! I come along mitout that, Nick Vedder. (*Sententiously.*) Good licker and water is like man and wife.

DERRICK and NICK. How's that, Rip?

RIP. (*laughing*) They don't agree together. I always like my licker single. Well, here's your good health, and your families', and may they live long and prosper! (*They all drink.*)

NICK. That's right, Rip; drink away, and drown your sorrow.

RIP. (*drolly*) Yes; but she won't drown. My wife is my sorrow, and you cannick drown her. She tried it once, but couldn't do it.

DERRICK and NICK. Why? How so?

RIP. (*puts down his cup and clasps his knee, still perched on the corner of the table*) Didn't you know that Gretchen like to got drowned?

DERRICK and NICK. No.

RIP. (*puts hat on*) That's the funniest thing of the whole of it. It's the same day I got married; she was comin' across the river there in the ferry-boat to get married mit me--

DERRICK and NICK. Yes.

RIP. Well, the boat she was comin' in got upsetted.

DERRICK and NICK. Ah!

RIP. Well, but she wasn't in it.

DERRICK and NICK. Oh!

RIP. (*explaining quite seriously*) No, that's what I say; if she had been in the boat what got upsetted, maybe she might have got drowned. (*More and more reflective.*) I don't know how it was she got left somehow or other. Women is always behind that way--always.

DERRICK. But surely, Rip, you would have risked your life to save such a glorious creature as she was.

RIP. (*incredulously*) You mean I would yump in and pull Gretchen out?

DERRICK. Yes.

RIP. Oh, would I? (*Suddenly remembering.*) Oh, you mean then--yes, I believe I would then. (*With simple conviction.*) But it would be more my duty now than it was then.

DERRICK. How so?

RIP. (*quite seriously*) Why, you see when a feller gets married a good many years mit his wife, he gets very much attached to her.

NICK. (*pompously*) Ah, he does indeed.

RIP. (*winks at Derrick and points at Nick with his thumb*) But if Mrs. Van Winkle was a-drowning in the water now, an' she says to me, "Rip, come an' save your wife!" I would say, "Mrs. Van Winkle, I will yust go home and think about it." Oh, no, Derrick, if ever Gretchen tumbles in the water, she's got to swim now, you mind that.

DERRICK. She was here just now, anxiously expecting you home.

RIP. I know she's keeping it hot for me.

NICK. What, your dinner, Rip?

RIP. No, the broomstick. (*Exit Nick into house, laughing.*) Derrick, whenever I come back from the mountains, I always stick the game-bag in the window and creep in behind.

DERRICK. (*sitting on table beside Rip*) Have you anything now?

RIP. (*dropping into the chair Derrick has left, leaning back, putting hands behind his head*) What for game? (*With humorous indifference.*) No, not a tail, I believe, not a feather.

DERRICK. (*touching Rip on the shoulder and shaking a bag of money*) Rip, suppose you were to hang this bagful of money inside, don't you think it would soothe her down, eh?

RIP. (*sitting up*) For me, is that?

DERRICK. Yes.

RIP. (*with a shrewd glance*) Ain't you yokin' mit me?

DERRICK. No, Rip, I've prospered with the lands you've sold me, and I'll let you have a loan on easy terms. I'll take no interest.

RIP. (*getting up and walking forward, with decision*) No, I'm afraid I might pay you again some day, Derrick.

DERRICK. And so you shall, Rip, pay me when you please.

   (*He puts the bag in Rip's hands and forces his fingers over it, turns, and goes to the table.*)

Say in twenty years--twenty years from this day. Ah, where shall we be then?

RIP. (*quizzically, and half to himself*) I don't know about myself; but I think I can guess where you'll be about that time. (*Sits down.*)

DERRICK. Well, Rip, I'll just step into the inn and draw out a little acknowledgment.

RIP. (*who has been leaning forward with elbows on knees, softly chinking the bag in his hand, looks up suddenly*) 'Knowledgment--for what is that?

DERRICK. Yes, for you to put your cross to.

RIP. (*indifferently*) All right; bring it along.

DERRICK. No fear of Gretchen now, eh, Rip?

RIP. (*plunged in thought*) Oh, no.

DERRICK. You feel quite comfortable now, don't you, Rip? (*Exit to inn.*)

RIP. Oh, yah! (*Suddenly serious and much mystified.*) Well, I don't know about that. Derrick! Derrick! (*Holding up bag and chinking it.*) It don't chink like good money neither. (*Grimly.*) It rattles like a snake in a hole.

GRETCHEN. (*inside the cottage*) Out with that lazy, idle cur! I won't have him here. Out, I say!

RIP. I'm glad I'm not in there now. I believe that's Schneider what she's lickin'; he won't have any backbone left in him. (*Sadly.*) I would rather she would lick me than the dog; I'm more used to it than he is. (*Gets up, and looks in at the window.*) There she is at the wash-tub. (*Admiring her energy, almost envying it.*) What a hard-workin' woman that is! (*With the air of a profound moral reflection.*) Well, somebody must do it, I suppose. She's comin' here now; she's got some broomstick mit her, too.

(*Rip snatches up his gun and slinks off around the corner of the house. Enter Gretchen with broomstick, followed by Hendrick and Meenie, carrying clothes-basket.*)

GRETCHEN. Come along, children. Now, you take the washing down to Dame Van Sloe's, then call at the butcher's and tell him that my husband has not got back yet, so I will have to go down myself to the marsh and drive up the bull we have sold to him. Tell him the beast shall be in his stable in half an hour; so let him have the money ready to pay me for it.

(*Rip has crept in and sat on the bench behind Gretchen.*)

Ah, it is the last head of cattle we have left. Houses, lands, beasts, everything gone--everything except a drunken beast who nobody would buy or accept as a gift. Rip! Rip! wait until I get you home!

(*Threatening an imaginary Rip with broomstick. With a comical grimace, Rip tiptoes back behind the house.*)

Come, children, to work, to work! (*Exit.*)

RIP. (*re-entering cautiously, laughing to himself*) She gone to look after the bull. She better not try the broomstick on him; he won't stand it.

(*Drops into the chair, with his back to the audience.*)

HENDRICK. Oh, Meenie, there's your father.

RIP. (*holds out his arms, and Meenie runs into them; taking her in his arms, and embracing her with great tenderness*) Ah, little gorl, was you glad to see your father come home?

MEENIE. Oh, yes!

RIP. (*holding her close*) I don't believe it, was you? Come here.

(*Getting up and leading her to the chair beside the table.*)

Let me look at you; I don't see you for such a long time; come here. I don't deserve to have a thing like that belong to me.

(*Takes his hat off as if in reverence.*)

You're too good for a drunken, lazy feller like me, that's a fact.

(*Bites his underlip, looks up and brushes away a tear.*)

MEENIE. (*kneeling by him*) Oh, no, you are a good papa!

RIP. No, I wasn't: no good father would go and rob his child; that's what I've done. Why, don't you know, Meenie, all the houses and lands in the village was mine--they would all have been yours when you grew up! Where they gone now? I gone drunk 'em up, that's where they gone. Hendrick, you just take warnin' by that; that's what licker do; see that? (*Holds up the skirt of coat.*) Bring a man to hunger and rags. Is there any more in that cup over there? Give it to me.

(*Rip makes this confession with a childlike simplicity. The tears come, and he brushes them away once or twice. When he asks for the cup at the end, it seems but the natural conclusion of his speech.*)

HENDRICK. (*hands him cup; Rip drinks*) Don't cry, Rip; Meenie does not want your money, for when I'm a big man I shall work for her, and she shall have all I get.

MEENIE. Yes, and I'll have Hendrick, too.

RIP. (*greatly amused*) You'll have Hendrick, too. (*With mock gravity.*) Well, is this all settled?

HENDRICK. Yes, Meenie and me have made it all up.

RIP. I didn't know, I only thought you might speak to me about it, but if it's all settled, Meenie, then get married mit him. (*Laughing silently.*) You goin' to marry my daughter? Well, now, that's very kind of you. Marry one another? (*Children nod. Rip speaks with immense seriousness.*) Well, here's your good health, and your family, may they live long and prosper. (*To Hendrick.*) What you goin' to do when you get married, and grow up and so? (*Leans forward.*)

HENDRICK. I'm not going to stop here with father; oh, no, that won't do. I'm going with Uncle Hans in his big ship to the North Pole, to catch whales.

RIP. Goin' to cotch wahales mit the North Pole? That's a long while away from here.

HENDRICK. Yes, but uncle will give me ten shillings a month, and I will tell him to pay it all to Meenie.

RIP. There! He's goin' to pay it all to you; that's a good boy, that's a good boy.

MEENIE. Yes, and I'll give it all to you to keep for us.

RIP. (*with one of his little explosive laughs*) I wouldn't do that, my darlin'; maybe if you give it to me, you don't get it back again. Hendrick! (*Suddenly earnest.*) You shall marry Meenie when you grow up, but you mustn't drink.

HENDRICK. (*slapping Rip on the knee*) I'll never touch a drop.

RIP. (*quite seriously*) You won't, nor me either; shake hands upon it. Now we swore off together. (*With a change of tone.*) I said so so many times, and never kept my word once, never. (*Drinks.*)

HENDRICK. I've said so once, and I'll keep mine.

DERRICK. (*outside*) Well, bring it along with you.

RIP. Here comes Derrick; he don't like some children; run along mit you.

   (*Exeunt children with basket. Enter Derrick, from inn, with document.*)

DERRICK. There, Rip, is the little acknowledgment. (*Handing it to him.*)

RIP. 'Knowledgment. (*Putting on hat.*) For what is that?

DERRICK. That is to say I loaned you the money.

RIP. (*lounging back in his chair*) I don't want that; I would lose it if I had it. (*Fills his cup from the bottle, and speaks blandly.*) I don't want it.

DERRICK. Don't you? But I do.

RIP. (*with simple surprise*) For what?

DERRICK. Why, for you to put your cross to. Why, bless me, I've forgotten my pen and ink. (*Enter Cockles.*) But luckily here comes my nephew with it. (*Aside.*) And in time to witness the signature.

RIP. Say, Derrick, have you been writing all that paper full in the little time you been in the house there?

(*Turns the paper about curiously. Pours out more schnapps.*)

DERRICK. Yes, every word of it.

RIP. Have you? (*With great simplicity.*) Well, just read it out loud to me.

DERRICK. (*aside*) Does he suspect? (*Aloud.*) Why, Rip, this is the first time you ever wanted anything more than the money.

RIP. (*clasping his hands behind his head with an air of lordly indifference*) Yes, I know; but I got nothing to do now. I'm a little curious about that, somehow.

COCKLES. (*aside to Derrick*) The fish has taken the ground bait, but he's curious about the hook.

DERRICK. (*aside*) I dare not read a word of it.

COCKLES. (*aside*) Nunky's stuck.

DERRICK. Well, Rip, I suppose you don't want to hear the formalities.

RIP. The what?

DERRICK. The preliminaries.

RIP. (*indolently*) I'll take it all--Bill, Claws, and Feathers.

(*Rip leans forward, rests his head on his hand, and looks at the ground.*)

DERRICK. "Know all men by these presents, that I, Rip Van Winkle, in consideration of the sum of sixteen pounds received by me from Derrick Von Beekman"--

(*Looks around at Cockles; they wink knowingly at each other. Continues as if reading. Watching Rip.*)

--"do promise and undertake to pay the same in twenty years from date."

(*Rip looks up; as he does so, Derrick drops his eyes to the document, then looks as if he had just finished reading.*)

There, now are you satisfied?

RIP. (*takes the document and speaks in childlike surprise*) Well, well, and does it take all that pen and ink to say such a little thing as that?

DERRICK. Why, of course it does.

COCKLES. (*aside to Derrick*) Oh, the fool! He swallows it whole, hook and all.

RIP. (*spreading the paper on the table*) Where goes my cross, Derrick?

DERRICK. (*pointing*) There, you see I've left a nice little white corner for you.

RIP. (*folds up paper in a leisurely manner and puts it in game-bag*) W-e-l-l, I'll yust think about it. (*Looks up at Derrick innocently.*)

DERRICK. Think about it? Why, what's the matter, Rip, isn't the money correct?

RIP. (*chuckling*) Oh, yes, I got the money all right. Oh! you mean about signing it. (*Rising. At a loss for a moment.*) Stop, yesterday was Friday, wasn't it?

DERRICK. So it was.

RIP. (*with an air of conviction*) Well, I never do nothing like that the day after Friday, Derrick. (*Rip walks away towards his cottage.*)

DERRICK. (*aside*) The idiot! What can that signify? But I must not arouse his suspicions by pressing him. (*Aloud.*) You are right, Rip; sign it when you please; but I say, Rip, now that you're in funds, won't you help your old friend Nick Vedder, who owes me a year's rent?

RIP. (*coming back to the table*) Oh, yah, I will wipe off my score, and stand treat to the whole village.

DERRICK. Run, boy, and tell all the neighbours that Rip stands treat.

RIP. (*leans on back of chair*) An', Cockles, tell them we'll have a dance.

COCKLES. A dance! (*Runs off.*)

DERRICK. And I'll order the good cheer for you. (*Exit.*)

RIP. So do! So do! (*Cogitating dubiously.*) I don't understand it.

(*Enter Hendrick with the basket over his head, followed by Meenie.*)

Oh, you've come back?

HENDRICK. Yes, we've left the clothes.

RIP. Meenie, you take in the basket. (*Exit Meenie into cottage.*) Hendrick, come here. (*Hendrick kneels between Rip's knees.*) So you are going to marry my daughter? (*Hendrick nods.*) So, so. That's very kind of yer. (*Abruptly.*) Why you don't been to school today, you go to school some times, don't you?

HENDRICK. Yes, when father can spare me.

RIP. What do you learn mit that school--pretty much something? (*Laughing at his mistake.*) I mean, everything?

HENDRICK. Yes; reading, writing and arithmetic.

RIP. Reading, and what?

HENDRICK. And writing, and arithmetic.

RIP. (*puzzled*) Writing and what?

HENDRICK. Arithmetic.

RIP. (*with profound astonishment and patting Hendrick's head*) I don't see how the little mind can stand it all. Can you read?

HENDRICK. Oh, yes!

RIP. (*with a serious affection of incredulity*) I don't believe it; now, I'm just goin' to see if you can read. If you can't read, I won't let you marry my daughter. No, sir. (*Drolly.*) I won't have nobody in my family what can't read. (*Taking out the paper.*) Can you read ritmatics like that?

HENDRICK. Yes, that's writing.

RIP. (*nonplussed*) Oh! I thought it was reading.

HENDRICK. It's reading and writing, too.

RIP. What, both together. (*Suspiciously looking at the paper.*) Oh, yes; I didn't see that before; go long with it.

HENDRICK. (*reads*) "Know all men by these presents"--

RIP. (*pleased, leaning back in his chair*) Yah! That's right, what a wonderful thing de readin' is; why you can read it pretty nigh as good as Derrick, yes, you do; go long.

HENDRICK. "That I, Rip Van Winkle,"--

RIP. (*taking off his hat, and holding it with his hands behind his head*) Yah, that's right; you read it yust as well as Derrick; go long.

HENDRICK. "In consideration of the sum of sixteen pounds received do hereby sell and convey to Derrick Von Beekman all my estate, houses, lands whatsoever"-- (*Hat drops.*)

RIP. (*almost fiercely*) What are you readin', some ritmatics what ain't down there: where you got that? (*Looking sharply at Hendrick.*)

HENDRICK. (*pointing*) There. Houses! Lands, whatsoever.

(*Rip looks not at the paper but at Hendrick very earnestly, as if turning over in his mind whether the boy has read it correctly; then satisfied of the deception Derrick has practiced upon him and struck by the humour of the way in which he has discovered it, he laughs exultantly and looks toward the inn-door.*)

RIP. Yes, so it is. Go long mit the rest.

(*He leans forward, and puts his ear close to Hendrick.*)

HENDRICK. "Whereof he now holds possession by mortgaged deeds, from time to time executed by me."

RIP. (*takes paper, and looks toward the inn, fiercely exultant*) You read it much better than Derrick, my boy, much better. (*After a pause, recollects himself. Kindly.*) That will do, run along mit you. (*Exit Hendrick.*) Aha, my friend, Derrick! I guess you got some snakes in the grass. Now keep sober, Rip; I dont touch another drop so long what I live; I swore off now, that's a fixed fact.

(*Enter Derrick, Vedder, Stein, and Villagers.*)

DERRICK. Come, Rip, we'll have a rouse.

RIP. (*seriously, half fiercely still*) Here, Nick Vedder, here is the gelt; wipe off my score, and drink away. I don't join you; I swore off.

NICK. Why, Rip, you're king of the feast.

RIP. (*absently, still intent of Derrick*) Am I dat?

OMNES. Swore off? What for?

RIP. I don't touch another drop.

STEIN. (*coming down towards Rip with cup*) Come, Rip, take a glass.

RIP. (*turning on him, almost angry*) Jacob Stein, you hear what I said?

STEIN. Yes.

RIP. (*firmly*) Well, when I said a thing, I mean it.

(*Leans back in his chair with his hands behind his head.*)

STEIN. Oh, very well.

(*Stein turns away; Nick holds cup under Rip's nose. Rip looks to see if they are watching him. He can resist no longer, and takes the cup.*)

RIP. (*laughing*) Well, I won't count this one. Here's your good health, and your families', may they all live long and prosper.

DERRICK. Here come the fiddlers and the girls.

(*Enter girls. Rip walks over and closes the shutter which has held his score, then returns and seats himself on a low stool, and keeps time to the music as the Villagers dance. Finally, the rhythm fires his blood. He jumps to his feet, snatches one of the girls away from her partner, and whirls into the dance. After a round or two, he lets go of her, and pirouettes two or three times by himself. Once more, he catches her in his arms, and is in the act of embracing her, when he perceives Gretchen over her shoulder. He drops the girl, who falls on her knees at Gretchen's feet. There is a general laugh at his discomfiture, in which he joins half-heartedly. As the curtain descends, Rip is seen pointing at the girl as if seeking, like a modern Adam, to put the blame on her.*)

ACT II.

Scene. The dimly lighted kitchen of Rip's cottage. The door and window are at the back. It is night, and through the window a furious storm can be seen raging, with thunder, lightning, and rain. A fire smolders on the hearth, to the right, and a candle gutters on the table in the center; a couple of chairs, a low stool, and a little cupboard, meagerly provided with cups and plates, complete the furniture of the room. Between the door and the window a clothes-horse, with a few garment hanging on it, forms a screen. To the left is a small door leading to the other rooms of the cottage. (*As the curtain rises, Meenie is seen sitting by the window, and Gretchen enters, takes off cloak, and throws a broomstick on the table.*)

GRETCHEN. Meenie! Has your father come yet?

MEENIE. No, mother.

GRETCHEN. So much the better for him. Never let him show his face in these doors again--never!

MEENIE. Oh, mother, don't be so hard on him.

GRETCHEN. I'm not hard; how dare you say so. (*Meenie approaches her.*) There, child, that father of yours is enough to spoil the temper of an angel. I went down to the marsh to drive up the bull. I don't know what Rip has been doing to the beast; he was howling and tearing about. I barely escaped with my life. (*Crash outside.*)What noise is that?

MEENIE. That's only Schneider, father's dog.

GRETCHEN. (*picking up a broomstick*) Then I'll Schneider him. I won't have him here. (*Exit through the door leading to the rest of the cottage.*) Out, you idle, vagabond cur; out, I say!

MEENIE. (*following her to the door, and crying*) Oh, don't, don't hurt the poor thing!

GRETCHEN. (*re-entering*) He jumped out of the window before I could catch him. He's just like his master. Now, what are your crying for?

MEENIE. Because my poor father is out in all this rain. (*A peal of thunder.*) Hark, how it thunders!

GRETCHEN. Serve him right--do him good. Is the supper ready?

MEENIE. Yes, mother; it is there by the fireside. Shall I lay the table?

GRETCHEN. Yes. (*Thunder.*) It's a dreadful night; I wonder where Rip is.

MEENIE. (*bringing cups and platters from the sideboard, together with a loaf of bread*) Shall I lay the table for two, mother, or for three?

GRETCHEN. For two, girl; he gets no supper here tonight. (*Another peal of thunder.*) Mercy, how the storm rages! The fool, to stop out in such a downpour. I hope he's found shelter. I must look out the old suit I washed and mended for him last week, and put them by the fire to air. The idiot, to stop out in such a downpour! I'll have him sick on my hands next; that's all I want to complete my misery.

(*She fetches clothes from the horse and hangs them on the back of the chair in front of the fire.*)

He knows what I am suffering now, and that's what keeps him out. (*Lightning.*) Mercy, what a flash that was! The wretch will be starved with the cold! Meenie!

MEENIE. Yes, mother.

GRETCHEN. You may lay the table for three. (*A knock at the outer door.*) There he is now. (*Enter Hendrick, shaking rain from his hat.*) Where's Rip? Is he not at your father's?

HENDRICK. No; I thought he was here.

GRETCHEN. He's gone back to the mountain. He's done it on purpose to spite me.

HENDRICK. (*going to the fire*) Shall I run after him, and bring him home? I know the road. We've often climbed it together.

GRETCHEN. No; I drove Rip from his house, and it's for me to bring him back again.

MEENIE. (*still arranging the supper table*) But, mother-- (*She pauses, with embarrassment.*) If he hears your voice behind him, he will only run away the faster.

GRETCHEN. Well, I can't help it; I can't rest under cover, while he is out in the storm. I shall feel better when I'm outside sharing the storm with him. Sit down, and take your suppers. I'll take my cloak along with me.

    (*Exit Gretchen. Meenie has seated herself by the window. Hendrick carries stool to the center of the stage, in front of the table.*)

HENDRICK. Meenie! Meenie!

MEENIE. Eh?

    (*Hendrick beckons to her. She runs to him. He stops her suddenly, then puts the stool down with great deliberation, and sits on it, while Meenie kneels beside him.*)

HENDRICK. (*in a very solemn tone*) I hope your father ain't gone to the mountains tonight, Meenie.

MEENIE. (*in distress*) Oh, dear! he will die of the cold there.

HENDRICK. (*suddenly*) Sh! (*Meenie starts.*) It ain't for that. (*Mysteriously.*) I've just heard old Clausen, over at father's saying, that on this very night, every twenty years, the ghosts--

MEENIE. (*catching his wrist*) The what?

HENDRICK. (*awed*) The ghosts of Hendrick Hudson, and his pirate crew, visit the Kaatskills above here. (*They look around, frightened.*)

MEENIE. Oh, dear! did he say so?

HENDRICK. Sh! (*Again they look around, frightened.*) Yes; and the spirits have been seen there smoking, drinking, and playing at tenpins.

MEENIE. Oh, how dreadful!

HENDRICK. Sh!

    (*He goes cautiously to the chimney, and looks up, while Meenie looks under the table; then he returns to the stool, speaking as he comes.*)

Yes; and every time that Hendrick Hudson lights his pipe there's a flash of lightning. (*Lightning; Meenie gives a gasp.*) And when he rolls the balls along, there is a peal of thunder.

> (*Loud rumbles of thunder. Meenie screams and throws herself into Hendrick's arms. He speaks with a manly effort to be courageous.*)

Don't be frightened, Meenie; I'm here.

> (*Re-enter Gretchen with her cloak.*)

GRETCHEN. Here, stop that!

> (*The children separate quickly. Hendrick looks up at the ceiling and whistles, with an attempt at unconsciousness, and Meenie assumes an innocent and unconcerned expession.*)

Now, don't you be filling that child's head with nonsense, but remain quietly here until I return. Hush, what noise is that? There is someone outside the window.

> (*She steps behind the clothes-horse. Rip appears at the window, which he opens, and leans against the frame.*)

RIP. Meenie!

MEENIE and HENDRICK. (*trying to make him perceive Gretchen, by a gesture in her direction*) Sh!

> (*Rip turns and looks around outside to see what they mean, then, discovering nothing, drops his hat in at the window, and calls cautiously.*)

RIP. Meenie!

MEENIE and HENDRICK. (*with the same warning gesture*) Sh!

> (*Gretchen shakes her fist at them; they assume an air of innocence.*)

RIP. What's the matter? Meenie, has the wildcat come home?

> (*Rip reaches in after his hat. Gretchen catches him by his hair, and holds his head down.*)

Och, my darlin', don't do that, eh!

HENDRICK and MEENIE. (*who run towards Gretchen*) Don't, mother! Don't, mother! Don't!

RIP. (*imitating their tone*) Don't, mother, don't! Don't you hear the children? (*Getting angry.*) Let go my head, won't you?

GRETCHEN. No; not a hair.

RIP. (*bantering*) Hold on to it then, what do I care?

HENDRICK and MEENIE. (*catching Gretchen's dress*) Don't, mother! Don't, mother! Don't!

> (*Gretchen lets go of Rip, and turns upon the children. They escape, and disappear through the door to the left. Rip gets in through the window and comes forward, apparently drunk, but jolly; and his resentment for the treatment he has just received is half humorous.*)

RIP. For what you do dat, hey? You must want a bald-headed husband, I reckon!

(*Gretchen picks up chair and bangs it down; Rip imitates her with the stool. She sits down angrily and slaps the table. Rip throws down his felt hat with a great show of violence, but it makes no noise. He seats himself on the stool.*)

GRETCHEN. Now, then!

RIP. Now, den; I don't like it den, neider.

(*When Rip is drunk, his dialect grows more pronounced.*)

GRETCHEN. Who did you call a wildcat?

RIP. (*with a sudden little tipsy laugh, and confused*) A wildcat--dat's when I come in at the window?

GRETCHEN. Yes; that's when you come in the window.

RIP. (*rising, and with a tone of finality*) Yes; that's the time I said it.

GRETCHEN. Yes; and that's the time I heard it.

RIP. (*with drunken assurance*) That's all right; I was afraid you wouldn't hear it.

GRETCHEN. Now who did you mean by that wildcat?

RIP. (*confused*) Who did I mean? Now, let me see.

GRETCHEN. Yes; who did you mean?

RIP. How do I know who-oo I mean? (*With a sudden inspiration.*) Maybe it's the dog Schneider I call that.

GRETCHEN. (*incredulously*) The dog Schneider; that's not likely.

RIP. (*argumentatively*) Of course it is likely; he's my dog. (*Conclusively.*) I'll call him a wildcat much as I please.

(*He sits down in the chair on which his clothes are warming.*)

GRETCHEN. And then, there's your disgraceful conduct this morning. What have you got to say to that?

RIP. How do I know what I got to say to that, when I don't know what I do-a, do-a? (*Hiccoughs.*)

GRETCHEN. Don't know what you do-a-oo! Hugging and kissing the girls before my face; you thought I wouldn't see you.

RIP. (*boldly*) I knowed you would--I knowed you would; because, because-- (*Losing the thread of his discourse.*) Oh-h, don' you bodder me.

(*He turns and leans his head against the back of the chair.*)

GRETCHEN. You knew I was there?

RIP. (*laughing*) I thought I saw you.

GRETCHEN. I saw you myself, dancing with the girl.

RIP. You saw the girl dancin' mit me.

(*Gretchen remembers Rip's clothes, goes over to see if he is wet, and*

pushes him towards the center of the stage. Rip mistakes her intention.)
You want to pull some more hair out of my head?

GRETCHEN. Why, the monster! He isn't wet a bit! He's as dry as if he'd
been aired!

RIP. Of course I'm dry. (*Laughing.*) I'm always dry--always dry.

GRETCHEN. (*examines the game-bag, and pulls out a flask, which she
holds under Rip's nose*) Why, what's here? Why, it's a bottle--a bottle!

RIP. (*leaning against the table*) Yes; it's a bottle. (*Laughs.*) You think I
don't know a bottle when I see it?

GRETCHEN. That's pretty game for your game-bag, ain't it?

RIP. (*assuming an innocent air*) Somebody must have put it there.

GRETCHEN. (*putting the flask in her pocket*) Then, you don't get it again.

RIP. (*with a show of anger*) Now mind if I don't get it again--well--all
there is about it-- (*Breaking down.*) I don't want it. (*With a droll air of
conviction.*) I have had enough.

GRETCHEN. I'm glad you know when you've had enough.

RIP. That's the way mit me. I'm glad I know when I got enough-- (*Laughs.*)
An' I'm glad when I've got enough, too. Give me the bottle; I want to put
it in the game-bag.

GRETCHEN. For what?

RIP. (*lounging off the table, and leaning his arms on Gretchen's shoulders*)
So that I can't drink it. Here's the whole business--

(*He slides his hand down to Gretchen's pocket and tries to find the
bottle while he talks to her.*)

Here's the whole business about it. What is the use of anybody--well--
wash the use of anybody, anyhow--well--oh--

(*Missing the pocket.*)

What you talkin' 'bout?

(*Suddenly his hand slips in her pocket, and he begins to pull the bottle
out, with great satisfaction.*)

Now, now I can tell you all 'bout it.

GRETCHEN. (*discovering his tactics, and pushing him away*) Pshaw!

RIP. If you don't give me the bottle, I just break up everything in the
house.

GRETCHEN. If you dare!

RIP. If I dare! Haven't I done it two or three times before? I just throw
everything right out of the window.

(*Rip throws the plates and cups on the floor and overturns a chair, and
seats himself on the table. Gretchen picks them up again.*)

GRETCHEN. Don't, Rip; don't do that! Now stop, Rip, stop!

(Gretchen bangs down a chair by the table and seats herself.)
Now, then, perhaps you will be kind enough to tell me where you've been for the last two days. Where have you been? Do you hear?

RIP. Where I've been? Well, it's not my bottle, anyhow. I borrowed that bottle from another feller. You want to know where I been?

GRETCHEN. Yes; and I will know.

RIP. *(good-humouredly)* Let's see. Last night I stopped out all night.

GRETCHEN. But why?

RIP. Why? You mean the reason of it?

GRETCHEN. Yes, the reason.

RIP. *(inconsequently)* The reason is why? Don't bother me.

GRETCHEN. *(emphasizing each word with a bang on the table)* Why--did--you--stop--out--all--night?

RIP. *(imitating her tone)* Because--I--want--to--get--up--early--in--the--morning. *(Hiccough.)* Come, don't get so mad mit a feller. Why, I've been fillin' my game-bag mit game.

(Rip gets down off the table, and Gretchen feels his game-bag.)

GRETCHEN. Your game-bag is full of game, isn't it?

RIP. *(taking her hand and holding it away from her pocket)* That? Why, that wouldn't hold it. *(Finding his way into her pocket.)* Now I can tell you all about it. You know last night I stopped out all night--

GRETCHEN. Yes; and let me catch you again.

(He is pulling the bottle out. Gretchen catches him, and slaps his hand.)
You paltry thief!

RIP. Oh, you ain't got no confidence in me. Now what do you think was the first thing I saw in the morning?

(Dragging a chair to the front of the stage.)

GRETCHEN. I don't know. What?

RIP. *(seating himself)* A rabbit.

GRETCHEN. *(pleased)* I like a rabbit. I like it in a stew.

RIP. *(looking at her, amused)* I guess you like everything in a stew--everything what's a rabbit, I mean. Well, there was a rabbit a-feedin' mit the grass--you know they always come out early in de mornin' and feed mit the grass?

GRETCHEN. Never mind the grass. Go on.

RIP. Don't get so patient; you wait till you get the rabbit. *(Humourously.)* Well, I crawl up--

GRETCHEN. Yes, yes!

RIP. *(becoming interested in his own powers of invention)* An' his little tail was a-stickin' up so-- *(With a gesture of his forefinger.)*

GRETCHEN. (*impatiently*) Never mind his tail. Go on.

RIP. (*remonstrating at her interruption*) The more fatter the rabbit, the more whiter is his tail--

GRETCHEN. Well, well, go on.

RIP. (*taking aim*) Well, I haul up--

GRETCHEN. Yes, yes!

RIP. And his ears was a-stickin' up so--

  (*He makes the two ears with his two forefingers.*)

GRETCHEN. Never mind his ears. Go on.

RIP. I pull the trigger.

GRETCHEN. (*eagerly*) Bang went the gun, and--

RIP. (*seriously*) And the rabbit run away.

GRETCHEN. (*angrily*) And so you shot nothing?

RIP. How will I shot him when he run away? (*Laughing at her disappointment.*) There, don't get so mad mit a feller. Now I'm going to tell you what I did shot; that's what I didn't shot. You know that old forty-acre field of ours?

GRETCHEN. (*scornfully*) Ours! ours, did you say?

RIP. (*shamefacedly*) You know the one I mean well enough. It used to be ours.

GRETCHEN. (*regretfully*) Yes; it used, indeed!

RIP. It ain't ours now, is it?

GRETCHEN. (*sighing*) No, indeed, it is not.

RIP. No? Den I won't bodder about it. Better let somebody bodder about that field what belongs to it. Well, in that field there's a pond; and what do you think I see in that pond?

GRETCHEN. I don't know. Ducks?

RIP. Ducks! More an' a thousand.

GRETCHEN. (*walking to broomstick*) More than a thousand ducks?

RIP. I haul up again--

GRETCHEN. (*picking up broomstick*) Yes, and so will I. And if you misfire this time-- (*She holds it threateningly over Rip's shoulder.*)

RIP. (*looking at it askance out of the corner of his eye, then pushing it aside*) You will scare the ducks mit that. Well, I take better aim this time as I did before. I pull the trigger, and--bang!

GRETCHEN. How many down?

RIP. (*indifferently*) One.

GRETCHEN. (*indignantly*) What! only one duck out of a thousand?

RIP. Who said one duck?

GRETCHEN. You did!

RIP. (*getting up and leaning on the back of the chair*) I didn't say anything of the kind.

GRETCHEN. You said "one."

RIP. Ah! *One.* But I shot more as one duck.

GRETCHEN. Did you?

RIP. (*sits on the low stool, laughing silently*) I shot our old bull.

    (*Gretchen flings down the broomstick, and throws herself into the chair at the right of the table, in dumb rage.*)

I didn't kill him. I just sting him, you know. Well, then the bull come right after me; and I come right away from him. (*With a vain appeal to her sense of humour.*) Oh, Gretchen, how you would laugh if you could see that-- The bull was a-comin', and I was a-goin'. Well, he chased me across the field. I tried to climb over the fence so fast what I could-- (*doubles up with his silent laugh*)--and the bull come up an' save me the trouble of that. Well, then, I rolled over on the other side.

GRETCHEN. And then you went fast asleep for the rest of the day.

RIP. That's a fact. That's a fact.

GRETCHEN. (*bursting into tears, and burying her head in her arms on the table*) Oh, Rip, you'll break my heart! You will.

RIP. Now she's gone crying mit herself! Don't cry, Gretchen, don't cry. My d-a-r-l-i-n', don't cry.

GRETCHEN. (*angrily*) I will cry.

RIP. Cry 'way as much as you like. What do I care? All the better soon as a woman gets cryin'; den all the danger's over.

    (*Rip goes to Gretchen, leans over, and puts his arm around her.*)

Gretchen, don't cry; my angel, don't.

    (*He succeeds in getting his hand into her pocket, and steals the bottle.*)

Don't cry, my daarlin'. (*Humourously.*) Gretchen, won't you give me a little drop out of that bottle what you took away from me?

    (*He sits on the table, just behind her, and takes a drink from the bottle.*)

GRETCHEN. Here's a man drunk, and asking for more.

RIP. I wasn't. I swore off. (*Coaxingly.*) You give me a little drop an' I won't count it.

GRETCHEN. (*sharply*) No!

RIP. (*drinking again*) Well, den, here's your good health, and your family, and may they live long and prosper! (*Puts bottle in his bag.*)

GRETCHEN. You unfeeling brute. Your wife's starving. And, Rip, your child's in rags.

RIP. (*holding up his coat, and heaving a sigh of resignation*) Well, I'm the same way; you know dat.

GRETCHEN. (*sitting up, and looking appealingly at Rip*) Oh, Rip, if you would only treat me kindly!

RIP. (*putting his arms around her*) Well, den, I will. I'm going to treat you kind. I'll treat you kind.

GRETCHEN. Why, it would add ten years to my life.

RIP. (*over her shoulder, and after a pause*) That's a great inducement; it is, my darlin'. I know I treat you too bad, an' you deserve to be a widow.

GRETCHEN. (*getting up, and putting her arms on Rip's shoulder*) Oh, Rip, if you would only reform!

RIP. Well, den, I will. I won't touch another drop so long as I live.

GRETCHEN. Can I trust you?

RIP. You mustn't suspect me.

GRETCHEN. (*embracing him*) There, then, I will trust you.
(*She takes the candle and goes to fetch the children.*)
Here, Hendrick, Meenie? Children, where are you?
(*Exit Gretchen through the door on the left.*)

RIP. (*seats himself in the chair to the right of the table, and takes out flask*) Well, it's too bad; but it's all a woman's fault anyway. When a man gets drinkin' and that, they ought to let him alone. So long as they scold him, he goes off like a sky-rocket.
(*Re-enter Gretchen and the children.*)

GRETCHEN. (*seeing the flask in Rip's hand*) I thought as much.

RIP. (*unconscious of her presence*) How I did smooth her down! I must drink her good health. (*About to drink.*) Gretchen, here's your good health.

GRETCHEN. (*snatching the bottle, and using it to gesticulate with*) Oh, you paltry thief!

RIP. (*concerned for the schnapps*) What you doin'? You'll spill the licker out of the bottle. (*He puts in the cork.*)

GRETCHEN. (*examining the flask*) Why, the monster, he's emptied the bottle!

RIP. That's a fac'. That's a fac'.

GRETCHEN. (*throwing down the flask*) Then that is the last drop you drink under my roof!

RIP. What! What!
(*Meenie approaches her father on tiptoe, and kneels beside him.*)

GRETCHEN. Out, you drunkard! Out, you sot! You disgrace to your wife and to your child! This house is mine.

RIP. (*dazed, and a little sobered*) Yours! Yours!

GRETCHEN. (*raising her voice above the storm, which seems to rage more fiercely outside*) Yes, mine, mine! Had it been yours to sell, it would have gone along with the rest of your land. Out then, I say--(*pushing open the door*)--for you have no longer any share in me or mine.

(*A peal of thunder.*)

MEENIE. (*running over, and kneeling by Gretchen*) Oh, mother, hark at the storm!

GRETCHEN. (*pushing her aside*) Begone, man, can't you speak? Are you struck dumb? You sleep no more under my roof.

(*RIP has not moved, even his arm remains outstretched, as it was when Meenie slipped from his side.*)

RIP. (*murmurs in a bewildered, incredulous way*) Why, Gretchen, are you goin' to turn me out like a dog?

(*Gretchen points to the door. Rip rises and leans against the table with a groan. His conscience speaks.*)

Well, maybe you are right.

(*His voice breaks, and with a despairing gesture.*)

I have got no home. I will go. But mind, Gretchen, after what you say to me tonight, I can never darken your door again--never--

(*Going towards the door.*)

I will go.

HENDRICK. (*running up to Rip*) Not into the storm, Rip. Hark, how it thunders!

RIP. (*putting his arm around him*) Yah, my boy; but not as bad to me as the storm in my home. I will go. (*At the door by this time.*)

MEENIE. (*catching Rip's coat*) No, father, don't go!

RIP. (*bending over her tenderly, and holding her close to him*) My child! Bless you, my child, bless you!

(*Meenie faints. Rip gives a sobbing sigh.*)

GRETCHEN. (*relenting*) No, Rip--I--

RIP. (*waving her off*) No, you have drive me from your house. You have opened the door for me to go. You may never open it for me to come back.

(*Leaning against the doorpost, overcome by his emotion. His eyes rest on Meenie, who lies at his feet.*)

You say I have no share in this house.

(*Points to Meenie in profound despair.*)

Well, see, then, I wipe the disgrace from your door.

(*He staggers out into the storm.*)

GRETCHEN. No, Rip! Husband, come back!

(*Gretchen faints, and the curtain falls.*)

ACT III.

Scene. A steep and rocky clove in the Kaatskill Mountains, down which rushes a torrent, swollen by the storm. Overhead, the hemlocks stretch their melancholy boughs. It is night. (*Enter Rip, almost at a run, with his head down, and his coat-collar turned up, beating his way against the storm. With the hunter's instinct, he protects the priming of his gun with the skirt of his jacket. Having reached a comparatively level spot, he pauses for breath, and turns to see what has become of his dog.*)

RIP. (*whistling to the dog*) Schneider! Schneider! What's the matter with Schneider? Something must have scared that dog. There he goes head over heels down the hill. Well, here I am again--another night in the mountains! Heigho! these old trees begin to know me, I reckon. (*Taking off his hat.*) How are you, old fellows? Well, I like the trees, they keep me from the wind and the rain, and they never blow me up; and when they lay me down on the broad of my back, they seem to bow their heads to me, an' say: Go to sleep, Rip, go to sleep. (*Lightning.*) My, what a flash that was! Old Hendrick Hudson's lighting his pipe in the mountains tonight; now, we'll hear him roll the big balls along.

(*Thunder. Rip looks back over the path he has come and whistles again.*) Well, I--no--Schneider! No; whatever it is, it's on two legs. Why, what a funny thing is that a-comin' up the hill? I thought nobody but me ever come nigh this place.

(*Enter a strange dwarfish figure, clad all in gray like a Dutch seaman of the seventeenth century, in short-skirted doublet, hose, and high-crowned hat drawn over his eyes. From beneath the latter his long gray beard streams down till it almost touches the ground. He carries a keg on his shoulder. He advances slowly towards Rip, and, by his gesture, begs Rip to set the keg down for him. Rip does so, and the Dwarf seats himself upon it. Rip speaks with good-humoured sarcasm.*) Sit down, and make yourself comfortable.

(*A long pause.*) What? What's the matter? Ain't ye goin' to speak to a feller? I don't want to speak to you, then. Who you think you was, that I want to speak to you, any more than you want to speak to me; you hear what I say?

(*Rip pokes the Dwarf in the ribs, who turns and looks up. Rip retreats.*) Donner an' Blitzen! What for a man is das? I have been walking over these mountains ever since I was a boy, an' I never saw a queer looking codger like that before. He must be an old sea-snake, I reckon.

(*The Dwarf approaches Rip, and motions Rip to help him up the mountain with the keg.*)

Well, why don't you say so, den? You mean you would like me to help you up with that keg? (*The Dwarf nods.*) Well, sir, I don't do it.

(*The Dwarf holds up his hands in supplication.*)

No, there's no good you speakin' like that. I never seed you before, did I?

(*The Dwarf shakes his head, Rip, with great decision, walking away, and leaning against a tree.*)

I don't want to see you again, needer. What have you got in that keg, schnapps? (*The Dwarf nods.*) I don't believe you.

(*The Dwarf nods more affirmatively.*)

Is it good schnapps? (*The Dwarf again insists.*) Well, I'll help you. Go 'long; pick up my gun, there, and I follow you mit that keg on my shoulder. I'll follow you, old broadchops.

(*As Rip shoulders the keg, a furious blast whirls up the valley, and seems to carry him and his demon companion before it. The rain that follows blots out the landscape. For a few moments, all is darkness. Gradually, the topmost peak of the Kaatskills becomes visible, far above the storm. Stretching below, the country lies spread out like a map. A feeble and watery moonlight shows us a weird group, gathered upon the peak--Hendrick Hudson, and his ghostly crew. In the foreground, one of them poises a ball, about to bowl it, while the others lean forward in attitudes of watchful expectancy. Silently he pitches it; and, after a momentary pause, a long and rumbling peal of thunder reverberates among the valleys below. At this moment, the Demon, carrying Rip's gun, appears over the crest of the peak in the background, and Rip toils after with the keg on his shoulder. Arrived at the summit, he drops the keg on his knee, gasps for breath, and glances out over the landscape.*)

I say, old gentleman, I never was so high up in the mountains before. Look down into the valley there; it seems more as a mile. I--

(*Turning to speak to his companion and perceiving another of the crew.*)

You're another feller! (*Second Demon nods.*) You're that other chap's brother?

(*The Demon again assents. Rip carries the keg a little farther, and comes face to face with a third.*)

You're another brother?

(*Third Demon nods. Rip takes another step, and perceives Hendrick Hudson in the center, surrounded by many Demons.*)

You're his old gran'father?

(*Hudson nods. Rip puts down the keg in perplexity, not untinged with alarm.*)

Donner and Blitzen! Here's the whole family; I'm a dead man to a certainty.

(*The Demons extend their arms to Hudson, as if inquiring what they should do. He points to Rip, they do the same.*)

My, my, I suppose they're speakin' about me!

(*Looks at his gun, which the first Demon has deposited on the ground.*)

No good shootin' at 'em; family's too big for one gun.

(*Hendrick Hudson advances, and seats himself on the keg, facing Rip. The Demons slowly surround the two. Rip looks about with growing apprehension.*)

My, my, I don't like that kind of people at all! No, sir! I don't like any sech kind. I like that old gran'father worse than any of them.

(*With a sheepish attempt to be genial, and appear at his ease.*)

How you was, old gentleman? I didn't mean to intrude on you, did I? (*Hudson shakes his head.*) What? (*No reply.*) I'll tell you how it was; I met one of your gran'children; I don't know which is the one-- (*Glancing around.*) They're all so much alike. Well--

(*Embarrassed and looking at one Demon.*)

That's the same kind of a one. Any way this one, he axed me to help him up the mountain mit dat keg. Well, he was an old feller, an' I thought I would help him. (*Pauses, troubled by their silence.*) Was I right to help him? (*Hudson nods.*) I say, was I right to help him? (*Hudson nods.*) If he was here, he would yust tell you the same thing any way, because--

(*Suddenly perceiving the Demon he had met before.*)

Why, dat's the one, ain't it? (*The Demon nods.*) Yes; dat is the one, dat's the same kind of a one dat I met. Was I right to come? (*Hudson nods approval.*) I didn't want to come here, anyhow; no, sir, I didn't want to come to any such kind of a place. (*After a pause, seeing that no one has anything to say.*) I guess I better go away from it.

(*Rip picks up his gun, and is about to return by the way he came; but the Demons raise their hands threateningly, and stop him. He puts his gun down again, grumbling to himself.*)

I didn't want to come here, anyhow--

(*Pulling himself together with an effort, and facing Hudson.*)

Well, old gentleman, if you mean to do me any harm, just speak it right out-- (*A little laugh.*) Oh! I will die game--(*glancing around, half to himself*)--if I can't run away.

(*Hudson extends a cup to Rip, as if inviting him to drink.*)

You want me to drink mit you?

(*Hudson nods. Rip approaches cautiously, unable to resist temptation.*)
Well, I swore off drinkin'; but as this is the first time I see you, I won't count this one--

(*He takes the cup. Hudson holds up another cup. Rip is reassured, and his old geniality returns.*)
You drink mit me? We drink mit one another?

(*Hudson nods. Rip feels at home and becomes familiar and colloquial.*)
What's the matter mit you, old gentleman, anyhow? You go and make so (*imitating the Demon*) mit your head every time; was you deaf? (*Hudson shakes his head.*) Oh, nein. (*Laughing at his error.*) If you was deaf, you wouldn't hear what I was sayin'. Was you dumb? (*Hudson nods.*) So? You was dumb? (*Hudson nods.*) Has all of your family the same complaint? (*Hudson nods.*) All the boys dumb, hey? All the boys dumb. (*All the Demons nod. Struck with an idea.*) Have you got any girls? (*Hudson shakes his head.*) Don't you? Such a big family, and all boys? (*Hudson nods.*) That's a pity. (*With profound regret.*) My, that's a pity. Oh, my, if you had some dumb girls, what wives they would make-- (*Brightening.*) Well, old gentleman, here's your good health, and all your family--(*turning and waving to them*)--may they live long and prosper.

(*Rip drinks. As he does so, all the Demons lean forward, watching the effect of the liquor. Rip puts his hand to his head. The empty cup falls to the ground. Rip speaks in an odd and ecstatic voice.*)
What for licker is that!

(*As he turns, half reeling, he sees Hudson holding out another cup. He snatches it with almost frantic eagerness.*)
Give me another one!

(*He empties it at a draught. A long pause follows: the effect of the liquor upon Rip becomes apparent; the light in his eyes fades, his exhiliration dies out, and he loses his grasp on the reality of his surroundings. Finally, he clasps his head with both hands, and cries in a muffled, terrified voice.*)
Oh, my, my head was so light, and now it's heavy as lead!

(*He reels, and falls heavily to the ground. A long pause. The Demons begin to disappear. Rip becomes dimly conscious of this, and raises himself on his elbow.*)
Are you goin' to leave me, boys? Are you goin' to leave me all alone? Don't leave me; don't go away. (*With a last effort.*) I will drink your good health, and your family's--

(*He falls back heavily, asleep--and the curtain falls.*)

ACT IV.

Scene 1. The same high peaks of the Kaatskills, and the far-stretching valley below, are disclosed in the gray light of dawn. (*Rip is lying on the ground, as in the last act, but he is no longer the Rip we knew. His hair and beard are long and white, bleached by the storms that have rolled over his head during the twenty years he has been asleep. He stirs and slowly rises to a half-sitting position. His former picturesque rags have become so dilapidated that it is a matter of marvel how they hold together. They have lost all traces of color, and have assumed the neutral tints of the moss and lichens that cover the rocks. His voice, when he first speaks, betrays even more distinctly than his appearance the lapse of time. Instead of the full round tones of manhood, he speaks in the high treble of feeble old age. His very hands have grown old and weather-beaten. He stares vacantly around.*)

RIP. I wonder where I was. On top of the Kaatskill Mountains, as sure as a gun! Won't my wife give it to me for stopping out all night? I must get up and get home with myself. (*Trying to rise.*) Oh, I feel very bad! Vat is the matter with my elbow?

(*In trying to rub it, the other one gives him a twinge, and he cries out.*)
Oh! the other elbow is more badder than the other one. I must have cotched the rheumatix a-sleepin' mit the wet grass. (*Rising with great difficulty.*) Och! I never had such rheumatix like that.
(*He feels himself all over, and then stands for a moment pondering, and bewildered by a strange memory.*)
I wasn't sleeping all the time, needer. I know I met a queer kind of a man, and we got drinkin' and I guess I got pretty drunk. Well, I must pick up my gun, and get home mit myself.
(*After several painful attempts, he succeeds in picking up his gun, which drops all to pieces as he lifts it. Rip looks at it in amazement.*)
My gun must have cotched the rheumatix, too. Now, that's too bad. Them fellows have gone and stole my good gun, and leave me this rusty old barrel.
(*Rip begins slowly to climb over the peak towards the path by which he had ascended, his memory seeming to act automatically. Reaching the highest point, looking out over the valley, he stops in surprise.*)
Why, is that the village of Falling Waters that I see? Why, the place is more than twice the size it was last night. I-- (*He sinks down.*) I don't know whether I am dreaming, or sleeping, or waking.
(*Then pulling himself together with a great effort, and calling up the*

image of his wife to act as whip and spur to his waning powers, he speaks with humourous conviction, as he get up painfully, again.)

I go home to my wife. She'll let me know whether I'm asleep or awake or not. (*Almost unable to proceed.*) I don't know if I will ever get home, my knees are so stiff. My backbone, it's broke already.

(*As the curtain falls, Rip stands leaning on the barrel of his gun as on a staff, with one hand raised, looking out over the valley.*)

Scene 2. A comfortable room in Derrick's house. (*Enter Meenie and Gretchen. Meenie is a tall young woman of twenty-six, Gretchen a matronly figure with white hair. They are well dressed, and have every appearance of physical and material prosperity.*)

GRETCHEN. I am sent to you by your father, Meenie.

MEENIE. Oh, don't call him so; he is not my father! He is your husband, mother; but I owe him no love. And his cruel treatment of you--

GRETCHEN. Hush, child! Oh, if he heard you, he would make me pay for every disrespectful word you utter.

MEENIE. Yes; he would beat you, starve and degrade you. You are not his wife, mother, but his menial.

GRETCHEN. My spirit is broken, Meenie. I cannot resent it. Nay, I deserve it; for as Derrick now treats me, so I treated your poor father when he was alive.

MEENIE. You, mother? You, so gentle? You, who are weakness and patience itself?

GRETCHEN. Yes; because for fifteen years I have been Derrick's wife. But it was my temper, my cruelty, that drove your father from our home twenty years ago. You were too young then to remember him.

MEENIE. No, mother, I recollect dear father taking me on his knee, and saying to Hendrick that I should be his wife; and I promised I would.

GRETCHEN. Poor Rip! Poor, good-natured, kind creature that he was! How gently he bore with me; and I drove him like a dog from his home. I hunted him into the mountains, where he perished of hunger or cold, or a prey to some wild beast.

MEENIE. Don't cry, mother!

(*Enter Derrick, now grown old and bent over his cane, and infinitely more disagreeable than before. He, too, has thriven, and is dressed in a handsome full suit of black silk.*)

DERRICK. Snivelling again, eh? Teaching that girl of yours to be an obstinate hypocrite?

MEENIE. Oh, sir, she--

DERRICK. Hold your tongue, Miss. Speak when you're spoken to. I'll have you both to understand that there's but one master here. Well, mistress, have you told her my wishes; and is she prepared to obey them?

GRETCHEN. Indeed, sir, I was trying to--

DERRICK. Beating about the bush, prevaricating, and sneaking, as you usually do.

MEENIE. If you have made her your slave, you must expect her to cringe.

DERRICK. (*approaching her threateningly*) What's that?

GRETCHEN. Meenie! Meenie! For Heaven's sake, do not anger him!

DERRICK. (*raising his cane*) She had better not.

MEENIE. (*defiantly*) Take care how you raise your hand to me, for I'll keep a strick account of it. And when Hendrick comes back from sea, he'll make you smart for it, I promise you.

DERRICK. Is the girl mad?

MEENIE. He thrashed your nephew once for being insolent to me. Go and ask him how Hendrick pays my debts; and then when you speak to me, you will mind your stops.

DERRICK. (*to Gretchen*) Oh, you shall pay for this!

GRETCHEN. No, Derrick, indeed, indeed I have not urged her to this! Oh, Meenie, do not speak so to him; for my sake forebear!

MEENIE. For your sake, yes, dear mother. I forgot that he could revenge himself on you.

DERRICK. As for your sailor lover, Hendrick Vedder, I've got news of him at last. His ship, the *Mayflower*, was lost three years ago, off Cape Horn.

MEENIE. No, no. Not lost?

DERRICK. If you doubt it, there's the *Shipping Gazette*, in on my office table. You can satisfy yourself that your sailor bully has gone to the bottom.

GRETCHEN. Oh, sir, do not convey the news to her so cruelly.

DERRICK. That's it. Because I don't sneak and trick and lie about it, I'm cruel. The man's dead, has been dead and gone these two years or more. The time of mourning is over. Am I going to be nice about it this time of day?

MEENIE. Then all my hope is gone, gone forever!

DERRICK. So much the better for you. Hendrick's whole fortune was invested in that ship. So there's an end of him and your expectations. Now you are free, and a beggar. My nephew has a fancy for you. He will have a share of my business now, and my money when--when I die.

GRETCHEN. Do not ask her to decide now!

DERRICK. Why not? If she expects to make a better bargain by holding off, she's mistaken.

GRETCHEN. How can you expect her to think of a husband at this moment?

DERRICK. Don't I tell you the other one is dead these two years?

GRETCHEN. (*leading Meenie away*) Come, my child. Leave her to me, sir; I will try and persuade her.

DERRICK. Take care that you do; for if she don't consent to accept my offer, she shall pack bag and baggage out of this house. Aye, this very day! Not a penny, not a stitch of clothes but what she has on her back, shall she have! Oh, I've had to deal with obstinate women before now, and I've taken them down before I've done with them. You know who I mean? Do you know who I mean? Stop. *Answer me! Do you know who I mean?*

GRETCHEN. (*submissively*) Yes, sir.

DERRICK. Then why didn't you say so before? Sulky, I suppose. There, you may be off. (*Exeunt.*)

Scene 3. The village of Falling Waters, which has grown to be a smart and flourishing town, but whose chief features remain unchanged. To the left, as of yore, is the inn, bearing scarcely any mark of the lapse of time, save the sign of George III has been replaced by a portrait of George Washington. To the right, where Rip's cottage used to stand, nothing remains, however, but the blackened and crumbling ruins of a chimney. A table and chairs stand in front of the inn porch. (*Into this familiar scene Rip makes his entrance, but not as before--in glee, with children clinging about him. Faint, weak, and weary, he stumbles along, followed by a jeering, hooting mob of Villagers; while the children hide from him in fear, behind their elders. His eyes look dazed and uncomprehending, and he catches at the back of a chair as if in need of physical as well as mental support.*)

KÄTCHEN. (*as Rip enters*) Why, what queer looking creature is this, that all the boys are playing--

SETH. Why, he looks as though he's been dead for fifty years, and dug up again!

RIP. My friends, *Kanst du Deutsch sprechen*?

FIRST VILLAGER. I say, old fellow, you ain't seen anything of an old butter-tub with no kiver on, no place about here, have you?

RIP. (*bewildered, but with simplicity*) What is that? I don't know who that is.

SECOND VILLAGER. I say, old man, who's your barber?

(*The crowd laughs, and goes off repeating, "Who's your barber?" Some of the children remain to stare at Rip; but when he holds out his hand to them, they, too, run off frightened.*)

RIP. Who's my barber; what dey mean by dat? (*Noticing his beard.*) Why is that on me? I didn't see that before. My beard and hair is so long and white. Gretchen won't know me with that, when she gets me home. (*Looking towards the cottage.*) Why, the home's gone away!

(*Rip becomes more and more puzzled, like a man in a dream who sees unfamiliar things amid familiar surroundings, and cannot make out what has happened; and as in a dream a man preserves his individuality, so Rip stumbles along through his bewilderment, exhibiting flashes of his old humour, wit, and native shrewdness. But with all this he never laughs.*)

SETH. I say, old man, hadn't you better go home and get shaved?

RIP. (*looking about for the voice*) What?

SETH. Here, this way. Hadn't you better go home and get shaved?

RIP. My wife will shave me when she gets me home. Is this the village of Falling Waters where we was?

SETH. Yes.

RIP. (*still more puzzled, not knowing his face*) Do you live here?

SETH. Well, rather. I was born here.

RIP. (*reflectively*) Then you live here?

SETH. Well, rather; of course I do.

RIP. (*feeling that he has hold of something certain*) Do you know where I live?

SETH. No; but I should say you belong to Noah's Ark.

RIP. (*putting his hand to his ear*) That I belong mit vas?

SETH. Noah's Ark.

RIP. (*very much hurt*) Why will you say such thing like that?

(*Then, with a flash of humour, and drawing his beard slowly through his fingers.*)

Well, look like it, don't I?

(*Beginning all over again to feel for his clue.*)

My friend, did you never hear of a man in this place whose name was Rip Van Winkle?

SETH. Rip Van Winkle, the laziest, drunken vagabond in the country?

RIP. (*somewhat taken aback by this description, but obliged to concur in it*)

Yah, that is the one; there is no mistaking him, eh?

SETH. I know all about him.

RIP. (*hopefully*) Do you?

SETH. Yes.

RIP. (*quite eagerly*) Well, if you know all about him; well, what has become of him?

SETH. What has become of him? Why, bless your soul, he's been dead these twenty years!

RIP. (*looking at Seth, aside*) Then I am dead, I suppose. (*Aloud.*) So Rip Van Winkle was dead, eh?

SETH. Yes; and buried.

RIP. (*humourously*) I'm sorry for that; for he was a good fellow, so he was.

SETH. (*aside*) There appears to be something queer about this old chap; I wonder who he is. (*Rising and taking chair over to Rip.*) There, old gentleman, be seated.

RIP. (*seating himself with great difficulty, assisted by Seth*) Oh, thank you; every time I move a new way, I get another pain. My friend, where is the house what you live in?

SETH. (*pointing at inn*) There.

RIP. Did you live there yesterday?

SETH. Well, rather.

RIP. No, it is Nick Vedder what live in that house. Where is Nick Vedder?

SETH. Does he? Then I wish he'd pay the rent for it. Why, Nick Vedder has been dead these fifteen years.

RIP. Did you know Jacob Stein, what was with him?

SETH. No; but I've heard of him. He was one of the same sort as Rip and Nick.

RIP. Yes, them fellows was all pretty much alike.

SETH. Well, he went off the hooks a short time after Rip.

RIP. Where has he gone?

SETH. Off the hooks.

RIP. What is that, when they go off the hooks?

SETH. Why, he died.

RIP. (*with an air of hopelessness*) Is there anybody alive here at all?
   (*With a sudden revulsion of feeling, convinced of the impossibility of what he hears.*)
That man is drunk what talks to me.

SETH. Ah, they were a jolly set, I reckon.

RIP. Oh, they was. I knowed them all.

SETH. Did you?

RIP. Yes, I know Jacob Stein, and Nick Vedder, and Rip Van Winkle, and the whole of them.

(*A new idea strikes him, and he beckons to Seth, and asks earnestly.*)

Oh, my friend, come and sit here. Did you know Schneider?

SETH. Schneider! Schneider! No, I never heard of him.

RIP. (*simply*) He was a dog. I thought you might know him. Well, if dat is so, what has become of my child Meenie, and my wife Gretchen? Are they gone, too? (*Turning to look at the ruins of the house.*) Yah, even the house is dead.

SETH. Poor old chap! He seems quite cast down at the loss of his friends. I'll step in and get a drop of something to cheer him up. (*Exit.*)

RIP. (*puzzling it out with himself*) I can't make it out how it all was; because if this here is me, what is here now, and Rip Van Winkle is dead, then who am I? That is what I would like to know. (*Very forlorn.*) Yesterday, everybody was here; and now they was all gone.

(*Re-enter Seth, followed by the Villagers.*)

SETH. (*offering Rip the cup*) There, old gent. There's a drop of something to cheer you up.

RIP. (*shaking hands with Seth and Kätchen*) Oh, thank you. I--I--swore off; but this is the first time what I see you. I won't count this one. (*His voice breaks.*) My friend, you have been very kind to me. Here is your good health, and your family's, and may they all live long and prosper!

SETH. I say, wife, ain't he a curiosity fit for a show?

RIP. (*aside*) That give me courage to ask these people anodder question. (*Beginning with difficulty.*) My friend, I don't know whether you know it or not, but there was a child of Rip--Meenie her name was.

SETH. Oh, yes; that's all right.

RIP. (*with great emotion, leaning forward*) She is not gone? She is not dead? No, no!

SETH. No; she is alive.

RIP. (*sinking back with relief*) Meenie is alive. It's all right now, all right now.

SETH. She is the prettiest girl in the village.

RIP. I know dat.

SETH. But if she wastes her time waiting on Hendrick Vedder, she'll be a middle-aged woman before long.

RIP. (*incredulously*) She's a little child, only six years old.

SETH. Six-and-twenty, you mean.

RIP. (*thinking they are making fun of him*) She's a little child no bigger than that. Don't bodder me; I don't like that.

SETH. Why, she's as big as her mother.

RIP. (*very much surprised that Seth knows Gretchen*) What, Gretchen?

SETH. Yes, Gretchen.

RIP. Isn't Gretchen dead?

SETH. No. She's alive.

RIP. (*with mixed emotions*) Gretchen is alive, eh! Gretchen's alive!

SETH. Yes; and married again.

RIP. (*fiercely*) How would she do such a thing like that?

SETH. Why, easy enough. After Rip died, she was a widow, wasn't she?

RIP. Oh, yes. I forgot about Rip's being dead. Well, then?

SETH. Well, then Derrick made love to her.

RIP. (*surprised, and almost amused*) What for Derrick? Not Derrick Von Beekman?

SETH. Yes, Derrick Von Beekman.

RIP. (*still more interested*) Well, and then?

SETH. Well, then her affairs went bad; and at last she married him.

RIP. (*turning it over in his mind*) Has Derrick married Gretchen?

SETH. Yes.

RIP. (*with a flash of his old humour but still with no laughter*) Well, I didn't think he would come to any good; I never did. So she cotched Derrick, eh? Poor Derrick!

SETH. Yes.

RIP. Well, here's their good health, and their family's, and may they all live long and prosper! (*Drinks.*)

SETH. Now, old gent, hadn't you better be going home, wherever that is?

RIP. (*with conviction*) Where my home was? Here's where it is.

SETH. What, here in this village? Now do you think we're going to keep all the half-witted strays that choose to come along here? No; be off with you. Why, it's a shame that those you belong to should allow such an old tramp as you to float around here.

VILLAGERS. (*roughly, and trying to push him along*) Yes; away with him!

RIP. (*frightened, and pleading with them*) Are you going to drive me away into the hills again?

FIRST VILLAGER. Yes; away with him! He's an old tramp.

(*Enter Hendrick, with stick and bundle, followed by village women.*)

VILLAGERS. Away with him!

HENDRICK. (*throwing down bundle*) Avast there, mates. Where are you towing that old hulk to? What, you won't? (*Pushing crowd aside, and going forward.*) Where are you towing that old hulk to?

SETH. Who are you?

HENDRICK. I'm a man, every inch of me; and if you doubt it, I'll undertake to remove the suspicions from any two of you in five minutes. Ain't you ashamed of yourselves? Don't you see the poor old creature has but half his wits?

SETH. Well, this is no asylum for worn out idiots.

VILLAGERS. (*coming forward*) No, it ain't!

HENDRICK. Ain't it?

OMNES. No, it ain't.

HENDRICK. Then I'll make it a hospital for broken heads if you stand there much longer. Clear the decks, you lubberly swabs!

    (*Hendrick drives them aside. Turns to Rip, who stands bewildered.*)
What is the cause of all this?

RIP. (*helplessly*) I don't know, do you?

HENDRICK. (*to Villagers*) Do any of you know him?

FIRST VILLAGER. No; he appears to be a stranger.

HENDRICK. (*to Rip*) You seem bewildered. Can I help you?

RIP. (*feebly*) Just tell me where I live.

HENDRICK. And don't you know?

RIP. No; I don't.

HENDRICK. Why, what's your name?

RIP. (*almost childishly*) I don't know; but I believe I know vat it used to be. My name, it used to be Rip Van Winkle.

VILLAGERS. (*in astonishment*) Rip Van Winkle?

HENDRICK. Rip Van Winkle? Impossible!

RIP. (*pathetically feeble, and old*) Well, I wouldn't swear to it myself. I tell you how it was. Last night, I don't know about the time, I went away up into the mountains, and while I was there I met a queer kind o' man, and we got drinkin'; and I guess I got pretty drunk. And then I went to sleep; and when I woke up this morning, I was dead. (*All laugh.*)

HENDRICK. Poor old fellow; he's crazy. Rip Van Winkle has been dead these twenty years. I knew him when I was a child.

RIP. (*clutching at a faint home*) You don't know me?

HENDRICK. No; nor anybody else here it seems.

    (*The Villagers, finding that there is to be no amusement for them, straggle off to their occupations.*)

SETH. (*as he goes into the inn*) Why, wife, he's as cracked as our old teapot.

RIP. (*with simple pathos*) Are we so soon forgot when we are gone? No one remembers Rip Van Winkle.

HENDRICK. Come, cheer up, my old hearty, and you shall share my breakfast.

(*Assists Rip to sit at the table. Rip has fallen into a dream again. Hendrick speaks to Kätchen.*)

Bring us enough for three, and of your best.

KÄTCHEN. That I will. (*Exit into inn.*)

HENDRICK. So here I am, home again. And yonder's the very spot where, five years ago, I parted from Meenie.

RIP. (*roused by the name*) What, Meenie Van Winkle?

HENDRICK. And she promised to remain true to Hendrick Vedder.

RIP. Oh, yah, that was Nick Vedder's son.

HENDRICK. (*turning to Rip*) That's me.

RIP. (*resentfully*) That was you! You think I'm a fool? He's a little child, no bigger than that—the one I mean.

HENDRICK. How mad he is!

(*Enter Kächen from inn with tray, on which is laid a breakfast. She puts tray on table. Exit Kätchen into inn.*)

There, that's right. Stow your old locker full while I take a cruise around yonder house, where, five years ago, I left the dearest bit of human nature that was ever put together. I'll be back directly. (*Aside.*) Who comes here? It's surely Derrick and his wife. Egad, I'm in luck; for now the old birds are out, Meenie will surely be alone. I'll take advantage of the coast being clear, and steer into harbor alongside.

(*Exit Hendrick. Enter Derrick, followed by Gretchen.*)

DERRICK. So you have come to that conclusion, have you?

GRETCHEN. I cannot accept this sacrifice.

RIP. (*starting from his reverie, and turning to look at her*) Why, that is Gretchen's voice.

(*As he recognizes her, and sees how aged she is.*)

My, my! Is that my wife?

DERRICK. Oh, you can't accept! Won't you kindly allow me a word on the subject?

RIP. (*aside, humourously*) No, indeed, she will not. Now, my friend, you are going to cotch it.

GRETCHEN. There is a limit even to my patience. Don't drive me to it.

RIP. (*aside, drolly*) Take care, my friend; take care.

DERRICK. Look you, woman; Meenie has consented to marry my nephew. She has pledged her word to do so on condition that I settle an annuity on you.

GRETCHEN. I won't allow my child to break her heart.

DERRICK. You won't allow? Dare to raise your voice, dare but to speak except as I command you, you shall repent it to the last hour of your life.

RIP. (*expectantly*) Now she'll knock him down, flat as a flounder.

DERRICK. (*sneeringly*) You won't allow? This is something new. Who are you; do you think you are dealing with your first husband?

GRETCHEN. Alas, no; I wish I was.

RIP. (*lost in wonderment*) My, my, if Rip was alive, he never would have believed it!

DERRICK. So you thought to get the upper hand of me, when you married me, didn't you?

GRETCHEN. I thought to get a home for my little girl--shelter, and food; want drove me to your door, and I married you for a meal's victuals for my sick child.

DERRICK. So you came to me as if I was a poor-house, eh? Then you can't complain of the treatment you received. You sacrificed yourself for Meenie, and the least she can do now, is to do the same for you. In an hour, the deeds will be ready. Now, just you take care that no insolent interference of yours spoils my plans; do you hear?

GRETCHEN. Yes, sir.

DERRICK. Why can't you be kind and affectionate to her, as I am to you. There, go and blubber over here; that's your way. You are always pretending to be miserable.

GRETCHEN. Alas, no sir! I am always pretending to be happy.

DERRICK. Don't cry. I won't have it; come now, none of that. If you come home today with red eyes, and streaky cheeks, I'll give you something to cry for; now you know what's for supper. (*Exit.*)

RIP. (*still amazed*) Well, if I hadn't seen it, I never would have believed it!

GRETCHEN. (*absorbed in her grief*) Oh, wretch that I am, I must consent, or that man will surely thrust her out of doors to starve, to beg, and to become-- (*Seeing Rip.*) Yes, to become a thing of rags and misery, like that poor soul.

RIP. She always drived the beggars away; I suppose I must go.

(*He is getting up, and starting to go.*)

GRETCHEN. (*taking penny from her pocket*) Here, my poor man, take this. It is only a penny; but take it, and may God bless you, poor wanderer, so old, so helpless. Why do you come to this strange place, so far from home?

RIP. (*keeping his face turned away from her*) She don't know me; she don't know me!

GRETCHEN. Are you alone in the world?

RIP. (*trying to bring himself to look directly at Gretchen*) My wife asks me if I'm alone.

GRETCHEN. Come with me. How feeble he is; there, lean on me. Come to yonder house, and there you shall rest your limbs by the fire.

> (*Gretchen takes his arm, and puts it in her own. As they move towards her house, Rip stops, and, with an effort, turns and looks her full in the face, with a penetrating gaze, as if imploring recognition, but there is none; and, sadly shaking his head, he shrinks into himself, and allows her to lead him tottering off.*)

Scene 4. The same room in Derrick's home as in Scene 2. (*Enter Derrick.*)

DERRICK. I don't know what women were invented for, except to make a man's life miserable. I can get a useful, hard working woman to keep my house clean, and order my dinner for me, for half that weak, snivelling creature costs me. (*Enter Cockles.*)

COCKLES. Well, uncle, what news; will she have me?

DERRICK. Leave it to me; she must, she shall.

COCKLES. If she holds out, what are we to do? It was all very well, you marrying Rip's widow, that choked off all inquiry into his affairs; but here's Meenie, Rip's heiress, who rightly owns all this property; if we don't secure her, we're not safe.

DERRICK. You've got rid of Hendrick Vedder; that's one obstacle removed.

COCKLES. I'm not so sure about that. His ship was wrecked on a lonely coast; but some of the crew may have, unfortunately, been saved.

DERRICK. If he turns up after your marriage, what need you care?

COCKLES. I'd like nothing better; I'd like to see his face when he saw my arm around his sweetheart--my wife. But if he turns up before our marriage--

DERRICK. I must put the screw on somewhere.

COCKLES. I'll tell you, Meenie will do anything for her mother's sake. Now you are always threatening to turn her out, as she turned out Rip. That's the tender place. Meenie fears more for her mother, than she cares for herself.

DERRICK. Well, what am I to do?

COCKLES. Make Gretchen independent of you; settle the little fortune on her that you are always talking about doing, but never keeping your word. The girl will sell herself to secure her mother's happiness.

DERRICK. And it would be a cheap riddance for me. I was just talking about it to Gretchen this morning. You shall have the girl; but I hope you are not going to marry her out of any weak feeling of love. You're not going to let her make a fool of you by and by?

COCKLES. I never cared for her until she was impudent to me, and got that sailor lover of hers to thrash me; and then I began to feel a hunger for her I never felt before.

DERRICK. That's just the way I felt for Gretchen.

COCKLES. 'T ain't revenge that I feel; it's enterprise. I want to overcome a difficulty.

DERRICK. (*chuckling*) And so you shall. Come, we'll put your scheme in train at once; and let this be a warning to you hereafter, never marry another man's widow.

COCKLES. No, uncle, I'll take a leaf out of your book, and let it be a warning to her. (*Exeunt.*)

Scene 5. A plain sitting-room in Derrick's house. A table stands in the center with several chairs around it. There are cups, a jug, and a workbasket on the table. (*As the curtain rises, Meenie is discovered seated by the table.*)

MEENIE. Why should I repine? Did my mother hesitate to sacrifice her life to make a home for me? No; these tears are ungrateful, selfish.

   (*The door at the back opens. Enter Gretchen, leading Rip, who seems very feeble and a little wild.*)

GRETCHEN. Come in and rest a while.

RIP. This is your house, your home?

GRETCHEN. Yes. Meenie, Meenie, bring him a chair.

RIP. (*turning aside so as to shield his face from Meenie*) Is that your daughter?

GRETCHEN. That is my daughter.

RIP. (*looking timidly at Meenie, as Gretchen helps him into a chair*) I though you was a child.

GRETCHEN. (*crossing to go into another room, and speaking to Meenie, who starts to follow her*) Stay with him until I get some food to fill his wallet. Don't be frightened, child, he is only a simple, half-witted creature whose misery has touched my heart.

   (*Exit Gretchen. Meenie takes her workbasket and starts to follow.*)

RIP. (*holding out his hand to detain her*) One moment, my dear. Come here, and let me look at you. (*Pathetically.*) Are you afraid? I won't hurt you. I only want to look at you; that is all. Won't you come?

(*Meenie puts down her workbasket, and Rip is relieved of his great fear that she might leave him. His excitement increases as he goes on in his struggle to make her recognize him.*)

Yes, I thought you would. Oh, yah, that is Meenie! But you are grown! (*Meenie smiles.*) But see the smile in the eyes! That is just the same Meenie. You are a woman, Meenie. Do you remember something of your father?

(*He looks at her as if on her answer hangs his reason and his life.*)

MEENIE. I do. I do. Oh, I wish he was here now!

RIP. (*half rising in his excitement*) Yah? But he isn't? No? No?

MEENIE. No; he's dead. I remember him so well. No one ever loved him as I did.

RIP. No; nobody ever loved me like my child.

MEENIE. Never shall I forget his dear, good face. Tell me--

RIP. (*eagerly and expectantly*) Yah?

MEENIE. Did you know him?

RIP. (*confused by her question, and afraid to answer*) Well, I thought I did. But I-- When I say that here, in the village, the people all laugh at me.

MEENIE. He is wandering. (*She starts to go.*)

RIP. (*making a great effort of will, and resolved to put the question of his identity to the test*) Don't go away from me. I want you to look at me now, and tell me if you have ever seen me before.

MEENIE. (*surprised*) No.

RIP. (*holding out his arms to her*) Try, my darlin', won't you?

MEENIE. (*frightened*) What do you mean? Why do you gaze so earnestly and fondly on me?

RIP. (*rising, in trembling excitement, approaching her*) I am afraid to tell you, my dear, because if you say it is not true, it may be it would break my heart. But, Meenie, either I dream, or I am mad; but I am your father.

MEENIE. My father!

RIP. Yes; but hear me, my dear, and then you will know.

(*Trying to be logical and calm, but laboring under great excitement.*)

This village here is the village of Falling Waters. Well, that was my home. I had here in this place my wife, Gretchen, and my child Meenie-- little Meenie--

(*A long pause, as he strives to reassemble his ideas and memories.*)

And my dog Schneider. That's all the family what I've got. Try and remember me, dear, won't you? (*Pleadingly.*) I don't know when it was-- This night there was a storm; and my wife drived me from my house; and I went away-- I don't remember any more till I come back here now. And see, I get back now, and my wife is gone, and my home is gone. My home is gone, and my child--my child looks in my face, and don't know who I am!

MEENIE. (*rushing into his arms*) I do! Father!

RIP. (*sobbing*) Ah, my child! Somebody knows me now! Somebody knows me now!

MEENIE. But can it be possible?

RIP. Oh, yah; it is so, Meenie! (*With a pathetic return of his uncertainty.*) Don't say it is not, or you will kill me.

MEENIE. No. One by one your features come back to my memory. Your voice recalls that of my dear father, too. I cannot doubt; yet it is so strange.

RIP. Yah, but it is me, Meenie; it is me.

MEENIE. I am bewildered. Surely mother will know you.

RIP. (*smiling*) No, I don't believe she'll know me.

MEENIE. She can best prove your identity. I will call her.

RIP. No. You call the dog Schneider. He'll know me better than my wife.
   (*They retire to a sofa in the background, where Rip sits with his arm around Meenie. Enter Derrick, with documents.*)

DERRICK. What old vagabond is this? (*Meenie starts to resent insult.*)

RIP. (*aside to Meenie*) Don't you say a word.

DERRICK. (*to Gretchen, who has entered, followed by Cockles*) Here, give him a cold potato, and let him go. Come you here, mistress. Here are the papers for the young couple to sign.

COCKLES. (*aside*) And the sooner the better. (*Aloud.*) Hush, Uncle, Hendrick is here.

DERRICK. Young Vedder? Then we must look sharp. (*To Gretchen.*) Come, fetch that girl of yours to sign this deed.

GRETCHEN. Never shall she put her name to that paper with my consent. Never.

DERRICK. Dare you oppose me in my own house? Dare you preach disobedience under my roof?

GRETCHEN. I dare do anything when my child's life's at stake. No, a thousand times no! You shall not make of her what you have made of me. Starvation and death are better than such a life as I lead.

DERRICK. (*raising cane*) Don't provoke me.

GRETCHEN. (*kneeling*) Beat me, starve me. You can only kill me. After all, I deserve it. (*Rising.*) But Meenie has given her promise to Hendrick Vedder, and she shall not break her word.

COCKLES. But Hendrick Vedder is dead.

(*The door is flung open, and Hendrick enters.*)

HENDRICK. That's a lie! He's alive!

GRETCHEN and MEENIE. (*rushing to him*) Alive!

HENDRICK. (*to Meenie*) I've heard all about it. They made you believe that I was dead. (*To Derrick.*) Only wait till I get through here. (*Embracing Meenie.*) What a pleasure I've got to come! (*To Derrick.*) And what a thrashing I've brought back for you two swabs.

DERRICK. (*angrily*) Am I to be bullied under my own roof by a beggarly sailor? Quit my house, all of you. (*He seizes Gretchen.*) As for you, woman, this is your work, and I'll make you pay for it.

GRETCHEN. Hendrick, save me from him. He will kill me.

HENDRICK. Stand off!

DERRICK. (*raising cane*) No; she is my wife, mine.

GRETCHEN. Heaven help me, I am!

(*Rip rises, comes forward, and leans against the table, one hand in his game-bag. He is fully awake and has recovered all his old shrewdness.*)

RIP. Stop. I am not so sure about that. If that is so, then what has become of Rip Van Winkle?

COCKLES. He's dead.

RIP. That's another lie. He's no more dead than Hendrick Vedder. Derrick Von Beekman, you say this house and land was yours?

DERRICK. Yes.

RIP. Where and what is the paper what you wanted Rip Van Winkle to sign when he was drunk, but sober enough not to do it?

(*Taking an old paper out of game-bag, and turning to Hendrick.*)

Have you forgot how to read?

HENDRICK. No.

RIP. Then you read that.

(*Hendrick takes the document from Rip, and looks it over.*)

DERRICK. What does this mad old vagabond mean to say?

RIP. I mean, that is my wife, Gretchen Van Winkle.

GRETCHEN. (*rushing to Rip*) Rip! Rip!

COCKLES. I say, Uncle, are you going to stand that? That old impostor is going it under your nose in fine style.

DERRICK. I'm dumb with rage. (*To the Villagers, who have crowded in.*) Out of my house, all of you! (*To Rip.*) Begone, you old tramp!

HENDRICK. (*to Rip*) Stay where you are. (*To Derrick.*) This house don't don't belong to you. Not an acre of land, nor a brick in the town is yours. They have never ceased to belong to Rip Van Winkle; and this document proves it.

DERRICK. 'Tis false. That paper is a forgery.

HENDRICK. Oh, no, it is not; for I read it to Rip twenty years ago.

RIP. Clever boy! Clever boy! That's the reason I didn't sign it then, Derrick.

DERRICK. (*approaching Hendrick*) And do you think I'm fool enough to give up my property in this way?

HENDRICK. No. You're fool enough to hang on to it, until we make you refund to Rip every shilling over and above the paltry sum you loaned him upon it. Now, if you are wise, you'll take a hint. There's the door. Go! And never let us see your face again.

RIP. Yah; give him a cold potato, and let him go.

(*Exit Derrick in a great rage. All the Villagers laugh at him. Hendrick follows him to the door.*)

COCKLES. (*kneeling to Meenie*) Oh, Meenie! Meenie!

HENDRICK. (*taking him by the ear*) I'll Meenie you!

(*He pushes Cockles out. Villagers laugh. Meenie gives Rip a chair.*)

GRETCHEN. (*kneeling beside Rip*) Oh, Rip! I drove you from your home; but do not desert me again. I'll never speak an unkind word to you, and you shall never see a frown on my face. And, Rip--

RIP. Yah.

GRETCHEN. You may stay out all night, if you like.

RIP. (*leaning back in his chair*) No, thank you. I had enough of that.

GRETCHEN. And, Rip, you can get tight as often as you please.

RIP. (*taking bottle and filling cup from it*) No; I don't touch another drop.

MEENIE. (*kneeling by the other side of Rip*) Oh, yes, you will, father. For see, here are all the neighbors come to welcome you home.

(*Gretchen offers Rip the cup.*)

RIP. (*with all his old kindliness and hospitality*) Well, bring in all the children, and the neighbors, and the dogs, and-- (*Seeing the cup which Gretchen is offering.*) I swore off, you know. Well, I won't count this one; for this will go down with a prayer. I will take my cup and pipe and tell my strange story to all my friends. Here is my child Meenie, and my wife Gretchen, and my boy Hendrick. I'll drink all your good health, and I'll drink your good health, and your families', and may they all live long and prosper!

CURTAIN.

Augustin Daly (1839-1899)
and *Under the Gaslight*

With his tremendous energy and almost total absorbtion in his work, Augustin Daly was the most influential man in American theatre during his lifetime. Drama critic, theatre manager, playwright, and adaptor, he became the first recognized stage director in America, a *regisseur* who exercised a fierce and tyrannical control over all aspects of his productions. His rules of conduct for actors and actresses imposed heavy fines for late appearances and forgotten lines and earned him the title "the autocrat of the stage."

Under the Gaslight was the first play in which Daly exploited his remarkable gift for sensational melodrama. In this play he also touched upon the social problems--poverty in cities, the system of justice, the treatment of Civil War veterans, the battle for women's rights--which would appear in his later plays such as *Divorce*, 1871, and *Undercurrent*, 1888. More memorable, though, were his vivid scenes: the fire and water spectacle in *A Flash of Lightning*, 1868; the hero's harrowing ordeal in the sawmill in *The Red Scarf*, 1868; and the train scene in *Under the Gaslight*, which Rose Eytinge, who played Laura in early productions, recorded in her memoirs: "I only remember that the situation of the piece is where I break down a door with an axe which I opportunely find, and rescue somebody who is lashed down on a railroad track."

In an essay entitled "The American Dramatist" (*North American Review*, 1886), Daly stressed "a plan of collaboration," an apt concept for Daly, whose brother Joseph contributed substantially to the plays Daly claimed as his own. His basic philosophy was to give audiences what they wanted. Consequently, he staged Shakespearean plays using bastard texts to display the particular talents of his performers. He ignored the plays of G.B. Shaw and Henrik Ibsen, and he did not actively promote American playwrights.

To Daly, Realism meant stage spectacle, and he is best remembered as a resourceful impressario and a conjurer of bold theatrical magic.

Augustin Daly in 1869

Under the Gaslight, Act III, Scene 3

UNDER THE GASLIGHT

(1867)

by Augustin Daly

CHARACTERS

Ray Trafford, a rich young man
Laura Courtland, his sweetheart
Pearl Courtland, her cousin
Fashionable Members of Society:
    Edward Demilt, Windel,
    Mrs. Van Dam, Miss Earlie
Snorkey, a messenger
Martin, a servant
Byke, a villain
Judas, his associate
Peachblossom, a servant
Negro servant
Ladies and Gentlemen

Street Sellers:
    Bermudas, Peanuts
Justice Bowling
Splinter, an attorney
Peter Rich, a vagrant boy
Policeman 999
Rafferdi, an organ-grinder
Sam, a negro
Police Sergeant
Officers of the police court
Policemen
Dock boys
Signalman

ACT I.

Scene 1. Parlour at the Courtlands, deep window at back showing snowy exterior-- Street lamp lighted-- Time, night-- The place elegantly furnished, chandelier, etc. (*Ray Trafford is discovered lounging on tête-à-tête, Pearl is taking leave of Demilt, Windel, Mrs. Van Dam, and Sue Earlie, who are all dressed and muffled to go out.*)

MRS. VAN DAM. Good night! Of course we'll see you on Tuesday.
PEARL. To be sure you will.
DEMILT. Never spent a jollier hour. Good night, Ray.
RAY. (*on sofa*) Good night.
MRS. VAN DAM. You won't forget the sociable on Tuesday, Ray?
RAY. Oh, I won't forget.
ALL. (*at door*) Good night--good night.
    (*Exeunt Demilt, Wendel, Mrs. Van Dam, and Miss Earlie.*)
PEARL. Good night. Oh, dear, now they're gone and the holiday's gone

with them. (*Goes to window.*) There they go. (*Laughter without.*) Ray, do come and look at the Van Dam's new sleigh. How they have come out.

RAY. Yes, it's the gayest thing in the park.

PEARL. I wonder where they got the money! I thought you said Van Dam had failed.

RAY. Well, yes. He failed to pay, but he continues to spend.

PEARL. (*as if to those outside*) Good night!

> (*Response from without as sleigh bells jingle "good night."*)

I wish I was in there with you. It's delightful for a sleigh ride, if it wasn't New Year's. Oh! there's Demilt over.

> (*Laughter outside, cracking of whips, Ray saunters up to window, sleigh bells jingle. Sleigh music heard to die away, Ray and Pearl wave their handkerchiefs. Pearl closes lace curtains.*)

Isn't it a frightful thing to be shut up here on such a beautiful night, and New Year's of all others? Pshaw, we've had nothing but mopes all day. Oh, dear, I hate mourning, though it does become me, and I hate everything but fun, larks, and dancing.

RAY. Where in the world is Laura?

PEARL. Oh, do forget her for a second, can't you? She'll be here presently. You're not in the house a minute but it's "Where's Laura?" "Why don't Laura come?"

RAY. (*taking her hand*) Well, if anybody in the world could make me forget her, it would be you. But if you had a lover, wouldn't you like him to be as constant as that?

PEARL. That's quite another thing.

RAY. But that doesn't answer my question. Where is she?

PEARL. I sent for her as soon as I saw you coming. She has hardly been down here a moment all this evening. Oh, dear! Now don't you think I'm a victim, to be cooped up in this way instead of receiving calls as we used to?

RAY. You forget that your mother died only last summer.

PEARL. No, I don't forget. Pshaw, you're just like Laura. She's only my cousin, and yet she keeps always saying "Poor aunt Mary. Let us not forget how she would have sorrowed for us."

RAY. Well, don't you know she would, too?

PEARL. I don't know anything about it. I was always at boarding school, and she only saw me once a year. Laura was always at home, and it's very different. But don't let's talk about it. To die--ugh! I don't want to die till I don't want to live--and that'll not be for a million of years. Come, tell me, where have you been today? How many calls did you make?

RAY. About sixty.

PEARL. That's all? You're lazy. Demilt and Windel made a hundred and thirty, and they say that's nothing. Won't you have a cup of coffee?

RAY. No.

PEARL. Ain't you hungry?

RAY. No--you torment.

PEARL. Oh, dear! I suppose it's because you're going to be married shortly to Laura. If there's one time that a man's stupid to his friends, it's when he's going to be married shortly. Tell me whom you saw.

(*Ray has sauntered off and is looking over cards on table.*)

Where are you? Oh, you needn't be so impatient to see her. Do be agreeable. Sit here and tell me something funny, or I shall drop down and fall asleep.

RAY. You witch! Why didn't I fall in love with you?

PEARL. (*laughing*) I don't know--why didn't you?

RAY. You never keep me waiting. (*Listening.*) Ah! that's her step. No.

PEARL. Do sit down.

RAY. (*sitting*) This calling's a great bore. But as you and Laura insisted I should go through it, I did. First, I--(*jumping up*)--I knew it was she. (*Goes to door, meets Laura, who enters.*) How you did keep me waiting!

(*Ray kisses both her hands.*)

LAURA. And you, sir, we have been looking for you since eight o'clock.

RAY. Oh, I was fulfilling your orders. I've been engaged in the business of calling from ten o'clock in the morning till now, ten at night.

LAURA. Well, you can make this your last one, for you have leave to spend a nice long hour chatting here before you go. Won't you have some supper?

RAY. I don't care if I do, I'm rather famished.

PEARL. Well, I declare! Did Laura bring your appetite with her?

(*Laura rings.*)

RAY. I don't know how it is, but she brings me a relish for everything in life, I believe. Laura, I think if I were to lose you, I'd mope to death and starve to death.

LAURA. Well, that's as much to say I'm a sort of life pill. (*Enter Martin.*) Martin, supper. (*Exit Martin.*)

RAY. You may joke about it, but it's so. You take the lounge.

(*Laura and Pearl sit on tête-à-tête.*)

PEARL. You don't want me to go away, do you?

(*Putting her head on Laura's shoulder.*)

LAURA. Certainly not. What an idea!

PEARL. I'm sure you'll have time enough to be alone when you are married. And I do so want to talk and be talked to.

LAURA. Well, Ray shall talk to you.

PEARL. He was just going to tell me about his calls today.

LAURA. That's exactly what we want to hear about. Did you call on everyone we told you to?

RAY. Everyone. There was Miss--

PEARL. Did you go to Henrietta Liston's first?

RAY. Yes, and wasn't she dressed!

PEARL. Speaking of dress, are you going to have your new pink for the sociable Tuesday?

LAURA. Yes, Pearl, and I will do credit to the occasion as it is our first for a year.

RAY. (*taking Laura's hand*) And *our* last.

PEARL. Our last!

RAY. Laura's and mine. For when we are married, you know, we shall be tabooed--where maids and bachelors only are permitted.

PEARL. Oh, bless me! (*Rising.*) How do you do, Mrs. Trafford?

LAURA. (*rising, sadly*) I wish you hadn't said that, Pearl. You know the old proverb, "Call a maid by a married name."

RAY. Nonsense! (*Putting his arm about Laura's waist.*) It's only a few days to wait, and we'll live long enough, you know. For nothing but death shall separate us. (*Martin appears at door.*)

PEARL. Oh, here's supper.

MARTIN. Beg pardon, Miss.

LAURA. What's the matter?

MARTIN. There's a person below, Miss, who says he's been sent with a bouquet for you, Miss, and must deliver it in person.

LAURA. For me? Who's servant is it?

MARTIN. I don't know, Miss, he looks like one of those soldier messengers, red hat and all that.

LAURA. Show him up here. (*Exit Martin.*)

PEARL. How romantic. So late at night. It's a rival in disguise, Ray.
(*Re-enter Martin, showing in Snorkey with an air of disdain. Snorkey has a large bouquet in his left hand, and his hat is under the stump of his right arm, which is cut off.*)

LAURA. You wished to see me.

SNORKEY. Are you Miss Laura Courtland?

LAURA. Yes.

SNORKEY. Then I was told to give you this.

LAURA. By whom?

SNORKEY. Now, that's what I don't know myself. You see, I was down by the steps of the Fifth Avenue Hotel taking a light supper off a small toothpick, when a big chap dressed in black came by, and says he, "Hallo, come with me if you want to earn a quarter." (*Confidentially to all.*) That being my very frame of mind, I went up one street and down another till we came here. "Just you take this up there," says he, "and ask for Miss Laura Courtland, and give it to her and no one else."

LAURA. It is some folly of our late visitors.

SNORKEY. I'm one of the soldier messengers, Miss. A South Carolina gentleman took such a fancy to me at Fredericksburg! Wouldn't have no denial--cut off my arm to remember me by; he was very fond of me. I wasn't any use to Uncle Sam then, so I came home, put a red band round my blue cap, and with my empty sleeve, as a character from my last place, set up for light porter and general messenger. All orders executed with neatness and dispatch.

LAURA. Poor fellow! Martin, be sure and give him a glass of wine before he goes.

SNORKEY. I'm much obliged, Miss, but I don't think it would be good for me on an empty stomach after fasting all day.

LAURA. Well, Martin shall find you some supper, too.

SNORKEY. Is this Martin? What a nice young man! Mayn't he have a drop of something, too? He must have caught cold letting me in, he has got such a dreadful stiffness in the back of his neck. (*Exit Martin.*)

RAY. (*giving pencilled address*) Call me at this place tomorrow, and you shan't regret it.

SNORKEY. All right, Cap'n. I haven't forgot the army regulations about punctuality and promotion. Ladies, if ever either of you should want a light porter, think of Joe Snorkey--wages no objection. (*Exit.*)

PEARL. (*who has been examining the bouquet*) Oh, Laura, only look, here's a billet-doux.

RAY. Nonsense, crazy-head, who would dare? (*Takes bouquet.*) A letter! (*Takes a paper from bouquet.*)

LAURA. A letter?

PEARL. I am crazy--am I?

RAY. "For Miss Laura Courtland. Confidential."

LAURA. (*laughs*) Ha, ha! From some goose who has made one call too many today. Read it, Ray.

RAY. "Dear Laura . . ." (*Refusing the letter and going to Pearl.*)

(*Laura looks at the letter a moment, when the whole expression of her face changes, then reads slowly and deliberately.*)

LAURA. " I respectfully beg you to grant me the favor of an interview tonight. I have waited until your company retired. I am waiting across the street now."

PEARL. (*runs to window*) A tall man in black is just walking away.

LAURA. " If you will have the door opened as soon as you get this, I will step over; if you don't, I will ring; under all circumstances I will get in. There is no need to sign my name; you will remember me as the strange man whom you once saw talking with your mother in the parlour, and who frightened you so much." What can be the meaning of this? Pearl-- no. (*Goes to bell on table and rings.*)

RAY. Laura, you--

LAURA. Ask me nothing. I will tell you by and by. (*Enter Martin.*)

MARTIN. Miss--

LAURA. Admit no one till you bring me the name.

MARTIN. I was about to tell you, Miss, that a strange man has forced himself in at the door and asks to see you, but will give no name.

RAY. Kick the rascal out.

PEARL. Oh, don't let him come here.

MARTIN. He's a very strange-looking person, Miss.

RAY. I'll find out what this means.

(*Ray is going to door when Byke appears at it, smiling and bowing.*)

BYKE. I'll spare you the trouble, if you'll hear me a minute.

RAY. (*violently*) Who are you, fellow?

BYKE. Don't, I beg you. Don't speak so crossly; I might answer back; then you'd kick me out, and you'd never forgive yourself for it as long as I lived.

RAY. Your business? Come, speak quickly and be gone.

BYKE. Business, on this happy day! I came for pleasure--to see Miss Courtland, my little pupil--grown so--only think, sir, I knew her when she was only a little child; I taught her music--she was so musical--and so beautiful--I adored her, and her mother told me I needn't come again.

(*To Laura, who is pale with terror, leaning on Pearl.*)

But I did, and her mother was glad to see me, wasn't she, little pupil? And begged me to stay--but I said no--I'd call occasionally--to see my dear little pupil and to receive any trifling contribution her mother might give me. Won't you shake hands, little pupil?

(*Advances suddenly, when Ray grasps him by the collar. Byke glares at him a moment, then quickly, as before.*)

Don't, please, don't; the stuff is old and I've no other.

RAY. The fellow's drunk. Leave the house.

BYKE. What, after sending that touching bouquet?

LAURA. It was you, then? I knew it.

BYKE. You see, she knows me. Ah, memory, how it blooms again when the plough of time has passed.

LAURA. Leave this house at once.

BYKE. Not until I have spoken to you.

RAY. (*seizing him*) You miserable rascal.

BYKE. Don't, pray don't. I weight a hundred and ninety-eight pounds, and if you attempt to throw me about, you'll strain yourself.

LAURA. Go; tomorrow in the morning I will see you.

BYKE. Thanks. I thank you, Miss, for your forbearance. I am also obliged to you, sir, for not throwing me out at the window. I am indeed. I wish you good night and many happy returns of the day.

(*Bows and turns to go, then familiarly to Martin.*)

Many calls today, John?

(*Exeunt Byke and Martin. Ray runs to Laura, who is pale and agitated.*)

LAURA. (*pointing after Byke*) See that he goes. (*Exit Ray. Laura, taking both of Pearl's hands in her own.*) Pearl, he must know everything.

PEARL. Oh, dear, this is dreadful. I do hate scenes.

LAURA. He must know everything, I tell you; and you must relate all. He will question, he will ponder--leave him nothing to ask.

PEARL. If you wish it, but--

LAURA. I desire it; speak of me as you will, but tell him the truth. (*Enter Ray, hastily.*) Stay with her, don't follow me. (*Exit Laura.*)

RAY. Pearl, what does this mean?

PEARL. Oh, it's only a little cloud that I want to clear up for you.

RAY. Cloud? How? Where?

PEARL. Don't I tell you I am going to tell you? Sit down here by me.

RAY. He said he knew her. And she gave him an interview for tomorrow. That drunken wretch--

PEARL. Do sit down. I can never speak while you are walking about so. Sit by me, won't you, for I've got something strange to tell you.

RAY. *You* serious? I'd as soon expect to see the lightning tamed. Well, I listen.

PEARL. I have something to say to you, Ray, which you must settle with your own heart. You love Laura, do you not?

RAY. Pearl, I do more; I adore her. I adore the very air that she breathes. I will never be happy without her, I can swear *that*.

PEARL. Laura is twenty now. How do you think she looked when I first saw her?

RAY. Were you at home when she first came into this earthly sphere?

PEARL. Yes.

RAY. Well then, I suppose she looked very small and very pink.

PEARL. She was covered with rags, barefooted, unkempt, crying, and six years old.

RAY. (*shocked*) Explain.

PEARL. One night father and mother were going to the opera. When they were crossing Broadway, the usual crowd of children accosted them for alms. As mother felt in her pocket for some change, her fingers touched a cold and trembling hand which had clutched her purse.

RAY. A pickpocket! Well?

PEARL. This hand my mother grasped in her own, and so tightly that a small, feeble voice uttered an exclamation of pain. Mother looked down, and there beside her was a little ragged girl.

RAY. The thief.

PEARL. Yes, but a thief hardly six years old, with a face like an angel's. " Stop!" said my mother, " what are you doing?" " Trying to steal," said the child. " Don't you know that it's wicked to do so?" asked my father. " No," said the girl, " but it's dreadful to be hungry." " Who told you to steal?" asked my mother. " She--there!" said the child, pointing to a squalid woman in a doorway opposite, who fled suddenly down the street. " That is Old Judas," said the girl.

RAY. Old Judas! What a name! But how does this story interest us?

PEARL. This child was Laura. My father was about to let her go unharmed, but my mother said, " No, it is not enough. We have a duty to perform, even to her," and acting on a sudden impulse, took her to our home. On being questioned there, the child seemed to have no recollection save of misery and blows. My mother persuaded father, and the girl was sent to a country clergyman's for instruction, and there she remained for several years.

RAY. Pearl, you are joking with me.

PEARL. In beauty, and accomplishments, and dignity, Laura, as mother named her, exceeded every girl of her age. In gratitude she was all that father could have wished. She was introduced, as you know, into society as my cousin, and no one dreams of her origin.

RAY. (*starting up*) Laura an outcast--a thief!

PEARL. (*rising*) No, that is what she might have been.

RAY. And this man--tonight?

PEARL. All I know about him is that four years ago this man came with a cruel-looking woman, to see mother. There was a fearful scene between them, for Laura and I sat trembling on the stairs and overheard some awful words. At last they went away, the man putting money into his pocket as he left.

RAY. But who were they?

PEARL. Laura never told me, and mother would not. But, of course, they must have been Laura's father and mother. (*Ray sinks on chair as if overcome.*) Mother made me promise never to tell anybody this, and you would have known nothing had not Laura made me speak. You see, she would not conceal anything from you. Ray, why don't you speak--shall I go after Laura? Shall I tell her to come to you? Why don't you answer? I'll go and tell her you want to see her. I'm going to send her to you, Ray. (*Goes off, still looking back at him.*)

RAY. (*starting up*) What a frightful story! Laura Courtland a thief! A drunken wretch who knows her history and a squalid beggar woman can claim her at any moment as their own child. And I was about to marry her. Yes, and I love her. But what would my mother think? My friends? Society? No--no--no--I cannot think of it. I will write her--I will tell her--pshaw! She knows, of course, that I cannot wed her now. (*Goes to the table.*) Here is paper. (*Sits.*) What am I about to do? What will be said of me? But I owe a duty to myself--to society--I must perform it. (*Writes.*) "Laura, I have heard all from your sister." What have I said? (*Crosses out last words.*) "From Pearl. You know that I love you, but my mother will demand of me a wife who will not blush to own her kindred, and who is not the daughter of obscurity and crime." It is just-- it is I who have been deceived. (*Addresses letter.*) I will leave it for her.

(*Puts on light overcoat which hangs on chair at back.*)

I must go before she returns. Her step--too late!

(*Ray crams the letter into pocket of overcoat. Enter Laura.*)

LAURA. (*gently*) Ray.

RAY. Miss--Miss Courtland.

(*Laura looks at him a moment, smiles, and then crosses without further noticing him, and sits down on tête-à-tête.*)

What have I said? What ought I to have said?

(*He takes a step towards her-- she rises, without looking at him, goes to the window, looks out, then looks over books on table.*)

Laura, I--

LAURA. Pshaw, where is my book?

RAY. What book do you want, Laura?

LAURA. Sir!

RAY. (*repulsed*) Oh--(*pause, then aside*)--I've been a fool. How lovely she looks. (*He follows her mechanically to table.*) Can I find it for you?

LAURA. (*picking up book and sitting*) Don't trouble yourself, I beg.

RAY. (*coming forward and leaning over her seat*) Laura.

LAURA. (*without lifting her head*) Well.

RAY. (*toying with her hair*) Look at me. (*Laura turns round and looks full at him.*) No, no, not that way--as you used to. You act as if I were a stranger.

LAURA. They are only strangers who call me Miss Courtland.

   (*Resumes reading.*)

RAY. Forgive me, I beg you to forgive me. I was mad--it was so sudden--this miserable story--but I don't care what they say. Oh, do listen to me. I thought you hated reading.

LAURA. I often wish that I were ugly, wretched, and repulsive, like the heroine in this story.

RAY. Why?

LAURA. Because then I could tell who really loved me.

RAY. And don't you know?

LAURA. No, I do not.

RAY. Well, I know.

LAURA. Do tell me then, please.

RAY. He has told you so himself a hundred times.

LAURA. You?

RAY. I!

LAURA. (*laughing heartily at him, then seriously*) How happy must those women be who are poor, and friendless, and plain, when some true heart comes and says " I wish to marry you!"

RAY. Laura, you act very strangely tonight.

LAURA. Will you put this book away?

RAY. (*throws it on table*) There, Laura. (*Seats himself beside her.*)

LAURA. (*rising*) There's Pearl calling me.

RAY. (*rising, taking her hand*) Laura, why don't you let me speak to you?

LAURA. About what?

RAY. About my love.

LAURA. For whom? Not me. This is only marriage and giving in marriage. I hate the very word.

RAY. You did not think so once.

LAURA. I wish I had. I am frightened now; I begin to understand myself better.

RAY. And I am frightened because I understand you less.

LAURA. Do not try to; good night. (*Stops by door as she is going out.*) Good night, Mr. Trafford. (*Exit Laura, laughing.*)

RAY. I've been an ass. No, I wrong that noble animal. The ass recognized the angel, and I, like Balaam, was blind. But I see now. After all, what have I to fear? (*Takes letter from pocket.*) No one knows of this. (*Puts it in his pocket again.*) Let things go on; we'll be married, go straight to Europe, and live there ten years. That's the way we'll fix it.

(*Exit Ray. Scene closes in.*)

Scene 2. 1st grooves-- The gentlemen's coat-room at Delmonico's-- Opening, C., for hats and coats. Chairs, L. Pier glass on flat. (*Enter Windel and Demilt, muffled, and with umbrellas; they proceed to disrobe.*)

DEMILT. Phew! Wet as the deuce, and cold, too. There'll be nobody here.

WINDEL. It's an awful night. The rooms are almost empty.

DEMILT. Sam! Where the dickens is that darkey?

(*Enter Sam, fetching in a chair, and boot-black box and brush.*)

SAM. Here, sah.

DEMILT. (*sitting in chair*) Hurry up with my boots. Who's here?

SAM. Berry few gemman, sah; only lebben overcoats and ten overshoes. Dem overshoes is spilin' the polishin' business.

DEMILT. Look out and don't give me any knocks.

WINDEL. (*handing in his coat at window and getting check for it*) I wonder if the Courtland girls have come yet.

DEMILT. What did Laura Courtland ever see in Trafford to fall in love with? The Van Dam party is my fancy.

WINDEL. (*brushing his hair at glass*) She's ten years older than you, and has a husband.

DEMILT. Yes, a fine old banker, on whom she can draw for everything but attention and affection. She has to get that by her own business tact.

(*Other parties enter, exchange good nights, and deposit their coats; some go out at once, some arrange themselves at glass.*)

DEMILT. That'll do, Sam, take my coat. (*Enter Ray Trafford.*)

WINDEL. Hallo, Trafford, this is a night, ain't it? Have the Courtlands come?

RAY. Not with me. Here, Sam, take my coat! (*His coat is pulled off by Sam, and four letters drop out.*) Stupid!

DEMILT. Save the pieces. Mind the love letters.

RAY. (*picking them up*) Look out well next time. (*Aside.*) There's that cursed letter I was going to send to Laura. Confound it, I must destroy it when I go home.

(*Puts letter back in overcoat pocket--gets his boots touched up.*)

DEMILT. I say, Trafford, what'll you take and let a fellow read those? Windel, I guess if the girls could get into the cloak-room, it would be better than the dead-letter office. What a time they'd have! Are you ready?

WINDEL. What's the use of hurrying? There's no life in the party till Laura Courtland comes. By jove, Trafford! You're in luck. She's the prettiest girl in New York.

RAY. And the best. (*March music heard.*)

DEMILT. There's the march music; let's go.

(*Gets a final brush as they all go off.*)

RAY. Come along. (*Exeunt.*)

SAM. (*picking up a letter dropped from Ray's pocket*) Dere's anoder of dem billy dooses; wonder if it am Mist Trafford's. Eh, golly! mustn't mix dem gemman's letter--mustn't mix 'em nohow--or nobody or nuffing wouldn't be able to stop fighting in dis city for de nex' month.

(*Exit, carrying a chair, etc.*)

Scene 3. The blue room at Delmonico's. Waltz music as the scene opens. (*Waltzes in motion-- Pearl is dancing with Mrs. Van Dam. Enter Ray Trafford, Demilt and Windel.*)

PEARL. There's Ray. I've had enough; I want to speak with him.

(*Bursts away from Mrs. Van Dam, runs up to Trafford. Demilt goes up to Mrs. Van Dam.*)

You lazy fellow, where have you been?

DEMILT. You're not tired, are you?

MRS. VAN DAM. I feel as fresh as a daisy.

DEMILT. Have a waltz with me.

(*Waltz music, piano, as they dance; Windel goes to Miss Earlie.*)

RAY. Where's Laura?

PEARL. She wasn't ready, and I was dying to come. Been fixing since eight o'clock; so I came with Miss Earlie. So you made it up with Laura?

RAY. Yes. Don't say anything more about the horrid subject. We've made it all up. But what on earth keeps her tonight? It's eleven already. Confound it, I tremble every moment she's out of my sight. I fear that terrible man and his secret.

MRS. VAN DAM. (*coming up, with Demilt*) Trafford, you look very uneasy; what's the matter?

RAY. Oh, nothing. I think I ought to go for Laura. I will, too. (*Servant passes at back.*) Here! go upstairs for my overcoat.

(*Ray gives the man a card, and he goes out.*)

MRS. VAN DAM. Nonsense! She'll be here in good time. You shan't leave us. Hold him, Pearl. We want a nine-pin quadrille; we haven't half enough gentlemen. Come, be jolly about it. You lovers are always afraid someone will carry your girls away.

RAY. (*uneasily*) I? I'm not afraid.

PEARL. Come, come! I never saw such a restless fellow.

SERVANT. (*entering with coat*) Here's your coat, sir.

MRS. VAN DAM. Give it to me. I'm determined you shan't go. (*Takes coat carelessly.*) I'll make you a promise-- If Laura isn't here in fifteen minutes, you shall have your coat, and may go for her.

RAY. Well, I suppose I'll have to wait.

MRS. VAN DAM. There, take him off, Pearl. (*Ray goes off with Pearl. To servant.*) Here, take this back. (*Flings coat to servant; letters drop from it.*) Well, there! (*Miss Earlie and another lady run and pick up letters.*) Love letters, of course! (*Smelling them.*) Perfumed to suffocation.

MISS EARLIE. Here's one for Laura, it's unsealed and not delivered.

(*Tremolo waltz music.*)

MRS. VAN DAM. A fair prize, let's see it. (*Music. She takes and opens it, puts on eye-glasses and reads.*) "Laura," well, come, that's cool for a lover, "I have heard all from"--something scratched out--ah! "your sister, Pearl--your obscure origin--terrible family connections--the secret of the tie which binds you to a drunken wretch--my mother, society--will demand of me a wife who will not blush to own her kindred--or start at the name of outcast and thief. Signed, Ray Trafford."

(*All stand speechless and look at each other-- all this time the rest have been dancing.*)

MISS EARLIE. What can it mean?

MRS. VAN DAM. It means that the rumours of ten years ago are proven. It was then suspected that the girl whom Mrs. Courtland brought every year from some unnamed place in the country, and introduced to everybody as her niece, was an impostor, which that foolish woman, in a freak of generosity, was thrusting upon society. The rumours died out for want of proof, and before Laura's beauty and dignity, but now they are confirmed; she is some beggar's child.

MISS EARLIE. What do you think we ought to do?
   (*Trafford surrenders Pearl to Demilt and comes down.*)
MRS. VAN DAM. Tell it--tell it everywhere, of course. The best blood
   of New York is insulted by the girl's presence.
RAY. What have you three girls got your heads together for? Some
   conspiracy, I know.
MRS. VAN DAM. (*to ladies*) Go, girls, tell it everywhere.
RAY. (*as the ladies distribute themselves among the groups*) What is it all
   about? Your face is like a portrait of mystery.
MRS. VAN DAM. (*showing letter*) Look at this, and tell me what it
   means.
RAY. (*quickly*) Where did you get this?
MRS. VAN DAM. It is you who must answer, and society that will
   question. So Laura is not a Courtland?
RAY. (*overcome*) You know, then--
MRS. VAN DAM. Everything! And will you marry this creature? You
   cannot, society will not permit your sacrifice.
RAY. This is not your business. Give me that letter.
MRS. VAN DAM. Certainly, take it. But let me say one word--its
   contents are known. In an hour every tongue will question you about
   this secret, every eye will inquire.
RAY. I implore you! Do not breathe a word for her sake.
   (*She turns scornfully away.*)
MRS. VAN DAM. The secret's not mine.
RAY. Who knows it?
MRS. VAN DAM. Look!
   (*She points to others who are grouped about whispering and motioning
   towards Ray. Enter Pearl and speaks to ladies and gentlemen.*)
RAY. (*wildly*) What will they do?
MRS. VAN DAM. Expose her! Expel her from society in which she is an
   intruder!
RAY. You dare not!
PEARL. Oh, Ray, what is the meaning of this?
RAY. (*bitterly*) It means that society is a terrible avenger of insult. Have
   you ever heard of the Siberian wolves? When one of the pack falls
   through weakness, the others devour him. It is not an elegant comparison, but there is something wolfish in society. Laura has mocked it
   with a pretense, and society, which is made up of pretenses, will bitterly
   resent the mockery.
MRS. VAN DAM. Very good! This handsome thief has stolen your

breeding as well as your brains, I see.

RAY. If you speak a word against her, I will say that what you utter is a lie!

MRS. VAN DAM. As you please, we will be silent. But you will find that the world speaks most forcibly when it utters no sound.

PEARL. Oh, go and prevent her coming here.

RAY. That I can do. (*Going up hastily, sees Laura entering.*) Too late. (*He retreats.*)

MRS. VAN DAM. Come, girls! Let us look after our things. They are no longer safe when an accomplished thief enters.

(*Music low, continues while all except Pearl and Ray pass out, eyeing Laura superciliously.*)

PEARL. Ray, Ray! why do you not come to her?

MRS. VAN DAM. (*surrounded by others*) Are you not coming with us, Trafford?

PEARL. (*to Laura*) Let us go home.

LAURA. No, stay with *him*!

(*Pointing to Ray, who has held off.*)

He shall not suffer the disgrace long.

(*About to faint; Ray runs forward, she proudly waves him away.*)

It is Heaven's own blow!

ACT II.

Scene 1. 2nd grooves-- Interior of a basement. Street and railings seen through window at back. Entrance door, L. Stove with long pipe in fire-place, R. Table with two windows at back, with flowers, etc.-- Humble furniture. Table, C. Three chairs. Closet, L. (*Peachblossom, a slip-shod girl, is discovered polishing stove.*)

PEACHBLOSSOM. (*singing*)
A lordly knight and a lovely dame were walking in the meadow.
But a jealous rival creeping came, a-watching in the shadow.
They heeded not, but he whett his knife and dogged them in the
    shadow;
The knight was brave, and the dame was true, the rival fared but
    badly;
For the knight he drew and ran him through, and left him groaning
    sadly.
The knight and dame soon wedded were, with bells a-chiming gladly.

The stove won't shine. It's the fault of the polish, I know. That boy that comes here just fills the bottles with mud, and calls it stove polish. Only let me catch him. Ah! Ah! (*Threatening gesture with brush.*) I declare I'd give it up if I didn't want to make everything look smart before Miss Nina comes in. Miss Nina is the only friend I ever had since I ran away from Mother Judas. I wonder where old Judas is now? I know she's drunk, she always was; perhaps that's why she never tried to find out what became of me. If she did, she could not take me away. Miss Nina begged me off a policeman. I belong to her. I wonder why she ain't got any other friends? She's awful mysterious. Tells me never to let any stranger see her. She's afraid of somebody, I know. It looks just as if she was hiding. I thought only bad girls, such as I, had to hide. If I was good and pretty like her, I wouldn't hide from the President.

(*Peachblossom is still polishing-- Judas appears at window with basket of ornaments, etc.*)

JUDAS. Hum! Is your ma in, my dear?

PEACHBLOSSOM. (*starting*) Oh! (*Aside.*) Old Judas! She's found me out at last. No, she hain't, or she'd have got me by the hair before she spoke, that's *her* way.

JUDAS. (*coming in at door-- Peachblossom keeps her back towards her*) Any old clothes to change for chany, my dear? Where's your ma's old skirts and shawls, my pet? Get 'em quick, before mother comes in, and I'll give you a beautiful chany mug or a tea-pot for them. Come here, my ducky--see the pretty-- (*Recognizes Peachblossom.*) Eh! why you jail-bird, what are you doing here? Are you sneakin' it? Answer me, or I'll knock your head agin the wall. (*Catches her by the hair.*)

PEACHBLOSSOM. You just leave me be. I'm honest, I am. I'm good!

JUDAS. You're good? Where's my shoe? I'll take the goodness out of you.

PEACHBLOSSOM. Oh, oh! please don't beat me. I ain't good. I'm only trying to be.

JUDAS. You're only trying to be, eh? Trying to be good, and here's me as was a-weeping every night, thinking as you was sent up for six months. Who're you living with--you ain't a-keeping house, are you?

PEACHBLOSSOM. I'm living with Miss Nina.

JUDAS. Nina, what's she? concert saloon girl?

PEACHBLOSSOM. No, she's a lady.

JUDAS. A lady--and have such baggage as you about? Where's my shoe? I'll make you speak the truth.

PEACHBLOSSOM. I don't know what she is. She met me when the police were taking me up for loafin' down Hudson Street, and she begged me off.

JUDAS. Has she any money?

PEACHBLOSSOM. No, she's poor.

JUDAS. Any nice clothes?

PEACHBLOSSOM. Oh, she's got good clothes.

JUDAS. Where are they?

PEACHBLOSSOM. Locked up, and she's got the key.

JUDAS. You're lying; I see it in your eye. You're always shamefaced when you are telling the truth, and now you're as bold as brass. Where's my shoe? (*Making a dash at her.*)

PEACHBLOSSOM. (*shouting*) There's Miss Nina! (*As if curtseying to someone behind Judas.*) Good morning, Miss.

JUDAS. (*changing her tone*) Ah, my pretty dear! What a good lady to take you in and give you a home. (*Turns and discovers the deception-- in a rage.*) You hussy! (*Peachblossom retreats.*) Wait till I get you in my clutches again, and it won't be long. Miss Nina takes care of you, does she? Who will take care of her? Let her look to it. (*Enter Laura, plainly dressed, at back.*) Beg pardon, Miss, I just called to see if you had any old clothes you'd like to exchange.

LAURA. No, I don't want anything, my good woman.

JUDAS. (*eyeing her sharply and going to door*) That's her--I'd know her anywhere! (*Malicious glance, and exit.*)

LAURA. You've been very good this morning, Blossom. The room is as nice as I could wish.

PEACHBLOSSOM. Please 'm, I try because you are so good to me. Shall I sweep out the airy? (*Aside.*) I guess I'd better--then she'll be alone, as she loves to be. (*Taking broom, exit.*)

LAURA. (*opening a package and taking out photographs*) No pay yet for colouring till I have practised a week longer. Then I shall have all the work I can do. They say at the photographer's I colour well, and the best pictures will be given me. The best! Already I have had beneath my brush so many faces that I know--friends of the old days. The silent eyes seem to wonder at me for bringing them to this strange and lowly home. (*Picking up letters from table.*) Letters, ah! answers to my advertisement for employment. No, only a circular "To the lady of this house." What's that! (*Starting.*) Only Blossom sweeping. Every time there is a noise I dread the entrance of someone that knows me. But they could never find me in New York. I left them all so secretly and suddenly. None of them can expect I would have descended to this. But it is natural, everything will find its level. I sprang from poverty, and I return to it. Poor Pearl. How she must have wondered the next morning--Laura gone! But three months have passed, and they have forgotten me. Ray will cheer her.

(Wrangling outside; Peachblossom bursts in, dragging Bermudas, with his professional tape, pins, blacking, and baskets.)

PEACHBLOSSOM. Here he is, 'm.

BERMUDAS. Leave go, I tell yer, or I'll make yer.

LAURA. What is the matter?

PEACHBLOSSOM. He's the boy that sold me that stove polish what isn't stove polish.

BERMUDAS. What is it then--s-a-a-y?

PEACHBLOSSOM. It's mud! It's mud at tenpence a bottle.

BERMUDAS. Ah, where could I get mud? Ain't the streets clean? Mud's dearer than stove polish now.

PEACHBLOSSOM. And your matches is wet, and your pins won't stick, and your shoe-strings is rotten, there now!

BERMUDAS. Well, how am I to live? It ain't my fault, it's the taxes. Ain't I got to pay my income tax, and how am I to pay it if I gives you your money's worth? S-a-a-y?

LAURA. Do let the boy alone, Blossom. Send him away.

(Enter Peanuts.)

PEANUTS. Extra! Hollo, Bermudas! how's your sister? Papers, Miss. Extra! Revolution in Mexico!

LAURA. Dear, dear, this is the way I'm worried from morning till night.

BERMUDAS. Here, just you get out! This is my beat.

PEANUTS. Vell, I ain't blacking or hairpins now, I'm papers. How'm I hurting you?

BERMUDAS. Vell, I'm papers at four o'clock, and this is my beat. Take care of me, I'm training for a fight. I'm a bruiser, I am.

PEANUTS. Hold yer jaw. *(They fight.)*

PEACHBLOSSOM. *(beats them with broom)* Get out with you, both of you! *(Grand escapade, and boys exeunt.)*

LAURA. Don't let's be troubled in this way again. Have you got the things for dinner?

PEACHBLOSSOM. Lor, no, Miss. It's twelve o'clock, and I forgot.

(Peachblossom gets shawl and big bonnet from hooks on the wall, basket from closet, while Laura opens her pocket-book for money.)

LAURA. What did we have for dinner yesterday, Blossom?

PEACHBLOSSOM. Beefsteak, 'm. Let's have some leg o' mutton today. We've never had that.

LAURA. But I don't know how to cook it. Do you?

PEACHBLOSSOM. No, but I'd just slap it on, and it's sure to come out right.

LAURA. Slap it on what?

PEACHBLOSSOM. The gridiron!

LAURA. (*giving money*) No, we'd better not try a leg of mutton today. Get some lamb shops; we know how to manage them.

PEACHBLOSSOM. (*as she is going*) Taters, as usual, 'mum?

LAURA. Yes; and stop, Blossom--while you're buying the chops, just ask the butcher--offhand, you know--how he would cook a leg of mutton, if he were going to eat it himself--as if you wanted to know for yourself.

PEACHBLOSSOM. Yes 'm, but I'm sure it's just as good broiled as fried.

(*Exit Peachblossom.*)

LAURA. Now to be cook. (*Laughing.*) The Tuesday Sociable ought to see me now. Artist in the morning, cook at noon, artist in the afternoon.

(*Snorkey raps at the door and enters.*)

SNORKEY. (*with letter*) Beg pardon, is there anybody here as answers to the name of A.B.C.?

LAURA. (*aside*) My advertisement for work. (*Aloud.*) Yes, give it to me.

SNORKEY. (*aside, seeing her face*) If I'd been taking something this morning, I'd say that I'd seen that face in a different sort of place from this.

LAURA. Is there anything to pay? Why do you wait?

SNORKEY. Nothing, Miss. It's all right. (*Going-- and aside.*) But it ain't all right, Snorkey, old boy.

(*Snorkey goes out after looking at her, stops at window, and gazes in.*)

LAURA. Yes, an answer to my advertisement. (*Reads.*) "To A.B.C.-- Your advertisement promises that you are a good linguist, and can teach children of any age. I have two daughters for whom I wish to engage your services while on a tour of Europe. Call at seven o'clock this evening, at No. 207 West 34th Street, Annersley." Hope at last, a home, and in another land soon. I was sure the clouds would not always be black above me. (*Laura kisses letter.*)

SNORKEY. (*re-entering*) Miss, I say, Miss? (*Laura starts.*) Sh--

LAURA. What do you want?

SNORKET. Only one word, and perhaps it may be of service to you. I'd do anything to serve you.

LAURA. And why me?

SNORKEY. I'm a blunt fellow, Miss, but I hope my way don't offend. Ain't you the lady that I brought a bouquet to on New Year's night-- Not here, but in a big house, all bright and rich, and who was so kind to a poor soldier?

LAURA. (*faint and leaning against chair*) Whoever you may be, promise to tell no one you saw me here.

SNORKEY. No fear, Miss. I promise.

LAURA. Sacredly?

SNORKEY. No need to do more than promise, Miss--I keeps my word. I promised Uncle Sam I'd stick to the flag--though they tore my arm off, and by darnation I stuck! I don't want to tell on you, Miss, I want to tell on someone else.

LAURA. What do you mean?

SNORKEY. They're looking for you.

LAURA. Who?

SNORKEY. Byke. (*Laura utters a loud cry and sinks on chair.*) He's on it day and night. I've got his money in my pocket now, and you've got his letter in your hand this minute. (*Laura drops the letter in dismay.*)

LAURA. This?

SNORKEY. Yes, it's his writin'--looks like a woman's, don't it? Lord! the snuff that man's up to would make Barnum sneeze his head off. He's kept me in hand, 'cause he thinks I know you, having seen you that once. Every day he reads the advertisements, and picks out a dozen or so, and says to me--"Snorkey, that's like my little pet," and then he sits down and answers them, and gets the advertisers to make appointments with him, which he keeps regularly, and regularly comes back cussing at his ill luck. See here, Miss, I've a bundle of answers to deliver as usual, to advertisers. I call's 'em Byke's Target Practice, and this time, you see, he's accidentally hit the mark.

LAURA. For heaven's sake, do not betray me to him! I've got very little money; I earn it hardly, but take it, take it--and save me. (*Offers money.*)

SNORKEY. No, Miss, not a cent of it. Though Byke is a devil and would kick me hard if he thought I would betray him.

LAURA. I don't want you to suffer for my sake; take the money.

SNORKEY. No, I stood up to be shot at for thirteen dollars a month, and I can take my chances of a kickin' for nothing. But Byke ain't the only one, Miss; there's another's looking for you.

LAURA. (*her look of joy changing to fear*) Another! Who?

SNORKEY. (*approaching smilingly and confidentially*) Mr. Trafford. (*Laura turns aside despairingly.*) He's been at me every day for more than six weeks. "Snorkey," says he, "do you remember that beautiful young lady you brought the bouquet to on New Year's night?" "Well," says I, "Cap'n, the young lady I slightly disremember, but the cakes and wine I got there that night I shall never forget." "Search for that young lady," says he, "and when you find her"--

LAURA. No, no, no; not even he must know. Do you hear--not he--not anyone. You have served them well; serve me and be silent.

SNORKEY. Just as you please, Miss, but I hate to serve you by putting your friends off the track--it don't seem natural-- Byke I don't mind but the Cap'n wouldn't do you any harm. Just let me give him a bit of a hint. (*Laura makes an entreating gesture.*) Well, I'm mum, but as I've only got one hand, it's hard work to hold my tongue. Not the least bit of a hint? (*Laura appeals to him and then turns away. Aside.*) They say when a woman says no she means yes. I wonder if I dare tell her that he's not far off. Perhaps I'd better not. But I can tell him. (*Exit.*)

LAURA. How shall I ever escape that dreadful man? And Ray searching for me, too. Our friends, then, remember us as well as our enemies.
  (*Enter Peachblossom, quickly, shutting the door behind her, with basket which she places on table.*)

PEACHBLOSSOM. Oh, Miss Nina, what ever is into the people? There's a strange man coming down the entry; I heard him asking that red cap fellow about you.

LAURA. Byke! Fasten the door, quick.
  (*Peachblossom runs to door, it is slightly open, she pushes it against someone on the other side.*)

PEACHBLOSSOM. Oh, dear, he's powerful strong; I can't keep it shut. Go away, you willin: Oh!
  (*The door is forced-- enter Ray Trafford.*)

RAY. Laura, it is I!

LAURA. Ray! (*Shrinks from him.*)

RAY. Dear Laura--
  (*He stops as he becomes conscious that Peachblossom, with her basket on her arm and her bonnet hanging on her back, is staring at him.*)
  I say, my girl, haven't you some particular business somewhere else to attend to?

PEACHBLOSSOM. (*seriously*) No, sir, I've swept the sidewalk and gone a-marketing, and now I'm indoors and I mean to stay.

RAY. And wouldn't you oblige me by going for a sheet of paper and an envelope? Here's a dollar--try and see how slow you can be.

PEACHBLOSSOM. (*firmly*) You can't sheet of paper me, Mister. I'm protecting Miss Nina, and I'm not to be enveloped.

LAURA. Go as the gentleman asks you, Blossom.

PEACHBLOSSOM. Oh! (*Takes money, fixes her bonnet. Aside.*) First, it's "keep the man out," now it's "let him stay in alone with me." But I suppose she's like all of us--it makes a great difference which man it is.
(*Exit Peachblossom.*)

RAY. (*after watching Peachblossom out*) Laura, when I approached you, you shrank from me. Why did you do so?

LAURA. Look around you and find your answer.

RAY. (*shuddering*) Pardon me, I did not come here to insult your misery. When I saw you, I forgot everything else.

LAURA. And now it's time for us to remember everything. I told you to look around that you might understand that in such a place I am no longer Laura Courtland, nor anything I used to be. But I did not ask your pity. There is no misery here.

RAY. Alone, without means, exposed to every rudeness, unprotected, is this not misery for you?

LAURA. (*laughing*) Oh, it's not so bad as that.

RAY. Laura, don't trifle with me. You cannot have exchanged everything that made you happy for this squalid poverty, and not feel it deeply.

LAURA. I have not time to feel anything deeply. (*Takes basket up, goes to table, busies herself about preparing dinner.*) I work from sunrise till night, and I sleep so soundly that I have not even dreams to recall the past. Just as you came in, I was about to cook our dinner. Only think-- lamb chops.

RAY. Lamb chops! It makes me shudder to hear you speak.

LAURA. Does it? Then wait till I get the gridiron on the fire and you'll shiver. And if you want to be transfixed with horror, stop and take dinner.

RAY. I will not hear you mock yourself thus, Laura. I tell you in this self-banishment you have acted thoughtlessly--you have done wrong.

LAURA. Why?

RAY. Because, let the miserable creatures who slandered you say what they might, you had still a home and friends.

LAURA. A home! Where the very servants would whisper and point, friends who would be ashamed to acknowledge me. You are mistaken. That is neither home nor friendship.

RAY. And you are resolved to surrender the past forever?

LAURA. The past has forgotten me in spite of myself.

RAY. Look at me.

LAURA. Well, then, there's one who has not forgotten me, but I desire that he may. You speak to me of bitterness. Your presence, your words, caused me the first pang I have felt since the night I fled unnoticed from my chamber, and began my life anew. Therefore, I entreat you to leave me, to forget me.

RAY. Laura, by the tie that once bound us!

LAURA. Yes, *once*. It *is* a long time ago.

RAY. What have I said? The tie which still--

LAURA. (*sharply turning*) Mr. Trafford, must I remind you of that night when all arrayed themselves so pitilessly against me, when a gesture from you might have saved me, and you saw me without stretching a finger to the woman who had felt the beating of your heart. No, you made your choice then--the world without me. I make my choice now-- the wide, wide, world without you.

RAY. I have been bitterly punished, for we are never so humiliated as when we despise ourselves. But, by the heaven above us both, I love you, Laura--I have never ceased to love you.

LAURA. I thank you. I know how to construe the love which you deny in the face of society to offer me behind its back.

RAY. Will you drive me mad? I tell you, Laura, your misery, your solitude is as nothing to the anguish I have suffered. The maniac who in his mental darkness stabs to the heart the friend he loved never felt in returning reason the remorse my error has earned me. Every day it says to me "You have been false to the heart that loved you, and you shall account for it to your conscience all your life. You shall find that the bitterest drops in the cup of sorrow are the tears of the woman you have forsaken." And it is true. Oh, forgive me--have pity on me.

LAURA. (*moved*) I forgive you. Yes, and I pity you--and so good-bye for ever.

RAY. Of course, I am nothing to you now; that is some comfort to me. I have only to be sorry on my own account, but I come to you on behalf of others.

LAURA. Whom?

RAY. My mother and Pearl, they ask for you. For them I have sought you, to urge you to return to them.

LAURA. Dear little Pearl.

RAY. Yes, she has been quite ill.

LAURA. She has been ill?

RAY. Think of those two hearts which you have caused to suffer and do not drive me from you. It is not only wealth, luxury, and refinement which you have surrendered--you have also cast away those greater riches, loving and devoted friends. But they shall persuade you themselves--yes, I'll go and bring them to you; you cannot resist their entreaties.

LAURA. No, no, they must not come here, they must never know where *I* hide my shame, and you must never reveal it.

RAY. I promise it if you will go to them with me. Think, they will insist on coming unless you do.

LAURA. Poor Pearl. If I go with you, you promise not to detain me--to permit me to come back and to trouble me and my poor life no more?

RAY. I promise, but I know you will release me from it when you see them. I will get a carriage, so that no one will meet you. Wait for me, I shall not be long. It is agreed?

LAURA. (*smiling*) Yes, it is agreed.

PEACHBLOSSOM. (*entering with a sheet of paper foolscap and some enormous envelopes*) Here they are.

RAY. That's a good girl, keep them till I come back. In half an hour, Laura, be ready. (*Exit.*)

PEACHBLOSSOM. (*with an air*) What's he going to do in half an hour?

LAURA. He's going to take me away with him for a little while, Peachblossom, and while I'm gone, I wish you to be a good girl, and watch the house and take care of it till I return.

PEACHBLOSSOM. I don't believe it, you won't return. (*Crying.*) That's what our Sal said when she went off with her young man, and she never came back at all. You shan't go; I hate him. He shan't take you away.

LAURA. (*who is getting ready, putting her hat on, etc.*) Blossom!

PEACHBLOSSOM. I don't care, if you go away, I'll go away; I'll bite and scratch him if he comes back. (*Fiercely tearing up the paper and envelopes.*) Let him come back--let him dare come back.

LAURA. Blossom, you're very wicked. Go into the corner this minute and put your apron over your head.

PEACHBLOSSOM. (*crying at Laura's feet*) Oh, please, Miss Nina, let me go with you and I'll be so good and not say a word to anyone. Do let me go with you. Let me ask him to let me go with you. (*Figure passes the window.*) Here he is; I see him coming.

LAURA. Run, run, open the door.

(*Peachblossom runs to door, throws it open, disclosing Byke-- Exclamation of horror from Laura.*)

BYKE. Ah, my dear little runaway, found you at last, and just going out. How lucky! I wanted you to take a walk with me.

LAURA. Instantly leave this place!

BYKE. How singular! You are alway ordering me out, and I am always coming in. We want a change. I will go out, and I request you to come with me.

LAURA. Blossom, go find an officer; tell him this wretch is insulting me.

BYKE. Blossom? Ah--exactly! Here, you Judas. (*Enter Judas.*)

PEACHBLOSSOM. Oh, Miss, save me!

BYKE. (*throws Peachblossom over to Judas, who drags her out*) Take care of that brat, and as for you, daughter, come with me.

LAURA. Daughter!

BYKE. Yes, it is time to declare myself. Paternal feeling has been too long smothered in my breast. Come to my arms, my child--my long-estranged child.

> (*Takes out dirty handkerchief and presses his eyes with pretended feeling.*)

LAURA. Heavens! Is there no help?

> (*She attempts to escape, Byke seizes her.*)

BYKE. What an unfilial girl; you take advantage of a father's weakness and try to bolt. (*Clutching her by the arm.*) Come, go with me and cheer my old age. Ain't I good to take you back after all these years?

> (*Drags her out, she calling "Help! Help!"*)

Scene 2. The Tombs Police Court. Long high desk with three seats across back, from R. to L., on platform. Railing in front, railing around L., with opening, L.C. In front of railing, a bench, R. and L.-- Gate in C. of railing. (*Judge Bowling seated and another Justice seated behind high desk, C., with clerk on his L. Justice is reading paper, with his feet upon desk, R. Policemen at R. and L. Policeman 999 at gate. Hard-looking set of men and women on benches, R. and L.-- Lawyer Splinter is talking to Rafferdi, an organ-man, who is in crowd. As the curtain rises, noisy buzz is heard.*)

BOWLING. Smithers, keep those people quiet. (*Policeman handling people roughly.*) Here, easy--Officer, treat those poor people decently. Well, whom have you got there?

POLICEMAN. (*dragging urchin within railing*) Pickpocket, your honour. Caught in the act.

BOWLING. What's he got to say for himself? Nothing, eh? What's his name?

POLICEMAN. (*stooping down to boy as if asking him*) Says his name is Peter Rich.

BOWLING. You stand a poor chance, Rich. Take him away.

> (*Bowling consults with another Justice, as the boy is taken off.*)

SPLINTER. (*to Rafferdi, who has his monkey and organ*) So you want to get out, eh? How much money have you got?

RAFFERDI. Be jabers! half a dollar in cents is all the money I'm worth in the world.

SPLINTER. Give it to me. I thought you organ fellows were Italians.

RAFFERDI. Divil doubt it! Ain't I got a monkey?

POLICEMAN. Here, you--come up here.

   (*Takes Rafferdi inside the railing.*)

BOWLING. Now then, what's this, Officer? (*Rafferdi takes stand.*)

POLICEMAN. Complaint of disturbing the neighborhood.

BOWLING. What have you got to say for yourself?

SPLINTER. If your honour please, I appear for this man.

BOWLING. Well, what have you got to say for him?

SPLINTER. Here is an unfortunate man, your honour--a native of sunny Italy. He came to our free and happy country, and became a votary of music, he bought an organ and a monkey, and tried to earn his bread. But the myrmidons of the law were upon him, and the Eagle of Liberty drooped his pinions as Rafferdi was hurried to his dungeon.

BOWLING. Rafferdi, you're an Irishman, ain't you? What do you mean by deceiving us?

RAFFERDI. Sure I didn't. It's the lawyer chap there. I paid him fifty cents, and he's lying out the worth of it.

BOWLING. You fellows are regular nuisances. I've a great mind to commit you.

SPLINTER. Commit him? If the court please, reflect--commit him to prison? What will become of his monkey?

BOWLING. Well, I'll commit him, too.

SPLINTER. You cannot. I defy the Court to find anything in the Statutes authorising the committal of a monkey.

BOWLING. Well, we'll leave out the monkey.

SPLINTER. And if the Court please, what is the monkey to do in the wide world, with his natural protector in prison? I appeal to those kindlier feelings in your honour's breast, which must ever temper justice with mercy. This monkey is perhaps an orphan!

BOWLING. (*laughing*) Take them both away, and don't let me catch you here again, Mr. Rafferdi, or you'll go to jail.

   (*Splinter goes down-- exit Rafferdi.*)

POLICEMAN. (*pulling Sam, a nigger, who is drunk, out of a crowd*) Get up here.

SAM. (*noisily*) Look yah--don't pull me around.

BOWLING. Silence there! What's all this noise about?

SAM. Whar's de court? I want to see de judge.

SPLINTER. My coloured friend, can I assist you?

SAM. Am you a Counseller-at-law?

SPLINTER. Yes, retain me. How much money have you got?

SAM. I ain't got no money, but I've got a policy ticket. It's bound to draw a prize.

SPLINTER. Got any pawn tickets?

SAM. Ob course. (*Giving him a handful.*)

BOWLING. Well, what's the charge?

POLICEMAN. Drunk and disorderly.

BOWLING. Well, my man, what have you to say?

SAM. Dis here gemman represents me.

SPLINTER. We admit, if the Court please, that we were slightly intoxicated, but we claim the privilege, as the equal of the white man.

BOWLING. (*to clerk*) Very good. Commit him for ten days.

SPLINTER. But this is an outrage, your honour.

BOWLING. (*to Officer, motioning to Sam*) Take him off.

(*Splinter sits down discomfited-- Sam very wroth.*)

SAM. What?

BOWLING. Take him away.

SAM. Look here, judge, hab you read the Civil Right Bill? You can't send dis nigger to prison, while dat bill am de law ob de land.

BOWLING. That'll do, remove him.

SAM. I ain't no gypsy. I'm one of de Bureau nigger, I am. Whar am de law? Don't touch me, white man! Dis am corruption--dis am 'ficial delinquency!

(*Policeman collars Sam and carries him off.*)

BOWLING. Any more prisoners? (*Noise.*) What noise is that?

(*Officer goes out. Enter Byke, followed by Officer, who escorts Laura.*)

BYKE. Where is the judge? Oh, where is the good, kind judge?

BOWLING. Well, my dear sir, what is the matter?

BYKE. Oh, sir, forgive my tears. I'm a broken-hearted man!

BOWLING. Be calm, my dear sir. Officer, bring this gentleman a chair.

(*Officer hands chair.*)

BYKE. Ah, sir, you are very good to a poor distressed father, whose existence has been made a desert on account of his child.

BOWLING. Repress your emotion, and tell me what you want.

BYKE. I want my child.

BOWLING. Where is she?

BYKE. She is here, sir--here--my darling, my beautiful child, and so unfilial--so unnatural.

BOWLING. How is this, young lady?

LAURA. (*standing inside railing*) It is all a lie. He is not my father.

BYKE. Not your father? Oh, dear, oh, dear, you will break my heart!

BOWLING. This needs some explanation. If not his child, who are you?

LAURA. I am-- I dare not say it. I know not who I am, but I feel that he cannot be my father.

BYKE. Oh, dear-- Oh!

BOWLING. (*sharply*) Silence! (*To Laura, sternly.*) You say you don't know who you are. Do you know this man?

LAURA. Yes.

BOWLING. Where and with whom do you live?

LAURA. I have lived alone for four months.

BOWLING. And with whom did you live before that?

LAURA. Oh, forgive me, if I seem disobedient--but I cannot tell.

BOWLING. Then I must look to this gentleman for information.

BYKE. And I will gladly give it. Yes, sir, I will gladly tell. She was taken from me years ago, when she was but a little child, by rich people who wanted to adopt her. I refused--they paid me--I was poor--I was starving--I forebore to claim her--she was happy, but they turned her forth four months ago into the street. I could not see her suffer--my child --the prop of my declining days. I begged her to come--she refused. My enemies had poisoned my daughter's mind against *me*, her father. I am still poor. I taught school, but I have saved a little money, only for her.

BOWLING. How old is she?

BYKE. Nineteen.

BOWLING. Your father is your legal guardian during your minority, and is entitled to your custody. Why are you so undutiful? Try to correct this.

BYKE. Oh, bless you, dear good judge for these words.

LAURA. Oh, have I no friends, must I go with him?

BOWLING. Certainly.

LAURA. Anything then. Exposure! Disgrace, rather than that!
    (*Judges consult. Enter Snorkey.*)

BYKE. (*aside*) Snorkey! the devil!

SNORKEY. Can I help you, Miss? Only tell me what to do, and if it takes my other arm off, I'll save you.

LAURA. Yes, yes, you can help me! (*To judges.*) Will you let me send a message?

BOWLING. You may do that.

LAURA. (*to Snorkey*) Run to that house--not my house--but the one in which you saw me first. Do you remember it?

SNORKEY. Don't I, and the wine and the cakes.

LAURA. Ask for Miss Pearl. Tell her where I am. Tell her to come instantly. (*Snorkey going.*) Stay--tell her to bring the ebony box in mother's cabinet. Can you recollect?

SNORKEY. Can I what? Gaze at this giant intellect and don't ask me! The ebony box--all right--I'm off. (*Exit.*)

BOWLING. It would have been as well, young lady, to have answered frankly at first.

BYKE. Oh, sir! Don't be harsh with her! Don't be harsh with my poor child.

BOWLING. Your father has a most Christian disposition.

LAURA. Sir, I have told you, and I now solemnly repeat it, that this man is no relation of mine. I desire to remain unknown, for I am most unfortunate; but the injustice you are about to commit forces me to reveal myself, though in doing so I shall increase a sorrow already hard to bear.

BOWLING. We sit here to do right, according to the facts before us. And let me tell you, young lady, that your father's statement is correct. Further, unless the witnesses you have sent for can directly contradict him, we shall not alter our decision.

LAURA. Let it be so. He says he gave me into the care of certain wealthy people when I was a little child.

BYKE. I am willing to swear it.

LAURA. Then he will be able to describe the clothes in which I was dressed at the time. They were safely kept, I have sent for them.

BYKE. Let them be produced--and I will recognize every little precious garment. (*Aside.*) This is getting ferociously hot for me! Ha!

(*Re-enter Snorkey with Ray, hastily.*)

SNORKEY. (*excitedly*) Here's a witness! Here's evidence!

(*Policeman admonishes him.*)

LAURA. (*as Ray takes her hand through the rail*) Ray!

BOWLING. Who is this?

RAY. I am a friend, sir, of this lady.

BYKE. He is a dreadful character--a villain who wants to lead my child astray! Don't--please don't let him contaminate her!

BOWLING. Silence! (*To Ray.*) Can you disprove that this young lady is his daughter?

RAY. His daughter?

LAURA. He knows nothing.

BOWLING. Let him answer. Come--have you any knowledge of this matter?

RAY. I have been told, sir, that-- (*Laura looks at him.*) No, I know nothing.

LAURA. Have you brought the ebony box? It contained the clothes which I wore when--

RAY. I understand; but in my haste, and not knowing your peril, I brought nothing. But can you not remember them yourself?

LAURA. Perfectly.

RAY. Right, then! (*Handing her a memorandum book and speaking to Bowling.*) Sir, this lady will hand you a description of those articles which she wore when she was found thirteen years ago. Then let this scoundrel be questioned--and if he fails to answer, I will accuse him of an attempted abduction.

BOWLING. That's the way.

BYKE. (*aside*) It will not be a great effort for me to remember.

BOWLING. (*taking the book from Ray*) Now, sir, I will listen to you.

(*Ray and Laura are eager and expectant.*)

BYKE. (*deliberately*) A soiled gingham frock, patched and torn.

(*Laura gives a shudder and turns aside.*)

BOWLING. What kind of shoes and stockings?

BYKE. Her feet were bare.

BOWLING. And the colour of her hood?

BYKE. Her dear little head was uncovered.

BOWLING. (*handing book back*) He has answered correctly.

LAURA. It is useless to struggle more. Heaven alone can help me!

RAY. You can see, sir, that this lady cannot be his daughter. Look at her and at him.

BOWLING. I only see that he has pretty well proven his case. She must go with him, and let her learn to love him as a daughter should.

RAY. She shall not! I shall follow him wherever he goes.

BYKE. (*taking Laura's hand*) I appeal to the Court.

BOWLING. Officer, take charge of that person, until this gentleman is gone.

(*Byke comes forward with Laura, who is dumb and despairing.*)

BYKE. My child, try and remember the words of the good judge. "You must learn to love me as a daughter should."

SNORKEY. (*to Ray*) Stay here, sir, I'll track him. No one suspects me.

(*Music-- Tableau-- closed in by next scene.*)

Scene 3. Exterior of the Tombs, with ballads on strings upon the railings. (*Enter Judas, followed by Peachblossom.*)

PEACHBLOSSOM. Only tell me where he has taken her, and I'll go with you--indeed, I will.

JUDAS. We don't want you, we wouldn't be bothered with you; she's our game.

PEACHBLOSSOM. What are you going to do with her?

JUDAS. Do! why we'll coin her. Turn her into dollars. We've had it on foot for a long time.

PEACHBLOSSOM. What? Is she the rich young lady I heard you and Byke speak of so often before I got away from you?

JUDAS. (*savagely*) Heard me speak of! What did you hear?

PEACHBLOSSOM. (*dancing off*) Oh, I know! I know more than you suppose. When you used to lock me up in the back cellar for running away, you forgot that doors had key-holes.

JUDAS. (*aside*) This girl must be silenced.

PEACHBLOSSOM. What are you muttering about? Don't you know how Byke used to throw you down and trample on you for muttering?

JUDAS. I'll have you yet, my beauty.

PEACHBLOSSOM. I think you are a great fool, Judas.

JUDAS. Likely, likely.

PEACHBLOSSOM. Why don't you give up Miss Nina to that handsome young gentleman? He'd pay you well for the secret. He'd give his whole fortune for her. I know, I saw it in his face. And he'd treat you better than Byke does.

JUDAS. Not yet, my chicken; besides, what does he care for her now? Isn't he going to marry the other girl--she's the one will pay when the time comes--but we intend to hold the goods till the price is high.

PEACHBLOSSOM. Then if you won't, I'll--I'll tell him all I used to overhear about babies and cradles, and he'll understand it, perhaps, if I don't.

JUDAS. (*aside*) Hang her--she'll make mischief. (*Aloud.*) Well, come along with me, my beauty, and I'll talk it over with you.

PEACHBLOSSOM. Don't touch me; I won't trust you with your hands on me. (*Judas makes a dart at her.*) I knew that was your game. But I'll be even with you yet.

   (*She dances off tantalisingly before Judas. Both exeunt. Enter Snorkey.*)

SNORKEY. (*despondingly*) I'm no more use than a gun without a trigger. I tried to follow Byke, but he smoked in a minute. Then I tried to make up with him, but he swore that I went against him in Court, and so he wouldn't have me at no price. Then I ran after the carriage that he got into with the lady, till a darn'd old woman caught me for upsetting her apple stand and bursting up her business. What am I to do now? I'm afraid to go back to the Cap'n; *he* won't have me at any price either, I suppose.

(*Gazing at ballads, hand in pocket-- going from one to the other. Enter Bermudas, with ballads in his hands, preparing to take others off the line, as if to shut up shop.*)

BERMUDAS. (*after gazing at Snorkey*) What are you a-doing of-- s-a-a-y? (*Snorkey takes no notice.*) This here's one of the fellows as steals the bread of the poor man. Reading all the songs for nothin', and got bags of gold at home. S-a-a-y!

SNORKEY. Well, youngster, what are you groaning about? Have you got the cholera?

BERMUDAS. Ah! what are you doing? Taking the bloom off my songs? You're read them 'ere ballads till they're in rags.

SNORKEY. I was looking for the "Prairie Bird."

BERMUDAS. Perary Bird, eh? There ain't no perary bird. There's a "Perary Flower."

SNORKEY. Now don't go into convulsions. I'll find it. (*Turns to songs.*)

BERMUDAS. S-a-a-y--you needn't look no further for that bird! I've found him and no mistake. He's a big Shanghae with a red comb and no feathers.

SNORKEY. He's dropped on me.

BERMUDAS. Ain't you a mean cuss, s-a-a-y? Why don't you come down with your two cents, and support trade?

SNORKEY. But I ain't got two cents. What's a fellow to do, if he hasn't got a red?

BERMUDAS. (*toning down*) Hain't you? Where's your messages?

SNORKEY. Haven't had one go today.

BERMUDAS. Where do you hang out?

SNORKEY. Nowheres.

BERMUDAS. My eye--no roost?

SNORKEY. No.

BERMUDAS. I tell you what, come along with us--we've got a bully place--no rent--no taxes--no nothin'.

SNORKEY. Where is it?

BERMUDAS. Down under the pier! I discovered it. I was in swimmin' and seed a hole and went in. Lots of room, just the place for a quiet roost. We has jolly times every night, I tell you, on the dock; and when it is time to turn in we goes below, and has it as snug as a hotel; come down with us.

SNORKEY. I will! These young rascals will help me to track that scoundrel yet.

BERMUDAS. Now, help me to take in my shop windows; it's time to shut up shop.

RAY. (*entering*) If what that crazy girl has told me can be true, Laura may yet be restored to her friends, if not to me, for I have dispelled that dream for ever. But that villain must be traced immediately, or he will convey his victim far beyond our reach or rescue.

(*Snorkey, helping to take down songs, sees Trafford.*)

SNORKEY. Hollo! Cap'n!

RAY. The man of all I wanted. You tracked him?

SNORKEY. They was too much for me, sir. Two horses was, but I saw them turn into Greenwich Street, near Jay.

RAY. This may give us a clue. I have learned from a girl who knows this fellow that he has some hiding-place over the river, and owns a boat which is always fastened near the pier where the Boston steamers are.

SNORKEY. Well, Cap'n, if anything's to be done, you'll find me at Pier-- What's the number of our pier, Shorty?

BERMUDAS. Pier 30! Downstairs!

SNORKEY. Pier 30. That's my new home, and if you want me, say the word.

RAY. You will help me?

SNORKEY. You bet, Cap'n. I was on Columbia's side for four years, and I'll fight for her daughters for the rest of my life, if you say so. If there's any fightin', count me in, Cap'n.

RAY. Thank you, brave fellow. Here, take this--no nonsense--take it. Pier 30, is it?

SNORKEY. Pier 30.

(*Exit Trafford.*)

BERMUDAS. (*eyeing money*) How much, Perary?

SNORKEY. One--two--three--four--four dollars.

BERMUDAS. Four dollars! S-a-a-y--don't you want to buy a share in a paying business? I'm looking out for a partner with a cash capital for the ballad business. Or I tell you what to do. Lay your money on me in a mill. I'm going to be a prize-fighter, and get reported in the respectable dailies. "Rattling Mill, 99th round, Bermudas the victor, having knocked his antagonist into nowheres."

SNORKEY. Come along, you young imp. I could floor you with my one arm, and then the report would be "25th round--Snorkey came up first, while his antagonist showed great signs of distress."

BERMUDAS. S-a-a-y, Perary, what are you going to do with all that money?

SNORKEY. I won't bet it on you, sure.

BERMUDAS. I'll tell you what to do; let's go and board at the Metropolitan Hotel for an hour.

SNORKEY. What will we do for toothpicks?

BERMUDAS. Oh, go along. You can't get anything to eat for four dollars.
   (*Exeunt Snorkey and Bermudas, squaring off.*)

Scene 4. Foot of Pier 30, North River-- Transparent set water pieces-- A pier projecting into the river. A large cavity in front. Bow of a vessel at back, and other steamers, vessels and piers in persective on either side. The flat gives view of Jersey City and river shipping by starlight. Music of distant serenade heard. (*Enter Byke, sculling a boat, which he fastens to the pier. Judas is on the pier, smoking pipe, looking down.*)

JUDAS. Have you fixed everything across the river?

BYKE. Yes, I have a horse and waggon waiting near the shore to carry her to the farm. Has anyone been around here?

JUDAS. Not a soul. I've been waiting here for an hour. What made you so long?

BYKE. I pulled down the river for a spell to throw any spies off the track. It was necessary after what you told me of that girl's threat to blab about the Boston pier.

JUDAS. Pshaw! she'd never dare.

BYKE. Never mind, it's best to be certain. Is the prize safe?

JUDAS. Yes, she was worn out, and slept when I came away. How her blood tells--she wouldn't shed a tear.

BYKE. Bah! If she'd been more of a woman and set up a screaming, we shouldn't have been able to get her at all. Success to all girls of spirit, say I.

JUDAS. Don't you think it might be worthwhile to treat with this young spark, Trafford, and hear what he has to offer?

BYKE. Satan take him, no! That'll spoil your game about the other girl, Pearl. He was making up to her all right, and if he gets this one back, he'll upset the whole game by marrying her. I tell you he's got the old feeling for her, spite of her running away. Now you can judge for yourself, and do as you please.

JUDAS. Then I do as you do--get her out of the city. When Pearl is married to him, we can treat for Laura's ransom by threatening them with the real secret.

BYKE. Then that's settled. (*Taking out flask.*) Here's the precious infant's health. Do you think she'll go easy, or shall we drug her?

JUDAS. Just tell her it's to meet her beau and get her ransom, or give her a reason and she'll be as mild as a lamb.

BYKE. Ha! let me get hold of her, and I'll answer she goes across, reason or no reason. (*Bermudas calls outside.*) There's a noise.

JUDAS. It's only the market boys coming down for a swim.

BYKE. Softly then, come along.

    (*Music-- Exeunt. Enter Bermudas, Peanuts, and two other boys.*)

BERMUDAS. Say, Peanuts, go down and see if any of the fellows is come yet.

    (*Peanuts scrambles down to hole in front on side of dock-- comes out again.*)

PEANUTS. There's nobody there.

SNORKEY. (*without*) Hollo!

BERMUDAS. Hollo! that's our new chum. Hollo! follow your front teeth, and you'll get here afore you knows it.

SNORKEY. (*entering, with more boys*) What a very airy location!

BERMUDAS. It's a very convenient hotel. Hot and cold salt water baths at the very door of your bedrooms, and sometimes when the tide rises, we has the bath brought to us in bed, doesn't we, Peanuts?

PEANUTS. That's so.

SNORKEY. Come, what do you do before you go to bed?

BERMUDAS. We'll have a swarry. Say, one of you fellows, go down and bring up the piany forty. (*Peanuts goes into hole and gets banjo.*) What'll I give you?

SNORKEY. Something lively.

    (*Music, nigger songs, and various entertainments-- trained dogs, street acrobats, etc., ending with dance by boys, given according to capacity and talent. At the end of it a general shout of jubilee.*)

SERGEANT. (*outside*) Here, boys! Less noise.

BERMUDAS. It's Acton and the police. Let's go to bed.

    (*Bermudas and boys get down into hole.*)

SERGEANT. (*entering in patrol boat*) If you boys don't make less noise, I'll have to clear you out.

BERMUDAS. (*on the pier*) It's an occasion, Mr. Acton; we've got a distinguished military guest, and we're entertaining him. (*Boat passes off.*) Come along, Perary, let's go to bed.

(*Snorkey is about to descend. Enter Ray Trafford on pier.*)

RAY. Is that you, Snorkey?

SNORKEY. (*quickly whispering*) Here, sir. Anything turned up?

RAY. Byke was overheard to say he intended crossing the river tonight. He will doubtless use that boat which he keeps by the Boston pier. The river patrol are on the watch for him, but I will meet him before he can embark.

SNORKEY. Which Boston pier is it, Cap'n? There are three on this river.

RAY. Three?

SNORKEY. Yes, one of them is two slips below. I tell you what, Cap'n; you get the officers, go by the shore way, search all the ships; I'll find a boat here, and will drop down the river, and keep an eye around generally.

VOICE. (*without*) This way, sir.

RAY. That's the patrol calling me. Your idea is a good one. Keep a sharp eye down the stream. (*Exit.*)

SNORKEY. (*alone*) Now for my lay.

BERMUDAS. (*popping his head up*) Say, can't I do nothin'? I'm the Fifth-Ward Chicken, and if there's any muss, let me have a shy.

SNORKEY. No; get in and keep quiet. (*Bermudas disappears.*) I wonder where I can find a boat. There ought to be plenty tied up about here. My eye! (*Discovering Byke's.*) Here's one for the wishin'--sculls, too. I'm in luck. Say, Bermudas, whose boat it this?

BERMUDAS. (*inside*) Yours, if you like. Turn it loose.

(*Snorkey jumps down, enters boat, pushes off.*)

Keep your toe out of my ear.

(*Pause. Enter Byke, Laura, and Judas, on pier.*)

LAURA. Is this the place? There is no one here; you have deceived me.

BYKE. Well, we have, but we won't do so any longer.

LAURA. What do you mean?

BYKE. (*drawing pistol*) Do you see this? It is my dog, Trusty. It has a very loud voice, and a sharp bite; and if you scream out, I'll try if it can't outscream you. Judas, unfasten the boat.

LAURA. What are you about to do? You will not murder me?

BYKE. No, we only mean to take you to the other shore, where your friends won't think of finding you. Quick, Judas!

JUDAS. The boat's gone.

BYKE. Damn you, what do you mean? Where is it? Here, hold her.

Where the devil is that boat?

SNORKEY. (*re-appearing in boat*) Here!

BYKE. Snorkey! We're betrayed. Come. (*Drags Laura away.*)

SNORKEY. The police are here. Turn, you coward, don't run away from a one-armed man!

BYKE. Judas, take her.

> (*Snorkey strikes at him with oar; Byke takes oar from him and strikes him-- he falls in boat.*)

SNORKEY. Help! Bermudas!

> (*The boys hear the noise, and scramble up at back. The patrol boat appears with lights.*)

BERMUDAS. Hi! Ninety-ninth round! First blood for Bermudas!

> (*Bermudas jumps at Byke.*)

BYKE. (*flinging Bermudas off*) Judas, toss her over.

> (*Judas throws Laura over back of pier. Enter Ray. Boys all get on pier and surround Byke, fighting him. Enter Officers-- Ray leaps into water after Laura-- Curtain-- Moonlight on during scene.*)

ACT III.

Scene 1. Long Branch. Ground floor of an elegant residence-- Open windows from floor to ceiling at back, opening upon a balcony or promenade. Perspective of the shore and sea in distance. Doors, R. and L. Sunset. (*The curtain rises to lively music. Enter Pearl, Mrs. Van Dam, Miss Earlie, and other ladies in summer costume, Demilt and Windel with them.*)

PEARL. And so the distinguished foreigner is in love with me? I thought he looked excessively solemn last night. Do you know, I can't imagine a more serious spectacle than a Frenchman or an Italian in love. One always imagines them to be unwell. (*To Mrs. Van Dam.*) Do fasten my glove--there's a dear.

MRS. VAN DAM. Where's Ray?

PEARL. Oh, he's somewhere. I never saw such another. Isn't he cheerful? He never smiles, and seldom talks.

MRS. VAN DAM. But the foreigner does. What an ecstasy he was in over your singing; sing us a verse, won't you, while we're waiting for Ray?

ALL. It will be delightful--do.

PEARL. Well! (*Sings.*)

Air. "When the War is Over, Mary."
Now the summer days are fading,
    Autumn sends its dreary blast
Moaning through the silent forest
    Where the leaves are falling fast.
Soon dread winter will enfold us--
    Chilling in its arms of snow,
Flowers that the summer cherished,
    Birds that sing, and streams that flow.

Say, shall all things droop and wither,
    That are born this summer day?
Shall the happy love it brought us--
    Like the flowers fade away?
Go; be still thou flutt'ring bosom--
    Seasons change and years glide by,
They may not harm what is immortal--
    Darling--love shall never die! *(Song ends.)*

Now, I've sung that to Ray a dozen times, and he never even said it was nice. He hasn't any soul for music; oh, dear, what a creature!

MRS. VAN DAM. Yes, and what a victim you will be, with a husband who has 600,000 dollars per annum income!

PEARL. That's some comfort, isn't it?

(Enter Ray Trafford, bowing to others.)

RAY. Going out, Pearl?

PEARL. Yes, we're off to Shrewsbury. Quite a party's going--four carriages--and we mean to stay and ride home by moonlight.

RAY. Couldn't you return a little earlier?

MRS. VAN DAM. Earlier! Pshaw! What's in you, Trafford?

(The ladies and gentlemen go up.)

RAY. You know that Laura will be quite alone, and she is still suffering.

PEARL. Well, she'll read and read, as she always did, and never miss me.

RAY. But at least she ought to have some little attention.

PEARL. Dear, dear, what an unreasonable fellow you are! Isn't she happy now--didn't you save her from drowning, and haven't I been as good to her as I can be--what more do you want?

RAY. I don't like to hear you talk so, Pearl, and remember what she and you were once. And you know that she was something else once--something that you are now to me. And yet how cheerful, how gentle she is. She has lost everything, and does not complain.

PEARL. Well, what a sermon! There, I know you're hurt and I'm a fool. But I can't help it. People say "she's good-looking, but she's got no heart!" I'd give anything for one, but they ain't to be bought.

RAY. Well, don't moan about it, I didn't mean to reprove you.

PEARL. But you *do* reprove me. I'm sure I haven't been the cause of Laura's troubles. I didn't tell the big ugly man to come and take her away, although I was once glad he did.

RAY. Pearl!

PEARL. Because I thought I had gained you by it. (*Ray turns away.*) But now I've got you, I don't seem to make you happy. But I might as well complain that you don't make me happy--but I don't complain, I'm satisfied, and I want you to be satisfied. There, *are* you satisfied?

MRS. VAN DAM. (*who, with others, has been promenading up and down the balcony*) Here are the carriages!

PEARL. I'm coming. Can't you get me my shawl, Ray?

(*Ray gets shawl from chair.*)

MRS. VAN DAM. And here's your foreign admirer on horseback.

(*Exeunt Miss Earlie, Demilt and Windel.*)

PEARL. Bye, bye, Ray. (*Exit Pearl.*)

MRS. VAN DAM. Are you not coming, Trafford?

RAY. I? No!

MRS. VAN DAM. Do come on horseback; here's a horse ready for you.

PEARL. (*without*) Ray! Ray!

MRS. VAN DAM. Pearl's calling you. Be quick or Count Carom will be before you, and hand her in the carriage.

RAY. (*taking his hat slowly*) Oh, by all means, let the Count have some amusement.

MRS. VAN DAM. (*taking Ray's arm*) You're a perfect icicle.

(*They exeunt. Noise of whips and laughter. Plaintive music as Laura enters, and gazes out at them.*)

LAURA. Poor Pearl. It is a sad thing to want for happiness, but it is a terrible thing to see another groping about blindly for it when it is almost within the grasp. And yet she can be very happy with him. Her sunny temper and her joyous face will brighten any home. (*Sits on table, on which are books.*) How happy I feel to be alone with these friends, who are ever ready to talk to me--with no longings for what I may not have--my existence hidden from all save two in the wide world, and making my joy out of the joy of that innocent child who will soon be his wife.

(Peachblossom appears at back, looking in cautiously, grotesquely attired.)

PEACHBLOSSOM. If you please.

LAURA. *(aloud)* Who's there?

PEACHBLOSSOM. *(running in)* Oh, it's Miss Nina! Oh, I'm so glad; I've had such a hunt for you. Don't ask me nothin' yet. I'm so happy. I've been looking for you so long, and I've had such hard luck. Lord, what a tramp--miles on miles.

LAURA. Did anyone see you come here? How did you find me?

PEACHBLOSSOM. I asked 'em at the hotel where Mr. Trafford was, and they said at Courtlands. And I asked 'em where Courtlands was and they said down the shore, and I walked down lookin' at every place till I came here.

LAURA. Speak low, Blossom. My existence is a secret, and no one must hear you.

PEACHBLOSSOM. Well, Miss, I says to Snorkey--says I--

LAURA. Is he with you?

PEACHBLOSSOM. No, Miss, but we are great friends. He wants me to keep house for him someday. I said to him--"I want to find out where Miss Nina's gone," and so he went to Mr. Trafford's and found he was come to Long Branch, but never a word could we hear of you.

LAURA. And the others--those dreadful people?

PEACHBLOSSOM. Byke and old Judas? Clean gone! They hasn't been seen since they was took up for throwing you into the water, and let off because no one came to Court agin 'em. Bermudas says he seen 'em in Barnum's wax-work show, but Bermudas is *such* a liar. He brought me up here.

LAURA. Brought you up here?

PEACHBLOSSOM. Yes, he sells papers at Stetson's; he's got the exclusive trade here, and he has a little waggon and a horse, and goes down to the junction every night to catch the extras from the express train what don't come here. He says he'll give me lots of nice rides if I stay here.

LAURA. But you must not stay here. You must go back to New York this evening.

PEACHBLOSSOM. Back! No, I won't.

LAURA. Blossom!

PEACHBLOSSOM. I won't, I won't, I won't! I'll never let you away again. I did it once and you was took away and chucked overboard and almost drowned. I won't be any trouble, indeed, I won't. I'll hire out at the hotel, and run over when my work is done at night, when nobody can see me, to look up at your window. Don't send me away. You're the only one as ever was good to me.

LAURA. (*aside*) It's too dangerous. She certainly would reveal me sooner or later. I must send her back.

PEACHBLOSSOM. Besides, I've got something to tell you. Dreadful! dreadful! about old Judas and Byke--a secret.

LAURA. A secret! What in the world are you saying?

PEACHBLOSSOM. Is it wicked to listen at doors when people talk?

LAURA. It is very wicked.

PEACHBLOSSOM. Well, I suppose that's why I did it. I used to listen to Byke and Judas when they used to talk about a rich lady whom they called Mrs. Courtland.

LAURA. Ah!

PEACHBLOSSOM. Judas used to be a nurse at Mrs. Courtland's, and was turned off for stealing. And wasn't she and Byke going to make money off her! And Byke was to pretend to be some beautiful lady's father. Then when they took you, Judas says to me: "Did you ever hear of children being changed in their cradles?"--and that you wasn't her child, but she was going to make money off the real one at the proper time.

LAURA. What do you tell me?

PEACHBLOSSOM. Oh! I'm not crazy. I know a heap, don't I? And I want you to think I'm somebody, and not send me away.

LAURA. (*to herself*) She must speak the truth. And yet if I were to repeat her strange words here, I should be suspected of forging the tale. No! Better let it rest as it is. She must go--and I must go, too.

PEACHBLOSSOM. You ain't mad with me?

LAURA. No, no; but you must go away from here. Go back to the hotel, to your friend--anywhere, and wait for me; I will come to you.

PEACHBLOSSOM. Is it a promise?

LAURA. (*nervously*) Yes, go.

PEACHBLOSSOM. Then I'll go; for I know you always keep your word--you ain't angry 'cause I came after you? I did it because I loved you--because I wanted to see you put in the right place. Honour bright, you ain't sending me away, now? Well, I'll go; goodbye! (*Exit.*)

LAURA. (*animated*) I must return to the city, no matter what dangers may lurk there. It is dangerous enough to be concealed here, with a hundred Argus-eyed women about me every day, but with this girl, detection would be certain. I must go--secretly if I can--openly if I must.

RAY. (*outside*) No, I shall not ride again. Put him up. (*Entering.*) Laura, I knew I should find you here.

LAURA. (*sitting and pretending composure*) I thought you had gone with Pearl.

RAY. I did go part of the way, but I left the party a mile down the road.

LAURA. You and Pearl had no disagreement?

RAY. No--yes; that is, we always have. Our social barometers always stand at "cloudy" and "overcast."

LAURA. And whose fault is that?

RAY. (*pettishly*) Not mine. I know I do all I can--I say all I can--but she--

LAURA. But she is to be your wife. Ray, my friend, courtship is the text from which the whole solemn sermon of married life takes its theme. Do not let yours be discontented and unhappy.

RAY. To be my wife; yes. In a moment of foolishness, dazzled by her airs, and teased by her coquettishness, I asked her to be my wife.

LAURA. And you repent already?

RAY. (*taking her hand*) I lost you, and I was at the mercy of any flirt that chose to give me an inviting look. It was your fault--you know it was! Why did you leave me?

LAURA. (*after conflict with her feelings*) Ray, the greatest happiness I have ever felt has been the thought that all your affections were forever bestowed upon a virtuous lady, your equal in family, fortune and accomplishments. What a revelation do you make to me now! What is it makes you continually at war with your happiness?

RAY. I don't know what it is. I was wrong to accuse you. Forgive me! I have only my own cowardice to blame for my misery. But Pearl--

LAURA. You must not accuse her.

RAY. When you were gone, she seemed to have no thought--no wish--but for my happiness. She constantly invited me to her house, and when I tried to avoid her, met me at every turn. Was she altogether blameless?

LAURA. Yes, it was her happiness she sought, and she had a right to seek it.

RAY. Oh! men are the veriest fools on earth; a little attention, a little sympathy, and they are caught--caught by a thing without soul or brains, while some noble woman is forsaken and forgotten.

LAURA. Ray, will you hear me?

RAY. (*looking at her hopefully*) Yes, speak to me as you used to speak. Be to me as you used to be.

LAURA. (*smiling sadly*) I cannot be that to you; but I can speak as the spirit of the Laura who is dead to you forever.

RAY. Be it as you will.

LAURA. Let the woman you look upon be wise or vain, beautiful or homely, rich or poor, she has but one thing she can really give or refuse--her heart! Her beauty, her wit, her accomplishments she may sell to you--but her love is the treasure without money and without price.

RAY. How well I have learned that.

LAURA. She only asks in return, that when you look upon her, your eyes shall speak a mute devotion; that when you address her, your voice shall be gentle, loving and kind. That you shall not despise her because she cannot understand, all at once, your vigorous thoughts and ambitious designs; for when misfortune and evil have defeated your greatest purposes--her love remains to console you. You look to the trees for strength and grandeur--do not despise the flowers, because their fragrance is all they have to give. Remember, love is all a woman has to give; but it is the only earthly thing which God permits us to carry beyond the grave.

RAY. You are right. You are always right. I asked Pearl to be my wife, knowing what she was, and I will be just to her. I will do my duty though it break my heart.

LAURA. Spoken like a hero.

RAY. But it is to you I owe the new light that guides me; and I will tell her--

LAURA. Tell her nothing--never speak of me. And when you see her, say to her it is she, and she alone, whom you consult and to whom you listen.

RAY. And you?

LAURA. You will see me no more.

RAY. You will leave me?

LAURA. Something of me will always be with you--my parting words-- my prayers for your happiness. (*Distant music heard.*)

RAY. (*falling on his knees*) Oh, Laura, you leave me to despair.

LAURA. No; to the happiness which follows duty well performed. Such happiness as I feel in doing mine.

(*Picture. During last of this scene the sun has set, and night comes on. Close in. Stage dark.*)

Scene 2. Woods near Shrewsbury Station. (*Enter Byke, shabbily dressed.*)

BYKE. It's getting darker and darker, and I'm like to lose my way. Where the devil is Judas? It must be nine o'clock, and she was to be at the bend with the waggon half an hour ago. (*Rumble of wheels heard.*) Humph--at last.

JUDAS. (*entering*) Is that you, Byke?

BYKE. Who did you suppose it was? I've been tramping about the wet grass for an hour.

JUDAS. It was a hard job to get the horse and waggon.

BYKE. Give me a match. (*Lights pipe and leans against a tree.*) Did you get the bearings of the crib?

JUDAS. Yes, it is on the shore, well away from the other cottages and hotels.

BYKE. That's good. Nothing like peace and quietness. Who's in the house?

JUDAS. Only the two girls and the servants.

BYKE. How many of them?

JUDAS. Four.

BYKE. It'll be mere child's play to go through that house. Have you spied about the swag?

JUDAS. They have all their diamonds and jewels there. Pearl wears them constantly; they're the talk of the whole place.

BYKE. We'll live in luxury off that girl all our lives. She'll settle a handsome thing on us, won't she? when she knows what we know, and pays us to keep dark--if t'other one don't spoil the game.

JUDAS. Curse her! I could cut her throat.

BYKE. Oh, I'll take care of that!

JUDAS. You always do things for the best, dear old Byke!

BYKE. Of course I do. What time is it?

JUDAS. Not ten yet.

BYKE. An hour to wait.

JUDAS. But, Byke, you won't peach on me before my little pet is married, will you?

BYKE. What's the fool about now?

JUDAS. I can't help trembling; nothing is safe while Laura is there.

BYKE. I've provided for that. I've had the same idea as you--while she's in the way, and Trafford unmarried, our plans are all smoke, and we might as well be sitting on the hob with a keg of powder in the coals.

JUDAS. That we might. But what have you thought to do?

BYKE. Why, I've thought what an unfortunate creature Laura is-- robbed of her mother, her home, and her lover; nothing to live for; it would be a mercy to put her out of the way.

JUDAS. That's it; but how--how--how--

BYKE. It's plain she wasn't born to be drowned, for the materials are very handy down here. What made you talk about cutting her throat? It was very wrong! When a thing gets into my head, it sticks there.

JUDAS. You oughtn't to mind me.

BYKE. Make your mind easy on that score.

JUDAS. (*alarmed, pointing off*) Byke, I heard someone in the bushes just there.

BYKE. (*nervously and quickly*) Who? Where?

JUDAS. Where the hedge is broken. I could swear I saw the shadow of a man.

BYKE. Stop here. I'll see. (*Goes off.*)

JUDAS. I begin to shiver. But it must be done or we starve. Why should I tremble? It's the safest job we ever planned. If they discover us, our secret will save us--we know too much to be sent to jail.

(*Re-enter Byke slowly.*)

BYKE. There are traces, but I can see no one. (*Looking off.*)

JUDAS. Suppose we should have been overheard!

BYKE. (*glaring at her*) Overheard? Bah! no one could understand.

JUDAS. Come, let us go to the waggon and be off.

BYKE. (*always looking off*) Go you, I will follow. Bring it round by the station, and wait for me in the shadows of the trees. I will follow.

(*Judas goes off. Byke, after a moment, still looking, buttons up his coat and hides behind wood.*)

Heigho! I must be off.

(*Enter Snorkey, slowly.*)

SNORKEY. Tracked 'em again! We're the latest fashionable arrivals at Long Branch. "Mr. Byke and Lady, and Brigadier-General Snorkey, of New York"; there's an item for the papers! With a horse and waggon, they'll be at the seaside in two hours; but in the train I think I'll beat 'em. Then to find Cap'n Trafford, and give him the wink, and be ready to receive the distinguished visitors with all the honours. Robbery; burglary; murder; that's Byke's catechism. "What's to be done when you're hard up? Steal! What's to be done if you're caught at it? Kill!" It's short and easy, and he lives up to it like a good many Christians don't live up to their laws. (*Looking off.*) They're out of sight. Phew! it's midsummer, but I'm chilled to the bone; something like a piece of ice has been stuck between my shoulders all day, and something like a black mist is always before me. (*Byke is behind tree.*) Just like old Nettly told me he felt, the night before Fredericksburg--and the next day he was past all feeling--hit with a shell, and knocked into so many pieces, I didn't

know which to call my old friend. Well--(*slapping his chest*)--we've all
got to go; and if I can save *them*, I'll have some little capital to start the
next world on. The next world! Perhaps I shan't be the maimed beggar
there that I am in this.

(*Takes out pistol, examines cap; goes off, Byke gliding after him.*)

Scene 3. Railroad Station at Shrewsbury Bend, R. Platform around it,
and door at side, window in front. At L., clump of shrubs and trees. The
railroad track runs from L. to R. View of Shrewsbury River in perspective. Night--moonlight. The switch, with a red lantern and a signalman's
coat hanging on it, L.C., the signal lamp and post beside it. (*Packages are
lying about, among them a bundle of axes. The Signalman is wheeling in a
small barrel, whistling at his work. Enter Laura, in walking dress, feebly.*)

LAURA. It is impossible for me to go further. A second time I've fled from
home and friends, but now they will never find me. The trains must all
have passed, and there are no conveyances till tomorrow.
SIGNALMAN. Beg pardon, ma'am, looking for anybody?
LAURA. Thank you, no. Are you the man in charge of this station?
SIGNALMAN. Yes, ma'am.
LAURA. When is there another train for New York?
SIGNALMAN. New York? Not till morning. We've only one more train
tonight; that's the down one; it'll be here in about twenty minutes--
express train.
LAURA. What place is that?
SIGNALMAN. That? That's the signal station shed. It serves for store-
room, depot, baggage-room, and everything.
LAURA. Can I stay there tonight?
SIGNALMAN. There? Well, it's an odd place, and I should think you
would hardly like it. Why don't you go to the hotel?
LAURA. I have my reasons--urgent ones. It is not because I want money.
(*Producing porte-monnaie.*) You shall have this if you let me remain here.
SIGNALMAN. Well, I've locked up a good many things in there
over-night, but I never had a young lady for freight before. Besides,
ma'am, I don't know anything about you. You know it's odd that you
won't go to a decent hotel, and plenty of money in your pocket.
LAURA. You refuse me--well--I shall only have to sit here all night.
SIGNALMAN. Here, in the open air? Why, it would kill you.
LAURA. So much the better.
SIGNALMAN. Excuse me for questions, Miss, but you're a-running

away from someone, ain't you?

LAURA. Yes.

SIGNALMAN. Well, I'd like to help you. I'm a plain man, you know, and I'd like to help you, but there's one thing would go agin me to assist in. (*Laura interested.*) I'm on to fifty years of age, and I've many children, some on 'em daughters grown. There's many temptations for young gals, and sometimes the old man has to put on the brakes a bit, for some young men are wicked enough to persuade the gals to steal out of their father's house in the dead of the night, and go to shame and misery. So tell me this--it ain't the old man, and the old man's home you've left, young lady?

LAURA. No, you good, honest fellow--no, I have no father.

SIGNALMAN. Then, by Jerusalem, I'll do for you what I can. Anything but run away from them that have not their interest but yours at heart. Come, you may stay there, but I'll have to lock you in.

LAURA. I desire that you should.

SIGNALMAN. It's for your safety as much as mine. I've got a patent lock on that door that would give a skeleton the rheumatism to fool with it. You don't mind the baggage; I'll have to put it in with you, hoes, shovels, mowing machines, and what is this? Axes--yes, a bundle of axes. If the superintendent finds me out, I'll ask him if he was afraid you'd run off with these. (*Laughs.*) So, if you please, I'll first tumble 'em in.

(*Signalman puts goods in house, Laura sitting on platform, looking at him. He comes towards her, taking up cheese-box to put it in station.*)

I say, Miss, I ain't curious, but, of course, it's a *young man* you're a-going to?

LAURA. So far from that, it's a young man I'm running away from.

SIGNALMAN. (*dropping a box*) Running away from a young man; let me shake hands with you. (*Shakes her hand.*) Lord, it does my heart good. At your age, too. (*Seriously.*) I wish you'd come and live in my neighborhood awhile--(*shaking his head*)--among my gals you'd do a power of good. (*Putting the box in station.*)

LAURA. (*aside*) I've met an excellent friend--and here at least I can be concealed until tomorrow--then for New York. My heart feels lighter already--it's a good omen.

SIGNALMAN. Now, Miss, bless your heart, here's your hotel ready.

(*Goes to switch and takes off coat, putting it on.*)

LAURA. Thanks, my good friend, but not a word to anyone till tomorrow, not even--not even to your girls.

SIGNALMAN. Not a word, I promise you. If I told my girls, it would be over the whole village before morning.

(She goes in-- he locks door. Laura appears at window facing audience.)

LAURA. Lock me in safely.

SIGNALMAN. Ah, be sure I will. There! *(Tries door.)* Safe as a jail. *(Pulls out watch and then looks at track with lantern.)* Ten minutes and down she comes. It's all safe this way, my noisy beauty, and you may come as soon as you like. Goodnight, Miss.

LAURA. *(at window)* Goodnight.

SIGNALMAN. Running away from a young man, ha! ha! ha!

(He goes to track, then looks down it, lights his pipe and is trudging off.)

SNORKEY. *(entering)* Ten minutes before the train comes, I'll wait here for it. *(To Signalman, who re-enters.)* Hallo, I say, the train won't stop here too long, will it?

SIGNALMAN. Too long? It won't stop here at all.

SNORKEY. I must reach the shore tonight; there'll be murder done unless I can prevent it.

SIGNALMAN. Murder or no murder, the train can't be stopped.

SNORKEY. It's a lie. By waving the red signal for danger, the engineer must stop, I tell you.

SIGNALMAN. Do you think I'm a fool? What, disobey orders and lose my place; then what's to become of my family? *(Exit.)*

SNORKEY. I won't be foiled; I will confiscate some farmer's horse about here and get there before them somehow.

(Enter Byke at back with loose coil of rope in his hand.)

Then when Byke arrives in his donkey cart, he'll be ready to sit for a picture of surprise.

BYKE. *(suddenly throwing the coil over Snorkey)* Will he?

SNORKEY. Byke!

BYKE. Yes, Byke. Where's that pistol of yours?

(Tightening rope round his arm.)

SNORKEY. In my breast pocket.

BYKE. *(taking it)* Just what I wanted.

SNORKEY. You ain't a-going to shoot me?

BYKE. No!

SNORKEY. Well, I'm obliged to you for that.

BYKE. *(leading him to platform)* Just sit down a minute, will you.

SNORKEY. What for?

(Laura appears horror-struck at window.)

BYKE. You'll see.

SNORKEY. Well, I don't mind if I do take a seat. *(Sits down, Byke coils the rope around his legs.)* Hollo, what's this?

BYKE. You will see. (*Picks the helpless Snorkey up.*)

SNORKEY. Byke, what are you going to do?

BYKE. Put you to bed. (*Lays him across the railroad track.*)

SNORKEY. Byke, you don't mean to-- My God, you are a villain!

BYKE. (*fastening him to rails*) I'm going to put you to bed. You won't toss much. In less than ten minutes you'll be sound asleep. There, how do you like it? You'll get down to the Branch before me, will you? You'll dog me and play the eavesdropper, eh? Now do it if you can. When you hear the thunder under your head and see the lights dancing in your eyes, and feel the iron wheels a foot from your neck, remember Byke. (*Exit.*)

LAURA. Oh, Heavens, he will be murdered before my eyes! How can I aid him?

SNORKEY. Who's that?

LAURA. It is I, do you not know my voice?

SNORKEY. That I do, but I almost thought I was dead and it was an angel's. Where are you?

LAURA. In the station.

SNORKEY. I can't see you, but I can hear you. Listen to me, Miss, for I've got only a few minutes to live.

LAURA. (*shaking door*) And I cannot aid you.

SNORKEY. Never mind me, Miss, I might as well die now and here, as at any other time. I'm not afraid. I've seen death in almost every shape, and none of them scare me; but for the sake of those you love, I would live. Do you hear me?

LAURA. Yes! yes!

SNORKEY. They are on the way to your cottage--Byke and Judas--to rob and murder.

LAURA. Oh, I must get out! (*Shakes window bars.*) What shall I do?

SNORKEY. Can't you burst the door?

LAURA. It is locked fast.

SNORKEY. Is there nothing in there? no hammer? no crowbar?

LAURA. Nothing. (*Faint steam whistle heard in the distance.*) Oh, Heavens! The train! (*Paralysed for an instant.*) The axe!!!

SNORKEY. Cut the woodwork! Don't mind the lock, cut round it. How my neck tingles!

(*A blow at door is heard.*)

Courage!

(*Another.*)

Courage!

(*The whistle again, nearer, and rumble of train on track-- another blow.*)

That's a true woman. Courage!

(*Noise of locomotive heard, with whistle. A last blow-- the door swings open, mutilated, the lock hanging-- and Laura appears, axe in hand.*)

Here--quick!

(*She runs and unfastens him. The locomotive lights glare on scene.*)

Victory! Saved! Hooray! And these are the women who ain't to have a vote!

(*Laura helps him from the track. The train of cars rushes past with roar and whistle.*)

ACT IV.

Scene 1. An elegant boudoir at Courtland Cottage, Long Branch. Open window and balcony at back-- Moonlight exterior-- Tree overhanging balcony. Bed is at L., toilette table R., armchair C., door L., lighted lamp on toilette table-- Dresses on chair by bed, and by window on R. Music.

PEARL. (*discovered, en negligée, brushing her hair at table before mirror*) I don't feel a bit sleepy. What a splendid drive we had. I like that foreigner. What an elegant fellow he is! Ray is nothing to him. I wonder if I'm in love with him. Pshaw! What an idea! I don't believe I could love anybody much. How sweetly he writes! (*Picks up letter.*) "You were more lovely than ever tonight--with one thing more, you'd be an angel!" Now that's perfectly splendid--"with one thing more, you'd be an angel-- that one thing is love. They tell me Mr. Trafford is your professed admirer. I'm sure he could never be called your lover, for he seems incapable of any passion but melancholy." It's quite true, Ray does not comprehend me. (*Another letter.*) "Pearl, forgive me if I have been cross and cold. For the future, I will do my duty, as your affianced husband, better." Now, did ever anyone hear such talk as that from a lover? Lover! Oh, dear! I begin to feel that he can love--but not me. Well, I'd just as soon break, if he'd be the first to speak. How sweet and fresh the air is. (*Turns down lamp.*) It's much nicer here, than going to bed.

(*Pearl settles herself in tête-à-téte for a nap. Pause. Moonbeams fall on Byke, who appears above the balcony. He gets over the rail and enters.*)

BYKE. Safely down. I've made no mistake--no, this is her room. What a figure I am for a lady's chamber. (*Goes to table, picks up delicate lace handkerchief, and wipes his face.*) Phew! Hot! Now for my bearings. (*Taking huge clasp-knife from his pocket.*) There's the bed where she's sleeping like a precious infant, and here-- (*Sees Pearl and steals round at back.*) It's so dark--I can't recognise the face. It's a wonder she don't feel me in the air and dream of me. If she does, she'll wake sure--but it's easy to settle that. (*Takes phial of chloroform from his pocket, saturates the handkerchief, and applies it.*) So--now my charmer, we'll have the earrings. (*Takes them out.*) What's here? (*Going to table.*) Bracelets--diamonds! (*Going to dresses, and feeling in the pockets.*) Money! That's handy. (*He puts all in a bag, and hands them over balcony.*) Now for the drawers; there's where the treasure must be. Locked? (*Tries them with keys.*) Patent lock, of course. It amuses me to see people buying patent locks when there's one key will fit 'em all. (*Produces a small crowbar. A shout is heard, and noise of waggon.*) What's that? (*Jumps, catching at a chair, which falls over.*) Damnation!

PEARL. (*starting up*) Who's there? What's that?

BYKE. Silence, or I'll kill you.

PEARL. Help! Help!

BYKE. (*running to bureau for knife*) You will have it, my pretty one.

PEARL. (*runs to door*) Save me! Save me!

 (*Byke pursues her, she dodges him. As Byke overtakes her, the door bursts open-- enter Ray and Laura. Byke turns and runs to balcony, and confronts Snorkey and Bermudas, who have clambered over.*)

LAURA. Just in time.

RAY. (*seizing Byke*) Scoundrel!

SNORKEY. Hold him, governor. Hold him!

 (*Assists Ray to bind Byke in chair.*)

BERMUDAS. Sixty-six and last round. The big 'un floored, and Bermudas as fresh as a daisy.

PEARL. Dear, dear Laura, you have saved me.

RAY. Yes, Pearl, from more than you can tell.

LAURA. No, no; her preservers are there. (*Pointing to Bermudas and Snorkey.*) Had it not been for the one, I should never have learned your danger, and but for the other, we could never have reached you in time.

SNORKEY. Bermudas and his fourth editions did it. Business enterprise and Bermudas' pony express worked the oracle this time.

BERMUDAS. The way we galloped! Sa-ay, my pony must have thought the extras was full of lively intelligence.

PEARL. Darling Laura, you shall never leave us again.

RAY. No, never!

SNORKEY. Beg pardon, Cap'n, what are we to do with this here game we've brought down?

RAY. The magistrates will settle with him.

SNORKEY. Come, old fellow.

BYKE. One word, I beg. My conduct, I know, has been highly reprehensible. I have acted injudiciously, and have been the occasion of more or less inconvenience to everyone here. But I wish to make amends, and therefore I tender you all, in this public manner, my sincere apologies. I trust this will be entirely satisfactory.

RAY. Villain!

BYKE. I have a word to say to you, sir.

SNORKEY. Come, that's enough.

BYKE. My good fellow, don't interrupt gentlemen who are conversing together. (*To Ray.*) I address you, sir--you design to commit me to the care of the officers of the law?

RAY. Most certainly.

BYKE. And you will do your best towards having me incarcerated in the correctional establishments of this country? (*Ray bows.*)

SNORKEY. How very genteel.

BYKE. Then I have to say, if you will, I shall make a public exposure of certain matters connected with a certain young lady.

LAURA. Do not think that will deter us from your punishment. I can bear even more than I have--for the sake of justice.

BYKE. Excuse me, I did not even remotely refer to you.

LAURA. To whom, then?

BYKE. (*pointing to Pearl*) To her.

RAY. Miss Courtland?

BYKE. Oh dear--no, sir. The daughter of old Judas--the spurious child placed in *your* cradle, Miss Laura Courtland, when you were abducted from it by your nurse.

PEARL. What does he say?

BYKE. That you're a beggar's child--we have the proofs! Deliver me to prison, and I produce them.

RAY. Wretch!

PEARL. Then it's you, dear Laura, have been wronged--while I--

LAURA. You are my sister still--whatever befalls!

PEARL. Oh, I'm so glad it's so! Ray won't want to marry me, now--at least, I hope so; for I know he loves you--he always loved you--and you will be happy together.

RAY. Pearl, what are you saying?

PEARL. Don't interrupt me! I mean every word of it. Laura, I've been very foolish, I know. I ought to have tried to reunite you--but there is time.

RAY. Dear Laura! Is there, indeed, still time? (*She gives her hand.*)

BYKE. Allow me to suggest that a certain proposition I had the honour to submit has not yet been answered.

RAY. Release him. (*Snorkey undoes his cords.*)

BYKE. Thank you--not so rough! Thank you.

RAY. Now, go--but remember, if you ever return to these parts, you shall be tried, not only for this burglary, but for the attempt to kill that poor fellow.

BYKE. Thank you. Good-bye. (*To Snorkey.*) Good-bye, my dear friend; overlook our little dispute, and write to me. (*Aside.*) They haven't caught Judas, and she shall make them pay handsomely for her silence yet. (*Enter Peachblossom.*)

PEACHBLOSSOM. Oh, Miss! Oh, such an accident--old Judas!

LAURA and BYKE. Well?

PEACHBLOSSOM. She was driving along the road away from here just now, when her horse dashed close to the cliff and tumbled her down all of a heap. They've picked her up, and they tell me she is stone dead.

BYKE. (*aside*) Dead! And carried her secret with her! All's up. I'll have to emigrate. (*Aloud.*) My friends, pardon my emotion--this melancholy event has made me a widower. I solicit your sympathies in my bereavement. (*Exit Byke.*)

BERMUDAS. Go to Hoboken and climb a tree! I guess I'll follow him and see he don't pick up anything on his way out. (*Exit Bermudas.*)

SNORKEY. Well, there goes a pretty moment of grief. Ain't he a cool 'un? If I ever sets up an ice-cream saloon, I'll have him for head freezer.

PEACHBLOSSOM. Oh, Miss Laura, mayn't I live with you now, and never leave no more?

LAURA. Yes, you shall live with me as long as you please.

SNORKEY. That won't be long if I can help it. (*Peachblossom blushes.*) Beg pardon. I suppose we'd better be going! The ladies must be tired, Cap'n, at this time of night.

RAY. Yes, it is night! It is night always for me.

　　(*He moves towards the door. Laura places one hand on his shoulder, taking his hand.*)

LAURA. But there is a tomorrow. You see, it cannot be dark forever.

PEARL. Hope for tomorrow, Ray.

LAURA. We shall have cause to bless it, for it will bring the long sought sunlight of our lives.

CURTAIN.

Bronson Howard (1842-1908)
and *Young Mrs. Wintrhop*

Bronson Howard's designation as the "Dean of American Drama" derived largely from his ability to support himself as a dramatist. He was, in fact, the first American to make a profession of writing plays. He lectured at Harvard College in 1886 on what he termed "the laws of dramatic composition," which in his mind were based upon an understanding of the sympathies of the audience and the expected motives and actions of the characters. To achieve a "satisfactory" and well constructed play, Howard believed, the dramatist had only to use common sense and remain in touch with human nature.

Howard came into the theatre at a time when American society, challenged by the strains upon it, was developing its own distinctive character. The United States needed dramatists who could not only entertain but stimulate emotion and thought, and Howard played a role in the transition from amusement to art. His first success was a farce, *Saratoga*, 1870, which ran for 101 nights at Daly's Fifth Avenue Theatre. With *The Banker's Daughter*, 1873, he began to develop his theories of the drama. In *Young Mrs. Winthrop* he consciously set his story of socio-economic and domestic conflict against a background of fashionable society. This play enjoyed an initial run of 180 performances and was hailed as "the great American drama so long and so ardently awaited."

Later, Howard would emphasize the idiosyncrasies of the American business world: *The Henrietta*, 1887, satirized life on the stock exchange; *Aristocracy*, 1892, extended his focus upon the business world to the international social scene. Ironically, *Shenandoah*, 1888, a romantic tale of the Civil War in the "horse-opera" genre, was his most successful play.

Howard founded the American Dramatists Club (forerunner of the Dramatists Guild) in 1891 but toward the end of his career weakened his position as a spokesman for American drama by joining the stable of playwrights of the Theatrical Syndicate. As a transitional dramatist and man of the theatre, however, anticipating the work of Clyde Fitch and Rachel Crothers, he helped establish the American dramatist as a professional if not a literary artist.

Bronson Howard

YOUNG MRS. WINTHROP

(1882)

by Bronson Howard

CHARACTERS

Mrs. Ruth Winthrop
Mr. Douglas Winthrop, her son
Constance Winthrop, his wife
Buxton Scott, a lawyer
Mrs. Dick Chetwyn, a lady of society
Edith, sister of Constance
Herbert
Dr. Mellbanke
A Maid

ACT I.

Scene. Interior of a private residence of a man of wealth in New York. Door, R.1E.; also R.U.E. A mantel and fire, R., near front. An easel with portrait of a beautiful little girl of four years, up C. Small stand or table down L.C. A number of presents for a child's birthday on chairs and other pieces of furniture, C. and L.C. Some of these presents must be such as referred to in the dialogue. Evening. Lights for ordinary family life. (*Discovered: Mrs. Ruth Winthrop, sitting before fire, down R. She has a doll, partly dressed, in her lap, and is working on its little bonnet. She is singing a lullaby, "Golden Slumbers" composed by Frank A. Howson, as she works, when the curtain rises.*)

MRS. RUTH. Golden slumbers kiss your eyes,
           Smiles await you when you rise;
           Sleep, little darling, do not cry.
           And I will sing a lullaby,
           And I will sing a lullaby,
           Lullaby, lullaby. (*Song ends.*)

There, Miss Dolly! (*Trying bonnet on the doll and holding it up.*) You will have a beautiful little mother to-morrow, and I shall be your great-grandmother. Your name is to be "Ruth"--after me. How do you like it? Your little mother has a very large family already, but I am sure she will love you more than any of the rest. (*Kisses the doll.*) Lie here, my pet. (*Holding the doll to her breast.*) You must go to sleep at once, for Mother Rosie will be up very early in the morning. (*Enter Douglas, up L.*) H-s-h. (*Sings as at rise of curtain, patting the doll.*)

DOUGLAS. (*at the back of her chair, leaning over her*) Playing with a doll, mother?

MRS. RUTH. Douglas! (*Looking up and laughing quietly.*) Yes. I had forgotten my gray hairs. I was a child again, like Rosie. We old folks grow young again in our grandchildren.

DOUGLAS. You've never grown old, Mother. You've always been living the same sweet loving life.

MRS. RUTH. (*with a quiet laugh*) Leave any woman alone with a doll five minutes, and she will be holding it to her heart without knowing it.

DOUGLAS. (*with a sigh, up C.*) Ah! Mother, I'm afraid some women outgrow it. Where is Constance?

MRS. RUTH. (*rising*) In her room.

DOUGLAS. Is she, too, at work for Rosie's birthday?

MRS. RUTH. Well--no--not just now. She is dressing for the reception at Mrs. Warrington's.

DOUGLAS. Ah! I did not know she was going.

MRS. RUTH. You have forgotten it? You have barely time to get ready.

DOUGLAS. Herbert will look after Constance. I have another engagement; I'm going to supper at the club. I must dress at once. Good night, Mother--if I do not see you again.

MRS. RUTH. Good night, my son.

(*He kisses her and moves to the door, up R.*)

DOUGLAS. (*stopping, aside*) I asked Constance not to go to-night.

(*Exit Douglas, up R.*)

MRS. RUTH. (*alone, looking after Douglas and shaking her head*) Douglas and Constance see less and less of each other every day. I am very anxious for them. "Business" and "the club," and the "duties of society," are changing them into mere acquaintances. Every time I have visited them, for the last two years, I have found them more indifferent, colder to each other. Love, even like theirs, cannot live. It is terrible--terrible! But I--I can only look on and be silent.

(*She sits, L.C. Enter Herbert, up R.*)

HERBERT. (*at C.*) Aunt Ruth!

MRS. RUTH. Herbert! What's the matter?

HERBERT. I've got to go to the ball to-night with Constance. Uncle Douglas isn't going. He says he has an engagement at the club. He always has an engagement at the club--or somewhere--and he always leaves me to go out with Constance. This is the fourth time in one week. I hate balls. (*Crossing, R.C.*)

MRS. RUTH. You hate balls! You were very fond of them last winter. You went nearly every evening.

HERBERT. It was different then. Where is Edith?

MRS. RUTH. Edith? (*Looking up significantly--then after a pause.*) She's with Rosie.

HERBERT. (*after a pause*) Aunt Ruth, how much income ought a man to have before he can get married; not enough to make a show on, but for him and his wife to live happily together?

MRS. RUTH. That depends, my dear boy, on how much they love each other. Two people who love each other very much can be exceedingly happy on a very moderate income.

HERBERT. Well--I'm sure I love her enough to be happy on nothing at all.

MRS. RUTH. Her?

HERBERT. Oh! Aunt Ruth--(*crossing to her*)--I can't talk to anyone else about it; but--(*taking her hand; she looking up in his face, smiling*)-- everybody can talk to you. I--I do love Edith.

MRS. RUTH. My dear boy, I know it.

HERBERT. My salary is only twelve hundred dollars a year; but Uncle Douglas told me to-day he will raise it to fifteen hundred after the first of March. That's because I have been working so hard--ever since I first began to--to feel that Edith might share it with me. I've saved five hundred dollars since then. I never saved a cent before. I have been wearing my old clothes, and I have my gloves cleaned--I don't care whether they smell of turpentine or not, when I go to balls, now, with Constance--and I've given up cigars. I do love Edith.

MRS. RUTH. You have chosen the very best way to make love to her: working hard and saving your money for her sake. But I will speak to you as if I were her mother, Herbert; for her own mother and her father lie side by side in the churchyard at Concord. Have you really thought what it means to marry a blind girl, like Edith?

HERBERT. (*with enthusiasm increasing as he proceeds*) It means, Aunt Ruth, that I shall always have to take care of her, as if she were a little child; it means that I shall be her whole world; I shall be her protector; she will depend upon me for everything; I shall have to work for her, and oh! how hard I shall work, when she is at our home thinking of me. I love her all the more for being blind.

MRS. RUTH. You *have* thought about it, my boy. If Edith loves you, even her blindness need not keep you apart.

HERBERT. If--she loves me. (*Sighs.*) I--I can never tell whether she does or not. She doesn't seem to know the difference between loving me and loving any of you. I might as well try to make love to little Rosie as to Edith.

MRS. RUTH. She knows as little about it as Rosie.

HERBERT. Yes. (*With a smile.*) That's because she's blind. I love her blindness.

MRS. RUTH. No one has ever spoken to her of love or marriage. She lives in a little world of her own. You must wait for her woman's nature to assert itself in her heart.

HERBERT. I thought, perhaps, you might help me a little.

MRS. RUTH. Help you?

HERBERT. If you would talk to her about it, just to let her know that when *I* tell her--I love her--it isn't quite the same thing--as--as any of you loving her, you know.

MRS. RUTH. It is awkward for a young lover, isn't it, Herbert? Perhaps I can do something for you. But you are only twenty-two and Edith is only seventeen. You can both wait.

(*Enter Constance, up R. She is in full evening dress, cloak over her arm, fan, etc. Crosses, C.*)

CONSTANCE. Are you ready, Herbert? Not dressed yet?

HERBERT. Eh? Oh! (*Suddenly bolting across stage.*) It won't take me ten minutes. (*Aside.*) I hate these balls. (*Exit, up R.*)

CONSTANCE. The boy is always late now. (*Taking up doll.*) You have finished Rosie's doll. What a sweet little lady she is. (*Laughs lightly-- then with a sigh.*) I could not finish the doll I was dressing for Rosie. I have had no time to do anything for my child's birthday. I was obliged to send down town at the last moment, this afternoon--and--and--buy a present for her. (*Sits, R.C.*)

MRS. RUTH. (*crossing, R.C.*) And here it is. Rosie will be delighted with it.

CONSTANCE. (*shaking her head sadly*) Rosie will love this doll better than that. Children seem to feel the difference between what is made for them with loving hands, and what is only bought with money. Rosie can look so far into one's heart with those great blue eyes of hers. I sometimes tremble when my child and I are together.

MRS. RUTH. (*tenderly*) When Rosie looks into your heart, Constance, I am sure she finds a great and true love there for her.

CONSTANCE. (*rises*) It is there--yes--it is there; but so many other things are there, too--I--I sometimes fear the child cannot always find it.

MRS. RUTH. We shall have a merry day to-morrow, Constance. Rosie will be awake long before breakfast. Edith and I have promised to be up as soon as she is, and bring her down to see the presents--and when you and Douglas come down--

(*Constance suddenly strikes bell on table, R.C.*)

CONSTANCE. I shall be up as early as you, Mother.

MRS. RUTH. Rosie will wake before six.

(*Enter Maid, up L.H.*)

CONSTANCE. (*to Maid*) Have me called at five o'clock to-morrow, Jeanette.

MAID. Yes, madam. (*Exit, up R.*)

MRS. RUTH. You will not be in bed before three.

CONSTANCE. If I can spare time for a fashionable ball to-night, I need not rob my child of it on her birthday. I, too, shall be with Rosie all day to-morrow.

MRS. RUTH. Oh! we shall have a happy day, all of us. But I fear Edith may have some difficulty in getting Rosie to sleep. The child has so many plans in her head for to-morrow. I will go to them. I hope you will have a pleasant time this evening, Constance. Good night. (*Crossing, R.*)

CONSTANCE. (*kissing her*) Good night, Mother dear. (*Exit Mrs. Ruth, R.1E.*) Shall I go to Mrs. Warrington's to-night? Douglas was very much in earnest when he asked me not to go. But he is going to his club. He is never at home. I *must* go. If I stay at home, I cannot help thinking. Oh! if I had died before his neglect began! I--(*slowly, as if a more painful thought had come into her mind*)--I sometimes feel that Douglas and I-- (*Sees the child's picture.*) No! Rosie! She belongs to us both! She will hold us together. (*Stands a moment in thought, then, smiling.*) How prettily she threw her arms about my neck and kissed me good-night just now. Shall I go to Mrs. Warrington's?

(*Enter Maid, up L., with a letter.*)

MAID. A letter for Mr. Winthrop--by messenger. No answer, madam.

CONSTANCE. I will give it to him. (*Taking letter. Exit Maid.*) Shall I go to-night? (*Looking at letter in her hand. Raises it to her face as if attracted by the odor.*) Violet! It is not a business letter. A lady's hand-writing! (*She turns the letter.*) A dove and a serpent as a crest-- H. D.--from Mrs. Hepworth Dunbar.

(*Constance leaves note on table, R.C., and crosses to L.   Enter Douglas, now in dress suit, up R.*)

DOUGLAS. Constance! (*Stopping, C.*)

CONSTANCE. (*at L.C.*) Douglas!

DOUGLAS. You are in full dress, I see.

CONSTANCE. Madam de Battiste's latest inspiration. Do you like it?

DOUGLAS. It is a very becoming costume, my dear.

CONSTANCE. You are in evening dress. You are going to accompany me?

DOUGLAS. I am engaged for a supper at the club with Dick Chetwyn.

CONSTANCE. Jeanette just brought in a note for you--it is on the table.

DOUGLAS. (*turning to table*) Ah!

(*Constance watches him as he opens and reads letter.*)

CONSTANCE. (*turning away with her back toward him*)   Anything important, Douglas?

DOUGLAS. (*after looking across at her quietly, then placing the letter in his pocket*) Merely a business matter. (*Turning to presents, C. and L.C.*) Rosie will be quite overwhelmed with her birthday presents to-morrow.

CONSTANCE. (*aside*) Business!

DOUGLAS. I ordered a little walnut bedstead--ah! here it is.   A dressing-table and mirror, with cut-glass perfumery bottles, and a box of cosmetics, and a tiny jewelry casket. (*Reads card.*) "Mrs. Richard Chetwyn." A very characteristic present. Here is a magnificent doll, in full ball costume, with real lace and a long train, and a coiffure. Another of our ultra-fashionable friends sent that, I suppose. It does seem a pity to put such ideas into the head of an innocent child. (*Leans over and reads card.*) "From Rosie's mamma." (*He glances at Constance.*) Forgive me, Constance, I was speaking thoughtlessly. Any expression of a mother's love is sacred to me. Constance--I--I am very sorry to see you in that costume to-night.

CONSTANCE. You did not wish me to go to Mrs. Warrington's.

DOUGLAS. Mrs. Warrington's house is a centre of a certain kind of fashionable society in New York. The men are rich and fast, and the wives vie with the men in the display of their riches. Constance, you have never cared for this extremely "fashionable" circle until within a year or two.

CONSTANCE. I had no reason to seek it.

DOUGLAS. Reason?

CONSTANCE. Some women find, in the gayeties of this society, something to compensate them for what they do not find at home.

DOUGLAS. (*quickly*) What do you mean, Constance?

(*Enter Maid with a card in an envelope.*)

MAID. Madam. (*Constance takes card. Exit Maid.*)

CONSTANCE (*reading card*) "Mrs. Richard Chetwyn"-- (*Turning card over.*) "Dick is going some where to-night, so I'll come around and go to Mrs. Warrington's with you."

DOUGLAS. Constance! (*Rising.*) It is my earnest wish that you should not go to the ball to-night. (*Pause.*) I--I am sorry that I am compelled to speak so strongly, but I--I insist.

CONSTANCE. Am I to understand that you command me not to go?

DOUGLAS. I did not use that word, Constance. I will never use it. I have too much respect for you to do that.

CONSTANCE. (*aside*) Respect!

(*She drops into a chair, her face in her hands, on the back of the chair. He crosses to her, looking down at her tenderly.*)

DOUGLAS. Constance--my wife! When we were married, six years ago, in the old church at Concord, as we knelt to receive the blessing of the pastor--your own dear father--a ray of bright sunshine coming through the window fell upon our heads. For many a month after, that sunlight seemed to rest upon us, and when Rosie came, the pastor's blessing seemed to be fulfilled. Constance, I--I have tried to be a kind husband to you.

CONSTANCE. A--kind--husband--yes.

DOUGLAS. And you have been a true, sincere, and devoted wife to me; yet, for the last two years or more, we have been drifting apart further and further. You speak of compensation in that fashionable world for something that you do not find at home. Are you likely to find anything there to compensate you for the happiness which you once found here? Does Mrs. Warrington, or Mrs. Maxwell, or Mrs. Dunbar fulfill your idea of a truly happy woman? No, Constance.

CONSTANCE. Mrs. Dunbar is a leader of the circle.

DOUGLAS. Yes. I believe she *is* the worst of the set. I am glad to know that you have no personal acquaintance with her. A woman who respects herself ought to avoid such a person. (*Crosses, R.*)

CONSTANCE. (*rising*) That is your opinion of Mrs. Hepworth Dunbar?

DOUGLAS. It is. And I trust that my wife will never be seen in her company. (*Looks at his watch.*) But I am late. Constance--I--I was wrong to use the word "insist," a moment ago. I feel sure that you will stay at home to-night, not because I "insist," but because it is my earnest--wish. Good night.

CONSTANCE. Good night.

(*Douglas is moving up, R. Constance stands, L. Enter Buxton Scott, up L., holding a huge package before him.*)

SCOTT. Ah! How is the happy mother--and the father--to-night?

CONSTANCE and DOUGLAS. Mr. Scott. (*Going to him.*)

SCOTT. Constance! (*Kissing her at one side of package.*) Douglas! (*Looking out at other side of package.*) I haven't a kiss for you.

CONSTANCE. Another present for Rosie!

DOUGLAS. From her godfather.

CONSTANCE. Let me help you.

SCOTT. Thank you. (*Putting it on chair, L.C. Constance begins to unwrap it.*) I brought that in my arms all the way. I was the proudest old bachelor in New York. I felt like a grandfather.

DOUGLAS. Constance and I almost feel that you *are* Rosie's grandfather.

CONSTANCE. Indeed we do.

SCOTT. So do I. In fact, I did have almost as much to do as either of her grandfathers with bringing her into the world. I helped along your courtship as much as a blundering old bachelor could. I patched up your lovers' quarrels and made peace between you--I think I may claim to be Rosie's grandfather.

CONSTANCE. A beautiful new baby-house, with furniture and carpets and mirrors, complete. I must kiss you again--for Rosie. (*Kissing him.*)

SCOTT. I shall drop in to-morrow if I can. You must let me have Douglas now for business. I'm his lawyer, you know, and we lawyers have to work night and day. (*Turns to Douglas, R.C., apart.*) I must speak with you at once.

DOUGLAS. (*apart*) Come into the library. (*Exeunt, up R.*)

CONSTANCE. (*pleasantly*) I'll not go to Mrs. Warrington's. I'll go to bed early and be up fresh and bright with Mother and Edith. Rosie and I will--

(*Stops suddenly, with expression changing suddenly from a smile to a look of pain.*)

What was that letter from Mrs. Dunbar to my husband? Not a word to me when he read it! (*Pause, C.*) No, no, no! I will not think of that. Douglas has become cold--but--I have never dreamed of anything like that. No! I--oh! if that, too, should come! If that, too, should come--I could not bear it.

(*Dropping into a chair, R.C., her head falling on her arms. Enter Mrs. Dick Chetwyn, in full evening dress, up L.*)

MRS. DICK. Constance, my dear!

CONSTANCE. (*suddenly arousing herself*) Ah! Barbara!

MRS. DICK. (*in a tone of great anxiety*) Something wrong with your new costume, my darling? Doesn't it fit?

CONSTANCE. (*brushing tears from her eyes*) It is not that.

MRS. DICK. Oh! I thought it was something serious. Your new dress is lovely, and your hair is perfection. Will your husband be ready soon? The men are always late. (*Crosses, C.*)

CONSTANCE. He is not going this evening.

MRS. DICK. O--h! That's what you're crying about. It's a long time since I cried because my husband wouldn't go with me anywhere. Dick says I've changed. He says I'm more likely to cry when he does go with me now. Dick goes one way, and I go the other, so we're both of us perfectly happy. Buxton Scott called to see Dick one day. I happened to meet him in the hall. "Ah!" said he, "you're at home; of course, your husband isn't. Good afternoon." Ha-ha-ha! We two widows must go to the ball by ourselves, I suppose.

CONSTANCE. Herbert is going. But didn't you know? Mr. Winthrop is engaged for a supper at the club with your husband.

(*She crosses, L., looking at toys, arranging them, etc.*)

MRS. DICK. Oh! is he? (*Crosses, R.*) Ha-ha-ha, I thought Dick was lying about it. He told me he was going to take supper with Mr. Winthrop at the club. After his telling me that, it was the last thing I dreamed of his doing. Poor Dick! It's a shame not to believe him when he does tell the truth; but I dare say they are both lying.

CONSTANCE. Oh! Barbara! How can you trifle about such serious things?

MRS. DICK. Well, you see, my dear, I know all about these men, and so'll you by the time you have had two husbands, as I have. My first husband was a physician; my second is a member of the bar. A doctor and a lawyer can teach you about all one woman needs to know on the subject of husbands. Dick makes up whatever Bob omitted in my education, and when I forget anything Bob taught me, Dick reminds me of it. Between Bob and Dick together, I'm a graduate--M.A.--Mistress of Arts.

CONSTANCE. Ah--I remember--your first husband's name was Robert.

MRS. DICK. M-m. Everybody called me Mrs. Bob then, just as they call me Mrs. Dick now. I never could rise to the dignity of my husband's full name. I dare say next time I shall be Mrs. Jack or Mrs. Tom. Yes, my dear, after you've married the second time, you'll know a great deal too much about these men to worry yourself about 'em. If your dress fits, and you haven't got a headache, no little matrimonial obscurities will ever affect your spirits. Keep your eyes open, my dear, and smile. I mean, keep one eye open and the other shut. When your husband gets round on the blind side of you, open that eye quietly, when he isn't looking. It's great fun! Ha-ha-ha. Bob told me one evening--it was the night of an Arion ball--no, that wasn't Bob--it was Dick. Dick said to me that evening--yes, it was Bob, too. It was four years ago--no--I was a widow then--one, two--(*counting on her fingers*)--three, four--that was six years ago. "Barbara, my dear," said Dick--I mean, said Bob--"I have an important engagement with a client--no--with a patient--to-night." "What sort of a lawsuit is it?" said I--I would say--"What disease is she suffering from?" said I. Then he quoted from some musty old law books--no, he ran over a lot of scientific medical terms. "Bob," said I, shaking my finger, "it won't do, you can't deceive me, Dick"--Bob--well, it was one of 'em. A woman that's been the wife of a doctor and a lawyer both gets awfully mixed up about professional engagements outside of business hours.

(*Constance is on her knees before doll-house, arranging furniture, etc.*)

CONSTANCE. (*rises*) Barbara--I--I don't think I'll go to the ball to-night.

MRS. DICK. Not go?

CONSTANCE. You know, to-morrow is Rosie's birthday. I wish to be as fresh and as bright as possible to enjoy the whole day with her. Herbert can go to Mrs. Warrington's with you.

MRS. DICK. Well, I've never had any children, but--

CONSTANCE. If you had, you would feel as I do. Ah, Barbara, Providence has denied to you the greatest blessing it ever brings to a woman. Heaven has been very kind to me. (*Turning to house and arranging it.*) I shall not go.

MRS. DICK. You'll break Madam de Battiste's heart if you don't appear in that costume to-night. Mrs. Dunbar--

CONSTANCE. (*looking up suddenly*) Mrs. Dunbar!

(*Mrs. Dick stops and looks at her inquiringly. Constance proceeds quietly.*)

What of her?

MRS. DICK. She has a new costume just arrived, direct from Paris. She is supposed to be the finest dressed woman in America. But Madam de Battiste told me that when you appeared in the same drawing-room with her to-night, Mrs. Dunbar and the Parisian dressmakers would lose their reputation. I told Madam de Battiste she might rob the Parisian dressmakers of their reputaitons, but Mrs. Hepworth Dunbar will never lose hers--again. By the by, my dear--ha-ha-ha-ha--speaking of Mrs. Dunbar--I'm jealous of you.

CONSTANCE. Jealous? Of me?

MRS. DICK. M--m. Mrs. Dunbar thinks a great deal more of your husband than she does of mine. (*Constance starts to her feet and moves down L.C. front.*) Everybody is talking about it. Dick was her favorite till a few weeks ago, you know; but his nose was put out of joint the moment Douglas appeared as a rival. Ha! ha! ha! We're all laughing at Dick. Ha! ha! ha! I had such a joke on him last evening. He told me he was going to drop in and see Mrs. Dunbar. I remarked that I was expecting a gentleman to call on me, and he departed with my blessing. Ha-ha-ha-ha. He was back in twenty minutes. "Wasn't she in?" said I. "Yes," said he, "she was, but just as I reached the front of the steps, Douglas Winthrop was entering the door. I thought I might be intruding. That's the second time this week. When I called on Tuesday, I found Winthrop in the parlor." Ha-ha-ha-ha. Your husband has cut mine out. You ought to be proud of him, my dear. The gentleman that was to call upon me--didn't. Dick and I spent the whole evening together. It wasn't so very bad either. It seemed novel to us, you know--we found each other quite interesting.

CONSTANCE. (*with suppressed feeling, L.*) You are quite sure that Mrs. Dunbar will be at Mrs. Warrington's this evening.

MRS. DICK. Sure of it. She ordered her costume by cable especially for this occasion.

CONSTANCE. (*aside*) If she and I should come face to face to-night, we would understand each other, without a word. (*Aloud suddenly.*) I will go to Mrs. Warrington's. (*Enter Herbert, up R.*) Oh! Herbert, you are ready. Mrs. Chetwyn is going with us. (*Gathering cloak, fan, etc., with nervous movement and speaking rapidly.*) We will send back your carriage, Barbara. Mine has been waiting this half hour. Come.

> (*Exit quickly and nervously, up L. Mrs. Dick is following her, also Herbert, who is pulling at his back collar-button, working at his wrist-bands, etc., and looking generally uncomfortable.*)

MRS. DICK. (*stopping and looking back at Herbert*) Herbert!

HERBERT. Mrs. Dick.

MRS. DICK. I know your secret. You're in love. Come here.

> (*Beckoning to him. He approaches her. She sniffs the air.*)

Benzine. Give me your hand.

> (*He looks at her in some surprise; then holds out his hand. She puts it daintily to her nose.*)

Economy--you're very much in love--mended all over--one place with black thread.

HERBERT. I did that myself just now--Aunt Ruth and Edith were both busy.

MRS. DICK. Is Edith busy now?

HERBERT. No.

MRS. DICK. You needn't go with us.

HERBERT. (*eagerly*) I needn't?

MRS. DICK. You follow us. I'll leave my carriage at the door for you. We'll give you ten minutes to make love. We'll wait for you in the cloak-room. By-bye-- (*Going--stops.*) Ha-ha-ha-- I saw it coming on you three months ago. I'm familiar with the symptoms. I've seen lots of men in love. I married two of 'em. (*Exit, up L.*)

HERBERT. Mrs. Dick is a nice woman. (*Looks out, R.*) Edith is coming. She has just left little Rosie. I wish she was half as fond of me as she is of Rosie.

(*Enter Edith, R.1E. Herbert stands, down L., beyond table, looking up at her. She touches the doorway lightly, feeling her way; then moving up, R.C., until her hand rests upon the back of a chair.*)

EDITH. (*to herself*) I thought the little thing never would go to sleep tonight. (*Laughing lightly.*) Ha-ha-ha-- She is so excited about her birthday. Now I can finish her present.

(*She crosses, touching another chair lightly on the way, and moves to table, L.C., taking up a little lace bed-spread.*)

HERBERT. (*aside, crossing*) She is smiling. Edith is always happy.

EDITH. (*facing Herbert, sewing*) I wonder what Herbert is doing now?

HERBERT. (*aside*) What pretty eyes she has!

EDITH. I always feel a little lonely when Herbert is away.

HERBERT. (*aside*) I wonder what she is thinking about.

EDITH. (*listening suddenly and smiling*) There's some one here.

(*Laughing lightly and holding out her hand.*)

Let me guess.

(*Herbert reaches forward his hand and touches the back of her hand gently with one finger.*)

Herbert! (*Pleased.*) I thought you had gone to the ball.

HERBERT. How do you always know when *I* touch your hand, Edith?

EDITH. Something tells me, Herbert.

HERBERT. Something tells you?

EDITH. I seem to feel that it is you. Your touch is always so different from the others. It seems so--so--gentle--and so--

HERBERT. So--tender--and--and--loving?

EDITH. Yes, Herbert.

HERBERT. I do love you, Edith.

EDITH. I'm glad of that, Herbert. I like to have you all love me.

HERBERT. Yes--of course, but--the others, you know--we all love you--certainly--but the rest of them--it's different with me. (*A slight pause as if waiting for her to speak.*) The rest of them--except Douglas, they're women, you know--and little Rosie.

EDITH. Well, can't they love me just as well as you?

HERBERT. Yes--they--of course they can love you as well as I--but--my love is a different kind of love from theirs.

EDITH. What do you mean--different--Herbert? (*She sits, L.C.*)

HERBERT. (*aside*) It's no use. I can't make love to her. (*Aloud.*) Ask Aunt Ruth what the difference is, Edith. Is that a present for Rosie?

EDITH. Yes. (*Breaking thread, etc.*) It is just finished. A little lace spread for the doll's bedstead her papa bought.

HERBERT. It is very pretty. I am going to take a holiday to-morrow, and spend the whole day with you and Rosie.

EDITH. Oh! I'm so glad. You are very fond of Rosie.

HERBERT. Yes, I'm very fond, indeed, of--Rosie.

EDITH. You spend all the time you can with her and me.

HERBERT. Yes--with her--and--and--you.

EDITH. What long soft hair Rosie has--and her face is as smooth as a peach, and it's as sweet, too. She is beautiful.

HERBERT. You see so many beautiful things, Edith! You never wish that you could see with your eyes, do you?

EDITH. Why should I? No, indeed! I am always happy--like everybody else in the world. I sometimes dream, Herbert, that there are people who are not happy. I dream that people are sometimes unkind to each other. Of course, I know it is only a dream; for when I wake up, everybody is so gentle and good, and so happy; but something whispers to me it is better to be as I am. I do not wish to see.

HERBERT. We all have eyes for you, Edith; even little Rosie--

EDITH. Oh! Rosie's eyes are mine. She leads me about everywhere and tells me of everything, all day long.

HERBERT. I wish I could lead you around everywhere, as Rosie does.

EDITH. You are not always with me.

HERBERT. I would like to be with you always.

EDITH. Would you, Herbert?

HERBERT. Edith--I--I hope to have a little home of my own some day.

EDITH. A home of your own? Do you mean--you--you will go away
from here?

HERBERT. Why--yes--I--I--I hope to have--a--wife.

EDITH. Wife! Oh! Herbert! (*With warm feeling, putting her arms about
his neck.*) You must never leave us.

HERBERT. Leave you? No--I--I don't want to leave you.

EDITH. Oh--can Rosie and I go with you to your little home? (*Sitting.*)

HERBERT. Well--you--of course, if--if Rosie--but--you--see--when a
young man gets married--I--I love Rosie very much--but--you--she--we--
you'd better ask Aunt Ruth about that, too, Edith. I must go now. Good
night.

EDITH. Good night, Herbert.

  (*Peaching up her face for him to kiss her. He leans down, about to kiss
  her lips; he hesitates, then raises her hand and kisses it gently.*)

HERBERT. Good night. (*Exit, up L.*)

EDITH. (*aside*) Herbert will never be lonely in his little home with so
many of us; but I--I--I wish that other one wouldn't be there.

  (*Enter Mrs. Ruth, R.1E., and crosses to Edith.*)

MRS. RUTH. It is long after bed-time, my darling. If Rosie should wake
up, she would miss you. You have finished the spread, I see.

  (*Taking spread from Edith, who sits in deep thought.*)

It is very nicely done, my dear.

EDITH. Mother?

MRS. RUTH. Edith.

EDITH. What--different kinds--(*rising*)--of love--are there?

MRS. RUTH. Different kinds of love? There are many kinds, my pet: a
mother's love; a father's, or a sister's, or a brother's, or a friend's. Then
there's another love, Edith--the love that two good people have for each
other when they are married.

EDITH. Do two people always get married when they love each other.

MRS. RUTH. Not always. They generally do.

EDITH. Why?

MRS. RUTH. They feel lonely. They want to be together--to comfort and
to take care of each other. But you mustn't sit up any longer. (*Walking
with her, R.*) I'll come to you as soon as I arrange the little bedstead.
(*Edith goes out, R.1E.*) I have given the little pet her first lesson in love.
(*Looking after her.*) That's quite enough for the present, I think.
(*Turning and crossing, up L.*) Herbert does need a little help.

  (*Kneeling at a toy bedstead, arranging spread, etc. Edith is heard
  calling "Mother!" without. Mrs. Ruth starts up. Re-enter Edith.*)

EDITH. Mother! Oh! Mother! (*Rushing across stage excitedly.*)

MRS. RUTH. (*intercepting her, L.C.*) My child.

EDITH. Rosie! Rosie! She is not asleep--nor awake--she is struggling--and--

MRS. RUTH. Calm yourself, my child. Rosie is dreaming, perhaps. She has been so excited all day.

EDITH. She is so cold and she breathes so hard.

MRS. RUTH. Come, Edith.

(*She goes out with Edith, R.1E. Enter Buxton Scott and Douglas, up R.*)

SCOTT. (*as he enters and passes, L.*) That's the only obstacle in our way now, Douglas. The directors of the bank are willing to settle it.

DOUGLAS. (*crossing down to table, L.C.*) I'll do all I can in the matter.

SCOTT. See you in the morning. (*Waving his hand.*)

DOUGLAS. (*waving his hand*) At nine.

(*Exit Scott, up L. Douglas takes note from his pocket.*)

What hour did she say? (*Reads.*) "Any time before eleven." I must send a line to Chetwyn--(*writes*)--and tell him it is impossible for me to join him at supper this evening.

(*Strikes bell. Enter Maid, up L. Douglas encloses note in envelope, directs it, and rises. Goes up and hands note to Maid.*)

Tell Morgan to take this to the Union Club--immediately.

(*Exit Maid. He looks at his watch.*)

Now for Mrs. Dunbar's.

(*Exit, up L.*)

ACT II.

Scene. The same. Night. A single lamp or drop-light upon table. (*At rise of curtain enter Douglas, up L., in some haste, and with expression of anxiety. He is still in evening dress and has his overcoat on his arm and hat in hand, as if having entered too hastily to throw them aside. He tosses them on chair as he proceeds. He is followed by Maid.*)

DOUGLAS. (*as he crosses, C.*) Eleven o'clock, you say?

MAID. Yes, sir. Miss Rosie was taken ill about the time you left the house, sir.

DOUGLAS. Did Dr. Mellbanke come promptly?

MAID. Yes, sir. And he is still here.

DOUGLAS. Still here! (*Looks at watch.*) Two o'clock. Dr. Mellbanke still here. (*Going quickly down R.*) It must be serious.

(*Dr. Mellbanke steps in, R.1E., raising his hand to check him.*)
The child, Doctor! Rosie!

DOCTOR. She is sleeping.

DOUGLAS. Is there danger?

DOCTOR. I hope for the best.

DOUGLAS. Ah! (*With a sigh of relief, walking L.*) What is it, Doctor?
(*The Maid goes out, with hat and coat.*)

DOCTOR. Just such an attack as she had two years ago.

DOUGLAS. She recovered from that in a few days.

DOCTOR. I trust she will do the same in this case.

DOUGLAS. Has she suffered much?

DOCTOR. She is now entirely free from pain.

DOUGLAS. Can I go to the room, Doctor?

DOCTOR. She is in a quiet sleep. We must take every advantage of it.

DOUGLAS. I might relieve her mother.

DOCTOR. The child's grandmother is with her.

DOUGLAS. Ah--Constance is resting.

DOCTOR. Mrs. Winthrop, herself, has not returned yet.

DOUGLAS. Not--returned?

DOCTOR. She is at Mrs.--Warrington's--I believe.

DOUGLAS. (*with a slight start*) At Mrs. Warrington's?

DOCTOR. Up to half an hour ago, I thought the case a very harmless one,
and I advised them not to send for Mrs. Winthrop. But it took a more
serious turn, and we sent for her. She has not arrived yet.

DOUGLAS. (*aside*) Constance *did* go!

DOCTOR. I thought it was she that entered, when I heard you at the
door. I came down stairs to ask her not to go to the child at present.
Mrs. Winthrop will be somewhat excited, of course--returning from a--a
social festivity--under such--such unusual circumstances.

DOUGLAS. Yes. (*With some bitterness.*) From a fashionable ball-room
to the bedside of a sick child is an abrupt change--for a mother.

DOCTOR. Will you kindly say to Mrs. Winthrop, for me, when she
arrives, that the little one is sleeping and the utmost quiet is necessary.
Her grandmother is taking every care of her. If Mrs. Winthrop will, for
the present, kindly refrain from coming to the room--

DOUGLAS. I will tell her.

DOCTOR. It will be better for the child. (*Exit, R.1E.*)

DOUGLAS. Better for the child!--that its mother should not enter its
sick-room in a rustling silk and a dragging train--fresh from the glare of
a ball-room. (*Enter Mrs. Ruth, R.1E.*)

MRS. RUTH. Douglas.

DOUGLAS. Mother. Rosie is still sleeping?

MRS. RUTH. Yes, gently, and without pain. The Doctor is with her now. I am glad the servant found you, Douglas. We sent to the club for you, at first.

DOUGLAS. I was not there. How--how did you know where I was, Mother?

MRS. RUTH. I happened to overhear you say to Mr. Scott that you would go to--to a Mrs.--a Mrs. Dunbar's.

DOUGLAS. Ah! yes, I see.

MRS. RUTH. When the servant returned and said you were not at the club, I thought you might be at that lady's house, so Dr. Mellbanke sent there for you.

DOUGLAS. Mother--I--I have a--a favor to ask of you. Say nothing to Constance about my having been at Mrs. Dunbar's to-night.

MRS. RUTH. Say--nothing--to--Constance! My son!

DOUGLAS. Do not misunderstand me, Mother.

MRS. RUTH. No, Douglas! Of course not. I heard Mr. Scott tell you that it was positively necessary for you to go to Mrs. Dunbar's--some business matter.

DOUGLAS. Yes, Mother, it was, and the cause of my going would bring deep pain to Constance, something, indeed, harder to bear than mere pain.

MRS. RUTH. Nothing can be so important, Douglas, as perfect confidence between husband and wife.

DOUGLAS. Mother, *please* do not say anything to her on this subject.

MRS. RUTH. Well, I--I promise you. I would not have mentioned it any way. Constance should have returned by this time.

DOUGLAS. It is too early, yet, to leave the most brilliant reception of the season.

MRS. RUTH. Early? With such a message? What do you mean, Douglas?
(*Enter Maid, up L.*)

MAID. Thomas is returning, madam.

MRS. RUTH. And Mrs. Winthrop?

MAID. Mrs. Winthrop had left the house before Thomas got there, madam.

MRS. RUTH. Ah. She has taken Mrs. Chetwyn home.
(*Exit Maid.*)

DOUGLAS. (*sitting, L.C.*) They are discussing the merits of the last new costumes.

MRS. RUTH. Douglas, I--I never heard you speak of your wife in a bitter tone.

DOUGLAS. My--wife--went to a "fashionable" woman's house, to-night, against the earnestly expressed desire of her husband. She is now away from her sick child. The physician has just requested me to ask her not to go to its bedside when she returns. I am a husband and a father! Do you wonder at my bitter tone?

MRS. RUTH. (*after a moment's pause*) Douglas--my son.

DOUGLAS. Mother.

(*She crosses to him and stands at his chair, looking down at him.*)

MRS. RUTH. May I speak frankly to you?

DOUGLAS. Need *you* ask me that?

MRS. RUTH. Even a mother fears to touch upon some subjects. I am long wished to say what is in my heart, but I--I have hesitated.

DOUGLAS. It *must* be good for me to know all there is in such a heart as yours. (*Taking her hand.*) Through childhood and manhood I have never found anything but love there.

MRS. RUTH. My darling boy!

DOUGLAS. I am a boy again, Mother. Speak to me--just as you used to.

(*He has placed her in the chair and is sitting on a stool beside her.*)

MRS. RUTH. I--I feel to-night, Douglas, that a crisis may be at hand, in the life of the two beings most dear to me in all the world. You are my only child--no!--my only *son*--for *she*, too, is my child--my daughter. I have known Constance since she was a little girl. I know how pure--how full of tenderness and love--her nature is. You were very happy--at first.

DOUGLAS. Very--at first.

MRS. RUTH. There was contentment and love in your home. A change has been gradually stealing over you both.

DOUGLAS. --Yes, Mother!--a change.

MRS. RUTH. Constance has become more and more what is called a "fashionable" woman.

DOUGLAS. Yes.

MRS. RUTH. Her child and her husband do not, now, receive all her attention, as they once did.

DOUGLAS. No.

MRS. RUTH. Her home has become less and less the center of her thoughts.

DOUGLAS. My dear mother! *Speak* to Constance. A single word from you--

MRS. RUTH. No--my son--it is to you that I will speak!

DOUGLAS. To--me?

MRS. RUTH. It is your fault, Douglas, not hers. If such a woman as Constance is not the wife and mother she should be, it is her husband's fault.

DOUGLAS. (*rising and crossing, C.*) My--fault!

MRS. RUTH. (*after a slight pause, assuming a lighter tone*) You did not dine at home this evening, Douglas. You dropped in at Delmonico's with a friend, you told me.

DOUGLAS. (*after looking up at her as if a little puzzled at the change of subject*) Yes! We had a matter of business to talk over.

MRS. RUTH. You were absent from home all *yesterday* evening.

DOUGLAS. A private meeting of our Board of Directors.

MRS. RUTH. You had a gentleman's dinner-party here on *Tuesday* evening.

DOUGLAS. Some capitalists to meet the president of a western railroad.

MRS. RUTH. You--you never return to your home in the daytime.

DOUGLAS. Business men never do that. (*Crosses, R.C.*) We lunch down-town, of course.

MRS. RUTH. Of course. On Monday evening--

DOUGLAS. I ran over to Philadelphia, Monday afternoon--a large contract for coal and iron. (*Sitting, R.C.*)

MRS. RUTH. (*rises and crosses to him*) I have now been here two months, Douglas. Your wife never sees you in the daytime, except on Sunday; and only three times since I came have you spent an evening quietly at home with her.

DOUGLAS. The constant pressure upon the time of a business man--

MRS. RUTH. Your *father* was a business man, Douglas! A successful one, too. He left you a large fortune, but he made *me* a very happy wife. *He* never forgot that his wife and child were more to him than all the triumphs of his business life. Remember your own childhood. Remember the many happy hours your father spent with you and me in our home. The trials of his daily work never made those hours less bright. Even your father's *successes* in business did not conflict with our domestic happiness.

DOUGLAS. Those times were different, Mother.

MRS. RUTH. No, my son! Domestic love in those days withered and died in the same hot fever as now. *You* have *caught* the disease and your father *escaped* it--that is all. Believe me, there are as many men to-day as then, rich and successful men, who do not neglect their families for the sake of making "money"--who do not sacrifice their wives and their children and all their own holiest affections--

DOUGLAS. Sacrifice!

MRS. RUTH. Yes, Douglas, sacrifice!

DOUGLAS. Surely you do not think that I--

MRS. RUTH. That is what *you* are doing, my son. Your wife has become almost a stranger to you. Her heart is slowly starving for want of your love. She is turning in her loneliness to the excitements of fashionable life. What effect *must* this daily separation have upon a woman like Constance? (*Goes up C.*) You have given her a magnificent house to live in, but you've given her no home.

DOUGLAS. Mother!

MRS. RUTH. For months you and she have been growing colder to each other every day.

DOUGLAS. Colder and colder--yes.

MRS. RUTH. Now-- (*She hesitates.*)

DOUGLAS. Now--well?

MRS. RUTH. Your child alone holds you together.

DOUGLAS. Our child! If she were to be taken away--!

MRS. RUTH. Then, Douglas, the holy grief of a father and mother would bring you and Constance together. If that great sorrow were ever to come upon you, it would bring its compensation. Two hearts never know all there is of love until they have *suffered* together.

DOUGLAS. (*after a pause, and holding her hand in both of his*) The same kind hand that led me when I was a boy shall lead me now, Mother. (*Rising.*) I have been cruel to Constance. She shall not be without a home hereafter. I will be her companion--her husband! As soon as she returns, I will confess the wrong I have done her. Our love shall have a new and a stronger life than ever--from this night.

MRS. RUTH. When you speak like that, I seem to hear your father's own voice.

DOUGLAS. (*walking R. with her, his arm about her waist*) I will try to honor his memory by making Constance as happy a wife as he made you. We shall both bless *you* for it, Mother!

MRS. RUTH. My boy!

(*Reaching up her face. He kisses her. Exit Mrs. Ruth, R.1E.*)

DOUGLAS. (*looking after her*) "Her children arise up and call her blessed."

(*Exit after her. A moment's pause. Enter Constance, up L.*)

CONSTANCE. Back again! (*With a weary air, throwing aside her cloak.*)

How quiet the house is! It's no use going to bed; I cannot sleep.

(*Dropping into chair before fire, R.*)

I wish these "social gayeties," as they call them, could go on forever. No matter how much I go out, or how bright the company is, it always ends in this; I am alone again, and I--I can't stop thinking. Oh! I wish I *could*--I *wish* I could. (*Looks into fire.*) Mr. Chetwyn was at the reception this evening. Douglas sent word to him he could not meet him at the club. He sent the message after receiving that note from Mrs. Dunlap--*she* was not there to-night! Oh! Why must I keep thinking--thinking?

(*Starting to her feet and moving C., pauses.*)

Perhaps I am wronging him. Yes. No--no! I will *not* believe it--I *have* not lost his love! There is something I do not understand. I will speak to Douglas about it in the morning. (*Smiling.*) It will all come right. I must get to sleep as soon as I can, to be up bright and early with Rosie. I will peep in at my little darling before I go to sleep.

(*Going toward door, R.1E. Enter Edith, R.1E.; also Herbert, up L.*)

Edith!

EDITH. Oh, Constance! you have come back.

CONSTANCE. Why are *you* up at this hour?

EDITH. I couldn't sleep. They told me to go to my room. But I was so unhappy about Rosie--

CONSTANCE. Rosie!

EDITH. Oh! You do not know?

CONSTANCE. Know what, Edith--I do not know what?

EDITH. The servant was sent to tell you--he--

CONSTANCE. Ah! (*A half-suppressed scream.*) Rosie! Rosie! She is not well!

(*She hurries past Edith and out, R.1.E., under great excitement.*)

HERBERT. (*joining Edith, up R.C.*) The servant must have missed us, Edith. What is it?

EDITH. Rosie is ill. The doctor is here. They sent me away.

(*Re-enter Mrs. Ruth, R.1E., leading Constance in, holding one of her hands, and her arm about her waist. Constance is under great emotion.*)

MRS. RUTH. You *must* calm yourself, my dear child. You must *calm* yourself! Dr. Mellbanke is right.

CONSTANCE. Yes--I know--I know. (*Moving up, L.C.*)

MRS. RUTH. You shall go to her, presently. But she is sleeping very quietly. The slightest noise might--

CONSTANCE. The doctor is right--he is right. I *am* excited! I have just returned from where people are dancing and laughing. I would endanger the life of my child! (*Sinking into chair at table, R.C.*) My own child! Douglas--my husband! Ask *him* to come to me, Mother; ask him to come to me.

MRS. RUTH. I will--I will.

CONSTANCE. Tell Douglas I want him near me--I want his arm about me, Mother.

MRS. RUTH. Whatever happens, trust to *his* love. It will always support and comfort you--my daughter!

(*Kissing her; she then turns to Herbert, C., speaking apart.*)

Herbert, Dr. Mellbanke wishes you to go for Dr. Holden--at once.

HERBERT. (*apart*) A consultation!

MRS. RUTH. H-s-h! (*Her finger to her lips.*) Dr. Mellbanke wishes to advise with him. (*Exit Herbert, L. Mrs. Ruth crosses, R.*) I will speak to Douglas, Constance. (*Exit, R.1.E.*)

CONSTANCE. (*taking off her jewels, etc., nervously, and dropping them on the table before her*) Oh, how I *hate* them! How I hate them! Why did I go to-night? My husband! I never longed for your love as I do now.

(*Edith makes her way across to Constance.*)

EDITH. Constance. (*Laying her hand on her shoulder.*)

CONSTANCE. Edith--sister!

EDITH. I am glad you have come back. Rosie was talking to me about you before she fell asleep.

CONSTANCE. *You* have been where *I* should have been to-night.

(*Taking Edith's hand and kissing it. Edith starts slightly and puts her other hand to Constance's cheek.*)

What did Rosie say, Edith?

EDITH. You are crying, Constance. (*Sinking to her knees beside her, with her arms about her.*) Don't cry. The last Rosie said, before she fell asleep, was "Mama." She loves you very much. She often, often tells me so. Don't cry, Constance.

CONSTANCE. Did her papa come home before she went to sleep?

EDITH. No. Mother sent to the club for him, at first, but he was not there. It took a long time to send to the other place, and Rosie was asleep when he came.

CONSTANCE. The--the other place--where?

EDITH. To--to some lady's house.

CONSTANCE. Some--some lady's--house?

EDITH. I forget the name--but you would know--Mrs.--Mrs.--Dun-- Dun--

CONSTANCE. Dunbar!

EDITH. Yes--that's the name.

CONSTANCE. Mother--sent--to see if--if Douglas was at--at Mrs. Dunbar's?

EDITH. Yes. Fortunately, he *was* there. I'm so glad you have both come back. It seems as if you *ought* to be together to-night. Don't cry, Constance.

> (*Reaching up with her arms about Constance's neck, as the latter sits rigidly looking away.*)

Rosie will be so glad to see you when she wakes up. The Doctor says she will soon get well.

> (*Her voice breaking, she drops her head into Constance's lap, weeping.*)

Don't cry.

CONSTANCE. You must go to bed, Edith, at once.

> (*Rising with arm about Edith and leading her up R., almost choking as she speaks, but controlling herself by an effort.*)

It is after two o'clock.

EDITH. Oh, I cannot sleep, Constance--I cannot sleep. Do not send me away.

CONSTANCE. You--you must go to your room, Edith.

EDITH. If you wish it, Constance.

CONSTANCE. Yes; good night.

EDITH. Good night.

> (*Kissing each other.   Exit Edith, up R.   Constance moves down and across, L.; supports herself by a chair, L.C.*)

CONSTANCE. I--I cannot breathe--I-- It is growing dark! I-- Douglas-- my husband--my heart is breaking!

> (*She buries her face in her hands. Enter Douglas, R.1E.*)

DOUGLAS. Constance--

> (*Sees her emotion and crosses to her rapidly.*)

My dear Constance! You are unstrung by this sudden news. You are nervous. Be seated.

> (*She drops into the chair.*)

Command yourself, my darling.

CONSTANCE. Yes-- (*Drawing up rigidly.*) I--I *will* command myself.

DOUGLAS. Let us hope for the best. Dr. Mellbanke says that Rosie may awake from her sleep refreshed and on the road to recovery.

CONSTANCE. (*aside*) Summoned from that woman's house to the bedside of his sick child!

DOUGLAS. This night will be the beginning of a new and a happy life for you and me, Constance--the beginning of a deeper and stronger love than we have ever known before. Rosie's future will be all the brighter for it. I have not been such a husband to you, of late years, as I ought. My feverish haste to make a larger fortune has led to what has seemed to you neglect--and it was nonetheless neglect because I was unconscious of it. I have allowed business considerations to outweigh all that is best in a man's life.

CONSTANCE. (*aside*) Business considerations! (*Rising.*)

DOUGLAS. Our love has been only flickering. It has not died out. We will be companions hereafter.

CONSTANCE. (*aside*) Companions!

DOUGLAS. You do not answer me, Constance.

(*A pause. She maintains her silence rigidly, looking away from him.*)
You are still silent?

(*Douglas stands looking at her a moment, and then crosses, R.C., slowly. He stops and looks down in thought.*)
Have I discovered my fault too late?

CONSTANCE. At that woman's house!

(*Enter Dr. Mellbanke, R.1E., stops, looks at Constance, then at Douglas.*)

DOUGLAS. (*turning to speak*) Constance--my--wife--I--

(*Dr. Mellbanke advances, taps him on the shoulder, and beckons to him quietly. Douglas starts and stops, as if a sudden fear checked him. Dr. Mellbanke glances at Constance and motions silence on his lips. Douglas starts with a short, quick breath. Constance turns suddenly at the sound, and looks at them both. The doctor beckons to Douglas out of room, quietly takes his arm and walks out with him, R.1E. Constance wavers a moment on her feet; then gives a quick, sharp scream, as if suddenly comprehending the truth. She staggers across R., front, trying to reach door at R.1E. Douglas reappears.*)

CONSTANCE. Rosie--not--not--

DOUGLAS. Be--be strong, my darling--be strong!

CONSTANCE. Rosie is--she is-- (*Staggering. Douglas supports her.*)

DOUGLAS. It--is--over.

(*She sinks into the chair at table. He stands over her, looking down tenderly.*)
She passed away in her sleep. My wife!

(*He bends down as if to embrace her. She looks up into his face with a cold, half-dazed expression, then turns from him and sinks with her head upon her arms. Douglas withdraws from her slowly, then speaks.*)
The last--link--broken!

ACT III.

Scene. Drawing-room. Door, up R., with hall or another apartment at back. Door, R.1E. (*Discovered: Constance sitting L.C. and Edith on a low stool by her side.   Constance is dressed in black; Edith in white, trimmed with black.*)

EDITH. I have been thinking about Douglas and you, Constance, almost all the time, to-day and yesterday. I dreamed about you last night. It seems very, very sad for Douglas to go away to Europe to-day--all by himself.

CONSTANCE. Yes, Edith; it *is* sad.

EDITH. He will be very lonely; and you will be lonely, too. Why don't you go with him?

CONSTANCE. Go with him? Why--I-- Never mind, my pet. Do not trouble your dear little head about Douglas and me. We--we do not find it convenient--to go together.

EDITH. How long will Douglas be gone?

CONSTANCE. I--I cannot tell.

EDITH. When I asked him, he said *he* didn't know.

CONSTANCE. Don't think about it, darling.

EDITH. I can't help it; I love you both so dearly, and I don't wish you to be unhappy. Mother told me that two people who loved each other enough to be married wished always to be together; and I know how I should feel if some one that I loved like that should go away.

CONSTANCE. Some one you loved?

EDITH. Love holds two people together so closely, that one is wretched without the other.

CONSTANCE. Why, my little innocent! How did *you* come to know anything of *that*?

EDITH. I--I don't know; I--I've been thinking about it for a long time. Sometimes I ask Mother. She always tells me to listen to my own heart. I--I *have* been listening to it. I--I *do* love some one, Constance!

   (*She drops her head into Constance's lap.*)

CONSTANCE. My child!

EDITH. I'm not a child any longer, sister.

CONSTANCE. I *see* you are not, my dear.

HERBERT. (*entering, up R.*) Edith!

   (*Edith starts up, rising and looking down with "consciousness" in her manner.*)

I've come up to go to the steamer with Uncle Douglas. Here's a bunch of violets. They're the first of the season; I've been watching for them.

EDITH. Oh! thank you.

HERBERT. It's half an hour yet before Douglas will go; and you are so fond of flowers--wouldn't you like to go into the conservatory?

EDITH. Yes, Herbert.

(*He leads her for a few steps. She returns and leans over Constance.*)

Sister, don't let Douglas go alone!

CONSTANCE. (*kissing her*) Go with Herbert, my darling.

(*Edith turns to Herbert, who leads her up and out, R.*)

No longer a child! I hope she will be happy.

(*Enter Maid, up R., with card which she gives to Constance, who reads.*)

"Mrs. Robert W. Mackenzie." (*Aside.*) One of Mother's friends, I suppose--from Boston, perhaps. (*Aloud.*) Take the card to Mrs. Winthrop, Jeanette.

(*Exit Maid, L.1E. Enter Mrs. Dick, up R.*)

Barbara!

MRS. DICK. Constance, my love! Your husband is going to Europe to-day, I hear.

CONSTANCE. Yes. (*Crossing, R., and sitting.*)

MRS. DICK. Business, I suppose. A married man never seems to care for the distance he has to travel--on business--when he's alone. Dick told me one day--there was a big law case in the West--no, that was Bob--it was a medical convention. "I've got to go to Chicago, my dear, on professional business," said he. "Oh, how *far*!" said I. "Merely a pleasant jaunt," said he. "*I'll* go *with* you, my love," said I. "My darling," said he, "it's *nine hundred miles*!" Ha-ha-ha-ha! First class in matrimonial geography: What is the exact distance between the city of New York and the city of Chicago? Answer: It depends on circumstances. Correct: Go to the head of the class. (*Enter Mrs. Ruth, L.1E.*) Ah! my dear Mrs. Winthrop, I came to tell Constance some news--you shall hear it, too.

MRS. RUTH. Thank you; I shall be very glad. But--(*looking across to Constance*)--you sent me a card, Constance--a Mrs. Mackenzie.

CONSTANCE. She is in the reception-room. Isn't she calling on you?

MRS. DICK. Why, *I'm* Mrs. Mackenzie!

CONSTANCE. You!

MRS. DICK. That's *my* card.

MRS. RUTH. (*confused*) But--your name--is--Chetwyn.

MRS. DICK. It was day before yesterday. Dick and I have got a divorce.

CONSTANCE. A divorce!

MRS. RUTH. Divorce!

MRS. DICK. M-m. That's my news. Sit down. I'll tell you all about it. (*They sit.*) We've been living in Connecticut for the past year, you know--except a few months in New York during the winter.

CONSTANCE. Yes--I know.

MRS. RUTH. (*with a bewildered air*) What has living in Connecticut to do with a--a divorce?

MRS. DICK. It has everything to do with it. They grant you a divorce there for incompatibility of temper.

MRS. RUTH. But I--I didn't know that you and your husband were incompatible.

MRS. DICK. Neither did *we*--till we went to live in Connecticut. We never knew we *had* any tempers to speak of, before. When we took a house in Stamford, we didn't dream of the effect it would have on a man and wife. Of course, Dick and I were both witnesses in the case.

MRS. RUTH. It must have been very sad.

MRS. DICK. Yes, it was--I had on a brocade--lavender and old gold-- lace to match the lavendar--and sleeves puffed above the elbows. The evidence was so comical.

MRS. RUTH. (*looking at her in bewilderment*) Comical!

MRS. DICK. You ought to have been there. Ha-ha-ha-ha! It was all about how Dick and I have been saying mean things to each other for a year--so as to obey the laws of the State. We called each other all sorts o' names. When we first married, Dick said I was a turtle-dove; after we got to Connecticut, he said I was a snapping turtle-dove. Ha-ha-ha-ha! I began by calling him a donkey--and then I called him a whole lot of animals. He told the judge, according to me he was a regular Noah's ark. I told the judge Dick called *me* animals, too. The judge said we seemed to be a happy family--and so he granted the divorce. I've gone back to my first husband's name.

CONSTANCE. Ah--I remember--Mackenzie.

MRS. DICK. I'm Mrs. Bob again, now. I gave Dick all the old cards I had left over--and the plate. I didn't want to keep Dick's name. If he should get married again, it'd be awkward, having two of us; we'd get mixed up. Of course, it doesn't make any difference to Bob. So Douglas sails to-day.

MRS. RUTH. (*rising*) Yes! And if you will kindly excuse me--

MRS. DICK. Certainly. (*Rising.*) I must run along, myself. Good morning.

MRS. RUTH. Good morning. (*Moving to her, speaking very earnestly.*) Believe me, my dear Mrs.--Mrs.--

MRS. DICK. Mackenzie.

MRS. RUTH. Mackenzie. I am very sorry that you and your husband are separated.

MRS. DICK. (*earnestly*) Thank you, my dear Mrs. Winthrop--but don't worry yourself about it: *we* don't. (*Mrs. Ruth turns, throwing up her hands, and goes out, L., shaking her head.*) Good by, Constance, my love-- I'm going to pop in and tell Mrs. Garnette--she's just got a divorce, too, you know. (*Kissing her and running up stage.*)

CONSTANCE. Good by.

(*She moves up into recess of window, L., and stands looking out.*)

MRS. DICK. (*stopping, up R.C., looking out, R.*) Here's Mr. Buxton Scott.

(*Scott appears from R. He and Mrs. Dick bow deeply to each other.*)

SCOTT. Mrs. Chetwyn.

MRS. DICK. Mrs.--Mackenzie--if you please!

SCOTT. (*turning and looking after her*) Eh? Mac--?

MRS. DICK. Dick and I are separated.

SCOTT. I never happened to meet either of you when you *weren't* separated.

MRS. DICK. We've got a divorce.

SCOTT. Ah! Then you and Dick will *see* something of each other. I congratulate you both. When were you divorced?

MRS. DICK. Day before yesterday.

SCOTT. And you've married a Mr. Mackenzie since?

MRS. DICK. Mr. Scott!

SCOTT. Oh! I beg your pardon; you've taken your first husband's name?

MRS. DICK. Yes. My maiden name was too far back. By the by, my darling old aunt, Miss Vandeveer, said the other day that she hoped you would come and see her.

SCOTT. With pleasure. She's a charming old lady. Give her my compliments. Tell her I hope to drop in often.

MRS. DICK. I will. I'm living with her.

SCOTT. (*in surprise, turning L.*) Eh?

MRS. DICK. You are still a bachelor?

SCOTT. I am.

MRS. DICK. I pity you, Mr. Scott. You should marry.

SCOTT. And pity myself? I prefer to have *you* pity me.

MRS. DICK. (*approaching him*) You really ought to make some woman happy.

SCOTT. (*aside*) She's after number three. (*Turning to her.*) My dear Mrs. Dick.

MRS. DICK. Bob.

SCOTT. Mrs. Bob. (*Looking down at her through his eye-glasses.*) I'll drop in on Dick and ask *his* opinion. He knows you *so* well.

MRS. DICK. Me! Bless you! I meant Aunt Jane.

SCOTT. Oh! (*Turning L.*)

MRS. DICK. I'm sure she'd make you happy. She's a charming old lady. Ha-ha-ha-ha-- (*Running R.--stops.*) Come and see Aunt Jane--often.

(*Exit Mrs. Dick, up R.*)

SCOTT. An old maid and a young grass widow. Two to one! I shall not call.

(*He turns, changing his tone and manner.*)

Constance.

(*She turns to him, giving both her hands. He holds them, looking at her with kindly interest, and speaking in an earnest, fatherly tone.*)

Douglas asked me to come and see him this morning, before he sailed.

CONSTANCE. He is in his room. I will send for him.

SCOTT. Thank you. (*He still retains her hands, looking steadily into her face.*) Constance, I have known you and Douglas since you were children. You have often called me your "second father."

CONSTANCE. You are the dearest friend we have in the world.

SCOTT. There is something on your heart.

CONSTANCE. On--my--heart?

SCOTT. I'm only a hard old bachelor, and a stony-hearted old warrior, but you may speak to me--as--as if I were really your father.

CONSTANCE. There are some things which one cannot--*will* not--talk about--to *any* one.

SCOTT. When you were a little girl, you used to bring all your troubles to me.

CONSTANCE. I am a woman now.

SCOTT. Constance, there is something wrong between you and your husband.

CONSTANCE. Something--wrong! Yes.

SCOTT. Will you confide in me?

CONSTANCE. I--I--(*hesitates--turns away*)--oh! I cannot! I cannot confide in *any* one.

SCOTT. I will not ask you to; but I will give you the advice which your own father would give if he were living. Whatever is on your heart, go to your husband--

CONSTANCE. To *him*! No, I am a humiliated wife. My natural pride compels me to be silent.

SCOTT. What can have happened to make you feel like this?

CONSTANCE. We will not talk about that. For two years and over, we have been growing more distant and more indifferent. I am worn out with such a life, at last. We--do not love each other now.

SCOTT. M-m-m. You do not love each other?

CONSTANCE. No; our love is a matter of the past.

SCOTT. How long will Douglas be gone?

CONSTANCE. I--I do not know.

SCOTT. M-m-m. Of course, now that your love is a matter of the past-- (*glancing at her shrewdly*)--it must be a great relief to you, too--to have Douglas go away.

CONSTANCE. Yes--it is--(*choking*)--a--a--great relief.

(*She bursts into tears.*)

SCOTT. (*approaching her, dropping one arm about her waist*) My child!

CONSTANCE. Father! (*Turning to him and hiding her face in his breast.*)

SCOTT. (*tenderly, yet half-humorously, patting her head*) I'm *sorry* you don't love each other any more. It is nearly time for Douglas to start, my dear; go and ask him to come to me.

CONSTANCE. Yes--I--I'll--(*going L.*)--I'll tell him you are here.

(*Exit Constance, L.1E., still crying.*)

SCOTT. (*looking after her, with a smile*) It's a pity they don't love each other any more. I shall make it my personal and professional duty to bring these two wrong-headed young people together--in spite of themselves. Providence, so to speak, has appointed me their attorney. I--*take*--the--case. The devil is the opposing counsel. He's a good lawyer; and highly respected by his fellow-members of the profession. He and I have frequently been on the same side of a case--I know his tricks. (*Sitting, R.*) I dare say a little lying will be necessary. If it is, I'll beat him at his own game. Even a lawyer must lie, now and then.

(*Enter Douglas, L.1E. He is in traveling suit.*)

DOUGLAS. (*taking Scott's hand*) My dear Scott!

SCOTT. Douglas!

DOUGLAS. I must apologize for asking you to come here; but I found it impossible, yesterday at the office, to say what I wanted. (*He strikes bell on table, R.C.*) I--I could not say it until the very last moment.

(*Enter Maid, up R.*)

Is the carriage at the door, Jeanette?

MAID. Yes, sir.

DOUGLAS. Tell Henry my trunk and valise are ready, and say to my mother and Miss Edith that I will be down in a few moments.

MAID. Yes, sir. (*Exit, up R.*)

DOUGLAS. (*turning to Scott*) I arranged yesterday for you to take the entire management of my property during my absence.

SCOTT. Yes.

DOUGLAS. I--I also hinted that I should ask you to make certain settlements of my estate. (*A pause.*) My departure for Europe, to-day, is the beginning of a final and absolute--separation--between my--wife-- and me.

SCOTT. A--final--separation! The *cause* of this, Douglas?

DOUGLAS. What makes a solid rock fall to pieces without any apparent cause? The silent and invisible power of a winter's frost. A frost like that has come upon Constance and me. (*A slight pause.*) It was my own fault. I gave myself up to the struggle for wealth. My wife lived alone and neglected, as many another rich man's wife lives--surrounded by everything a husband's *money* can furnish to make her happy. One night--not many weeks ago--my mother told me how cruelly I had neglected Constance--how I had robbed her of a home. I confessed my wrong to my wife at once. I spoke to her lovingly. She was silent. At that very moment, the Angel of Death passed upward with the soul of our little one in his arms. My child--and my wife's love--were both-- dead; it seemed as if we buried them in the same grave. Since that night, Constance has been--respectful--and kind to me--but cold and distant-- never the loving wife. We have both lived within ourselves--strangers to each other in our own home--husband and wife only to the world. We are nothing to each other now but--ice.

SCOTT. M-m. (*Glancing at him, then rather carelessly.*) I hope you'll have a pleasant voyage, Douglas--and a happy time, on the other side.

DOUGLAS. Happy? Can *you* say "happy"? You--who knew us both when we were happy indeed! How can you mock me like that? You are cruel, Scott--you are cruel.

(*He drops his face into his hands.*)

SCOTT. (*approaching and taking one of his hands*) Douglas--I see you are quite right. You are both of you nothing--but--ice.

(*Looking into Douglas' face with a keen glance, still holding his hand; Douglas turns away, L. Scott continues, aside, turning R.*)

Mount Hecla is nothing but ice--on the outside. But it's a tolerable live volcano, for all that; there's plenty of heat inside.

DOUGLAS. I wish you to--to draw up the papers for an equal division of my property, between my wife and me--and such other papers as our--legal--separation--may involve.

SCOTT. No, Douglas! I cannot. I love you both too much.

DOUGLAS. I should not have asked you. We must call upon a stranger, after all. (*Sitting, L.C.*)

SCOTT. No!--not to a stranger. If--if it must be done, you may leave it in my hands. How long will you be away?

DOUGLAS. I cannot tell; years, perhaps. I feel now as if I could *never* return to America.

SCOTT. You must.

DOUGLAS. Must?

SCOTT. (*aside*) Now for my first lie in the case. (*Aloud.*) I cannot possibly make a division of your property unless you are in this country.

DOUGLAS. You have my power of attorney.

SCOTT. In such a case as this, a power of attorney would be utterly useless. (*Aside.*) He doesn't know anything about law. If another lawyer overheard my advice, he'd think *I* didn't. (*Aloud.*) Can't you come back--in three months?

DOUGLAS. Three months? Impossible!

SCOTT. I shall be obliged to leave New York in four months, for the Sandwich Islands--an important case for the United States Government. I may be gone two years. (*Aside.*) The opposite counsel himself can't meet that.

DOUGLAS. I cannot confide this matter to any one but you.

SCOTT. Well, then--you must return--in three months.

DOUGLAS. (*after a pause*) Well, I will.

SCOTT. (*aside*) I've gained the first point in the case. The sooner I can bring them together, the harder it'll be for the devil to keep them apart. (*Aloud.*) Constance, of course, understands my relations to--

DOUGLAS. We have never spoken on the subject of our final separation.

SCOTT. Ah!

DOUGLAS. Of course, we both understand the situation. But we bade each other good by, a moment ago, without a word.

SCOTT. You have said good by already?

DOUGLAS. Yes. (*Rising and going up.*) I am simply flying from a life which I can endure no longer. We can write to each other on the subject. We cannot trust our tongues. You, of course, can communicate with Constance, as my representative.

SCOTT. My dear Douglas--you do not understand the law.

DOUGLAS. The law? No.

SCOTT. (*aside*) I don't intend he shall. (*Aloud.*) It is a legal impossibility for me to act in any capacity whatever between you and your wife, unless you meet her again, personally--at once--and come to an exact mutual understanding as to your respective intentions. De Vinculo Matrimonii--Chapter thirty-seven--section two hundred and thirty-nine--revised statutes--1878. (*Aside.*) Lie number three. (*Striking bell and rising.*) If I leave them alone together, it's twenty to one he won't go to Europe at all. (*Enter Maid, R.*) Please ask Mrs. Winthrop if she will kindly come here. (*Exit Maid, L.1E.*) Good by, Douglas.

DOUGLAS. You will remain?

SCOTT. I have an immediate engagement. (*Taking out watch.*) It is now after eleven o'clock. I have a case before the Supreme Court at eleven-thirty. (*Aside.*) If I keep on lying at this remarkable rate, and with such perfect ease, I'll begin to suspect I'm the devil himself.

(*He offers Douglas his hand.*)

DOUGLAS. Good by, old friend!

SCOTT. Good by.

(*Douglas turns to table, R.C. Scott turns up C., aside.*)

If the good angels ever do help a lawyer--when he happens to be on their side--I'll win my case.

(*Exit, up R. Douglas has taken a miniature from the table, R.C. He raises it to his lips and is looking at it as Constance enters, L.1E.*)

CONSTANCE. Douglas.

DOUGLAS. Ah--Constance. (*Leaves miniature on the table.*) I have just had an interview with Mr. Scott. I desired to leave a--a very important matter--affecting us both--in his hands. But he has just assured me that he cannot possibly act as our legal adviser in any way whatever unless we come to a--a full mutual understanding as to--as to--the--the relation which we--which we intend to--to bear to each other--hereafter.

CONSTANCE. A--a mutual understanding--yes.

DOUGLAS. We may be perfectly frank with each other now. We will speak at last what we have both understood for many weeks in our hearts. My departure is only a cloak, of course, to hide the truth for a little time from our friends, and from the world. We--we are about to--to separate--forever.

CONSTANCE. Separate--for ever! (*With emotion, almost staggering.*)Yes.

DOUGLAS. I find it necessary to return in three months. We can then make such--final--and permanent--arrangements--concerning our--our merely legal relations--as we may mutually agree upon. I--I take it for granted that you, no more than I, desire any form of--divorce.

CONSTANCE. No--not that.

DOUGLAS. We can both trust Mr. Buxton Scott.

CONSTANCE. Yes!

DOUGLAS. He can draw up a mutual agreement of--separation--in the usual legal form. We *must* meet--once more--to sign it--and--and--that will be the--end.

CONSTANCE. The--end--yes. (*Sinks in chair, L.C.*)

DOUGLAS. While I am away, you will remain in this house; and I shall have it transferred to you in the final division of the property. It has many sad memories for both of us; but we have passed some very happy hours in it, too. The voice of our child, now silent, has made its walls sacred. The ashes of our own love have become cold upon the hearthstone; but *her* little spirit may still hover about our former home; and it seems right that it should always find her mother here. (*Moving to her and extending his hand.*) Good by, Constance.

(*She rises, turns toward him, and places her hand in his, looking down.*)

CONSTANCE. Good by, Douglas.

(*He holds her hand a moment; then turns up stage. He stops and moves down to the table, R.C., taking the child's picture.*)

DOUGLAS. Constance, you have other pictures of Rosie. I, too, have another with me. But this one has a value in my eyes that no one else, not even you, could understand. May I take it with me?

CONSTANCE. Yes. Her memory will belong to both of us forever.

DOUGLAS. (*aside*) I see her face in this--mother and child in one.

(*He then moves up, R. She looks after him, making a sudden movement as if to go to him, which she checks. He passes out rapidly, without looking back.*)

CONSTANCE. Child and husband--both gone!

ACT IV.

Scene. Same as that of ACT I; without the child's toys, and with some changes in the arrangement of the furniture. Small table, a little left of C., front, with inkstand and pens. The portrait of Rosie is absent. No fire. It is now spring. Afternoon. (*Edith and Herbert discovered. She is sitting near C., sewing. He sits near her, L.C., with a book in his hand, in a thoughtful attitude, as if he had stopped reading, losing himself in revery.*)

EDITH. It's a very pretty story. Go on, Herbert. I like to hear you read. You've been silent for a long time.

HERBERT. I've been thinking.

EDITH. What about?

HERBERT. About *you*.

EDITH. I must go to my room. I haven't given the canary his bath to-day, and I must see how the old cat and the new kittens are getting on.
   (*She rises.*)

HERBERT. No; please don't go. (*She resumes her seat.*) Edith, you are so different from what you used to be. You always run away from me, now --except when some one is with us, or when I am reading to you--and whenever I try to tell you what is in my heart, you change the subject.

EDITH. I must thread my needle again.

HERBERT. (*after a glance and a pause*) I'll thread it for you.

EDITH. You! (*Laughing, taking thread from spool.*) I haven't time to wait.

HERBERT. Oh, I *can* thread it. Every young bachelor learns how to do that. I often have to sew on buttons and things.

EDITH. Well, you may do it.

HERBERT. (*taking needle and thread*) Whew!

EDITH. What's the matter?

HERBERT. It's sharp.

EDITH. (*laughing*) Didn't you know that before? I knew you'd get into trouble. Mind you thread the right end.

HERBERT. You *like* the story I am reading?

EDITH. Yes. The part I like best is where love is gradually growing in her heart--without her knowing why--or where it came from--or what it is.

HERBERT. I can't see anything of that kind in the story.

EDITH. You *can't!*

HERBERT. She doesn't seem to love him at all, yet.

EDITH. Oh, yes, she does!

HERBERT. She always avoids him; and whenever he tries to make love to her, she finds an excuse for leaving him--or talks about something else.

EDITH. Why, that's the very sign she loves him.

HERBERT. (*eagerly*) Is it, Edith?

EDITH. Of course! Don't you understand that? I'm *sure* she loves him. I feel it, as you go along in the book.

HERBERT. (*significantly--looking at her earnestly*) That's just the way *you* act to *me*.

EDITH. Is the needle threaded?

HERBERT. One moment.

(He suddenly begins to thrust the thread at the eye of the needle.)

EDITH. How are you getting on?

HERBERT. Splendidly! We're having a regular set-to. This is such a little fellow!

EDITH. Ha-ha-ha-ha.

HERBERT. I can always get ahead of a big one.

EDITH. Ha-ha-ha. Hadn't *I* better do it, Herbert?

HERBERT. No. *(With a vigorous thrust.)* I can *do* it.

EDITH. *(after a pause)* Isn't the hero of the story funny, Herbert?

HERBERT. Funny? how?

EDITH. He was so frank and bold at first. But now that she really loves him, he never seems to know what to do or say.

HERBERT. Oh, *I* understand *him* well enough.

EDITH. He seems almost afraid of her.

HERBERT. Of course he does. That's the way with any man, when he really loves a woman. *(Earnestly.)* I'm almost afraid of *you*.

EDITH. Is the needle ready?

HERBERT. I'll hit it in the eye in a moment.

> *(Beginning to thrust at the needle again. He goes on, keeping his eye intently on the needle, and trying to thread it with a variety of motions, ranging from quiet efforts to desperate thrusts.)*

Of course, a man can't talk to a woman he loves--*(needle)*--as easily as he can--*(needle)*--to a woman he doesn't love.

EDITH. In the last chapter you read they were alone together for nearly an hour, and he never said a word about love.

HERBERT. He was coming to the subject half a dozen times--*(needle)*--and she always turned him off.

EDITH. But she was *thinking* about it.

HERBERT. How could he tell that?

EDITH. He might have guessed it.

HERBERT. I don't see how he could guess that she was *thinking* about love--*(paying great attention to needle)*--when she was *talking* about her old cat and new kittens--*(needle)*--or her canary's bath.

EDITH. I don't remember that in the book.

HERBERT. Eh? Oh! No.

EDITH. There's nothing about a cat or a canary in the story you were reading.

HERBERT. *You* know the story I am *thinking* about. *(Rising and leaning over her, earnestly.)* Do you remember, Edith, one night last winter, I told you I hoped to have a little home of my own?

EDITH. (*dropping her head*) Yes.

HERBERT. And I said, I--I hoped to get--married.

EDITH. Yes.

HERBERT. You didn't know what I meant--when I told you--I loved you.

EDITH. I--I never dreamed of such a thing as love till that night.

HERBERT. I tried to teach you what it was.

EDITH. (*rising, turning R.*) It seems as if I have lived years since then.

HERBERT. (*with deep earnestness*) Edith--I love you--with all my soul! But I feel as if *I* could learn from *you* now. I hardly dare ask for your love. It could not be stronger than mine--but it would be better and sweeter and purer.

EDITH. (*after a slight pause*) You need not ask for it. It belongs to you.

HERBERT. My darling! (*Embracing her.*) I shall be your guide and your protector through life!

EDITH. (*her head resting on his breast*) Oh, Herbert--I am so happy!

HERBERT. Whew!

EDITH. (*starting up*) What is it, Herbert?

HERBERT. That needle.

EDITH. (*sympathetically*) O--h, where is it?
(*Taking his hand, which he puts in hers, and touching different parts with her finger.*)
Here?

HERBERT. No.

EDITH. Here?

HERBERT. No.

EDITH. Here?

HERBERT. Yes--there.

EDITH. A--h! (*Putting his hand to her lips.*)

HERBERT. We can look after the old cat and the new kittens, now.
(*Exeunt, R.1E. Enter Constance, up R. She moves down, R.C., glancing at clock on mantel.*)

CONSTANCE. Will the time never come? Oh! I wish to-day were past.
(*Enter Mrs. Ruth, up L., in bonnet, etc.*)

MRS. RUTH. Constance! I have just left Douglas--at his hotel. He has told me the worst! This afternoon you are to sign the papers that separate you forever.

CONSTANCE. Yes. *I* could not tell you.

MRS. RUTH. When Douglas did not come to his own home, I knew, for the first time, how wide the gulf between you had become. Is it too late?

CONSTANCE. Yes! Too late. (*Crossing, R.*)

MRS. RUTH. Douglas said the same.

(*Passing Constance, and moving toward the door, R.1E.*)

My heart is full.

(*She stops with her hands over her face; rouses herself and turns.*)

I--I shall always love you, Constance, as my own child!

CONSTANCE. Mother! (*Going to her.*)

MRS. RUTH. (*embracing her*) My daughter!

(*She kisses her and goes out, R.1E. Enter Maid, up L., with a card.*)

CONSTANCE. I can see no one to-day, Jeanette--(*takes card*)--except--Mr. Buxton Scott will be here--you may admit him at once. (*Exit Maid, up L. Constance reads card.*) "Mrs.--Richard--Chetwyn."

MRS. DICK. (*putting her head in a door, up L.*) How d' y' do?

CONSTANCE. Barbara?

MRS. DICK. Dick and I have got married again. I'm using the same old cards. May I come in?

CONSTANCE. Certainly.

MRS. DICK. I'll tell you all about it. (*Sitting beside her.*) It was private. We found that being divorced was worse than being incompatible. We were both awfully lonely. Ha-ha-ha! Dick and I went through our courtship all over again, just as if we'd never been married at all. Poor Aunt Jane had another dreadful time with me.

CONSTANCE. What do you mean?

MRS. DICK. Aunt Jane Vandeveer brought me up, you know. The dear old maid! I've always been her favorite niece. She's going to leave me all her money. I went to stay with Aunt Jane again after Dick and I were separated. She was more particular with me than she was when I was a young lady. Ha-ha-ha! One day Aunt Jane and I passed Dick on Madison Avenue. Of course, we didn't bow to each other. But Dick winked at me. Aunt Jane saw it. She was fearfully indignant. The next time we met--Aunt Jane was on the opposite side of me--and *I* winked at *Bob*--I mean *Dick.* After that we carried on a regular flirtation with each other. He used to pass the house and wave his handkerchief. Aunt Jane always closed the parlor shutters with a bang, and I kissed my hand to him out of the second story window. Ha-ha-ha! Then Dick sent me a secret note by one of the servants. We arranged a clandestine meeting in Stuyvesant Square; and we went down to Long Beach together. Dick said sweet things to me all the afternoon, just as he did when we first fell in love, and after it was dark, we wandered off on the beach by ourselves, in the moonlight--and I had tears in my eyes--and Dick kissed me--and the next day we ran away and got married.

CONSTANCE. You--you ran away--with your own husband?

MRS. DICK. I *had* to. Aunt Jane says she'll never forgive us. But she *will*. I always did run away to get married. Dick and I are having another honeymoon.

CONSTANCE. I--I am very glad you are happy again, Barbara.

MRS. DICK. Thank you, my dear; I knew you would be. (*In a serious tone.*) I--I wish *you* were happy, too, Constance.

CONSTANCE. I?

MRS. DICK. Forgive me, Constance--but--I--I know things aren't quite as they should be. Perhaps I know more than I ought to. Women always *do*. Your husband hasn't been here since he landed; and that was two weeks ago. I am so happy now with Dick--I don't like to see you miserable; and I feel as if *I* might have had something to do with it.

CONSTANCE. You?

MRS. DICK. I was always such a thoughtless creature! One night last winter I told you how Dick found Douglas at Mrs. Dunbar's house once or twice. I thought it was great fun then; but I shouldn't think so now. When I was a grass widow, I often met Mrs. Dunbar. She's a grass widow, too, you know. Grass widows always do meet each other; and they always talk about the infelicities of married life. That's one reason I'm glad to join the army of married women again. Mrs. Dunbar told me that it was nothing but a *business* connection with Mr. Winthrop and her. (*Enter Maid, up L.*)

MAID. Mr. Scott is here, madam.

MRS. DICK. He's the very man.

CONSTANCE. Ask him to come in here, Jeanette. (*Exit Maid.*) What do you mean, Barbara?

MRS. DICK. Mrs. Dunbar said Buxton Scott knew all about it. Ask *him*, my dear, at once. I'll leave you with him. Is your mother in?

CONSTANCE. Yes.

MRS. DICK. I'll run and tell her about Dick and me. I know she'll be glad to hear it.

(*Exit, R.1E. Enter Buxton Scott, up L.*)

SCOTT. Constance, my dear! I am very sorry to come on such an errand. (*Taking her hand.*) Is there anything you wish to say to me before Douglas arrives?

CONSTANCE. Yes; I wish to ask you a question. Have you ever had any business connection with--Mr. Winthrop--and--and Mrs. Hepworth Dunbar?

SCOTT. Mrs.--Dunbar? (*Aside.*) Of course! I might have known a woman would pop up somewhere in this case. (*Aloud.*) Yes, Constance, I had. But that is a professional confidence.

CONSTANCE. As you please, Mr. Scott. It is not a matter that can now effect the future relations of Mr. Winthrop and me. We can never come together again. But it is not too late for me to--be--just--if I have wronged him.

SCOTT. (*aside*) I'll be hanged if I give the devil a single point in the case--even for the sake of my professional honor; *he* doesn't care a rap for *his* professional honor. (*Aloud.*) I'll tell you the whole truth, Constance. Your brother Clarence--

CONSTANCE. Clarence! what of him?

SCOTT. He was a confidential clerk, and he speculated in stocks--like many another young man. The result--a defalcation--fifty thousand dollars.

CONSTANCE. Defalcation!

SCOTT. Douglas *saved* him from imprisonment and disgrace--(*she starts*)--by meeting the whole amount himself, out of his own fortune.

CONSTANCE. Imprisonment--(*sinking in chair, R.C.*)--disgrace!

SCOTT. It was impossible to prevent the *criminal arrest* of Clarence without the consent of *all* the creditors. The only one that refused was Mrs. Hepworth Dunbar, to whom a large amount of the misplaced securities belonged. She had certain social grudges to make good; Mr. Douglas Winthrop had declined to allow his wife to be introduced to Mrs. Dunbar. She had now an opportunity to disgrace the family. Your husband was compelled to call upon her--frequently--in person. His last call was late one night. Clarence would have been arrested the next day. Douglas' appeal was in vain. He was called suddenly from her house that night by a messenger from home. On the following morning I called on Mrs. Dunbar myself. I told her that the child of Douglas Winthrop had died the night before. Even a woman like that has a heart. Mrs. Dunbar had lost a child herself; and the memory of her own sorrow made her merciful. Your brother was saved. His--fault--is a secret!

(*Enter Douglas, up L. Scott turns.*)

Douglas.

(*Nodding and moving up C. Douglas bows to him. Constance turns, and they look at each other a moment; then Douglas moves to her, extending his hand frankly, and taking her hand and holding it a moment.*)

Constance.

(*He drops her hand; both standing a moment in silence, looking down.*)

CONSTANCE. Douglas--I--I have this moment heard of a great kindness you have done my brother and--me.

(*Douglas glances sharply up at Scott.*)

Do not blame *him*. I *asked* him to tell me. I--(*with deep feeling*)--I *thank* you, Douglas.

DOUGLAS. I only did what *any* man of proper feeling would have done under the same circumstances.

(*A long silence, both looking down. Douglas crosses, L.*)

Mr. Scott, we will proceed with the business before us.

(*Scott, up C., looks from one to the other, alternately, several times; then moves down to table, near C., front.*)

SCOTT. I have drawn up four documents. (*Taking papers from his pocket.*) These two are duplicates. (*Reads endorsement on one paper.*) "Douglas Winthrop and Constance Winthrop--Deed of Separation."

(*Douglas and Constance sit, L. and R. Scott sits at table; opens the paper; and reads in a rapid, business-like tone.*)

"This indenture, made the seventh day of May, 1882, by and between Douglas Winthrop, of the city and State of New York, party of the first part, and Constance Winthrop, of the same place, party of the second part--Witnesseth: whereas the said parties of the first and second parts were lawfully united in wedlock on the twenty-eighth day of June, in the year"--

(*He stops suddenly in his quick reading; the tone of his voice changing, and speaking slowly, with natural feeling.*)

I remember that day perfectly. We all drove to the church together from the old homestead near Concord. The marriage service never seemed so beautiful to me as it did that morning. Your dear old father's voice, Constance, had more than a pastor's tenderness in it as he uttered the words which you both repeated after him--"for better, for worse, in sickness and in health, to love and to cherish, until death us do part."

(*Constance and Douglas rise, showing signs of rising emotion.*)

When you knelt at the chancel rail before him, his voice was trembling as he repeated that beautiful prayer: Send thy blessing upon these thy servants; that they may ever remain in perfect love and peace together.

(*Constance and Douglas drop their heads sadly.*)

As he pronounced the blessing--of a pastor and father in one--the sun came from behind a cloud--and light streamed through the window on your heads. Douglas' *mother* was leaning on my arm.

(*Constance and Douglas turn up stage, R. and L., standing with backs to audience and their heads bowed deeply.*)

There were tears in her eyes, but a smile shone through them; as if the love of a mother's heart was pouring *its* blessing upon both her children --like the sunshine through the window.

(*His voice is a little broken, and he brushes a tear from his eye with his handkerchief.*)

But--(*brushes away another tear, leaving handkerchief on table*)--hem--this is a digression. We will proceed with the business before us.

DOUGLAS. (*with choking voice*) Please read the papers as rapidly as possible, Mr. Scott.

CONSTANCE. We--(*choking*)--we need not delay more than is-- absolutely--necessary.

SCOTT. (*resuming his rapid business tone; reading*) "And whereas said parties of the first and second parts"--but we shall not sign this instrument until we have considered the *other* papers. We will dispose of them at once.

(*Putting down the Deed, taking up another paper and rising.*)

This is a deed whereby Douglas Winthrop conveys in fee simple to Constance Winthrop the old homestead where she was born near Concord, Massachusetts. (*Pause.*) Some of the happiest hours of my life were passed there. Constance was a perfect little tom-boy. Ha-ha-ha! You both gave me a particularly warm reception, one day, when I had just arrived from New York. I was going up the gravel walk. Your father was coming down the steps to meet me. Constance came bounding around the corner, and you after her. She was *running* one way and *looking* the other. As your father was helping me to my feet, he remarked that those children were *always* upsetting something. Ha-ha! Five minutes after that, Douglas was in the cherry-tree, and you were holding up your little apron for the fruit--the old cherry-tree down in the corner, near the summer-house.

CONSTANCE. Oh, no--the cherry-tree was in the *other* corner.

DOUGLAS. Over near the old well.

SCOTT. So it was. When you both grew older, I often saw you walking arm in arm on the lawn--after the stars came out. Constance was always explaining to me that you were giving her lessons in-- astronomy. You were quite as likely to be telling her where the stars were in the afternoon as at night. Those were delightful days at the old homestead.

DOUGLAS and CONSTANCE. (*with thoughtful manner, as if the force of old memories is beginning to influence them*) Delightful!

SCOTT. You had a lover's quarrel about that time. Constance had given you a pair of slippers she had been working for you. When you quarrelled, she took them away from you, and gave them to *me*. I remember, Constance had a little dark bay pony.

CONSTANCE. Oh, no! (*Moving to R.C., near Scott.*) It was gray.

DOUGLAS. With a black spot on the left shoulder. (*Moving down, L.C.*)

SCOTT. Dappled gray--so it was. His name was Jack.

CONSTANCE. Oh, no!

DOUGLAS. No!

CONSTANCE. It was Jenny.

SCOTT. Oh, yes--of course--Jenny. The first time Douglas helped you to mount--Jenny--(*turning to Douglas*)--you gave her too strong a lift!

DOUGLAS. (*with a smile*) Yes.

SCOTT. (*to Constance*) You fell over on the other side!

CONSTANCE. Yes.

(*Constance and Douglas laugh gently and pleasantly. Scott laughs with them quietly, moving back as step.*)

SCOTT. The old family carriage horse--*his* name was Jack.

DOUGLAS. *He* was dark bay. (*To Constance.*) You used to drive Jack for your father--(*stepping to her in front of Scott*)--when he made his pastoral visits.

(*Scott gradually retires up stage, L.*)

CONSTANCE. I always sat in the carriage, to keep the flies off Jack.

DOUGLAS. I often met you on the road; and I used to think you were doing as pious a work outside, making the old horse comfortable, as your father was doing inside.

CONSTANCE. Old Jack was one of the family. Dear old Jack!

DOUGLAS. Dear old Jack!

SCOTT. (*up L.C.*) Dear old Jack!

(*He stands, up. L., pretending to look over deed, but watching them.*)

DOUGLAS. Do you remember one such afternoon, Constance? You were sitting in front of the little house where the old sexton's widow lived.

CONSTANCE. (*smiling*) How often we used to run down there when we were children! (*Sitting, front.*)

DOUGLAS. Yes--she always had fresh doughnuts for us, on Saturdays.

(*Sitting at her side near the table. Constance nods, smiling.*)

But we had grown older, at the time I am thinking of now. I joined you in the carriage. I--I asked you a question, that afternoon. (*Taking her hand.*) Do you remember your answer?

CONSTANCE. (*as if lost in memory*) Yes.

DOUGLAS. That was the very word! I asked you to be--my--wife. Oh, Constance! I was the happiest man in the world.

SCOTT. (*aside*) They're doing very well *without* a lawyer. (*Exit, up L.*)

DOUGLAS. We were in the shade of the great elm. Old Jack turned his head and looked back at us, as if he was giving us his consent. This ring--(*referring to one on her finger*)--was the pledge of the promises we made to each other that day. Our initials are engraved inside of it.

CONSTANCE. And the word--"Forever."

DOUGLAS. When I placed it on your finger in the dear old home--(*gradually extending his arm about her waist*)--I drew you to me--(*raising her hand toward his lips*)--and I--

(*He suddenly stops; his eye resting upon the Deed of Separation on the table near him. He slowly withdraws his arm and drops her hand; reaches forward and takes the paper; finally holding it in both hands before him and looking at it steadily. Constance looks at the paper, draws up, rises, and walks R. Douglas starts to his feet, drops the paper upon the table, and turns up, L., under strong emotion. He stands for a moment, before speaking, as if collecting his thoughts and bringing his feelings under control.*)

We--we were losing ourselves in--in *dreams* of the past.

CONSTANCE. We had forgotten the--the *present.*

DOUGLAS. (*as if suddenly seeing Scott, beckoning with a nervous movement*) Ah--Mr. Scott--Mr. Scott!

(*Douglas walks down, L., a few steps. Re-enter Scott, up L. The deed, folded, is still in his hand. Scott stops, C., and looks R. and L.*)

SCOTT. I beg your pardon. I left my handkerchief in my hat outside.

(*Moving down C. He discovers his handkerchief on the table; picks it up quickly, and thrusts it into his pocket, glancing each way. He then begins to read very rapidly from the deed in his hand.*)

"Said party of the first part does by these presents grant, sell, remise, release, convey and confirm"--m--m--m--"heirs and assigns forever the premises hereinafter described"--m--m--m--m--"namely, to wit--South side of the Boston High-road--intersection of the county line--fence in a southernly direction along the western bank of the Coolsac Creek"--

(*Dropping suddenly to a conversational tone.*)

Speaking of the Coolsac Creek, by the by, I saw the same old clump of willows on the opposite bank, when I was there last summer. That was a sort of meeting-place for young lovers. I remember, one day--I met Douglas and a lady there. You remember it, Douglas--what *was* her name? It was Douglas and Miss--

(*Turning to Constance, who draws up sharply and looks around; Douglas looks in surprise.*)

That particular friend of yours, Constance--Miss--Kate--Miss--really, I--

CONSTANCE. Kate Fairfield!

SCOTT. Yes--that's the name. Douglas was arranging a bunch of violets in her hair. But this is a digression. I beg your pardon. (*Reads rapidly.*) "With all and singular the tenements, hereditaments, and appurtenances thereunto belonging; and the said party of the first part"--

DOUGLAS. Pardon me, Mr. Scott--but you are mistaken--I was never at the place you refer to with Miss Kate Fairfield.

CONSTANCE. (*with great dignity and signs of rising jealousy*) Mr. Scott's memory may be more accurate than yours.

DOUGLAS. But I protest--I--

CONSTANCE. You were saying, Mr. Scott?

SCOTT. Let me see--it was--no--ah--now I think again--I get you young people so mixed up when I recall those days--it was Mr. Lawrence Armytage--and--Constance.

(*Douglas and Constance both start.*)

CONSTANCE. (*moving down, R., a few steps, indignantly*) Nothing of the kind!

(*Scott turns up stage, C., standing with his back to the audience and looking at a picture on the wall.*)

DOUGLAS. Mr. Lawrence Armytage was *frequently* at the house when *I* called.

CONSTANCE. Kate Fairfield lived on the highroad between your house and mine.

DOUGLAS. Mr. Armytage always dropped in--to see--your *father*.

CONSTANCE. Whenever you were late--you--(*choking*)--you always said it was the old sexton's widow! (*Angrily, crossing to him, L.*) I saw you, myself--talking with Kate Fairfield, over the gate--while I was passing in the carriage with father--the very day before I took away your slippers and gave them to Mr. Scott--and I'm *glad* I *did* it!

(*She draws up before him angrily; then turns her back on him and returns R., with a dignity in absurd contrast with the words and situation.*)

DOUGLAS. (*following her R.*) And the very day after that, you discovered that I was only asking Miss Fairfield if *her* mother would lend *my* mother the hemmer of her sewing-machine! And you took the slippers away from Mr. Scott and sent them back to *me*!

CONSTANCE. Oh!

   (*Douglas returns L., triumphantly. She turns toward him.*)

  I *didn't* send them back to you!

DOUGLAS. You? (*Turning suddenly.*) Mr. Scott!

   (*He appeals earnestly to Scott, up stage.*)

SCOTT. (*jumping around suddenly*) Eh?

CONSTANCE. (*to Scott*) He says *I* sent those slippers back to him. You *know* I didn't--don't you?

SCOTT. (*starting down C.*) Certainly, you didn't.

DOUGLAS. The package was addressed in *her* handwriting.

SCOTT. Yes--(*still moving down*)--Constance wrote the address.

CONSTANCE. Mr. Scott *sent* it--by the boy--himself.

SCOTT. (*at C, front*) Yes--I *sent* it.

DOUGLAS. It is quite immaterial; I dare say you sent another pair to Mr. Armytage!

CONSTANCE. (*bursting into sobs, R.C.*) O--o--o--o--o--h!

   (*Douglas stands, L.C., with his arms folded. Scott looks from one to the other a moment.*)

SCOTT. Ah, by the way, it has just occurred to me: it was Mr. Armitage and Miss Fairfield I saw together under the willows.

CONSTANCE. Oh. (*Looking up from her sobs.*) It wasn't *either* of us.

SCOTT. When I saw Douglas in the lane--*you* were with him, Constance.

DOUGLAS. Oh. It was *both* of us.

SCOTT. (*to Douglas*) You had been gathering some water-lilies for Constance.

CONSTANCE. (*brightly, with sudden recollection*) Oh, yes!

SCOTT. (*to Constance*) It was the day he fell into the pond.

DOUGLAS. Yes!

SCOTT. He got into the mud up to the knees.

CONSTANCE. I remember!

DOUGLAS. So do I!

SCOTT. (*to Douglas*) Constance tried to pull you out of the water; and-- (*to Constance*)--he pulled you *in*!

   (*Constance and Douglas burst into a merry laugh, nodding at each other across Scott.*)

We will proceed with the business before us.

   (*Their faces suddenly drop. They turn up stage, R. and L.*)

Returning to the original Deed of Separation.

   (*Taking up the Deed. Constance and Douglas look at each other across the stage, at back; then drop their eyes. Scott reads.*)

"The said Douglas Winthrop and the said Constance Winthrop, his wife, have by mutual consent agreed to live separate and apart from each other--and whereas the aforesaid"-- (*Enter Edith, R.1E.*)

SCOTT. Edith!

EDITH. Mr. Scott!

SCOTT. (*going to her*) I have some news for you, Edith. Your brother Douglas is here.

EDITH. Oh! Where is he?

(*Scott leads her to Douglas, who meets her, L.C.*)

Douglas! (*Throwing her arms about his neck.*)

DOUGLAS. Edith--my little sister!

EDITH. Oh--I am so *glad* you have come home--so glad! We shall all be happy, now.

DOUGLAS. Happy! Yes.

EDITH. Constance has missed you so much, Douglas--so much! You won't go away from us again--will you?

DOUGLAS. I--I--

SCOTT. My little pet!

(*He takes her from Douglas, who turns up stage a few steps.*)

EDITH. H'm!

SCOTT. I know you have a great deal to tell Douglas, but not now. (*Leading her to seat, L.*) Sit down, Edith.

EDITH. Oh, very well--I will wait. But I *am* so glad Douglas is home again.

DOUGLAS. (*apart--in Scott's ear*) We--we *cannot* go on with this--in *her* presence.

SCOTT. (*apart, to him*) I need not read the rest of the paper. You and Constance can sign it--in silence.

(*Douglas retires up C., a little to the R., dropping his head. Constance stands, R., partly upstage. Scott returns to the table, near C., front; takes up the Deed of Separation and turns, facing Constance and Douglas.*)

There is one piece of property not mentioned in any of these deeds: a burial lot in Greenwood Cemetery, with one little grave.

(*A pause, Constance and Douglas looking down, with bowed heads.*)

EDITH. Mother and I went to Greenwood yesterday, Douglas. You and Constance must go with us next time. The place where Rosie lies is covered with flowers.

(*Constance and Douglas give way to their tears, both dropping their faces into their hands.*)

SCOTT. Even a lawyer cannot divide that property, nor the memories of

a father and mother that cluster about the grave of their child--and there
is a little soul that belongs to you both.

(*He turns over the leaves of the Deed to the last page.*)

You--you will both sign--here--if you please.

(*He takes up the pen, dips it into the ink, and turns, holding it toward
them. During this action they have rushed into each other's arms,
weeping. Picture. Scott turns and drops the pen, taking the Deed and
tearing it.*)

I have won the case.

(*He walks up C. Enter Mrs. Ruth, R.1E. She starts, with an exclamation, looking at Douglas and Constance, with her back to the audience.
Douglas meets her, embracing her. Enter Herbert, up L. Places a ring
upon Edith's first finger. Enter Mrs. Dick, R.1E., sailing in rapidly.*)

MRS. DICK. I've been away from Dick for nearly two hours.

(*She turns, C., seeing Douglas, and goes to him and takes his hand.*)

Mr. Winthrop!

DOUGLAS. (*smiling*) Mrs. Dick!

MRS. DICK. (*turning to Constance*) Constance! I really must go. Dick'll
be lonely. We haven't been separated so long since we've been married--
this time. Good by, all.

(*Going up, L., nods to Scott as she passes him, up C.*)

Ah--Mr. Scott.

SCOTT. Mrs. Mackenzie!

MRS. DICK. (*stopping, up L.C., turning*) Mrs. Chetwyn.

SCOTT. Eh?

MRS. DICK. Dick and I have got married again.

SCOTT. Married? You and-- Allow me.

(*Offers her a card.*)

My professional card.

MRS. DICK. Thank you--no. We've had quite enough of the law; and if
we ever go anywhere by way of Connecticut, we'll take through tickets.
Call on us, Mr. Scott--any evening--Dick and I are always at home.

(*Exit Mrs. Dick, up L.*)

SCOTT. The devil has lost that case, too.

(*Douglas, with one arm about Constance's waist, raises her hand in his
and looks at the ring on her finger. He then speaks to Mrs. Ruth.*)

DOUGLAS. Dear Mother, our hearts have conquered us. (*Turning to
Constance.*) We can trust to them hereafter.

CONSTANCE. (*looking down at the ring*) Yes, Douglas, "forever."

CURTAIN.

Denman Thompson (1833-1911)
and *The Old Homestead*

Over the years, critics have made many disparaging remarks about the play, but anyone interested in letting "the scarlet runners chase ye back to childhood" can drive this very summer to West Swanzey, New Hampshire, and enjoy performances of *The Old Homestead* at the Potash Bowl, where Denman Thompson is still revered as "a famous theatrical trouper."

As a boy of seventeen, Thompson left his home in Swanzey for Boston, where he became a circus acrobat. Taking a variety of odd jobs and eventually becoming an itinerant player, he specialized in Irish roles for a while and traveled to Toronto, London, and back to America. After working as a song and dance man in variety theatre, he gained some experience playing Uncle Josh, a New England farmer, in a sketch called *The Female Bathers; or, Peeping Tom at Long Branch*. When an attack of rheumatism put him to bed for several weeks in 1875, he occupied himself by writing a two-scene sketch about a Yankee farmer--*Joshua Whitcomb*.

When Thompson took his thirty-minute skit on tour, it was an immediate hit, and, with the help of his business manager, George W. Ryer, he expanded it into a full-length play entitled *The Old Homestead*, which opened at the Boston Museum on April 5, 1886. After that, Thompson, with his benevolent face, snowy hair, and totally unsophisticated manner, played Uncle Josh back and forth and up and down the country, earning a considerable fortune in the process.

The Old Homestead was successful for a number of reasons in addition to Thompson's acting. The Yankee character continued a long tradition. The contemporary interest in realism and local color induced such a serious critic as William Dean Howells to wax enthusiastic over this "sweetest and simplest of plays." The production kept pace with the times, and new scenes and scenery were added during the 1890's and afterwards. There was nothing in the play to offend contemporary audiences, and a number of dramatic genres-- comedy, farce, melodrama, variety theatre, and the minstrel show--were represented in a sentimental and humorous fashion.

Denman Thompson's
New Play

SETH.   JOSH.   CY.

"JOSH" THERE DON'T YOU FEEL BETTER NOW?

THE OLD HOMESTEAD

THE OLD HOMESTEAD

(1886)

by Denman Thompson

CHARACTERS

Joshua Whitcomb	Pat Clancey
Cy Prime	Francois Fogarty
Happy Jack	A Porter
Frank Hopkins	A Drunken Man
Eb Ganzey	Aunt Matilda Whitcomb
John Freeman	Rickety Ann
Henry Hopkins	Miss Annie Hopkins
Judge Patterson	Miss Nellie Freeman
Seth Perkins	Maggie O'Flaherty
Reubin Whitcomb	Mrs. Henry Hopkins
The Hoboken Terror	Mrs. Murdock
The Dude	Mrs. Maguire
Doyle, the Policeman	Miss Nellie Patterson
U. S. Letter Carrier	Miss Elinor Stratton
Len Holbrook	The Misses Stratton

ACT I.

Scene. Homestead farm of the Whitcombs'. The back scene, or drop, depicts undulating farm lands and in the foreground a typical stone wall is seen. A cosy farmhouse, with or without flowered porch, stands R. of stage. Entrance to house is made by step through screened door. A curtained window above door and one facing audience. Beneath upper window, a common bench with milk pans and pails. At down stage R. corner of house, a rain spout and rain barrel parallel to footlights. At R. of barrel--below window, facing audience--a low wash bench with bar of common soap. A common chair stands L. of rain barrel--at corner of house. At L. side of stage either a barn or granary, or simple wood wings. A square, old-fashioned well with windlass, bucket and dipper, down stage, at L.C., with a small bench in front and a common chair at R. of it. Between well and L. of stage, a wood-saw, saw-horse, wood-block, split kindling wood and chips. Grass mats and farming implements can give further atmosphere to typify the farm yard and homestead. (*Mixed Quartette sings "Lawn Tennis," or other lively selection, off R. Matilda and Rickety Ann discovered listening. Matilda is sitting on bench in front of well and Rickety is standing up stage looking off R., at singers.*)

MATILDA. Our visitors are enjoying themselves. Well, I like to see it. Shows they are happy. Sent word to Joshua by the Bennets boy to come up to the house. He's down in the meadow helping the hired men--wish he'd come. Suppose he wants to get all his hay mowed up in case it should rain before morning. (*Crosses to Rickety.*) What's that they are playn' over there, Rickety Ann? Some new kind of a ball game, ain't it?

RICKETY. Guess it 'tis, Aunt Tildy--never seed one like afore. Come near breaking a window a while ago, too.

MATILDA. Did they? Well, now, that's dreadful careless. You tell them, Rickety Ann, that they must be careful. (*Goes down to porch steps.*)

RICKETY. Yes'm. (*Calling off, to singers.*) Say, you folks, Aunt Tildy says if you break a window, she'll make you pay for it.

FRANK. (*outside--off R.*) You don't say so.

MATILDA. Why, Rickety Ann, I didn't say nothin' o' the sort.

RICKETY. Well, if you didn't, you thought it.

(*Rickety comes down to L. of Matilda.*)

MATILDA. Never mind what I think--you do what I say.

RICKETY. All right, Aunt Tildy; but I didn't mean nothin'.

MATILDA. (*mounting porch*) All right then, bring in the wood and we'll finish getting the supper. (*Going into house, R.*) Come!

(*Rickety crosses, going to wood-block, L, kneeling and picking up split kindling wood and chips, piling it up on one arm, speaking as she does.*)

RICKETY. Well, that new hired girl don't know enough to blow hot soup. Put the ice in the well the other day to cool the water. (*Laughs.*) She don't know nothin'.

MATILDA. (*inside house*) Rickety Ann!

RICKETY. Yes'm, I'm comin'.

(*Cross to house, R., with wood. Enter Frank and Annie Hopkins followed by John and Nellie Freeman. They variously group about, C., and point at Rickety--all laughing.*)

What are you laughing at? (*Turning around.*) Is there anything on me?

FRANK. Quite a wild flower, isn't it?

JOHN. A daisy I should say. (*All laugh.*)

RICKETY. Now what are you laughing at me for?

FRANK. Oh, nothing in particular, but we must have something to laugh at. (*All laugh.*)

RICKETY. Think they're smart. I bet they don't know beans when the bag's untied. (*Exit into house, R.*)

FRANK. Well, we are doing very well. Only been here two hours, lawn tennis up, trunks in our rooms and by Jove! I'm hungry as a hunter.

ANNIE. (*comes down to R. of well*) So am I.

JOHN. (*has taken position at L. of well*) If supper isn't ready pretty soon, I am going to ask for a piece of bread and butter.

NELLIE. (*has taken position at L. of John*) Well, if I have to wait much longer, I shall faint.

FRANK. (*going to door of house*) Come over here and get a whiff of this.

ALL. What is it? (*All going to house.*)

FRANK. Fried pork.

ALL. Oh, doesn't it smell good!

FRANK. Yes, and I never could bear it at home.

ALL. Nor I.

RICKETY. (*entering from behind house, shouting*) Look out for snakes!
  (*Runs to back of well, laughing. The girls scream. Annie runs across and jumps on chair near lower corner of house, Frank on her L. Simultaneously, Nellie leaps on bench in front of well, with John on her L. Josh runs on from up L., hat in hand; enter Matilda from house--same business of jumping as Josh stands R.C.*)

JOSH. Hello! Hello! Hello! What's all this hollerin' about?

ALL. Snakes!

JOSH. Snakes? (*Jumps around and looks on ground.*) Git out! I don't see any snakes!

FRANK. (*pointing to Rickety*) Well, that sunflower over there said there was.

RICKETY. Oh, I didn't nuther! I said look out for snakes.

FRANK. (*helping Annie down from chair and same business for John and Nellie*) What did you say that for?

RICKETY. Well, I got to have something to laugh at, hain't I?
  (*All laugh but Josh and Matilda. Exit Rickety, up C., back of barn.*)

JOSH. Want to know if you're Henry Hopkins' boy!

FRANK. Yes, Mr. Whitcomb.

JOSH. How de-do? (*Shakes hands with Frank.*) Knowed your father first rate; he and I used to go to school together.

MATILDA. Looks a little mite like Henry used to, don't you think so, Joshua?

JOSH. Yes, a little mite, his hair ain't quite so red.

(*Frank crosses to Nellie and John, quietly communicating his delight. Josh turns to Annie.*)

I want to know if you are Henry's daughter?

ANNIE. Yes, Mr. Whitcomb. (*Crosses and shakes hands.*)

JOSH. Well, it beats all natur imazingly how these youngsters do grow.

MATILDA. She favors the Richardsons.

JOSH. So she does.

MATILDA. I can see it, she looks like her mother. Knowed your mother first rate when she was a gal.

(*Annie and Matilda retire up, R.C.; Annie explains the use of the racket which she holds in her hand.*)

JOSH. So did I, too.

FRANK. Mr. Whitcomb, this is Mr. Freeman and his sister.

JOSH. How de-do, sir? How de-do, Miss? Glad to see yer.

(*He shakes hands with Nellie and John, in front of well.*)

FRANK. They were on their way to the White Mountains, and I took the liberty of asking them to stop over a day or two.

JOSH. That's right! That's right! We'll stow 'em away somewhere. Now I want to call you all to order on one p'int.

ALL. What is it? (*Matilda and Annie come down R.*)

JOSH. Call me uncle and Matilda aunt; then we'll get acquainted quicker.

ALL. Why, certainly!

JOSH. Gosh! You are all dressed up like a circus, ain't you?

FRANK. These are lawn tennis suits.

JOSH. Little too slick to hay in. You'll have to get on your old clothes to-morrow.

FRANK. But we're all going fishing in the morning.

JOSH. Gosh! I thought so. I see yer net stuck up to dry over on the grass there. (*Pointing off, up R.*) Now what do you expect to catch in a scoop like that? (*Pointing to tennis racket in Frank's hand.*)

FRANK. What you see over there is a lawn tennis net, and this is a racket.

JOSH. Want to know.

FRANK. A new one on you, isn't it?

JOSH. Shouldn't wonder a mite.

MAGGIE. (*entering from house, R.*) If ye plaze, mum, shall I peel the potatoes or bile them with their jackets on? (*Exit into house.*)

MATILDA. That girl will be the death of me. (*Exit into house.*)

JOSH. Bile the potatoes with their jackets on? It won't surprise me if she biled them with their overcoats on--not a mite.

RICKETY. (*entering, L., speaking mysteriously to visitors*) Hush, don't say a word, but if any on you have got any gold watches, you'd better hide 'em, for I just seed the awfullest looking tramp running around one of the haystacks that I ever seed in all my life.

ANNIE. A tramp! Why, we'll all be robbed. Come, Nellie and John.

(*Exit Annie into house, followed by Nellie and John, quickly--back of well.*)

JOSH. Here! Here! Here! There ain't no danger, not a mite!

(*Turns to Rickety, who has crossed behind him.*)

What's the matter with ye, want ter scare everybody to death?

RICKETY. Well, if he ain't a robber, I jist bet he's a wild man escaped out of a menagerie.

(*Frank goes up stage, looking off L.; then leisurely down to L.C, at R. of well--in time for speech.*)

JOSH. Well, stop yer yawpin' and go get me a towel, and I'll wash up out here. (*Exit Rickety into house.*) And you help Aunt Tilda get supper ready.

(*Throws hat and glasses on chair at R. and puts glasses in hat. Then, going to steps--rolling up shirt sleeves--calls off, into house.*)

And tell Miss O'Flaherty to get her milking done before night.

FRANK. How is the fishing around here, Uncle Josh?

(*Enter Rickety with towel, places it on bench by rain barrel and house, and exit back into house.*)

JOSH. Gosh! I don't know! Ain't been fishin' since I was a boy.

FRANK. How is that?

JOSH. Ain't had time.

(*Goes to bench, takes tin wash bowl, dips water out of barrel at corner of house while he speaks; soaps his hands with a piece of brown soap and washes his face--after speaking; and then comes to R.C. with one eye closed to keep out soap, drying hands and face with towel.*)

FRANK. No? (*Sitting on R. edge of bench at well.*)

JOSH. No, we have to scratch around up here like a hen with forty chickens to pay taxes and keep out of the poor house. We don't have much time for fishin', I can tell you. How's your father?

FRANK. Quite well, thanks.

JOSH. Got rich, I hear. (*Crosses to wash bench, throwing down towel.*)

FRANK. Yes, rated at over a million.

JOSH. (*amazed, crossing to C.*) Christopher Columbus! A million dollars?

FRANK. Quite a sum of money, isn't it?

JOSH. Gosh! I guess it is. Only think on't, he and I sit on the same bench together in the district school.

FRANK. Yes; I've often heard him speak of it.

JOSH. You can see the old schoolhouse down there just over the tops of them trees. (*Points off L.*) Stands right across from that old barn with a load of hay on it.

FRANK. (*looking off L.*) Yes, I see it.

JOSH. 'Twas a new building then, but age is beginning to tell on it. We are growing old together. Many's the time that your old dad and I got our jackets tanned there, I can tell you.

FRANK. I suppose so.

JOSH. New York must be a pretty smart sort of a village, I guess, ain't it?

FRANK. Well, I should say it is. Were you never there?

JOSH. No, sir. Never sot foot in it.

　　(*Goes to chair, R, takes hat and glasses and puts them on.*)

But I'm going there one of these days to look for my boy.

FRANK. (*rising*) Why, have you a son in New York?

JOSH. (*reflectively*) I don't know--I did have four or five months ago. Ain't heard nothin' from him since.

FRANK. He went there thinking to make his fortune, I suppose?

JOSH. Well, not exactly. Might as well tell you first as last, 'cause you're sure to hear on't, and I want you to hear on it right! Pull up a chair and sit down. (*Gets chair at R. and bringing it R.C., sits.*)

FRANK. Yes, thank you, I will.

　　(*Takes chair near well and sits, R.C, about three feet L. of Josh.*)

JOSH. About a year ago now he was cashier in the Cheshire Bank in Keene, a few miles from here. Well, it seems one day, a party of sharps from Boston went to Keene and went into the bank and when some of them were talking to Reub, one of the mean sneaks got into the vault and stole a lot of money.

FRANK. He did?

JOSH. Gosh! Yes. It all came out on the trial. Well, they pitched on to my boy and had him arrested right before a lot of visitors from Boston on suspicion of robbing the bank; but they let him go again pretty quick, I can tell you. When I think on't, I get so mad I perty near froth. Charged with stealing something he didn't know no more about than the man in the moon.

FRANK. What a shame!

JOSH. I guess it was. And he felt it dreadfully, too. I don't believe the boy has had a good night's rest since. He always imagined people p'inted at him and was down-hearted and low-spirited, so one day he packed his trunk and started for New York.

FRANK. So you think of going there to look for him, do you?

JOSH. I certainly shall.

FRANK. Why not go back with us?

JOSH. Gosh! I will if my new boots are done in time.

FRANK. And I will assist you to look for your boy in every way I can.

JOSH. Thank 'ee, thank 'ee. Now I am going to ask you something, and I know you will laugh at me.

FRANK. Why should I?

JOSH. Because it is so foolish. (*Looking mysteriously to house.*) Say, do you believe in dreams? (*Frank laughs.*) That's right, laugh--I don't blame you a mite.

FRANK. Why do you ask?

JOSH. Because I've had 'em about my boy lately--so nat'ral that it almost seems as though they must be true.

FRANK. That is the result of constantly thinking of him--nothing more, believe me.

JOSH. I hope not--I hope not.

RICKETY. (*entering from house*) Say, Uncle, Aunt Tildy says to ask you if you won't come in and cut some dried beef for supper.

JOSH. Why, sartin. (*Rises.*) Won't you come in the house, young man?

FRANK. (*rises and takes chair, replaces it by well*) No thanks--I'll stop out here and look around if you have no objections.

JOSH. Oh, no; make yourself at home. I don't care what you do as long as you don't set on my beehives-- (*Goes to steps, R.*) Be careful about that! (*Exit Josh into house.*)

RICKETY. (*looking about mysteriously*) Say, who be you anyway? I didn't know you was comin'.

FRANK. No? Then there must be something wrong about it, isn't there?

RICKETY. Oh, I don't know.

FRANK. Well, I'm Frank Hopkins, and I am from New York. Now who are you?

RICKETY. Oh, well, I ain't very bright, folks say. My name is Mary Ann Maynard, but they call me Rickety Ann.

FRANK. What for?

RICKETY. I don't know--guess 'cause I had the rickets when I was little.

FRANK. Indeed!

RICKETY. (*looking about before speaking*) Say, do you know what?

FRANK. No, what is it?

RICKETY. Well, I can climb a tree jist as good as a boy. Want to see me?
(*She turns up stage as if to look for a tree.*)

FRANK. (*stopping her*) No, no! I'll take your word for it.

RICKETY. (*admiringly--surveying Frank*) Say, do you know you're awful nice lookin'?

FRANK. Thanks.

RICKETY. Yes, you be.

FRANK. Say, Rickety Ann, have you always lived here?

RICKETY. No, I was borrowed out o' the poor house jist to help Aunt Tildy while the visitors are here. But I guess I'll never go back there any more.

FRANK. No?

RICKETY. Aunt Tildy says if I am a good girl I may stay here jist as long as I want to, and I'm going to try and be good. Wouldn't you?

FRANK. I certainly should.

RICKETY. Say, you never lived in the poor house, did you?

FRANK. No indeed.

RICKETY. Oh, you wouldn't like it a bit, I bet!

FRANK. No.

RICKETY. 'Cos you don't get half enough to eat only on prize days!

FRANK. What do you get on prize days?

RICKETY. Well, on prize days the one that eats the most puddin' and milk gets a piece of pumpkin pie; and that last time I eat the most puddin' and milk.

FRANK. And you got the pie, of course.

RICKETY. No; eat so much puddin' and milk couldn't eat no pie. (*Cow bells heard, off.*) Oh, here comes the cows--I must go and drive them in the barnyard.
(*Exit Rickety, up L., calling "Co boss, co boss, co boss,"--calling cows.*)

FRANK. (*crossing to R.*) Good-bye.
(*Enter Maggie from house, crossing R. to L., singing an Irish ditty, looking around now and then at Frank in a flirting way and exit, up L. Frank in meantime is following her up, returning the flirtation.*)

ANNIE. (*appearing at door of house*) There, there! That will do, young man! Come and lift the tray out of my trunk. (*Exit into house.*)

FRANK. (*up L., speaking as he crosses R.*) Very well, Annie, but the next time I come to the country, I come alone.
(*Exit Frank into the house. Enter Matilda from house, who takes chair, R.C., and picks the stems from strawberries, which she has, from one pan to the other.*)

MATILDA. Well, I guess I'll pick the berries out here--a little mite cooler than it is inside.

(*Enter Rickety, up L.*)

RICKETY. (*crosses to R., singing*) "Cy Prime had a wife but I guess he killed her, now I guess he's comin' over to court Aunt Tilda."

MATILDA. (*rising indignantly*) What's that? What's that?

(Exit *Rickety hastily into house, laughing, and Matilda sits, busy with strawberries. Enter Cy, up L., with a small tin pail with berries, singing "Roll on, silvery moon, guide the traveller on his way."--*)

CY. (*sees Matilda--speaks aside, L.C.*) There she is--the smartest woman that every fried a nut cake or turned a flapjack. I hev been trying for nigh on to thirty years to ask Tildy to have me for better or worse, but could never muster up courage enough to pop the question; but I'll do it now or bust my galluses. I got a bran new speech all rit out that I'm going to speak to her--hev been studying it for the past six months. (*Aloud.*) Well, Tildy, how de-do--how de-do? (*Comes down R.*)

MATILDA. (*looking up, sees Cy*) How de-do, Cyrus?

CY. Here, I brought you a leetle mess o' rasberries. Found some pretty nice ones, and I thought I might as well bring them to you.

(*He hands small can of berries to Matilda.*)

MATILDA. Thank you, Cyrus. (*Takes berries and turns them into can she has.*) Come in awful handy. Had some, but we got company, and I was a leetle might afraid they wouldn't go around.

CY. Yes. Met Dr. Baxter--he told me you'd got company.

MATILDA. Been perty warm to-day, ain't it?

CY. Warm? Should think it was! Been hotter than mustard. Oh, it got so hot to-day over to the store that the mercury jumped right up and knocked the top off the thermometer!

MATILDA. (*smiling*) Oh, I guess not!

CY. Oh, I guess yes!

MATILDA. (*looking archly at Cy*) Oh, I guess not!

CY. (*hitching trousers and scraping ground with toe of boot*) Well, that's what I was told; but folks lie so nowadays you can't believe more'n half you hear.

MATILDA. I should think so!

CY. (*aside*) If she keeps on talking about the weather, I sha'n't get any chance to speak my new speech!

MATILDA. Cyrus, git a chair and sit down.

CY. Yes, don't care if I do. As I said before, it has been perty hot, and I've had a long walk and I'm nigh on tuckered out. (*Going to porch, near steps, sees cucumbers.*) Well, by jinks! That's a nice mess of cucumbers you've got there, to be sure. (*Takes up biggest one.*) That's a whopper, ain't it? Got some nice tomatoes, too.

(*Picks one up--then replaces it. He crossed down to L. of Matilda and speaks bashfully and hesitatingly.*)

Say, Tildy, I can remember when folks around here used to call them things love apples.

MATILDA. Yes, so can I.

(*Cy crosses to well--takes chair L. of Matilda after several movements as to proximity. He finally sits about two feet away.*)

CY. And they'd no more think of eatin' one o' them in them days than they ud think o' eatin' a toadstool now. (*Aside.*) I wonder how in Sam Hill my new speech begins? (*Thinks.*) Oh, oh yes--I know! (*Business.*) Well, Tilda--

(*She looks up at him as soon as he speaks, which knocks the lines out of his head.*)

MATILDA. Well, Cyrus?

CY. (*weakening, aside*) 'Tain't no use--I can't do it. She's knocked the first lines of my new speech clean out o' my head. (*Recovering.*) Well, Tildy, as I was going to say--

(*Enter Eb Ganzey from L. entrance, down stage. He crosses slowly from L., behind the well, to upper R. entrance, whistling "Devil's Dream," or other tune, in country style. Cy is obviously nervous at the interruption and follows Ganzey's movements till he goes off, up R., back of house, then he speaks.*)

Tildy, what's that Ganzey doin' around here?

MATILDA. Well, he's been helpin' the hired men down in the meadow and chorin' around here.

CY. Well, I don't s'pose you have to pay him nothin', do you?

MATILDA. Oh, yes! Guess Joshua gives him a little suthin'. Why?

CY. Well, I should think it would be a pretty tough match to get work enough out o' him to pay for what he eats.

MATILDA. Oh, well, he's growin', you know.

CY. Growin'! Well, I should think he was! He's longer than a shootin' match! Well, Tilda, I thought I'd come over here to-day to see if you-- that is, I thought I'd come over to ask you if you thought that--Tildy, what kind o'--what kind er--

(*Re-enter Ganzey, from above house, R., whistling softly and with an ear to the dialogue. He has an empty pail--goes to well--draws bucket of water--fills pail, and waits for cue.*)

MATILDA. What kind o' what?

CY. Paint would you put on a house if you wanted to make it look yaller.

MATILDA. Yaller paint, of course!

CY. Yes, that would be a good idea. Wonder I didn't think of it before.

GANZEY. (*from well, taking bucket in hand*) And if you want the house to look green, put on green paint. (*Exit, whistling, up R., above house.*)

CY. (*commencing to get angry and watching Ganzey off*) Tildy, does that boy whistle all the time?

MATILDA. Pretty much; he's got to be a chronic whistler.

CY. A comic whistler?

MATILDA. Chronic whistler!

CY. Oh, yes! A chronic whistler! Well, if he comes fooling around where I be agin, I'll give him somethin' that'll cure him of his chronicness.
    (*Continues speaking as he takes soiled paper of speech from pocket and gazes at it sideways, unobserved by Matilda.*)
Yes, Tilda, I thought I'd get some yaller paint and put it on my house and make it look yaller; and then I'd get some dark green paint and put on the door and make that look green; and then I'd get a new brass knocker and put that on the front door and make that look brassy; then get a half a dozen new cane seat chairs and put them in the parlor.
    (*Enter Rickety from house; whispers to Matilda; both exeunt hurriedly into house.*)
I been laying awake pretty nigh all night thinkin' I'd come over here to-day and ask you to have me for better or worse, there!
    (*Business of astonishment, etc. Gets up from chair and looks all around for missing Matilda.*)
Well, I guess I'm about as fur off as ever and, if anything, a little mite further off, but never mind, I've made up my mind to it and that's all there is about it.
    (*Sits again. Enter Matilda from house and sits in chair.*)

MATILDA. Well, Cyrus, what do you think?

CY. I don't know, Tilda, what is it?

MATILDA. My cake is all crisp.

CY. (*aside*) Well, I'm afraid mine is all dough.

MATILDA. That gal has gone and let that cake get all burned up and makes me so plaguey mad!

CY. Oh, well, I wouldn't get mad if I was you. She couldn't help it--she was born that way, wasn't she?

MATILDA. But we ain't got no cake in the house. Now what'll folks think on't to see no cake on the table for supper?

CY. Well, that's a pretty serious question, Tilda, I must confess; but if I was in your place, I'd put on plenty of applesass and nut cakes; then I don't think they'd miss the cake much. And I was goin' to tell you furthermore, Tilda, I got a new kitchen stove put up in my kitchen, too!

MATILDA. Sho', have yer?

CY. Yes, the old one is pretty nigh all burned out, and I got my old horse and wagon all painted up fresh, and my sister Betsy was asking me this very morning what I was gettin' things so all fired slicked up for, so I told her right out plump and plain that I was comin' over here and I was goin' to say to you--

(*Enter Rickety from house, down steps.*)

RICKETY. Supper is ready. (*Goes up stage and exit, R., above house.*)

CY. (*aside*) Supper is ready. So am I pretty nigh ready for the crazy house.

MATILDA. (*rising and placing chair at corner of house, down stage*) All right! Cyrus, come now and we'll set right down to supper.

(*Exit Matilda into house.*)

CY. Yes, Tilda, but before we go to supper I'd like to git a question o' mine answered. (*Arises from chair, disgusted. Places chair at R. of well.*) Now I'd like to know how a man supposed to have his head full of green paint and yaller paint and brass knockers and cane seat chairs--

(*Ganzey whistling, off. Cy goes to cucumbers--picks them up and lays for him. Enter Ganzey. As he crosses to well, Cy pelts him with cucumbers. Ganzey runs off, dropping pail. Cy kicks pail and cries.*)

Oh!!

MATILDA. (*entering from house*) Well, Cyrus, what's the matter?

CY. What's the matter? Why, it's all over with me.

MATILDA. Nonsense!

CY. Yes; I have just kicked the bucket.

MATILDA. Come in to supper.

(*Exeunt both into house. Re-enter Ganzey, up L, looks around cautiously while whistling--picks up pail and goes to well to draw water.*)

MAGGIE. (*entering, up. L., crosses down to R.C.*) Hey, sonny! Mind yourself or you'll fall in the well and spile the water!

GANZEY. That's all right! You're going to catch it!

MAGGIE. And for what?

GANZEY. The cake is all burnt up!

MAGGIE. And what if it is? What have I got to do with it? I can't watch the cake and milk the cows all at one time, can I? I wonder do they think I'm twins?

(*Exit Maggie into house. Enter Quartette as farmers from up R., behind house, and crosses to well, leaving rakes and pitchforks up stage.)*

GANZEY. *(crossing to R.C.)* Say, boys, you'll have to wait a little while for supper. Uncle Josh has got visitors and the first table is full.

FIRST MAN. That's all right, we're in no hurry. I guess we can wait if you can. *(All laugh.)*

GANZEY. *(laughing mockingly)* I can wait as long as any on ye, come right down to it. *(Exit, up R., behind house.)*

FIRST MAN. *(drinking water which he dips from bucket)* That tastes good. I tell you, boys, there's nothing like water out of the bucket in a tin dipper--beats all your tomfool drinks in the country. It's as good as the song--as the old bucket itself. Let's sing it while we're waiting for supper?

(They sing "Old Oaken Bucket," "Hard Times Come Again No More." During encore enter Ganzey and Rickety from above house, R. Rickety sits on doorstep while Ganzey stands by barrel, looking into it. Extra ladies may enter from above house, during first song, as if they had been berrying. They stand, C., listening, and exeunt, up L., after singing is over. Exit Quartette, R., back of house.)

GANZEY. Oh, Rickety, come here! *(Looking earnestly into barrel.)*

RICKETY. *(going to barrel)* What do you want?

GANZEY. Look! There's wigglers in the water barrel.

(Tramp heard singing "White Wings," off L. Ganzey and Rickety both go to up L. entrance and look off. Ganzey runs off, up R. Rickety runs toward house until stopped by Tramp. Enter Happy Jack, up L.)

RICKETY. *(in doorway, startled)* I'll tell Uncle!

JACK. One moment, my pretty gazelle.

RICKETY. What's that?

JACK. Come here.

RICKETY. *(timidly)* What do you want?

JACK. I would banquet, fair maid. I'm a prestidigitator.

RICKETY. *(awed--dropping down a step)* A what-a-ta-tor?

JACK. That is, I make things disappear.

RICKETY. *(starts to go into house)* Well, I thought so!

JACK. Stay! For instance, I take a couple of slices of bread thusly-- *(pretends to palm pieces of bread)*--place a piece of cold meat between them, presto change! Gone!

RICKETY. Sho'! That's nothing! Anybody can do that.

(She tries to imitate him.)

JACK. Well, to be plainly spoken, I would eat, ma amie.

RICKETY. *(starts to go into house)* No, you won't eat me, nuther!

JACK. Stay! Don't light a fire for me! Just plain every-day bread and a little cold meat will do; don't care for turkey.

RICKETY. Well, you won't get nuthin' here. (*Exit into house.*)

JACK. No? Then I'll score my first failure. (*Strikes chest.*) Happy, old boy, how is your high C?

(*Business running scale and breaking into "Nobody's Darling," or other song. He crosses to well, L.C. Enter Josh from house and crosses to R.C.. Matilda and Rickety enter from house and group at doorstep.*)

JOSH. (*amused*) I can't help that.

JACK. (*very polite*) Probably you would like something different.

(*Starts "Sixteen Dollars on My Inside Pocket" or other popular air.*)

JOSH. Tut! Tut! I got visitors. I don't want none o' that!

JACK. (*very polite*) All right!

JOSH. How'd you get here?

JACK. (*laughs*) Came in on a hot wave.

JOSH. Who be you?

JACK. (*bows low*) A man without a home; poor, but a gentleman still.

JOSH. You're a tramp, I guess, ain't you?

JACK. Well, vulgarly speaking, yes; properly, no!

JOSH. What be you?

JACK. A natural result.

JOSH. Of what?

JACK. Drink!

(*Matilda throws hands up in horror and quietly goes into house.*)

JOSH. By gum! You look like it.

JACK. (*bows low*) Thanks!

JOSH. You seem pretty sober now.

JACK. It's a dead force though, I can assure you.

JOSH. Shouldn't wonder. You've got one thing in your favor, Mr.--

JACK. What is it, sir?

JOSH. You ain't afraid to tell the truth.

JACK. (*bows low*) Thank you. (*Crosses to L. of well, "sprucing up."*)

JOSH. (*turning to Rickety*) Politer than a pair o' sugar tongs. (*To Jack.*) Git a chair and set down. (*Aside.*) Somethin' good about this fellow, if he ain't a hypocrite. If he is, I'll find him out pretty quick.

(*Josh takes chair from R., places it R.C. and sits. Jack has gone above well--look in--takes dipper--then turns to Josh.*)

JACK. Old gentleman, can I have a drink?

JOSH. Certainly, help yourself. Pitch right in.

JACK. Won't you join me?

(Business. Jack laughs--drinks mouthful--makes face.)

JOSH. That's pretty good--out o' my own well, too. What's the matter? Don't like it, do you?

JACK. Well, it tastes a little weak.

JOSH. 'Tain't quite so strong as you're used to drinking.

JACK. You struck it right the first time, old gentleman.

(He turns water from dipper into bucket by well and puts dipper in bucket. Takes chair by well and, placing it a few feet of Josh, sits.)

JOSH. I thought so. Now, are you hungry?

JACK. Well, I think I could manage to eat a tart if it were not too large.

RICKETY. *(back of Josh, R.C.)* Well, if that ain't cheek. Guess I'd better shut up the hens.

(She starts to cross up to L. entrance. Josh stops her--she comes back with a suspicious eye on Jack.)

JOSH. Here, Rick, come here. You go and tell Aunt Tildy to git a couple slices o' bread and butter and bring them here.

(Rickety starts for house slowly.)

JACK. *(rising--to Rickety)* Skip!

(Exit Rickety quickly. Jack coughs as Josh is stooping to look at Jack's boots. Jack coughs violently over him, at which Josh, rising, jumps away and puts handkerchief over top of head as it to protect himself.)

JOSH. You got a cold, ain't you?

JACK. *(coughing)* Yes, a slight one. Guess I must have left the bars down last night.

JOSH. Where did you stop?

JACK. *(crossing to front of well)* At Widow Green's.

JOSH. At Widow Green's?

JACK. Yes.

JOSH. *(innocently)* I don't know no Widow Green around here.

JACK. *(advancing to Josh at R.C.)* Why, my dear old unsophisticated--

JOSH. Here, here! That'll do!

JACK. We knights of the road call a hayfield "Widow Green."

JOSH. Oh, you do, do you?

JACK. Yes, I guess I must have crawled in the north side of a stack. The fact is, I am getting heedless of late. *(Feeling inside coat pocket.)* Haven't got a cigarette about you, have you?

JOSH. *(decisively, as he sits)* No, sir, I don't smoke.

JACK. *(sits in his chair)* Quite right--it's a pernicious habit, anyways. The fact is I only smoke occasionally.

JOSH. Well, why don't you carry a pipe?

JACK. No; it makes your clothes smell.

JOSH. I guess you're kind of a comic, ain't you?

JACK. Well, there's no use crying over spilt milk, so I use a little philosophy now and then.

JOSH. Philosophy is all well enough in sunshine; but I should think you would want something a little more substantial in rough weather.

JACK. You're right there, old gentleman.

JOSH. Do you know, I often wonder how you fellows get along?

JACK. Yes?

JOSH. And what you think of, if you ever do think. What your aim in life is.

JACK. (*rising, walking to well and turning*) Well, I merely log along, grab on when I can. I'm acclimated and adjusted to all countries and climes, weather in the everglades of Florida or on the snowy ranges of the Sierras; it's all the same.

    (*Pause, as he crosses back to chair--puts R. foot on same--and chants.*)

I'm often drunk and seldom sober, win or lose I take my booze, for I'm Happy Jack the rover.

JOSH. Well, I declare! You are a good one to speak a piece! I guess you're a good deal like a singed cat: you feel better than you look.

JACK. (*laughing*) That's a good one, old gentleman. Well, there's no use denying what everybody can see, is there?

JOSH. No, that's so.

    (*Jack looks in front of him as if he sees coin, then picks it up.*)

JACK. Is this yours?

JOSH. What is it?

JACK. A ten-cent piece.

JOSH. Guess not. Ain't in the habit of carrying money around loose in my pockets. Maybe you dropped it yourself?

JACK. (*feeling inside pockets*) No, my money is all right. I might have lost my reputation or a trifle like that: but ten cents? Never!

JOSH. Never mind, keep it--it might come in handy.

JACK. (*sitting down*) Why, what would that little thing buy?

JOSH. A bar of soap.

JACK. Say, old gentleman, what are you trying to give me anyway?

JOSH. A little advice.

JACK. A little advice, eh?

JOSH. Yes, sir.

JACK. Advice is good. Say, did you ever try to live on it?

JOSH. Don't know as I ever did.

JACK. Well, try it and you will find it an excellent substitute for anti-fat.

JOSH. What's your name.

JACK. Jack.

JOSH. Jack what ?

JACK. Happy Jack.

JOSH. By gosh! It fits you, don't it?

JACK. (*laughs*) Like a glove.

JOSH. Where do you come from?

JACK. Nowhere.

JOSH. Where do you live?

JACK. Everywhere.

JOSH. Sho'! I want to know!

JACK. I am the champion deadhead of America, the star truck rider of the world. (*Rises, takes off hat, bows, and sits again.*)

JOSH. What do you mean by that?

JACK. That I ride from one end of the country to the other, without a dollar.

JOSH. What on?

JACK. The cars.

JOSH. Don't they put you off?

JACK. They don't see me.

JOSH. What's the reason they don't?

JACK. I ride underneath on the trucks.

JOSH. O-ho!

JACK. I don't travel on a train unless they run a sleeper.

   (*Josh whistles low in surprise.*)

They are better than common passenger cars--the trucks are wider and more comfortable and don't come quite so near your head.

JOSH. By gum! It must be pretty risky business, ain't it?

   (*Music cue for sympathetic music pp. in orchestra.*)

JACK. (*with pathos*) Yes. Not a day passes that some poor fellow is not either killed or maimed. Now last winter on our way south, my partner lost his life. I was riding on the rear truck and he was on the front. In rounding a curve the brace of the truck bent and caught him between the truck and the brace and smashed him to death. I had to ride nearly thirty-two miles listening to his pitiful cries for help, but I couldn't reach him, so he said: "Jack, old pard, you'll have to get another pal. I'm called in," and all was over with poor Tom. A higher power had put on the brakes. The engine of life was stopped.

   (*Jack buries face in old dirty handkerchief. Enter Matilda, from house, with two slices of bread, gives them to Josh and exit into house.*)

JOSH. (*rises, handing bread to Jack, and sits again*) Here, here!

JACK. (*rises, takes bread and puts in pocket as he speaks*) Thank you; I will not eat this now.

JOSH. Are your parents living?

JACK. (*wipes eyes with handkerchief*) One of them, sir.

JOSH. Which one?

JACK. My mother. (*Crossing a few steps, L., to hide emotion.*)

JOSH. Where?

JACK. In New York City.

JOSH. Poor?

JACK. No, sir, rich.

JOSH. Why, what made you leave home?

JACK. Simply because I couldn't have my own way.

JOSH. Well, you look as though you had had it lately. Now, why don't you go home?

JACK. Have you any sons?

JOSH. Yes, sir--one.

JACK. Where?

JOSH. In New York, I believe; he was there the last time I heard on him.

JACK. (*crossing back to chair*) Well, why doesn't he come home?

JOSH. Now by gosh! You have got me!

JACK. I'll tell you why I don't go home. Because I'm ashamed to! I'm no good--a wreck at thirty--look fifty, don't I?

JOSH. Pretty near.

JACK. Yes.

JOSH. Do you ever think?

JACK. Think of what?

JOSH. (*with pathos*) Your mother. How she watched you all through the cares and dangers of childhood; worked for you; prayed for you. I tell you, boy, you owe that mother more than you can ever repay. Her care may have saved your life a dozen times--you can't tell.

JACK. (*sits, penitently, with lowered head*) Say, old gentleman, you've set me thinking.

JOSH. I'm glad of it if I have. Now look here, will you go home if I give you money enough to pay your fare?

JACK. Yes.

JOSH. And stop drinking?

JACK. Whew! Say, old gentleman, that's a corker, but I'll try it.

(*Jack rises, puts chair back by well, then comes resolutely back to Josh.*)

JOSH. All right, sir--there's a ten-dollar bill. (*Gives ten-dollar bill to Jack.*) It won't break me, and it may make you. You can take a train and go as far as New Haven, then take a boat and be home in the morning.

JACK. Ten dollars, eh? (*Music stops.*)

JOSH. Yes, sir.

JACK. (*reflectively and with wonder*) Ten great big dollars! Say, old gentleman, if you had set the dog on me, it would have been more in my way.

JOSH. Why, what good would that do?

JACK. Oh, no good! It would seem more natural, that's all.

JOSH. I suppose so, poor fellow.

JACK. (*starts up stage to L.C. musingly*) Go home, yes! Stop drinking? (*Returns to Josh.*) Say, old gentleman-- (*Offering money.*) You had better take this money back. I don't honestly believe I can do as I have agreed.

JOSH. (*rising*) Well, you can try, can't you?

JACK. Yes, I can try.

JOSH. (*putting hand on Jack's shoulder*) That's right! Go home and try to be somebody; it ain't too late.

JACK. (*with determination*) Well, I will! And if I don't win, I'll give old John Barleycorn the toughest scuffle he ever had for the underhold. Good-bye, old friend, good-bye!

  (*Jack shakes hands and exit, up L., walking as if footsore.*)

JOSH. Good-bye, sir! (*Sits in chair, R.C., reflecting.*) Maybe I have done a foolish thing. Well, never mind--if he don't profit by it, it won't be my fault. But I kind of think he will. A man who can express so much feeling at another's misfortune must have a kind heart.

  (*Josh gazes meditatively in front. Mixed Quartette, off R., sings "Oh, Where Is My Boy To-night," pp., then gradually f. till finish of song and slow curtain.*)

ACT II.

Scene. A parlor of the Hopkins' mansion, New York City. A C. opening, or arch, at back through which is seen a corridor. In the C. of the corridor stands a large statue of Venus of Melos on a pedestal. The statue is flanked by palms, or flowering plants. Up stage, in the R. wall, a door leads off to the smoking and billiard room. Down stage in the L. wall is another door. A sofa, or divan, with pillows occupies the C. of the room, and back of it stands a library table with books, papers, a shaded lamp and a tap bell. In front of the sofa lies a white, or black, bear rug. Down stage R. stands a piano and stool. An easy chair, or armchair, stands to the L. of piano and a trifle above. A footrest, without legs, upholstered in the same material is in front of the armchair. Above the piano a standing piano lamp with shade. At L. C. a so-called "self rocker" rocking chair with a small table at L. of it on which is a vase of flowers. Down below L. door a chair. Above L. door a reception-hall chair. At back, R. of C. arch, a bookcase. At back, L. of C. arch, a writing desk and chair. Pictures on walls. Curtains on C. arch. Flowers in vases. The whole set symbolizes refined taste and culture. (*Mrs. Hopkins is seated at piano, R., playing. Mr. Henry Hopkins reclines on sofa, C., reading New York paper. Enter Francois, dressed in livery, from L. with a card on a tray, and presents same to Mrs. Hopkins. She stops playing--looks at card and replaces it on tray. Exit Francois, C. to L. Mrs. Hopkins rises and comes to R.C. Henry rises, folds paper, and throws it on table back of sofa.*)

HENRY. Who is it, Lizzie?

MRS. HOPKINS. Judge Patterson and his daughter.

HENRY. Oh, I am glad of that. I was thinking of the Judge just a moment ago. I want his opinion regarding some real estate I think of purchasing.
    (*Henry crosses down to L.C., awaiting arrivals. Enter Nellie Patterson and Judge Patterson. Mrs. Hopkins, goes up stage, kisses Nellie and shakes hands with Judge. Mrs. Hopkins and Nellie stand R.C. up stage until Judge and Henry sit, later, up L.*)

JUDGE. (*as he enters*) Good-evening, Mrs. Hopkins.

MRS. HOPKINS. Good evening, Judge.

HENRY. Well, Judge, how are you?

JUDGE. (*coming down to R. of Henry*) Splendid. We have just returned from a drive through the park, and Nellie insisted upon calling to see if Frank and Annie had returned.

HENRY. I am very glad you did, as I desire your opinion regarding that 85th Street property belonging to the Lennox estate.
    (*Business: going up stage, L. Judge sits on reception chair above L. door and Henry, drawing chair from writing desk, sits beside him. Mrs. Hopkins and Nellie come down and sit on sofa.*)

MRS. HOPKINS. We received a dispatch from the children this morning. They will be home this evening. The coachman has driven to the station to meet them--expect them every moment.

NELLIE. Why, how long have they been absent? A week or more, is it not?

MRS. HOPKINS. A fortnight yesterday and how we have missed them!

NELLIE. I am sure you must have! How tanned Annie will be! I do so long to see her!

(*Door-bell rings, off L. Mrs. Hopkins and Nellie rise; Nellie goes up stage R.; Mrs. Hopkins turns R. and goes to arch.*)

MRS. HOPKINS. That must be the children. Henry, they are here!

(*Enter Frank and Annie. Annie kisses Mrs. Hopkins., followed by Frank. Henry and Judge arise. Annie kisses Henry and bows to Judge and Nellie--then back to Mrs. Hopkins., who leads her to sofa, speaking as they go and sit. Frank sits in armchair, R., Nellie sits on piano stool.*)

Now then, Annie, come tell me. What kind of a time did you have?

ANNIE. Just lovely!

MRS. HOPKINS. And how is dear old Matilda?

ANNIE. She's splendid.

HENRY. And Uncle Joshua?

JOSH. (*outside*) How do you git in here, anyway?

FRANK. Here he is--he can answer for himself.

ANNIE. We brought him with us. He is awfully odd, but you can't help liking him, he's so good. (*Going up stage to door and looking off.*) No, no--not up stairs; this way, Uncle Josh. (*At entrance of Josh, all rise.*)

JOSH. (*entering, taking Annie's right hand in his left*) I hain't got the hang o' the schoolhouse yit, but I'll fetch it. Annie, you got visitors, hain't ye?

ANNIE. This is my father, Uncle.

JOSH. (*shaking hands heartily*) You ain't Henry Hopkins--Hank Hopkins, Red-headed Hank!

HENRY. (*laughs*) Yes, the very same.

JOSH. How de-do? Glad to see ye.

HENRY. (*introducing*) My wife.

JOSH. (*shaking hands*) I want to know if you are Henry's wife?

MRS. HOPKINS. Yes, Mr. Whitcomb.

JOSH. Let me see--you was a Richardson, warn't ye?

MRS. HOPKINS. Yes, Mr. Whitcomb.

JOSH. Betsy Richardson!

MRS. HOPKINS. (*haughtily*) Elizabeth Richardson!

JOSH. Yes, I remember we just to call you Bets, for short. I can remember the first time I ever saw you just as well as if 'twas yesterday.

MRS. HOPKINS. Indeed!

JOSH. Yes. You druv down to the store with your father on a load of wood. I never will forget how pretty you looked that day in your new calico frock and sunbonnet and new yarn stockings, hanging down over that load of maple.

(*As Mrs. Hopkins appears annoyed, Frank takes Josh by arm and leads him to where Judge stands.   Henry laughs heartily, angering Mrs. Hopkins, who seats herself, R., as Henry follows, stands behind her chair, and tries to pacify her.*)

FRANK. (*introducing*) Judge Patterson, Mr. Whitcomb.

JUDGE. (*shakes hands*) How do you do?

JOSH. How de-do? Let me see, you ain't any relation of old Judge Patterson that used to keep the soap factory at Chesterfield, be you?

JUDGE. (*laughs*) No, sir--

JOSH. Well, but I didn't know but what you was.

JUDGE. No, sir; no, sir!

(*Josh looks up casually and sees the statue of Venus, jumps up and runs off, C., returning immediately to stare at statue.*)

JOSH. Henry--

HENRY. Well?

JOSH. Was she a New York lady before she died? (*All laugh heartily.*)

MRS. HOPKINS. (*annoyed*) Henry, for goodness' sake, take him away or I shall go frantic.

HENRY. Where shall I take him?

MRS. HOPKINS. Anywhere--to the stables!

JOSH. What's that about stables? What kind of a barn hev you got anyway, Henry?

HENRY. A perfect beauty! Would you like to have a look at it?

JOSH. Sartin. I wanted to help your man onharness and fodder, but he said he guessed he could do it all right. (*Looking at Mrs. Hopkins.*) They won't be mad if Henry and I go out to the barn, will they?

MRS. HOPKINS. (*sarcastically*) No; I don't think they will!

JOSH. Well, I hope not. Frank, look out for my trunk.

FRANK. I'll attend to that, Uncle.

JOSH. Hev you milked yet?

HENRY. (*laughs*) Oh, long ago! Come along with me; I'll show you a beautiful barn. (*They exeunt, C. arch to L.*)

JUDGE. Oh, there, never mind, Mrs. Hopkins--don't feel annoyed. We understand your position perfectly; let us treat it in the proper spirit. (*Laughing.*) I know it's terribly embarrassing, but it's awfully funny.

MRS. HOPKINS. Well, I suppose I might as well laugh as cry. (*Laughs.*)

JUDGE. Certainly. But it's too funny for anything, isn't it? (*Laughs.*)

ANNIE. Frank and I are really to blame. Ma and Pa knew nothing of his coming. We brought him with us because he wanted to see New York, and to find his son who left his home about a year ago. He has not heard from him for a long time, and the fear that something happened to him constantly worries him. He didn't look half so funny in the country.

JUDGE. I suppose not.

FRANK. And, Mother, we wished to surprise you with old recollections.

MRS. HOPKINS. (*rising*) You have been entirely successful. (*All laugh.*)

ANNIE. Come, Nellie, I have so much to tell you about Swanzey and Chesterfield.

(*Exeunt Nellie and Annie, followed by Mrs. Hopkins.*)

FRANK. Now, Judge, won't you come with me into the smoking room and join me in a cigar?

JUDGE. The very thing, my boy. "Was she a New York lady before she died?"

(*Judge and Frank exeunt, up R., laughing, as Henry and Josh enter, L., laughing.*)

JOSH. I knowed you'd laugh when I told you about it. (*Looking around.*) Hello! Where's all the visitors gone?

HENRY. Oh, they are about the house somewhere. Come, Joshua, sit down. (*Sits on sofa, offering Josh a seat.*)

JOSH. You don't set on that, do you?

HENRY. Why, certainly.

JOSH. Go 'long--it'll spile it, won't it?

HENRY. No--no.

JOSH. No danger of going through, is there?

HENRY. No--no. (*Josh sits, then jumps up suddenly.*) What's the matter?

JOSH. Gosh! I thought I sot on a cat. (*Sits.*)

HENRY. (*laughs*) Well, Joshua, I suppose the old farms at Swanzey are pretty well worn out by this time?

JOSH. Well, the yield ain't quite so good as they used to be, and it's been a leetle worse this year than ever. Then we hev had a good deal to contend with--the season's been dry and we've had two circuses and a balloon ascension, and a wrestling match, and one thing and another; and old Abe Hill always contended such things hurt crops worse than grasshoppers.

HENRY. Joshua, is the old meetin' house there yet?

JOSH. The main part on't is--they got it raised up; new stained windows in, new belfry on, and one thing and another, so it don't look much as it did when you and I had our marriages published on the front of it.

HENRY. No, I suppose not. Is the old house still standing.

JOSH. Our old house?

HENRY. Yes.

JOSH. Jist the same. You remember the old kitchen, don't you?

HENRY. Indeed I do.

JOSH. And the old fireplace where you and I and brother Bill and Eb and Dad Cross used to sit around cold winter nights, when we was boys popping corn and telling Injun stories.

HENRY. (*laughing*) And we use to get so frightened we were almost afraid to go to bed.

JOSH. Bill was a master hand to tell stories, warn't he?

HENRY. Indeed he was. Tell me, Joshua, are the Shaw boys living?

JOSH. All dead--every one o' them.

HENRY. You don't say so!

JOSH. Yes.

HENRY. And the Pattersons?

JOSH. All living but Bill, and I guess he'd 'a' ben if he'd 'a' stayed to home.

HENRY. How is that?

JOSH. Well, Bill always had a kind o' roving turn o' mind, and he got oneasy and went out west somewhere, out to Montanny, I guess it was; and he got tangled up with politics and whiskey and a piece of rope and kind 'o discouraged him a leetle mite. Henry, I guess you must remember the Divine boys?

HENRY. (*thinking*) Divine boys?

JOSH. You must remember the youngest--Deuteronomy?

HENRY. Yes, of course, I do.

JOSH. Well, he got a new glass eye.

HENRY. (*laughs*) No!

JOSH. Yep--don't wear it only Sundays though. (*Henry laughs.*) You see, Deut lost an eye during the war, and he never felt able to get one till t'other day he went up to Keene and got one o' the jewelers to send down to Boston and get him one. When he got it home, it didn't fit very well-- was a leetle mite too big, I guess. However, he put it in his eye and started for meetin' the fust Sunday he got it, and he come pretty near breakin' the meetin' up before he got home.

HENRY. How was that?

JOSH. Well, it appears Deut got to sleep during sarvice and commenced to snore.

HENRY. Yes.

JOSH. And old Mrs. Munsel sot in the pew right in front him and she turned around to nudge him and there was Deut fast asleep, one eye shut and the new one wide open. (*Both laugh heartily.*) Scart the old woman so she squaked right out in meetin', like a guinea hen.

HENRY. I don't suppose Deut ever wore it again.

JOSH. Oh, yes, he did--he took it to the blacksmith's and got it filed down and it works fust rate now.

HENRY. Oh, go along! (*Shoving Josh with left hand.*) Joshua, whatever became of Nick Ludlow?

JOSH. Dead.

HENRY. (*surprised*) No!

JOSH. Yes; died last April.

HENRY. You don't say so! What complaint?

JOSH. No complaint--everybody satisfied. (*Henry laughs heartily.*) Now, Henry, I'm going to ask you suthin' jist to see if you remember it.

HENRY. (*turns half back to Josh*) Well, go on.

JOSH. Now look out!

HENRY. Well, I'm waiting for you.

JOSH. Do you remember the first circus you and I ever went to see?
   (*Both laugh heartily--Josh falls back on sofa, recovers himself, rubs top of head with both hands, and sinks back, laughing as though exhausted.*)

HENRY. And how we laughed at the old clown!

JOSH. And et ginger bread!

HENRY. Yes.

JOSH. Henry, do you remember that?

HENRY. Remember it? I shall never forget it as long as I can remember anything.

JOSH. Me nuther! I spent forty-one cents that day!

HENRY. We went together, don't you remember?

JOSH. So we did!

HENRY. I called for you at your house.

JOSH. There! That's right.

HENRY. It was the first you ever wore a round-about suit.

JOSH. (*proudly*) So it was!

HENRY. Oh, you were dressed to kill that day!

JOSH. Gosh! I guess I was! You had on a new store hat and I had to wear the old one Til braided. You beat me on the hat but I kind o' cut you out on the clothes. (*Chucks Henry in ribs--both laugh.*)

HENRY. Yes.

JOSH. Both on us barefoot.

HENRY. Yes, both of us. (*Josh gives Henry affectionate shove.*) And away we both started for Keene and the circus. (*With pathos.*) And don't you remember, Joshua, that when we got on top of that little hill near Jackson's we looked back and there was your dear old mother standing in the doorway. (*Rising and folding his hands in pantomime.*) Her hands wound up in her apron, with her head thrown back, the way she had a way of doing, looking at us through her big, bowed spectacles, wondering, I suppose, which one of us would be president first. (*Sits.*)

JOSH. (*with feeling, shaking hands and looking over glasses*) Happy days, Henry!

HENRY. Happy, indeed, Joshua.

JOSH. (*with pathos*) No use talking, children little know the anxiety parents have for them. I've got a boy all alone in this great city and I'm dreadfully worried about him.

HENRY. Don't you know where he is stopping?

JOSH. No, I don't.

HENRY. And hasn't he written you?

JOSH. Not for four or five months.

HENRY. Oh, well--we must hunt him up for you. What was he doing when you last heard from him?

JOSH. He warn't doin' nothin'. Said he expected to get something to do before long and writ a little mite as though he was discouraged. And when I answered I guessed he'd better come back again--but you know how it is with boys when they go away from home to make their living, they hate to come back and have folks say they warn't smart enough to do it; and Reub is kind o' proud-spirited. I don't know as I blame him much--like as not he's out o' money--maybe he's sick and perhaps he's--

(*He puts handkerchief to eyes and completely breaks down.*)

HENRY. (*patting Josh on back soothingly*) Come, come--old friend, this won't do--cheer up! We'll find him for you yet.

JOSH. (*brightening*) Think so?

HENRY. I know it.

JOSH. (*grasping Henry's hand warmly*) Henry, I'll sleep all the better to-night for them few words of encouragement.

HENRY. I hope so.

JOSH. (*wiping eyes*) I feel sure on 't.

HENRY. By the way, Joshua, I had almost forgotten to ask you if you had your supper yet.

JOSH. No; I don't want any nuther. I ate two plates of beans at Springfield as I come along, and besides my carpet-bag is about half full of nut cakes, and I have been nibbling on them the biggest part of the way. Henry, I ain't very particular about my eatin' but if you could manage it so I can sleep somewhere near the earth, I would like it fust rate. The fact on it is, I am a leetle mite skittish about fires, and I'd like to be where I can step right out in case of a flare-up. I am a poor hand to shin down a lightning rod.

HENRY. (*laughs lightly*) Oh, well, we can arrange that for you very readily--(*pointing at door down L.*)--you can sleep in my private office right on the ground floor here.

JOSH. No; can I though?

HENRY. Yes.

JOSH. That'll suit me fust rate.

(*Henry reaches back and strikes gong on table. Josh is startled.*)

Gosh! It ain't one o'clock, is it?

HENRY (*laughs*) One o'clock! What an idea!

(*Enter Francois from L. Josh rises and bows very low to him. Henry, astonished, rises and pushes Josh back gently on sofa.*)

FRANCOIS. Yis, sur!

HENRY. (*sitting*) Where is Mrs. Hopkins?

FRANCOIS. In the library, sur.

HENRY. Very well. Tell Christina to have the folding bed in my private office let down for Mr. Whitcomb, who will occupy that room to-night.

FRANCOIS. Yis, sur!

JOSH. (*watching him off*) Who is that, Henry?

HENRY. My servant, Francois.

JOSH. Gosh! I thought it was some foreign lord!

HENRY. (*laughs*) Oh, no; oh, no! (*Door-bell rings.*)

JOSH. Got his trousers gallused up pretty high, ain't he?

HENRY. He has indeed.

JOSH. Outgrowed them a leetle mite, I guess.

HENRY. It looks like it, very much.

(*Re-enter Francois, from L., same business of presenting card on tray.*)

JOSH. There's the plate! Meetin's commenced.

(*Dives in pocket for change. Henry sees mistake, takes card, laughing. Josh covers face with handkerchief and leans back against sofa..*)

HENRY. (*looking at card*) Commissioner Nichols, eh?

FRANCOIS. Yis, sur. He says he won't detain you but a moment if you will jist step to the door.

HENRY. Very well. Excuse me, Joshua, for a moment. (*Rises.*) I have a little private business to transact and will join you presently. (*Exit, L.*)

JOSH. That's all right, Henry. Frenchy and I will visit here. (*To Francois.*) Come, sit down.

FRANCOIS. No, sur! It's against the rules.

JOSH. What's agin the rules?

FRANCOIS. To sit down.

JOSH. (*standing up*) I want to know! It ain't agin the rules for me to stand up and talk to you a little while, is it?

FRANCOIS. No, sur!

JOSH. (*going R.C. to Francois*) We ain't got very well acquainted, hev we? (*Striking Francois playfully with handkerchief.*)

FRANCOIS. Well, not very well, sur.

JOSH. What's your politics?

FRANCOIS. What do you think?

JOSH. Well, I'm a leetle mite divided in my opinions. (*Places handkerchief across Francois's throat.*) From here down--(*business*)--you look like a Republican; but from here up, you look like a Democrat.

FRANCOIS. Now I'll lay you can't tell what I am, and I'll give you two guesses.

JOSH. I bet I can.

FRANCOIS. Well, go on then.

JOSH. You're a Democrat.

FRANCOIS. No, sur!

JOSH. Republican?

FRANCOIS. (*approaching Josh--whispering*) Hi-ber-ni-an!

JOSH. (*surprised*) Well, that's the fust one of them critters I've seen. What makes you wear your trousers so short?

FRANCOIS. Sure an they make me!

JOSH. Who makes you?

FRANCOIS. The boss.

JOSH. Must be pretty rough on you in fly time.

FRANCOIS. Faith an' you're a funny man, Mr. Whitecomb.

JOSH. Whitecomb? My name is Whitcomb!

FRANCOIS. Fitcomb!

JOSH. Gosh! If I didn't know you was French, I'd think you was Irish.

FRANCOIS. Oui-oui; certe mong!

JOSH. Hello, hello! What kind o' lingo is that?

FRANCOIS. Shure, that's Frinch. I do be hearin' so much o' that kind o' talk I don't often know whether I am a New York French Irishman or an Irish French Canadian New Yorker, or a Bulgarian.

JOSH. Well, you'll get so mixed up some o' these days, they will have to run you through a separating machine.

(*Accidentally puts hand on gong on table--jumps back surprised; then*

walks slowly up stage until sees statuette; then jumps away.)
Now I don't want to ask any foolish questions, but I would like to know what they hev got that wax figger stuck up there for?

FRANCOIS. Werra, man, dear--that's not wax, that's alabaster marble.

JOSH. I want to know!

FRANCOIS. Why, certainly!

JOSH. What do you do with it when the minister comes?

FRANCOIS. We don't do nothin' at all with it.

JOSH. You don't?

FRANCOIS. No, sur!

JOSH. I'll bet ten dollars if I put that up in my corn field, I'd be arrested before night. (*Exit Francois.*) It's darn lucky I didn't bring Matilda with me, she'd put for home jist as soon as she seed any sich sight as that.

HENRY. (*entering, L, putting hand on Josh's shoulder*) Joshua, wouldn't you like to join us in the smoking room and have a little chat before you retire?

JOSH. (*winding old-fashioned watch*) No; I guess not, Henry. I'm kind o' tired and sleepy, and I'll go to bed so as to be up bright and arly and look for Reub, you know.

HENRY. Is there anything I can do for you before going?

JOSH. Let me see--yes, you can ask your hired man if he won't bring my trunk up into my room--wish you would--if he ain't too busy.

(*Henry goes to table, strikes bell and rejoins Josh. Enter Francois.*)

HENRY. (*laughs*) Have Mr. Whitcomb's trunk brought up immediately.

FRANCOIS. Yis, sur. (*Exit.*)

HENRY. Now, Joshua, excuse me a moment or two, and I'll see you before you retire.

JOSH. That's all right, Henry. I want to look around here a little while before I go to bed, anyway.

(*Exit Henry. Josh observes square footrest in front of armchair, upholstered in same material as the furniture. He looks about and sees all chairs supplied with cushions except the reception chair.*)

Somebody must have knocked the cushion out of one of the chairs.

(*He picks up footrest and, crossing, places it in reception chair and, gaping about, exit, down L. Enter Francois, followed by a porter with old-fashioned trunk on shoulder. Francois stands L. while porter deposits trunk in Josh's room, then both exeunt, L. Enter Josh in shirt-sleeves, looking about as if in search for something. A slight pause. Enter Henry, Judge, and Frank from door, up R.*)

HENRY. Well, Judge, you're not going so soon?

JUDGE. Am very sorry but we must be going.

HENRY. *(sees Josh and puts hand on Josh's shoulder)* Why, Joshua, what are you doing here?

JOSH. I'm looking for a boot-jack. *(All laugh.)*
There! I suppose I've made some mistake agin.
(Sits on "self-rocker," which tips forward, and he falls on floor. Gets up, sits way back, and falls backward. Chair and all is caught behind by two foot high stool. Frank runs to his assistance each time he falls and helps him up. All laugh.)
Henry, rears up like a two-year-old, don't it? I know what I'd do with it if 'twas mine.

HENRY. What?

JOSH. Put martin gills on it.

HENRY. Joshua, we don't use boot-jacks here.
(All laugh.)

JOSH. *(still sitting in chair)* You don't?

HENRY. No.

JOSH. How do you get your boots off?

HENRY. We have them made so they will come off easy.

JOSH. Well, that is what our shoemaker never learnt yet.
(Crosses R. leg over L. knee and holds up boot.)
Henry, straddle that boot--why, you've done it lots o' times.
(Henry appears surprised at first, then, remembering old times, crosses to Josh, turns his back--Josh puts his foot between Henry's legs and with L. foot braces himself on Henry's back. Same business with other foot. When boots off, Henry crosses to Judge and places hand on Judge's shoulder, who is watching action. All laugh heartily. Josh picks up boot, crosses to C. and steps on white bear rug, which tickles his foot, and jumps off hurriedly and stands looking at Judge.)
What's the matter, Judge? That's the fust boot-jack you ever see like that, I guess, ain't it?

JUDGE. *(laughing heartily)* No; but it's the first one I have seen in a great many years.

JOSH. I suppose so. Some good leather in them boots, Henry.

HENRY. Yes.

JOSH. Now I'm all ready to tumble into bed.

HENRY. That's right.

JOSH. You tell the women folks I got kind o' sleepy and went to bed, won't you?

HENRY. Certainly.

JOSH. Might as well leave a sasser o' taller alongside o' the fireplace. I may want to grease my boots before you get up in the morning.

HENRY. All right.

JOSH. Good-night, Judge. (*Exit, L., into room.*)

HENRY. Good-night. Hope you will sleep soundly. Now, Frank, tell your mother to come in. (*Exit Frank, through arch.*) Dear old Joshua, he is the very embodiment of honesty and rural simplicity.

JUDGE. He is indeed, Henry.

(*Enter Annie, Nellie, Mrs. Hopkins, and Frank. Frank and Mrs. Hopkins remain at up C. Nellie sits on sofa. Annie crosses, C.*)

ANNIE. Well, father, how do you like Uncle Josh?

HENRY. First rate, daughter--first rate! I like a man, I don't care what shape he is.

ANNIE. Thank you. (*Goes R., sits on piano stool.*)

NELLIE. Father, don't you think it is time we said good-night?

JUDGE. Presently, dear.

HENRY. (*looking at watch*) Why this haste? It is scarcely ten.

JUDGE. Henry, call at the house some time next week, and we will look at the Lennox property together.

HENRY. Very well, what day do you propose?

JUDGE. Say Tuesday.

HENRY. There! That will suit me to a T. Now, Judge, before you go will you oblige me by singing my old favorite?

JUDGE. Certainly, Henry.

HENRY. Thank you.

JUDGE. (*going to piano*) Miss Annie, will you kindly play for me?

ANNIE. Why, certainly. What shall I play?

JUDGE. Your father's favorite.

(*Annie plays, he sings.*)

> The hush of midnight weaves its spell--
>> In peace the throbbing city lies;
> When lo!--afar, a distant bell
>> Gives echo through the wintry skies.
> Awake! Awake! the warning tolls,
>> There's danger lurking--dread and dire--
> Awake! Awake! the warning rolls:
>> The town's afire! The town's afire!

Chorus.

> Lo! the engine's clang and the pulsing roar
>> Of a thousand throats rise higher and higher;

Till the welkin swells the clamorous bells
    Of Fire!--Fire!--Fire!
(*During the song, when Judge sings "Fire!--Fire!--Fire! enter Josh, L.,
in his night dress, boots in R. hand, dragging his trunk with his L.,
shouting "Fire!" at the top of his voice. Henry runs in front of him to
stop him. Frank catches hold of the end of his trunk, holding Josh back,
who is struggling to get out of door, C. All laugh.*)

P.S. *At the end of this act there is generally a call. Josh slips off his
long night gown, pulls on his boots, goes before curtain in his shirt
sleeves, bows awkwardly--never stepping out of his character--is
always Joshua.*

ACT III.

Scene. Exterior of Grace Church, Broadway and Tenth Street, New
York, at night. The drop representing the church is hung about six feet
from the curtain line, admitting of entrances, R. and L. A lamp post,
without the framework, glass, or lamp, stands R.C. near the curtain line.
A U.S. letter box is attached to the lamp post. (*Chime of bells, off L. When
chimes stop, an organ is heard with mixed Quartette singing the "Psalms,"
or other selection, off, in church. Near the conclusion, enter Josh and Henry
and stand with backs to audience, listening to singing of choir.*)

JOSH. That's good music, Henry.
HENRY. First class, Joshua, first class.
JOSH. That's a good melodeon they've got in there. What meetin' house is
    this, Henry?
HENRY. Grace Church.
JOSH. (*looking up at spire*) By gum! It's a whopper, ain't it?
HENRY. It is indeed grand, Joshua. In my mind this is one of the prettiest
    sights in New York City. Especially by moonlight, as you see it now.
JOSH. Pretty and no mistake; beats the old Baptist meetin' house at
    Swanzey all holler, don't it?
HENRY. Comes pretty close to it, and we used to think that beat the
    world.
JOSH. So we did, Henry, so we did.
    (*In taking handkerchief out of pocket, pulls a letter with it.*)
There's that letter I wrote to Til and I forgot to put it in the post-office.
Have to do it the first thing in the morning, just as soon as I get up.

HENRY. No, no! Save yourself all that trouble; put it in the letter box. (*Points R.*) There.

JOSH. Is that a letter box?

HENRY. Yes.

JOSH. Gosh! Thought it was a knapsack strapped on there. (*Hesitating.*) No; I guess not! (*About to put letter in pocket.*) Somebody will hook it.

HENRY. No! No! It will be perfectly safe there.

JOSH. (*going to box and trying to lift the top*) How do you get the lid up?

HENRY. Oh, no; not that way! Here, I'll show you how.

(*Henry crosses to box, lifts lid, and Josh drops letter in.*)

JOSH. By gum, that's handy, ain't it?

HENRY. It is indeed.

JOSH. How they do improve now-a-days!

HENRY. Wonderful, perfectly wonderful!

JOSH. I suppose that's in the post-office by this time. Well, Henry, another day is pretty near gone and we ain't found Reuben yet.

HENRY. Well, well! Don't get discouraged; New York is a large place. We'll run across him yet.

JOSH. I don't know; I got my doubts about it now.

HENRY. (*comforting*) Come! Come, old friend, you mustn't be dis-heartened, we shall certainly find him. Now, Joshua, don't you think you'd better go home with me and have a good night's rest and you can start out nice and fresh in the morning.

JOSH. (*gratefully*) Henry, it's real good of you to help me look for Reuben, and I know I ought to do just as you say; but I would like to hang around a little while longer. It's right in the shank of the evening and I might run across him.

HENRY. Very true; but you know that I--

JOSH. I know that you got visitors up to the house and you want to go and visit with them, so you run right along home and I won't be long.

HENRY. Very well. You haven't forgotten the way there, have you?

JOSH. Well, I guess I ain't; let me see. (*Thinks.*) I go right straight up the road until you come to the first open lot.

HENRY. Yes, Union Square.

JOSH. Go right straight through that and keep right on till I get up as far as the Waldorf Tavern.

HENRY. That is right.

JOSH. Then keep straight ahead to where I see the stage go out this morning--

HENRY. The tallyho from the Plaza.

JOSH. Then cross over and it is a little ways up on the right-hand side.

HENRY. That's correct. You'll not get lost.

JOSH. Well, I guess not! I didn't live in Boston two weeks, last summer, for nothin'.

HENRY. No?

JOSH. No! Streets so crooked there pretty near made me cross-eyed afore I got home.

HENRY. (*laughing*) They must be crooked indeed.

JOSH. Crooked! I guess they was. I had to get Jack Martin's boy to put a halter on me and take me up to the Common every morning and let me go. Didn't make no difference with way I struck out, I always fetched up on Boston Common.

HENRY. Yes; but how did you get home at night?

JOSH. Same boy there with the halter and a hand full o' oats.

HENRY. (*laughingly*) Oh, Joshua, not quite so bad as that, I guess!

JOSH. Well, perhaps not, Henry; but it warn't far from it.

HENRY. (*starting off*) Well, I must be going.

JOSH. All right. Tell the folks I won't be out late.

HENRY. See that you're not. Good-bye for the present. Good-bye.

   (*Exit Henry, R.1E.*)

JOSH. Good-bye, Henry. Guess folks must think I'm crazy--staring at everybody as though I never see nothin' afore. I got to do it to look for Reub, and they go by so fast sometimes it almost makes me dizzy. I am like a dog that has lost its owner: I trot after one a little ways and then back and after another, and that's the way I go it from morning till night.

   (*Enter, R., apple woman--Mrs. Maguire--crying "Apples! Apples!"*)

MRS. MAGUIRE. Do you wish to buy any apples, sir?

JOSH. No; I ain't hungry.

MRS. MAGUIRE. Well, buy some to take home with you.

JOSH. I hain't got no home here; I'm visitin'.

MRS. MAGUIRE. Buy some to take to your friends, thin.

JOSH. My friends are better able to buy them than I be.

MRS. MAGUIRE. Faith and you're smart, ain't ye?

JOSH. Well, I manage to get along without taking up a collection, I guess.

MRS. MAGUIRE. Well, thin, take my advice about one thing.

JOSH. What's that?

MRS. MAGUIRE. Don't go to Philadelphia.

JOSH. Why not?

MRS. MAGUIRE. For the Cintinnial is over. Apples! Apples! (*Exit, L.*)

JOSH. Well, I must look all fired green when folks think I'm on my way to the Centennial, a year after it is over. I did not go there at all; wish I had now; they say it was worth seeing. I bet a ninepence I don't miss the next one!

(*Enter Dude, R., crossing, bumps his L. shoulder against Josh's R. Turns, taps Josh with cane. Josh puts his hand on his watch. Dude crosses to L.C. and makes the same motion with cane. Josh takes off his hat and makes motion as if to shoo Dude off. Exit Dude, L.*)

Shoo! Shoo! Gosh! I like to run over a goslin'.

(*Exit Josh, R.1E. Enter Happy Jack in evening dress, top coat, gloves and cane, L. He crosses to C.*)

JACK. Well, there's no use talking, fine feathers make fine birds. By Jove! I must look like a winner!

(*Hums "After the Opera Is Over," or other song, and crosses to exit, R., when he is stopped by voices of Policeman and Reuben, off L.*)

POLICEMAN. Come on, you've been sitting here long enough.

REUBEN. Hold on, officer! I haven't done anything!

(*Enter Reuben and Policeman, L.1E.; Policeman precedes Reuben, his hand on Reuben's coat collar.*)

POLICEMAN. Come on; you can't stop here.

REUBEN. Hold on, officer--let me explain.

POLICEMAN. You can tell the judge all about that in the morning.

JACK. (*to Policeman*) Say, what are you going to do with him?

POLICEMAN. (*roughly*) Is that any of your business?

JACK. Oh, no! Oh, no; it is not any of my business, but he's a friend of mine.

POLICEMAN. Oh, he's a friend of yours, is he?

JACK. Yes, he isn't a bad sort of fellow, officer.

(*Takes note from breast pocketbook and presses it in Policeman's hand.*) He's all right.

(*Policeman, keeping R. hand that holds a club down by side, takes sly glance at note and changes tone.*)

POLICEMAN. Oh, well, if he is a friend of yours, of course that makes all the difference in the world. (*Exit, L.1E., swinging club.*)

REUBEN. That was very kind of you, sir.

JACK. Don't mention it.

REUBEN. Do you know me?

JACK. No, sir.

REUBEN. How do you know that I'm worthy of your friendship?

JACK. Well, I'll take chances that you are.

REUBEN. I'm afraid you're taking long chances.

JACK. Never mind, I am used to it. Racing is a weakness of mine, and I play a short horse occasionally if I think it a good one. Now tell me what the King of Clubs want to take you in for?

REUBEN. (*pointing L.1E.*) I fell asleep in that doorway.

JACK. A little tired out, I suppose?

REUBEN. Yes; partly that.

JACK. A little discouraged, eh?

REUBEN. (*nervously*) No, sir; I was sleeping off a drunk.

JACK. I thought so. (*Feeling Reuben's arm.*) Why, look here, old fellow, you're all over ashake!

REUBEN. Yes; I know it.

JACK. You need a good strong milk punch to brace you up.

REUBEN. I think that would do me good.

JACK. Have you got the price?

REUBEN. Not a cent. (*Feeling in pockets.*)

JACK. Oh! Well, here's a dollar note for you. (*Taking bill from vest pocket.*) Now go and take a good bracer; get a shave; have your head rubbed; get something to eat and after that sit down and think a while.

REUBEN. (*gratefully shaking hands with Jack*) Thank you, sir, thank you! (*Exit, R.1E.*)

JACK. (*looking after him*) There he goes, poor fellow; struck a bee line for the nearest dive. Now, he may take my suggestion about bracing up and he may not. Well, never mind, if a man can make a dollar note win once in a hundred times in such a case he ought to feel himself well paid.

(*Exit Jack, R.1E. Enter Mrs. Maguire, L.1E., followed by Policeman.*)

MRS. MAGUIRE. Apples! Apples!

POLICEMAN. Well, Mrs. Maguire!

MRS. MAGUIRE. (*turning and making curtesy*) Good-evening, sir.

POLICEMAN. How is business to-night?

MRS. MAGUIRE. Och! Surely there's nothing at all doing; I am jist waitin' for the weddin' party to come out of the church; thin I expect to sell out and go home.

POLICEMAN. Nice apples you have there. (*Handling apples.*)

MRS. MAGUIRE. Faith an' they are splendid.

POLICEMAN. (*putting hands in pants pockets*) How do you sell them?

MRS. MAGUIRE. (*hands apple*) Och! Nothin' at all to you, sir; take one.

POLICEMAN. Thank you. (*Crosses to R.*)

MRS. MAGUIRE. Don't mention it.

POLICEMAN. You are very kind. (*Salutes Mrs. Maguire and exit, R.*)

MRS. MAGUIRE. (*looking after him*) Faith an' I am. Nice man is Mr.

Doyle if you trate him decent and lave him eat all yer apples. Apples!
(*Exit Mrs. Maguire, R. Enter Josh, R.1E., followed by Policeman.*)

JOSH.   Well, I guess I'll have to do as Henry says, give it up for to-night and take a fresh start in the morning; can't find Reuben nowhere. (*To Policeman.*) Good-evening, neighbor.

POLICEMAN.   Good-evening, sir.

JOSH.   You are a constable here, I guess.

POLICEMAN.   No, sir, I'm a policeman!

JOSH.   Same thing, we call 'em constables up our way.

POLICEMAN.   Indeed?

JOSH.   Yes. How long have you held office here?

POLICEMAN.   Well, let me see, I've been on the force about six years.

JOSH.   How long you lived in New York?

POLICEMAN.   All my life; was born here.

JOSH.   How old be you?

POLICEMAN.   Thirty.

JOSH.   And you ain't killed yet?

POLICEMAN.   (*laughing*) Nary a kill.

JOSH.   Well, that beats all! Had an idea man couldn't live in New York all his life without getting killed.

POLICEMAN.   Ha! Ha! Ha!

JOSH.   You must know most everybody 'round here, I guess?

POLICEMAN.   Yes, I know a good many.

JOSH.   You know Henry Hopkins?

POLICEMAN.   Henry Hopkins? What does he do?

JOSH.   Don't do nothin' and got rich at it.

POLICEMAN.   Henry Hopkins--can't say that I do.

JOSH.   Well, that beats all! Thought everybody knew Henry. He's lived here more'n thirty years.

POLICEMAN.   Well, you're not in the country now, old gentleman.

JOSH.   No, I wish I was.

POLICEMAN.   Why so?

JOSH.   My feet are pretty near worn out walking over these stone pavements.

POLICEMAN.   Tires you, eh?

JOSH.   Yes. You have to sot up all night, I suppose?

POLICEMAN.   Yes, sir.

JOSH.   Gosh! I never could do that!

POLICEMAN.   Oh, that's nothing; you would soon get used to it.

(*Exit Policeman, L.1E.*)

JOSH. Well, I guess not. I never sot up all night but once or twice in my life and that was just before I got married. Darned if I ain't gettin' hungry; had nothing to eat since noon. Henry and I went into a tavern where they had a printed schedule of what they had to eat. Couldn't read it any more'n you could hog latin, not a mite! I didn't see only two Down-east names on it, Baked Beans a la Boston. I took a mouthful but I spit them right out again. The "a la" they put in them just spiled them. Henry eat the beans and I had some ice cream and clams.

(*Enter Terror, R., with hat pulled down over eyes; cigar lit and touching rim of hat. He crosses to back of Josh and knocks into R. shoulder with his L. shoulder as he passes and then turns to Josh.*)

TERROR. Get out of the way! Do you want the whole sidewalk?

JOSH. Well, why don't you bump agin somebody? Who be you anyway?

TERROR. I'm de Hoboken Terror!

JOSH. Well, yer hat'll catch fire there if you ain't careful!

TERROR. What doo you soi? (*Approaching Josh from L.*)

JOSH. I say, if you cock your cigar up like that you'll get your hat on fire.

TERROR. Oh, what's de matter wid you?

(*He grabs Josh's hat from head and throws it on stage in front of him. Then flicks ashes from cigar--restores it, and assumes tough attitude.*)

JOSH. Well, I lasted longer than I thought I would. I expected to get scalped the first day I got here. (*Picking up hat slowly and deliberately.*) What did you do that for?

TERROR. Just for fun!

JOSH. Well, I ain't got no objection to your havin' a little fun, but I don't want yer to have it all to yourself.

(*He knocks Terror's hat off and squares off at him, country style-- jumping about and moving backwards to R.C.*)

TERROR. (*dumbfounded*) Look here! If you wasn't an old man, I'd come over there and make it pleasant for you.

JOSH. Well, I'll be right here when you come!

(*Enter Policeman, L.1E. He stands L. of Terror, who turns and sees him, crosses to him, stops, throws R. lapel of coat back bravado style, and blows cloud of smoke out. Exit Terror, L.1E. Josh crosses to L.C.*)

If that fellow ain't careful, he'll scare somebody.

POLICEMAN. You ran against a wrestler that time, old gentleman.

(*Exit Policeman, L. Enter Mrs. Maguire, R.*)

JOSH. So did he, too. Don't you worry about that.

(*Off L., the bass drum, tamborines, and singing of a stirring hymn.*)

Sounds like Fourth of July.

(*Enter, from L., the Salvation Army, consisting of bass-drummer--in advance--followed by two women beating tamborines, a flag bearer, and four other women. Army exits, singing and playing, R. Josh looks on in wonder.*)

MRS. MAGUIRE. Apples! Apples!

(*She trips over to L.C. to the music. Re-enter the Salvation Army, R. and crosses stage, followed by a drunken man, and exit, L.*)

Apples! Apples!

(*These lines are spoken as the Army passes. Re-enter Army from L., still singing and playing, and followed by the drunken man and the Hoboken Terror. All exeunt, R. Singing and music die out in the distance.*)

JOSH. What's the militia out to-night for?

(*Enter Postman, R.1E., takes out key, opens box, places mail in bag.*)

MRS. MAGUIRE. Wusha, man dear, they ain't soldiers.

JOSH. No?

MRS. MAGUIRE. No. That's the Salvation Army.

JOSH. Gates of Garra! I want ter know?

MRS. MAGUIRE. Apples! (*Exit, L.1E.*)

JOSH. That beats all I ever see. (*Discovering Postman.*) Robbing the mail, by gosh! Here! Here! You can't do that!

(*He seizes Postman and turns around to L. Both struggle for bag.*)

I've got him! I've got him!

(*Enter Policeman, L.1E., running in and separating them.*)

POLICEMAN. Here! Here! What's the matter here?

JOSH. Catch him! Catch him! He took my letter out of that box!

POLICEMAN. Why, this man's appointed by the Government to collect the mail.

JOSH. Gosh all fish hooks! (*Hides behind lamp post.*) Now I'd sell out pretty cheap.

POSTMAN. What's the matter with the old jay?

POLICEMAN. Oh, that's all right. It's only a mistake. (*Exit Postman, L.*) Say, look here, old gentleman, you'll have to be a little more careful in the future.

JOSH. That's all right. I didn't know he was the postmaster. (*Exit Policeman, L.1E., laughing.*) No business to go 'round without a guide-board on. That was a pretty narrow escape for me. Guess I had better go home before I get in the lock up.

(*Enter Jack, R.1E., stops C. surprised at seeing Josh. Looks Josh all over. Josh puts R. hand on watch and L. hand in pocket.*)

JACK. (*astonished*) Why, no!

JOSH. What's the matter?

JACK. It is.

JOSH. How do you know it is?

JACK. My preserver!

JOSH. Sho'!

JACK. Why, you saved my life!

JOSH. Well, that's the first time I ever knew I looked like a life preserver.

JACK. I met you in Swanzey.

JOSH. (*very slowly and knowingly*) Well, I guess not! I have had that two or three times before.

> (*He turns up stage and balances first on one toe and then on other in a country smart way as much as to say, "I know a thing or two!"*)

JACK. (*laughing*) Yes, I did. About three weeks ago. Don't you remember?

JOSH. No--the next Centennial ain't begun yet.

JACK. Your name is Whitcomb.

JOSH. Now, look here, Appetite Joe, I have heard on you; I have been tackled by about a dozen of you fellers since I have been here, and I'm gittin' kind o' tired on't. Now if you don't want ter get your feathers ruffled up, you go look for squashes somewhere else! I just hitched up to a feller and I feel pretty darn "kinky." Ain't quite so green as you think I be. I take the papers. Play none o' yer "hunker slidin' on me," by gosh!

> (*Same business up stage.*)

JACK. Let me put you right.

JOSH. Oh, I'm all right! Don't you worry!

JACK. Don't you remember about three weeks ago giving a poor miserable wretch money enough to go to his home?

JOSH. (*puzzled*) Now how did you find that out?

JACK. I am the man.

JOSH. You be darned! You ain't?

JACK. I can convince you.

JOSH. (*putting his hands in his pockets*) Well, that's what you'll have to do before I talk to you much longer.

JACK. I can tell you the last words you said to me.

JOSH. Well, let's hear them.

JACK. Go home and try and be somebody. It isn't too late.

JOSH. (*taking hands from pockets and slapping them together*) By gum! That's what I said!

> (*Jack holds out hand to shake. Josh puts hands in pockets quickly.*)

Hold on! Hold on! Tell me what you said and then I'll give up.

JACK. I told you I would try and if I didn't win, I'd give old John Barleycorn the toughest scuffle he ever had for the underhold.

JOSH. Well, that's just what you said.

(*Shakes hands and returns his hand to his pocket, still on his guard.*)

And there's my hand. I'm glad to see you.

JACK. And I am glad to see you, old gentleman and old friend.

(*Taking ten-dollar bill from pocket and handing to Josh.*)

Allow me to return your ten dollars.

JOSH. (*taking money*) Now, by gosh! I know it's you. How de-do! (*Shaking hands.*) I guess your mother was glad to see you, wasn't she?

JACK. Yes, overjoyed!

JOSH. I knowed she'd be!

JACK. Did you find your boy yet, Mr. Whitcomb?

(*Organ plays piano--some very pretty church service.*)

JOSH. (*with feeling*) No, sir; I didn't, and I have been trampin' up and down these streets for more'n a week searching for him everywhere; and I have seen more wickedness and misery in that time than I ever thought could exist in a civilized community. I am dreadfully afraid he has been led off, and took to drink.

JACK. What makes you think so?

JOSH. Because I have seen so much of it since I have been here. Henry Hopkins says drink is the ruination of more than half the young men of New York.

JACK. Well, Henry Hopkins isn't far from being right.

(*Organ stops. Commotion outside, R.1E.*)

JOSH. There's a row! Don't go too near or you'll get stabbed. A lot of rowdies outside--

JACK. Here comes my dollar investment and about as drunk as they make them.

(*Voices outside: "Good-night, old feller," etc. Enter Reuben, staggering R.1E. to C. He falls into Josh's arms and then falls on his knees.*)

JOSH. (*bending over him*) My boy Reub! Reub! Reub!

(*When Reuben falls, Policeman runs on, L.1E., and Jack, who is L.C., stops him and then crosses back of Josh to R.C.*)

Why, it's my boy Reub!

Organ in church plays "Wedding March" piano, till curtain, and then forte till final curtain. Second Curtain: Policeman, L.C., with head bowed. Reuben stands with his head on Josh's shoulder. Jack removes his hat and with bowed head stands at R.C.

ACT IV.

Scene. Kitchen in the Old Homestead. A door up R.C. opening off to outside. At R. of door--in corner--a wood box. At L. of door a kitchen chair. An old-fashioned fireplace C. with andirons, fire logs lit, bellows, fire shovel, and tongs. A mantel on which an old lantern in lit, two candlesticks, an almanac, and Josh's hat and mittens. In front of fireplace a rag rug and a plain rocking chair. At L. of fireplace a tall grandfather's clock with key inside. L. of clock a curtained window, the panes of which suggest snow on the outside. A small table below window. Midway at L. wall a kitchen cupboard--shelves papered--and filled with crockery. Leaning against cupboard a broom whose handle has been partly cut through the middle. Down stage L. a door leading into the "front" room. Midway on R. wall hangs a series of pegs on which hang Ganzey's hat and mittens, Cy's hat and comforter, and Seth's hat and scarf. Down stage at R. a door. An old-fashioned cradle stands in R. corner and a kitchen chair to L. of it. Two kitchen chairs stand near cupboard at L. Below door L. a black hair-seated "front-room" chair. A few common pictures adorn the walls. (*Cy Prime and Seth Perkins are seated near cupboard, L., with checkerboard on knees, playing. Josh is standing R. of them watching the game. Matilda is at fireplace talking to two of the Stratton girls. Eb Ganzey and Rickety Ann are conversing over R. with the Quartette and others. Elinor Stratton is seated L. of cradle, down R. Cy moves a "man" and laughs.*)

JOSH. What's the matter, Cy, got him penned?

CY. Yes; he can't make a move without losing two men. I sot a trap for him and he stepped right into it. I knowed he would.

ELINOR. (*sitting by cradle*) Uncle Josh, what is the cradle doing here?

JOSH. Got it down to rock Stocky's baby in, when he was on here visiting from Wesconsin--ain't used it sence Reub was a baby. Come now, let's all go into the front room, we've got a table sot in there. We'll have some pumpkin pie, cookies, and games, playin' on the melodeon and one thing and another.

MATILDA. Joshua, has the fire got to going in the stove?

JOSH. Rearin' away like a mill dam.

MATILDA. Come on, boys and girls, come! (*Exit, L.*)

JOSH. Come on, all on ye.

(*Exeunt all except Seth, Cy, Rickety, and Ganzey. Ganzey, eating almonds, going down C. Cy rises, goes up by fireplace, and Seth rises and places checkerboard on cupboard.*)

RICKETY. Say, Eb, what you eatin'?

GANZEY. Almonds. Oh, here's a double one!

RICKETY. Gimme one?

GANZEY. Will if you play philophene.

RICKETY. All right, I will. (*Ganzey gives almond.*) Five or take, yes or no.

GANZEY. Yes or no.

RICKETY. All right. Now remember if I ask you anything and you say yes or no, I ketch you.

GANZEY. All right. Say, Rickety, goin' to dance with me to-night?

RICKETY. Oh, you jist want me to say yes so you can ketch me.

    (*Exit Rickety, L., laughing. Ganzey whistles; goes up stage. Cy picks up iron shovel to strike him--exit Ganzey hurriedly, L.*)

CY. (*laughing*) You play checkers! Ho, ho, ho!

SETH. Ho, ho, ho! Why don't you laugh?

CY. Well, I be a-laughing, ain't I?

SETH. That's all right, go it--keep it up! It'll be my turn one of these days.

CY. What do you mean by that?

SETH. I mean that I consider it pretty darn small potatoes when a man pens another playin' checkers to holler right out before the hull room full then laugh at him!

CY. Oh, you do, do you?

SETH. Yes, I do!

CY. Well, that ain't no wuss than what you done.

SETH. What did I do?

CY. Didn't you blat right out before everybody that you could beat anybody in the house playin' checkers?

SETH. No, I didn't, nuther!

CY. Yes, you did, tuther!

SETH. Said I'd play anybody in the house.

CY. I took you up, didn't I?

SETH. Yes.

CY. An' I beat you, didn't I?

SETH. Yes; and you crowed about it.

CY. Well, supposin' I did?

SETH. That's all right. (*Sneeringly.*) You put me in mind of an old rooster I've got. He's always fightin'; wins one battle in about fifty and then crows so durn loud you can hear him all over town.

CY. Oh, he do, do he?

SETH. Yes; that's what he do do.

CY. Ha! Ha! Well, I won't tell you what you put me in mind on. But you'd better take my advice and not go through that pasture where the Hennesy folks keep their goats. (*Sits.*)

SETH. Why?

CY. Because they're liable to put a bell on you.

SETH. (*angrily*) Cy Prime, I've stood your slurs about my personal appearance about as long as I'm going to. You ain't got nothin' to brag on. There ain't no more meat on you than there is on a hoe handle, not a mite. You ain't heavy enough to sink a fish line. You're that kind o' calf that lives all winter and dies in the spring.

CY. Why, you gol darn picter out of a comic almanac, what are you talking about? (*Rises and goes toward Seth.*)

SETH. That's what I said. (*Firmly.*) And so are you, too!

CY. (*throwing off coat, displaying sleeveless arms*) Well, don't say it again, for I don't like it.

(*Cy threatens Seth. Enter Josh, L., followed by Matilda and Ganzey.*)

JOSH. (*going up to fireplace*) Here! Here! What you got your coat off for, Cy?

(*Cy moves to R.C. Matilda and Ganzey are at L.*)

CY. Well, I was jist showing Seth where I got vaccinated, that's all.

(*Cy shows vaccinated arm and then puts on coat.*)

MATILDA. What is it, what is it?

(*Josh takes hat and mittens from mantelplace and puts them on.*)

JOSH. Oh, these two boys quarreling again, that's all.

SETH. Well, he commenced it.

CY. I didn't nuther.

SETH. Now, Cy, you know very well--

JOSH. (*comes down between them*) Boys! boys! boys! Stop it now!

(*Seth goes up stage and stands by window, L.C., while Cy crosses to R.*)

MATILDA. Where you goin', Joshua?

JOSH. Goin' out to the barn to see if the cattle's all right. Ebenezer, get your mittens on.

(*Ganzey goes up to pegs, R., and puts on hat and mittens.*)

Run down the road and tell Len Holbrook to come up here and bring his fiddle.

(*Matilda sits in armchair at fireplace and knits.*)

GANZEY. S'pose he's in bed?

JOSH. Tell him to get up.

GANZEY. All right. (*Hands Josh lighted lantern from shelf.*)

JOSH. Come, Cy, fill your wood box, it's gettin' late.

CY. All right, Joshua, all right. (*Exeunt Josh and Ganzey, door R.*) I snum!
I forgot all about my wood for night. By Jinks! But never mind, I kin git
it jist as well now as any other time. (*Puts on hat and comforter from
pegs.*) Don't make any difference. (*Sees Seth at window.*) Now there is
some manoeuverin' goin' here and I know it. That fellow is tryin' to pull
the wool over my eyes. He's no more lookin' out that winder than he's
lookin' up the chimley. (*Exit, R.*)

SETH. (*coming down R. of Matilda*) Tildy, do you know--
    (*Enter Cy cautiously, sees Seth talking to Matilda; goes down stage and
    stands beside him. Seth turns, sees Cy, puts hand to mouth and goes up
    to window again.*)

CY. I knowed it! I'll keep my eye on that Swanzey dude!
    (*Exit Cy, R. Melodeon heard, off L., with Quartette singing "I'll meet
    her when the sun goes down," or other melody.*)

SETH. The young folks in the front room 'pear to be enjoyin' theirselves,
don't they, Tildy?

MATILDA. Yes, they do. Why don't you go in, Seth?

SETH. (*takes chair R. of fireplace and sits on her R.*) No, no! Most too old
to play games and cut up didoes as I used to.

MATILDA. (*knitting*) Yes, that's so--both on us gettin' pretty old now.

SETH. Yes, yes--

MATILDA. So I thought arter the young folks get started playin' games
and one thing another, I'd jist come out here and knit a spell.

SETH. Glad you did; glad you did.

MATILDA. Seth, why don't you come round here and see us oftener? I
believe 'twas more'n a month sence you was here last.

SETH. I would come round oftener but you see it makes old Cy Prime so
hoppin' mad.

MATILDA. Well, you mustn't mind him.

SETH. Well, I don't much. He's allus throwin' out slurs about my
sneakin' 'round here to see you.

MATILDA. Go long!

SETH. Yes. Warn't more'n a week ago, he twitted me right out before the
hull store about the time I took you up to Keene to see old blind Dexter's
wax figgers.

MATILDA. Why, Seth! That was thirty year ago or more!

SETH. I know that; but the mean way he said it made me so plaguey mad,
I throwed a ten penny nail at him and broke his new clay pipe all to

smash. (*Laughs.*) Guess we'd 'a' had a pitch battle right then and there if the neighbors had not interfered. Phew! Phew! That fire o' yours is pretty hot, don't you think it is, Tildy?

MATILDA. Pretty warm, Seth. Cold night outside and it takes considerable fire to warm up the house.

(*Enter Cy, R.C. Sees Seth sitting by Matilda--throws bundle of wood which he carries in wood box, R. Seth jumps up, crosses down to R.C., startled. Cy comes down C.*)

CY. Well, Seth Perkins, couldn't keep on your own side of the fence, could you? What you doin' 'round here, anyhow?

SETH. Well, I ain't doin' chores for my board.

CY. Nor I, nuther, ain't doin' chores for my board. I'm stoppin' here this winter with Joshua, 'cause my sister Betsy's gone out west visitin' and you know it, too, gol darn ye.

(*Both square off to fight--country style. Enter Josh, R.C., hastily throwing hat and mittens on mantel and comes down between Cy and Seth, while Matilda rises and goes down to L.C.*)

JOSH. Here--here! Stop this, or I'll put you both in the trundle bed. What's this all about, Til?

MATILDA. I don't know.

JOSH. Well, you go into the front room and turn the damper in the stove-pipe; I'm afraid it'll draw all the heat up the chimney--the sparks are flyin' out like fury.

MATILDA. Be they! (*Exit, L.*)

JOSH. Yes, I'll settle this business pretty quick. It's ben goin' on jist about as long as it orter. Seth, you go over there and set down--you go over there and set down, Cy.

(*Seth in meantime goes up to wood box and gets a chip of wood, places it on his L. shoulder. Cy sees it and goes and knocks it off. Both pretend to fight again. Josh interferes and stops it. Seth sits, R.C., and Cy takes chair from up C. and brings it down L. of Seth, slams it and sits.*)

Stop slammin' the chairs around--I won't have it.

(*Sees a black hair-seated chair, L., goes over, takes it up.*)

Who brought this front-room chair out in the kitchen, I'd like to know.

(*Cy and Seth look at each other. Josh takes chair off L., leaves it and returns.*)

Now, what's the matter with you two old fools?

(*Takes chair and sits, L.C.*)

You've been snappin' and snarlin' at each other for more'n thirty years; and ain't ye ashamed o' yourselves and you boys together raised on jinin' farms. Cy, don't you remember when you and Seth was barefooted boys ridin' saw logs 'round the mill pond; how you fell in one day where it was over your head and you would have drownded if it hadn't ben for him? He jumped in and saved you. You couldn't swim and he could. Hev you forgot that, Cy? I hev heard your father tell it lots o' times. (*Looking at Seth.*) And, Seth--

SETH. Eh?

JOSH. Don't you remember when your brother Bill came home from New Orleans sick, a good many years ago, and everybody thought he had the yellow fever and was afraid to go near him, how Cy jumped up in the store and said, "Hang yellow fever--I ain't afraid of it! Sha'n't leave no neighbor o' mine alone, I'll tend to him." And he did tend to him for a good many long weeks.

(*Seth fills up and wipes eyes with handkerchief.*)

Hev you forgot that, Seth?

SETH. (*rises and takes Josh's hand, who also rises*) No, Josh; I ain't and I never will either. (*Goes up C.*)

JOSH. That's right, that's right!

CY. (*crying*) Well, I ain't got nuthin' agin Seth and I could prove it, too, if old Bill Jones was alive. (*Rises and goes to Josh.*)

SETH. (*coming down to C.*) If Cy was taken sick, I'd watch over him jist the same as he did my brother Bill; I would if it killed me!

JOSH. I know that, I know that. Come now, shake hands and be friends.

(*Josh puts Cy's hand in Seth's, crossing to back of them.*)

CY. And, Seth, if you should fall overboard and was goin' to git drownded, I'd jump in and save your live, and I can't swim a lick!

JOSH. There now! Don't you feel better? (*Patting both on backs.*)

SETH. I do; a durned sight.

JOSH. Of course you do.

CY. And so do I. If I had a dipper o' cider, I'd stay up till ten o'clock.

JOSH. Here! Don't get reckless! There, boys, go and fill your wood box.

CY. All right, Joshua.

(*Josh goes to C. Cy replaces his chair R. of fireplace, gets hat and comforter, and comes down R.C. Seth gets hat and scarf from peg, puts them on, and goes to Cy.*)

SETH. Hold on, Cy, I'll help you bring in your wood.

CY. Will you, Sethy?

JOSH. (*laughs*) Seth-y!

SETH. What's the use o' us two fallin' out?

CY. Oh, not a bit o' use at all.

SETH. We're a couple o' ninny hammers.

CY. Yes, we ain't got as much gumption as a sick woodchuck!

SETH. Have an apple? (*Takes apple from coattail pocket, hands to Cy.*)

CY. Yes, don't care if I do.

SETH. Come along now, and I'll help you bring in your wood.

CY. Will you? (*Exit, R., running, followed by Seth.*)

JOSH. How true it is, once a man, twice a child. When they commenced to fill up, I came near sloppin' over myself.

MATILDA. (*entering, L.*) Have they made up, Joshua?

JOSH. Better friends than ever.

MATILDA. Well, I'm glad of that--so much better than always hectorin' one another.

    (*Cy and Seth outside, laughing.*)

JOSH. (*goes to window and knocks on pane*) Boys! Boys!

SETH and CY. What is it?

JOSH. March up here!

    (*Seth and Cy come to window.*)

Now stop your wrestling and get your wood in.

    (*They pretend to wrestle, Seth calling to Cy to stop. Josh laughs.*)

Darned if Cy hain't flopped him flatter than a flounder in the snowbank.

Well, no use talking, boys will be boys. By gum! It's sharp out to-night.

    (*Josh goes and stands with back to fireplace.*)

MATILDA. (*sitting in rocker*) Pretty cold, I guess.

JOSH. Cold and crisp as a new dollar bill.

MATILDA. Do you think the pigs hev got straw enough in the pen?

JOSH. Yes; pitched in a fresh bundle jist afore I come in. Had the wust time a little while ago with that old brindle heifer you ever seen in your life.

MATILDA. What's she ben doin' now?

JOSH. Got loose agin and got on to the barn floor and was havin' a cotillion with the fannin' mill.

MATILDA. Well, of all things! How does she manage to git loose so often?

JOSH. I don't know unless she unties herself.

MATILDA. No, Joshua, that's impossible.

JOSH. I don't know about that. Cy says he saw her pick the padlock on the corn crib door the other day with her horn.

MATILDA. Well, Cyrus says more'n his prayers.

JOSH. Shouldn't wonder a mite.

MATILDA. Did you shet the hen house door?

JOSH. Yes. Everything's all snugged up--not a critter on the place but what'll sleep as warm as a meadow mouse under a haystack.

MATILDA. Well, I'm glad o' that. Hate to know there's anything sufferin' belonging to us.

JOSH. Did you wind the clock?

(*Melodeon plays "Grandfather's Clock," off L.*)

MATILDA. Not yet. Elinor Stratton's playin' the melodeon--

JOSH. Plays fust rate, too, for a gal that's got as bad a cold as she has.

(*Goes to clock, L.C., and winds slowly--during which Matilda fills up and puts handkerchief to eyes, rises and comes L.C.*)

What's the matter, Til?

MATILDA. Nothin'--nothin' much.

JOSH. (*comes down C.*) Yes, there is, too. What you snivellin' about?

MATILDA. Well, I was worrying a little mite about Reuben. Do you think he'll come home to-night, Joshua?

JOSH. (*takes chair at L.C. and sits*) Jist as sartin as the world. Didn't his letter say, "Father, I'll be home New Year's if I'm spared my health"? Ain't his friends and schoolmates here to meet him? He's comin' by way o' Boston; train may be late comin' into Keene. Then he's got to drive six miles, you must remember that.

MATILDA. Yes, I know all that, Joshua; but why didn't you bring him home with you when you was in New York?

JOSH. Well, I'll tell you, Til. He did start to come but when he got as far as the depot, I noticed something troubled him. He hung back a leetle mite, and I said to him--"Reuben, don't you want to go home with me?" And he says, "Yes, Father, I do; but I hate to go back and have Swanzey people say that Reuben Whitcomb went away to make his own living and his father had to go and bring him back again." (*With pathos.*) And, Til, when he hung down his head and his eyes filled up with tears, and his voice was kind o' choked, he says, "Father, let me stick it out a little while longer"--I says, "Go it!" "Thank you," he says, "I'll be home by New Year's"; and he'll be here to-night, you see if he ain't.

MATILDA. I hope so.

JOSH. I feel sure on't. (*Rises and wipes eyes.*) Guess I'd better go down in the cellar and set my mouse trap before I go to bed.

(*Exit Josh, down stage R. door. Enter Cy, R.C. door, throwing wood in box and warming himself at fireplace. In meantime Matilda takes chair at C. up stage at L. and sits knitting.*)

CY. Well, I tell you what it is--pretty cold night out to-night, Tildy.

MATILDA. Yes, Cyrus.

CY. (*coming down to R.C.*) I'll bet it's as cold to-night as it was the night

Washington crossed the Delaware.

MATILDA. Now what do you know about Washington crossing the Delaware?

CY. What do I know about it? Well, I know old Bill Jones put him up to it--that's what I know about it.

(*Enter Seth and throws wood in box, then goes C.*)

SETH. There, there! I s'pose you ben tellin' Til how you flopped me over in the snow, ain't ye?

CY. No, I never said a word about it, did I, Tildy?

MATILDA. No, you didn't.

SETH. He done it though--fair and square. S'pose you'll crow about that for the next twenty years.

(*Enter Josh, R, crosses up to fireplace and sits in rocking-chair.*)

CY. No, I won't--I won't say a word about it; I guess your foot slipped, anyway.

SETH. (*crosses to Cy*) No, it didn't, I was throwed fair.

CY. Well, you know how it is with me, when I get that grape-vine lock o' mine sot--suthin's got to come.

(*Cy seizes Seth about the waist--legs entwined--illustrating grape-vine lock. An approaching sound of sleigh bells is heard, off R.*)

JOSH. Whose bells be them outside?

SETH. Sounded a leetle like Deacon Frosser's.

CY. More like David Wilson's.

JOSH. (*rising*) You're both wrong. They don't belong around here, for I can tell every string of bells in town.

(*Outside, "Whoa!" Enter Ganzey hurriedly.*)

GANZEY. Reub is here!

(*Enter Reuben. Josh clasps him to his breast and turns him over to Matilda, who does the same.*)

JOSH. (*excitedly*) There he is! I told you he would come. (*Exit Ganzey.*)

MATILDA. My boy--my boy!

JOSH. Take him right in the front room. (*Exeunt Matilda and Reuben, L.*) All your friends and schoolmates there. (*Excitedly.*) Put the shed under the hoss, throw a blanket over the barn. Fly around! (*Exit, L.*)

SETH. Did you ever hear anything like that in all your born days?

CY. (*laughing*) So I'm to put the shed under the hoss, be I?

SETH. An' I'm to throw a blanket over the barn.

CY. Well, never mind. Josh's so tickled to think Reuben's got home that he don't know whether he's on his head or his heels, do he?

(*Cy picks up broom--goes up--sweeps around fireplace.*)

SETH. (*crosses to L. and sits in chair*) No; his heart's sot on that boy.
  (*Enter Ganzey and Jack, R.C. door.*)

GANZEY. Come right in, Mister--I'll tell Uncle Josh.

JACK. All right, thank you.
  (*In passing Cy, Ganzey whistles--Cy tries to strike him with broom but he is too quick for him; exit Ganzey, L., hurriedly.*)
  Good-evening, gentlemen.
  (*Jack takes off his hat and coat, hangs them on pegs, crosses, stands in front of the fire, and warms his hands.*)

CY. How de-do? (*Places broom above door, L., comes down and sits.*)

SETH. (*seated R. of Cy*) Good-evenin', good-evenin'.

CY. Did you drive Reub down from Keene?

JACK. Yes, came from New York with him.

CY. How you talk! (*Snickers.*)

SETH. Purty cold weather out to-night, eh, stranger?

JACK. Yes, sir; it's a little tough on mosquitoes. (*Laughs.*)

CY. Skeeters! (*Laughs and nudges Seth.*)

JACK. But then we didn't mind it much--young blood, you know.

SETH. That's so. Cold weather don't bother us youngsters much, does it, Cy? (*Chuckling quietly and nudging Cy.*)

CY. Not a hooter. (*Hits breast and coughs.*)

SETH. (*aside*) Citified lookin' chap, ain't he, Cy? (*Nudges Cy.*)

CY. (*aside*) Yes, one o' them cute New Yorkers, I guess. Say, Seth, tell him some sort o' whopper to pay him off for that skeeter joke o' his.

SETH. (*aside*) Hadn't you better tackle him?

CY. (*aside*) No; you can lie better than I can.

SETH. Stranger--

JACK. Beg pardon--

SETH. Be you one o' the Hopkins o' New York?

JACK. No, sir, my name is Hazard.

SETH. Oh! Any relation to Hap Hazard?
  (*Both laugh. Cy and Seth both poke each other playfully as if they had said something smart. They rise and go up L.C., chuckling.*)

JOSH. (*off L.*) Where is he? Where is he? (*Enter, L.*) Happy Jack, sure as a gun!

JACK. (*shaking hands*) How do, how do, Mr. Whitcomb?

JOSH. How de-do? I'm glad to see you.

JACK. Thank you. On time, you see. I told you we would be here on New Year's Eve.

JOSH. So you did. I'd take your word for a million.

JACK. Thank you.

JOSH. (*crossing to L.C., calling*) Til, come here.

MATILDA. (*entering*) What is it, Joshua?

JOSH. Mr. Hazard.

MATILDA. Mr. Hazard?

JOSH. Why, you don't know him, do you? He is the young man who was so good to Reub and me in New York--the one I was tellin' you about--here last summer; turned over a new leaf in life--that's him!

MATILDA. Oh, there now--you ain't the young man who was here last summer, be you?

JACK. The very same.

MATILDA. (*shakes hands heartily with Jack*) Well, how do you do? I'm glad to see you.

JACK. Thank you.

MATILDA. (*looking Jack over*) Of all things--how you have changed.

JOSH. Fooled me, too, and I've travelled most all over the world.

JACK. Yes, Miss Whitcomb--it was under the old elm at the corner of the lane I first began my reformation. I couldn't help drawing a mind picture of it as I passed by coming to the door; and, old friend, I owe it all to you. (*Crossing to Josh.*)

JOSH. Don't say another word about it; if you do, I'll knock you down. Come into the front room and get acquainted.

(*Josh and Jack exeunt, L. Matilda follows them to L. door when knock is heard at R.C. door.*)

MATILDA. Come in.

(*Enter Len Holbrook, takes off scarf and hat, hangs them R.*)

LEN. How de-do, Aunt Tilda!

MATILDA. How do you do, Mr. Holbrook? (*Exit, L.*)

LEN. Hello, Cy!

CY. Hello, Len!

LEN. How are you, Seth?

SETH. How de-do; how de-do?

CY. Pretty cold out to-night, ain't it, Len?

LEN. Yes, it's pesky cold.

SETH. Brought your old fiddle with you, I see.

LEN. Yes. Jist goin' to bed when the Ganzey boy came and said Joshua was going to hev a frolic and wanted me to fiddle--so here I be.

CY. That's right; that's right.

LEN. Hope they won't serve me the same as they did over at Richmond t'other night.

CY. How's that?

LEN. Greased my bow! Didn't get it out for more'n two days. (*Exit, L.*)

CY. Greased his bow! That's Richmond all over! (*Knock at door, R.C.*) Come in! (*Seth joins Cy at R.*)

SETH. Hello, hello! More company, more visitors!

CLANCEY. (*entering, pipe in mouth*) Hello, boys!

(*He sits by fire, throws hat and mittens on floor, and warms his hands.*)

CY. Why, how are you, Mr. Clancy?

CLANCEY. How are you?

SETH. What's the news?

CLANCEY. Oh, nothin' strange--me hens has stopped layin', that's all.

CY. No wonder. Pretty cold weather out.

CLANCEY. Faith an' it is. (*Rising.*) It's terribly frosty--the fire in my pipe is frozen stiff.

CY. Why don't you wear an overcoat?

CLANCEY. Overcoat, is it? Wusha, now! I have been in this country twenty-seven years, and I never wore an overcoat but the one you see on me now.

CY. You're a tough little man, Mr. Clancey!

CLANCEY. I'll warrant you. Faith an' there's not a man my heft around here that will weigh within tin pounds o' me.

CY. Well, you hev done well in this country.

CLANCEY. Oh, jist about as well as them that ha' done no better.

CY. It's a wonder to me that you don't go over to Ireland once more jist to see the old folks.

CLANCEY. Is it me go over to Ireland? Why, man, I've been out here so long and I have got so Yankified I'm afraid they wouldn't understand what I'd be sayin'.

CY. (*chuckling*) Yankified? So is a tater!

CLANCEY. Say, Cy, O'Rourke, the horseshoer, was tellin' me Joshua's boy is home agin from New York.

CY. Yes, that's right.

CLANCEY. Faith an' I'm glad to know that. Well, I just thought I'd come over and wish him welcome home agin. He thought a great deal about me.

MATILDA. (*Entering, L.*) How do you do, Mr. Clancey?

CLANCEY. Well, well, Miss Whitcomb, how are you?

MATILDA. I'm pretty well, thank you.

CLANCEY. Faith an' you're lookin' well.

MATILDA. You've just come in time.

CLANCEY. Yes.

MATILDA. We have got the table sot in the front room an' all the neighbors are there to welcome Reuben home. Go right in with the rest of them, Mr. Clancey.

CLANCEY. Why, certainly, of course. Say, whisper, I'm bashful, you know, in company, but if there's any ateing goin' on, I'm at home with ye.

(*Exit Clancy, L. Knock at door, R.C.*)

MATILDA. Come in!

(*Enter Mrs. Murdock, with baby wrapped in small blanket.*)

Well, how are you, Mrs. Murdock? Glad to see you.

MRS. MURDOCK. How do--how do, Aunt Matilda? Good-evenin', Cyrus.

CY. Good-evenin', Anna Maria.

MRS. MURDOCK. How-do--how do, Mr. Perkins?

SETH. Good-evenin', Mrs. Murdock, good-evenin'.

(*Seth and Cy cross up back to L.C.*)

MRS. MURDOCK. Wanted to see Reuben so bad, couldn't wait till mornin'. Knew he'd got home, 'cause I see him drive by. Had to bring baby long 'cause everybody has gone to watch-meetin' but me, and couldn't leave him alone, you know.

MATILDA. Of course not, Anna Maria. How he does grow, don't he? Fast asleep, too. Well, take him right into my room, put him between the blankets and let him have his sleep out.

MRS. MURDOCK. Now, Tildy, if there's anything you want me to do, just let me know, and I'll roll up my sleeves and pitch right in. (*Exit, L.*)

MATILDA. Thank you, Anna Maria, you're real good, but I guess I can get along pretty well now. (*Exit, L.*)

SETH. (*comes down L., taking broom which stands above door at L.*) I bet you I--I bet you I can--

CY. Oh, no; no-no! You think you kin pull me up with that broomstick--why, you couldn't pull up a hill o' taters.

(*Cy goes to C. Seth comes to C. with broom.*)

SETH. Set down, then, I'll show ye--if this stick holds out, I'll yank ye more'n forty rods.

(*Both sit on floor, feet together, catching hold of broom handle.*)

Now, Cy, you pull fair.

(*Both pull hard and stick breaks; both fall over backwards. Enter Josh, Reuben, and Jack, L. door.*)

JOSH. Hello, hello, hello. What's all this about?

(*Seth jumps up and rushes off, L. Cy puts broom portion of his broken half up his coattails and ties scarf over it; puts on hat and rushes off, C.*)

Up to some o' their capers, I'll warrant you.

REUBEN. Father, you haven't said anything about--

JOSH. Not a word to a soul--not even to your aunt.

REUBEN. Thank you. (*Shakes hands.*)

JOSH. Let bygones by bygones. That's the best way, ain't it, Jack?

JACK. Right you are, Mr. Whitcomb. (*Takes Josh's hand.*)

JOSH. You two boys ought to be brothers as long as you live.

JACK. It can be done.

JOSH. How?

JACK. (*laughing*) Mother is still a widow.

JOSH. I never thought of that.

REUBEN. It's worth thinking of, Father.

JOSH. Tut, tut, boys! Don't put sich nonsense in my head.

GANZEY. (*entering, L.*) Uncle, the gals and boys are goin' to slide down hill, and they want to know if they can pile into your old sleigh?

JOSH. Yes; have the new one if they want.

GANZEY. Can they?

JOSH. Yes.

GANZEY. (*going to door, L.*) Say, come on, all on ye--Uncle says you can hev the sleigh, come on, come on. Say, Reub, won't you go with us?
(*Enter Seth, Elinor, Rickety, Stratton girls, and Quartette, who cross up stage and exeunt, R.C.--all dressed for out of doors.*)

REUBEN. No; I'll stay here with Father.

ELINOR. (*pausing*) Come, Reuben, I brought your hat and coat.
(*Reuben takes hat and coat and follows Elinor off, R.C.*)

JOSH. Run along and have a good time. Jack and I'll keep house till you come back. There they go as happy as robins in spring. Well, Mr. Hazard, how do you like driving over our New Hampshire hills?

JACK. (*taking chair R. of fireplace, sits*) I think it's delightful. It's great to get the blood circulating.

JOSH. (*sits in rocker*) I guess it is!

JACK. Why, it beats the Turkish bath out of sight.

JOSH. So it does. I tell you, for health, give me a good old-fashioned New England winter. I have seen the time, boy, when I was at your age, I used to jump into a sled behind a pair o' steers, in my shirt sleeves and my hat off, and go flying over the snow when it was cold enough to freeze the hinges off the barn door. Ben to dancing school lots o' times on a bob sled. We didn't used to hev dyspepsa them days. We didn't used to pull our chairs up to the table and say, "What hev you got for dinner?" but "How much hev you got?" Worked hard, lived plain, slept well, money was scarce and luxuries a good sight scarcer.

JACK. Well, you are none the worse for it.

JOSH. All the better! Hard as a hickory nut and spry as a kitten at sixty-four.

MATILDA. (*entering, L.*) Josh, I wish you'd come and help me put the table back. (*Exit, L.*)

JOSH. (*rises*) Sartin. Come, Jack, I want to talk to you about your mother.

JACK. (*exit, L., with Josh*) Oh-ho!

(*Enter Rickety and Ganzey, R.C. They stand by fireplace.*)

RICKETY. Well, if that ain't the meanest thing I ever knowed! Got the sleigh out from under the barn, helped them draw it up the hill, then they wouldn't let us go at all. Told us we could take hold o' hands and slide standin' up! It's mean, that's just what it is!

GANZEY. Mean! Well, I guess it is, come right down to it.

RICKETY. Now you jist wait till they ask me to do anything agin, that's all--jist wait now! Wouldn't let us slide with them 'cause we weren't dressed good enough, I s'pose.

GANZEY. Ain't them mittens pretty? (*Shows mittens.*)

RICKETY. Oh, they're awfully nice.

GANZEY. Mother knit 'em.

RICKETY. Honest?

GANZEY. Goin' to hev sleeve buttons when I'm big enough.

RICKETY. No!

GANZEY. It's all that Ed Bogus's fault. He's awful stuck up ever sence he went to Saratogy last summer and stayed all night. He thinks he can order folks around jist as he's a mind to. Jist you wait till I get him alone! Jist you wait! You'll see!

RICKETY. Well, I jist would! Oh, say, let's put red pepper on the popcorn.

GANZEY. No, I'll tell you something better than that!

RICKETY. What?

GANZEY. Let's eat up all the pie.

RICKETY. Oh, all right. Say, Eb, do you like me?

GANZEY. Yes.

RICKETY. Philophene! (*Exit, up R.C., laughing.*)

GANZEY. (*whistles; hears organ off L., goes to L. door--listens*) Oh, the baby's awaked up--I better hide or they'll make me rock the cradle.

(*Ganzey hides in corner, up C. Enter Mrs. Murdock with baby, which she places in cradle, R. She sings a lullaby, during which enter Seth, Cy, Elinor, Rickety Ann, and the Stratton girls, R.C., laughing. Mrs.*

Murdock holds up a warning finger. The characters tiptoe softly and exeunt, L. Enter Quartette, R.C., and, standing by fireplace, joins chorus of lullaby and quietly exit, L., at finish. Pause. Enter Matilda.)

MATILDA. Well, Anna Maria, is the baby asleep?

MRS. MURDOCK. Yes.

MATILDA. Why, what's the matter? You ben cryin', ain't you?

MRS. MURDOCK. Yes; the boys jist sung such a sweet song. It made me feel bad. I boo-hoo dreadful easy and always did, from a gal.

MATILDA. Never mind, Anna Maria, I wouldn't cry.

CY. *(entering, L. door)* Say, Tildy--

MATILDA. What?

CY. You better come in here and pat Seth Perkins on the back.

MATILDA. Why?

CY. *(standing by fireplace)* Because he's jist swallowed a fork.

(Enter Josh and Reuben, followed by Jack, Seth, Clancey, Ganzey, Holbrook, Quartette, Rickety, Elinor, Stratton girls, and neighbors. Jack crosses, gazing at Elinor, who sits at cradle. Seth joins Cy. Rickety and the two Stratton girls go up R.C. Quartette goes up L.C. with women neighbors. Clancey, Ganzey, and Holbrook, with violin, remain L.)

JOSH. Here, Til, it's all settled. Reub and I hev had a good talk--we hev agreed on every pint--he works the old farm on shares, takes possession to-morrow, New Year's Day--what do you think of that?

MATILDA. Oh, tell me all about it. *(Reuben and Matilda go up stage.)*

JACK. Mr. Whitcomb--

JOSH. What is it?

JACK. Who were those young ladies Reuben introduced me to? I have really forgotten their names.

JOSH. They are the Stratton gals.

JACK. And the one sitting at the cradle?

JOSH. That's Elinor.

JACK. She's a very pretty girl.

JOSH. And a proper good gal, too. Shin up to her and I'll lend you my front room to spark in, and you can burn all the wood you want to.

JACK. All right, thank you. *(Jack crosses, R., and is greeted by Elinor.)*

JOSH. Now move your chairs and we'll have a dance.

(Everyone becomes alert and active, removing chairs and rugs aside. Len Holbrook and another fiddler tune up while Clancey and Ganzey rush on the small, portable melodeon from off L. The musicians sit while Ganzey, back of them, manipulates a jew's harp. Josh stops them.)

Hold on! I want to say a word to our neighbors before they go. Now, you fathers that hev got wild boys, I want you to be kind o' easy with 'em. If they are kind o' foolish now and then, forgive 'em. Like as not, it is as much your fault as 'tis theirs--they might have inherited it, you can't tell. And, mothers--well, what's the use of saying anything to you, bless your smilin' faces. Your hearts are always biling over with love and kindness for the wayward child! Now don't let this be your last visit to the Old Homestead. Come up in June when all natur' is at her best--come on, all on ye, and let the scarlet runners chase ye back to childhood.

Music cue. The musicians strike a few chords while the characters, amid laughter and jollity, seek partners and positions for the Virginia Reel. The couples form in two lines down the middle of the room, gentlemen on one side facing their lady partners in the opposite line. The respective partners down stage are as follows: Josh and Mrs. Murdock; Jack and Elinor; Reuben and Rickety; Cy and Matilda; Seth and Stratton girl; one of Quartette and other Stratton girl. Len Holbrook, or one of the Quartette, mounting a chair, can call the figures of the dance, which progresses with hilarity and enthusiasm till finish and . . .

CURTAIN.

DENMAN THOMPSON
—— 1833 - 1911 ——

A famous theatrical trouper who lived and died in West Swanzey. He gained a national reputation by his portrayal of the character, "Joshua Whitcomb," the New Hampshire farmer on a trip to Boston. From this he subsequently evolved "The Old Homestead," a play of long runs before enthusiastic audiences.

James A. Herne (1839-1901)
and *Margaret Fleming*

After theatre managers refused to stage *Margaret Fleming* following tryout performances in Lynn, Massachusetts, in July 1890, William Dean Howells and other prominent literary figures helped James Herne rent Chickering Hall in Boston, where his play opened on March 4, 1891, for a three-week run. Produced in New York in December, it failed because, as more than one critic pointed out, it did not "give pleasure."

Nothing in Herne's earlier career, including his collaboration with David Belasco, gave evidence of his later accomplishments. It was *Drifting Apart*, 1888, a temperance drama concerned with a sailor's family in Gloucester, Massachusetts, that brought him to the attention of American literary realists--Howells, Hamlin Garland, and Stephen Crane. Herne's reading of the works of Henrik Ibsen, Thomas Hardy, and Émile Zola, and his acceptance of social determinism in the writings of Charles Darwin and Henry George, eventually moved him to express his thoughts in "Art for Truth's Sake in the Drama" (*Arena*, 1897). In this essay he asserted that *truthfulness* was the "superior quality" of all drama, which must "interest" and "instruct."

The melodramatic plot of *Margaret Fleming* does not explain the "epoch-marking" quality that critics have attached to Herne's play, nor does the then shocking scene when Margaret unbuttons her dress to nurse the newborn child. More relevant is the emphasis upon the forces of science and democracy which challenged late 19th century American thought: Herne's use of weather to set the mood, his reference to glaucoma, his awareness of double standards, his symbolic introduction of the roses, his expression of social Darwinism through Dr. Larkin, and Margaret's Ibsenian cry that the truth has killed her.

Just as American audiences were offended by a production of Ibsen's *Ghosts* in 1889, they rejected *Margaret Fleming*. Turning his hand to sentimental melodrama, Herne wrote *Shore Acres*, 1892, featuring a kind-hearted and tolerant man of selfless character--and realized a million dollars for his efforts.

James A. Herne as Joe Fletcher

Katharine Corcoran Herne as Margaret

MARGARET FLEMING

(1890)

by James A. Herne

CHARACTERS

Philip Fleming, mill owner	Charlie Burton
Dr. Larkin	Margaret Fleming
Joe Fletcher	Maria Bindley, a nurse
Mr. Foster, manager of the mill	Mrs. Burton
Williams, foreman	Hannah, the cook
Bobby, office boy	Jane, a maid

ACT I.

Scene 1. The action takes place in Canton, Massachusetts, in 1890. It is morning in Spring in Philip Fleming's private office at the mill. Bright sunlight floods the room at first. Later it becomes cloudy until at the end of the scene rain is falling fitfully. The room is handsomely furnished. There is a table in the center at the back between two windows. Above the table and attached to the wall is a cabinet with a mirror in the door. In the right corner is an umbrella stand and hat-rack beside a door leading to the street. There are two windows below the door. A little to the right of the center of the room is an armchair, and in the same position on the left is a flat-top office desk, with a chair on either side. Behind it on the left is a door leading to the mill. There is a bunch of flowers on the desk, and two silver frames holding pictures of Margaret and Lucy. There are also pictures on the wall, including one of the mill and one of Philip's father as a young man. (*As the curtain rises, Bobby enters from the left with a desk-basket of mail, which he places on the desk. He rearranges the chairs slighty. As he is about to go out, a key is heard in the door on the right. Bobby pauses expectantly. Philip Fleming, carrying an umbrella and a rain-coat, enters from the street door on the right. He is a well dressed, prosperous, happy-looking man about thirty-five. He hangs up his hat and coat, and places his umbrella in the stand. Then he glances carelessly into the hat-rack mirror and runs his hand lightly over his hair.*)

PHILIP. (*in a friendly manner*) Good morning, Bobby.

BOBBY. (*grinning appreciatively*) Good morning, sir.

(*Philip goes to his desk and, shifting one or two articles out of his way, begins the duties of the day.*)

PHILIP. Did you get wet this morning in that big shower?

BOBBY. Yes, sir, a little, but I'm all right now.

(*Philip glances rapidly through the letters and with an eager manner selects two large envelopes, opens one, glances through a document it contains, and places it in his inside coat-pocket with a satisfied smile.*)

PHILIP. (*chatting, continuing his work*) Still doing the four mile sprint?

BOBBY. Yes, sir. Oh, I like it, sir--when it don't rain.

(*Philip opens other letters rapidly, glancing with a quick, comprehensive eye through each before placing it on the growing heap on the desk.*)

PHILIP. How about the bicycle?

BOBBY. Well, sir, Mr. Foster says he thinks he'll be able to recommend me for a raise pretty soon, if I keep up my record.

PHILIP. (*looking at him quizzically*) A raise, Bobby?

BOBBY. Yes, Mr. Fleming, and my mother says I can save all I get, and I guess I'll have a bicycle pretty soon then.

PHILIP. How long have your been here?

BOBBY. Six months the day after tomorrow.

PHILIP. (*smiling kindly*) I guess I'll have to talk to Foster, myself.

BOBBY. Oh, thank you, Mr. Fleming.

(*Philip opens a letter which appears to disturb him. He pauses over it with a worried frown.*)

PHILIP. Ask Mr. Foster to come here at once, please. (*As Bobby starts to go.*) And tell Williams I want to see him.

BOBBY. Yes, sir.

(*Bobby goes out the door on the left. There is a moment's pause, and then Foster enters from the same door. He is a bright, active young man about twenty-eight or thirty.*)

PHILIP. Good morning, Foster.

FOSTER. Good morning, Mr. Fleming.

PHILIP. Here's a letter from the receiver for Reed and Vorst. He wants to know if we'll accept an immediate settlement of forty per cent.

FOSTER. (*becoming serious*) Gee, Mr. Fleming, I don't see how we can. I was depending on at least fifty per cent to carry us through the summer. It's always a dull season, you know, and--

PHILIP. Why, we have more orders now than we had this time last year.

FOSTER. Yes, I know, sir. But, I was going to speak to you. The Cotton Exchange Bank doesn't want to renew those notes.

PHILIP. Doesn't, eh? Well, then, we'll have to accept Reed and Vorst's offer.

FOSTER. I think it would be a mistake just now, sir. If we hold out, they've got big assets.

PHILIP. Can't be helped. I'm hard-pressed. We're short of ready money.

FOSTER. I don't understand it. We've had a better winter than we've had for years.

PHILIP. (smiling) That last little flier I took wasn't as successful as the former ones.

FOSTER. You've been too lenient with the retailers.

PHILIP. "Live and let live" 's my motto.

FOSTER. I'd hate to see anything happen to the mill.

PHILIP. Nothing's going to happen. Let me do the worrying. Our credit's good. I'll raise the money tomorrow.

FOSTER. I hope so, sir. Anything else?

PHILIP. (giving him the letters) Wire the answers to these right away. That's all.

FOSTER. All right, sir.

(Foster goes out. Philip takes up a large sheet of paper which contains a report from one of the departments of the mill. He scans it closely and makes some calculations upon a sheet of paper. Williams enters.)

PHILIP. (looking up) Good morning, Williams.

(Williams is quite an old man, but has the attitude of one who knows his business and can do things. He stands with bent shoulders and arms hanging limp. He is chewing tobacco, and speaks with a quick, sharp, New England accent.)

WILLIAMS. Good morning, Mr. Fleming.

PHILIP. (holding the report in his hand) Williams, a short time ago you told me that the main supply belt in the finishing room was only repaired a few times during the last six months. I find here from your report that it has broken down about twice a week since last January. How long does it take to make a repair?

WILLIAMS. Oh, sometimes about ten minutes--other times again, twenty minutes. We have done it in five minutes.

PHILIP. There are about one hundred and ten operators in that room?

WILLIAMS. One hundred and seven.

PHILIP. Why, you should have reported this condition the first week it arose. Poor economy, Williams.

(*He makes a few, rapid calculations upon the back of a report.*)

Twelve hundred dollars lost time. (*He shakes his head.*) We could have bought a new belt a year ago and saved money in the bargain.

WILLIAMS. I told Mr. Baker several times, sir, in the beginning, and he didn't seem to think anything of it.

PHILIP. Well, report all such details to me in the future.

(*He writes a few lines rapidly and rings the bell. Bobby enters briskly.*)

Tell Mr. Foster to get those firms over long distance, and whichever one can make the quickest delivery to place orders there--see?

BOBBY. Yes, sir.

(*He has a soiled card in his hand, which he offers to Philip with a grin.*)

A man outside told me to hand you his visiting card.

WILLIAMS. Is that all, sir?

PHILIP. Yes. (*He smiles as he reads the card.*) Joe Fletcher! Tell him to come in. (*Philip resumes work at his desk. Williams goes out.*)

BOBBY. Yes, sir.

(*He follows Williams. After a moment Joe Fletcher enters. He is a man of middle age, well made but heavy and slouching in manner. He has a keen, shrewd eye in a weak and dissipated face, which is made attractive, nevertheless, by a genial and ingratiating smile. He is wearing a shabby linen coat called a "duster," which hangs, crushed and limp, from his neck to his ankles. Strung from his left shoulder is a cord hung with sponges of various sizes. Several lengths of chamois are dangling with the sponges across his breast and back, draping his right hip and leg. In one hand he has a weather beaten satchel. He carries by a leather thong a heavy stone hanging from a cracked plate. There are two holes in the rim of the plate, through one of which runs the thong by which it is carried. To the other, the big stone is fastened to it with a piece of chain. He carries it unconscious of its weight. There is a pervading sense of intimacy between the man and his equipment, and from his battered hat to his spreading shoes the stains of the road, like a varnish, bind them together in a mellow fellowship.*)

PHILIP. Hello, Joe. (*He looks at him with humorous curiosity.*)

JOE. (*light-heartedly*) How de-do, Mr. Fleming.

(*Joe's voice is broken and husky. He gives a little, dry cough now and then in an ineffectual attempt to clear it. He crosses to the corner of the table, and shows by his step that his feet are sore and swollen.*)

PHILIP. What are you doing now, Joe?

(*Indicating his effects, Joe places the stone against a corner of the table*) *on the floor, and puts the valise on the edge of the table.*)

JOE.   Traveling merchant; agent for Brummell's Giant Cement; professional corn doctor--soft and hard corns--calluses--bunions removed instantly, ingrowing nails treated 'thout pain or loss of blood--or money refunded. Didn't ye read m'card?

PHILIP. *(laughing)* Well, not all of it, Joe.

JOE. *(reminiscently)* Inventor of Dr. Fletcher's famous cough mixture, warranted to cure coughs--colds, hoarseness and loss o' voice. An infallible remedy fur all chronic conditions of the *pull-mon*-ary organs. *(He coughs again.)* When not too fur gone.

> (*He takes a labeled bottle containing a brown mixture from his inside pocket, shakes it, and holds it up proudly before Philip.*)

Kin I sell ye a bottle? (*He smiles ingratiatingly.*)

PHILIP. *(smiling but shaking his head)* No, Joe, I guess not today.

JOE. *(opening the satchel insinuatingly)* Mebbe a few boxes o' corn salve? It's great. (*Philip shakes his head.*) Would ye like to consider a box o' cement?

PHILIP. *(still smiling)* No, but I'll take one of those big sponges.

JOE. I thought I could sell ye something.

> (*He unhooks a large sponge and lays it upon the desk. Philip hands him a bill. He takes it carelessly, looks at it, shakes his head regretfully, and puts it into his pocket. Then he feels in his other pocket and taps his vest pockets.*)

Gosh, I'm sorry, but I ain't got a bit of change.

PHILIP. Oh, never mind the change, Joe. (*He laughs indulgently.*)

JOE. *(regretfully)* Well, I'd feel better if I *hed* the change. Kin I set down fur a minnit, Mr. Fleming? M'feet gets so tired.

PHILIP. Yes, Joe, sit down.

JOE. I got pretty wet a while ago in that shower. My, but it did come down.

PHILIP. *(warmly)* Perhaps you'd like a hot drink?

> (*Philip indicates, with a nod of the head, the cabinet back of Joe, as the latter is about to sit down. Joe shows a lively interest.*)

JOE. *(glancing at Philip with a shy twinkle in his eye)* Oh, kin I, Mr. Fleming? Thank ye.

> (*He shuffles over to the cabinet, opens the door, and gloats over the vision of joy which greets him. He selects a bottle.*)

PHILIP. Hold on, Joe. Wait for some hot water.

JOE. *(hastily)* No, thank ye. I'm afraid I'd be like the Irishman in the dream.

PHILIP. What was that, Joe?

JOE. (*as he pours out a generous portion*) Well, the Irishman was dreaming that he went to see the priest, and the priest asked him to have a drink. "I will, thank ye kindly," says Pat. "Is it hot or cold, ye'll have it?" says the priest. "Hot, if ye plaze, yer Riverence," says Pat, and while they were waiting for the hot water, Pat wakes up. "Bad luck to me," says he, "why didn't I take it cold?"

(*He drains the glass, smacks his lips, and chuckles.*)

My, but that's good stuff! Mr. Fleming, are ye as fond of it yourself as ye used to be?

PHILIP. (*smiling and shaking his head*) No, Joe. I've got through with all that foolishness. I've sewed my wild oats.

JOE. (*chuckling as he sits in the chair*) You must have got a pretty slick crop out o' yourn.

PHILIP. Every man gets a pretty full crop of those, Joe, before he gets through.

JOE. Ye've turned over a new leaf, eh?

PHILIP. Yes--married.

JOE. Married?

PHILIP. Yes, and got a baby.

JOE. Thet so! Did ye marry out'n the mill?

PHILIP. Oh, no. She was a Miss Thorp, of Niagara.

(*He shows the picture of the child to Joe.*)

JOE. (*showing interest immediately and gazing at the picture, while gradually a gentle responsive smile plays over his features; he speaks admiringly*) By George! That's a great baby!

(*He gives a chuckling laugh.*)

Boy?

PHILIP. (*proudly*) No. Girl!

JOE. Thet so! Should a thought you'd a wanted a boy.

(*With sly significance, and chuckling at his own joke.*)

Ye've hed so many girls.

PHILIP. (*laughing lightly*) Tut, tut, Joe, no more of that for me.

(*He hands him the frame containing Margaret's picture.*)

My wife.

JOE. (*his expression becoming grave as the sweetness and dignity of the face touch him, he takes a long breath*) My, but that's a fine face. Gee, if she's as good as that, you're a lucky man, Mr. Fleming.

PHILIP. Yes, Joe, I've got more than I deserve, I guess. (*He becomes serious for the first time and a shadow flits over his face. He sighs.*)

JOE. (*sympathetically*) Oh, I understand just how you feel. I'm married m'self.

(*He sits down facing the audience, his hands clasped, his thumbs gently rolling over each other. A far-away tender look comes into his eye.*)

PHILIP. (*surprised*) Married? (*Joe nods his head.*) Where's your wife?

JOE. Left me. (*He gives a sigh of self pity.*)

PHILIP. (*touched*) Left you!

(*He shakes his head compassionately, then the thought comes to him.*)

If my wife left me, I'd kill myself.

JOE. (*philosophically*) Oh, no, no, ye wouldn't. You'd get over it, just as I did. (*He sighs.*)

PHILIP. How did it happen? What did you do?

JOE. (*innocently*) Not a durn thing! She was a nice, German woman, too. She kept a gent's furnishing store down in South Boston, and I married her.

PHILIP. (*recovering himself and speaking gaily*) Oh, Joe. (*He shakes his head in mock reproval.*) You married her for her money, eh?

(*He laughs at Joe.*)

JOE. (*ingenuously*) No, I didn't, honest. I thought I might get a whack at the till once in a while, but I didn't.

PHILIP. (*quizzing him*) Why not, Joe?

JOE. She fixed me up a pack and sent me out on the road to sell goods, and when I got back, she was gone. There was a new sign on the store, "Isaac Litchenstein, Ladies' and Gents' Dry Goods."

(*He draws a big sigh.*)

PHILIP. And you've never seen her since?

JOE. (*shaking his head sadly*) No, siree, never!

PHILIP. (*serious again, impressed by Joe*) That's pretty tough, Joe.

BOBBY. (*entering*) Dr. Larkin would like to see you, sir.

JOE. (*gathering himself and his merchandise together*) Well, I guess I'll get out and drum up a few sales. Much obliged to you, Mr. Fleming.

PHILIP. Oh, stop at the house, Joe. Mrs. Fleming might want something. It's the old place on Linden Street.

JOE. Got a dog?

PHILIP. Yes.

JOE. That settles it.

PHILIP. Only a pug, Joe.

JOE. Oh, a snorer. I'll sell him a bottle of cough mixture. (*As Dr. Larkin enters.*) Hello, Doc! How are you? Raining?

(*Joe goes to the door on the right, crossing the Doctor, who is walking toward Philip on the left.*)

DOCTOR. (*looking at him, mystified*) Good morning, sir. No, it's not raining.

(*Joe goes out. Dr. Larkin is a tall, gaunt man who looks older than he is, with quite a stoop in his shoulders. He has dark brown hair and a beard, streaked with gray, and soft, kind blue eyes. He carries the medicine satchel of a homeopathic physician. His manner is usually distant and cold but extremely quiet and gentle. In the opening of this scene he is perturbed and irritated; later, he becomes stern and authoritative.*)

PHILIP. Good morning, Dr. Larkin.

DOCTOR. (*turning to Philip*) Who is that fellow?

(*He looks after Joe as he goes out.*)

PHILIP. Don't you remember him? That's Joe Fletcher.

DOCTOR. Is that Joe Fletcher? Why, he used to be quite a decent sort of fellow. Wasn't he a foreman here in your father's time?

PHILIP. Yes, he was one of the best men in the mill.

DOCTOR. (*shaking his head*) He is a sad example of what liquor and immorality will bring a man to. He has indulged his appetites until he has no real moral nature left.

PHILIP. (*lightly*) Oh, I don't think Joe ever had much "moral nature."

(*The sunlight leaves the room; it is growing cloudy outside.*)

DOCTOR. Every man has a moral nature. In this case it is love of drink that has destroyed it. There are some men who are moral lepers, even lacking the weakness of the tippler as an excuse.

PHILIP. Have you been to the house, Doctor? About midnight Margaret thought little Lucy had a fever. She was going to call you up--but--

DOCTOR. (*abruptly*) She would not have found me in at midnight.

PHILIP. Ah, is that so? Someone very ill? (*The telephone rings.*) Excuse me, Doctor. Hello. Oh, is that you, Margaret? How is Lucy now? Good! I knew she'd be all right. Yes, of course. Do--bring her. (*To the Doctor.*) She's bringing baby to the 'phone. Hello, Lucy. Many happy returns of the day. Good-bye. Yes, I'll be home at twelve sharp. Apple pie? Yes, of course, I like it. That is, *your* apple pie. (*He leaves the phone with a joyous air.*) This is baby's birthday, you know, Doctor.

DOCTOR. I've just left a baby--(*bitterly, looking at Philip significantly*)-- that should never have had a birthday.

PHILIP. (*without noticing the Doctor's manner, he goes to the cabinet and, taking a box of cigars, offers the box to the Doctor*) Why, Doctor, you're morbid today. Take a cigar; it will quiet your nerves.

(*The rain begins to fall, beating heavily against the windows.*)

DOCTOR. No, thank you. (*With a subtle shade of repugnance in his tone.*)
I'll smoke one of my own.
> (*Philip smiles indulgently, goes to the desk, sits in a chair to the left of
> it, lights a cigar, leans back luxuriously with his hands in his pockets
> and one leg over the other, and tips back the legs of the chair.*)

PHILIP. (*carelessly*) What's the matter, Doctor? You used to respect my
cigars.

DOCTOR. (*hotly*) I used to respect you.

PHILIP. (*rather surprised but laughing good-naturedly*) Well, Doctor,
don't you now? (*He is bantering him.*)

DOCTOR. (*quietly but sternly*) No, I don't.

PHILIP. (*smoking placidly*) Good lord--why?

DOCTOR. (*his satchel resting upon his knees, his hands clasping the metal
top, he leans over a trifle and, looking impressively into Philip's face,
says, in a low, calm voice*) At two o'clock last night Lena Schmidt gave
birth to a child.

PHILIP. (*becoming livid with amazement and fear, and staring blankly
before him, the cigar dropping from his parted lips*) In God's name, how
did they come to send for you?

DOCTOR. Dr. Taylor--he called me in consultation. He was frightened
after the girl had been in labor thirty-six hours.

PHILIP. (*murmuring to himself*) Thirty-six hours! Good God! (*There is
a pause; then he partly recovers himself.*) I suppose she told you?

DOCTOR. She told me nothing. It was a lucky thing for you that I was
there. The girl was delirious.

PHILIP. Delirious? Well, I've done all I could for her, Doctor.

DOCTOR. (*his tone is full of scorn*) Have you?

PHILIP. She's had all the money she wanted.

DOCTOR. (*in the same tone*) Has she?

PHILIP. I tried to get her away months ago, but she wouldn't do it. She
was as stubborn as a mule.

DOCTOR. Strange she should want to remain near the father of her
child, isn't it?

PHILIP. If she'd done as I told her to, this thing would never have
happened.

DOCTOR. You'd have forced some poor devil to run the risk of state's
prison. By God, you're worse than I thought you were.

PHILIP. Why, Doctor, you must think I'm—

DOCTOR. I don't think anything about it. I know just what brutes such
men as you are.

PHILIP. Well, I'm not wholly to blamé. You don't know the whole story, Doctor.

DOCTOR. I don't want to know it. The *girl's* not to blame. She's a product of her environment. Under present social conditions, she'd probably have gone wrong anyhow. But you! God Almighty! If we can't look for decency in men like you--representative men--where in God's name are we to look for it, I'd like to know?

PHILIP. If my wife hears of this, my home will be ruined.

DOCTOR. (*scornfully*) Your home! Your home! It is just such damned scoundrels as you that make and destroy homes.

PHILIP. Oh, come now, Doctor, aren't you a little severe?

DOCTOR. Severe! Severe! Why, do you realize, if this thing should become known, it will stir up a stench that will offend the moral sense of every man, woman, and child in this community?

PHILIP. Well, after all, I'm no worse than other men. Why, I haven't seen the girl for months.

DOCTOR. Haven't you? Well, then suppose you go and see her now.

PHILIP. (*he springs to his feet*) I'll do nothing of the sort.

DOCTOR. Yes, you will. She shan't lie there and die like a dog.

PHILIP. (*walking around the room, greatly perturbed*) I tell you I'll not go!

DOCTOR. Yes, you will.

PHILIP. (*coming over to the Doctor and looking down upon him*) What'll you do if I don't?

DOCTOR. I don't know, but you'd best go and see that girl.

PHILIP. (*turning away*) Well, what do you want me to say to her?

DOCTOR. Lie to her as you have before. Tell her you love her.

PHILIP. I never lied to her. I never told her I loved her.

DOCTOR. Faugh!

PHILIP. I tell you, I never did!

DOCTOR. (*rising from his chair*) You'd better get Mrs. Fleming away from here until this thing blows over. When I think of a high-minded, splendid little woman like her married to a man like you--ugh!

(*The Doctor goes out quickly. Philip, left alone, walks about like an old man, seems dazed for a moment, then goes mechanically to the telephone.*)

PHILIP. Linden, three seven two one. Margaret. (*He speaks in a broken, hushed voice.*) Margaret! Yes, it's I, Philip. Yes! Well, I'm tired. No, I can't come home now. I will not be home to luncheon. I have a business engagement. No, I cannot break it off. It's too important. Eh? Why, with a man from Boston. Yes, certainly, I will, just as soon as I can get away.   Yes, dear--I will--good-bye. (*Just before he finishes, Foster enters.*) Hello, Foster.

FOSTER. (*consulting a memorandum*) I couldn't get the Harry Smith Company, New York, until noon, sir. They say that the belting can be shipped by fast express at once. The Boston people want ten cents a square foot more than they asked, but we can save that in time and express rates.

PHILIP. When would the New York shipment get here?

FOSTER. At the earliest, tomorrow afternoon.

PHILIP. White and Cross can ship at once, you say?

FOSTER. Yes, sir.

PHILIP. Well, give them the order. Their stuff is better, anyhow. Have a covered wagon at the station for the four-ten train. Keep enough men overtime tonight to put it up.

FOSTER. Yes, sir, the sooner it's done, the better.

PHILIP. Yes, Williams is getting old. He's not the best man for that finishing room. Put him where you can keep an eye on him. He's all right. I have an appointment and will not be in the office again today. Get the interest on those notes off.

FOSTER. Yes, I've attended to that already. Anything else?

PHILIP. No.

FOSTER. All right, sir. Good morning.

(*Philip, who has braced himself for this, relaxes again. The rain continues. He goes about the room, lights a cigar, puts on a rain-coat, looks at his watch, buttons his coat, all the while sunk in deep thought. He takes his umbrella and hat and goes out quickly, shutting the door so that the click of the latch is heard, as the curtain falls.*)

Scene 2. The scene is the living room in Margaret's home. At the back, large glass doors open on to a spacious porch with a garden beyond. There is a fire-place with logs burning, in the corner on the left, and beside it a French window opening on the garden. Below it is a door leading to another room. There is another door on the right going to the main part of the house. There is a table in the center, a baby grand piano on the lower right, and a baby carriage close by the doors at the back. The room is furnished in exquisite taste showing in its distinct character the grace and individuality of a well-bred woman. (*Margaret is seated in a low rocking-chair near the fire with the baby in her lap. A large bath towel is spread across her knees. She is exquisitely dressed in an evening gown. Maria Bindley, the nurse-maid, is dressed in a black dress, cap, and* apron. *She is a middle-aged German woman, dark in complexion, and of medium build and height. She speaks with a not too pronounced German accent. She is gathering up the baby's garments, which are scattered about Margaret's feet. She is furtively weeping and makes an occasional effort to overcome her emotion. Margaret is putting the last touches to the baby's night toilet. She is laughing and murmuring mother talk to her. A shaded lamp is burning on the table to the right. The effect of the light is subdued. The glare of the fire is the high note, making a soft radiance about Margaret and the child. Maria is in the shadow, except as she flits into the light whenever she moves near Margaret. The sound of the rain beating against the windows is heard now and then.)*

MARGARET. (*in a low, laughing tone*) No--no--*no!* You little beggar. You've had your supper! (*She fastens the last two or three buttons of her dress.*) No more! Time to go to sleep now! No use staying awake any longer for naughty father. Two whole hours--late! No, he doesn't care a bit about you; not a bit! (*She shakes her head.*) No, nor me either. Never mind, darling, we'll punish him well for this. Yes, we will. Perhaps we'll leave *him* some day, and then we'll see how he likes being left alone. Naughty, bad father--isn't he? *Yes, he is!* Staying away all day! Never mind, ladybird--hush, go to sleep now--Mother loves her! Go to sleep--close your eyes.
   (*This is all said in a cooing, soothing voice. She begins to sing a lullaby.*)
Go--to--sleep--blossom--go to sl--
   (*Maria comes close to Margaret and picks up two little socks. As she rises, she sniffs in an effort to suppress her tears. This attracts Margaret's attention and immediately she is all commiseration.*)
Don't cry, Maria--please don't. It distresses me to see you cry.
MARIA. (*smiling a little at Margaret's sympathy, she talks as she smooths the socks and folds them*) I cannot help it, Mrs. Fleming--I am an unhappy woman. I try not to cry, but I cannot keep back de tears. (*She puts the socks in the basket on the table.*) I have had an unhappy life--my fadder vas a brute. (*She picks up the dress and shakes it.*) My first husband, Ralph Bindley, vas a goot, honest man. (*She puts the dress in the basket.*) Und my second husband vas dot tramp vot vas here dis morning. Vat I have told you aboudt already. (*She gathers together the other garments.*) Und now my sister--my little Lena--is dying.
MARGARET. (*in dismay*) Dying! Why, you didn't tell me *that*, Maria!
MARIA. Vell, she is not dying just this very moment, but the doctor says she vill never leave dot bed alive. My sweet little Lena! My lovely

little sister. I have nursed her, Mrs. Fleming, yust like you nurse your baby now.

MARGARET. (*holding the child to her breast*) What did you say her name was?

MARIA. (*working mechanically and putting the things neatly away*) Lena--Lena Schmidt. She does not go by my name--she goes by my fadder's name.

MARGARET. And, you say, she ran away from you?

MARIA. Ya--I tried to find her every place. I hunted high und low, but she does not come, und von day I meet an olt friend on Vashington Street, Chris Anderson, und Chris, he tell me that two or three weeks before he see her by the public gartens. Und she vas valking by the arm of a fine, handsome gentleman--und she looked smiling and happy, und Chris, he says dot he knows *dot* gentleman--*dot* he vas a rich man vot lives down in Canton where Chris vonce worked when he comes to dis country first.

MARGARET. And didn't you ask the man's name?

MARIA. Ach, I forget. Und Chris go back to de olt country, und I never found out. Und den I tink maybe she is married to dot man--und she is ashamed of me and dot miserable husband of mine. I say to myself, "I vill go and see--und find oudt if she is happy." Den I vill go far away, where she vill never see me again. Und I come here to Canton, und at last I find her--und Ach Gott! She is going to be a mutter--und she is no man's vife!

(*Maria has been weeping silently but has continued to work, only pausing at some point in her story that moved her.*)

MARGARET. (*deeply touched*) Did she tell you the man's name?

MARIA. Ach! No! You could not drag dot out of her mit red hot irons. She says she loves dis man, und she vill make him no trouble. (*Beside herself with vindictive passion.*) But, by Gott, I vill find dot man oudt, und I vill choke it from his troat.

MARGARET. (*terrified at her ferocity and crushing her child to her breast*) Oh, Maria--don't--please don't! You frighten me!

MARIA. (*at once all humility*) Excuse me, Mrs. Fleming. I did not mean to do dot.

MARGARET. (*kindly*) You need not remain any longer. I can manage baby myself. You had best go to your sister at once. If I can be of any help to you, please tell me, won't you?

MARIA. Ya, Mrs. Fleming, I tank you und if she is vorse maybe I stay all night.

MARGARET. Yes, certainly. You need not come back tonight.

MARIA. (*very softly and humbly*) I am much obliged to you, Mrs. Fleming.

MARGARET. (*as Maria is going*) Oh! You had best take my rain-coat.

MARIA. Ah, you are very goot, Mrs. Fleming.

> (*She has finished her work and is going but hesitates a moment and turns back.*)

If you please, don't tell Mr. Fleming about me und my poor sister!

MARGARET. (*slightly annoyed*) Decidedly not! Why should I tell such things to him?

MARIA. Vell--men don't have sympathy mit peoples like us. He is a fine gentleman, und if he knowed about *her*--he might not like to have *me* by his vife und child. He might tink *I* vas as badt as she was. Good night, Mrs. Fleming.

MARGARET. Good night, Maria. No need to hurry back in the morning.

> (*There is a wistful sympathy in Margaret's face. As her eyes rest upon the door through which Maria has passed, she is lost in thought. Presently a door slams, then she is all alert with expectation. There is a moment's pause; she listens, then quickly puts the child in the baby carriage and runs to the door.*)

Is that you, Philip?

JANE. (*outside*) No, ma'am, it is not Mr. Fleming. It was only the post man.

> (*Margaret turns away with a sigh of disappointment, goes to the French window and peers out at the rain. Jane enters with several letters, leaves them on the table, and goes out. Margaret turns from the window, brushes the tears away impatiently, and drifts purposelessly across the room toward the right, her hands clasped behind her back. Finding herself at the piano, she listlessly sits before it and plays a plaintive air, softy. Then suddenly she dashes into a prelude to a gay love song. As she sings half through a stanza, the song gradually loses spirit. Her hands grow heavy over the keys, her voice breaks, and the words come slow and faltering. She ends by breaking into tears, with her head lowered and her fingers resting idly on the keys. The child attracts her and she goes quickly to her. She laughs through her tears into the wide-open eyes, and begins scolding her for not going to sleep. Soft endearing notes come and go in her voice. A tender joy takes possession of her spirit. She takes the child in her arms.*)

MARGARET. Well, my lady, wide awake! Come, come, no more nonsense, now! No! Go to sleep! Late hours--will--certainly spoil--your beauty. Yes! Close up your eyes--quick! Come! There, that's nice. She's a sweet, good child! (*She hums.*) Go--to--sleep!

> (*She sways slowly from right to left, then swinging with a rhythmic*)

step with the lullaby, she lilts softly.)
Blow, blow, blossom go--into the world below--I am the west wind, wild and strong--blossoms must go when they hear my song.

(*She puts out the lamp, leaving the room in the warm glare of the firelight.*)
Go, little blossom, go--into the world below. Rain, rain, rain is here. Blossoms must learn to weep.

(*She reaches the French window. As she turns, Philip is seen through the filmy curtains. He enters unnoticed.*)
I am the east wind, bleak and cold, poor little blossoms their petals must fold. Weep, little blossoms, weep, into your cradles creep.

(*She is unconscious of Philip's presence. His rain-coat and hat are dripping wet. He is pale and weary, his manner is listless and abstracted, and he looks as though he had been wandering about in the rain for hours. He drifts into the room. Margaret turns around and takes a step, her eyes upon the child, then her lullaby grows indistinct as she notices that the baby is asleep. Another step takes her into Philip's arms. She gives a cry of alarm.*)
Oh, Philip! You frightened me! Why did you do that?

PHILIP. Why are you in the dark, Margaret? (*He goes toward her as if to take her in his arms.*) Dearest!

MARGARET. (*drawing back from him with a shade of petulance*) You're all wet. Don't come near baby. She was wakeful. I've put her to sleep. Where have you been all day?

PHILIP. Didn't I tell you over the 'phone I had an engagement?

MARGARET. (*as she flits swiftly into the room on the left*) Did it take you all day to keep it?

(*Margaret remains in the room long enough to put the child in the crib and then returns.*)
PHILIP. Yes. A lot of things came up--that I didn't expect. I've been detained. (*He is still standing where she left him.*)

MARGARET. (*turning up the lamp*) Why, dear, look! Your umbrella is dripping all over the floor.

PHILIP. (*noticing the little puddle of water*) Oh, how stupid of me!

(*He hurries out the door on the right, removes his hat and rain-coat, leaves the umbrella, and returns quickly. Margaret, meanwhile, has mopped up the water. Then she turns on a lamp.*)
MARGARET. (*reproachfully*) We've been awfully lonesome here all day, baby and I!

PHILIP. (*by the fire*) Forgive me, sweetheart. I've had a very hard day.

MARGARET. Did you forget it was Lucy's birthday?

PHILIP. (*smiling gravely*) No, I didn't forget. You have both been in my mind the whole day.

MARGARET. (*glowing with love and a welcome that she refused to give until now*) Oh, Philip! (*She throws herself in his arms.*) It's good to get you back. So good! (*After a moment, she rings the bell. Jane answers.*) Jane, I wish you would serve dinner in here.

JANE. Yes, Mrs. Fleming. (*Exit Jane.*)

PHILIP. (*drawing Margaret close to him again, as though a long time had passed since he parted from her*) Dear little wife!

JANE. (*coming in with a tray containing food and silver, and going to the center table*) Shall I lay the table here, Mrs. Fleming?

MARGARET. No--here--cosy--by the fire.

(*Jane dresses the table deftly and without bustle. She goes away and returns with the dinner.*)

You need not return, Jane. I'll ring if we need you.

JANE. Very well, Mrs. Fleming. (*She goes off.*)

PHILIP. (*sitting to the right of the table, and taking a large envelope from his pocket, he withdraws a bank book and hands it to Margaret, who is about to sit down on the left*) Here, Margaret--I want you to look over that.

MARGARET. (*taking the book and reading the cover*) "Margaret Fleming in account with Boston Providence Savings Bank." (*She opens the book and reads.*) "By deposit, May 3, 1890. $5,000." Five thousand dollars! Oh, Philip!

PHILIP. (*smiling complacently*) There's something else.

MARGARET. Yes? (*Philip nods his head, and hands her a large envelope which he has taken from his pocket. She looks at it and reads.*) "Margaret Fleming, guardian for Lucy Fleming." (*She takes a document from the envelope.*) A certificate for $20,000 worth of United States bonds, maturing 1930. Why, Philip! How wonderful! But, can you afford it? (*He smiles and nods his head, and then begins to serve the dinner. Margaret, in childish joy, rushes to the door of the room where the child is.*) Oh, baby! Lucy! You are rich, rich! (*She stops and peeps in.*) Oh, my, I must not wake her. *The little heiress!*

(*She sits at the table and begins to serve.*)

PHILIP. (*handing her another envelope, tenderly*) For you, Margaret!

MARGARET. (*taking it and becoming breathless as she reads it*) It's a deed for this house and all the land! Ah, Philip, how generous you are, and this is what has kept you away all day! And I was cross with you.

(*Tears come to her eyes.*) Forgive me, dear, please do. (*She goes to him and kneels by his side.*) But, why do you do all this? What need? What necessity for me to have a deed of property from you?

PHILIP. Well, things have not been going just our way at the mill. The new tariff laws may help, but I doubt it. At all events, before anything serious--

MARGARET. (*a little awed*) Serious?

PHILIP. Well, you never can be sure. At any rate, in times of stress a business man should protect his family.

MARGARET. Is there danger--of--trouble?

PHILIP. No! I hope not. I think I'll be able to tide it over.

MARGARET. But, dear--you--this property, is worth a lot of money. Why not sell it? Wouldn't that be a great help? A resource in case--

PHILIP. Sell the home?

MARGARET. No, sell the house. The home is where we are. (*She rises and stands back of his chair with her arms about his neck.*) Where *love* is-- no matter *where*, just so long as we three are there together. A big house--a little house--of course, I do love this place, where you were born, and baby-- (*Taking a long breath.*) It's very precious--but-- (*She has moved to the head of the table and now lays down the deed.*) I cannot take it, dear. It frightens me. It's too valuable--all this--land--no-- let us guard it together and if bad times come, it will be--a fine thing to have--

PHILIP. (*protesting*) Now, my dear!

MARGARET. I don't want the responsibility. Suppose something happened to me. (*She sits at the table, on the left.*)

PHILIP. Ah--Margaret--

MARGARET. (*laughing*) Well--I just said "suppose."

PHILIP. (*laughing*) Well--*don't say it*. We'll think of nothing "suppose." *Nothing*, but bright--*beautiful* things.

MARGARET. Come, dear, eat. I should think you were famished. You've touched nothing yet.

PHILIP. I don't feel hungry. I'm tired--awfully tired.

MARGARET. No wonder, after all you've been through today. I'll make you a cup of tea. (*She rings the bell. Jane enters.*) Boiling water, Jane, please, and bring the tea things. (*Exit Jane. While Margaret is busy over the tea things, she stops and looks at him quizzically.*) Who was that tramp you sent here this morning?

PHILIP. (*innocently*) What tramp?

MARGARET. Why, the one with the plate and the big stone--the cough medicine--the sponges and--(*she imitates Joe*)-- the voice.

PHILIP. (*laughing*) Ah, he's not a tramp--that's Joe Fletcher.

MARGARET. Did you know that he was Maria's husband.

PHILIP. (*amazed*) What! Maria's husband? What did he say to her?

MARGARET. (*smiling reminiscently*) He didn't say much-- *She* did all the talking.

PHILIP. What did *she* say?

MARGARET. I don't know. She spoke in German. I think, she was swearing at him. When I came, she had him by the ears and was trying to pull his head off. Then she got him to the floor and threw him down the front steps. It was the funniest thing I ever saw. I couldn't help laughing; yet my heart ached for her.

PHILIP. Poor Joe! That's the second time she's thrown him out.

MARGARET. She never did that before?

PHILIP. He says she did.

MARGARET. Well, she didn't. He robbed her and left her.

PHILIP. What?

MARGARET. She went out on the road to sell goods and left him in charge of the shop. When she came back, he was gone and he had sold out the place to a secondhand dealer.

PHILIP. (*in wonderment*) What a liar that fellow is!

MARGARET. Well, if he told you any other story--he certainly is. (*She notices a change in his face.*) Why, Philip! You look awfully white! Are you ill? Are you keeping anything from me? Oh, please tell me--do. (*She goes to him, and puts her arms about his shoulders, with her face against his as she finishes the last line.*) Let me share your trouble.

PHILIP. No--no--dear heart--nothing! There's nothing more to tell. I'm very tired.

MARGARET. Oh, how selfish of me. You should have gone to bed the moment you came.

PHILIP. I'll be all right in the morning. I must have caught a chill. (*He shudders.*) My blood seems to be congealed.

MARGARET. (*alarmed*) Oh, my dear--my poor boy! It was a dreadful thing you did. (*He starts guiltily.*) Going about in the rain all day.

(*She goes swiftly into the room on the left and returns with a handsome dressing gown and slippers. She fusses over Philip, helps him to get into his dressing gown, and warms his slippers by the fire.*)

I must give you some aconite. A hot drink--a mustard foot bath.

PHILIP. I don't think I need anything, dear, but a hot drink, perhaps, and a night's rest. I'll be all right in the morning. I think I'll take a little brandy.

MARGARET. (*quickly*) I'll get it for you, dear. Keep by the fire.
> (*She rushes out the door on the right, and returns quickly with a silver tray holding a cut-glass decanter of brandy and a glass. She pours out some and holds up the glass.*)

Is that enough?

PHILIP. Plenty--thank you! (*He drinks it, while Margaret replaces the tray on a small table.*) Now, dear, I'll look after that mustard bath.

PHILIP. Oh, Margaret, please don't bother. I really don't need it.

MARGARET (*laughing*) Yes, you do. (*She shakes her finger threateningly.*) You might just as well make up your mind that you've got to have it.

PHILIP. (*smiling resignedly*) All right--"boss."

MARGARET. (*laughing at him as she starts to go*) You know, Philip dear, you gave me the strangest feeling when you stood there--the rain dripping from you--you didn't look a bit like yourself. (*She gives an apologetic laugh.*) You gave me a dreadful fright. Just like a spirit! A lost spirit. (*She laughs again.*) Now, wasn't that silly of me?
> (*She runs off to the right, still laughing. Philip sits in the fire light looking sadly after her as the curtain falls.*)

ACT II.

The scene is the same as the second scene of the first act. The large doors at the back are open, showing a luxuriant garden in brilliant sunshine. (*The baby is in her carriage by the garden door. Margaret, in a dainty house dress, is seated in a low chair in the center of the room, mending one of the baby's dresses. Dr. Larkin, sitting at the table on the left with his back turned to her, is folding little packages of medicine. Margaret looks happy and contented as she chats with him.*)

DOCTOR. You say you have no pain in the eyes?

MARGARET. No pain at all . . . only, once in awhile there is . . . a . . . sort of a dimness.

DOCTOR. Yes, a dimness.

MARGARET. As if my eyes were tired.

DOCTOR. Yes!

MARGARET. When I read too long, or . . .

DOCTOR. (*turning about and looking at her*) Do you know what would be a good thing for you to do?

MARGARET. What, Doctor?

DOCTOR. Wear glasses.

MARGARET. Why, Doctor, aren't you dreadful! (*She laughs at him.*) Why, I'd look a sight.

DOCTOR. Well, it would be a good idea, all the same. You should wear glasses when you are reading or sewing, at least.

MARGARET. (*laughing gaily at him*) Well, I'll do nothing of the sort. Time enough for me to wear glasses, years and years from now.

DOCTOR. (*smiling indulgently*) It would be a good thing to do now. How is "Topsy" this morning?

MARGARET. (*glancing proudly in the direction of the baby*) Oh, she's blooming.

DOCTOR. Mrs. Fleming, any time you want to sell that baby, Mrs. Larkin and I will give you ten thousand dollars for her.

MARGARET. (*laughing and beaming with pride*) Yes . . . Doctor . . . when we *want* to sell her. How is Mrs. Larkin?

DOCTOR. She's doing very nicely. I'm going to try to get her up to the mountains this summer. (*He finishes the packages.*) There . . . take one of these powders three times a day. Rest your eyes as much as possible. Don't let anything fret or worry you, and keep out-doors all you can.

(*He closes the bag after putting a couple of bottles and a small medicine case in it.*)

MARGARET. Oh, Doctor, aren't you going to leave something for Philip?

DOCTOR. (*giving a dry little grunt*) Hum! I forgot about him.

(*Standing by the table, he takes a small case from his satchel, removes two large bottles of pellets from it, fills two phials from them, and makes a number upon the cork of each with a fountain pen.*)

You say he was pretty wet when he came home last night?

MARGARET. Yes, and tired out. He had a very hard day, I think. I never saw him so completely fagged. It seemed to me he had been tramping in the rain for hours. I gave him a good scolding, too, I tell you. I doctored him up as well as I could and put him to bed. (*Smiling contentedly.*) He's as bright as a lark this morning, but all the same, I insisted upon his remaining home for a rest.

DOCTOR. (*beaming kindly*) You take good care of him, don't you?

MARGARET. (*playfully*) I've got to . . . He's all I have, and men like Philip are not picked up every day, now, I tell you.

DOCTOR. (*drily*) No, men like Philip Fleming are certainly not to be found easily.

MARGARET. I hope there's nothing wrong with him. I was worried last night. You know, he has been working awfully hard lately.

DOCTOR. (*kindly*) Now, don't fret about imaginary ills. He's probably a little over-worked. It might be a good idea to have him go away for a week or two.

MARGARET. (*entering into the suggestion*) Yes . . . a little trip somewhere would help him a lot, I'm sure.

DOCTOR. (*holding up his finger*) But, you must go with him, though.
   (*Margaret, by this time, is standing up, with the baby's dress tucked under her arm. She takes stitches as she talks.*)

MARGARET. (*eagerly*) Of course! I wouldn't let him go alone. Somebody might steal him from me. (*She smiles.*)

DOCTOR. (*snapping the clasp of his satchel, vehemently murmurs under his breath*) Hum! They'd bring him back mighty quick, I guess. (*Returns to her.*) Give him these. Tell him to take two alternately every hour.

MARGARET. (*taking the phials and nodding her head as if to remember*) Two every hour--thank you.
   (*Philip enters from the garden, gaily humming an air. He has a freshly plucked rose in his hand.*)

PHILIP. Good morning, Doctor.

DOCTOR. (*coldly*) Good morning.

MARGARET. (*regretfully*) Oh, Philip, you plucked that rose.

PHILIP. Yes, isn't it lovely? It's the first of the season. (*He smells it.*)

MARGARET. Yes, and I've been watching it. I wanted it to open yesterday for baby's birthday.

PHILIP. (*playfully*) It saved itself for today for baby's mother.
   (*He puts it on her breast.*)

MARGARET. (*pleased*) Well, I'd rather it had bloomed yesterday for her. Excuse me, Doctor, I must run into the kitchen. We have a new cook and she needs watching.

PHILIP. (*gaily*) And she's a dandy. (*He breaks into a chant.*) Oh, I'm glad we've got a new cookie. I'm glad we've got a new cook. She's . . .

MARGARET. (*laughing at him*) Hush! Hush! Philip, stop--be quiet!
   (*She puts her hand over his mouth. He tries to sing through her fingers.*)
She'll hear you. Oh, Doctor, isn't he terrible? He's poking fun at her all the time, but she is funny, though. (*She runs off joyously to the right.*)

PHILIP. What a glorious morning, after yesterday.

DOCTOR. (*eyeing him coldly*) Yes--it is--you're in high feather this morning, eh?

PHILIP. (*cheerily*) Of course I am. What's the good in worrying over things you can't help?

DOCTOR. Have you seen . . .?

PHILIP. (*quickly*) Yes. (*In a low voice.*) I've made arrangements for her to go away as soon as she is well enough.

DOCTOR. *Humph!*

PHILIP. It's a terrible mess. I'll admit I never realized what I was doing, but, I shall make things all right for this girl and her child. (*He sits on the edge of the table to the left. The Doctor is standing to the right of him.*) Doctor, I'm going to tell my wife this whole, miserable story.

DOCTOR. (*aghast*) What?

PHILIP. (*hastily interrupting*) Ah, not now--in the future. When we both have grown closer together. When I have shown her by an honest and decent life that I ought to be forgiven--when I feel sure of her faith and confidence--then I shall confess and ask her to forgive me.

DOCTOR. (*shaking his head*) That would be a mighty hazardous experiment. You would draw a woman's heartstrings closer and closer about you--and then deliberately tear them asunder. Best keep silent forever.

PHILIP. There would be no hazard. I know Margaret--of course, if she found me out now--I admit it--it would be a terrible thing, but--

DOCTOR. (*abruptly*) You'd better get Mrs. Fleming away from here for a few weeks.

PHILIP. (*surprised*) Away? (*He smiles confidently.*) What need?

DOCTOR. She is threatened with a serious affection of the eyes.

PHILIP. (*his smile fading away, then recovering quickly and laughing lightly*) Aren't you trying to frighten me, Doctor?

DOCTOR. (*annoyed*) I don't care anything about you, but, I tell you, your wife has a tendency to an affection of the eyes called glaucoma.

PHILIP. (*interested*) Glaucoma? Affection of the eyes? Why, Margaret has magnificent eyes.

DOCTOR. Yes, she has magnificent eyes, but, her child is the indirect cause of the development of an inherent weakness in them.

PHILIP. In what way?

DOCTOR. Conditions incident to motherhood. Shock. She is showing slight symptoms now that if aggravated would cause very serious consequences.

PHILIP. (*puzzled*) I do not understand.

DOCTOR. The eye--like other organs, has its own special secretion, which keeps it nourished and in a healthy state. The inflow and outflow of this secretion is equal. The physician sometimes comes across a patient of apparently sound physique, in whom he will find an abnormal condition of the eye where this natural function is, through some inherent weakness, easily disturbed. When the patient is subject to illness, great physical or mental suffering, the too great emotion of a sudden joy or sorrow--the stimulus of any one of these causes may produce in the eyes a super-abundant influx of this perfectly healthy fluid and the fine outflowing ducts cannot carry it off.

PHILIP. Yes. What then?

DOCTOR. The impact continues--until the result--is--

PHILIP. Yes? What is the result?

DOCTOR. Blindness.

PHILIP. (*awed*) Why--that is horrible! Is there no remedy?

DOCTOR. Yes. A very delicate operation.

PHILIP. Always successful?

DOCTOR. If performed under proper conditions--yes.

PHILIP. And my wife is in danger of this?

> (*He walks up and down the room.*)

DOCTOR. There is no danger whatever to Mrs. Fleming, if the serenity of her life is not disturbed. There are slight but nevertheless serious symptoms that must be remedied at once, with ordinary care. She will outgrow this weakness. Perhaps you will understand now how necessary it is that she leave Canton for a few weeks.

PHILIP. (*deeply impressed*) Yes, I do. I will set about getting her away at once. I can leave the mill for a while in Foster's hands.

DOCTOR. Yes, he is an honest, capable fellow. Above all things, do not let Mrs. Fleming suspect that there is anything serious the matter. Keep her cheerful.

PHILIP. Ah, Margaret is the sunniest, happiest disposition--nothing troubles her.

DOCTOR. Well, you keep her so. (*Philip takes out his cigar case and offers it; the Doctor refuses laconically.*) Thank you, I have my own.

> (*He has taken a cigar from his vest pocket. Philip strikes a match and offers it to the Doctor. At the same time, the Doctor is lighting his cigar with his own match, ignoring Philip's attention. Philip shrugs his shoulders indulgently, lights his cigar, and good-naturedly watches the Doctor, who takes up his satchel and leaves the room hastily with a curt farewell.*)

Good morning.

PHILIP. (*genially*) Good morning, Dr. Larkin.

> (*He sits in the armchair to the right and comfortably contemplates the convolutions of the cigar smoke. The closing of the front door is heard. Joe Fletcher appears at the French window, stealthily peering into the room. He sees Philip and coughs.*)

JOE. Hello, Mr. Fleming!

PHILIP. (*looking up*) Hello, Joe--come in.

JOE. (*in a whisper*) Is it safe?

PHILIP. (*laughing*) Yes, I guess so.

JOE. (*slouching inside*) Where's Maria?

PHILIP. Gone out.

JOE. (*relieved*) Say, that was a damn mean trick you played on me yesterday.

PHILIP. What trick?

JOE. Sending me up here--you knew durn well she'd go fer me.

PHILIP. (*laughing*) I didn't know Maria was your wife, honest I didn't.

JOE. Oh, tell that to the marines. I want my sign. (*As Philip looks puzzled.*) The sample of Giant's Cement with the plate.

PHILIP. (*remembering*) Oh, yes.

(*He chuckles to himself, goes to the door at the right and brings back the cracked plate with the big stone hung to it. Joe takes it and turns to go.*)

Why did you lie to me yesterday?

JOE. I didn't lie to you.

PHILIP. You told me your wife ran away from you.

JOE. So she did.

PHILIP. *She* says you robbed her and left her.

JOE. She's a liar, and I'll tell her to her face.

PHILIP. (*laughing*) Come, Joe, you wouldn't dare.

JOE. She's a liar. I'm not afraid of her.

PHILIP. She made you run yesterday.

JOE. (*holding up the sign*) Didn't she have this? What chance has a fellow got when a woman has a *weapon* like this?

PHILIP. (*laughing at him*) And you were in the war.

JOE. Yes, I was in the war! The Johnnies didn't fight with things like this.

PHILIP. Come, Joe, I believe she'd make you run without that.

JOE. She's a liar. I can lick her. (*With conviction.*) I have licked her. (*He grows bolder.*) An' I'll lick her again.

PHILIP. (*laughing heartily*) Come, Joe, that'll do. The best way for you to lick 'er is there.

(*He points to the decanter upon the side table. Joe gazes upon it tenderly and chuckles with unctuous satisfaction.*)

JOE. That's a great joke, Mr. Fleming. Kin I?

(*He shuffles over to the decanter.*)

PHILIP. Yes, go ahead.

(*Joe pours the liquor into a glass. Maria walks hastily in through the window and sees Philip.*)

MARIA. (*diffidently*) Excuse me, Mr. Fleming, I did not know you vas here. I always come in dot way mit de baby.

(*Joe is in the act of carrying the glass to his lips. He hears Maria's voice and stands terrified. Maria sees him and becomes inflamed with indignation. She puts her hands on her hips and glares at him.*)

Vell, you dom scoundrel!

JOE. (*soothingly extending a hand to her*) There now, Maria, keep cool. Don't lose your temper.

MARIA. (*mocking him*) Yah, don't lose my temper. Didn't I tell you never to darken dis house again? *Du teufel aus Hölle!*

(*She makes a lunge at him. He dodges and hops on tip-toe from side to side in a zig-zag.*)

JOE. Just a minute, Maria! (*He gulps.*) I can--I can explain--the whole--thing.

(*He makes a desperate bolt, but Maria is on his heels. He stumbles and falls sprawling upon his hands and face, with his head to the front, in the center of the room. She swoops upon him, digs her hands into the loose folds of his coat between the shoulders and drags him to his feet. He limps with fright, puffing and spluttering, awkwardly helping himself and dropping the sign.*)

Maria, for God's sake, don't! I ain't ever done anything to you.

MARIA. (*dragging him toward the window*) Ach, Gott! No, you have never done nutting to me.

JOE. I'll make it all right with you. Let me go. I want my sign! Ugh!

(*She throws him through the French window. He stumbles and staggers out of sight. Maria picks up the sign and flings it after him. All the time she is scolding and weeping with anger.*)

MARIA. Don't you dare come here no more to a decent house, you loafer. You can't explain nutting to me, you tief--you loafer--

(*She sinks into the chair at the right of the table, leans her arms across the table, buries her face in them, and sobs bitterly. All her fury has vanished and she is crushed and broken.*)

PHILIP. (*laughing and calling after Joe*) Joe, come back! Joe! (*He goes out through the window.*) Joe!

MARGARET. (*rushing in and up to the garden door, afraid some harm has come to the child*) What on earth is the matter? An earthquake?

MARIA. (*sobbing*) No, Mrs. Fleming. It was dot miserable husband of me.

MARGARET. What?

MARIA. Yah, I yust came in now, und I find him dere drinking of Mr. Fleming's brandy.

MARGARET. Good gracious--what did you do, Maria?

MARIA. I skipped dot gutter mit him, I bet my life. (*She is still weeping.*)

MARGARET. (*a smile flickering about her lips*) There, Maria, don't cry. Don't let him trouble you so. How is your sister?

MARIA. Vorse, Mrs. Fleming.

MARGARET. Worse. Oh, I'm so sorry.

MARIA. Yah. I don't tink she vill ever leave dot bed alive. My poor little Lena. Mrs. Fleming, I ask you--mebbe you vill come to see her. She talks about you all de time now.

MARGARET. Talks about me? Why, how does she know me?

MARIA. Vell, she ask about you--a lot--und I tell her of you and your beautiful home und your little baby, und now she says she'd like yust once to look into your face.

MARGARET. (*hesitating a moment*) Well, I'll go. If I only could do anything for her, poor girl.

MARIA. Yah, she is a poor girl, Mrs. Fleming. Mebbe she vill tell you the name of this man vot--

MARGARET. (*with repugnance*) Oh, no, no! I don't want to know the brute or his name.

MARIA. (*vindictively*) Oh, Gott! If I vould know it--

MARGARET. (*breaking in upon her, kindly*) But, I'll go to see her.

MARIA. Tank you, Mrs. Fleming. You are a goodt lady.

MARGARET. Where did you say she lives?

MARIA. (*still quietly weeping*) Forty-two Millbrook Street. By Mrs. Burton's cottage.

MARGARET. Very well. (*Philip's voice is heard outside, laughing.*) Oh, there's Mr. Fleming. Come, Maria, don't let him see you crying. Come, go to the kitchen and tell Hannah--

(*She has urged Maria to her feet and is pressing her toward the door.*)

MARIA. Is dot new girl come?

MARGARET. Yes.

MARIA. Hannah is her name?

MARGARET. (*pressing her*) Yes, tell her to make you a nice cup of tea, and then you'd best go back to your sister.

MARIA. Tank you, Mrs. Fleming. I don't want no tea. Mebbe she needs me. I go right back to her. You'll come sure, Mrs. Fleming?

MARGARET. (*putting her through the door on the right as Philip comes in through the window on the left*) Yes, I'll come in a little while.

PHILIP. Oh, Margaret, I wish you'd been here. (*He begins to laugh.*) Such a circus. The funniest thing I ever saw.

MARGARET. Yes, Maria told me. Poor thing. I'm sorry for her.

  (*Philip laughs. Margaret goes to her work basket on the center table, takes out the two phials, and goes to him.*)

  Here, dear--some medicine Dr. Larkin left for you.

PHILIP. (*pushing her hand away gently*) Oh, I don't want any medicine. There's nothing the matter with me. (*He begins to chuckle again.*) If you could--

MARGARET. (*shaking him by the lapels of his jacket*) Yes, there is a great deal the matter with you. (*She looks at him seriously and he becomes serious.*) Doctor says you're all run down. You've got to have a rest. Here, now, take two of these pellets, alternating every hour. (*He takes the phials and puts them in his vest pocket.*) Take some now!

PHILIP. Oh! Now? Must I?

MARGARET. (*shaking him*) Yes, this minute. (*He takes two pellets and pretends to choke. She shakes him again.*) Look at your watch. Note the time.

PHILIP. Yes'm.

MARGARET. Well, in an hour, take two from the other phial.

PHILIP. Yes'm. (*He lights a fresh cigar. Margaret gives a cry of reproval.*)

MARGARET. Philip! What are you doing? (*She rushes at him and takes the cigar from him.*) Don't you know you mustn't smoke when you are taking medicine.

PHILIP. Why not?

MARGARET. It'll kill the effect of it. You may smoke in an hour.

PHILIP. I've got to take more medicine in an hour!

MARGARET. Well, I guess you'll have to give up smoking.

PHILIP. What!

MARGARET. Until you're well.

PHILIP. But, I'm well now.

MARGARET. (*going through the door on the left*) Until you have stopped taking those pellets!

PHILIP. All right. I'll forget them.

MARGARET. Philip!

PHILIP. (*going to the baby in the garden doorway*) The cigars! What are you doing?

MARGARET. Changing my gown. I'm going out.

PHILIP. Where are you going?

MARGARET. Oh, just a little errand.

PHILIP. Well, hurry back.

MARGARET. Yes, I won't be long. (*She gives a little scream.*) Oh!

PHILIP. What's the matter?

MARGARET. Nothing. Stuck a pin into my finger, that's all.

PHILIP. My! You gave me a shock.

   (*He puts his hand to his heart playfully.*)

MARGARET. (*laughing*) Sorry. Did you see my gloves?

PHILIP. Yes.

MARGARET. Where?

PHILIP. On your hands, of course.

MARGARET. Now, don't be silly!

PHILIP. (*playing with the baby*) Margaret, you know, baby's eyes are changing.

MARGARET. No.

PHILIP. Yes. They're growing like yours.

MARGARET. Nonsense. She has your eyes.

PHILIP. (*eyeing the baby critically*) No, they're exactly like yours. She's got my nose, though.

MARGARET. (*giving a little cry of protest*) Oh, Philip--don't say that.

PHILIP. Why?

MARGARET. It would be terrible if she had your nose. Just imagine my dainty Lucy with a great big nose like yours.

PHILIP. (*feeling his nose*) Why, I think I have a very nice nose.

MARGARET. (*coming in, laughing*) Oh, yes, it's a good enough nose--as noses go--but-- (*She touches the bell.*)

PHILIP. (*noticing her gown*) Your new suit?

MARGARET. (*gaily*) Yes. Like it?

PHILIP. It's a dandy. Turn around. (*She dances over to him and twirls about playfully.*) Wait, there's a thread.

   (*He plucks it off her skirt. Jane enters.*)

MARGARET. Jane, please tell Hannah to come here.

JANE. Yes, ma'am. (*She goes off. Philip begins to chuckle.*)

MARGARET. Now, Philip, I implore you to keep still. Please don't get me laughing while I'm talking to her.

PHILIP. (*indignantly*) I'm not going to say anything.

   (*Hannah appears. She is very large, stout, and dignified.*)

MARGARET. (*hurriedly, in haste to be off*) Hannah! I'm going out and I shall not be able to look after the baking of the bread. When the loaves have raised almost to the top of the pans, put them in the oven.

HANNAH. (*who has been studying admiringly Margaret's costume*) Yes,

ma'am. I does always put the bread in when it's almost up to the top in
the pans.

MARGARET. And bake them just one hour.

HANNAH. Ah! Yes, ma'am. I always bakes 'em an hour.

(*Philip smothers a laugh in a cough. Margaret stares at him.*)

MARGARET. And have luncheon on at half past twelve, please.

HANNAH. Yes, I always has the lunch on at half past twelve, sharp.

MARGARET. (*putting on her gloves*) Thank you, Hannah, that's all.
Well, I'm off. (*To Philip.*) Good-bye, dear. (*She starts off hastily.*)

HANNAH. Good-bye, ma'am. (*She goes out.*)

MARGARET. (*pausing to look at Philip as he plays with the baby in the
carriage*) Oh, how dear you both look there together.

PHILIP. (*looking at his watch*) You'd best hurry if you want to get back
at--(*he imitates Hannah*)--half past twelve, sharp.

MARGARET. (*rapturously gazing at them*) Oh, if I could paint, what a
picture I would make of you two!

PHILIP. Are you going?

MARGARET. Yes, I'm going. (*She notices Philip giving the baby his
watch, and giving a little scream of alarm, she rushes at him.*) Philip,
what are you doing?

PHILIP. That's all right. She won't hurt it.

MARGARET. Suppose she'd swallow it.

PHILIP. Well!

MARGARET. (*mocking him*) Well! There, put it in your pocket. And
have some sense. (*She picks up the rattle and the big rubber ball and puts
them in his hands.*) There, you can play with these.

(*They both laugh with the fun of it all.*)

PHILIP. Oh! Go on, Margaret, and hurry home.

MARGARET. (*kissing him and the baby*) All right. Won't be long. Don't
forget your medicine, and please don't smoke when my back is turned.

(*She dances out through the French window, overflowing with fun and
animation. This scene must be played rapidly, with a gay, light touch.*)

ACT III.

The scene is a neat, plainly furnished sitting-room in Mrs. Burton's
cottage. The walls are covered with old-fashioned wall paper of a faded
green color. Sunlight streams in through two windows at the back. In
one there is a small table holding a few pots of geraniums, and in the
second, a hanging basket of ivy. A few straggling vines creep about the

window frame. There are doors at the left center, down left, and on the right. In the center of the room stands a table with a chair to the right of it, and a few hair-cloth chairs are here and there. A sofa stands against the left wall below the door, and there is a low rocking-chair on the left. (*The room is empty and after a moment the stillness is broken by the wail of an infant. The hushed notes of a woman's voice are heard from the open door on the left, soothing the child. A low knock is heard at the door to the right. The door opens slowly and Dr. Larkin enters. Mrs. Burton emerges from the room on the left with a tiny baby wrapped in a soft white shawl in her arms. She is a motherly woman, large and placid, with a benign immobility of countenance. She speaks with a New England drawl.*)

MRS. BURTON. Good morning, Doctor. I didn't hear ye knock.

DOCTOR. How is your patient this morning?

MRS. BURTON. Why, ain't yer seen Doctor Taylor? Didn't he tell ye?

DOCTOR. No. She's--?

MRS. BURTON. (*nodding her head*) Yes.

DOCTOR. When did it happen?

MRS. BURTON. About an hour ago. She seemed brighter this morning. After her sister went out, she slept for a while. When I came in the room, she opened her eyes and asked me for a pencil and paper. I brought 'em to her and she writ for quite a spell. Then she lay back on the pillow. I asked her if she wouldn't take a little nourishment. She smiled and shook her head. Then she gave a long sigh--an'--an'--that was all there was to it.

DOCTOR. How's the child?

MRS. BURTON. Poor little critter-- (*She looks down at it.*) I can't do nothing for it. I've tried everything. It ought to have mother's milk-- that's all there is to it. Be quiet, you poor little motherless critter.

DOCTOR. It would be better for it if it had gone with her.

MRS. BURTON. Why, Doctor, ain't ye awful?

DOCTOR. Why, what chance has that child got in this world? I'll send you something for it. (*He turns to go.*)

MRS. BURTON. Don't ye want to see her?

DOCTOR. No! What good can I be to her now, poor devil?

   (*Charlie Burton, a sturdy lad of ten, breaks boisterously into the room from the door on the right, carrying a baseball and bat.*)

CHARLIE. Ma! Ma! Here's a woman wants to see Mrs. Bindley.

MRS. BURTON. (*reprimanding him*) Lady! And take your hat off.

   (*Dr. Larkin and Mrs. Burton look expectantly toward the door.*)

Margaret enters slowly, her eyes bent upon her glove which she is unfastening. Dr. Larkin is dumbfounded at the sight of her. She takes a few steps toward him and looks up.)

MARGARET. Why, Doctor! I didn't know that you were on this case.

DOCTOR. (*confused*) I'm not. Dr. Taylor--he--called me in consultation. But, what in the name of all that's wonderful brings you here?

MARGARET. Maria!

DOCTOR. What Maria? Not--

MARGARET. Yes, our Maria--this sick girl is her sister.

  (*She removes her hat and places it with her gloves on the table.)*

DOCTOR. (*in consternation*) Her sister! Then you know?

MARGARET. I know that there is a poor sick girl here who wants--

DOCTOR. (*going to her, brusquely*) Mrs. Fleming, you'd best not remain here--the girl is dead. Go home.

MARGARET. (*pityingly*) Dead? Poor thing!

DOCTOR. Yes. Does your husband know you are here?

MARGARET. (*shaking her head*) Oh, no!

DOCTOR. Come, you must go home.

  (*He almost pushes her out of the room in his urgency.)*

MARGARET. (*resisting him gently*) Ah, no, Doctor. Now that I am here, let me stay. I can be of some help, I know.

DOCTOR. No, you can be of no use. Everything has been done.

MARGARET. Well, I'll just say a word to Maria. Where is she?

DOCTOR. I don't know--I don't know anything about Maria.

MRS. BURTON. She's in there.

  (*She nods toward the door on the left. The Doctor has crowded Margaret almost through the door in his eagerness to have her out of the house. She is reluctantly yielding to him, when Mrs. Burton's voice arrests her. She turns quickly and, looking over the Doctor's shoulder, notices the child in Mrs. Burton's arms. She impulsively brushes the Doctor aside and goes toward her, her face beaming with tender sympathy.)*

MARGARET. Oh, is this the baby?

MRS. BURTON. Yes'm.

MARGARET. (*going close to her on tip-toes and gazing with maternal solicitude down upon the child*) Poor little baby! What a dear mite of a thing it is.

MRS. BURTON. Yes'm.

MARGARET. (*impulsively*) Doctor, we must take care of this baby.

DOCTOR. (*impatiently*) You've got a baby of your *own*, Mrs. Fleming.

MARGARET. Yes, and that's why I pity this one, I suppose. I always did love babies, anyhow. They are such wonderful, mysterious little things, aren't they?

MRS. BURTON. Yes'm.

DOCTOR. (*spurred by a growing sense of catastrophe*) Mrs. Fleming, there is danger to your child in your remaining here.

MARGARET. (*alarmed*) Oh, Doctor!

DOCTOR. I hated to tell you this before--but--there is contagion in this atmosphere.

MARGARET. (*hastily taking her hat from the table*) Doctor, why didn't you--

(*She is hurrying away when she is checked by a poignant moan. She turns a frightened face and sees Maria coming from the room on the left with a letter in her hand. Maria's face is distorted by grief.*)

MARIA. Ah, Mrs. Burton, I have found out who dot man is. He is-- (*She sees Margaret and smiles bitterly upon her.*) So, you have come, Mrs. Fleming?

MARGARET. (*making a movement of sympathy*) Maria!

MARIA. Vell, you may go back again. You can do nutting for her now. She is dead. (*Perversely.*) But, ven you do go, you vill take dot baby back mit you. He shall now have two babies instead of one.

MARGARET. (*smiling*) What do you mean, Maria? Who shall have two babies?

MARIA. (*fiercely*) Philip Fleming--dot's who.

(*Margaret stares at her, only comprehending half what Maria means. Dr. Larkin goes quickly to her.*)

DOCTOR. Come away, Mrs. Fleming--the woman is crazy.

(*He tries to draw her away.*)

MARIA. (*contemptuously*) No, I ain't crazy! (*She shakes the letter at Margaret.*) You read dot letter and see if I vas crazy!

(*Margaret, in a dazed way, reaches for the letter, and tries to read it, turning it different ways.*)

MARGARET. I cannot make it out. (*She hands it to the Doctor, and speaks helplessly.*) Read it--to me--Doctor--please.

DOCTOR. (*beside himself and snatching the letter*) No, nor shall you.

(*He makes a motion to tear the letter.*)

MARIA. (*threateningly*) Don't you tear dot letter, Doctor.

MARGARET. (*putting her hand out gently*) You must not destroy that letter, Doctor. Give it back to me.

(*Dr. Larkin returns the letter reluctantly. Margaret attempts to read it, fails, become impatient, and hands it to Maria, helplessly.*)

You read it to me, Maria.

(*Maria, whose passion has subsided, takes the letter in an awed manner and begins to read it. The Doctor is in a daze. Margaret sinks into the chair to the right of the table. She has recovered her calm poise, but does not seem to be at all the same Margaret.*)

MARIA. (*reading in a simple, unaffected manner*)

"Canton, June 10.

Dear Mr. Fleming:

You was good to come to see me, and I thank you. I will not trouble you no more. I am sorry for what has happened. I know you never loved me and I never asked you to, but I loved you. It was all my fault. I will never trouble you no more. You can do what you like with the baby. I do not care. Do not be afraid, I shall never tell. They tried to get me to, but I never shall. Nobody will ever know. No more at present, from your obedient servant, Lena Schmidt."

MARGARET. (*turning to the Doctor, who is standing close to her chair*) Did you know--anything of this--Doctor?

DOCTOR. (*evasively*) Well--I knew--something of it--but, this girl may be lying. Such as she is--will say anything sometimes.

MARIA. (*fiercely*) Don't you say dot, Doctor. She would not tell nutting to hurt him, not to save her soul.

DOCTOR. (*with finality*) Well, now that you know the worst, come away from here--come home.

MARIA. Oh! Ya! She can go home. She have alvays got a home und a husband und fine clothes, because she is his vife, but my poor sister don't have any of dese tings, because she is only de poor mistress. But, by Gott, she shall not go home unless she takes dot baby back mit her.

DOCTOR. She shall do nothing of the sort.

MARIA. Vell, den, I vill take it, und fling it in his face.

MARGARET. (*calmly, and rising from the chair*) You shall not go near him. You shall not say--one word to him!

MARIA. Von't I? Who is going to stop me? I vould yust like to know dot?

MARGARET. (*quite calmly*) I am!

MARIA. (*mockingly*) You--you vill take his part, because you are his vife! (*Fiercely.*) Vell! (*She draws a pistol from her dress pocket.*) Do you see dot gun? Vell, I buy dot gun, und I swore dot ven I find out dot man I vill have his life. Und, if you try to stop me, I vill lay you stiff und cold beside her.

MARGARET. (*calmly, pityingly, holding out her hand as though to quiet*) *her*) Maria! Stop! How dare you talk like that to me? Give me that pistol. (*Maria, awed by Margaret's spirit, meekly hands her the weapon.*) You think--I--am happy--because I am his wife? Why, you poor fool, that girl--(*pointing to the door on the left*)--never in all her life suffered one thousandth part what I have suffered in these past five minutes. Do you dare to compare her to me? I have not uttered one word of reproach, even against her, and yet she has done me a wrong, that not all the death-bed letters that were ever written can undo. I wonder what I have ever done to deserve this.

(*Margaret loses control of herself and sinks sobbing into the chair, her arms upon the table, and her head dropping upon them.*)

DOCTOR. (*overcome by the situation, throws his arms about her and tries to draw her to her feet*) For God's sake, Mrs. Fleming, let me take you out of this hell.

MARGARET. (*gently resisting him*) Ah, Doctor, you cannot take *this hell* out of my breast.

(*Suddenly her manner changes. She speaks with quick decision.*)

Maria, get me a sheet of writing paper. Doctor, give me a pencil.

(*Dr. Larkin puts his hand into his vest pocket. Maria, who seems dazed, looks helplessly about as though the paper might be within reach. Then suddenly thinking of the letter in her hand, she tears off the blank half of it and quickly lays it on the table before Margaret.*)

DOCTOR. (*giving her the pencil*) What are you going to do?

MARGARET. Send--for *him!*

DOCTOR. No--not here!

MARGARET. Yes--here-- (*She writes nervously, mumbling what she writes.*) "Philip: I am waiting for you, here. That *girl* is *dead.*" (*She folds the letter.*) Where's that boy?

(*Maria and Mrs. Burton both make a movement in search of Charlie.*)

MARIA. Charlie! (*She goes to the door at the back and calls again in a hushed voice.*) Charlie! (*Charlie enters. She whispers to him that the lady wants him.*) You, go quick! (*Charlie goes to Margaret.*)

MARGARET. (*intense nervousness*) Charlie, do you know Mr. Fleming?

CHARLIE. Yes'm.

MARGARET. Do you know where he lives?

CHARLIE. Yes'm--on Linden Street.

MARGARET. Yes--go there--don't ring the bell--go through the garden-- you will find him there, playing with the baby. Give him this.

CHARLIE. Any answer?

MARGARET. (*at nervous tension*) No! Go quick! Quick! (*Charlie goes;*

Margaret springs to her feet.) Now, Doctor--I want you to leave me!

DOCTOR. Mrs. Fleming, for God's sake, don't see him here.

MARGARET. Yes, here--and--alone! Please go. (*The Doctor does not respond.*) I don't want you or any other living being to hear what passes between him and me, and--(*pointing to the room*)--*that dead girl*. Please go!

DOCTOR. Mrs. Fleming, as your physician, I order you to leave this place at once.

MARGARET. No, Doctor--I must see him, *here.*

DOCTOR. (*with gentle persuasion*) Mrs. Fleming, you have no right to do this. Think of your child.

MARGARET. (*remembering*) My baby! My poor, little innocent baby! Oh, I wish to God that she were dead.

> (*She is beside herself and not realizing what she says. She crosses to the left.*)

DOCTOR. (*following her*) Mrs. Fleming, in God's name, calm yourself! I have tried to keep it from you, but I am forced to tell you-- (*He is so deeply moved that he is almost incoherent.*) If you continue in this way, dear lady, you are exposing yourself to a terrible affliction--this--trouble--with your eyes. You are threatened with--if you keep up this strain--a sudden blindness may fall upon you.

MARGARET. (*appalled*) Blind! Blind! (*She speaks in a low, terrified voice.*) Oh, no, Doctor, not *that*--not *now*--not until after I've seen him.

DOCTOR. Not only that, but if you keep up this strain much longer, it may cost you your life.

MARGARET. I don't care--what happens to me, only, let me *see* him, and then, the sooner it all comes the better.

> (*She crosses to the left with the Doctor following her.*)

DOCTOR. (*growing desperate, and throwing his arms about her*) Mrs. Fleming, you must leave this place! Come home.

MARGARET. No. Doctor, please leave me alone. (*She draws herself from him.*) I tell you I've got to see him here. (*Then with a sweet intimacy, she goes to him. She speaks brokenly.*) A woman has a strange feeling for the physician who brings her child into the world--I love you--I have always obeyed your orders, haven't I?

DOCTOR. (*quietly*) Always.

MARGARET. Then, let me be the doctor now, and I order you to leave this house at once.

DOCTOR. (*hopelessly*) You are determined to do this thing?

MARGARET. (*with finality*) Yes.

DOCTOR. Very well then--good-bye.

(*He holds out his hand, which she takes mechanically. He holds her hand warmly for a moment. She clings to him as though afraid to let him go, then slowly draws away.*)

MARGARET. Good-bye!

(*The Doctor leaves the room quickly. Margaret takes a step after him until she touches the table in the center. She stands there gazing into space, the calmness of death upon her face. The sunlight streaming through the window falls upon her. Mrs. Burton is sitting in a rocking-chair in the center of the room. Maria is sitting on the sofa, weeping silently, with clasped hands, her arms lying in her lap, her body bent.*)

MARIA. (*making a plaintive moan*) Ah--Mrs. Fleming, you must not do dis ting. Vat vas I--vat vas she, I'd like to know--dot ve should make dis trouble for you? You come here, like an angel to help us, und I have stung you like a snake in dot grass. (*She goes to Margaret and falls upon her knees.*) Oh, Mrs. Fleming, on my knees I ask you to forgive me.

(*Margaret stands immobile at the table, her right hand resting upon its edge--her left hand partly against her cheek. She is lost in spiritual contemplation of the torment she is suffering. She shows impatience at the sound of Maria's voice, as though loath to be disturbed. She replies wearily.*)

MARGARET. I have nothing to forgive. Get up, Maria. You have done nothing to me--go away!

MARIA. (*in a paroxysm of contrition*) Oh, I beg, Mrs. Fleming, dot you vill take dot gun and blow my brains out.

MARGARET. Don't go on like that, Maria! (*Maria's weeping irritates her.*) Get up! Please go away. Go away! I say.

(*Maria slinks away quietly into the back room. Margaret takes a long, sobbing breath, which ends in a sigh. She stares into space and a blank look comes into her face as though she were gazing at things beyond her comprehension. Presently the silence is broken by a low wail from the infant. It half arouses her.*)

What is the matter with that child?

(*Her voice seems remote. Her expression remains fixed.*)

Why don't you keep it quiet?

MRS. BURTON. (*in a hushed voice*) It's hungry.

MARGARET. (*in the same mood, but her voice is a little querulous*) Well, then, why don't you feed it?

MRS. BURTON. I can't get nothing fit for it. I've tried everything I could think of, but it's no use. (*She gets up and places the child upon the sofa to*

the left.) There, be still, you poor little critter, an' I'll see what I ken get fer ye. (*As she goes through the door at the back, Margaret speaks warily.*)
MARGARET. Bring a lamp--it's getting dark here.

(*She is still in the same attitude by the table. There is silence; then the child's wail arouses her. She half turns her head in its direction--and tries to quiet it.*)

Hush--child--hush--

(*Then she reaches out her hand as if to pat it.*)

There--there--poor little thing. Don't fret--it's no use to fret, child--be quiet now--there--there, now.

(*She turns and slowly gropes her way to the sofa, sits on the edge of it, and feels for the child and gently pats it. She murmurs softly.*)

Hush--baby--go to sleep.

(*There is a silence while a soft flood of sunshine plays about her. A pitying half smile flits across her face. She utters a faint sigh and again drifts away into that inner consciousness where she evidently finds peace. Again the child is restless--it arouses her and, hopeless of comforting it, she takes it in her arms. After a moment, she rises to her feet and stumbles toward the table. She knocks against the low chair. At the same moment, Philip Fleming dashes breathlessly into the room through the door on the right. He pauses in horror as Margaret raises her head, her eyes wide open, staring into his--her face calm and remote. She hushes the child softly, and sits in the low chair. Philip stands in dumb amazement, watching her. The child begins to fret her again. She seems hopeless of comforting it. Then, scarcely conscious of what she is doing, suddenly with an impatient, swift movement, she unbuttons her dress to give nourishment to the child, when the picture fades away into darkness.*)

ACT IV.

The scene is the same as ACT II. The doors and window leading into the garden are open. (*Maria is seated close to the open door, sewing. She occasionally looks into the garden as if guarding something. She is neatly dressed, fresh and orderly looking. Her manner is subdued. A bell rings and a closing door is heard. Then Dr. Larkin enters. Maria goes to meet him and scans his face anxiously.*)

MARIA. Goot morning, Doctor.
DOCTOR. Good morning. Well! Any news?

MARIA. (*losing interest, shaking her head sadly*) No, Doctor. No vord from him yet. It is seven days now--I hoped--mebbe you might have some.

DOCTOR. No--nothing. How is Mrs. Fleming?

(*Maria sits down to the left and the Doctor to the right.*)

MARIA. Yust the same as yesterday, und the day before, und all the udder days. Ach, so bright, und so cheerful, but I tink all the same she is breaking her heart. Ach, ven I look into her sad eyes--vot cannot see me--I am ashamed to hold my head up. (*She brushes away the tears.*)

DOCTOR. Does she talk about him at all?

MARIA. No, she never speaks his name.

DOCTOR. How is the child?

MARIA. (*brightening*) She is fine. Dot little tooth came trough dis morning und she don't fret no more now.

DOCTOR. And, the other one?

MARIA. (*indifferently*) Oh, he's all right. I put him beside Lucy in her crib dis morning und she laughs and pulls at him und plays mit him yust like he vas a little kitten. Dis is no place for him, Doctor. Ven Mr. Fleming comes home, he vill fix tings, und I vill take him away by myself--vere she no more can be troubled mit him.

DOCTOR. Things will come out all right. You'd best keep quiet. Have nothing whatever to say in this matter.

MARIA. Ya. I make enough trouble already mit my tongue. You bet I keep it shut in my head now. Shall I call Mrs. Fleming? She is in the garden.

DOCTOR. She's there a great deal now, isn't she?

MARIA. Ya, she is always dere by the blossoms und the babies. (*She goes to the door and speaks in slow, deferential voice.*) Mrs. Fleming, Dr. Larkin is here.

MARGARET. (*outside*) Yes, I'll come.

(*She slowly emerges from the garden into the doorway, her arms filled with flowers. She is daintily dressed and there is a subtle dignity and reserve about her. She smiles cheerily.*)

Good morning, Doctor. Maria, there are some daffodils out by the yellow bed. Bring them, please.

(*She slowly enters the room. The Doctor goes to her and gently leads her to the table on the right, where she puts the flowers, after carefully locating a place to lay them.*)

DOCTOR. Well, well, where did you get such a lot of roses? I couldn't gather so many in a month from my scrubby bushes. The bugs eat 'em all up.

MARGARET. Why don't you spray them? (*Maria brings a large, loose bunch of daffodils.*) Bring some jars, Maria.

DOCTOR. I did spray them.

MARGARET. When?

DOCTOR. When I saw the rose bugs.

MARGARET. (*smiling*) That's a fine time to spray bushes. Don't you know that the time to prevent trouble is to look ahead? From potatoes to roses, spray before anything happens--*then* nothing *will* happen.

DOCTOR. (*laughing*) Yes, of course, I know, but I forgot to do it until I saw two big, yellow bugs in the heart of every rose and all the foliage chewed up.

MARGARET. There's no use in it now. You are just wasting time. Start early next year before the leaves open.

DOCTOR. (*admiringly*) What a brave, cheery little woman you are.

MARGARET. What's the use in being anything else? I don't see any good living in this world, unless you can live right.

DOCTOR. And this world needs just such women as you.

MARGARET. What does the world know or care about me?

(*The bell rings and the door opens and shuts.*)

DOCTOR. Very little, but it's got to feel your influence.

(*He pats her hand. Jane enters.*)

JANE. Mr. Foster wishes to see you for a moment, Mrs. Fleming.

MARGARET. Tell him to come in. (*Jane goes out. In a moment Foster enters, flurried and embarrassed.*) Good morning, Mr. Foster. (*She holds out her hands to him.*) Anything wrong at the mill?

FOSTER. Good morning, Mrs. Fleming. Oh, no--not at all, not at all. How do you do, Doctor?

(*He shakes hands with the Doctor with unusual warmth.*)

DOCTOR. (*somewhat surprised, looking at him quizzically*) Hello, Foster.

MARGARET. Will you sit down, Mr. Foster?

FOSTER. Thank you--yes, I will. What beautiful flowers! Mother says you have the loveliest garden in Canton.

MARGARET. (*pleased*) That's awfully nice of her. I had a delightful visit with her yesterday.

FOSTER. (*nervously*) Yes, she told me so.

MARGARET. We sat in the garden. What a sweet, happy soul she is.

FOSTER. (*fussing with his hat and getting up and moving his chair close to the Doctor's*) Yes. Mother always sees the bright side of the worst things.

MARGARET. She's very proud of you.

FOSTER. (*laughing foolishly*) Oh, yes, she is happy over anything I do.

(*He looks at Margaret furtively, then at the Doctor. He evidently has something to say. Suddenly in a tense whisper, he speaks to the Doctor.*) Mr. Fleming has come back.

DOCTOR. Hush! Where is he? At the mill?

FOSTER. No. Here--outside.

DOCTOR. How does he look?

FOSTER. He's a wreck. He wants to see her.

DOCTOR. Well, tell her--I'll go-- (*He rises.*)

FOSTER. No! (*He grabs him by the coat.*) For God's sake, don't go. You tell her--you're her doctor.

(*Margaret, who has been busy with the flowers, becomes suddenly interested.*)

MARGARET. What are you two whispering about?

FOSTER. (*laughing nervously*) Oh, just a little advice, that's all. (*He goes to Margaret.*) I'll say good morning, Mrs. Fleming. Glad to see you--er--looking--ah--so well.

(*Foster shakes hands and rushes out. Margaret stands a little mystified. The Doctor approaches her gently.*)

DOCTOR. (*very tenderly*) Mrs. Fleming--I have something to say to you.

MARGARET. (*standing tense, with ominous conviction*) Philip is dead!

DOCTOR. No. He is not dead.

MARGARET. Where is he?

DOCTOR. *Outside.*

MARGARET. Why doesn't he come in?

DOCTOR. He's ashamed--afraid.

MARGARET. This is his home. Why should he be afraid to enter it? I will go to him.

(*She starts toward the door, and then staggers. The Doctor puts an arm around her.*)

DOCTOR. There now. Keep up your courage. Don't forget, everything depends upon you.

MARGARET. (*brokenly*) I'm brave, Doctor. I--perhaps it's best for you to tell him to come here.

DOCTOR. (*patting her on the shoulder*) Remember, you are very precious to us all. We cannot afford to lose *you.*

(*Dr. Larkin goes out. Margaret stands by the table, calm and tense. Philip comes in from the right, carrying his cap in his hands. He looks weary and broken. He crosses behind Margaret to the center of the stage and, standing humbly before her, murmurs her name softly.*)

PHILIP. Margaret.

MARGARET. Well, Philip. (*After a slight pause.*) You have come back.

PHILIP. (*humbly*) Yes.

MARGARET. (*gently*) Why did you go away?

PHILIP. (*overwhelmed with shame*) I couldn't face you. I wanted to get away somewhere, and hide forever. (*He looks sharply at her.*) Can't you see me, Margaret?

MARGARET. (*shaking her head*) No!

PHILIP. (*awed*) You are blind! Oh!

(*Margaret sits down in a chair by the table. Philip remains standing.*)

MARGARET. Don't mind. I shall be cured. Dr. Norton sees me every day. He will operate as soon as he finds me normal.

PHILIP. You have been suffering?

MARGARET. Oh, no. (*After a pause.*) Philip, do you think that was right? To run away and hide?

PHILIP. I did not consider whether it was right or wrong. (*Bitterly.*) I did not know the meaning of those words. I never have.

MARGARET. Oh, you are a man--people will soon forget.

PHILIP. (*fiercely*) I do not care about others. It is you, Margaret--will you ever forget? Will you ever forgive?

MARGARET. (*shaking her head and smiling sadly*) There is nothing to forgive. And, I want to forget.

PHILIP. (*bewildered by her magnanimity but full of hope*) Then you will let me come back to you? You will help me to be a better--a wiser man?

MARGARET. (*smiling gently*) Yes, Philip.

(*A quick joy takes hold of Philip. He makes a warm movement to go to her, then checks himself, and approaches her slowly while speaking, overcome by the wonder and beauty of her kindness.*)

PHILIP. All my life, Margaret, I will make amends for what I have done. I will atone for my ignorance-- Oh, my wife--my dear, dear wife.

(*He hangs over her tenderly, not daring to touch her. At the word "wife" Margaret rises, shrinking from him as though some dead thing was near her. A look of agony flits across her face.*)

MARGARET. No! Philip, not that! No!

(*She puts out her hands to ward him off.*)

PHILIP. (*beseechingly*) Margaret!

MARGARET. (*her face poignant with suppressed emotion, she sinks into her chair and confesses, brokenly*) The wife-heart has gone out of me.

PHILIP. Don't--don't say that, Margaret.

MARGARET. I must. Ah, Philip, how I worshipped you. You were my idol. Is it my fault that you lie broken at my feet?

PHILIP. (*with urgency*) You say you want to forget--that you forgive! Will you--?

MARGARET. Can't you understand? It is not a question of forgetting, or of forgiving-- (*For an instant she is at a loss how to convince him.*) Can't you understand, Philip! (*Then suddenly.*) Suppose--I--had been unfaithful to you?

PHILIP. (*with a cry of repugnance*) Oh, Margaret!

MARGARET. (*brokenly*) There! You see! You are a man, and you have your ideals of--the--sanctity--of--the thing you love. Well, I am a woman--and perhaps--I, too, have the same ideals. I don't know. But, I, too, cry "Pollution!" (*She is deeply moved.*)

PHILIP. (*abashed*) I did not know. I never realized before, the iniquity-- of my--behavior. Oh, if I only had my life to live over again. Men, as a rule, do not consider others when urged on by their desires. How you must hate me.

MARGARET. No, I don't--I love you--I pity you.

PHILIP. Dear, not now--but in the future--some time--away in the future--perhaps, the old Margaret--

MARGARET. Ah, Philip, the old Margaret is dead. The truth killed her.

PHILIP. Then--there is no hope for me?

(*There is a dignity and a growing manliness in his demeanor.*)

MARGARET. (*warmly*) Yes. Every hope.

PHILIP. Well, what do you want me to do? Shall I go away?

MARGARET. No. Your place is here. You cannot shirk your responsibilities now.

PHILIP. I do not want to shirk my responsibilities, Margaret. I want to do whatever you think is best.

MARGARET. Very well. It is best for us both to remain here, and take up the old life together. It will be a little hard for you, but you are a man--you will soon live it down.

PHILIP. Yes--I *will* live it down.

MARGARET. Go to the mill tomorrow morning and take up your work again, as though this thing had never happened.

PHILIP. Yes. All right. I'll do that.

MARGARET. Mr. Foster, you know, you have an unusually capable man there?

PHILIP. Yes, I appreciate Foster. He's a nice chap, too.

MARGARET. He has carried through a very critical week at the mill.

PHILIP. Don't worry, Margaret, everything will be all right there now. I will put my whole heart and soul into the work.

MARGARET. Then, you must do something for your child.

PHILIP. Yes, our dear child.

MARGARET. No, not our child--not Lucy. Your son.

PHILIP. My son?

MARGARET. Yes.

PHILIP. Where is he?

MARGARET. Here.

PHILIP. (*resentfully*) Who brought him here?

MARGARET. I did.

PHILIP. (*amazed*) You brought that child here?

MARGARET. Yes, where else should he go?

PHILIP. You have done that?

MARGARET. What other thing was there for me to do? Surely if he was good enough to bring into the world, he is good enough to find a shelter under your roof.

PHILIP. (*moved*) I never dreamed that you would do that, Margaret.

MARGARET. Well, he is here. Now, what are you going to do with him?

PHILIP. (*helplessly*) What can I do?

MARGARET. Give him a name, educate him. Try to make atonement for the wrong you did his mother. You must teach him never to be ashamed of her, to love her memory--motherhood is a divine thing--remember that, Philip, no matter when, or how. You can do fine things for this unfortunate child.

PHILIP. (*contemptuously*) Fine things for him! I am not fit to guide a young life. A fine thing I have made of my own.

MARGARET. There is no use now lamenting what was done yesterday. That's finished. Tomorrow? What are you going to do with that?

PHILIP. There does not seem any "tomorrow" worth while for me. The past--

MARGARET. The past is dead. We must face the living future. Now, Philip, there are big things ahead for you, if you will only look for them. They certainly will not *come* to *you*. I will help you--we will fight this together.

PHILIP. Forgive me, please. I'll not talk like that any more.

MARGARET. Of course, there will be a lot of talk--mean talk--but they will get tired of that in the end. Where have you been all this time?

PHILIP. In Boston.

MARGARET. What have you been doing?

PHILIP. Nothing--I've been--in the hospital.

MARGARET. (*stretching out her arms to him with an infinite tenderness*) Ah, Philip, you have been ill?

PHILIP. No!

MARGARET. What was it? (*He is silent.*) Please tell me.

PHILIP. (*rather reluctantly reciting his story*) I was walking across the bridge over the Charles River one night--I was sick of myself--the whole world--I believed I should never see your face again. The water looked so quiet, it fascinated me. I just dropped into it and went down. It seemed like going to sleep. Then I woke up and I was in a narrow bed in a big room.

MARGARET. (*breathless*) The hospital?

PHILIP. Yes.

MARGARET. Oh, that was a cruel thing to do. Were they kind to you there?

PHILIP. Yes. There was an old nurse there--she was sharp. She told me not to be a fool, but to go back to my wife. She said--"If she's any good, she will forgive you." (*He smiles whimsically.*) Margaret, some day I am going to earn your respect, and then--I know, I shall be able to win you back to me all over again.

MARGARET. (*smiling sadly*) I don't know. That would be a wonderful thing. (*She weeps silently.*) A very wonderful thing. (*Then suddenly she springs to her feet.*) Ah, dreams! Philip! Dreams! And we must get to work.

(*Philip is inspired by her manner, and there is a quickening of his spirit, a response to her in the new vibration in his voice.*)

PHILIP. Work! Yes--I'll not wait until tomorrow. I'll go to the mill now.

MARGARET. That's fine. Do it.

PHILIP. Yes, I'll take a bath and get into some fresh clothing first.

MARGARET. Do. You must look pretty shabby, knocking about for a week without a home.

PHILIP. Oh, I'll be all right. I'd like to see Lucy. (*He looks about.*) Where is she?

MARGARET. (*at the table, occupied with the flowers*) They are both out there. (*She indicates with a turn of her head.*) In the garden.

(*Philip goes quickly to the door opening upon the garden and gazes out eagerly. Margaret, at the table, pauses in her work, gives a long sigh of relief and contentment. Her eyes look into the darkness and a serene joy illuminates her face. The picture slowly fades out as Philip steps buoyantly into the garden.*)

CURTAIN.

Charles H. Hoyt (1859-1900)
and *A Trip to Chinatown*

Theatre was a business for Charles Hoyt. He worked hard at it, too, and in a good year would earn nearly half a million dollars. Although his methods were unorthodox, combining sloppiness with meticulous care, he created a market for his farces and without them the theatre of the 1890's would have been much the poorer.

A reporter with the *Boston Post*, Hoyt became a playwright who capitalized on the events, fads, and trends of his day-- sports, politics, the temperance movement, the militia, women's rights. He made notes on scraps of paper, jotted down remarks he heard, and remembered strange names and peculiar people. After creating a script and putting it into rehearsal, he would travel with the company and watch audience reactions night after night, constantly changing the play. Sometimes he kept a piece on the road for months, perfecting gags and business, before opening it in New York, where critics seldom failed to find audiences in "gales of merriment."

Hoyt had his first New York production with *A Bunch of Keys*, 1883. When his operetta, *The Maid and the Moonshiner*, 1886, was a dismal failure, he vowed never again to begin a title with the word "the." The "hilarious confusion" for which Hoyt was famous, however, continued throughout the 1890's, with satires on politics (*A Texas Steer*, 1890), the home guard (*A Milk White Flag*, 1893), and baseball (*A Runaway Colt*, 1895). A mixture of slapstick and music with an awareness of social foibles, a number of his plays exist in manuscript form in the New York Public Library. Even so, it is difficult to know what actually happened on stage. The text of *A Trip to Chinatown* printed here combines the first two acts of a version in the Poultney Collection (University of San Francisco) with Act III of the NYPL script to make a coherent play. It is clear that characters, settings, and actions changed as the play toured the country and Hoyt and/or actors made revisions.

In 1898 Hoyt's second wife died, and his health began to decline. In July 1900 he was declared an incurable paretic and committed to an asylum. Released to the custody of the town of Charlestown, N.H., in August, he died on November 20.

Charles H. Hoyt

A TRIP TO CHINATOWN
Or, An Idyl of San Francisco

(1891)

by Charles H. Hoyt

CHARACTERS

Welland Strong, a man with one foot in the grave
Ben Gay, a wealthy San Francisco bachelor, of the Union Club
Slavin Payne, a servant to Ben
Rashleigh Gay, Ben's nephew
Tony Gay, Ben's niece
Wilder Daly, Rashleigh's friend
Flirt, Wilder's sister
Mrs. Guyer, a widow from Chicago, not too strenuous on culture
    but makes up for it with a "biff"
Noah Heap, waiter at The Riche

The scene is laid in the city of San Francisco.

ACT I.

Scene. Reception room in Ben Gay's house. (*Discovered: Slavin Payne.*)

SLAVIN. (*reads the superscription on an envelope in his hand*) "Mr. R. Gay!" I haven't a doubt that it's an "R," and it's meant for Mr. Rashleigh. Besides, it's from a lady. The shape, the perfume--(*smells it*)--the handwriting, all prove it to be from a lady, and the old gentleman never receives notes from ladies. There's no doubt in my mind it's for Rashleigh. Still, the "R" looks enough like a "B," I think, to warrant me in giving it to Uncle Ben. He'll open it and I hope find out from it how the young man is going on. I'll give it to the old man.
WILDER. (*entering*) Slavin, has Mr. Rashleigh come it?
SLAVIN. No, Mr. Daly.
WILDER. When do you expect him?
SLAVIN. I don't expect him, sir. I would not dare take the liberty of expecting him, sir. I know my place, sir.

RASHLEIGH. (*entering*) Hullo, Wilder, old man! You here? I was over at your house looking for you.

SLAVIN. Is anything required of me?

RASHLEIGH. Yes. Get out! (*Exit Slavin.*)

WILDER. Now, Rashleigh, you know the masquerade ball tonight. Well--

RASHLEIGH. I know! I'm going to be there.

WILDER. Yes. But the girls are going. Flirt is up in Tony's room now. The scheme's all fixed.

RASHLEIGH. They're going! Why, how? I can get out, but Uncle Ben'll hear of it--and your father'll never let Flirt go.

WILDER. To the ball, no! But we're not supposed to be going there. We have got permission to go on a night tour of Chinatown. That will account for our being out late. Well, instead of going to Chinatown, we all meet at The Riche, have a jolly supper. Our masks will be sent there; we'll put them on and go to the ball. Being en masse, nobody'll know us, and when we get home, the old folks will never suspect we haven't been to Chinatown. See?

RASHLEIGH. That's all very well, if it works. How did Flirt get your father to consent to her going through Chinatown?

WILDER. Oh, he consented when Mrs. Guyer said she'd go as chaperone. Didn't you get a note from her telling you all about it?

RASHLEIGH. No. Did she send me one?

WILDER. Yes. She sent it by messenger from our house.

RASHLEIGH. I never got it. Very strange!

WILDER. Now, does it all go?

RASHLEIGH. Why, yes. If Uncle Ben will consent to Tony's going through Chinatown.

WILDER. Leave the girls to coax him.

RASHLEIGH. But, say, if the widow's going along, we'll need a third fellow to balance the party. You bet she doesn't go without a fellow all to herself.

WILDER. The widow! Well, hardly! She's the one who got up this whole scheme, my boy. The trip to Chinatown story and all! And you bet she's taken care the party isn't short on men. She's got Towne Painter to go as Flirt's escort, so you can devote yourself entirely to the widow.

RASHLEIGH. Well, that suits me! The widow's more fun than any girl I know. Say, Wilder, I don't believe a woman is ever at her best till she becomes a widow.

WILDER. The boys all seem to think she's in her prime anyway. That's a great song Billy Parker wrote and dedicated to her. (*Starts to sing.*)

      Duet. RASHLEIGH and WILDER. *"The Widow."*
Do you know? Have you met her?
If so, you'll ne'er forget her--
The pretty little widow with the laughing eyes of brown.
Demure in her sobriety,
Severe in her propriety,
But the life of all society,
The jolliest thing in town.
No giddiness or giggle,
No shyness and no wiggle,
That makes the budding maiden such a nuisance and a bore.
So bright in conversation,
So free from affectation,
You can bear no hesitation,
And you hasten to adore!

      Chorus.
But when you come to tell her how you love her,
As never was a woman loved before!
Do not think you can deceive,
Don't expect her to believe,
She has heard it in the days of yore!

Most likely she'll refuse you,
Most likely 'twill amuse you,
She's got so many clothes in black, to mourning she must cling;
But if your pray'r impresses,
And besides, she rather guesses,
But along with her addresses,
A husband is the thing;
She'll breathe hard for a minute,
But, my boy, there's nothing in it;
It's only strict propriety that makes her tremble so.
She long ago has brooded
On the question, and concluded,
Very likely before you did,
If you'd be the man or no?

Chorus.

But when you come to put your arms around her,
And squeeze her till you can't squeeze any more,
If you think she's going to faint,
She will fool you, for she ain't!
She has been there several times before! (*Voices heard outside.*)

WILDER. It's the girls and your uncle. (*Enter Ben, Flirt, and Tony.*)

BEN. I don't care if night trips to Chinatown are the fashion! I say, no!

TONY. But, Uncle, I've lived here in San Francisco all my life and have never been through the China quarter, and this is such a good chance. We'll have a whole party together, and of course a policeman. And we'll ask Mrs. Guyer to chaperone us.

BEN. I don't see that she'd make any difference.

FLIRT. Why, she's a widow.

BEN. Yes, and is always sniveling about it. Why doesn't she get married again? I suppose because no man's fool enough to yield to her blandishments. I know I wouldn't!

TONY. But if she goes--

BEN. She goes alone! I won't have you out all night chasing through Chinatown. That settles it! (*Tony bursts into tears.*)

TONY. I think you're just as mean as you can be! (*Exit Tony, crying.*)

FLIRT. (*crying*) Poor Tony! (*Exit Flirt, crying.*)

RASHLEIGH. Come, Wilder. (*Exeunt Rashleigh and Wilder.*)

BEN. Now I'm an infernal old beast, I suppose. Well, I can't help it. They're my sister's children, and I'll do my duty as their guardian, if I earn their everlasting hatred!

SLAVIN. (*entering with a letter*) Letter for you, sir, by messenger boy.

BEN. (*looks at it*) For me!

SLAVIN. Yes, sir. Anything I can do for you, sir?

BEN. Yes. Go away! (*Exit Slavin.*) Looks like a woman's letter. What woman would write to me? (*Opens letter and reads.*)

"My dear old boy!" (*Look.*)

"You must take me to the grand masquerade ball tonight! Even if I am in mourning, I'm bound to go on the strict QT, and you are the only man I dare to trust. You get the masks--it wouldn't do for me to order them--meet me at The Riche, don our masks and drive to the ball, and nobody'll know anything about it. Don't fail, for I'm dying for a good time. Yours----,

P.S. If you want to make it a party of four, I can bring Flirt."

Well, I'll be--! Well, that letter's plain enough. These widows know what they want and are not afraid to declare themselves. But this to me! Why, I know she's been running to the house to see Tony, but I never suspected it was me she was after! Damn bright woman, that widow! I'll not disappoint her. But how can I stay out all night without the family knowing it? Change my mind. Let 'em go to Chinatown! By jove, how lucky it comes!

(*Orchestra begins.*)

There's that cussed street band. Playing dance music, too. That's suggestive. I hope I haven't forgotten how to shake my feet.

(*Dances. At close, enter four young people and catch him.*)

TONY. Why! Uncle Ben!

BEN. I--was only thinking. I've turned matters over in my mind.

TONY. I should think you must have with such violent exercise.

BEN. I've decided to let you go to Chinatown. It's highly proper that you should see it thoroughly. Promise me you will go. Go early and stay late!

YOUNG PEOPLE. We will! (*Exit Ben, R.*) Well!

FLIRT. There's a change of mind for you. I wonder what did it.

TONY. I don't know nor care. We go to the ball! That's the point!

(*All burst into chorus during which Widow enters.*)

WIDOW. And for it all, you can thank me!

TWO GIRLS. Our chaperone!

WIDOW. That will do, young ladies! Rashleigh, why didn't you answer my note?

RASHLEIGH. Because I didn't get it.

WIDOW. Didn't get it? How stupid of you!

RASHLEIGH. Oh, I know what it said. And it's all right. So you can dispense with those black looks.

WIDOW. Not for twenty-nine days. You must remember I'm a widow.

WILDER. Still mourning for poor Jack?

WIDOW. Bitterly! I shall wear a black mask at the ball. Wilder, don't forget that in ordering the masks.

SLAVIN. (*entering with a letter, to Rashleigh*) Note for you, sir. (*Gives letter.*) Can I oblige you, sir?

RASHLEIGH. Yes! Go and hide yourself! (*Exit Slavin.*) It's a note from Painter. (*Reads.*)

> "Dear Rashleigh:
>   May be a little late, but will join you at The Riche. Will inquire for Mr. Gay's room. Wait for me. Yours, Towne Painter."

That settles it! Our party of six is complete! Of course we'll wait for him. You wouldn't care to go with the party one man short?

WIDOW. Care to? I just wouldn't!

BEN. (*entering*) Now, Tony-- Why, Mrs. Guyer! Good morning! How do you do?

WIDOW. (*rather surprised*) Good morning, sir!

BEN. (*aside*) I see! Discretion!

TONY. Uncle, she's going to chaperone us!

BEN. Is she? That's nice! But if she changes her mind--(*winks at Widow*)--you can go just the same. (*Aside.*) She's throwing 'em off. Sly woman! I must speak to her. (*Aloud.*) Tony, I want you four young people to get 'round the piano and sing me my favorite quartette.

TONY. Anything to oblige. (*The four gather around the piano.*)

BEN. Mrs. Guyer, sit down. (*Seats her. Aside to her.*) Of course, you mean to keep your appointment tonight?

WIDOW. Most surely! Why?

BEN. Oh, I shouldn't let the young folks go out, only for that.

WIDOW. You flatter me! (*Aside.*) What ails the man?

TONY. We can't find the quartette, but here's a quintette. Come, Mrs. G., help us out. (*Widow goes to piano to sing.*)

BEN. (*aside*) Rats! I asked 'em to sing so I could talk to her. Well, I'll be--!

    Quintette. "Push Dem Clouds Away."
If you want to get to Heaven on de nickel-plated road,
Just push dem clouds away!
Bring along all yer baggage and check it to de Lord,
When you push dem clouds away!
If de train am a-speedin' an' you can't catch on,
When you push dem clouds away!
You're a coon dat's gone, and wuss dan none,
When you push dem clouds away!

    Chorus.
Just push!
Don't shove!
Just push dem clouds away!
Keep a-pushin' an' a-shovin', an' a-pushin' an' a-shovin'
Till you push dem clouds away!

Oh, de chickens up dere don't have to scratch,
When you push dem clouds away!
All green and yaller is dat water-million patch,
When you push dem clouds away!
If de people am a-yellin' for pie and milk,
Just push dem clouds away!
De angels dere all dress in silk,
When you push dem clouds away!

There'll be no boys a-puffin' cigarettes,
When you push dem clouds away!
They'll all have wings, those mammy's little pets,
When you push dem clouds away!
Old Gabriel's horn will toot and roar,
When you push dem clouds away!
There'll be no dudes around the stage door,
When you push dem clouds away!

FLIRT. Does that satisfy your craving for music?
BEN. Entirely. I don't care if I never hear you sing again!
WIDOW. That's nice! Now, I must run home and get rested for tonight.
 Good-by, all.
BEN. (*opens portières; aside to Widow*) Everything's okay?
WIDOW. I hope so.
BEN. You and I are all right, but no Flirt!
WIDOW. Certainly not! (*Exit.*)
BEN. Young ladies, there's a woman whose example you ought to follow.
TONY. You don't know how hard we try to, sir.
SLAVIN. (*entering with a telegram*) Telegram, sir! (*Hands it.*) Any
 service I can perform, sir?
BEN. Yes. Leave the room! (*Exit Slavin. Ben reads telegram.*)
   "You will probably see me before this reaches you, for I am at
   Oakland. Will reach your house in an hour. Welland Strong."
 Whew! I didn't expect him till tomorrow.
FLIRT. Who is he? A nice young fellow, or an old codger like--oh, lots
 of folks.
BEN. He is a dying man, an old and dear boyhood friend of mine on
 whom Death has fixed its clutch. He comes here as my guest in the hope
 that our glorious climate may prolong his existence. Poor fellow, he
 used to be the picture of health. I dread to see him, hollow-chested,
 cheeks hectic, flushed, and glassy-eyed. And he, my boyhood's dearest

friend! Say, he's liable to be here any minute. We must--(*rings*)--make ready to receive him. Get a lounge ready. (*Girls obey.*)

SLAVIN. (*entering*) Did you ring?

BEN. Ring? I next thing to turned in a fire-alarm! Get a glass of wine ready on this table. Bring fans and smelling salts. Have a man help you bring him from the carriage. (*Everybody bustling to get everything fixed.*) He'll probably faint after his long journey. Now, is everything ready?

STRONG. (*entering with cat and parrot*) Ah, there! (*All turn to him.*)

BEN. What? Welland Strong?

STRONG. Yes! Welland Strong!

BEN. Why, how do you do?

STRONG. I may die before night! (*Business.*)

BEN. Sit down! Here, Slavin! Take the gentleman's wraps! Have a glass of wine? (*Exit Slavin with wraps.*)

STRONG. I will! Wine is harmful to me. It shortens my life. But I'll take it! (*Drinks.*)

BEN. You don't look badly, old man!

STRONG. No! That's the exasperating thing about it!

WILDER. Which lung is affected, sir?

STRONG. Neither as yet. But the left one probably will be by Saturday night.

RASHLEIGH. Do you cough much?

STRONG. Not at all! That's a very serious feature. My malady is so deep-seated that I can't bring the cough to the surface. But instead I feel a sensation which, in a well man, would be called a thirst for liquor.

TONY. And what do the doctors say?

STRONG. No two agree.

BEN. And who shall decide when doctors disagree?

STRONG. Usually the coroner. Why, I had seven of them. One fool said that nothing ailed me. Do you know, the only man who really understood my case was a horse doctor! He said if I stayed in Boston, I'd die in sixty days. Out here I'd live two years if I obeyed certain rules. Here's the book of rules, and it tells just how much I shorten my life each time I break one. That glass of wine shortened it nineteen hours.

SLAVIN. (*entering*) Shall I take the gentleman's game to his room, sir?

STRONG. He may as well.

SLAVIN. Anything else I can do?

BEN. Yes! Keep out! (*Exit Slavin with pets.*)

STRONG. By the way, can you give me the address of a good horse doctor?

BEN. Why, yes. But hadn't you better see our family physician?

STRONG. Oh, no! He's no good! None of these M.D.'s are! They're used to catering to their patients' whims. Giving them what they want to take. A horse doctor don't try to please his patients. He gives them what they need. I'll never trust any but a horse doctor.

BEN. Well! Well! I'll see you have one. I know a man who cured my mules of cholic.

STRONG. That's the man I want. He'll keep me going along, if anyone can.

TONY. What feature of our climate do you rely on to help you?

STRONG. The earthquakes!

ALL. The earthquakes?

STRONG. Yes. They're very invigorating.

BEN. Have you ever seen an earthquake?

STRONG. I was chased three miles by one once.

BEN. Now, old man, you've got two or three years anyhow and we'll try to make you comfortable. After dinner we'll sit down and talk over old times. (*Aside.*) I forgot! I've got to be out tonight. What'll I do with him? (*Aloud.*) We'll have the house all to ourselves, for the young people are going out to see Chinatown by night. You'd enjoy it if you were only able to go with them.

(*The four young people look at each other, startled.*)

TONY. But he isn't, Uncle. It's a very fatiguing trip.

STRONG. I don't know! I have sworn to see Chinatown, and, fading daily as I am, I shall never again be so able as tonight. It will, of course, shorten my life, but I'll go if the young people will take me!

BEN. Why, of course! Just delighted to have you go! Aren't you?

YOUNG PEOPLE. Oh, yes.

STRONG. Then I'll sacrifice--(*looks in book*)--ten days of my life and go!

(*Cats heard outside. Enter Slavin, all scratched.*)

SLAVIN. Your cats got at our cat, sir! You'd better come, sir!

(*Exeunt Strong and Ben, excited. Brief cat fight outside.*)

WILDER. Damn!

FLIRT. M-m-m!

TONY. M-m-m!

FLIRT. This is a nice fix!

TONY. We're dished on going to the ball, and we've got to put in a night toting that old fool all over Chinatown!

FLIRT. It's bad enough to lose the ball.

TONY. But toting him around is such a cheerless task.

WILDER. What's to be done?

YOUNG PEOPLE. Ask the widow!

WIDOW. (*entering*) What? How to get out of this new scrape?

GIRLS. You know--?

WIDOW. Just met your uncle in the hall. He told me this Mr. Strong would go with us to Chinatown, so I need have no compunctions about not going. And then--then he winked most mysteriously.

TONY. Uncle winked at you! I can't understand what he meant!

WIDOW. Neither can I, and I'm a widow!

FLIRT. But this dying creature that's tucked upon us! What are we going to do with him?

WIDOW. Take him along!

YOUNG PEOPLE. To Chinatown?

WIDOW. No! To the ball!

TONY. But if we tell him where we're going, he will go straight to Uncle with the story.

WIDOW. But don't tell him where he's going; just take him along.

TONY. But when he comes home, he'll tell on us.

WIDOW. Then he'll have to tell on himself, too! I don't know this Mr. Strong, but if he isn't as deep in this scrape as we are before we get home, then may I always remain a widow.

TONY. But he'll make four men to three ladies. Some girl with have to manage two beaux.

WIDOW. I think somebody will prove equal to that emergency!

TONY. On the whole, I'm rather glad he's going. We'll have a lot of fun with him.

WIDOW. He's got an exciting evening in store for him.

STRONG. (*entering*) The excitement of that cat fight has taken a week off my life.

TONY. Here he is. Oh, Mr. Strong, I want to introduce you to our charming young widow, Mrs. Guyer.

WIDOW. (*curtsies*) I am honored.

STRONG. (*pathetically*) A widow and a woman!

WIDOW. Those affiliations usually go together.

STRONG. How pathetic! In the flower of youth to be bereft of sweet companionship! To be doomed henceforth forever to tread life's pathway unaided and alone!

WIDOW. Ye-yes. But, say--there's no law against her marrying again.

WILDER. Well, if I left a widow--

WIDOW. You'd be pig enough to want her to stay one. That's a man. He thinks it's a slur on him for his widow to marry. Nothing of the sort.

It's a compliment. Shows he made married life so happy that she wants more of it.

RASHLEIGH. When I marry, I think I shall marry a widow.

FLIRT. Oh, Rashleigh! Why?

RASHLEIGH. I'm too lazy to do any of the courting myself.

WIDOW. We will change the subject. Mr. Strong, is your visit to San Francisco for pleasure?

STRONG. I came here to die.

WIDOW. To die!

STRONG. Yes! It's a sure thing. The remedy I am taking for my lung trouble contains dynamite. If the disease conquers the remedy, why, I die of the disease. If the remedy conquers the disease, I shall be so full of dynamite eventually that I'll go off with a bang--(*Widow startled*)--like a torpedo dropped from the roof on a policeman's head! Think, I may suddenly vanish with a loud report--(*Widow screams*)--before your eyes! (*Widow screams again.*) And it may happen any moment! Now!!! (*Widow shrieks wildly and faints in chair.*) Great heavens! She's fainted! Send for the horse doctor!

WIDOW. (*springs up and glares at him*) What!

ACT II.

Scene. "The Riche" Restaurant. The stage is divided into three compartments: C., private supper room; R., the office with desk, etc.; L., another private supper room. (*Discovered: Noah Heap in C. room.*)

NOAH. Mr. Rashleigh Gay's party of six. Well, that means up all night for me and plenty of wine on ice. But it also means five dollars for a tip. Mr. Gay may sometimes forget some of the commandments, but he always remembers the waiter. He'll go to Heaven. (*Voices outside.*) Here they are. (*Opens door, C.*) Right this way, Mr. Gay. This is your room.

(*Enter three ladies, Rashleigh, and Wilder.*)

TONY. Number 10, with a piano. I'm glad we've got that!

FLIRT. But what's that orchestra?

WILDER. They have one that plays every night in this restaurant from eight to twelve.

NOAH. (*points R.U.E.*) The ladies' dressing room in there! (*Points L.U.E.*) The gentlemen's here. The dresses are in the room.

FLIRT. Let's go and get dressed at once while they're getting supper so we'll lose no time. Come on, Tony. (*Exeunt Tony and Flirt, R.U.E.*)

WILDER. (*to Widow*) What shall we order for supper?

WIDOW. Oh, some Pommery. (*Exit, R.U.E.*)

RASHLEIGH. Mr. Painter's not here yet?

NOAH. No, sir.

WILDER. We'll have to wait for him; he's got our tickets to the ball.

RASHLEIGH. Couldn't we buy others?

WILDER. No, none are sold at the door. So we've got to wait for him. We'll go ahead with supper--though--sa-say! Where's our dying companion, Strong?

STRONG. (*entering*) Here I am!

RASHLEIGH. What's happened?

STRONG. The hackman said five dollars. I said two!

WILDER. What did you agree upon?

STRONG. Five! Tell me! Do we stop here long?

WILDER. Our friend, Mr. Painter, who is to meet us here, hasn't arrived, and he has the tickets.

STRONG. Tickets! For Chinatown?

WILDER. Ye-yes. Of course.

RASHLEIGH. Oh, you're not let into Chinatown without tickets. (*To Noah.*) Isn't that so?

NOAH. Yes, sir. Fifty cents, please. (*Rashleigh gives Noah a coin.*)

STRONG. Supper! (*Consults book.*) Eating at night shortens my life ten days!

RASHLEIGH. Well, you can sit and see us eat.

STRONG. You're very kind. But I'll not impose upon your courtesy. Lend me a pencil till I put down--(*writes*)--"Late supper, ten days off." What's ten day's life to me? Here, waiter, my hat and coat!

　(*Exit Noah with wraps.*)

WILDER. Now, Rashleigh, we must be getting dressed. But, say, we haven't ordered supper.

RASHLEIGH. That's so. Mr. Strong, what would you like? Won't you give the order?

STRONG. I fear the taste of a dying man may not exactly suit your fancies.

WILDER. I don't know. I never tasted one. But you go ahead and order the supper.

RASHLEIGH. The wines we get out here are harmless.

　(*Exeunt Rashleigh and Wilder, L.U.E.*)

STRONG. I don't quite understand all this! (*Enter Noah, C.*) Oh, waiter! I hope you were careful of my coat. There was a large bottle of medicine in each pocket.

NOAH. Yes, sir.

STRONG. If the medicine's got mixed, they would explode.

NOAH. Why didn't you say so before? (*Grabs carafe and drinks.*)

STRONG. Waiter, I will order the supper. Give us--(*pantomimes business of ordering the supper*)--and, waiter, could you give me a glass of whale's milk?

NOAH. Whale's milk?

STRONG. Why, yes. My doctor recommends it.

NOAH. Well, you tell him to go milk a whale and get some. It ain't on our bill of fare.

STRONG. Too bad! Say, waiter, will you do me a favor? There's a porous plaster between my shoulders that's driving me crazy. Will you kindly reach down my back and pull it off?

NOAH. Certainly, sir. (*Puts hand down Strong's back.*) How do you like your agony, sir?

STRONG. Take it slow. There's not a bit of hurry.

NOAH. I know, sir. A hair's breadth at a time. I won't hurt you, sir.

STRONG. Easy! Easy!

(*A bell rings in outer office. Noah bolts for the door, R., taking porous plaster with him. He leaves Strong quivering with pain. Noah enters outer office and looks at annunciator.*)

He took skin and all!

(*Re-enter Noah in room, C., with plaster stuck to his fingers.*)

NOAH. I'll swear I heard a bell ring. Didn't you?

(*Business with plaster.*)

STRONG. No, sir! I wasn't listening for bells.

NOAH. Here's your plaster, sir. (*It sticks to Strong's hands.*)

STRONG. I don't want it. I never save these things as souvenirs. You throw it out.

NOAH. Excuse me! I've got to get supper.

(*Exit, C. and re-enters room, R., the office.*)

STRONG. (*business with plaster; gets badly stuck up and in desperation goes off, C., calling*) Waiter! Waiter!

(*Meanwhile Noah has gone behind office desk. Enter Ben, office, R.*)

BEN. Has a lady been here inquiring for Mr. Gay?

NOAH. No, sir.

BEN. I'm in time. Show me to a private supper room for two.

NOAH. Certainly, sir. This way. (*Exeunt Noah and Ben.*)

WIDOW. (*entering, wearing Hamlet dress, from R.U.E.*)   It seems I am to go to the ball in the guise of a man. I was forced to it. A man among women! Well, that's what I always wanted to be! What sort of a young fellow shall I be to catch the girls? The very English young man: "Good morning, dear boy. Awfully pleased, awfully! Beastly weather this--in London, you know. Come 'round to the club, old chappie! Have a brandy and soda. We've new windows in our club now--special glass, magnificent fog effect! Brightest day makes you feel right at home in London, dear boy." And there's the young freshman in college: "We boys--ha! ha! ha!--have lots of--ha! ha! ha!--fun. We've had a cow in the president's chair twice, and--ha! ha! ha!--we've had a cane rush--ha! ha! ha!--and three men had broken bones, and it was lots of fun, and--ha! ha! ha! Let's waltz! What! Engaged for the next? And all the rest? And here comes Mr. Winner. Yes, he's a senior, and I'll have to excuse you! Oh!" Or I might be one of those dear, delightful toughs: "Say, dere sis, come and do a toin! What's dat? Engaged, be blowed! If he says a woid, I'll t'row him out, see?" But I guess I'll do best as just the average young man right up to date. (*Sings.*)

> WIDOW.   *"The Chaperone."*
> A crisp young chaperone,
> Who is always bright and gay;
> And when they dare not go alone,
> They always take a chaperone
> To take the curse away,
> To take the curse away.
> Although it's far from pleasing
> To be severe and hurt,
> I'm chaperone this evening,
> That all of you may flirt.
> A crisp young chaperone,
> Who is always bright and gay;
> And when they dare not go alone,
> They always take the chaperone
> To take the curse away,
> To take the curse away.
>
> A gay young chaperone,
> Who is always bright and gay;
> And captivating at a glance,
> Will set your sluggish heart adance:
> And eyes that fire and flash,

And eyes that fire and flash.
But still she's oft demurely,
Quite shy, reserved and plain;
Perhaps you think so surely,
Her heart and hand you'll gain.
A crisp young chaperone,
Who is always bright and gay;
And when they dare not go alone,
They always take the chaperone
To take the curse away,
To take the curse away.

(*A dance, and exit, R.U.E. Enter Ben and Noah, room L.*)

BEN. This will do. When the lady calls, show her right in. And, say, you'd better have supper all ready. I shan't have to wait long for her.

NOAH. Yes, sir. Champagne, and what else, sir?

BEN. The best of everything. A corking supper, my boy! Nothing's too good!

NOAH. Yes, sir. Like to look at the evening paper, sir?

BEN. No. No paper for me! (*Exit Noah.*) I'll just sit and think of what a lucky dog I am. I wonder how Strong's enjoying Chinatown.

(*Ben sits, smoking.   Enter Widow and the two girls in costume, R.U.E.*)

WIDOW. I think you are very unkind, girls, to make any such remarks. You know I won't be out of mourning for twenty-nine days yet, and it's the only black dress of the lot.

(*Strong enters, C., sees Widow; exit Strong, C., and coughs outside.*)

Here comes Mr. Strong! I--I-- Where's my mask? (*Dons mask.*) Now to win him over to our frolic. I wonder if he's got a mask.

STRONG. (*looking out, C.*) May I come in?

WIDOW. Certainly, Mr. Strong. I want to ask you a question. Are you stuck?

STRONG. Not now!

WIDOW. But you have been!

STRONG. (*aside*) That waiter told her. (*Aloud.*) Yes.

WIDOW. And you may be again some day.

STRONG. Not if I know it!

TONY. (*exhibits costume*) Will these do? (*Sees Strong.*) Oh!

STRONG. Bless my soul! What does all this mean?

WIDOW. Girls, we may as well throw aside all attempts at concealment. (*Strong turns to go.*) Mr. Strong--(*removes mask*)--we are not going to

Chinatown. We are going to the masquerade! We expect you to go with us, to join in the fun with us--and when we get home, we rely on your sense of honor to swear that we've been to Chinatown!

STRONG. But, my dear--

WIDOW. Swear as an honest man that you will do this.

STRONG. But I don't think your uncle would deceive me!

(*The girls offer him a glass of wine.*)

BEN. (*in the other room*) I wonder what Strong would say if he knew I was here.

WIDOW. Swear it!

STRONG. I do.

TONY. Ah, I knew he was a thoroughbred!

STRONG. Say! Come to think of it, it's a mighty good joke on the old fellow! (*Laughs.*) One moment. (*Produces book.*) This means two weeks more off my life--but let her rip! (*Enter two boys, L.U.E.*)

FLIRT. Are you dressed at last?

RASHLEIGH. We are! Now for the supper, and then we're ready to start.

WILDER. Mr. Strong, perhaps we ought to explain.

STRONG. It might be as well, but if you've got a really good lie fixed up for me, I don't mind hearing it.

TONY. He knows us, and he's with us.

TWO YOUNG MEN. He is? Good boy!

(*One each side of him and sing "We'll Show You 'Frisco!" Then they all sing, the girls between them.*)

"*Out for a Racket!*"
Out for a racket, racket up to here!
Out for a racket, racket up to here!
Out for a high old frolic,
Strictly alcoholic,
Wine or whiskey, ale or lager beer!
Out for a racket, racket up to here!
Out for a racket, racket up to here!
Out for a high old frolic,
Strictly alcoholic,
Out for a racket up to here!

WIDOW.   In me, a modest maid you see!
Of course you know I'm college bred!

I've learned to calm my ecstasy,
To worldly joys seem dead!
This air demure is all put on,
I love to romp and make a noise!
My mamma thinks I'm an angel, but--
You ought to see me with the boys!
I love to romp and make a noise,
And you should see me with the boys! Ah!

Although, you see, I'm scarce of age,
I love to have a high old time!
Just now this seems to be the rage,
To me it is divine!
A cigarette, a glass of wine,
With lots of fun and lots of noise!
I would not be an angel when
I have a night out with the boys!
I love to romp and make a noise,
And you should see me with the boys! Ah!

BEN. (*looks at watch*) Ten minutes of ten! By jingo, she ought to be here. It's prolonging the agony. (*Rings. Enter Noah.*) Waiter, are you sure that lady hasn't called?

NOAH. Sure, sir! Supper's ready to serve when you want it.

BEN. I don't want it till she gets here. She can't be long now.

NOAH. Patience is a great thing in these cases, sir. Don't you want the evening paper, sir?

BEN. No, no! I didn't come here to read the evening paper. Bring me a cocktail. (*Exit Noah.*)

FLIRT. Say, let's not wait for Mr. Painter. I'm starved.
    (*Enter Noah, C., with tray.*)

RASHLEIGH. Waiter, you can bring the supper.
    (*Music begins.*)

TONY. There's the orchestra. Say, we're losing time! What's the matter with dancing right here?

FLIRT. That's so! Come on! Mr. Strong, you'll dance?

STRONG. If you can bear the spectacle of a man with one foot in the grave trying to be merry with the other, I'll do my best.
    (*Minuet. To finish it, Noah, who has been setting table, drops tray. Strong falls in chair. Exit Noah, C.*)
There goes that lung!

FLIRT. Why, no! The waiter dropped a tray of dishes.

STRONG. I thought that lung had busted, sure. It's likely to at any minute.

BEN. Some pack of hoodlums in that next room! By jove, this is getting monotonous.

NOAH. (*entering with four cocktails*) You didn't say what kind of cocktail, so I brought four.

BEN. You know your business.

NOAH. I can take three of them back.

BEN. Over my dead body! (*Takes tray.*)

NOAH. Hadn't you better look at the evening paper, sir?

BEN. No, sir! I had not!

(*Exit Noah. Three men gather about Widow. Tony and Flirt are alone.*)

FLIRT. Will you look at that!

TONY. Excuse me! I'd rather not see it.

FLIRT. I don't know why men go crazy over widows! It's enough to drive one--

TONY. To marrying some man and then poisoning him. This man Strong's only going to live two years. I've a mind to make love to him. With what I'd keep him out nights, I think I could shorten his existence to six months.

FLIRT. And she--

TONY. She's doing her duty as chaperone. Taking care we don't get familiar with the gentlemen.

FLIRT. Yes, and taking great satisfaction in it. I can see she's laughing at us!

TONY. I vow I'll break it up. (*Aloud.*) Mrs. Guyer, how long did Mr. Guyer last after you were married?

WIDOW. Only six months. (*Men draw away.*)

TONY. I--I heard he died from the effects of a blowing up!

WIDOW. (*unruffled*) Yes. Excursion boat. Dear boy! He was insured for fifty thousand dollars! (*Men right back around her.*)

TONY. (*aside to Flirt*) I wish I was a man or a parrot! I want to swear! Say, Flirt, sing a song. They'll have, in common decency, to listen.

FLIRT. I can't.

TONY. Then ask me to.

FLIRT. (*aloud*) Say, everybody. Tony knows this song the orchestra's playing. I want you all to listen to it.

(*Tony sings "Never To Know." Business of weeping with the song.*)

STRONG. Beautiful! How touching! How much we miss in this life by

476 ON STAGE, AMERICA!

not daring to speak out. I went thirsty two days in a prohibition town because I didn't dare to ask the landlord for a drink. (*Weeps again.*) Forgive these tears! But that song has turned all my thoughts to sadness. The separation of two fond beings makes me think of the fast approaching day when one of my lungs will be withered and vanished, leaving the other desolate, alone, and overworked. I have often in the still watches of the night pondered on this and at last my sad musings took the form of a little poem.

TONY and WIDOW. Oh, give it to us.

STRONG. (*takes drink, makes memorandum in book*) It's called the "Lay of the Lingering Lung." I wish that band would play a soft, tuneful melody.
  (*Recitation with music by Strong. As they break up, Strong goes to Tony, and Rashleigh to Flirt. Widow sizes up situation.*)

WIDOW. Ahem! Have you heard the latest scandal?
  (*Every man rushes up to her.*)

THREE MEN. What is it?

TONY. What have you been doing today?

WIDOW. That remark was contemptible. Now, you shan't hear the story. (*Tells story to men in dumb show.*) It isn't long. (*To girls.*) And I really am not trying to monololize the gentlemen entirely. I shall probably insist, as a favor to me, that they devote themselves to you.
  (*She goes on with a cry. Makes gestures.*)

TONY. There they are again! I vow I'll be a widow within a year.

FLIRT. I know what it is. It's the dress.
  (*Widow makes parenthetical gesture.*)

TONY. Did you see that gesture? I'll bet I know what she said. A widow'll say anything. Come, Flirt. (*They rise.*) Gentlemen, we wish to use your dressing room just a moment. (*Exeunt, L.U.E. Ben rings.*)

WIDOW. I'll bet I know what they're up to. (*Rises.*) Pray excuse me.
  (*Exit Widow, R.U.E. Noah enters Ben's room.*)

BEN. Fill 'em up again all 'round.

NOAH. (*takes tray*) Yes, sir. I have the evening paper.

BEN. Keep it! (*Exit Noah.*) By thunder, that widow takes her time!
  (*During the above, Rashleigh has filled glasses and passed them.*)

STRONG. Gentlemen, you ought not to tempt me like this. (*Drinks and reaches for bottle.*) Every glass of this stuff is a day off my life. (*Drinks.*) You are aiding and abetting suicide. (*Produces book.*) Has anybody kept tab on me?

WILDER. That last one was seven, I think.

STRONG. A week gone! I've wasted five weeks of my life tonight, and I

came here for my health. My first night in San Francisco reminds me of
the first night I struck New York. (*Sings.*)

STRONG. *"The Bowery."*
Oh! The night that I struck New York,
I went out for a quiet walk;
Folks who are "on to" the city say,
Better by far that I took Broadway;
But I was out to enjoy the sights,
There was the Bowery ablaze with lights;
I had one of the devil's own nights!
I'll never go there any more!

Chorus.
The Bow'ry, the Bow'ry!
They say such things and they do strange things
On the Bow'ry! The Bow'ry!
I'll never go there any more!

I had walked but a block or two,
When up came a fellow and me he knew;
Then a policeman came walking by,
Chased him away and I asked him, "Why?"
"Wasn't he pulling your leg?" said he;
Said I, "He never laid hands on me!"
"Get off the Bow'ry, you yap!" said he;
I'll never go there any more!

I went into an auction store,
I never saw any thieves before;
First he sold me a pair of socks,
Then, said he, "How much for the box?"
Someone said, "Two dollars!" I said, "Three!"
He emptied the box and gave it to me;
"I sold you the box, not the socks," said he.
I'll never go there any more!

I went into a concert hall,
I didn't have a good time at all;
Just the minute that I sat down
Girls began singing, "New Coon in Town."

I got up mad and spoke out free,
"Somebody put that man out!" said she.
A man called a bouncer attended to me.
I'll never go there any more!

I went into a barber shop,
He talked till I thought he would never stop;
I said, "Cut it short." He misunderstood,
Clipped down my hair as close as he could;
He shaved with a razor that scratched like a pin,
Took off my whiskers and most of my chin;
That was the worst scrape I ever got in.
I'll never go there any more!

I struck a place that they call a "dive,"
I was in luck to get out alive;
When the policeman heard my woes,
Saw my black eyes and my battered nose,
"You've been held up!" said the "copper" fly!
"No, sir! But I've been knocked down!" said I.
Then he laughed, but I couldn't see why!
I'll never go there any more!

    Chorus.
    The Bow'ry, the Bow'ry!
    They say such things and they do strange things
    On the Bow'ry! The Bow'ry!
    I'll never go there any more!
(*Enter Noah with note and four cocktails on tray, C.*)

WILDER. What's that?
NOAH. Cocktails. The gentleman in the next room ordered them.
RASHLEIGH. Very good of him. (*Passes glasses.*)
STRONG. (*takes glass*) That man's bent on my murder. (*All drink.*)
BEN. (*rings*) I wonder what's become of my cocktails.
RASHLEIGH. Tell the gentleman we're very much obliged.
NOAH. Yes, sir. A note, sir. (*Gives note. Exit, C.*)
RASHLEIGH. (*reads note*) It's from Painter. "Unavoidably detained. See
  you very soon."
    (*Noah enters Ben's room.*)

BEN. Where's my cocktails?

NOAH. Gentlemen in the next room drank them, sir, and sent in their compliments.

BEN. They did! Well, I like their nerve! You go back quick and get me four more. Stop! Make it eight! And, sir! Are you sure that lady hasn't got here?

NOAH. Sure, sir. Only ladies here are with the party next room. I rather think, sir--

BEN. Think what?

NOAH. You're shook!

BEN. Shook?

NOAH. Hadn't you better eat your supper alone, sir?

BEN. No, sir. She'll be here, sir! You get those cocktails!

NOAH. The evening paper!

BEN. Damn the evening paper! (*Exit Noah.*) Shook! Me shook!

WILDER. Mr. Strong, this isn't the first time you've been out for a pleasant evening. I see by the way you handle that bottle.

STRONG. When I was on earth, I was not obtuse to the redeeming features of wine, women, and song.

RASHLEIGH. Well, be a boy again. We have the wine and the women. Give us the song.

STRONG. If you care to listen to a voice from the grave, I'll--let me see-- give you a little story of the course of true love.

(*Strong sings "2:15." He and the two boys are drunk.*)

BEN. I'm having a devil of a good time. This is what you get for trusting a widow. (*Enter Noah with cocktails.*)

NOAH. Cocktails, sir! Shall I put them down?

(*Strong, in the other room, is getting a bit loaded.*)

BEN. No, I'll do that. (*Takes tray.*)

NOAH. The evening paper!

BEN. (*somewhat jagged*) Give it to me! (*Takes paper. Tears it up.*) Now, are you easy in your mind? I came here to have supper with a lady! Do you think I'll be satisfied with an evening paper?

NOAH. What about that supper, sir?

BEN. I'll eat it. Bring it up.

NOAH. The evening paper, sir, had a whole page about a scandal in high life.

BEN. (*looks at fragments*) It did? Well, I'll be dashed! Have you got another copy?

NOAH. No, sir.

(Exit Noah. Ben gets on floor and tries to piece paper together. Enter, into other room, the two girls in shape dresses.)

TONY. Now can we have a little attention?

(Enter Noah at C. Musical introduction. Tony and Flirt sing. Then the two boys join them. As they go up, Widow enters, R.U.E., in white Chinese dress and does Chinese specialty. Then Strong, pretty drunk, joins Widow and sings with her. All join in chorus and dance at finish.) The widow in white! Have the twenty-nine days gone by so soon?

WIDOW. *(bursts into tears)* Oh, Tony! How cruel of you! To think I'd forget the respect due poor Jack! Don't you see this is a Chinese dress, and the Chinese for mourning wear white. I know my business.

NOAH. Supper is served.

WIDOW. Come on! Let's get it over before you boys get to making love to each other's girls and the quarrels begin.

(They sit at table, filling time while Ben speaks in the other room.)

BEN. I can't put it together. It's all mixed up with the market reports. *(Reads.)* "The infuriated husband, revolver in hand, rushed madly after a drove of prime western hogs just arrived." Oh, rats! *(Rises, pretty drunk; kicks at paper. Falls in chair.)* By jove, I'm drunk! *(Rises and tries himself.)* Drunker'n a boiled oil! That's a good one! I'll just keep it up and get paralyzed. I'll have some fun out of this racket yet. *(Rings.)*

WIDOW. Please pass the salt.

RASHLEIGH. With all my heart.

WIDOW. Just the salt, please.

TONY. *(rises)* Well, here's to all of us!

ALL. Drink hearty! *(They sing.)*

"Reuben and Cynthia."
Reuben, Reuben, I've a notion
If the men were sent away,
Far beyond the stormy ocean,
Female hearts would all be gay.
Cynthia, Cynthia, I've been thinking,
If the men should take that trip,
All the women in creation,
Right away would take that ship.

Reuben, Reuben, I've been thinking,
What a strange thing that would be,
If the streams of drinking water,
All turned salty as the sea.

Cynthia, Cynthia, I've been thinking,
You can safely take my word,
More than half the population,
Wouldn't know it had occurred.

Reuben, Reuben, I've been thinking,
Will you tell me where or when,
Women will be forced to stop this,
Doing things just like the men?
Cynthia, Cynthia, I've been thinking,
And can answer with dispatch;
She must cease her mannish methods,
When she comes to strike a match.

Reuben, Reuben, I've been thinking,
Why do people risk their gold,
Betting on the wicked races,
Knowing they are bought and sold!
Cynthia, Cynthia, I've been thinking,
That is where the laugh comes in;
Each man thinks that he has fixed it,
So the horse he backs will win.

STRONG. Anybody have some cold meat? Mutton or beef?

FLIRT. Which is the best?

STRONG. (*smells each*) It appears to be a case of horse and horse!
Waiter, this knife is very dull.

NOAH. Permit me, sir. (*Takes knife; gets behind Strong; imitates sharpening knife.*) Try that, sir.

STRONG. (*tries it*) Much better!

NOAH. Anything else you want, sir?

STRONG. What have you got?

NOAH. Anything on earth.

STRONG. If there's anything you have not got, I want it.

NOAH. I can give you anything from a train of cars to a dog fight.

ALL. Give us a dog fight!

(*Noah's imitations. At start of dog fight, Ben in next room starts looking for it. Afterwards, exit Noah.*)

STRONG. (*rises*) Ladies and gentlemen--

WIDOW. He's going to make an after-dinner speech! Stop him!

RASHLEIGH. Head him off!

ALL. Come on! (*Medley. At end of medley, all off.*)

BEN. (*rings, after entering from hall, where he has been looking for dog fight*) She's here! I've found this handkerchief in the hall and it's hers. (*Enter Noah.*) You demented lizard, do you see that? It's her handkerchief! She's here! Now, trot her out!

NOAH. Was that the lady you were waiting for?

BEN. Yes! Well?

NOAH. Why, we thought it was your wife! We said you weren't here!

BEN. Well!

NOAH. And she went away!

BEN. (*grabs him*) While I've waited, she's been here and you sent her away!

NOAH. I regret it, sir.

BEN. Regret it! Regret it! I'd kill you where you stand, only I don't want to become known as a foolkiller! But I'll make it cost you your job. I'll give you a character at the office!

(*Ben bolts out. Exit Noah, after him. Strong enters, L.U.E., and crosses to R.U.E.*)

STRONG. (*bows*) Did any of you ladies bring a corn knife?

TONY. (*looks out*) No. Will a curling iron do?

STRONG. No, thanks! I can't curl my corns.

(*Exit Strong, R.U.E. Enter Ben at office, followed by Noah, who goes behind counter.*)

NOAH. What is it, sir?

BEN. I want to see somebody in authority.

NOAH. Gaze right on me!

BEN. You! You're in authority! Well, I want to tell you that the waiter I've had is a blear-eyed tramp, a bandy-legged idiot, and a foul hedgehog!

NOAH. I'll make a note of it. Anything else, sir?

BEN. Yes. Your place is a dive, and I'll never set foot in it again.

(*He starts to go.*)

NOAH. (*locks door*) Hadn't you better settle your bill first?

BEN. I forgot, how much is it?

NOAH. One hundred dollars.

BEN. One hundred dollars! What for?

NOAH. Well, there's sixty-five dollars for the supper.

BEN. But I haven't had supper.

NOAH. But you ordered it.

BEN. All right! I deserve it! I--I--(*business of looking for pocketbook*)--why, I've--I've lost my pocketbook. I'll send you the money tomorrow.

NOAH. We don't do business that way.

BEN. But I'm perfectly good.

NOAH. What name?

BEN. Excuse me! But you shall have your money.

NOAH. I mean to--before you go.

BEN. But, my boy--

NOAH. Send home for it!

BEN. Send for the money to pay for a racket here! Impossible! Now, my dear boy--

NOAH. No! I'm a blear-eyed tramp, and I get that money, or you go to jail. See?

STRONG. (*entering, L.U.E.*) I'll see why they don't answer that bell!
    (*Exit Strong, C.*)

NOAH. Do I get it, or do I ring for the police?

BEN. My very dear boy, I'm a respectable citizen. Don't arrest me! The story'll be all over town.

NOAH. Yes, but you won't be all over to hear it. You'll be in the jail.
    (*Strong enters office.*)

STRONG. You hyena, I want--
    (*Strong and Ben look at each other. Both yell. Strong turns to run.*)

BEN. Here! I want you! (*Starts after Strong.*)

NOAH. Here! Come back, you!
    (*Noah starts after them. Grand chase. As they rush through C. room, everybody exclaiming: "What's the matter?," etc. Strong yells, "Murder!" and "Help!" Ben and Noah ad lib. Everybody working up excitement. At finish Ben overtakes Strong in room C. and grabs him.*)

BEN. Now, I've got you!

STRONG. I'm a dying man! Mercy!

BEN. Mercy! Not a damned bit! Lend me a hundred dollars!

ACT III.

Scene. Private gymnasium in the house of Ben Gay. (*Discovered: Tony and Flirt in wrappers.*)

FLIRT. I think we're the first ones up. And I had a good mind not to get up at all.

TONY. This settles the "out for a racket" business for me, Flirt. Do you realize that we're in an awful scrape? Of course, Uncle can't do anything worse to you than tell your father.

FLIRT. That's so. He couldn't do anything worse. I'd rather he'd whip me. I guess it does settle the "out for a racket" business. Oh, Tony, isn't there anything to keep him from telling? I'll get killed.

TONY. I don't know of any. We'll all have to suffer except the widow. And she's the only one who had any fun. The way the men devoted themselves to her ruined my evening. Flirt, I've made up my mind. I'm going to be a widow!

FLIRT. Oh, Tony! But you've got to be a wife first, and your husband may live forever.

TONY. No, he won't! I shall marry Mr. Strong! Heaven has sent him here, I feel, to my relief. (*Enter Wilder and Rashleigh.*)

FLIRT. Oh, Wilder, did you send home that we were here?

WILDER. I did. And, say, it's lucky we didn't go to the ball. It was closed by the police.

RASHLEIGH. And Painter was arrested! That's why he didn't come to The Riche.

WIDOW. (*entering*) Good morning, everybody!

ALL. Good morning.

TONY. To what are we indebted for this early call?

WIDOW. I've come over first, to have a little practice with the foils. (*Throws off cloak, disclosing fencing costume.*) Second, to get you out of the scrape.

FLIRT. Oh, can you?

WIDOW. Well, you know me! What do you think?

WILDER. We'll bet on you every time.

WIDOW. Last night after I reached home, I began to think that you were in a fix. "They've got to tell some story to get out of it," said I. "And they're not good at telling stories," said I. "They may lay the blame on me," said I. "Then my reputation will be in the laundry, and a widow has to be careful of her reputation. I must go over there and tell a story that will get us all out of it," said I. And here I am!

TONY. One word for us, and two for yourself! You're very good!

WIDOW. Now, am I in time?

RASHLEIGH. I think so. Neither Uncle nor Mr. Strong are up yet.

WILDER. That Strong's a thoroughbred, after all.

WIDOW. A delightful man! It's a pity he's got to die so soon!

TONY. Nothing of the sort! I--I mean--perhaps he hasn't. (*Aside.*) But I'm sure he has!

FLIRT. Well, say, what story are we to tell Uncle?

WIDOW. I don't know yet. But there's a way out of this scrape, and I know how to find it. I've only got one favor to ask. Don't mix in and spoil things. How soon will they be up?

RASHLEIGH. Nobody knows.

WIDOW. I've got to be at my dressmaker's in an hour. Can't you call them?

TONY. Not for worlds!

WIDOW. Then we must make a racket so they'll have to get up! Where are their rooms?

TONY. (*points R. and L.*) There and there! Come, Flirt, let's get our gymnasium suits on. (*Exeunt two girls.*)

WIDOW. We may as well start the racket! Come on!

>(*Medley, during which the two girls return in gymnasium suits. At finish, all exeunt. Enter Strong from R., Ben from L. They look like wrecks. Neither knows what to say. Strong has a bowl of ice and offers some to Ben.*)

STRONG. Have a piece.

BEN. (*takes ice*) Thanks! Don't you think a little absinthe would do us good? (*Rings.*)

STRONG. It can't shorten my life much!

>(*Slavin heard singing below. Comes upstairs, still singing "Out for a Racket."*)

SLAVIN. (*pretty drunk*) Here I am!

BEN. Slavin! Sirrah! What does this mean?

SLAVIN. I've been right with you. Drunk as a boiled owl! I knew everybody else was on a toot, so I filled up! Three very pretty jags we three gentlemen had! (*Exit.*)

STRONG. What a beastly fellow!

BEN. That is strictly between us! My catching you was an accident. I went to The Riche to have supper with a lady.

STRONG. You old rascal!

BEN. But if my family knew that, I'd lose their respect forever.

STRONG. Why, you didn't do anything wrong, did you?

BEN. No, damn it! The widow didn't--

STRONG. The widow didn't what?

BEN. Why--er--that's--that's something you didn't understand. What I was going to say is this: That loan of a hundred dollars squares you, but in order to save my own reputation, I must make these youngsters believe that I followed them there, and I must punish them accordingly.

It's rough on them, but–

STRONG. Don't make it too rough. Remember we used to enjoy a little racket in the days gone by when we were their age.

BEN. By thunder, we did!

(*Duet. "Days Gone By." Enter Slavin with three drinks.*)

SLAVIN. Here we are, brother sufferers.

BEN. (*takes drink*) If you don't stop your impudence, I'll discharge you!

(*Ben and Strong drink.*)

SLAVIN. That's what I want! I'm drunk and I'm glad of it! I'm a whale!

STRONG. A whale! No!

SLAVIN. This is the first time in forty years I've dared to open my head and now I'm going to let 'er go. I'm looking to get kicked out of the house!

BEN. You shall be! (*Exit downstairs, kicking Slavin.*)

STRONG. He'll just give it to those children to prove his own probity. I think I'll take to bed till the affair's over.

TONY. (*entering, in gymnasium dress*) Oh, there he is! Oh, if I can get him to marry me! Black is so becoming to me. Ahem! Good morning! Mr. Strong, how do you feel this morning?

STRONG. I think I shall live until dinner time.

TONY. Oh, I hope so. We should miss your cheery "Yes, thanks," when the wine is served. Oh, Mr. Strong, do you know, everything about you interests me. Have you got a wife?

STRONG. A wife? No.

TONY. Then you're a jolly bachelor!

STRONG. No! Not a bachelor!

TONY. Not a bachelor! Oh, forgive me if I've touched a tender spot in your heart. You are a widower!

STRONG. No, not a widower!

TONY. Excuse me, Mr. Strong, you say you're not a single man!

STRONG. I am not.

TONY. Nor a married man nor a widower! Will you kindly tell me what you are?

STRONG. Well, if you must know, I'm a divorced man!

TONY. A divorced man! How romantic!

STRONG. Yes, and very expensive.

TONY. And when are you going to--try it again?

STRONG. Never!

TONY. Never? Oh, don't say that!

STRONG. Why, I'm a dying man!

TONY. That's it! With such a glorious opportunity to make a woman a widow, you have no right to remain single a minute. You ought to marry the first woman you can lay your hands on!

STRONG. (*puts his hands behind him and shies away*) But I don't want a wife!

TONY. You do! To wear mourning for you! Now, you must--

STRONG. But the divorce forbade me to marry. It would be contempt of court.

TONY. Then contempt the court! Positively despise it!

STRONG. And go to prison? Say, it's time to take my medicine! Excuse me! (*Exit, L.*)

TONY. Well, I declare!

WILDER. (*entering*) Sweetheart, I want to--

TONY. Oh, go away!

WILDER. What?

TONY. Go away! You weary me!

WILDER. Weary you? Why, I thought you loved me!

TONY. I do, but you won't do! You're not going to die in two years!

WILDER. I hope not!

TONY. Then that lets you out. You're not in it. So don't bother me!
   (*She rushes out.*)

WILDER. Well, I declare! (*Terrible crash below.*)

THREE LADIES. (*entering, ad lib*) What's that?
   (*Etc.; Slavin enters, coming upstairs, singing. Girls much alarmed.*)

SLAVIN. (*has parrot and cat; to Wilder*) You're wanted below. (*Throws Wilder downstairs.*) That's two! (*Girls scream.*) I'm going to do 'em all! I've been discharged, and before I go I'm going to lick every man in the house! Then I'll kiss all the women. (*Women scream and exeunt, Widow into Ben's room.*) I'm a whale! Where's that dying man? He's my pie! I'll make him eat his own game! (*Going out.*) I'll give you your medicine!
   (*Tremendous crash, R. Enter Tony, Flirt, and Rashleigh.*)

RASHLEIGH. What is it?

FLIRT. Slavin is in there killing Mr. Strong!

TONY. Go save him! (*Crash, R.*)

RASHLEIGH. Give me something to hit him with! (*Grabs Indian club.*) That's too heavy! (*Drops it. Crash, R.*)

TONY. (*hands him the same club*) Here, try this!

RASHLEIGH. That's too light! (*Crash, R.*) Where's my ball bat?

FLIRT. Locked up in the locker! The key's downstairs.

RASHLEIGH. Go get it! (*Exit Flirt, downstairs. Tremendous crash, R.*) Oh, wait till I get something to hit him with! (*Crash.*)

TONY. Oh, he'll be killed! Take the Indian club!

RASHLEIGH. No, I can't! I must have the bat! (*Crash.*)

TONY. Oh, Rashleigh, save him! He'll surely be killed!

RASHLEIGH. Then I'll avenge him! (*Enter Flirt from downstairs.*)

WIDOW. (*entering, L.*) What's the matter?

TONY. Slavin is killing Mr. Strong!

(*Grand crash. Widow and girls yell. Enter Strong, dragging in Slavin, who is all torn up; handful of parrot feathers.*)

STRONG. I have shortened my life one year!

SLAVIN. You've shortened mine fifty! I'll never be able to digest that parrot!

ALL. The parrot!

SLAVIN. He made me swallow it! (*All laugh.*) That's right! And damn it! How I hate feathers! (*Spits some out.*) Ladies and gentlemen, is there anything I can do for you?

ALL. Yes! Get out! (*Exit Slavin.*)

WIDOW. Mr. Strong, you are a brave man!

STRONG. I know it!

WIDOW. Hadn't somebody better go and see if the others are hurt?

STRONG. With pleasure! (*Exit, C.*)

WIDOW. Tell me, whose room was that I ran into?

TONY. Why, Uncle Ben's.

WIDOW. (*bursts out laughing*) I see it all. You're out of your scrape! Oh, this is funny! (*Laughs. Enter Wilder, C.*)

ALL. What *is* it?

WIDOW. Only a letter I saw lying on his desk! (*Laughs.*) But I shan't tell you a word more, only back me up in all I say to him, and I'll get you out of your scrape. But, listen, we must all seem very merry, and when he comes in, all laugh at the good joke on him.

FLIRT. But what is the joke?

WIDOW. You'll see! Come on. Start a chorus or something. What, must I start it? Very well!

(*Specialty, Widow and Quartette. Enter Strong, C.*)

STRONG. The servant has apologized to everyone but me. He says he hasn't done anything to me, and I agree. By the way, your uncle's coming. (*Enter Ben, C. All laugh at him.*)

BEN. Oh, that's the way you feel, is it? I suppose you consider this affair of last night a laughing matter?

WIDOW. Decidedly! With the laugh on you!

ALL. With the laugh on you!

BEN. On me? We'll see about that!

WIDOW. Gently, now, Mr. Gay, we want you to settle a bet.

BEN. I never settle bets.

STRONG. How about loans? I have the check here as evidence.

WIDOW. (*grabs check*) Just what I wanted. Now, Mr. Gay, listen! Your niece here, poor innocent Tony, was telling us what a good man you were, and I laughed at her.

BEN. Very nice of you!

WIDOW. I offered to bet her a supper at The Riche that if any decent-looking woman asked you to take her to the masquerade, you'd do it.

BEN. (*aside*) I've been buncoed!

WIDOW. She took the bet, and so I wrote this note which I have just picked up in your room--(*shows note*)--for you to meet me at The Riche. Then we all went to The Riche to see if you were there. And you were!

WILDER. (*to Tony*) What a corking lie! She's a wonder!

TONY. Oh, Uncle, I never thought it of you!

   (*Widow speaks to Tony. Exit Tony, L.*)

FLIRT. What will my father say when I tell him?

BEN. (*yells*) Hold on! I--I-- Why, that letter made me think that you had all gone to The Riche; so I went there to catch you, and I did! Ha! Ha!

WIDOW. How did you happen to run up such a big bill. (*Looks at check.*) What is this item for supper ordered for self and lady? (*All laugh.*)

TONY. (*entering with masks*) And what did you want of these two masks?

BEN. Why, I--you understand?

WIDOW. Mr. Gay, don't you think I've won that bet?

BEN. Oh--I--don't think anything about it! Don't one of you dare to mention this affair again as long as you live! (*To Flirt.*) Especially to your father!

WIDOW. But about that supper at The Riche?

BEN. Oh, I'll pay for that and we'll all have a good time together. Eh, Strong?

STRONG. It will shorten my life a year, but I'm with you!

Chorus. "Out for a Racket."

Finale.

CURTAIN.

David Belasco (1853-1931)
and *The Girl of the Golden West*

David Belasco insisted upon calling himself a playwright rather than a dramatist because, he wrote, "My plays are all written to be acted, not to be read." He found very little relationship between the *theatre* and *literature*. A man of definite ideas, he wrote essays about the playwright, the box office, acting, staging techniques, and, of course, himself. He had, according to Stark Young, a critic for the *New Republic*, a "true theatrical temperament."

Indeed, at the beginning of the 20th century no one was more admired as a total man of the theatre: actor, playwright, collaborator, adaptor, stage manager, director, producer, and theatre owner. His forté was melodrama--the exciting if artificial world of romance, suspense, and spectacle; in all he contributed more than sixty plays to the American stage. By the 1920's, however, a new generation of theatre artists had begun to explore the contradictions and complexities of character, motivation, and action that Belasco's melodramatic methods could hardly accommodate.

No play better illustrates the wizardry of Belasco than *The Girl of the Golden West*. As director and producer, he created the visual and aural effects which established the mood of western America in 1849. The blizzard in Act II, with the raging wind and fine powdered snow driven through the cracks of The Girl's cabin, required a crew of thirty-two highly trained stage hands.

Five years earlier, Giacomo Puccini had persuaded Belasco to allow him to write an opera based on *Madame Butterfly* by Belasco and John Luther Long, one of a dozen people with whom Belasco collaborated. Now, once again, Puccini was fascinated, and, with Belasco as stage director, *La Fanciulla del West* opened at the Met on December 10, 1910, with Emmy Destinn as The Girl, Pasquale Amato as Rance, and Enrico Caruso as Dick Johnson. The response was astounding: fourteen curtain calls at the end of Act I, nineteen at the end of Act II, and twenty at the final curtain. The audience was applauding the singers, Puccini, conductor Arturo Toscanini, and the genius of David Belasco.

David Belasco

Blanche Bates and Robert Hilliard, 1905

THE GIRL
OF THE GOLDEN WEST

(1905)

by David Belasco

CHARACTERS

The Girl
Wowkle, the fox, Billy Jackrabbit's squaw
Dick Johnson, a stranger
Jack Rance, gambler and sheriff
Sonora Slim
Trinidad Joe
Nick, bartender at the Polka
The Sidney Duck, a faro-dealer
Jim Larkens
Happy Halliday
Handsome Charlie
Deputy Sheriff
Billy Jackrabbit, an Indian
Ashby, Wells-Fargo Agent
José Castro, member of Ramerrez's band
Rider of the Pony Express
Jake Wallace, a traveling camp minstrel
Bucking Billy, from Watson's
The Lookout
A Faro-Dealer
The Boy from the Ridge
Joe, concertina player
Citizens of the Camp and Boys of the Ridge

Time: During the days of the gold fever, 1849-50.
Place: Cloudy Mountain, California, a mining camp.

ACT I.

Scene. A glimpse of Cloudy Mountain, in the Sierras. The peak is white, the sky above very blue, and the moon, which seems strangely near, shines on the steep trail leading to the cabin of The Girl. A lamp, placed in the cabin window by Wowkle, the squaw, shows that The Girl has not yet come home from her place of business, the Polka Saloon.

Scene. An exterior view of the Polka Saloon and the miners' cabins at the foot of Cloudy Mountain. The cheerful glow of kerosene lamps, the rattle of poker chips, and an occasional "whoop," show that life in the Polka is in full swing. The strains of "Dooda Day" are heard from within, the singer accompanying himself on the concertina:

> Camptown ladies sing this song, Dooda! Dooda!
> Camptown racetrack, five miles long, Dooda! Dooda! Day.
> G'wine to run all night,
> G'wine to run all day,
> Bet my money on a bob-tail nag,
> Somebody bet on the bay.

Scene. The interior of the Polka: a large square bar-room, built of rough pine boards. A pair of scales for weighing gold-dust and a dice-box used to "shake for drinks" are on the bar. Behind the bar on a shelf are liquors, cigars, and shewing tobacco. The bar contains one and two bit pieces, Mexican dollars, and slugs of gold ($50). The safe is made out of an empty whiskey keg. Boxes and cans of provisions lie on the floor, and strings of red peppers hang from the rude rafters. A stuffed grizzly bear graces the scene, a small green parasol in one paw, a battered old silk hat on its head. An odd collection of hats and caps are stuck on the prongs of a pair of elk antlers on the wall, and several saddles lie on the floor under the antlers. The furniture is composed of pine chairs, a faro table, a poker table, and an old whittled desk at which the miners write their rare letters to those at home. A $5000 reward for the road-agent Ramerrez, or information leading to his capture, signed by Wells-Fargo, is tacked to the back of the door. The platform on which a camp minstrel is singing "Dooda Day" is protected by a piece of sheet iron which the musician can lift as a shield to ward off stray bullets in case of a sudden quarrel. The room is heated by a blazing pine log fire in an adobe fireplace. A square opening in the wall leads to the dance-hall, L.; a ladder, resting against a balcony over the bar, enables the bartender to ascend in case of trouble and cast a quick glance over both rooms.

(*As the interior of the bar-room is disclosed, Sonora Slim, a tall, lanky miner with an emphatic manner, and Trinidad Joe, his partner, are playing at faro. The dealer is "Sid," an Australian known as "Sidney Duck," fat, greasy, unctuous, and cowardly. He is an expert at fancy shuffling. His even voice is heard from time to time, murmuring below the dialogue, as the game goes on. A case-keeper and lookout complete the group at the faro table. Billy Jackrabbit, a full-blooded Indian, lazy, shifty and beady-eyed, wearing moccasins, odds and ends of a white man's costume, and a quantity of brass jewelry, is watching the game. He frequents the bar-room, picking up cigar butts, and occasionally, when an opportunity presents itself, steals a drink. Handsome Charlie, a big picturesque miner, is drinking at the bar with Happy Halliday, a long-legged fellow, high-booted and spurred. Nick, the bartender, is busy during the act carrying drinks into the dance-hall and returning to those in the bar-room. He wears "'Frisco trousers, very high-heeled boots, a flashy necktie, a gay velvet vest. He combs his hair over his forehead in a cowlick.*)

SONORA. (*joining the singer, who is accompanying himself on the concertina*) "Dooda! Dooda! Day!" (*To the faro-dealer.*) What did that last eight do?

SID. Lose.

SONORA. Well, let the tail go with the hide.

    (*Nick, who has entered, sets a few fresh candles about and gives a drink to the concertina player, who goes into the dance-hall.*)

TRINIDAD. How many times did the ace win?

SID. Three times.

BILLY JACKRABBIT. Give Billy Jackrabbit four two dolla--Mexican-- chips.

    (*Sidney gives some chips to the Indian. As the music starts in the dance-hall, and the shuffling of feet is heard, Happy, unable to resist, gives a long whoop.*)

HAPPY. Root hog or die!

    (*With another whoop, Happy joins the dancers. Handsome would follow him, but decides to remain to take another drink.*)

SONORA. (*suspiciously*) See here, gamboleer Sid, you're too lucky.

TRINIDAD. You bet! More chips, Australiar.

    (*Sid gives some chips to Trinidad. The Proprietor of a wheel-of-fortune, which is set up in the dance-hall, calls.*)

PROPRIETOR. (*in a professional voice*) And round goes the wheel!

HAPPY. (*above the music*) Git, you loafer!

(*A muffled shot. The music stops abruptly.*)

VOICE. (*from the dance-hall*) Missed!

(*Nick hastens off, not forgetting to take a bottle and glasses with him. During the excitement, Billy Jackrabbit steals four cigars from a box on the bar.*)

PROPRIETOR. The lone star now rises!

(*The music starts again. Nick re-enters, giving the Indian a suspicious glance. Billy Jackrabbit decides to take himself off for a short time.*)

NICK. (*explaining as loud whoops are heard*) Boys from the Ridge--cuttin' up in the dance-hall. Hy're you, Jim?

(*Jim Larkens, shabby and despondent, a miner who has not struck it rich, returns Nick's greeting, gets paper, a pen and ink from the bar, and sits at the desk to write the usual sad letter to his family in the East.*)

SONORA. (*looking towards the dancers with disgust*) I don't dance with men for partners. When I chassay, Trinidad, I want a feminine piece of flesh and blood--with garters on!

TRINIDAD. You bet!

SONORA. I say, Nick. (*Going up to the bar, confidentially.*) Has The Girl said anything more about me to-day?

NICK. (*lying as usual*) Well, you got the first chance.

SONORA. (*grinning*) Yes? Cigars for the boys.

(*Nick brings a box of cigars to the faro table, and the men smoke.*)

FIDDLER. (*calling in time to the dance music*)

First lady swing with the right hand gent,
With the left hand gent, with the right hand gent,
First lady swing with the left hand gent,
And--lady in the center, and gents all around!

(*During this, two men from the rival mining-camp at the Ridge enter, dancing up to the bar.*)

SID. Hello, boys! 'Ow's things at the Ridge?

RIDGE MAN. (*defiantly*) Wipes this camp off the map.

(*All jump to their feet, save Sid. The insult calls for immediate punishment.*)

SONORA. What ?

TRINIDAD. Say it again!

(*Nick persuades the Ridge boys to retire to avert bloodshed, and they disappear with a final defiant whoop as Jake Wallace, a favorite camp minstrel, who journeys from one camp to another, is heard on the road outside, playing on his banjo and singing.*)

JAKE WALLACE. (*outside*) Wait for the wagon--

Wait for the wagon--

Wait for the wagon and we'll all take a ride.

Wait for the wagon and we'll all take a ride.

NICK. (*in extravagant style*) Aw! Here he is, boys--just up from the Ridge--Jake Wallace, the camp favorite!

(*Jake Wallace enters, carrying a banjo, his face half blackened. He wears a long minstrel's duster over his heavy coat, flapping shoes, and a "stove-pipe" hat. He is the typical camp minstrel.*)

SONORA. Howdy, Jake!

HANDSOME. Hello, Jake, old man! How be you?

TRINIDAD, SID, and CASE-KEEPER. Hello, Jake!

JAKE. (*nods, smiling, seats himself on the musician's stand, in the musician's chair*) Hello, boys! My first selection, friends, will be "The Little--"

SONORA. Aw--give us "Old Dog Tray," Jake. (*Jake tunes up.*)

TRINIDAD. (*apart to Nick*) Nick, have you saw The Girl?

NICK. (*confidentially*) Well, I gave her your message. You've got the best chance. (*Digs him playfully in the ribs and winks at him.*)

TRINIDAD. Whiskey for everybody.

(*Nick sets out whiskey and glasses, and the men drink.*)

JAKE. (*strikes a chord, announcing impressively*) "Old Dog Tray, or Echoes from Home."

(*During the song, Billy Jackrabbit, who has followed Jake on, sits on the floor playing solitaire. The miners continue to gamble.*)

How often do I picture

Them old folks down to home;

And often wonder if they think of me!

(*Larkens, dropping his letter in the box on the floor, chokes back a sob.*)

SONORA. Slug's worth of chips. (*Sid gives chips to Sonora.*)

JAKE. Would angel mother know me,

If back there I did roam?

Would old dog Tray remember me?

(*Pauses to take a drink from Nick.*)

Now, boys!

ALL. (*joining in the chorus, keeping time with their feet*)

Oh, mother, angel mother, are you a-waitin' there,

Beside the littul cottage on the lea?

JAKE. On the lea--

ALL. How often would she bless me, all in them days so fair--

Would old dog Tray remember me?

SONORA. Remember me!

> (*Larkens breaks down and sobs. All stop playing and turn in their chairs, looking at him.*)

Why, Jim . . .

LARKENS. Say, boys--I'm homesick and I'm broke, and I don't give a damn who knows it. I want to go home again. . . . I'm tired o' drillin' rocks. . . . I want to be out in the fields again. . . . I want to see the grain growin'. . . . I want the dirt in the furrows at home. . . . I want old Pennsylvany. . . . I want my folks. . . . I'm done! I'm done! I'm done!

> (*He sobs on the bar, his face buried in his hands.*)

JAKE. (*quite used to these scenes, singing*)

> Oh, mother, angel mother, are you a-waitin'--

> (*Sonora motions Jake to stop singing. Jake, understanding, smilingly makes a gesture as though touching an imaginary hat brim, and collects his money.*)

SONORA. Here, Jake. (*Tosses a coin to Jake.*) Boys, Jim Larkens allows he's goin' back East. Chip in.

> (*The Miners and Gamblers throw money on the table. When the cash is handed to Sonora, he gives it to Larkens.*)

Here you are, Jim.

JIM. (*deeply touched*) Thank you, boys--thank you.

> (*Crying, he stumbles out of the room.*)

TRINIDAD. (*suddenly making a lunge at Sid's card box*) That ain't a square deal--he's cheating!

> (*Billy Jackrabbit picks up a chair, and holds it up to protect himself; Jake Wallace hides behind the shield. The lookout steals out. Nick re-enters with a large tray of whiskey and glasses. Handsome and a Gambler sieze Sid and bring him down to the front of the table.*)

SONORA. Lift his hand!

TRINIDAD. Heist his arms! (*Taking the deck, throwing it on the table.*) There!

SONORA. String him up!

TRINIDAD. You bet!

SID. (*whining*) For 'eaven's sike!

NICK. Chicken lifter!

TRINIDAD. String him!

SID. Oh, boys! Boys!

> (*Rance comes in, stands impassively watching the scene. He is the cool, waxen, deliberate gambler. His hands, almost feminine in their whiteness, are as waxen as his face. He has a very black moustache. He wears*

the beaver hat of the times, and an immaculate suit of broadcloth. His boots are highly polished, long and narrow with high heels, his trousers strapped over them. He wears a white puffed shirt, with a diamond stud held by side chains, and a large diamond flashes on his hand. He smokes the Spanish cigarros.)

RANCE. Well, gentlemen, what's this?

SONORA. Ah! Here's Jack Rance.

TRINIDAD. *(threatening Sid)* The sheriff!

RANCE. What's the matter with the cyards?

(He takes out his handkerchief, delicately unfolding it, and flicks it over his boots.)

SONORA. The Sidney Duck's cheated.

TRINIDAD. String him! *(To Sid.)* Come on, you!

RANCE. Wait a minute. Don't be hasty, gentlemen. I've got something to say about this. I don't forget, although I am Sheriff of Manzanita County, that I'm running four games. It's men like him cast reflections on square-minded sporting men like myself; and worse--he casts reflections on the Polka, the establishment of the one decent woman in Cloudy.

NICK. *(indignant)* You bet!

SONORA. A lady, damn it! *(Turning on Sid.)* You lily-covered skunk!

TRINIDAD. String him up!

HANDSOME. Come on!

(There is a general movement towards Sid.)

RANCE. Hold on! Hold on! After all, gents, what's death? A kick and you're off. I've thought of a worse punishment. Give him his coat.

(Handsome gives a coat to Sid, who puts it on.)

Stand him over here.

(Sid is pushed forward.)

Hand me the deuce of spades.

(Sonora gives Rance the card. Rance takes a pin from Sid's cravat, and pins the card over Sid's heart.)

I place it over his heart as a warning. He can't leave the camp, and he never plays cyards again. Handsome, pass the word to the boys.

(Handsome goes into the dance-hall to spread the news.)

SID. *(sniffs imploringly)* Ow--now! Don't say that! Don't say that!

NICK. *(pointing to the door)* Git! Git!

(Sid leaves hurriedly, followed by Billy Jackrabbit, who is never quite comfortable when the sheriff is laying down the law. Jake Wallace, one eye on the would-be lynchers, is softly playing "Pop Goes the Weasel.")

RANCE. *(coolly, as though nothing had occurred)* Well, gentlemen, a little game of poker, just for social recreation? Nick, chips.

SONORA. Ha! I'm your Injun!

(*Sonora goes to the poker table as Nick brings down the poker chips.*)

TRINIDAD. (*joining Rance*) That's me!

(*But before the game can proceed, a Deputy Sheriff enters, a gaunt, hollow-cheeked, muscular man, with a heavy, sweeping moustache, his hair in a cowlick--wearing a pale, faded beaver hat and a heavy overcoat, his pistol and powder flask in his belt.*)

DEPUTY. Sheriff, Ashby of Well-Fargo just rode in with his posse.

RANCE. Ashby? Why, what's he doing here?

DEPUTY. He's after Ramerrez.

RANCE. Ramerrez? Oh, that polite road-agent that's been visitin' the other camps?

DEPUTY. Yes, they say he has just turned into our county.

(*Nick gives the Deputy a drink.*)

SONORA. (*apprehensively*) What? Our county?

(*Ashby enters--a man to remember--nervous, dogged, white and closely-cropped hair, very black eyebrows--thin lips. He wears 'Frisco clothing, which shows the wear and tear of the road. He is suave in his greetings, but quick in action and speech. He is never sober, never drunk, but continually drinking.*)

ASHBY. (*greeting Rance*) Hello, Sheriff!

RANCE. Boys, Mr. Ashby of Well-Fargo.

(*Ashby shakes hands with Trinidad and Sonora, then makes for the bar.*)

ASHBY. Hello, Nick!

NICK. Hello, Ash!

ASHBY. (*to the Deputy*) How are you, sir?

(*Deputy returns Ashby's greeting and passes off as Ashby shakes hands warmly with Nick.*)

Nick, give us a drink.

NICK. Sure.

(*He takes four glasses and a bottle of whiskey to the poker table and then hastens off into the dance-hall.*)

ASHBY. Everybody'll have the same.

(*Jake joins the group as Rance pours the whiskey.*)

Well, gentlemen, I trust The Girl who runs the Polka is well?

SONORA. Fine as silk, Mr. Ashby. How long you been chasin' up this here road-agent?

ASHBY. Oh, he only took to the road three months ago. Wells-Fargo have had me and a posse busy ever since. He's a wonder.

SONORA. Must be, to evade *you.*

ASHBY. Yes, I can smell a road-agent in the wind; but, Rance, I expect to get that fellow right here in your county.

RANCE. Is this Ramerrez a Spaniard?

ASHBY. No, can't prove it. Heads a crew of greasers and Spaniards. His name's assumed.

RANCE. They say he robs you like a gentleman.

ASHBY. (*lifting his glass*) Well, look out for the greasers up the road.
(*All drink.*)

RANCE. We don't let 'em pass through here.

ASHBY. Well, boys, I've had a long ride. Wake me up when the Pony Express goes through.
(*He takes off his coat, goes up to a table, and, setting a bottle of whiskey in a convenient spot, lies down on the table.*)

NICK. (*bringing in a kettle of hot water and glasses containing whiskey and lemon*) Regards of The Girl. Hot whiskey with lemming extract.
(*He pours the hot water into the glasses.*)

RANCE. (*accepting a glass*) Gentlemen, The Girl! The only girl in the camp—the girl I mean to make Mrs. Jack Rance!
(*Nick catches Sonora's eye, also Trinidad's.*)

SONORA. That's a joke, Rance. She makes you look like a Chinaman.

RANCE. (*rising, at white heat*) You prove that!

SONORA. In what particular spot will you have it?
(*Instantly Rance's right hand creeps towards his pistol as Sonora, anticipating his movement, has reached for his weapon. Trinidad runs to the bar and drops behind it as Nick crouches out of sight at one end of it. Jake Wallace hides behind the shield.*)

NICK. (*seeing The Girl coming in through the dance-hall*) The Girl. . . .
(*Coaxingly.*) Aw--take your drinks.
(*Trinidad and Jake venture to peep out. The quarrel is over.*)

RANCE. Ha! Ha! Ha! Once more, friends, The Girl!

ALL. The Girl!
(*They drink. Ashby snores peacefully. The Girl enters. The character of The Girl is rather complex. Her utter frankness takes away all suggestion of vice--showing her to be unsmirched, happy, careless, untouched by the life about her. Yet she has a thorough knowledge of what the men of her world generally want. She is used to flattery-- knows exactly how to deal with men--is very shrewd--but quite capable of being a good friend to the camp boys. Handsome follows her and stands leaning agains the bar, watching her admiringly.*)

GIRL. Hello, boys! How's everything? Gettin' taken care of?

SONORA. (*who melts whenever he sees her*) Hello, Girl!

GIRL. Hello, Sonora!

TRINIDAD. Hello, Girl!

GIRL. Hello, Trin.

SONORA. Mix me a prairie oyster.

GIRL. I'll fix you right up, Sonora. (*As shots are heard in the dance-hall.*) Say, Nick--you quiet things down. (*Exit Nick.*) They've had about enough. Look here, Sonora: before I crack this egg, I'd like to state that eggs is four bits apiece--only two hens left.

(*Giving a little push to Handsome, who has been leaning on the bar.*)

Oh, run away, Handsome.

(*Handsome sits, watching The Girl.*)

SONORA. Crack the egg--I'll stand it.

NICK. (*re-entering, grinning, pouring out a drink, going to The Girl*) Regards of Blond Harry.

GIRL. (*taking it*) Here, give it to me--(*pouring it back into the bottle*)--and say it hit the spot.

NICK. (*whispering*) Say, Min, throw around a few kind words--good for the bar.

GIRL. (*good-naturedly*) Oh, you! (*Exit Nick.*) Ha! Ha! (*As Ashby awakens.*) Hello, Mr. Ashby!

ASHBY. (*rousing and gallantly picking up his glass, goes to the bar to toast The Girl*) Compliments of Wells-Fargo!

GIRL. Thank you. (*Shaking Sonora's drink.*) You see we live high shouldered here in Cloudy.

SONORA. You bet!

ASHBY. What cigars have you?

GIRL. Regalias, Auroras, and Eurekas.

ASHBY. Any'll do.

NICK. (*entering hurriedly*) Man jest come in threatenin' to shoot up the furniture.

GIRL. (*quietly, giving Ashby a cigar*) Who is it?

NICK. Old man Watson.

GIRL. Leave him shoot. He's good for it.

VOICE. (*from the dance-hall*) Nick! Nick!

(*Nick hastens off as several shots are heard. In the excitement, Billy Jackrabbit, who has re-entered, quietly steals down to the faro table and drains a glass of whiskey which has been left standing there.*)

GIRL. Here, you Billy Jackrabbit: what are you doing? Did you marry my squaw yet?

BILLY JACKRABBIT. (*going to the bar*) Not so much married squaw yet.

GIRL. Not so much married? Come here, you thieving redskin--with a pocketful of my best cigars! (*Taking the cigars from him.*) You git up to my cabin and marry my squaw before I get there. Git! (*Billy Jackrabbit goes out.*) With a papoose six months old--it's awful! Here, Sonora-- (*bringing him the drink*)--here's your prairie oyster. Hello, Rance!

RANCE. Hello, Girl!

SONORA. (*giving her a bag of gold-dust*) Here, Girl, clear the slate out of that.

NICK. (*re-entering with a bottle*) Say, they's a fellow in there wants to know if we can help out on provisions.

GIRL. Sure. What does he want?

NICK. (*putting the cigar-box and bottle back on the shelf*) Bread.

GIRL. (*behind the bar*) Bread! Does he think we're runnin' a bakery?

NICK. Then he asked for sardines.

GIRL. Sardines! Great Gilead! You tell him we have nothing but straight provisions here: we got pickled oysters, smoking tobacco, an' the best whiskey he ever saw.

NICK. Yes'm.

TRINIDAD. You bet!

GIRL. Sonora.

> (*She gives him his change and cleans the slate on which she keeps the record of the drinks. She then hands Ashby some coins.*)

Mr. Ashby--change.

ASHBY. (*throwing the money back on the bar*) Keep the change. Buy a ribbon at the Ridge. Compliments of Wells-Fargo.

GIRL. (*sweeping it into the drawer*) Thank you.

SONORA. (*going up to the bar*) Girl, buy *two* ribbons at the Ridge.

> (*Throwing down a stack of silver dollars, facing Ashby. Insinuatingly.*)

Fawn's *my* color! . . .

GIRL. Thank you.

RANCE. Play cyards.

ASHBY. (*changing--raising his finger warningly*) You, Girl! You must bank with us oftener, and then if this road-agent, Ramerrez, should drop in, you won't lose so much.

SONORA. The devil!

TRINIDAD. (*thoughtfully*) Ha!

GIRL. Oh, go on! I keep the specie in an empty keg now, but personally I've took to banking in my stocking.

NICK. (*who has brought in an armful of wood and mended the fire*) Say, we've got an awful pile this month--makes me sort o' nervous.

(*Pointing to a keg at the end of the bar.*)

Why, Sonora alone has got ten thousand in that keg for safe keepin'.

ASHBY. And Ramerrez's band everywhere!

GIRL. Bet if a road-agent come in here, I could offer him a drink an' he'd treat me like a perfect lady.

SONORA. You bet he would, the darned old halibut!

NICK. Tobacco.

GIRL. Solace or Honeydew?

NICK. Dew.

(*He takes it and is about to exit when the Deputy enters wildly.*)

DEPUTY. Boys! Boys! Pony Express!

(*The sound of the approaching pony has grown louder, and now stops quickly.*)

DRIVER OF THE PONY EXPRESS. (*off*) Hello! (*Nick runs out.*)

DEPUTY. (*outside*) Hello!

DRIVER. (*unseen, speaking through the open door as though on horseback*) Big hold-up last night at the Forks.

TRINIDAD. Hold-up?

DRIVER. Ramerrez!

(*Enter Nick with several letters and one newspaper. He gives the mail to The Girl and goes to the bar.*)

SONORA. Ramerrez!

ASHBY. (*to The Girl*) You see?

DRIVER. (*still out of sight*) Look sharp! There's a greaser in the trail.

RANCE. A greaser? Deputy, go find him.

GIRL. (*looking over the mail*) Sonora, you got a newspaper.

(*Sonora receives it joyously.*)

DRIVER. So long!

ASHBY. (*going to the door--calling*) Pony Express! I want you!

HANDSOME. (*leaning over Sonora--enviously*) Sonora's got a newspaper.

SONORA. Yes--damn thing's two months old.

HANDSOME. (*wistfully*) Still, he *did* get a newspaper.

(*The Driver enters, coming quickly towards Ashby. He is a thin young fellow of twenty--his skin deeply tanned by the wind--smooth-faced but unshaven. His clothing is weather-beaten and faded by wind, rain, dust, and alkali. A leather patch is stitched over the seat of his breeches. His shabby leather gloves proclaim hard service. He is booted and spurred,*) *and has a pistol in his belt. He carries a mail pouch.*)

ASHBY. You drop mail at the greaser settlement?

DRIVER. Yes, sir--tough place.

ASHBY. Know a girl there named Nina Micheltoreña?

GIRL. (*laughs*) Nina Micheltoreña? Oh, they all know her. Whoo! She's one of them Cachuca girls, with droopy Spanish eyes. Oh, you ask the boys about her!

> (*She slaps Handsome and Trinidad on the back. The music starts in the dance-hall and The Girl runs off to see that her patrons are enjoying the evening. Handsome, Sonora, and Trinidad follow her off.*)

ASHBY. (*to the Driver*) Hold her letters.

DRIVER. Yes, sir. (*He hastens off to ride to the next camp.*)

ASHBY. Sheriff, I expect to see this Nina Micheltoreña to-night--here--in the Polka.

RANCE. You do? Well, the boys better look out for their watches. I met that lady once.

ASHBY. She wrote about that five thousand reward I offered for Ramerrez.

RANCE. What! She's after that? (*Shuffling the cards.*)

ASHBY. (*getting his coat*) She knows something. (*To The Girl, who has re-entered and gone behind the bar.*) Well, I'll have a look at that greaser up the road. He may have his eye on the find in that stocking of yours.

GIRL. (*good-naturedly*) You be darned! (*Ashby goes out.*)

RANCE. Say, Minnie--

GIRL. (*polishing glasses*) H'm?

RANCE. Will you marry me?

GIRL. Nop.

RANCE. (*going to the bar*) Why not?

GIRL. 'Cause you got a wife in Noo Orleans--or so the mountain breezes say.

RANCE. Give me some cigars.

GIRL. (*handing him cigars from a certain box*) Them's your kind, Jack.

RANCE. (*putting the cigars in his case*) I'm stuck on you.

GIRL. (*lightly*) Thank you.

RANCE. I'm going to marry you.

GIRL. Think so?

RANCE. H'm . . . (*Lighting a cigar.*)

GIRL. They ain't a man here goin' to marry me.

NICK (*entering hurriedly*) One good cigar.

GIRL. (*handing a cigar to Nick*) Here's your poison. Three bits. (*To*

Rance.) Why, look at 'em! There's Handsome: got two wives I know of somewhere East--(*turning suddenly to Nick*)--who's that cigar for?

NICK. Tommy!

GIRL. Give it back. He don't know a good cigar when he's smoking it.

(*She puts the cigar back in the box, takes another and hands it to Nick.*)

Same price. (*Nick goes off.*) And Trin with a widder in Sacramento; and you--Ha! Not one of you travelin' under your own name.

NICK. (*comes back, grinning*) One whiskey.

GIRL. (*pouring out the whiskey and giving it to Nick*) Here you be.

NICK. With water.

GIRL. (*putting the bottle back*) No, no, you don't; no fancy drinks here.

NICK. Feller just rode in from the Crossin'--says he wants it with water.

GIRL. He'll take it straight, or git!

NICK. But he won't git.

GIRL. You send him to me--I'll curl his hair for him!

NICK. Yes'm. (*Exit.*)

RANCE. (*earnestly*) Give you a thousand dollars on the spot for a kiss.

GIRL. Some men invite bein' played.

RANCE. Well, what are men made for? (*Putting down a gold piece.*)

GIRL. (*taking it*) That's true.

RANCE. You can't keep on running this place alone--it's getting too big for you. Too much money circulating through the Polka. You need a man behind you. Marry me.

GIRL. Nop.

RANCE. My wife won't know it.

GIRL. Nop.

RANCE. Now, see here, Min--

GIRL. (*firmly*) No--take it straight, Jack--nop! Ah, come along. Start your game again, Jack. Come along. (*Going to the faro table,.*) Whoop la! Mula! Good Lord, look at that faro table!

RANCE. (*following her*) Listen, we may not have another chance.

GIRL. Look here, Jack, let's have it right now. I run this Polka alone because I like it. My father taught me the business, and--well, don't worry about me--I can look after myself. I carry my little wepping-- (*touching her pocket to show that she has a pistol*)--I'm independent--I'm happy--the Polka's paying an'--ha!--it's all bully! Say, what the devil do you mean proposin' to me with a wife in Noo Orleans? Now, this is a respectable saloon--an' I don't want no more of that talk.

RANCE. I didn't say nothin'.

GIRL. (*tidying the faro table*) Push me that queen.

(*Rance slowly hands the card to her and, going to the table, leans thoughtfully against a chair.*)

Thank you, Jack. No offense, Jack; but I got other ideas of married life from what you have.

RANCE. Aw! Nonsense!

GIRL. (*leaning against the faro table, facing Rance*) I dunno about that. You see, I had a home once, and I ain't forgot it. A home up over our little saloon in Soledad. Ha! I ain't forgot my father an' mother an' what a happy married couple they was. Lord! How they loved each other--it was beautiful!

SID. (*entering, snivelling*) Ow, Miss . . .

GIRL. Say--I've heard about you--you git!

(*Sid hastily takes his departure. The Girl turns to Rance.*)

I can see Mother now . . . fussin' over Father an' pettin' him, an' Father dealin' faro--Ah, but he was square . . . and me, a kid as little as a kitten, under the table sneakin' chips for candy. Talk about married life! That was a little heaven. I guess everybody's got some remembrance of their mother tucked away. I always see mine at the faro table with her foot snuggled up to Dad's an' the light of lovin' in her eyes. Ah, she was a lady! No--(*leaving the table and going behind the bar*)--I couldn't share that table an' the Polka with any man--unless there was a heap o' carin' back of it. I couldn't, Jack, I couldn't.

RANCE. (*restraining anger*) Oh, the boys were right! I *am* a Chinaman!

GIRL. No, you're not, Jack.

RANCE. (*following her*) But once when I rode in here, it was nothing but Jack--Jack--Jack--Jack--Jack Rance! God! I nearly got you then.

GIRL. (*with playful sarcasm*) Did you?

RANCE. Then you went on that trip to Sacramento and Monterey . . . and you changed. . . . Who's the man?

GIRL. Ha! Ha! Ha! Ha!

RANCE. One of them high-toned Sacramento shrimps? (*As she laughs.*) Do you think he'd have *you*?

GIRL. (*suddenly serious*) What's the matter with me? Anythin' about me a high-toned gent would object to? Look here, Jack Rance, ain't I always been a perfect lady?

RANCE. Oh, Heaven knows your character's all right.

(*He goes back to the faro table.*)

GIRL. (*sarcastically*) Well, that ain't your fault. Adios.

(*She starts to leave the room, then pauses and looks at him.*)

Jack . . .

(*As he will not look at her, she turns again to go into the dance-hall, but, looking off, she sees an unexpected guest and exclaims in surprise.*)

H'mp! Utopia!

(*She goes behind the bar. Mr. Johnson enters the room from the dance-hall. He is a young man of about thirty--smooth-faced, tall. His clothing is bought in fashionable Sacramento. He is the one man in the place who has the air of a gentleman. At first acquaintance, he bears himself easily but modestly, yet at certain moments there is a devil-may-care recklessness about him. He is, however, the last man in the world one would suspect of being the road-agent, Ramerrez.*)

JOHNSON. Where's the man who wanted to curl my hair?

(*Rance turns to look at the stranger.*)

GIRL. (*who remembers Johnson as a man she met on the road to Monterey*) Hello--er--stranger. (*Johnson looks at The Girl.*)

RANCE. We're not much on strangers here.

JOHNSON. I'm the man who wanted water in his whiskey.

GIRL. You, eh? (*To Nick, who comes back with a bottle and glasses.*) Oh--er--Nick, this gentleman takes his whiskey as he likes it.

NICK. Moses!

JOHNSON. (*coming to the bar*) In the presence of a lady--I will take--nothing. (*Bows to her with formality.*) Pardon me, but you seem to be almost at home here. (*Nick laughs softly.*)

GIRL. (*amused*) Who--me? (*Leaning on the bar.*)

NICK. (*laughing*) Why, she's The Girl who runs the Polka.

(*He passes off, still laughing.*)

JOHNSON. (*staring at The Girl*) You?

GIRL. Yep.

JOHNSON. (*meditating*) The Girl who runs the Polka. . . .

(*There is a merry twinkle in The Girl's eye as she looks at Johnson, but he is disconcerted. This news interferes with Mr. Johnson's plans.*)

GIRL. Yes.

RANCE. You're from the Crossing, the bartender said. I don't remember you.

JOHNSON. You're mistaken. I said that I road over from the Crossing. (*Turning to The Girl again.*) So you are The Girl?

GIRL. Yes.

RANCE. (*aggressively*) No strangers allowed in this camp.

(*A pause. The Girl and Johnson speak in such low tones that Rance is unable to hear them.*)

Perhaps you're off the road.

(A pause. The Girl and Johnson are still talking. Sneeringly.)
Men often get mixed up when they are visiting Nina Micheltoreña on the
back trail.

GIRL. Rance!

JOHNSON. *(sharply to Rance)* I merely stopped in to rest my horse--and
perhaps try a game of--*(coming to the table)*--er--poker.

(He picks up a pack of cards.)

GIRL. *(calls)* Nick, bring in his saddle.

(As Nick goes for the saddle, Rance rises, annoyed.)

RANCE. A game, eh? I haven't heard your name, young man.

GIRL. *(laughs)* Oh! Names out here!

JOHNSON. My name's Johnson. *(Throwing down the cards.)*

GIRL. *(cynically)* Is--how much?

JOHNSON. Of Sacramento.

GIRL. Of--how much?

(Coming down and shaking hands--not believing a word he says.)
I admire to know you, Mr. Johnson of Sacramento.

JOHNSON. Thank you.

RANCE. *(angrily)* Say, Minnie--I--

GIRL. *(aside to Rance, lightly)* Oh--set down.

(He indignantly sits on the end of the faro table. She turns to Johnson.)
Say, do you know what I think of you? I think you staked out a claim in
a etiquette book. So you *think* you can play poker?

JOHNSON. That's my conviction.

GIRL. Out of every fifty men who *think* they can play, one ain't mistaken.

JOHNSON. *(following The Girl to the bar)* You may be right.

GIRL. Say, try a cigar.

JOHNSON. Thank you.

GIRL. Best in the house--my compliments. *(She lights a match.)*

JOHNSON. Thank you--you're very kind. *(In a lower tone.)* So you
remember me?

GIRL. If you remember me.

RANCE. *(muttering to himself, glancing over his shoulder)* What the
devil are they talking about, anyway?

JOHNSON. I met you on the road to Monterey--

GIRL. Goin' an' comin'. You passed me up a bunch of wild syringa over
the wheel. You asked me to go a-berryin', but I didn't see it.

JOHNSON. I noticed that.

GIRL. And when you went away, you said--*(embarrassed)*--oh, I dunno.

JOHNSON. Yes, you do--yes, you do. I said: "I'll think of you all the time!" Well, I've thought of you ever since.

GIRL. Ha! Somehow I kinder thought you might drop in, but as you didn't . . . of course--(*with a sense of propriety*)--it wasn't my place to remember you—first.

JOHNSON. But I didn't know where you lived . . . I--

GIRL. (*confidentially*) I got a special bottle here. Best in the house. Will you?

JOHNSON. Why--

GIRL. (*gets a bottle and a glass*) My compliments.

JOHNSON. You are *very* kind. Thanks.

　(*Rance rises and, going to the bar, proceeds to dash the glass to the floor as Mr. Johnson is about to take it.*)

RANCE. (*livid*) Look here, Mr. Johnson! Your ways are offensive to me--damned offensive. My name's Rance--Jack Rance. Your business here--your business! (*Calling.*) Boys! Boys! Come in!

　(*Trinidad, Handsome, Sonora, and Happy come in.*)

There's a man here who won't explain his business--he--

SONORA, TRINIDAD, HAPPY, and HANDSOME. (*at the same time*) What? Won't he? Oh, we'll see! Guess we'll make him.

GIRL. Wait a minute. I know him.

THE BOYS. (*as one man*) Eh?

GIRL. (*to Rance*) Yes, I didn't tell you, but I know him.

RANCE. (*to himself*) The Sacramento shrimp, by God!

GIRL. (*comes from behind the bar*) Boys, I vouch to Cloudy for Mr. Johnson.

　(*All the men except Rance salute Johnson.*)

JOHNSON. (*making a sweeping gesture*) Boys. . . .

THE BOYS. Hello, Johnson.

SONORA. Boys, Rance ain't runnin' the Polka yet.

　(*A waltz is played as Nick enters.*)

NICK. (*to The Girl*) The boys from the Ridge invites you to dance with them.

JOHNSON. May I have the honor of a waltz?

　(*Trinidad, Sonora, and Handsome are overcome by Johnson's manners.*)

NICK. Moses! (*Retreats to the dance-hall.*)

GIRL. Me, waltz? Me? Ha! Oh, I can't waltz. Ha!--But I can polky.

JOHNSON. Then may I have the pleasure of the next polka?

SONORA. (*to the boys*) He's too flip.

GIRL. Oh, I dunno. Makes me feel kind o' foolish--you know--kind o' retirin' like a elk in summer.

JOHNSON. (*amused*) Yes, they *are* retiring.

GIRL. (*unconsciously wipes her hands on her dress*) Well . . . I don't like anybody's hand on the back of my waist; but somehow--

(*She looks at Rance recklessly. Johnson offers her his arm. Unused to this formality, she looks at his proffered arm two or three times, half ashamed, then at the boys, who are watching her with twinkling eyes.*) Oh, Lord, must I? (*Then making up her mind.*) Oh, come along.

JOHNSON. Thanks.

GIRL. (*dances off with Johnson, calling to the fiddler*) A polky!

(*In the dance-hall they are acclaimed by loud whoops.*)

SONORA. (*to Rance*) Chink!

RANCE. Ha! Ha! Cleaned out, by God! by a high-toned, fair-haired dog named Johnson. Well, I'll be damned! (*As Nick comes in with a saddle.*) What's that?

NICK. Johnson's saddle.

RANCE. (*knocking the saddle out of Nick's hands*) You know, Nick, I've got a great notion to walk out of this door, and--

NICK. (*scenting the loss of a good customer*) Aw, she's only kiddin' him.

(*He removes the saddle to a place of safety.*)

ASHBY. (*outside*) Boys!

RANCE. What's that?

TRINIDAD. Why, that's--

NICK. That's Ashby.

ASHBY. (*outside*) Come on--you!

TRINIDAD. What's the matter?

DEPUTY. (*calling*) Run him in.

(*He enters with Ashby and several men. They bring in José Castro. Billy Jackrabbit follows them on. Castro is an oily, greasy, unwashed Mexican greaser of a low type. His clothing is partly Mexican. He is yellow, sullen, wiry, hard-faced, tricky, and shifty-eyed. He has the curved legs of a man who lives on a broncho. Ashby is completely transformed. His hat is on the back of his head, his hair is ruffled and falls over his forehead in straggling locks; his coat is thrown open and his face is savage and pitiless.*)

ASHBY. The greaser in the trail.

RANCE. (*takes Castro by the hair, throwing him over and forcing his head back*) Here, you--give us a look at your face.

ASHBY. Nick, come--give us a drink. (*Going to the bar.*)

RANCE. Tie him up.

(*Billy Jackrabbit goes to the fireplace and gets the lariat as Rance pushes*

Castro to the floor.)

ASHBY. (*inviting all to drink*) Come on, boys.

(*The boys, with the exception of Sonora, join Ashby at the bar.*)

CASTRO. (*seeing Johnson's saddle on the floor--to himself*) Ramerrez's . . .
(*He pauses--overcome.*) Taken . . .

ASHBY. (*to Sonora, who is watching The Girl dance*) Say, my friend, don't
you drink?

SONORA. Oh, occasionally. (*He joins Ashby.*)

RANCE. (*looking off at The Girl*) Polkying!

(*Nick lets down the pelts which screen off the dance-hall, as Billy
Jackrabbit and the Deputy throw Castro into a chair. Castro, who has
caught a glimpse of Johnson dancing with The Girl, is relieved.*)

ASHBY. (*having tasted his drink--going to Castro*) Come now, tell us
what your name is.

HAPPY. You bet!

ASHBY. Speak up! Who are you?

SONORA and HANDSOME. Speak up! What's your name?

(*Rance, eyeing Castro, sits at the faro table, his legs crossed.*)

CASTRO. José Castro, ex-padroña of the bull-fights.

RANCE. But the bull-fights are at Monterey. Why do you come to this
place?

CASTRO. To tell the Señor Sheriff I know where ees--Ramerrez.

(*The men would surround Castro, but Rance motions them back.*)

RANCE. You lie! (*Raises his hand for silence.*)

CASTRO. Nay, plaanty Mexican vaquero--my friends Peralta--Vellejos
--all weeth Ramerrez--so I know where ees.

RANCE. (*pointing at him quickly to take him off his guard*) You're one of
his men yourself!

CASTRO. (*quickly, with childlike innocence*) No--no . . .

RANCE. (*pointing to Ashby*) That's Ashby--the man that pays out that
reward you've heard of. Where is Ramerrez's camp?

CASTRO. Come weeth me one mile, and, by the soul of my mother--the
blessed Maria Saltaja--we weel put a knife into hees back.

RANCE. One mile, eh?

SONORA. If I thought . . .

RANCE. Where is this trail?

CASTRO. Up the Madroña Canyada.

A MAN. (*entering from the dance-hall*) Hello, boys! What's--

ALL. (*warning the new-comer to silence*) Sh! Git! Git out! Shut up! Git!

RANCE. Go on.

CASTRO. Ramerrez can be taken, if many men come weeth me . . . forty
minutes there and back--

RANCE. What do you think?

ASHBY. Curious. . . . This is the second warning we have had from here.

RANCE. (*to Ashby*) This Nina Micheltoreña's letter to you? You say she
is coming here to-night? (*As Ashby nods.*) Looks as though he was
known around here.

ASHBY. All the same, I wouldn't go.

SONORA. What! Risk losin' him?

RANCE. Boys, we'll take the chance. (*He rises.*)

NICK. Want a drink?

(*He goes up to the bar, clearing off the bottles and glasses. Ashby has
gone out. The men put on their overcoats, hats, etc. and prepare to leave
in search of the road-agent.*)

MEN. (*exclaiming*) Ready, Sheriff! Come on, boys! Come on, Happy!
Careful, boys!

RANCE. (*at the open door, sniffing the air*) I don't like the smell of the air.
Snow. (*He goes out.*)

DEPUTY. Load up.

TRINIDAD. Get out the horses.

HAPPY. We'll get this road-agent.

SONORA. (*as he passes Castro*) Come on, you oily, garlic-eating, red-
peppery, dog-trottin', sun-baked son of a skunk!

(*The men hasten off, followed by Billy Jackrabbit, leaving Castro, Nick,
and the Deputy in the bar-room.*)

DEPUTY. Come on, you!

CASTRO. (*his teeth chattering*) One dreenk--I freeze--

DEPUTY. Give him a drink, Nick. Watch him. (*He goes out.*)

NICK. (*contemptuously*) What'll you have?

CASTRO. (*rises*) Geeve me--

(*Suddenly facing the dance-hall and speaking so loudly that his voice
may be heard by Johnson.*)

--aguardiente!

NICK. Set down!

(*Castro, looking off, seeing that Johnson has seen him, sits, as Johnson
hastens in from the dance-hall.*)

JOHNSON. So--you did bring my saddle in, eh, Nick?

CASTRO. (*in a low voice*) Ramerrez! . . . Master . . .

JOHNSON. Don't talk . . .

CASTRO. I let them take me, according to your beeding.

JOHNSON. (*looking towards Nick*) Careful, José . . .

   (*He puts the saddle on the table.*)

NICK. (*coming down with a drink for José, who bolts it*) Here.

VOICES. (*from the dance-hall*) Nick! Nick!

NICK. Oh--the Ridge boys goin'.

   (*He goes back to the bar with the glasses-- then speaks to Johnson.*)

Say--keep your eye on him a minute, will you?

JOHNSON. Certainly. You tell The Girl you pressed me into service, will you? (*Touches his pistol pocket.*)

NICK. Sure. Say, she's taken an awful fancy to you.

JOHNSON. No!

NICK. Yes. Drop in often--great bar.

JOHNSON. It certainly is. (*Nick hastens off.*) Ha! Ha! Ha! (*To Castro.*) Go on . . .

CASTRO. Bueno! Our men lie in the bushes near. I lead the Sheriff far off . . . then I slip away. Queeckly rob thees place now and fly. It is death for you to linger. Ashby ees here.

JOHNSON. (*without looking*) Ashby! Wait a minute.

   (*As Nick sticks in his head to cast a watchful glance at Castro.*)

All right, Nick. Yes, everything's all right.

   (*Nick goes out again as a cachuca is gaily played.*)

CASTRO. By to-morrow twilight, you must be safe in your rancho.

JOHNSON. No--we'll raid on.

CASTRO. An hundred men on your track--

JOHNSON. One minute's start of the devil does me, José.

CASTRO. I fear the woman, Nina Micheltoreña . . . teeribly I fear. Close at hand . . . knowing all . . . fresh from your four weeks' quarrel with her . . . still loving you.

JOHNSON. Loving me? Oh, no. Like you, Nina loved the spoils, not me. No, I raid on.

SONORA. (*outside*) Bring along the greaser, Dep.

   (*The boys are heard off stage, and the glare of torches is seen through the windows.*)

DEPUTY. (*outside*) All right.

CASTRO. (*to Johnson*) We start. Queeckly geeve the signal.

GIRL. (*calling in the dance-hall*) Good-night, boys--good-night. (*The music ends.*) Remember me to the Ridge.

RIDGE BOYS. (*off stage*) You bet! So long! Whoop! Whooppee!

CASTRO. All gone. Only the woman there--and her servant. . . . Antonio waits your signal.

DEPUTY. (*entering*) Come on.

CASTRO. Adios.

JOHNSON. Adios.

DEPUTY. Come on.

(*He drags Castro off. The boys move away. Johnson takes up his saddle.*)

GIRL. (*entering from the dance-hall*) Nick, you can put the lights out.

(*Nick puts out the candle over the table.*)

Put the lights out here, too. (*To Johnson.*) Oh, you ain't goin'?

JOHNSON. Not yet, no, but . . .

GIRL. I'm glad of that. Don't it feel funny here? It's kind of creepy. I suppose that's because (*Putting a chair in place.*) I never remember seeing the bar so empty before.

NICK. (*putting out the candle on the mantelpiece*) I'm goin' to close the shutters. (*He closes the shutters.*)

GIRL. (*crossing to the table*) What for--so early?

NICK. (*in a half whisper*) Well, you see, the boys is out huntin' Ramerrez --and they's too much money here.

GIRL. Oh, all right. Cash in. Don't put the head on the keg. I ain't cashed in m'self yet.

NICK. (*rolling out the keg*) Say, Min . . .

GIRL. Huh?

NICK. (*looking uneasily at the keg, and then darting a quick glance towards Johnson*) Know anything about--him?

GIRL. Oh, sure.

NICK. All right, eh?

GIRL. Yes.

(*Nick blows out the lights at the door, and goes into the dance-hall.*)

Well, Mr. Johnson, it seems to be us a-keepin' house here to-night, don't it?

JOHNSON. Strange how things come about. . . . (*Sitting on the table.*) Strange to be looking everywhere for you, and to find you at last at the Polka.

GIRL. Anything wrong with the Polka?

JOHNSON. Well, it's hardly the place for a young woman like you.

GIRL. How so?

JOHNSON. It's rather unprotected, and--

GIRL. Oh, pshaw! I said to Ashby only to-night: "I bet if a road-agent come in here, I could offer him a drink an' he'd treat me like a perfect lady." (*Going back of the bar for a bottle.*) Say, won't you take something?

JOHNSON. No, thank you. I'd like to ask you a question.

GIRL. I know what it is--every stranger asks it, but I didn't think *you* would. It's this: am I decent? Yep, I am--you bet!

JOHNSON. Oh, Girl: I'm not blind--that was not the question.

GIRL. (*leaning over the bar, looking at him*) Dear me suz!

JOHNSON. What I meant to say was this: I am sorry to find you here almost at the mercy of the passer-by . . . where a man may come, may drink, may rob you if he will; and where I dare say more than one has even laid claim to a kiss.

GIRL. They's a good many people claimin' things they never git.

(*She is putting her money in a cigar-box.*)

I've got my first to give.

JOHNSON. (*studying her*) You're clever. Been here long?

GIRL. Yep.

JOHNSON. Live in the Polka?

GIRL. Nop.

JOHNSON. Where do you live?

GIRL. Cabin up the mountain a little ways.

JOHNSON. You're worth something better than this.

GIRL. What's better'n this? I ain't boastin', but if keepin' this saloon don't give me a sort of position around here, I dunno what does. Ha! Look here! Say, you ain't one of them exhorters, are you, from the missionaries' camp?

JOHNSON. My profession has its faults, but I am not an exhorter.

GIRL. You know I can't figger out jest exactly what you are.

JOHNSON. Try.

GIRL. Oh, I can tell--I can spot my man every time. I tell you, keepin' a saloon is a great educator. (*Sitting.*) I dunno but what it's a good way to bring up girls. They git to know things. Now, I'd trust you.

JOHNSON. You would trust me?

GIRL. Notice I danced with you to-night?

JOHNSON. Yes.

GIRL. I seen from the first you was the real article.

JOHNSON. I beg pardon.

GIRL. Why, that was a compliment I handed to you.

JOHNSON. Oh . . .

GIRL. (*confidentially*) Your kind don't prevail much here . . . I can tell--I got what you call a quick eye.

JOHNSON. I'm afraid that men like me--prevail, as you say, almost everywhere.

GIRL. Go on! What are you giving me? Of course they don't. Ha! Before

I went on that trip to Monterey, I thought Rance here was the genu*ine* thing in a gent--but the minute I kind o' glanced over you on the road--I--I seen he wasn't. Say--take your whiskey--and water. (*She rises.*)

JOHNSON. No.

GIRL. (*calling*) Nick? (*Changing her mind.*) No, I'll help you to a drink myself.

JOHNSON. No, thank you.

GIRL. (*leaning against the bar, studying him*) Say, I've got you figured out: you're awful good, or awful bad. . . .

JOHNSON. (*half amused*) Now, what do you mean by that?

GIRL. Well, so good that you're a teetotaler--or so bad that you're tired o' life an' whiskey.

JOHNSON. (*rising and going to her*) On the contrary, although I'm not good--I've lived, and I've liked life pretty well, and I am not tired of it: it's been bully! (*Leaning on the bar.*) So have you liked it, Girl, only you haven't lived--you haven't lived.

(*He attempts to take The Girl's hand, but she retreats.*)

Not with *your* nature. You see, I've got a quick eye, too.

(*Nick enters slowly and prepares to seat himself back of the poker table.*)

GIRL. Nick, git!

(*Nick casts an inquisitive glance at the pair and hastens out.*)

Say, what do you mean by--I haven't lived?

JOHNSON. (*insinuatingly, half under his breath*) Oh, you know.

GIRL. No, I don't.

JOHNSON. Yes, you do.

GIRL. Well, say it's an even chance I do and an even chance I don't.

JOHNSON. (*in a low voice*) I mean life for all it's worth . . . to the utmost . . . to the last drop in the cup . . . so that it atones for what's gone before, or may come after.

GIRL. No, I don't believe I do know what you mean by them words. Is it a--

(*She crosses to the poker table and sits down on her revolver, which is in her pocket. She rises hastily.*)

Oh, Lord! Excuse me--I set on my gun. (*Impulsively.*) I can't pass you on the road. I take your dust. Look here: I'm goin' to make you an offer.

JOHNSON. An offer?

GIRL. It's this: if ever you need to be staked--

JOHNSON. Eh?

GIRL. Which, of course, you don't--name your price--jest for the style I'll git from you an' the deportment.

JOHNSON. Deportment? Me?

NICK. (*re-entering*) Oh, er--I'd like to say--

GIRL. (*annoyed*) Oh! (*Nick goes off hurriedly.*)

JOHNSON. Well, I never heard before that my society was so desirable. Apart from the financial aspect of the matter--I--

GIRL. (*admiringly, half to herself*) Ain't that great? Ain't that great? Oh, you got to let me stand treat. (*Calls.*) Nick?

(*She slips down from the table where she has been seated.*)

JOHNSON. No, really. Say, Girl, you're like finding some new kind of flower.

GIRL. You know the reason I made you that offer is--we're kind of rough up here, but we're reaching out. Now, I take it that what we're all put on this earth for--every one of us--is to rise ourselves up in the world-- to reach out.

JOHNSON. (*with a change of manner*) That's true--that's true. I venture to say there isn't a man who hasn't thought seriously about that. I have. If only a man knew how to reach out for something he hardly dare even hope for. It's like trying to catch the star shining just ahead.

GIRL. That's the cheese. You've struck it. (*Nick enters.*)

NICK. I *have* been a'tryin' to say--

GIRL. What *is* it, Nick?

NICK. I jest seen an ugly lookin' greaser outside a winder.

GIRL. (*going up to the door*) A greaser? Let me look.

JOHNSON. (*knowing that it is his man awaiting the signal--speaking with an air of authority*) I wouldn't.

GIRL. Why not?

NICK. I'll bolt all the winders.

(*Nick goes off. A whistle outside. Johnson recognizes the signal.*)

GIRL. Don't that sound horrid? (*Getting behind the counter.*) I'm awful glad you're here. Nick's so nervous. He knows what a lot of money I've got. Why, there's a little fortune right in that keg.

JOHNSON. (*crossing over to the keg and looking at it*) In that keg?

GIRL. The boys sleep round it nights.

JOHNSON. But when they're gone--isn't that a careless place to leave it?

GIRL. (*coming down to the keg*) Oh, they'd have to kill me before they got it.

JOHNSON. I see--it's *your* money.

GIRL. No, it belongs to the boys.

JOHNSON. Oh, that's different. Now, I wouldn't risk my life for that.

GIRL. (*putting the bags of gold-dust in the keg, and closing the keg and standing with her foot on it*) Oh, yes, you would--yes, you would--if you seen how hard they got it. When I think of it--I--I nearly cry. You know there's somethin' awful pretty in the way the boys hold out before they strike it--awful pretty--in the face of rocks and clay and alkali. Oh, Lord, what a life it is, anyway! Why, they eat dirt--an' they sleep dirt, an' they breathe dirt till their backs are bent, their hands twisted, their souls warped; they're all wind-swept an' blear-eyed--an' some of 'em jest lie down in their own sweat beside the sluices, an' they don't never rise again. I've seen 'em there. I got some money of old Brownie's. (*Pointing to the keg.*) He was lyin' out in the sun on a pile of clay two weeks ago an' I guess the only clean thing about him was his soul--an' he was quittin'--quittin' right there on the clay--an' quittin' hard. . . . (*Remembering the scene with horror.*) Oh, he died--jest like a dog . . . you wanted to shoot him to help him along quicker. Before he went, he sez: "Girl, give it to my old woman." An' he--left. She'll git it. (*Slight pause.*) An' that's what aches you. They ain't one of these men workin' for themselves alone. The Almighty never put it in no man's heart to make a beast or pack-horse of himself--except for some woman, or some child. Ain't it wonderful? Ain't it wonderful, that instinct, ain't it--what a man'll do when it comes to a woman? Ain't it wonderful? Yep, the boys use me as a--ha!--sort of lady bank. (*She wipes her eyes.*) You bet I'll drop down dead before anyone'll get a dollar of theirs outer the Polka.

JOHNSON. (*after a short pause*) That's right. (*Taking The Girl's hand.*) I'm with you. I'd like to see anyone get that.

(*They shake hands over the keg--not heroically, but very simply.*)

Girl, you make me wish I could talk more with you, but I can't. By daybreak I must be a long way off. I'm sorry. I should have liked to call at your cabin.

GIRL. (*wistfully*) Must you be movin'--so--soon?

JOHNSON. I'm only waiting till the posse gets back and you're safe. (*Listening.*) There. . . . They're coming now. . . .

GIRL. I'm awful sorry you got to go. I was goin' to say--(*rolling the keg up stage, she takes a lantern off the bar and sets it on the keg*)--if you didn't have to go so soon, I'd like to have you come up to the cabin to-night, and we would talk of reaching out up there. You see, the boys will come back here. . . . We close the Polka at one--any time after that.

JOHNSON. I--I should ride on now--but--I'll come.

GIRL. Oh, good! (*Giving the lantern to Johnson.*) You can use this lantern. It's the straight trail up--you can't miss it. Say, don't expect too much of me--I've only had thirty-two dollars' worth of education.

(*Her voice breaks, her eyes fill with tears.*)
P'raps if I'd had more--why, you can't tell what I might have been. Say, that's a turrible thought, ain't it? What we--might have been? And I know it when I look at you.

JOHNSON. (*touched*) God knows it is! What we might have been--and *I* know it when I look at *you*, Girl--I know it when I look at you.

GIRL. (*wipes away a tear*) You bet!

(*Suddenly collapses, burying her face on her arm on the bar, sobbing, speaking through her tears.*)
Oh, 'tain't no use--I'm ignorant--I don't know nothin' an' I never knowed it till to-night. The boys always told me I knowed so much--but they're such damned liars.

JOHNSON. (*coming up and leaning on the bar, speaking earnestly, with a suggestion of tears in his voice*) Don't you care--you're all right, Girl-- you're all right. Your heart's all right--that's the main thing. As for your looks--to me you've got the face of an angel. I--I'll just take a glance at my horse.

(*He takes up his saddle, crosses to the door, and then turns back. To himself.*)
Johnson, what the devil's the matter with you?

(*He goes out hastily, carrying the lantern, and slamming the door behind him. The Girl stands immovable for a moment, then calls suddenly.*)

GIRL. Nick! Nick!

(*Nick enters quickly. She turns her face away, wiping off a tear.*)
You run over to the Palmetter rest'rant an' tell 'em to send me up two charlotte rusks an' a lemming turnover--just as quick as they can--right up to the cabin for supper. (*Nick goes off.*) Ha!

(*She crosses to the poker table and sits on the edge, the light above shining down on her face. Strumming on a guitar and mandolin is heard as though the musicians were tuning up for the boys.*)
He says. . . . He says. . . . (*Sentimentally.*) I have the face of an angel.

(*A little pause, then turning her face away.*)
Oh, hell!

ACT II. "Two people who came from nothing."

Scene. The home of The Girl on Cloudy Mountain. One o'clock in the morning. The interior of the cabin has but one room, square and made of logs. It is half papered as though the owner had bought wall-paper in camp and the supply had given out. There is but one door, and that leads to the trail. This door, in the center at back, is double boarded and fastened by a heavy bar. It opens on a rough vestibule, built to keep out the storms and cold. The windows, at which are calico curtains, are provided with heavy wooden shutters and bars. There is an air of security, as though the room could be made into a little fortress.

The furniture is rather primitive. A bed, screened off by calico curtains, stands at the right. Below it is a bureau covered by a Navajo blanket on which a few crude toilet articles are set about. A cheap black framed mirror, decorated with strings of Indian beads and white cambric roses, hangs over the bureau. A wash-stand, backed by a "splasher" of white oilcloth, is near the bed. On the opposite side, a pine wardrobe, rudely painted by a miner, contains most of The Girl's clothing. A sunbonnet and shawl hang on a peg driven into the side of the wardrobe. A gay hat-box from Monterey and a small basket grace the top of the wardrobe. A calico curtain covers a few garments hanging on pegs. In an angle formed by a fireplace, is a row of shelves holding tin cups, Indian baskets, two plates, a tin can, knives, forks, and spoons. A rocking-chair, made of a barrel set on rockers and dyed by blueing, is embellished with calico cushions and an anti-macassar. There are four other chairs in the room.

Near the center is a pine table covered with a red cloth and over this a white table-cloth. Three dishes are on the table; one contains the charlotte "rusks," one the "lemming" turnover, and the other bisquits and chipped beef. A bowl of brown sugar is in the center of the table. A fire burns in a fireplace which has an iron hood, a big back log, and a smaller log in front. A pile of wood lies on the floor, close at hand. A kettle hangs over the fire and a coffee-pot is on a log. A few china ornaments, a bunch of winter berries stuck in a glass jar, and a bottle of whiskey with two glasses are on the mantel. A box nailed on the wall forms a book-shelf for a few well-worn old books. A wolf skin and moccasins are in front of the bureau, a large bear-skin rug is on the floor opposite the fireplace. A few pictures taken from *Godey's Lady's Book*, one or two old prints, and a large sombrero hat hang on the wall. A horseshoe over the door and the head of a small antelope, an old pair of snowshoes over the window and a lady's night-dress on a peg complete the decorations.

Above is a loft reached by a ladder which is swung up out of the way. By standing on a chair and reaching up, one may pull the ladder down to the floor. Some old trunks and a few little boxes are neatly piled on the floor of the loft. Blankets screen off one end of the attic. A lamp hangs from an arm (swinging from the loft above) and shines down on the table. The winter is now beginning, and although there is no evidence of snow in the early part of the act, the cabin windows are heavily frosted. When the curtain rises, the scene is lighted by the lamps and the glow from the fireplace. The moon is shining brightly through the window.

(*At the rise of the curtain, Wowkle, a squaw, is seated on the floor, singing, her papoose on her back. She is dressed in a long cloth skirt, a short red calico skirt hanging over it. She wears moccasins. Her hair is parted in the middle and drawn into two tight little blue-black braids, crossed in the back, low in the neck. She wears a number of glass bead necklaces and small silver hoops in her ears. She is young, beady-eyed, sweet-faced, and rather plump--the lax uncorseted, voluptuous type of squaw. She is perfectly good-natured, at time quizzical, but utterly unreliable and without any ideas of morality. Billy Jackrabbit enters.*)

BILLY JACKRABBIT. Ugh!

WOWKLE. Ugh!

(*As Billy comes towards Wowkle, he sees the food, looks at it greedily, picks up a plate, and is about to stick his finger into the contents.*)

Charlotte rusk--Palmetto rest'rant. Not take.

BILLY JACKRABBIT. (*putting the plate back on the table*) H'm . . . H'm . . . Me honest.

WOWKLE. Huh!

(*Billy stoops and picks up a piece of paper to which some of the food, which has been wrapped in it, still clings. He rubs his fingers over the paper and licks them during the conversation.*)

BILLY JACKRABBIT. (*grunting, sitting down beside Wowkle*) Send me up from Polka--say p'raps me marry you. . . . Huh?

WOWKLE. (*impassively*) Me don't know. (*Pause.*)

BILLY JACKRABBIT. Me don't know.

(*A slight pause. They are sitting side by side on the floor--unlike lovers--just as two Indians.*)

Me marry you, how much me got give fatha--Huh?

WOWKLE. (*indifferently, with a black look*) Huh! Me don't know.

BILLY JACKRABBIT. Me don't know. (*Pause.*) Me give fatha four dolla --(*indicating with his fingers--licking one*)--and one blanket.

WOWKLE. Betta me keep um blanket for baby.

BILLY JACKRABBIT. (*grunts*) Me give fatha three dolla and baby.

WOWKLE. We keep um baby.

BILLY JACKRABBIT. (*tearing off a piece of the sticky paper and handing it to Wowkle*) Tawakawa.

WOWKLE. Toanimbutuc.

(*Billy offers to let the baby lick the paper, but she draws the child away.*)
Aie! Missionary woman at Battla Ridge him say marry first--then baby.

BILLY JACKRABBIT. (*who has licked paper clean, and is now smoking his pipe*) Huh!

WOWKLE. Me say baby first . . . him say all right, but marry--get plenty bead.

BILLY JACKRABBIT. (*eyeing her beads and giving his pipe to Wowkle who takes a puff*) You sing hymn for get those bead?

WOWKLE. Me sing--

(*She sings softly in a fairly high-pitched voice with a slight nasal tone.*)
My days are as um grass--

BILLY JACKRABBIT. (*recognizing the air, he gives a grunt and joins in*)
Or as um faded flowa--
Um wintry winds sweep o'er um plain,
We pe'ish in--um--ow-a--

(*Taking his pipe from Wowkle.*)
By Gar, to-morrow we go missionary--sing like Hell--get whiskey.

(*Rises and sings.*)
Pe'ish in um ow-a.

(*He goes up to the door and stands there.*)
Al-right--go missionary to-morrow--get marry--huh?

WOWKLE. Billy Jackrabbit-- (*She rises.*) P'raps me not stay marry with you for long time.

BILLY JACKRABBIT. (*unimpressed*) Huh! How long--seven monse?

WOWKLE. Six monse.

BILLY JACKRABBIT. (*taking a red handkerchief from his pocket and sticking it between the papoose and the board*) Um . . . for baby. (*Nudging Wowkle with his elbow.*) You come soon?

WOWKLE. Girl eat suppa first--me come.

BILLY JACKRABBIT. (*nudging her again--then going into the vestibule*) Huh! Girl come.

(*The Girl appears outside the door, holding up a lantern. There is a suppressed excitement in her manner as she enters, yet she shows a new thoughtfulness and speaks quietly. She looks about as though to see what effect this little cabin will have on Johnson.*)

GIRL. (*hanging her lantern on the outer door*) Turn up the lamps--quick.
  (*Wowkle turns up the lamp on the table.*)
  Hello, Jackrabbit. Fixed it?

BILLY JACKRABBIT. Me fix.

GIRL. That's good. Now, git!
  (*Exit Billy Jackrabbit. The Girl goes to the table.*)
  Wowkle, it's for two to-night.

WOWKLE. Ugh!

GIRL. Yep.

WOWKLE. Come anotha? Neva before come anotha.

GIRL. Never you mind. He's coming--he's coming. Pick up the room.
  (*Hanging up her coat.*) What time is it, Wowkle?
  (*She shakes Wowkle. Wowkle gets plates, cups, etc.*)
  Wowkle, what did you do with them red roses?

WOWKLE. (*pointing to the bureau*) Ugh.

GIRL. Good.
  (*She finds the roses and arranges them in her hair.*)
  No offense--but I want you to put your best foot forward--
  (*She takes a pistol out of her pocket and puts it on the lower end of the bureau.*)
  --when you're waitin' on table to-night. This here comp'ny of mine is a
  man of idees. Oh, he knows everything--sort of a damn-me style.
  Wowkle, how's the papoose? Father really proposed to you?

WOWKLE. Yep--get married.

GIRL. (*taking a ribbon from a drawer*) Here! You can have that to fix the
  baby up for the weddin'. Hurry, Wowkle. I'm going to put these on--
  (*She sits on the floor and puts on a pair of new slippers which she has
  taken from the bottom drawer.*)
  --If I can get 'em on. Remember what fun I made of you when you took up
  with Billy Jackrabbit? "What for?" says I. Well, p'raps you was right.
  P'raps it's nice to have someone you really care for--who really belongs
  to you. P'raps there ain't so much in the saloon business for a woman,
  after all--an' you don't know what livin' really is. Ah, Wowkle, it's nice
  to have someone you can talk to, someone you can turn your heart inside
  out to--(*a knock sounds on the window*)--Oh, Lord! Here he is, Wowkle!
  (*She tries to conceal herself behind the foot of the bed--one slipper in her
  hand. Sid opens the window and peers in.*)

WOWKLE. Ugh!

GIRL. (*disgusted at seeing Sid*) What are you doin' here, you Sidney
  Duck! You git!

SID. Beg pardon, Miss. I know men ain't allowed up here.

GIRL. No.

SID. But I'm in grite trouble. The boys are 'ot. They missed the road-agent, Ramerrez--and now they're tiking it out on me. (*Sniffs.*) If you'd only speak a word for me, Miss.

GIRL. No! Wowkle, shut the winder.

SID. (*pleading*) Ow, don't be 'ard on me.

GIRL. Now, look here! They's one kind of men--(*gesticulating with a slipper*)--I can't stand--a cheat an' a thief, an' you're it. You're no better than that road-agent, Ramerrez. (*Putting on the other slipper.*) Wowkle, close the winder. Close the winder.

SID. Public 'ouse jide! (*He slams the window and disappears.*)

GIRL. I got 'em on! (*Rising with difficulty.*) Say, Wowkle, do you think he'll like 'em? How do they look? Gosh! They're tight. Say, Wowkle, I'm going the whole hog.

(*She has taken a lace shawl from the bureau drawer and puts it on; then she sprinkles some perfumery over a large lace handkerchief and starts to draw on a pair of one-button gloves.*)

Look here, Wowkle, does it look like an effort?

WOWKLE. (*understanding at last*) H'm! Two plate . . .

(*There is a knock on the door. The Girl hastily adjusts her belt, pulls up her stocking, and opens the door.*)

JOHNSON. (*surprised*) Hello!

GIRL. (*embarrassed*) Hello, Mr. Johnson . . .

JOHNSON. (*noticing her gloves*) Are you going out?

GIRL. Yes--no--I don't know. Oh, come on in.

JOHNSON. (*setting his lantern on the table and attempting to put his arms around her*) Thank you!

WOWKLE. (*shutting the door, which Johnson has left open*) Ugh!

JOHNSON. (*eyeing Wowkle*) I beg your pardon. I didn't see--

GIRL. You stop jest where you are, Mr. Johnson.

JOHNSON. I--I apologize. But seeing you standing there, and looking into your lovely eyes--well, the temptation to take you in my arms was so great--that I--I took it.

(*Wowkle, blowing out Johnson's lantern, goes into the cupboard with her papoose.*)

GIRL. You must be in the habit of taking things, Mr. Johnson. I seen you on the road to Monterey, goin' an' comin'--I seen you come since, an' passed a few words with you; but that don't give you no excuse to begin this sort of game. Besides, you might have prospected a bit first, anyway.

JOHNSON. I see how wrong I was. May I take off my coat? (*She does not answer.*) Thank you. (*Laying his coat on a chair.*) What a bully little place you have here--awfully snug. And I've found you again! Oh, the luck! (*Holding out his hand.*) Friends, Girl?

GIRL. (*withholding her hand*) Are you sorry?

JOHNSON. No, I'm not sorry.

GIRL. (*bashfully, half to herself*) That damn-me style! Well, look here--(*going towards the chair at the table*)--down to the saloon to-night, you said you always got what you wanted. Well, of course, I've got to admire you for that--I guess women always do admire men for gettin' what they want. But if huggin' me is included, cut it out, Mr. Johnson.

JOHNSON. (*facing her across the table*) That was a lovely day, Girl, on the road to Monterey, wasn't it?

GIRL. Was it? Oh, take a chair an' set down.

JOHNSON. Thanks. (*But he does not sit.*)

GIRL. Say, look here! I been thinkin' . . . You didn't come to the saloon to see me to-night. What brought you?

JOHNSON. It was Fate.

GIRL. Was it Fate--or--the back trail?

JOHNSON. (*coming to the table, attempting to embrace her*) It was Fate.

GIRL. (*retreating to a corner*) Wowkle, git the coffee. (*To Johnson.*) Oh, Lord, take a chair.

(*The Girl starts to place a chair near the table; Johnson intercepts her before she can pick up his coat, which lies across the back of the chair.*)

JOHNSON. Careful, please! Careful!

GIRL. (*peering at the revolvers in his coat pockets*) How many guns do you carry?

JOHNSON. (*hanging his coat on the peg*) Oh, several--when travelling through the country.

GIRL. (*apprehensively*) Set down. (*He sits.*)

JOHNSON. Ha! It must be strange, living all alone way up here in the mountains. Isn't it lonely?

GIRL. Lonely? Mountains lonely? Ha! Besides--(*sitting in the barrel rocking-chair*)--I got a little pinto, an' I'm all over the country on him--finest little horse you ever throwed a leg over. If I want to, I can ride right down into the summer at the foothills, with miles of Injun pinks jest a-laffin'--an' tiger lilies as mad as blazes. There's a river there, too--the Injuns call it a "water road"--an' I can git on that an' drift an' drift, an' I smell the wild syringa on the banks--M'm! And if I git tired o' that, I can turn my horse up grade an' gallop right into the winter an' the lonely pines an' firs a'whisperin' an' a-sighin'. Oh, my mountains! My beautiful peaks! My Sierras! God's in the air here, sure. You can see Him layin' peaceful hands on the mountain tops. He seems so near, you want to let your soul go right on up.

JOHNSON. (*nodding his head slightly in appreciation*) When you die, you won't have far to go, Girl.

GIRL. (*after a pause*) Wowkle, git the coffee.

(*The Girl and Johnson sit at the table. Wowkle pours the coffee into the cups and sets the pot back in the fireplace.*)

JOHNSON. But when it's cold up here--very cold and it snows?

GIRL. Oh, the boys come up an' dig me out of my front door--ha!--like--a-- (*She spears a bisquit with her fork.*)

JOHNSON. Little rabbit, eh?

GIRL. I git dug out nearly every day when the mines is shet down an' the Academy opens.

JOHNSON. (*surprised*) Academy? Here? Who teaches in your Academy?

GIRL. Me. I'm her. I'm teacher.

JOHNSON. You teach? Oh--

GIRL. Yep, I learn m'self--(*putting sugar in Johnson's coffee*)--an' the boys at the same time. But, of course, Academy's suspended when they's a blizzard on--

JOHNSON. (*seeing that she is continuing to put sugar in his coffee*) Hold on . . . hold on . . .

GIRL. --'cause no girl could git down the mountain then.

JOHNSON. Is it so very severe here when there's a blizzard on?

GIRL. Oh, Lordy! They come in a minute--all of a sudden--an' you don't know where you are. It's awful! (*Offering a dish with an air of pride.*) Charlotte Rusks!

JOHNSON. (*surprised*) No!

GIRL. And lemming turnovers!

JOHNSON. Well!

GIRL. Will you have one?

JOHNSON. You bet! Thank you. Let me send you some little souvenir of to-night--something you'd love to read in your course of teaching at the Academy. What have you been reading lately?

GIRL. Oh, it's an awful funny book, about a couple. He was a classic an' his name was Dant.

JOHNSON. He was a classic, and his name was Dant. Oh, Dante! Yes, I know. And did you find it funny? Dante funny?

GIRL. I roared. You see, he loves a lady-- (*Rising to get the book.*)

JOHNSON. Beatrice--

GIRL. How?

JOHNSON. Go on.

GIRL. He loves a lady. It made me think of what you said down to the saloon to-night about livin' so you didn't care what come after. Well, he made up his mind--this Dant--Dantee--that one hour of happiness with her was worth the whole da--(*correcting herself*)--outfit that come after. He was willin' to sell out his chances for sixty minutes with her. Well, I jest put the book down and hollered!

JOHNSON. Of course you did. All the same, you knew he was right.

GIRL. (*putting the book back on the shelf*) I didn't.

JOHNSON. You did.

GIRL. Didn't.

JOHNSON. You did.

GIRL. Didn't.

JOHNSON. You know he was right!

GIRL. I don't.

JOHNSON. Yes, you do. You do.

GIRL. I don't. That a feller could so wind himself up as to say--(*sitting at the table*)--"Jest give me one hour of your sassiety--time ain't nothin'--nothin' ain't nothin'--only to be a da--darn fool over you." Ain't it funny to feel like that? Yet I suppose there are folks who feel like that; folks that love into the grave, and into death--and after. Golly! It jest lifts you right up by your boot-straps to think of it, don't it?

JOHNSON. (*looks at her intently, not smiling; he is fascinated*) It does have that effect.

GIRL. Yet p'raps he was ahead o' the game. Ha!--I dunno. Oh, say, I jest love this conversation with you. I love to hear you talk. You give me idees. Wowkle, bring the candle.

(*Wowkle gives the candle to Johnson.*)

Say, look here: one of your real Havanas.

(*Wowkle knows now that Johnson is the chosen man. She eyes him with great curiosity.*)

JOHNSON. No, I--

GIRL. (*handing him the cigar*) Go on.

JOHNSON. (*looking her through and through, his eyes half closed*) Thank you. How I would love to know you, Girl!

GIRL. You do know me.

JOHNSON. (*lights his cigar*) Not well enough.

GIRL. What's your drift?

JOHNSON. To know you as Dante knew the lady. To say: "One hour for me--one hour--worth the world."

GIRL. (*drinking her coffee*) He didn't git it, Mr. Johnson.

JOHNSON. All the same, there are women we can die for. . . .

GIRL. How many times have you died?

JOHNSON. (*lays the cigar down on the table*) That day on the road to Monterey I said: "Just that one woman for me." (*Taking The Girl's hand.*) I wanted to kiss you then.

(*She rises, pulls her hand away, and starts to clear the table.*)

GIRL. Wowkle, heist the winder.

(*Wowkle goes to the window and stands there.*)

Mr. Johnson, some men think so much of kisses, that they don't never want a second kiss from the same girl.

JOHNSON. That depends on whether they love her or not. All loves are not alike.

GIRL. No, but they all have the same aim--to git her, if they can.

JOHNSON. You don't know what love is.

GIRL. Nop, I don't. My mother used to say, Mr. Johnson, "Love's a tickling sensation at the heart that you can't scratch."

(*Johnson rises and goes up to the door, laughing heartily.*)

We'll let it go at that.

JOHNSON. (*turns to embrace The Girl*) Oh, Girl, you're bully!

(*Wowkle clears the table.*)

GIRL. (*retreating*) Look out or you'll muss my roses.

JOHNSON. Hadn't you better take them off, then?

GIRL. Give a man an inch, an' he'll be at Sank Hosey before you know it.

JOHNSON. (*following The Girl*) Is there anyone else?

GIRL. (*taking off her roses*) A man always says: "Who was the first one?" But the girl says: "Who'll be the next one?"

JOHNSON. But the time comes when there will never be a next one.

GIRL. No?

(*She takes off one of her gloves, blows into it, and puts it in the bureau drawer.*)

JOHNSON. No.

GIRL. I'd hate to stake my pile on that! Git to your wigwam, Wowkle.

(*She takes off the other glove. Wowkle, who has put the dishes in a pail, grunts, hangs the papoose on her back, and puts on her blanket.*)

JOHNSON. Must I go, too?

GIRL. Mm--not just yet. You can stay--a--a hour or two longer.

JOHNSON. Yes? Well, I'm like Dante: I want the world in that hour, because I'm afraid the door of this little paradise may be shut to me afterwards. Let's say that this is my one hour--the hour that gives me that kiss.

GIRL. Go long . . .

(*Wowkle has reached the door and opened it. A gust of wind, and a little snow blows in. The wind has been rising for some time, but The Girl and Johnson have not noticed it.*)

WOWKLE. Ugh--come snow.

(*The Girl and Johnson do not hear her. All through the following scene, they are so engrossed in each other, that they don't notice Wowkle.*)

GIRL. (*to Johnson*) You go to grass.

JOHNSON. (*embracing her--trying to kiss her*) Listen . . .

WOWKLE. Ugh! It snow . . . See . . .

GIRL. Why, if I let you have one, you'd take two.

JOHNSON. No, I wouldn't.

WOWKLE. Very bad.

JOHNSON. I swear I wouldn't.

WOWKLE. Ugh! (*She is disgusted and goes out, closing the door.*)

GIRL. (*retreating*) Oh, please . . .

JOHNSON. (*steps back a little and stands with his arms open*) One kiss-- only one.

GIRL. 'Tain't no use. I lay down my hand to you.

(*She runs into his arms.*)

JOHNSON. (*embracing and kissing her*) I love you!

(*The wind blows the snow against the windows. The vestibule doors slam. The curtains of the bed flap in the wind. A small basket on the wardrobe blows down. A flower-pot topples over. The blankets in the loft flap. The lamps flicker. Suddenly the wind dies down. The clock on the mantel strikes two. The wind begins to rise again. The Girl and Johnson are absolutely oblivious to the storm. After a little pause, Johnson speaks, still holding her in his arms.*)

What's your name, Girl--your real name?

GIRL. Min--Minnie. My father's name was Smith.

JOHNSON. Oh, Minnie Sm—

GIRL. But 'twasn't his right name.

JOHNSON. No?

GIRL. His right name was Falconer--

JOHNSON. Minnie Falconer. That's a pretty name. (*He kisses her hand.*)

GIRL. I think that was it--I ain't sure. That's what he said it was. I ain't sure of anything--only--jest you. (*She snuggles closer.*)

JOHNSON. I've loved you ever since I first saw you. . . . So you're sure of me--sure. (*He gently puts her away, remembering what he is.*) You turn your head away, Girl, and don't you listen to me, for I'm not worth you. Don't you listen. You just say, "No--no-no!" (*He turns away.*)

GIRL. Say, I know I ain't good enough for you, but I'll try hard. If you see anything better in me, why don't you bring it out? I've loved you ever since I saw you first . . . 'cause I knowed that you was the right man.

JOHNSON. (*conscience-smitten*) The right man. Ha, ha!

GIRL. Don't laugh.

JOHNSON. (*seriously*) I'm not laughing.

GIRL. Of course, every girl kind o' looks ahead.

JOHNSON. Yes.

GIRL. And figgers about--bein'-- Well-- Oh, you know--

JOHNSON. Yes, I know. (*He is standing so that she cannot see his face.*)

GIRL. She figgers about bein' settled . . . and when the right one comes-- why, she knows him--jest as we both knew each other standin' in the road to Monterey. I said that day: "He's good--he's grand--he can have me!"

JOHNSON. (*meditatively, with longing--turning to her*) I could have you . . . (*With sudden resolve.*) I have looked into your heart, Girl, and into my own, and now I realize what this means for us both--for you, Girl, for you--and knowing that it seems hard to say good-bye--as I should . . . and must . . . and will. (*He kisses her, then turns to go.*)

GIRL. What do you mean?

JOHNSON. (*collecting himself*) I mean it's hard to go--and leave you here. The clock reminded me that long before this, I should have been on the way. I shouldn't have come up here at all. God bless you, dear--I love you as I never thought I could.

GIRL. (*troubled*) But it ain't for long you're goin'?

JOHNSON. For long? (*Resolving not to tell her the truth.*) No--no; but I've got to go now while I have the courage. (*Taking her face in his hands--kissing her.*) Oh, Girl! Girl! (*Kissing her hands.*) Good-bye . . .

(*He gets his hat and coat, opens door and looks out.*)

Why, it's snowing!

(*As the door opens, all the sounds of the snow-swept woods are heard-- the whispering and rocking of the snow-tossed pines, and the winds howling through a deep cañon. The Girl runs up and closes the outside and inside doors, goes to the window, pulls back the curtain, wipes the frost from the window pane, trying to peer out.*)

GIRL. Snowing . . . It's the first snow this winter. You can't see an inch ahead. That's the way we git it up here. Look! Look!

JOHNSON. (*looking through the window*) This means-- No . . . it can't mean that I can't leave Cloudy to-night. I must.

GIRL. (*turning to him*) Leave Cloudy? You couldn't keep to the trail. It means you can't git off this mountain to-night.

JOHNSON. (*thinking of the posse*) But I must!

GIRL. You can't leave this room to-night--you couldn't find your way three feet from this door--you, a stranger. . . . You don't know the trail anyway, unless you can see it.

JOHNSON. (*apprehensively*) But I can't stay here.

GIRL. Why not? It's all right. The boys'll come up an' dig us out to-morrow or day after. Plenty of food here--and you can have my bed.

JOHNSON. I couldn't think of taking it.

GIRL. I never use it cold nights. I always roll up in my rug in front of the fire. (*Amused.*) Think of it snowing all this time, an' we didn't know it!

JOHNSON. (*pre-occupied--gravely*) But people coming up and finding me here, might . . .

GIRL. Might what?

(*Two shots, fired in quick succession, in the distance at the foot of the mountain.*)

JOHNSON. What's that? . . . What's that?

GIRL. Wait . . .

(*More shots in the distance, fired at intervals.*)

They've got a road-agent . . . It's the posse. P'raps they've got Ramerrez or one of this band.

(*Johnson rushes to the window, vainly trying to look out.*)

Whoever it is, they're snowed in--couldn't git away.

(*Another shot.*)

I guess that time another thief crept into camp. (*Meaning eternity.*)

JOHNSON. (*wincing*) Poor devil! But, of course--as you say--he's only a thief.

GIRL. (*who has thrown her pillow in front of the fire*) I ain't sorry for him.

JOHNSON. (*after a slight pause*) You're right!

(*Then, as though he had made up his mind, he takes down his overcoat and puts it on.*)

Girl, I've been thinking . . . I've got to go--I've got to go. I have very important business at dawn--imperative.

GIRL. Ever sample one of our mountain blizzards? In five minutes you wouldn't know where you was. Your important business would land you at the bottom of a cañon--about twenty feet from here. You say you

believe in Fate. Well, it's caught up with you. You got to stay here.
(*She puts the tablecloth in the cupboard as though putting the house in order for the night.*)

JOHNSON. Well, it is Fate--my Fate--(*throwing down his coat*)--that has always made it easy for me to do the thing I shouldn't do. As you say, Girl, if I can't go, I can't . . . (*looking at her intently*)--but I know now as I stand here, that I'll never give you up.

GIRL. (*not quite understanding*) Why, what do you mean?

JOHNSON. (*deliberately--above the crying of the wind*) I mean . . . suppose we say that's an omen--(*pointing as though to the falling snow*)--that the old trail is blotted out and there's a fresh road. . . . Would you take it with me, a stranger--who says: "From this day I mean to be all that you would have me"? Would you take it with me? Far away from here--and--forever?

GIRL. Well, show me the girl who would want to go to Heaven alone. (*Johnson kisses her hand.*) I'll sell out the saloon. I'll go anywhere with you--you bet!

JOHNSON. You know what that means, don't you?
(*He sits by the table, looking at The Girl.*)

GIRL. Oh, yes. They's a little Spanish Mission Church here . . . I pass it 'most every day. I can look in an' see the light burnin' before the Virgin--an' all the saints standin' round with glassy eyes an' faded satin slippers--an' I often thought: what'd they think if I was to walk right in to be made--well, some man's wife. That's a great word, ain't it--wife? It makes your blood like pin-points thinkin' about it. There's somethin' kind o' holy about love, ain't there? Say, did you ever ask any other woman to marry you?
(*She sits down on the floor, leaning towards Johnson, in his arms.*)

JOHNSON. No.

GIRL. Oh, I'm glad! Ah--take me--I don't care where--as long's it's with you. Jest take me.

JOHNSON. So help me Heaven, I'm going to, Girl. You're worth something better than me, Girl; but they say love works miracles every hour: it weakens the strong and strengthens the weak. With all my soul I love you. . . . (*Noticing that she is dozing.*) Why, Minnie . . . Minnie . . .

GIRL. (*waking with a start*) I wasn't asleep. . . . I'm jest happy an' let down, that's all. Say, I'm awful sorry--I've got to say good-night.

JOHNSON. Good-night.
(*He kisses her. They rise.*)

GIRL. That's your bed over there.

JOHNSON. I hate to take it. Hadn't you better take the bed and let me sleep by the fire?

GIRL. Nop.

(*She moves the barrel rocking-chair away from the fireplace.*)

JOHNSON. Are you sure you will be more comfortable there?

GIRL. You bet I will--don't worry.

JOHNSON. (*throwing his hat and coat on the bed*) Very well.

GIRL. (*as she spreads rugs on the floor in front of the fire*) This beats a bed any time. There's one thing--(*reaching up and pulling down a quilt from the loft*)--you don't have to make it up in the morning.

(*She puts a lighted candle on the hearth, blows out the lamps on the mantel, the stand, and the bureau. She climbs up on the table, turns down the hanging lamp, steps to the floor, notices that she has turned it too low, glances at Johnson, making sure that he does not see her, gets up on the table again, turns the wick higher, then goes into the wardrobe where she makes her toilet for the night.*)

Now, you can talk to me from your bunk, and I'll talk to you from mine.

JOHNSON. Good-night.

GIRL. Good-night.

(*Johnson starts to go to bed--turns quickly, listens--then goes towards the bed--pauses--runs to the door and listens. His face is full of resolve. He shows the desperado's ability to meet all emergencies. He speaks quietly--in fact, the scene between these two, from this moment until the door is opened, must be done in the lowest audible tones--to convey the impression that those outside do not hear.*)

JOHNSON. What's that?

GIRL. That's snow slidin' . . . Good night.

JOHNSON. God bless you, Girl. Thank you.

(*He goes behind the curtains of the bed. A pause.*)

H'm . . . There *is* something out there . . . sounded like someone calling.

GIRL. That's only the wind. (*Coming out of the wardrobe.*) It's gettin' colder, ain't it?

(*She sits on the floor, takes off her slippers, and puts on moccasins, then rises and comes down to the fire, arranges the rugs and pillow, says a brief prayer, lies down and tucks herself in.*)

Good-night again.

JOHNSON. Good-night.

GIRL. (*lifting up her head*) Say, what's your first name?

JOHNSON. Dick.

GIRL. (*sentimentally*) So long, Dick.

(She snuggles down again in the folds of the rug.)

JOHNSON. So long, Girl.

GIRL. *(half rising)* Say, Dick, are you sure you don't know that Nina Micheltoreña?

JOHNSON. *(after a slight pause)* Sure.

GIRL. *(with a satisfied air)* Good-night. *(She lies down again.)*

JOHNSON. Good-night.

> *(Suddenly a voice is heard to call and some one knocks on the door. The Girl rises and sets the candle on the table. Johnson throws open the curtains and pulls his revolvers from his pockets.)*

GIRL. There *is* some one calling.

NICK. *(outside)* Hello!

GIRL. Listen! What could that--

JOHNSON. *(in a low voice)* Don't answer.

GIRL. Who can it be?

JOHNSON. You can't let anybody in here--they wouldn't understand.

GIRL. Understand what?

> *(She goes to the window. It never occurs to her that the situation is compromising.)*

JOHNSON. Sh!

GIRL. It's the posse. How did they ever risk it in this blizzard? What can they want?

JOHNSON. *(low, but very distinctly, above the rising wind, his hands on his pistols)* Don't answer.

NICK. *(outside)* Min! Minnie! Girl!

GIRL. *(calling through the door)* What do you want? *(Turning quickly to Johnson.)* What did you say?

JOHNSON. Don't let them in.

SONORA. *(outside)* Are you all right, Girl?

GIRL. *(calling loudly through the door)* Yes, Sonora, I'm all right. *(Turning again to Johnson.)* Jack Rance is there. . . . If he wants to see you here--he's that jealous--I'd be afraid of him. *(Listening at the door.)* And Ashby's there and--

JOHNSON. *(now sure that they are after him)* Ashby!

NICK. *(outside)* We want to come in.

JOHNSON. No.

GIRL. *(glibly, calling)* You can't come in. *(To Johnson.)* What will I say?

JOHNSON. *(quietly)* You've gone to bed.

GIRL. Oh, yes. *(To Nick, outside.)* I've gone to bed--I'm in bed now.

ASHBY. *(outside)* We've come to warn you.

GIRL. They've come to warn me.

NICK. (*outside*) Ramerrez . . .

GIRL. (*calling through door*) What?

NICK. (*outside*) Ramerrez is on the trail.

GIRL. Ramerrez is on the trail. (*To Johnson.*) I got to let 'em in.

(*Johnson gets behind the curtains of the bed, where he is entirely concealed.*)

I can't keep 'em out such a night. (*Calling to the men.*) Come on it, boys.

(*She opens the door, and the men enter--Rance first. Rance, wearing a luxurious fur overcoat, his trousers tucked into his high-heeled boots, goes to the candle, warming his hands over it, taking off his gloves, brushing the snow off with his handkerchief. Sonora, in a buffalo overcoat, cap, ear muffs, and high boots, comes to the fireplace. Ashby follows with a lighted lantern. He wears an overcoat over the one in which he first appeared. Nick comes down to The Girl, then crosses to the fire; he has pieces of blanket tied round his legs and feet. Rance turns up the wick of the hanging lamp. All are snow-covered.*)

SONORA. (*going to the fireplace*) Ow! Glad you are safe. I'm froze!

(*He stamps his feet and rubs his hands together.*)

NICK. The Polka has had a narrow squeak, Girl.

GIRL. (*seated*) Why, what's the matter, Nick?

RANCE. (*suspiciously*) It takes you a long time to get up--and you don't seem to have so much on you, either.

GIRL. (*indignantly*) Well, upon my--

(*She rises and, picking up a rug from the floor, wraps it round her knees and sits. The wind rises and falls, crying in the cañons.*)

SONORA. We thought sure you was in trouble. My breath jest stopped--

GIRL. Me--in trouble?

RANCE. See here--that man Johnson--

SONORA. Fellow you was dancin' with--

RANCE. (*with a grimace of pleasure, spreading his stiffened fingers before the blaze*) Your polkying friend Johnson is Ramerrez.

GIRL. (*blankly*) What'd you say?

ASHBY. I warned you. Bank with us oftener.

GIRL. (*dazed*) What did you say?

RANCE. We say--Johnson was a--

GIRL. What?

RANCE. Are you deef? The fellow you've been polkying with is the man that has been asking people to hold up their hands.

GIRL. (*lightly, yet positively*) Go on! You can't hand me out that.

RANCE. You don't believe it yet, eh?

GIRL. (*rising, imitating his "yet"*) No, I don't believe it yet, eh? I know he isn't.

RANCE. Well, he *is* Ramerrez, and he *did* come to the Polka to rob it.

GIRL. But he didn't rob it.

SONORA. That's what gits me--he didn't.

GIRL. I should think it would git you.

ASHBY. We've got his horse.

SONORA. I never knew one of these men to separate from his horse.

RANCE. Oh, well, if we've got his horse, with this storm on, we've got him. The last seen of Johnson he was heading this way. You seen anything of him?

GIRL. Heading this way?

SONORA. So Nick said. (*The Girl gives Nick a glance.*)

NICK. He was. Sid says he saw him, too.

RANCE. But the trail ends here--and if she hasn't seen him--(*looking at The Girl*)--where was he going?

(*Nick spying Johnson's cigar, recognizes it as one of their rare dollar Havanas. The Girl's eyes follow Nick's glance. Unseen by Rance, there is a glance between Nick and The Girl.*)

NICK. (*to himself*) Oh, my God!

SONORA. (*answering Rance's question*) Yes, where was he going?

(*Rance looks at The Girl, now intercepting Nick's glance.*)

NICK. Well, I thought I seen him--I couldn't swear to it. You see, it was so dark. Oh, that Sidney Cove's a liar, anyway.

(*Nick puts the tell-tale cigar in his pocket, looking furtively about to make sure that he is not seen.*)

ASHBY. He's snowed under. Something scared him off, an' he lit off without his horse.

GIRL. (*sitting down*) Ha! How do you know that man is a road-agent?

SONORA. (*warming his hands and breathing on his fingers*) Well, two greasers jest now was pretty positive of it before they quit.

GIRL. (*with scorn*) Greasers! Oh!

RANCE. But the woman knew him--she knew him. (*Sitting on the table.*)

GIRL. (*quietly, for the first time impressed*) The woman? What'd you say?

SONORA. It was the woman who first told us that Ramerrez was here-- to rob the Polka.

RANCE. She's down at the Palmetto now.

ASHBY. It will cost us the reward.

RANCE. But Ramerrez is trapped.

GIRL. Who is this woman?

RANCE. (*as though to excite her jealousy*) Why, the woman from the back trail. That damn--

GIRL. Nina Micheltoreña?

RANCE. H'm, h'm.

GIRL. Then she knows him. She *does* know him . . . (*She rises again.*)

RANCE. He was the sort of man who polkas with you first--then cuts your throat.

GIRL. (*turning on Rance*) It's my throat, ain't it?

RANCE. Well, I'll be--

NICK. (*going to Rance and speaking to him in a low voice*) Say, she's cut up because she vouched for him. Don't rub it in.

GIRL. Nina Micheltoreña . . . How did she know it?

SONORA. Why, from what she said--

RANCE. She's his girl. She's--

GIRL. His girl?

RANCE. Yes, she gave us his picture--(*taking a picture from his pocket and turning it over*)--with "Love" on the back.

GIRL. (*takes the picture, looks at it, and laughs*) Nina Micheltoreña, eh? Ha! I'm sorry I vouched for him, Mr. Ashby.

RANCE. Ah!

GIRL. (*so that Ashby shall not suspect*) I suppose they had one of them little lovers' quarrels that made her tell you, eh? He's the kind of man that sort o' polkys with every girl he meets. Ha! Ha! Ha! Ha!

RANCE. What are you laughing at?

GIRL. (*turning to Rance again*) Oh, nothing--only it's kind o' damn funny how things come out--ain't it? Took in! Nina Micheltoreña! Nice company he keeps. One of the Cachuca girls with eye-lashes at half mast, ha! And she sold him out--for money. Ah, you're a better guesser than I am, Jack.

RANCE. (*grimly*) Yes.

GIRL. Well, it's gittin' late. Thank you. Good-night, boys.

SONORA. Hell, boys! Come on and let a lady go to bed. Good-night, Girl.
(*He goes to the door. Ashby follows Sonora, then Rance and, last, Nick. When the door opens, all the lamps flicker in the wind.*)

GIRL. Good-night, Sonora. Good-night, Mr. Ashby. Good-night, Jack.

SONORA. Lordy! Will we ever git down again?

NICK. (*as the others are outside, meaningly*) You want *me* to stay?

GIRL. (*going to the door*) No. Good-night.

(The men all go out calling "Good-night," etc. The Girl shuts the door, and stands with her back against it. With a change of manner, her eyes blazing.)

Come out of that--step out there!

(Johnson appears between the curtains of the bed.)

You came here to rob me.

JOHNSON. *(quietly)* I didn't.

GIRL. *(viciously)* You lie!

JOHNSON. I don't.

GIRL. You do.

JOHNSON. I--I admit that every circumstance points to--

GIRL. Stop! Don't you give me any more of that Webster dictionary talk--but get to cases. If you didn't come here to steal--you came to the Polka to rob it, didn't you?

JOHNSON. *(with sudden determination)* Yes, I did, but when I knew it was you who-- *(He goes towards her.)*

GIRL. Wait! Wait! *(Johnson pauses.)* Don't you take a step--look out, or I'll-- A road-agent . . . a road-agent! . . . Well, ain't it my luck? Wouldn't anybody know to look at me that a gentleman wouldn't fall my way? A road-agent . . . Oh! Oh! Oh! *(With a revulsion of feeling.)* You can git now--git! You--you thief! You imposer on a decent woman. I ought to have told the boys--but I wasn't goin' to let on I could be so took in. I wasn't goin' to be the joke of the world, with you behind the curtain, an' me eatin' charlotte rusks an' lemming turnovers an' a-polkering with a road-agent. Ha! But now you can git! Now you can get!

(She sits on the table, looking straight before her as though to forget the sight of the man.)

JOHNSON. *(in a low voice)* One word--only one word. . . . I'm not going to say anything in defense of myself. It's all true--everything is true, except that I would have stolen from you. I am called Ramerrez--I have robbed--I am a vagabond--a vagabond by birth--a cheat and a swindler by profession. I'm all that--and my father was all that before me. I was born, brought up, educated, thrived on thieves' money--but until six months ago, when he died, I didn't know it. I lived in Monterey-- Monterey, where we met. I lived decently. I wasn't the thing I am to-day. I only learned the truth when he died and left me with a rancho and a band of thieves--nothing else--nothing for us all--and I . . . I was my father's son--no excuse . . . it was in me--in the blood . . . I took to the road. I didn't mind much after--the first time. I only drew the line at killing. I wouldn't have that. And that's the man I am--the blackguard I am. (*With feeling.*) But, so help me God, from the moment I kissed you to-night, I meant to change. I meant to change.

GIRL. (*sniffling*) The devil you did!

JOHNSON. (*advancing a step*) I did, believe me--I did. I meant to go straight and take you with me--but honestly . . . when I could do it honestly. I meant to work for you. Every word you said to me to-night about being a thief cut me like a knife. Over and over again, I said to myself: "She must never know." Now . . . (*a slight pause*)--well--I've finished.

GIRL. Is that all?

JOHNSON. No. Yes. What's the use? That's all.

GIRL. (*half crying*) Well, there's jest one thing you've overlooked explainin', Mr. Johnson. It shows jest exactly what you are. It wasn't so much bein' a road-agent I got against you--it's this: you kissed me. You kissed me. You got my first kiss.

JOHNSON. Yes, damn me!

GIRL. You said you'd been thinkin' of me ever since you saw me at Monterey--an' all the time you'd walked straight off and been kissin' that other woman. You've got a girl. It's that I've got against you. It's my first kiss I've got against you. It's that damned Micheltoreña that I can't forgive. But now you can git--you can git! (*Rushing to the door and opening it.*) If they kill you, so much the better. I don't care--I don't care--I don't care!

JOHNSON. You're right. You're right. By God! You're right.

(*He takes out a pistol, but, not much caring whether he lives or dies, he looks at the pistol and puts it back in his pocket and goes out empty-handed--his head bowed.*)

GIRL. That's the end of that--that's the end of that. (*She goes to the door and closes it.*) I don't care--I don't care. I'll be like the rest of the women I've seen. I'll give that Nina Micheltoreña cards an' spades. (*Wiping her nose.*) They'll be another huzzy around here. (*A shot outside, close at hand.*) They've got him . . . (*With a bravado toss of her head.*) Well, I don't care--I don't care.

(*Johnson falls against the door outside. The Girl, with a revulsion of feeling, rushes to the door, opens it, and he staggers in, her arms about him. Johnson leans against the wall, the Girl closes the door.*)

JOHNSON. (*holding his hand to his right side*) Don't lock the door . . . I'm going out again . . . I'm going out . . .

(*He swings round, lurches, and nearly falls as The Girl pushes him onto a chair.*)

Don't bar the door. Open it . . . open it . . . by God! I won't hide behind a woman.

GIRL. (*leaning over Johnson*) I love you an' I'm goin' to stand by you. You asked me to go away with you. (*Crossing for the whiskey bottle and a glass.*) You get out of this, an' I will. If you can't save your own soul--

(*There is a rap on the window. Rance is peering through, but he cannot see Johnson. The Girl sets down the bottle and glass and pauses. She looks up at the ladder to the loft, gets on a chair, and lets it down. Rance goes from the window to the door.*)

--I'm goin' to save it for you. You're the man that had my first kiss.

(*In a lower voice, never pausing, she urges Johnson to the loft.*)

Go up there!

JOHNSON. (*his handkerchief pressed to his side*) No--no--no--no-- Not here.

GIRL. Do you want them to see you in my cabin? Hurry . . . Hurry . . .

JOHNSON. No--no--

(*There is a rap on the door. She gives him a push, and with an effort Johnson gradually climbs up the ladder, reeling as he goes.*)

GIRL. Yes, you can do it. You can--you're the man I love. You've got to show me the man that's in you. Go on . . . go on. . . .

(*A second rap on the door.*)

Just a step--a step.

JOHNSON. I can't . . . I can't.

(*He reaches the loft, collapses, falling to his knees. He lies on the floor of the loft, one outstretched hand holding the handkerchief. The Girl swings the ladder up.*)

GIRL. (*looking up, calling softly*) You can. Don't move.

(*Another rap on the door.*)

The cracks are wide--take that handkerchief away.

(*He draws the handkerchief out of sight.*)

That's it.

(*Another knock. The Girl calls off.*)

Yes, yes, in a minute. (*In a whisper to Johnson.*) Don't move.

(*The door opens and Rance appears. He slams the door behind him.*)

Well, what do you want now? You can't come in here, Jack Rance.

RANCE. No more Jack Rance. It's the Sheriff after Mr. Johnson.

GIRL. What?

RANCE. I saw him coming in here. (*He cocks his revolver.*)

GIRL. It's more than I did.

(*Rance glances at the bed, opening the curtain.*)

An' the door was barred. Do you think I want to shield a man who tried to rob me? If you doubt my word, go on--search the place; but that ends your acquaintance with the Polka. Don't you ever speak to me again--we're through!

RANCE. Wait a minute . . . What's that?

(*He listens--the wind is calling. After a slight pause, Rance comes to the table. The Girl is leaning against the bureau. Rance uncocks his revolver, puts it in the holster, takes off his hat, shakes the water from it, and drops it on the table. His eyes never leave The Girl's face.*)

I saw someone standing outside--there--(*crossing to the fireplace*)-- against the white snow. (*Taking off his overcoat.*) I fired. (*Shaking the coat.*) I could have sworn it was a man.

GIRL. Go on--go on--finish your search--then never speak to me again.

RANCE. (*seeing that he has gone too far*) Say, I--I don't want to quarrel with you.

GIRL. Go on--go on--and then leave a lady to herself to git to bed. Go on and git it over. (*She goes to the bureau, her back to Rance.*)

RANCE. I'm crazy about you. I could have sworn I saw-- You know it's just you for me--just you--and damn the man you like better! I--I-- Even yet I--I can't--(*starting to put on his coat*)--get over the queer look on your face when I told you who that man really was. You don't love him, do you?

(*A pause. He throws the coat on the floor and advances towards her.*)
Do you?

GIRL. (*lightly*) Who? Me?

(*With a forced laugh, she eyes Rance disdainfully.*)

RANCE. (*somewhat relieved, takes a step towards her*) Say, was your answer to-night final about marrying me?

GIRL. (*coyly, flirting*) I might think it over, Jack.

(*Another somewhat artificial laugh.*)

RANCE. Minnie . . . (*Coming close to her.*) I love you . . . (*Putting his arms about her, kissing her.*) I love you.

(*She struggles to escape from him, and, picking up the bottle from the table, raises it to strike him, then sinks to the floor, sobbing.*)

GIRL. (*nervously*) Oh, my God, I-- (*Rance stands looking down at her.*)

RANCE. (*with the nasty laugh of a man whose vanity is hurt*) Ha! Ha! Ha! God! I--I didn't think it was that bad--I didn't. I am much obliged to you. Thank you. (*Taking up his coat.*) Good-night. Much obliged. Can't you--can't you even say good-night?

(*His coat is in his left hand, his cap in his right. The Girl rubs her*) *hands on her dress and comes towards him. He drops his cap.*)

GIRL. Yes. Good-night, Jack Rance. Good-night, Jack Rance, I--

(*As he holds out his hand, a drop of blood from the loft falls on it.*)

RANCE. (*slowly, after a pause*) Look at my hand--(*pulling out his handkerchief and wiping his hand*)--my hand. That's blood.

GIRL. Yes, I must have scratched you jest now. I'm awfully sorry.

RANCE. There's no scratch there. There isn't a mark.

(*More blood falls on the outstretched hand holding the handkerchief.*)

GIRL. (*quickly*) Yes, but there will be in the morning, Jack. You'll see it in the morning.

(*Rance looks towards the loft. Placing his hand on his pistol, he puts his handkerchief in his pocket.*)

RANCE. He's up there.

GIRL. (*holding his hand which grasps the revolver*) No, he isn't, Jack. No, he isn't. No, he--

RANCE. You go straight to the devil.

(*Rance picks up a chair to climb up--then sees the ladder.*)

GIRL. (*trying to stop him*) No, he isn't, Jack. Not there, Jack. Not there, Jack. He is not there--

RANCE. (*drawing down the ladder*) Mr. Johnson, come down.

GIRL. Wait a minute, Jack . . . Wait a minute . . .

RANCE. (*as Johnson moves towards the ladder*) Come down, or I'll--

GIRL. Wait jest a minute, Jack! Jest a minute . . .

RANCE. (*his revolver levelled at Johnson*) Come down here!

(*Step by step, Johnson comes down the ladder, his eyes fastened on Rance. The Girl stands watching Johnson. Johnson's hands, which are up, slowly fall, and, with unseeing eyes, he lurches to the chair behind the table, falls forward, his head resting on the table--unconscious, half in the shadow. Rance puts his revolver in the holster.*)

GIRL. Don't you see he can't hold up his hands? Oh, Jack, don't make him-- Don't you see he can't? Oh, Jack, don't make him. No, no, wait, Jack, jest a minute--wait!

RANCE. (*leaning over Johnson*) Wait a minute? What for? (*Laughs--a low, unctuous laugh.*) So you dropped into the Polka, Mr. Johnson, to play me a little game of poker to-night? Ha! Ha! Ha! Funny how things change about in an hour or two. You think you can play poker? That's your conviction, is it? Ha! Ha! Ha! Well, you can play freeze-out as to your chances, Mr. Johnson, of Sacramento! It's shooting or the tree. Speak up--which will you have?

GIRL. (*who has picked up her pistol--in a low voice, quiet but tense*) You better stop that laughing, or you'll finish it in some other place where things ain't quite so funny.

(*Something in her voice strikes Rance, and he stops laughing.*)

He doesn't hear you. He's out of it. But me--me--I hear you--I ain't out of it. You're a gambler--he was, too--so am I.

(*Having engaged Rance's attention, she throws the pistol back into the drawer.*)

I live on chance money--drink money--card money--saloon money. We're gamblers--we're all gamblers! (*Leaning over towards Rance.*) You asked me to-night if my answer to you was final. Now's your chance! I'll play you a game--straight poker. It's two out of three for me. Hatin' the sight of you--it's the nearest chance you'll ever git for me.

RANCE. Do you mean--

GIRL. With the wife in Noo Orleans, all right. If you're lucky, you git him an' me; but if you lose, this man settin' between us is mine--mine to do with as I please--an' you shut up and lose like a gentleman.

RANCE. (*looking in her eyes*) You must be crazy about him.

GIRL. (*briefly*) That's my business.

RANCE. Do you know you're talking to the Sheriff?

GIRL. I'm talkin' to Jack Rance, the gambler.

RANCE. (*quietly, coolly*) You're right. (*Standing upright.*) And I'm just fool enough to take you up. (*Looking for a chair.*) Ah! (*Placing a chair before the table.*) You and the cards have got into my blood. I'll take you.

(*He pulls off the table-cover and throws it on the floor.*)

GIRL. Your word?

RANCE. I can lose like a gentleman.

(*She starts to draw back her hand, but he grasps it.*)

But, my God! I'm hungry for you--and, if I'm lucky, I'll take it out on you so long as God lets you breathe.

GIRL. (*draws away from him*) Fix the lamp.

(*Rance, his eyes still on her, reaches up to the lamp, does not find it at first, looks up, turns up the wick.*)

Wait jest a minute--(*going into the wardrobe with the candle*)--jest a minute.

RANCE. What are you waiting for?

(*He takes a pack of cards from his pocket, sits at the table, and shuffles.*)

GIRL. (*in the wardrobe*) I'm jest gittin' the cards, an' kind o' steadyin' my nerves.

RANCE. I've got a deck here.

GIRL. (*coming out of the wardrobe, blowing out the candle, and throwing it *on the floor*) We'll use a fresh deck. (*Laying a fresh pack on the table.*) There's a good deal dependin' on this, Jack Rance.

(*The Girl sits. Rance looks at her, then lays aside his own cards and takes hers.*)

Are you--ready?

RANCE. Ready? Yes, I'm ready. Cut for deal. (*She cuts. Rance shuffles.*) This is a case of show-down.

GIRL. Show-down.

RANCE. Cut. (*Begins to deal.*) The best two out of three.

GIRL. Best two out of three.

RANCE. (*as he glances over the cards he has drawn--in a low voice-- colloquially*) What do you see in him?

GIRL. What do you see in me, Jack? (*Taking up her cards.*) What have you got?

RANCE. King high.

GIRL. King high.

RANCE. (*showing her the hand*) Jack next.

GIRL. (*showing her hand to Rance*) Queen next.

RANCE. (*throwing down his hand*) You've got it. (*As she shuffles.*) You've made a mistake on Johnson.

GIRL. (*dealing*) If I have, Jack, it's my mistake. What have you got?

RANCE. (*showing her the cards*) One pair--Aces.

GIRL. (*throwing down her cards*) Nothing.

RANCE. (*shuffles*) We're even. We're even.

GIRL. It's the next hand that tells, Jack, ain't it?

RANCE. Yes.

GIRL. I'm awfully sorry it's the next hand that tells. I--I--want to say that no matter how it comes out--

RANCE. Cut.

(*She cuts the cards and he picks them up and deals.*)

GIRL. --that I'll always think of you the best I can, and I want you to do the same for me.

RANCE. You heard what I said.

(*The Girl starts to draw her cards towards her. He reaches across, places his hand over hers and over the cards.*)

GIRL. Yes.

RANCE. But I have got a feeling that I win--that in one minute I'll hold you in my arms.

(*He spreads out his cards, still holding her hand and looking at her. Then, as though resolved to face the consequences, he looks at his cards.*

She is leaning forward and her hand is being drawn towards him. As he sees his cards, he smiles. The Girl collapses with a shudder. He leans forward. Very calmly.)

I win.

GIRL. (*very anxiously*) Think so?

RANCE. Three Kings and it's the last hand. (*Showing her his cards.*)

GIRL. Oh, Jack, quick--get me something--I'm faintin'!

RANCE. (*throwing the cards face down on the table*) Where? Where?

GIRL. There.

RANCE. (*finding the bottle, but not the glass*) Oh, yes, here it is--here's the bottle. Where's the glass? Where's that damn glass?

(*As Rance turns away, she puts her cards in the bosom of her dress and draws five cards from her stocking.*)

GIRL. Hurry . . . hurry . . .

RANCE. (*dropping the bottle, turning and leaning forward as if to impress her, his arm round her neck*) You're fainting because you've lost!

GIRL. (*rising, laying down her hand on the table*) No, Jack--it's because I've won--three Aces and a pair.

(*He looks at her hand. A slight pause.*)

RANCE. Good-night.

(*Always the gambler, he picks up his hat and coat and goes. The Girl drops the cards and takes Johnson in her arms.*)

ACT III.

Scene. The interior of a typical mining-camp dance-hall of the period. The walls are of rough boards nailed across upright beams. The mines are closed on account of the weather, and the hall is decorated in honor of the opening of the "Academy." Garlands of pine and wreaths of red berries hang over the doors and windows. Yellow curtains hang at the windows. Eagles' wings, as well as wings of smaller birds, are tacked to the wall. Antlers (on which the miners hang their hats when the "Academy" is in session) are fastened to the wall, also birds' wings and a motto, painted on an old weather-beaten piece of wood, "Live and Learn." A stuffed game-cock and a candle lamp with a reflector are over a door at R. A horseshoe is fastened over the door to the exterior. A lamp hangs from the center of the ceiling, and stuck into its cheap iron brackets are flags whose stars indicate the number of States of that period.

At the back, towards the R., is a platform on which the teacher's home-made desk stands. It is decorated with a garland of pine. A bunch of red and white berries, a ruler, chalk, a whiskey bottle, glass and bell are on the desk. A box is used for the teacher's seat. A black-board is at the back, standing on the floor and resting against the table. An old sheet-iron stove, heavily dented, is below the desk. The fire is burning brightly. The stove has an iron railing fastened to the base, on which the miners rest their feet. The stove-pipe goes up through the ceiling. Whittled benches are arranged about the room and two or three chairs.

Sonora's coat is lying on a chair, and Trinidad's jacket is on the bench against the wall at back. Doors lead to the bar-room, which we saw in the first act, and a glimpse of the bar is shown. Fastened to the frame of one of these doors is a large hand, rudely painted, the index finger pointing to the words, "To the bar!" A red curtain cuts off the balcony on the same side of the room. Another door, on the opposite side of the room, leads to a lean-to in which there is a door leading to the exterior. A door at back opens directly upon the trail, and, when this door is ajar, one sees the snow-covered country and the green firs of Cloudy Mountain heavily weighted by snow. It is a bright winter's morning.

(*At the rise of the curtain, Jack Rance is sitting near the fire--worn, pale, and waxen. He has not slept, and his eyes are red and half closed as he sits thinking. He is no longer immaculate in dress--his necktie is partly undone, his waist-coat is unfastened, his boots unpolished, his hair is ruffled, and the cigar in his hand has gone out. Nick, standing near the foot of the platform, seems troubled as he looks towards the window as though towards The Girl's cabin.*)

NICK. I'd be willin' to lose the profits of the bar, if we could git back to a week ago--(*pouring out a drink*)--before Johnson walked into this room.

RANCE. (*showing feeling*) Johnson! By--(*taking off his hat*)--week--a week . . . A week in her cabin--nursed and kissed . . .

NICK. (*remonstrating*) Oh, say, Rance!

RANCE. You bet she kissed him, Nick. It was all I could do to keep from telling the whole camp he was up there.

NICK. But you didn't. If I hadn't been let into the game by The Girl, I'd a-thought you were a level Sheriff, looking for him. Rance, you're my deal of a perfect gent.

RANCE. What did she see in that Sacramento shrimp to love?

(Nick puts his foot on a chair and hands the drink to Rance.)

NICK. Well, you see, I figger it out this way, boss: love's like a drink that gits a-holt on you, an' you can't quit . . . it's a turn of the head, or a touch of the hands, or it's a half sort of smile--an' you're doped--doped with a feelin' like strong liquor runnin' through your veins--

(Rance drops the hand which holds the glass.)

--an' there ain't nothin' on earth can break it up, once you've got the habit. That's love. I've got it--you've got it--the boys've got it--The Girl's got it--the whole damn world's got it! It's all the Heaven there is on earth, an' in nine cased out of ten, it's Hell.

(A pause. Rance, in deep thought, lets his glass tip and his whiskey drip to the floor. Nick touches Rance's arm, points to the whiskey. Rance takes out his watch, glances at it, hands the glass back to Nick, who goes towards the door leading to the bar.)

RANCE. *(looking at his watch)* Well, Nick, her road-agent's got off by now.

NICK. Left Cloudy at three o'clock this morning--five hours off.

(Rance takes out a match, strikes it on the stove, then lights his cigar.

RIDER OF THE PONY EXPRESS. *(suddenly calling, outside)* Hello!

NICK. Pony Express! Got through at last!

(Nick goes to the bar-room. The Rider of the Pony Express comes in from bar-room, muffled up to his eyes.)

RIDER. Hello, boys!

(The Rider gives a letter to the Deputy Sheriff, who comes in from the lean-to.)

Letter for Ashby. Well, boys, how'd you like bein' snowed in for a week?

RANCE. Ashby ain't up yet. Dep, call Ashby.

(The Deputy goes off to the L.)

RIDER. *(at the stove)* Boys, there's a rumor up at the Ridge that you all let Ramerrez freeze, an' missed a hangin'. Say, they're roarin' at you boys. So long!

(Sonora and Trinidad, who have appeared from the bar-room, give the Rider a hard glance as he goes out through the bar.)

SONORA. *(calling after the Rider)* Wait! Says you to the boys at the Ridge as you ride by--the Academy at Cloudy is open to-day--says you-- full blast.

(A door slams as the Rider goes on his way.)

TRINIDAD. *(calling after the Rider)* Whoopee! Whoop! They ain't got no Academy at the Ridge.

NICK. (*bringing in whiskey for Trinidad and Sonora*) Here, Sonora.

RANCE. (*with a sneer*) Academy! Ha! Ha! Academy!

SONORA. What's the matter with you, Rance, anyway? We began this Academy game together--we boys an' The Girl--an' there's a--(*spits on the floor*)--pretty piece of sentiment back of it. She's taught some of us our letters an'--

TRINIDAD. He's wearin' mournin' because Johnson didn't fall alive into his hands.

SONORA. Is that it?

TRINIDAD. (*to Rance*) Ain't it enough that he must be lyin' dead down some cañon with his mouth full of snow?

SONORA. You done all you could to git him. The boys is all satisfied he's dead.

> (*Nick gives Sonora a sharp look, then turns guiltily to Rance. He picks up the empty glasses.*)

RANCE. (*rising, walking about restlessly*) Yes--he's dead. (*Going to the window and glancing out.*) The matter with *me* is, I'm a "Chink."

ALL. Ha! Ha! Ha! Ha!

RANCE. Boys, it's all up with The Girl and me.

TRINIDAD. (*self-consciously*) Throwed him!

SONORA. (*in a low voice to Nick*) As sure's you live, she's throwed him over for me.

> (*Nick hastily leaves the room with the glasses--coming back at once.*)

TRINIDAD. (*singing in his glee*) Will old dog Tray remember me.

SONORA. (*crossing to the door at the L.*) The percession will now form to the Academy wood-pile, to finish splittin' wood for teacher.

TRINIDAD and SONORA. (*singing*) Old dog Tray remember me.

SONORA. (*chuckling, to himself*) For me!

> (*Sonora and Trinidad go out to the lean-to.*)

DEPUTY. (*entering excitedly*) Ashby's out with a posse. (*Rance turns quickly.*) Got off jest after three this morning. (*Closes the door.*)

NICK. What?

RANCE. (*aside to Nick, with much excitement*) He's after Johnson!

NICK. Help yourself, Dep. (*The Deputy goes into the bar-room.*)

RANCE. Ashby's after Johnson! He was watching that horse--took him ten minutes to saddle up. Johnson has ten minutes' start. (*Hopefully.*) Oh, God! (*Going towards the bar.*) They'll never get him. Johnson's a wonder on the road. You got to take your hat off to that damn cuss.

> (*Rance passes off. Approaching miners whoop, coming to school. Sonora enters with an armful of wood, which he puts on the floor near*)

the stove. Trinidad enters, runs to the door at the back and opens it, then puts on his jacket. The Deputy strolls in from the bar.)

SONORA. Boys gatherin' for school.

(Handsome, Happy, Joe, a Gambler, and a Miner come into the room, playing leap-frog as they enter, talking and laughing. Their boots are covered with snow. Happy goes up to the teacher's desk and picks up a book tied in a red handkerchief.)

HAPPY. Here, Trin--here's the book.

(He throws it to Trinidad, who throws it to Sonora, Sonora to Joe, Joe to Handsome, Handsome to Sonora. Bucking Billy, a new scholar from Watson's Camp, comes in.)

DEPUTY. Sh, boys! Noo scholar from Watson's.

(Indicating Bucking Billy, a large, awkward miner, wearing an overcoat, muffler, and top boots with brass tips. He carries a dinner pail which contains a sandwich and whiskey flask. He has a slate under his arm. All stare at him.)

SONORA. Did you ever play lame soldier, m'friend?

BUCKING BILLY. No.

SONORA. We'll play it after school. You'll be the stirrup. *(To the others--with a wink.)* We'll initiate him.

NICK. *(up at the window)* Boys, boys, here she is.

HAPPY. *(looking of the window)* Here comes The Girl.

SONORA. Fix the seats.

(All save Nick, Trinidad, and a Miner hasten off.)

TRINIDAD. *(confidentially)* Here, Nick, you don't think to-day'd be a good time to put the splice question to her?

NICK. *(dubiously)* I wouldn't rush her. You got plenty of time.

(Nick hangs the blackboard on the wall. Sonora enters with a cask. The miner gets another cask. Handsome enters with a plank, which he lays across the two casks. This forms a long table for the students. Sonora picks up his coat, which is lying on a chair, and puts it on hurriedly. Happy, the Deputy, and the miner arrange more benches.)

TRINIDAD. Hurry up, boys, hurry up! Git everything in order.

(The Girl enters. She is carrying a small book of poems. The men take off their hats.)

BOYS. *(all speaking together)* Hello, teacher!

GIRL. Hello!

(Sonora crosses to The Girl and hands her a bunch of berries.)

TRINIDAD. Hello, teacher! *(He hands her an orange.)* From 'Frisco.

(Happy comes down with a bunch of berries, which he gives her.)

HAPPY. Regards!
>   (*Nick takes off The Girl's moccasins.*)
GIRL. (*quietly*) Hello, boys! How's everything?
>   (*With a guilty look, she glances from one to another, to see if they suspect her. She goes to the desk.*)
HANDSOME. Bully!
SONORA. Say--we missed you. Never knew you to desert the Polka for a whole week before.
GIRL. No, I--(*laying the berries and the orange on the desk*)--I--
HAPPY. Academy's opened.
GIRL. Yes . . . (*Taking off her gloves.*) I see . . .
SONORA. Here's a noo pupil--Bucking Billy from Watson's.
GIRL. How do you do, Bucking Billy?
BUCKING BILLY. (*coming forward, shyly*) How do!
GIRL. (*starting and looking out the window*) What's that?
NICK. Log fell in the stove.
GIRL. Oh . . . (*Pulling herself together.*) I guess I'm kind of nervous to-day.
>   (*She exchanges glances with Nick as she takes off her coat and hands it to him.*)
SONORA. No wonder. Road-agent's been in camp . . . and we missed a hangin'. I can't get over that.
GIRL. Well, come on, boys, and let me see your hands. (*Emphatically.*) Let me see them! (*After looking at the outstretched hands.*) Git in there and wash them.
SONORA. Yes'm. Been blackenin' my boots. (*He points to his boots.*)
GIRL. Yes, an' look at them boots--an' them boots--an' them boots! Git in there, the whole lot of you, an' clean up--an' leave your whiskey behind.
>   (*The boys go into the lean-to. Untying the strings of her cap, she takes it off and hands it to Nick.*)
Have you heard anything? Did he git away safe?
NICK. Yes.
GIRL. I was watchin' an' I seen him go . . . but suppose he don't git through . . . suppose . . .
NICK. He'll git through, sure. We'll hear he's out of this country before you know it.
>   (*Nick hangs up The Girl's wraps. Rance enters.*)
GIRL. Jack Rance. I want to thank you.
RANCE. Oh, don't thank me that he got away. (*In a low voice.*) It was them three Aces and the pair you held.

GIRL. (*in confidence*) About them three Aces--I want to say--

RANCE. But he better keep out of my country.

(*The Girl and Rance look intently at one another.*)

GIRL. Yes . . .

(*She rings the bell. The boys enter. Rance sits down by the stove, paying no attention to the others. Happy enters, carrying the slates, which are in a very bad condition--some have no frames, some have very little slate left--one or two have sponges hanging from the frames on strings, and all have slate-pencils fastened to the frames. Happy gives out the slates as the others march by.*)

HAPPY. Come on, boys--git your slates.

TRINIDAD. Whoop!

GIRL. Trin, you're out of step, there. Git in step, Happy.

(*The boys all march forward in the manner of school children. As each one gets his slate, he takes his seat. The Girl sits back of her desk on the platform. With a sickly laugh, trying to take interest in the scholars.*)

Now, boys, what books have we left over from last year?

HAPPY. (*rising*) Why, we scared up jest one whole book left--and the name of it is--

SONORA. (*taking the book out of his pocket, and reading the title*) "Old Joe Miller's Jokes."

GIRL. That will do nicely.

SONORA. (*rising*) Now, boys, before we begin, I propose no drawin' of weppings, drinkin', or swearin' in school hours. The conduct of certain members wore on teacher last term. I don't want to mention no names-- but I want Handsome and Happy to hear what I'm sayin'. Is that straight?

ALL. You bet it is!

GIRL. (*timidly*) Last year you led off with an openin' address, Jack.

ALL. Yes! Yes! Yes! Yes! Go on, Sheriff!

TRINIDAD. Let her go, Jack.

(*There is a pause. Rance looks at The Girl, then turns away.*)

RANCE. I pass.

GIRL. (*quickly and with anxiety*) Then Sonora?

SONORA. (*embarrassed at being called upon to make a speech*) Oh, Hell! I--

ALL. Sh! Sh! Sh! Go on! Go on! Go on!

SONORA. (*abashed*) I didn't mean that, of course.

(*As he rises, he shifts his tobacco and unconsciously spits on Bucking Billy's new boots. Bucking Billy moves away.*)

I look upon this place as somethin' more than a place to set around an' spit on the stove. I claim they's culture in the air of California--an' we're here to buck up again' it an' hook on.

ALL. (*pounding upon the desks enthusiastically*) Hear! Hear! Hear!

SONORA. With these few remarks I--I set.

GIRL. (*with deep feeling*) Once more we meet together. There's been a lot happened of late that has learned me that--

> (*Rance turns slightly in his seat. Nick looks at Rance, Rance at The Girl.*)

--p'raps--I don't know so much as I thought I did--and I can't learn you much more. But if you're willin' to take me for what I am--jest a woman who wants everybody to be all they ought to be--why, I'm willin' to rise up with you, an' help reach out--

> (*Handsome raises his hand.*)

--an'-- What is it, Handsome?

HANDSOME. Whiskey, teacher. I want it so bad! Just one drink 'fore we start.

> (*The boys all stand up, raising their hands and calling: "Teacher." The Girl puts her fingers in her ears.*)

GIRL. No! . . . and now jest a few words on the subject of not settin' in judgment on the errin'--(*as the boys all sit down again*)--a subject near my heart.

> (*The Sidney Duck opens the door. The card is still pinned on his coat.*)

ALL. Git! Git!

GIRL. (*as Sid is about to retreat*) Boys! Boys! I was jest gettin' to you, Sid, as I promised. Come in. (*Sid enters.*)

SONORA. What--here? Among gentlemen? Git!

ALL. Eh? What? Git! Git!

TRINIDAD. Why, this fellow's a--

GIRL. I know--I know . . . but of late a man in trouble has been on my mind–

ALL. Eh?

GIRL. (*catching Rance's eye*) Sid--of course, Sid--

ALL. Oh . . .

GIRL. --an' I fell to thinkin' of the Prodigal Son--he done better at last, didn't he?

SONORA. I never heard that he was a card sharp.

TRINIDAD. No.

GIRL. (*overcome with guilt, nervously*) But suppose there was a moment in Sid's life when he felt called upon to find an extra Ace. (*A slight pause.)* Can't we forgive him? He says he's sorry. Sid?

SID. Oh, yes, Miss, I'm sorry. Course if I 'adn't got caught, things would 'a been different. I'm sorry.

GIRL. Sid, you git your chance.

(The boys mutter. The Girl takes the card off Sid's coat.)

Now go and set down.

(The Girl sits. Happy strikes Sid as he attempts to sit.)

HAPPY. Git out of here!

GIRL. Happy! Happy!

(Sonora, as Sid passes him, puts out his foot and trips him.)

Sonora!

(Sid sits on a stool in a corner. Everyone moves away as far as possible.)

TRINIDAD. *(rises)* Say, Girl, You mean to say that honesty ain't the best policy? Supposin' my watch had no works, an' I was to sell it to the Sheriff for one hundred dollars. Would you have much respect for me?

GIRL. If you could do it, I'd have more respect for you than for the Sheriff.

(Billy Jackrabbit and Wowkle enter quietly and sit on the bench by the wall under the blackboard. They take no part, but listen stupidly. Wowkle has the papoose on her back.)

RANCE. *(rising)* Well, being Sheriff, I'm careful about the company I keep. I'll set in the bar. Cheats--*(looking at Sid)*--or road-agents aren't jest in my line. *(Turning, starting to go.)* I walk in the open road, with my head up--(as *The Girl looks down)*--and my face to the sun; and wherever I've pulled up, you'll remark I've always played square and stood by the cyards.

(He pauses in the doorway.)

GIRL. *(sitting)* I know--I know--an' that's the way to travel--in the straight road. But if ever I don't travel that road--or--you--

NICK. You always will, you bet!

ALL. You bet she will! You bet!

GIRL. But if I don't--I hope there'll be someone to lead me back to the right road. 'Cause remember, Rance, some of us are lucky enough to be born good--others have to be directed. *(Rance goes out.)*

SONORA. *(touched)* That's eloquence.

(Sid sobs. Happy takes out a bottle of whiskey and puts it to his lips. The boys all reach for it. The Girl takes the bottle away.)

GIRL. Give me that and set down.

(The boys sit down immediately. The Girl goes back to her desk, hands the bottle to Nick, and sits. Nick puts the bottle on the shelf of the desk.)

Now, if somebody can sing "My Country 'Tis"--Academy's opened.
Sonora?

SONORA. No--I can't sing.

> (*The boys all try to make each other sing. While they are chaffing each other, Wowkle and Billy Jackrabbit rise and sing.*)

BILLY JACKRABBIT and WOWKLE. (*singing*)

> My country 'tis of thee,
> Sweet land of liberty,
> Of thee I sing!

SONORA. Well, if that ain't sarkism!

BILLY JACKRABBIT and WOWKLE. (*singing*)

> Land where our fathers died . . .

SONORA. (*quickly, between the two lines*) You bet they died hard!

BILLY JACKRABBIT and WOWKLE. (*singing*)

> Land of the Pilgrim's pride,
> From every mountain-side
> Let freedom ring!

> (*When the song is ended, the Indians sit down again.*)

GIRL. Thank you, Billy and Wowkle. Now, them that can read, read.

TRINIDAD. This is us! Old Joe Miller!

SONORA. (*reading from the book*) "Can Feb-u-ary March? No, but--A-pril May."

GIRL. Now, Trin.

> (*As Trinidad laboriously reads the ancient joke, Sid, who has noticed Bucking Billy's dinner-pail, reaches out with his feet, pulls the pail over to him, helps himself to food and a small flask of whiskey. He pushes the pail back and starts to eat and drink, glancing at the others furtively to see if he has been caught.*)

Now, then, boys, we mustn't forget our general infla--information. Trin, who killed Abel?

TRINIDAD. (*in a surprised tone--thinking of some local character*) Why, I didn't know he was dead.

GIRL. Bucking Billy, you count up to ten.

BUCKING BILLY. (*rising*) 1, 2, 3, 4--

SONORA. Pretty good! I didn't think he knowed that much.

BUCKING BILLY. 5, 6, 7, 8, 9, 10, Jack, Queen--

> (*All laugh. Bucking Billy discovers that his pail has been opened.*)

Somebody stole my lunch!

SONORA. (*rising*) Who?

BUCKING BILLY. (*pointing to Sid*) Him!

ALL. Put him out! Git out! Put him out!

GIRL. Boys! Boys!

(*Sonora, Trinidad, and Handsome throw Sid out and return to their seats. The Girl looks out through the window for a moment, then turns and opens a book.*)

I will read you a little verse from a book of pomes.

No star is ever lost we once have seen,

We always may be what we might have been.

(*She rests her hand on the desk and breaks down, sobbing quietly. Nick rises and goes to her.*)

SONORA. Why, what's the--

ALL. Why--what's--

GIRL. Nothin' . . . nothin' . . . only it jest came over me that we mustn't be hard on sinners an' . . . (*Breaking down completely.*) Oh, boys . . . I'll be leavin' you soon--how can I do it? How can I do it?

SONORA. What?

TRINIDAD. What did she say?

SONORA. What'd you say? (*Going to her.*) Why, what's the matter?

GIRL. (*raising her head*) Nothin'--nothin'--only I jest remembered I've promised to leave Cloudy soon, an' p'raps we--might never be together again--you an' me an' the Polka. Oh, it took me jest like that--when I seen your dear old faces--your dear, plucky old faces--and reelized that--

(*She drops her head on the desk again. Rance enters.*)

SONORA. (*after a pause*) What! You leavin' us?

HAPPY. Leavin' us?

NICK. (*softly, that the others do not hear*) Careful, Girl, careful!

GIRL. It's bound to happen soon.

SONORA. Why, I don't quite understand. Great Gilead! We done anythin' to offend you?

GIRL. Oh, no, no!

SONORA. Tired of us? Ain't we got--(*casting about for a word*)--style enough for you?

HAPPY. (*rising*) Be you goin' to show them Ridge boys we're petered out an' culture's a dead dog here?

TRINIDAD. Ain't we your boys no more?

SONORA. (*with sentiment, looking like a large cherub*) Ain't I your boy? Why, what is it, Girl? Has anybody--tell me--perhaps--

GIRL. (*raising her head and drying her eyes*) We won't say no more about it. Let's forget it. Only--when I go away--I want to leave the key of my cabin with old Sonora here. An' I want you all to come up sometimes, an' to think of me as the girl who loved you all, an' some-where is wishin' you well--an'--(*putting her hand on Nick's shoulder*)--I want to think of little Nick here runnin' my bar, an' not givin' the boys too much whiskey.

SONORA. Hold on! They's jest one reason for a girl to leave her home an' friends . . . only one. Some other fellow away from here--that she--she likes better than she does any of us. Is that it?

GIRL. (*raising her head again*) Likes in a different way--yes.

HAPPY. Well, so help me!

  (*Sonora goes sadly back to his seat. The boys form a pathetic picture.*)

TRINIDAD. Sure you ain't makin' a mistake?

GIRL. Mistake? No, no, boys--no mistake. Oh, boys, if you knew--

  (*She rises, hesitates a moment, then goes to them.*)

Trin . . .

  (*Putting her hands on Trinidad's shoulder.*)

Ah, Sonora . . .

  (*She kisses Sonora on the cheek, turns and exits into the bar-room, sobbing.*)

SONORA. Boys, Academy's busted. . . . (*A pause.*)

RANCE. (*sitting down in front of the stove*) Ha! Ha! Ha! Ha! Well, the right man has come at last. Take your medicine, gentlemen.

SONORA. Rance, who's the man?

RANCE. (*casually*) Oh--Johnson.

TRINIDAD. Holy--!

SONORA. Great--!

TRINIDAD and SONORA. You lie!

  (*During the following speeches, some of the boys move the benches and desks back against the walls. Bucking Billy and the Miner leave.*)

RANCE. Ask Nick. (*Trinidad and Sonora look at Nick.*)

SONORA. Why, you told me I had the first chance.

TRINIDAD. He told me the same thing.

SONORA. Well, for a first class liar!

TRINIDAD. You bet!

SONORA. But Johnson's dead. (*Suddenly, after a short pause.*) He got away . . .

RANCE. (*shaking the ashes from his cigar*) Yes, he got away . . .

  (*A pause as they realize the situation. Sonora comes to Rance, followed by Trinidad and Happy.*)

SONORA. Jack Rance, I call on you, as Sheriff, for Johnson. He was in your county.

HAPPY. You hustle up an' run a bridle through your pinto's teeth, or your boom for re-election's over, you lily-fingered gambler!

TRINIDAD. (*shaking his fist at Rance*) You bet!

RANCE. (*coolly*) Oh--I--don't know as I give a--

TRINIDAD. No talk! We want--

ALL. (*save Rance and Nick*) Johnson!

ASHBY. (*outside*) Boys!

NICK. Why, that's--

RANCE. That's Ashby! Oh, if--

(*In his face is the hope of Johnson's capture. To Ashby, who is still outside.*)

You've got him?

(*Ashby enters, his face cool, triumphant. He stands near the door. The Deputy hastens out. This entire scene is played easily and naturally-- no suggestion of dramatic emphasis.*)

ASHBY. Yes--we've got him!

SONORA. Not--

ASHBY. Johnson.

(*All look at each other with meaning glances. Nick alone is sorry that Johnson is caught.*)

TRINIDAD. Alive?

ASHBY. You bet!

RANCE. (*with a short, brutal laugh, the veneer of the gambler disappearing*) Well, I didn't do it. I didn't do it. Now, he be damned!

(*Johnson enters, his arms bound, pale, but with the courage of a man who is accustomed to risking his life. He is followed by the Deputy.*)

There's an end of him. How do you do, Mr. Johnson? I think, Mr. Johnson, about five minutes will do for you.

(*Trinidad takes out his watch.*)

JOHNSON. I think so.

SONORA. (*sarcastically*) So this is the gentleman The Girl loves?

RANCE. That's the gentleman.

GIRL. (*outside*) Nick? Boys?

(*Nick holds the door open. The Girl appears on the threshold of the bar-room. Ashby steps between The Girl and Johnson, so that The Girl does not see him.*)

I forgot . . . it's recess. They can have a drink now.

(*The Girl moves away from the door.*)

JOHNSON. Lock that door, Nick.

(*Nick shuts the door to the bar and locks it.*)

RANCE. Why the hell--

JOHNSON. Please!

SONORA. (*threateningly*) Why, you--

RANCE. (*to Sonora*) You keep out of this. I handle the rope--I pick the tree.

SONORA. Then hurry.

TRINIDAD. You bet!

(*Ashby nods in approval.*)

SONORA. Come on.

(*There is a general movement towards the door leading to the trail.*)

RANCE. Deputy?

(*The Deputy comes forward.*)

JOHNSON. One minute . . .

RANCE. Be quick, then.

JOHNSON. It's true . . . I love The Girl.

RANCE. (*brutally*) Well--you won't in a minute. You--

JOHNSON. (*as Rance makes a movement to strike him*) Oh, I don't care what you do to me. I'm prepared for death. That's nothing new. The man who travels my path faces death every day--for a drink of water or ten minutes' sleep. You've got me, and I wouldn't care . . . but for The Girl.

TRINIDAD. You've jest got three minutes.

SONORA. Yes.

JOHNSON. I don't want her to know my end. That would be an awful thought--that I died out there, close at hand. She couldn't stay here after that--she couldn't, boys, she couldn't.

RANCE. (*briefly*) That's understood.

JOHNSON. I'd like her to think that I got away--went East--and changed my way of living. So you jest drag me a long way from here before you-- And when she grows tired of looking for letters that never come, she will say: "He has forgotten me," and that will be about enough for her to remember. She loved me before she knew what I was . . . and you can't change love in a minute.

RANCE. (*striking him in the face*) Why, you . . .

JOHNSON. I don't blame you! Strike me again--strike me! Hanging is too good for me. Damn me, body and soul--damn me! Why couldn't I have let her pass? Oh, by God, I'm sorry I came her way; but it's too late now-- it's too late! (*He bows his head. A pause.*)

RANCE. Is that your last word? (*Johnson does not answer.*) That your last word?

(*Trinidad snaps his fingers to indicate that time is up.*)

Dep.

(*The Deputy comes to Johnson. Rance moves away, but Nick steps to Johnson's side.*)

NICK. Good-bye, sir . . .

JOHNSON. Good-bye, Nick. You tell The Girl--no, don't say anything.

HAPPY. Come on, you!

(*They start to go.*)

NICK. (*his voice trembling*) Boys, when Alliger was hanged, Rance let him see his sweetheart. I think--considerin' as how she ain't goin' to see no more of Mr. Johnson here--an' knowin' The Girl's feelin's--I think she ought to have a chance to--

ALL. No! No! No!

RANCE. No!

JOHNSON. I've had my chance--inside of ten minutes I'll be dead, and it will be all your way. Couldn't you let me? I thought I'd have the courage not to ask, but--oh, couldn't you?

NICK. (*goes to the door as though hearing a sound*) Here's The Girl, boys.

RANCE. No!

JOHNSON. All right. Thank you, Nick.

NICK. You must excuse Rance for bein' so small a man as to deny the usual courtesies, but he ain't quite himself.

JOHNSON. Come, boys, come.

(*He starts for the door, L. Sonora pushes him back. The Deputy and one of the miners step between Johnson and the door.*)

RANCE. Wait a minute. (*A pause. Johnson slowly turns to face Rance.*) I don't know that I'm so small a man as to deny the usual courtesies, since you put it that way. I always have extended them. But we'll hear what you have to say--that's our protection; and it might interest some of us to hear what The Girl will have to say to you, Mr. Johnson. After a week in her cabin, there may be more to know than--

JOHNSON. (*in a low voice*) Why, you damned--

NICK. (*moving toward Rance*) Rance, you--

(*The boys all look at Rance angrily, showing that they resent his words.*)

SONORA. Now, Rance, you stop that!

RANCE. We'll hear every word he has to say.

SONORA. You bet! He puts up nothin' noo on us.

ASHBY. (*looking at his watch*) Well, boys, you've got him safe--I can't wait. I'm off. (*He goes off.*)

GIRL. (*outside*) Nick? Nick?

NICK. Here's The Girl, boys.

RANCE. Deputy . . . (*Untying Johnson.*) Circle around to the bar, boys.

Trin, put a man at that door. Sonora, put a couple of men at those windows.

(*Sonora, Happy, the Deputy, and the Gambler go outside. Handsome and Trinidad go into the lean-to. Nick stands at the bar-room door.*)

Johnson, if you can't think of something pleasant to tell The Girl, lie to her.

JOHNSON. I'll let her think I came back to see her again. She needn't know it's the last time.

GIRL. (*outside*) Nick? Nick?

(*Rance goes out. He, Trinidad, and Handsome pass the windows. Johnson steps behind the door. Nick unbars the door. The Girl enters.*)

What you got the door barred for, Nick? (*Looking around.*) Where are the boys?

NICK. Well, you see, the boys--the boys--has--has--

GIRL. Has what?

NICK. (*as though struck by a bright idea*) Has gone.

GIRL. Gone where?

NICK. Why, to the Palmetter. Oh, say, Girl--

(*He crosses over to her and puts his hands on her shoulders.*)

I like you. You've been my religion--the bar an' you. You don't never want to leave us. Why, I'd drop dead for you!

GIRL. (*somewhat surprised and touched*) Nick!

(*She goes up to her desk as Johnson knocks on the door.*)

JOHNSON. (*appearing*) Girl! (*He holds out his arms to her.*)

GIRL. You? You? Look outside an'--

(*Nick closes the door, bars, and holds it.*)

JOHNSON. Don't say a word.

GIRL. (*in Johnson's arms*) You shouldn't have come back.

JOHNSON. I had to--to say good-bye once more.

NICK. (*lying with effort*) It's all right--it's all right.

(*During Nick's speech, The Girl draws the curtains.*)

The boys--why, the boys--they are good for quite a little bit yet. Don't git nervous. I'll give you warning. (*Nick steps into the bar.*)

JOHNSON. Don't be afraid, Girl.

GIRL. But you can't go now without being seen.

JOHNSON. (*with a smile*) Yes--there's one way out of Cloudy--and I'm going to take it.

GIRL. (*attempting to move from him*) Then go! Go!

JOHNSON. Just remember that I am sorry for the past--and don't forget me.

GIRL. Forgit you? How could--

JOHNSON. I mean . . . till we meet.

GIRL. (*apprehensively*) Did he call?

JOHNSON. No. He will--he'll warn me . . . Don't forget me.

GIRL. Every day that dawns I'll wait for a message from you. I'll feel you wanting me. Every night, I'll say: "To-morrow"--an' every to-morrow I'll say: "To-day!" For you've changed the whole world for me. I can't let you go . . . but I must. Dick--Oh, I'm afraid!

(*She hides her head on Johnson's shoulder.*)

JOHNSON. You mustn't be afraid. In a few minutes, I shall be quite free.

GIRL. And you'll make a little home for me where you're goin'--soon-- with you?

(*She is overcome. Johnson merely nods.*)

A strange feelin' has come over me. A feelin' to hold you, to cling to you--not to let you go. Somethin' in my heart says, "Don't let him go."

JOHNSON. Girl, it's been worth life just to know you. You've brought me nearer Heaven. You--to love a man like me!

(*He covers her face with his hands, breaks down and sobs.*)

GIRL. Don't say that. Don't! Suppose you was only a road-agent--an' I was a saloon-keeper: we both came out of nothin' an' we met, but, through lovin', we're goin' to reach things now--that's us! We had to be lifted up like this, to be saved.

(*Nick enters. As he opens the door, the boys are seen outside, but The Girl has her back to them.*)

NICK. (*backing off, closing the door again*) It's all clear now.

JOHNSON. Good-bye.

GIRL. (*in Johnson's arms*) You act as though we was never goin' to meet again, an' we are, ain't we?

JOHNSON. Why, surely--we are.

GIRL. I want you to think of me here jest waitin'. You was the first . . . they'll never be anyone but you. All that Mother was to Father, *I'm* goin' to be to you. You're the man I'd want settin' across the table, if they was a little kid like I was, playin' under it. I can't say more than that! Only--you--you will--you must git through safe--an', well, think of me here jest waitin' . . . jest waitin' . . . jest waitin' . . .

(*He stands looking at her. After a little pause, she puts her face in his arm and weeps.*)

JOHNSON. Oh, Girl, Girl! That first night I went to your cabin--I saw you kneeling--praying. Say that in your heart again for me--now. Perhaps I believe it--perhaps I don't. I hope I do. I want to. But say it--

say it, Girl--just for the luck of it. Say it.

(*He kneels at her feet, his head bowed. The Girl prays silently, crossing herself before she begins, and, at the end of the prayer, they embrace. Sonora opens the door quietly.*)

God bless you! Good-bye. . . . Good-bye, Girl!

(*Sonora is followed by the other boys. Rance is the last to enter. Johnson, looking over The Girl's shoulder, sees them. He kisses her hands.*)

GIRL. Good-bye . . .

JOHNSON. Girl! Girl! (*He goes off.*)

GIRL. He's gone--Nick.

(*Sobbing, she makes a movement to follow Johnson, then goes to Nick and sobs in his arms. Suddenly, she sees the men.*)

NICK. (*soothingly*) Girl! Girl!

GIRL. (*in alarm*) You--you knew. . . . You all knew . . . You had him--you had him all the time . . . An' you're goin' to kill him--but you sha'n't!

(*Running over to the door, L., she throws herself against it--her back to it, then sobs convulsively.*)

No! You sha'n't kill him--you sha'n't--you sha'n't!

SONORA. (*advancing*) Girl . . . the boys an' me ain't perhaps reelized jest what Johnson stood for to you, Girl--an', hearin' what you said, an' seein' you prayin' over the cuss--

RANCE. Damned cuss!

SONORA. Yes, the damned cuss, I got an idee maybe God's back of this here game.

GIRL. (*with much anxiety*) You're not goin' to pull the rope on him?

RANCE. (*to the men*) You mean I am to set him free?

GIRL. (*a gleam of hope in her heart*) You set him free?

RANCE. I let him go?

SONORA. That's our verdict, an' we're prepared to back it up.

GIRL. Dick--Dick--you're free!

(*She rushes out and her voice is heard outside.*)

You're free! You're free!

(*There is a pause. The men stand silently looking at each other.*)

NICK. The Polka won't never be the same, boys--The Girl's gone.

ACT IV. "Oh, my beautiful West! Oh, my California!"

Scene. The boundless prairies of the West. On the way East, at dawn, about a week later. In the far background are foothills with here and there a suggestion of a winding trail leading West. The foliage is the pale green of sagebrush--the hills the deeper green of pine and hemlock. In the foreground is a little teepee made of two blankets on crossed sticks. The teepee is built against a grass mound and is apparently only a rude shelter for the night. Back of the tent is an old tree stump which stands out distinctly against the horizon. Here and there are little clumps of grass, bushes, and small mounds of earth and rocks. A log fire is burning to the L. of the teepee, a Mexican saddle lies beside the fire.

(*As the curtain rises, the stage is in darkness. Johnson is lying on the grass, leaning against his saddle, smoking a cigarette. The Girl is inside the teepee. Gradually the dawn begins to break. As the scene becomes visible, The Girl pushes aside the blanket and appears in the opening.*)

GIRL. Dick, are you awake?

JOHNSON. (*turning to her*) Another day . . . the dawn is breaking.

GIRL. (*looking towards the unseen hills in the distance*) Another day. . . . Look back . . . the foothills are growing fainter every dawn--farther away. Some night when I am going to sleep, I'll turn--and they won't be there--red and shining. That was the promised land.

JOHNSON. (*rising*) We must look ahead, Girl, not backwards. The promised land is always ahead.

   (*A glimmer of the rising sun is seen on the foliage of the foothills.*)

GIRL. Always ahead. . . . Yes, it must be.

   (*She comes out of the teepee and goes up the path.*)

Dick, all the people there in Cloudy--how far off they seem now--like shadows in a dream. Only a few days ago, I clasped their hands; I saw their faces--their dear faces! An' now they are fadin'. In this little, little while, I've lost them. . . . (*There are tears in her voice.*) I've lost them.

JOHNSON. Through you, all my old life has faded away. *I* have lost that.

GIRL. Look! (*Pointing to the East as she notices the sunrise.*) The dawn is breakin' in the East--far away--fair an' clear.

JOHNSON. A new day. . . . Trust me. (*Stretching out his hands to her.*) Trust me. . . . A new life!

GIRL. A new life. (*Putting her hands in his.*) Oh, my mountains-- I'm leavin' you-- Oh, my California, I'm leavin' you-- Oh, my lovely West-- my Sierras!-- I'm leavin' you! Oh, my--

   (*Turning to Johnson, going to him and resting in his arms.*)

--my home.

CURTAIN.

Other Books from
Feedback Theatrebooks & Prospero Press

An Outline History of American Drama, 2nd Edition

A Chronological Outline of World Theatre

The Playwright's Companion, An Annual
A Practical Guide to Script Opportunities in the U.S.A.

Professional Playscript Format Guidelines & Sample

The Theatre Lover's Cookbook
Recipes from 60 Favorite Plays

The Musical Theatre Cookbook
Recipes from Best-Loved Musicals

Prospero's Almanac, First Edition
The Theatre Lover's Guide to the World at Large

Acting Editions

The Contrast
Metamora
The Stage-Struck Yankee
Fashion
Glance at New York
Rip Van Winkle
Under the Gaslight
Young Mrs. Winthrop
The Old Homestead
Margaret Fleming
A Trip to Chinatown
The Girl of the Golden West